P9-DDE-394

SOLOMON ISLANDS VISITORS PERMIT
Subject to the Immigration Act
permitted to enter and remain until
Two month
NTA CRUZ Date of Entry 13-8-82
Immigration Officer
holder of this permit is not to
e in any employment without
written sanction of the
ssioner of Labour.

11 JUL 1980
PERMITTED TO ENTER AND
REMAIN IN SINGAPORE
FOR FOURTEEN DAYS FOR
SOCIAL VISIT ONLY FROM
DATE SHOWN ABOVE

PENDARATAN TRANSIT
IMMIGRATION NGURAH RAI, BALI
I N D O N E S I A
PERMITTED TO STAY 30 DAYS
From 3 0 JAN 1983
Holder of this permit
1. to be engaged in any employment, paid or unpaid
2. to enter any educational institution.
This permit cannot be converted into stay permit

EN UN ARRIVAL DEPARTURE
HONIARA
SOLOMON ISLANDS
26 / 13 / 9 / 82
igration Office

(VSI) VISITOR permitted to remain
until 1 Feb 78

HONG KONG
CANCELLED
OCT 1977
IMMIGRATION
OFFICER

-3 MAY 1981
IMMIGRATION SINGAPORE
Immigration Regulations, 1972
PERMITTED TO ENTER AND
REMAIN IN SINGAPORE
FOR FOURTEEN DAYS FOR
SOCIAL VISIT ONLY FROM
DATE SHOWN ABOVE

VANUATU IMMIGRATION
PERMITTED TO ENTER AS
PERMIS D'ENTREE COMME
VISITEUR/VISITOR
-4 AUG 1982
AND REMAIN FOR
DUREE DU SEJOUR
INTERDICTION DE TRAVAILLER
EMPLOYMENT PROHIBITED

AUSTRALIA
-6 MAY 1981
SYDNEY KINGSFORD-SMITH

IMMIGRATION

LANGUAGES
OF ASIA
AND THE
PACIFIC

LANGUAGES OF ASIA AND THE PACIFIC

A TRAVELLERS' PHRASEBOOK

Charles Hamblin

ANGUS & ROBERTSON PUBLISHERS

Angus & Robertson Publishers
London • Sydney • Melbourne

First published in Australia by Angus & Robertson Publishers, 1984
First published in the United Kingdom by Angus & Robertson (UK) Ltd, 1984

© Charles Hamblin 1984

National Library of Australia
Cataloguing-in-publication data.

Hamblin, Charles.
    Languages of Asia and the Pacific.

    ISBN 0 207 13628 9

    1. Asia — Languages — Terms and phrases.
    2. Pacific area — Languages — Terms and phrases.
    I. Title.
409'.5

Typeset in Great Britain by William Clowes & Sons Ltd, Beccles and London
Printed in Hong Kong

CONTENTS

INTRODUCTION

From Turkey west, you are well provided with phrasebooks; from Iran east, only one or two languages are easily accessible to the traveller. It is, of course, a Great Truth of modern travel that "you can go anywhere with English"; but it is a truth that assumes that you never wish to venture far out of sight of an international hotel or a tourist bus. The real facts of linguistic geography are sketched below in "Languages by Countries," (page 407).

This book makes possible basic communication with most of the population of South and East Asia, Indonesia, the Pacific and Latin America. It is complementary to books such as the excellent *Languages of Europe* of Archibald Lyall or one of its successors. In fact it follows Lyall's format, though it gives more grammar.

Basic communication with Asians and Oceanians is neither easier nor more difficult than with anyone else. To learn a language thoroughly takes years of study, but you can be speaking a sentence or two within five minutes. You do not have to start with a new alphabet or difficult phonetics. You may need to form some new habits of pronunciation, but they are hardly more difficult than those required for, say, French.

This book has really (of course) had some thirty authors, association with whom has made the task of collating their work a very great pleasure. They are: Mrs Victoria Yaganagi (Persian); Mr Mohammed Kazim and Mrs Sashi Rani Goel (Urdu and Hindi); Mr Mohammed Habibullah Khan (Bengali); Dr Kingsley Goonewardane (Sinhalese); Mr Suresh Eswaran (Tamil); Ko Lay Myint (Burmese); Mr Chainarong Engkagul (Thai); Miss Douang Samone Sriratanakoul (Lao); Miss Chantou Boua (Kampuchean); Mr Tai Nguyen Anh (Vietnamese; Mrs Lily Hsiao Lee (Mandarin); Miss Rosaline Young Wai Shan (Cantonese); Mr Ho Soon Cheng (Hokkien); Miss Haruko Murakami (Japanese); Mr Don'o Kim and Mr Wonho Chong (Korean); Mr Andreas Hadiwidjaja and Mr Othman Mohamad (Indonesian and Malay); Mr Policarpio J. Dangalio and Miss Lina Valcarcel (Tagalog); Mrs Elsie Manley (Spanish); Mr Julius Repper (Portuguese); Dr Véra Sauran (French); Mr Austin Sapias (New Guinea Pidgin); Mr Tupeni L. Baba (Fijian); Mr Pesalili Fekitoa (Tongan); Mr Samata Elia (Samoan); and Mrs Lorna Miriama Brotherton Canning (Tahitian). Numerous other friends and colleagues have been unstinting in their help.

Charles Hamblin

HOW TO USE THIS BOOK

LEARNING PRONUNCIATION Guides to pronunciation are printed against the phrases, numerals and sentences for each language, so that the book can be used alone, without other aid. These guides are, naturally, only an approximation, and they are best used for initial orientation only.

Read and re-read the section on pronunciation in the grammar, and aim to do without the printed pronunciation guide as soon as possible. In the case of most of the languages in this book, the ordinary (romanised) text is a good guide to pronunciation once the values of the letters are understood.

Practise reading *aloud,* without at first worrying about meaning, from the ordinary text.

Take every opportunity to listen to native speakers or to get their help. In the absence of anything else, try to find some radio broadcasts to listen to.

FIRST STEPS AT GRAMMAR Use the sentences for practice. For each one:

1. Work out the meaning word by word, referring to the grammar and the vocabulary. (A sentence here or there may defeat you, but don't get hung up on it. Concentrate on picking out what you can.)
2. Read the sentence repeatedly aloud, now thinking of what it means, until you feel familiar with it.
3. Finally, look at the English and see if you can translate it into the language.

SUBSEQUENT STUDY This book has no "drill" of the kind most textbooks have. But it is not hard to make up your own. How much of this you do will naturally depend on your time and aims.

Unless you are that rare person who can memorise vocabulary by the page, your best plan is to concentrate on mastering simple sentence forms and rely on looking up the vocabulary as you need it.

For each grammatical point, write down ten or a dozen illustrations with varied vocabulary. Keep the sentences simple and practical and vary just a word or two at a time. (Your "model" sentences may contain mistakes, but they will not have as many as you would make if you didn't do the study.) Come back to them on subsequent occasions, read them over with understanding, dramatise them to yourself and add to them. The secret of language learning at any level is constant, constructive repetition within a plan that ensures you are covering the right ground.

Here is a possible plan of study. (It may need to be varied slightly depending on the language.)

1. Greetings and set phrases.
2. Numerals. (Learn these especially thoroughly; you will need them more than anything else.)
3. Numerals before nouns, and expressing distances and amounts of money.
4. Questions "How many ... ? ," "How much ... ? ," and their answers.
5. Questions "Is this ... ? ," "Is that ... ? ," and their answers "This is/is not ..."
6. The question "Is there ... ? ," and its answers "There is a/no ... ," "There are (so many) ..."
7. The question "Where is ... ? ," and its answers "... is (not) here/there," "... is (not) in ..."
8. Pronouns in equational sentences "I am a ... ," "Is he a ... ?"
9. Possession, "That is (not) the ... of the ... ," "That is (not) my ... ," etc.

10. Polite imperatives with simple verbs, "Please sit down/come/ . . . ," "Please don't . . ."
11. Imperatives with direct and indirect objects, "Please give/send/bring/pay . . ."
12. "I would like to . . . ," "I want a . . . ," and similarly with other pronouns.
13. "Is it possible to . . . ? ," "Can you . . . ?" and answers.
14. Present tense with noun subjects and objects.
15. Present tense with pronoun subjects and objects.
16. Time-words, "now," "at . . . o'clock."
17. Past tense, future tense.
18. Adjectives attached to nouns and predicated of them, "The . . . is . . ."
19. Comparatives and superlatives.
20. "All," "some," "not all," "many"; also "always," "somewhere," etc.

Other special points requiring practice can be picked up from the grammar notes for any particular language. The notes have been written with the needs of this kind of programme in mind, but, if the precise point you want is not included, you should try to think up an alternative way of getting your meaning across for use when you need to.

CONVERSATION PRACTICE As a tourist you will get this on the nearest street-corner, once you are started. But a half-hour session with a patient teacher can work wonders in the early stages. Ask him/her all your burning questions. (Don't waste time talking English; ask them in the language!)

TONAL LANGUAGES (Burmese, Thai, Lao, Vietnamese, Mandarin, Cantonese, Hokkien) The "tone," or pitch-level, of a word may be as important to its meaning as the sounds that go to make it up. To pronounce one of these languages correctly you must first break English speech habits in which pitch-variations are used for emphasis and to indicate division into clauses. Words are emphasised in these languages by being pronounced more loudly or slowly. Questions are distinguished not by a rise in pitch at the end but by a generally higher pitch or by an increased range.

For orientation, find your normal speech-range and think of it as the first five notes of a musical scale; say, C to G. Then "sing" a high tone as G, a low-falling one as E down to C, and so on. Make no distinction for questions or imperatives. These rules are, of course, very rough; above all, copy a native speaker.

ADDITIONAL HELP A tape to guide pronunciation of the languages in this book can be purchased from:
> Tape Correspondence Service
> Division of Post-graduate Extension Studies
> University of New South Wales
> Kensington, N.S.W., Australia 2033

The tape, on two cassettes, gives, for each language, the Everyday Phrases, Numerals, Days of the Week, Months, and Sentences, spoken by a native speaker.

SPECIAL NOTE FOR THOSE WITH LIMITED HORIZONS Avoid the tendency to put languages in a pecking order, with your own at the top. You can say anything in any language. Nearly every language in this book is the vehicle of a substantial literary culture, and the speakers of the others are hard at work building.

PART I

PERSIAN
HINDI AND URDU
BENGALI
SINHALESE
TAMIL

PERSIAN

Persian is the national language of Iran and one of the two principal languages of Afghanistan. It is spoken by a significant minority in Pakistan. It is written in the Arabic alphabet. There is no completely standard romanisation and this book uses its own.

PRONUNCIATION Vowels:

Long Ā is like *aw*, and I and U have the long sounds *ee* and *oo*.
Other vowels, including ordinary A, are short and lightly sounded.
At the end of a word, E has lip-spread (like French *é*).
Diphthongs AE, AI, UI and OU are approximately *eigh, igh, wee* and *owe*.

Consonants are generally as in English, but

ZH, KH, GH are the sounds in "pleasure," "loch," "Ugh!"
The sign ' represents a glottal stop as in the Cockney pronunciation of "bottle" as "bo'l."
H is sounded even at the end of a word; hence *Shāh* as in the middle of "I sure hope."
S is always *ss* not *z*.
R is rolled.

Pronounce double consonants double; for example, *ammā*, "but," as *am-mā*.
Stress is on the last syllable of each word, except in the case of certain suffixes.

NOUNS Form plurals by adding *-hā*, and always stress the plural ending: *kif*, "bag"; *kifhā*, "bags." For living things, alternatively add *-ān* (*-yān* after a vowel), similarly stressed: *mard*, "man"; *mardhā* or *mardān*, "men."

There are no articles "a" or "the," and nouns very often stand alone; but *in*, "this, these," *ān*, "that, those," or *yek*, "one," may be used: *in zan*, "this woman"; *yek ketāb*, "one book," "a book."

The word *rā* placed after a word or phrase that is the object of a verb gives it a definite sense: *Mard rā didam*, "I saw the man." Use *rā* also when the object is preceded by *in* or *ān*.

The suffix *-i* added to any noun gives it a very indefinite sense: *mardi*, "some man or other."

ADJECTIVES and other qualifiers follow the noun, and the qualified noun takes the very lightly sounded suffix *-e* (*-ye* after a vowel): *marde khub*, "good man"; *zane irāni*, "Iranian woman"; *doktore zan*, "woman doctor."

When the qualifier is a noun it may also represent a possessor, so that *-e* can be translated directly as "of": *kife mard*, "bag of the man," "the man's bag." For explicitness, or to remove ambiguity, insert the word *māl*, "property": *kif māle mard*.

To form the comparative, add *-tar* to the adjective; for a superlative, *-tarin*. Only exceptions: *khub, behtar, behtarin*, "good, better, best"; and *ziād* (or *kheili*), *bishtar, bishtarin*, "much, more, most."

In comparison, "than" is *az*: *bozorgtar az mard*, "bigger than the man."

ADVERBS Adjectives can be used as adverbs without change of form.

PRONOUNS

man, "I"	*mā*, "we"
shomā, "you" (singular or plural)	
u, "he, she"	*ishān*, "they" (people)

3

ān, "it"   *ānhā*, "they" (things)

In object position add *-rā*: *shomārā*, "you"; *urā*, "him, her," etc., except that "me" has the short form *marā*.

Possession can be indicated as for nouns: *kife man* or *kif māle man*, "my bag" — but a more usual construction uses suffixes:

-am, "my"   *-emān*, "our"
-etān, "your"
-esh, "his, her, its"   *-eshān*, "their"

Hence *kifam*, "my bag." Insert *-y-* if the noun ends in a vowel: *ketābhāyetān*, "your books."

VERBS The verb comes at the end of the sentence.

The infinitive ends in *-tan* or *-dan*. Since many verbs have an irregular present stem, the third person singular present is shown in parentheses in the vocabulary.

The present tense has stressed prefix *mi-*, and endings as in the following example:

miravam, I go"   *miravim*, "we go"
miravid, "you go"
miravad, "he, she, it goes"   *miravand*, "they go" (people)

Use the singular *miravad* also for "they go" in the case of things. Pronoun subjects need not be expressed.

The past tense stem is formed very regularly from the infinitive by deleting *-an*. This directly gives the third person singular and inanimate plural form: *raftan*, "to go," *raft*, "he (etc.) went." For the remaining forms, add endings *-am*, *-id*, *-im*, *-and* corresponding with the present: *raftam*, "I went," etc.

The verb *budan*, "to be," has a past tense *budam*, . . . , but also a present stem *hast-* giving present tense *hastam*, "I am," . . . ; the third person singular has the special form *ast*, "he/she/it is," often pronounced just *e*, or attached to the preceding word as a suffix *-st*: *Ketāb khub ast*, "The book is good." The form *hast* is preserved to mean "There is": *Ketābe khub hast*, "There is a good book."

For a negative verb, prefix *na-* (with short *a*, strongly stressed): *naraft*, "he (etc.) did not go"; *namiravam*, "I am not going." The negative of *hastam*, . . . is *nistam*, . . . (third person singular and inanimate plural *nist*): *Ān bozorg nist*, "It is not big."

Use a negative verb even when the sentence has another negative such as *hich kas*, "no one": *Hich kas injā nist*, "There is no one here."

Note that Persian has many compound verbs consisting of a noun followed by a verb such as *kardan*, "to do"; for example, *pāk kardan*, "to clean." The two parts of the verb should not be separated by other words.

QUESTIONS have no special sentence form, but *Āyā* is often used to introduce yes/no questions: *Āyā kifetān bozorg ast?*, or just *Kifetān bozorg ast?*, "Is your bag big?"

IMPERATIVES use a subjunctive verb form: replace *mi-* of the second person present by *be-* (stressed), or by *na-* for a negative: *shomā midehid*, "you are giving"; *Bedehid*, "Give"; *Nadehid*, "Don't give."

For "Let's," form a similar first person plural: *Beravim*, "Let's go."

NUMERALS Use the singular form of the noun after a numeral, inserting *nafar* when indicating numbers of people, *tā* when indicating numbers of things: *do nafar mard,* "two men"; *se tā otāgh,* "three rooms." No special word is needed in time or money expressions.

CURRENCY In Iran: a single unit, the *ri'āl*; but 10 *ri'āl* is called 1 *tomān.* In Afghanistan: 1 *afghāni* = 100 *puli.*

FORMS OF ADDRESS Note the traditional Muslim greeting *Salām aleikom* and reply *Aleikom-os-salām.* But a common modern greeting is *Shādzi.*

Address men as *āghā,* "sir," women as *khānom,* "madam." Prefix these, with *-e* ending, also to titles, for example, *āghāye doktor.* Further prefix *jenāb* to indicate special respect: *jenābe āghāye doktor.*

There are various polite substitutes for pronouns; note *bande* ("servant") for "I, me"; and *ghorbān* or *jenābe āli* for "you."

The verb *farmudan (mifarmāyad),* "command," often replaces *kardan* or *dādan* in the second person as an auxiliary verb.

KIN TERMS

pedar, "father"
barādar, "brother"
pesar, "son"
shouhar, "husband"

mādar, "mother"
khāhar, "sister"
dokhtar, "daughter"
zan, "wife"

NAME OF LANGUAGE
Persian's name for itself is *Fārsi.*

HINDI AND URDU

Hindi is an official language (with English) of India, spoken as a first language by 150 million in the northern provinces and by a substantial minority elsewhere.

Urdu is (with English and Bengali) official in Pakistan, and has fifty million speakers there and in India.

The two languages are fundamentally the same, and their speakers can understand one another. The differences are that

1. Hindi is written in the Sanskrit alphabet, Urdu in the Arabic;
2. In vocabulary, Hindi speakers often prefer Sanskrit-derived words where Urdu speakers (mostly Muslims) lean to Arabic and Persian.

We here use, as far as possible, a common style and vocabulary in a direct romanisation of the Hindi script. Where necessary, Urdu alternatives are shown in square brackets [ ].

PRONUNCIATION Vowels:

Long vowels AA, E, II, O, UU as *ah, eh, ee, oh, oo.*
Short vowels A, I, U as in English "cut," "bit," "look."
AI as short *a* in "bat": AU as short *o* in "lot."
Ã, Ẽ, Ĩ, Õ, Ũ AĨ, AŨ are corresponding nasalised vowels, namely, pronounced in such a way that part of the air escapes through the nose. They are always fairly long.

Consonants make several distinctions which require careful observation and practice:

T, D are pronounced with the tongue spread against the top teeth as if for English *th.*
Ṭ, Ḍ are pronounced with the tongue curled back against the roof of the mouth.
Ṭ, Ṭ, P, K are made without any rush of breath, that is, like unvoiced D, Ḍ, B, G. C is, similarly, like unvoiced J.
TH, ṬH, PH, KH, ĊH are "aspirated" sounds, in which the H is separately sounded as a rush of air (stronger than in English) following the initial consonant. DH, ḌH, BH, GH, JH are similar "voiced" sounds. In general, always pronounce H as a strong separate sound.
N before K, G or H is like *ng,* and NG hence has a following *g* sound as in English "finger."
R is trilled behind the top teeth.
Ṛ is flapped, with tongue curled back.
Ś is like English *sh.*
K̲H̲ is as in English "loch" (shown by underlining).
G̲ and G̲H̲ are as in "Ugh!" (shown by underlining).

Pronounce double consonants double.
Stress is more even than in English.

NOUNS are of two genders, masculine and feminine. The genders of nouns denoting inanimates must be learnt with the words.

The following table gives "direct" and "oblique" cases, in singular and plural, of nouns of the various classes. Direct case is used as subject or indefinite object, oblique case with prepositions.

		Masculine Nouns		Feminine Nouns	
		in -*aa*	other	in -*ii*	other
S.	D.	*kamraa*	*ghar*	*larkii*	*kitaab*
	O.	*kamre*	*ghar*	*larkii*	*kitaab*
Pl.	D.	*kamre*	*ghar*	*larkiyā*	*kitaabe*
	O.	*kamrõ*	*gharõ*	*larkiyõ*	*kitaabõ*
		"room"	"house"	"girl"	"book"

In a few nouns the base changes to accommodate the ending.

Prepositions follow the noun: *kamre kaa*, "of the room"; *kamre mẽ*, "in the room"; *kamrõ mẽ*, "in the rooms," etc.

There are no articles, and nouns may stand alone: *kitaab*, "a book" or "the book." The word *ek*, "one," may be used for "a, an."

ADJECTIVES Some adjectives ending in -*aa* agree in number and gender with their nouns, forming masculine singular -*aa*, -*e*, masculine plural -*e*, -*e*, feminine in all cases -*ii*: *aćchaa kamraa*, "good room"; *aćche kamre mẽ*, "in the good room"; *aćchii larkii*, "good girl"; *aćchii larkiyõ kaa*, "of the good girls."

Adjectives not in -*aa*, as well as some in -*aa* marked "inv." (invariable) in the vocabulary, do not change their form: *laal kursii*, "red chair"; *laal kursiyā*, "red chairs."

Form comparative with *aur*, superlative with *sabse*: *baraa*, "big," *aur baraa*, "bigger," *sabse baraa*, "biggest." Exception: *aćchaa*, "good," has *behtar*, "better," *behtarin*, "best," both invariable.

"Than" is *se* with the oblique case, preceding the adjective: *kamre se aur baraa*, "bigger than the room."

PRONOUNS (with oblique case in parentheses) are

mã [*mujh*], "I, me"
aap [*aap*], "you" (singular or plural)
yeh [*is*], "this"
voh [*us*], "that"

ham [*ham*], "we, us"

ye [*in*], "these"
ve [*un*], "those"

There are no third person pronouns apart from the words for "this," etc., and these are used for people as well as things. (They can also be used before nouns as demonstratives.)

The possessives *meraa*, "my," *aapkaa*, "your," *hamaraa*, "our," are declined like adjectives; similarly *iskaa*, "belonging to this (person or thing)," *uskaa*, "belonging to that," *inkaa*, "belonging to these," *unkaa*, "belonging to those": *meraa saamaan*, "my baggage"; *aapkii ćaabiyā*, "your keys"; *unke kamre mẽ*, "in their room."

VERBS The verb comes at the end of the sentence.

The verb *honaa*, "to be," has present tense *maĩ hũ, aap haĩ, yeh hai, ham haĩ, ye haĩ*; and in the past tense first and third singular *thaa*, otherwise *the*: *Kamraa baraa hai*, "The room is big"; *Bas thaa*, "It was the bus" (or "There was a bus").

For other verbs, form the present or past tense by altering the infinitive ending -*naa* to -*taa* and adding the present or past tense of the verb "be." The form in -*taa* is a present participle and must agree with the subject like an adjective: *dekhnaa*, "to see"; *Maĩ dekhtaa hũ* (man speaking) or *Maĩ dekhtii hũ* (woman speaking), "I see"; *Aadmii dekhtaa hai*, "The man sees"; *Aurtẽ dekhtii the*, "The women saw."

Although these have the form of English "is seeing" (etc.) they are ordinary present and past tenses. To translate English "He is seeing" say *Yeh dekh rahaa hai,* where *rahnaa* is the verb "to remain." Use this form also to render future tense.

Hindi has a number of other inflected verb-forms, but these are adequate to simple purposes.

Auxiliary verbs generally follow the infinitive of the main verb: *ćaahnaa,* "to want," *Maĩ dekhnaa ćaahtaa hũ,* "I want to see" (man speaking).

An indefinite object takes the direct case: *Maĩ gaạriyā dekhtaa hũ,* "I see (some) cars." A definite object takes the oblique case followed by *ko: Maĩ gaạriyõ ko dekhtaa hũ,* "I see the cars"; *Voh gaạrii ko ćalaataa the,* "He drove the car."

The same construction marks the indirect object of a verb such as *denaa,* "to give": *Voh laarke ko ketaab detaa the,* "He gave the boy a book." (Use *ko* for both objects if necessary.)

Personal pronouns also take *ko,* but *maĩ* and *ham* instead have special endings: *mujhe, hamẽ.*

For a negative, place *nahĩ* (sometimes *na*) before the verb, and in the present tense omit the verb "be": *Maĩ nahĩ dekhtaa,* "I do not see" (man speaking); *Voh nahĩ dekhtii thaa,* "She did not see"; *Ve gaarii ko dekhnaa nahĩ ćaahte,* "They do of a verb to -*nevaalaa: kitaab ko paṛhnevaalaa,* "book reader," "person reading a Note that a reflexive pronoun, of any person or number, is usually *aap: Maĩ aapne saamaan ko dekhtaa hũ,* "I see my luggage."

Note the formation of nouns meaning "one who does ..." by changing the -*naa* of a verb to -*nevaalaa: kitaab ko paṛhnevaalaa,* "book reader," "person reading a book."

QUESTIONS A yes/no question can have the same form as the corresponding statement, or may be introduced by *Kyaa: Kyaa aap bhuukhe haĩ?,* or just *Aap bhuukhe haĩ?,* "Are you hungry?"

An interrogative word such as *kab,* "when?," generally immediately precedes the verb: *Aap kab jaa rahii haĩ?,* "When you are going?"

IMPERATIVES have a polite form in -*iye* that makes "Please" unnecessary: *Rahiye,* or *Aap rahiye,* "Please stay."

For "Don't," use *Na: Na jaaiye,* "Please don't go."

For "Let's," use the ending -*ẽ* and include the pronoun *Ham: Ham jaaẽ,* "Let's go."

NUMERALS The list of numerals up to ninety-nine contains many irregularities, and it is reluctantly recommended to the beginner that he confine himself to those tabulated, otherwise resorting to specification figure by figure.

After numbers above one, use the plural of the noun as in English: *do kamre,* "two rooms."

In writing, Urdu speakers may prefer Arabic numerals to Western. (See tabulation under Persian.)

CURRENCY 1 *ruupii* (f.) = 100 *paise* (m. pl.): the names are the same in India and Pakistan.

FORMS OF ADDRESS Use *saahab* for "sir" or "madam."

In India, "Mr," "Mrs" and "Miss" are *Srii, Sriimatii* and *Kumaarii,* before surnames. In Pakistan, use *saahab,* following the name, for either sex; or, as the equivalent of "Mrs" for a married woman, *Begam* before or after the surname.

The polite word *jii* is often added to a name used when addressing its bearer; and in the polite form *Jii hã* (or just *Jii*) for "Yes."

Gestures commonly replace words in conveying greetings, thanks, etc.

KIN TERMS Urdu terms are in square brackets where they differ from Hindi:

"father," *baap* or *baapuu*, or the more respectful *pitaa [vaalid]*

"mother," *mã*, or the more respectful *maataa [vaalida]*

"husband," *pati [śauhar]*

"wife," *patnii [biivii]*

"son," *betaa*; "daughter," *betii*

"brother," *bhaaii*; "sister," *bahn*

But a younger brother and sister are usually explicitly *ćhotaa bhaaii* and *ćhotii bahn*.

NAME OF LANGUAGE

Hindi is *Hindii* (f.) and Urdu is *Urduu* (f.). India is *Bhaarat* (m.).

BENGALI

Bengali is the national language of Bangladesh (fifty million speakers) and a major language also in India (thirty-five million speakers in the state of West Bengal, which includes the city of Calcutta).

It is written in its own version of the Sanskrit alphabet. Romanisation is straightforward.

PRONUNCIATION Vowels:

A, I, U are pronounced *ah, ee, oo*.

E is like short English *e* in "bet," or between this and short *a* as in "bat."

Ō is a pure vowel approximately as English *oh* (but not necessarily long).

O is a short *aw*.

Diphthongs OI, UI, AI, AE, OU are combinations of the sounds of the individual vowels.

Ã, Ẽ, Ĩ, Õ, Ũ are nasalised versions of the plain vowels; that is, they are pronounced in such a way that part of the air escapes through the nose.

Consonants involve some special distinctions:

T, D are pronounced with the tongue spread against the upper teeth as if for English *th*.

Ṭ, Ḍ are pronounced with the tongue curled back against the roof of the mouth.

T, Ṭ, P, K are made without any rush of breath, that is, like unvoiced D, Ḍ, B, G. Ć is, similarly, like unvoiced J.

TH, ṬH, PH, KH, ĆH are aspirated; that is, a rush of air (strong separate H sound) follows the other consonant.

DH, ḌH, BH, GH, JH are similar voiced sounds: and, in general, H is strongly sounded and voiced.

NG is as in "singer," not as in "finger."

Ṛ is a flapped retroflex (tongue curled back).

Ś is like English *sh*.

Pronounce double consonants double.

Stress is more even than in English.

NOUNS

The plain form of the noun serves as subject, direct object or indirect object in the singular, except that living things add *-ke* for direct or indirect object: *baṛi*, "house" (subject or object); *ćhele*, "boy" (subject); *ćheleke*, "boy" (object), or "to the boy."

Add *-r* for possessive (*-er* after a consonant): *baṛir*, "of the house"; *ćheler baṛi*, "boy's house."

Add *-e* to denote "in" or "at," or *-te* in the case of a word of more than one syllable and ending in a vowel: *baṛite*, "in the house."

Plural forms are generally used only in the case of living things, and then only when there is no other indication of plurality. In the case of living things, add *-ra* for plural subject, *-der* (or *-eder*) for all other purposes: *ćhelera*, "boys" (subject); *ćheleder*, "boys," "of boys," etc.

Prepositions follow the noun, which, in the case of living things, is usually in the possessive: *ćheler theke*, "from a boy."

There is no definite or indefinite article, but the particle *-ṭa* (or *-ṭi*, considered "polite") is commonly attached to a noun to give definiteness: *ćheleṭi*, "the boy." Possessive endings may be added: *ćheleṭir*, "of the boy."

The numeral *ek*, "one," with *-ṭa* attached, is used if necessary as an indefinite article: *ekṭa baṛi*, "a house."

BENGALI

PRONOUNS The essential pronouns are: *ami,* "I"; *apni,* "you" (singular, polite); *tini,* "he, she" (polite); *śe,* "he, she, it" (ordinary). Pronouns take endings, including plural endings, like nouns:

	"I"	"you"	"he, she"	"he, she, it"
S.	ami	apni	tini	se
	amake	apnake	tãke	take
	amar	apnar	tãr	tar
	"we"	"you"	"they"	"they"
Pl.	amra	apnara	tãra	tara
	amader	apnaker	tãder	tader

The demonstratives *e,* "this, these," and *ō,* "that, those," precede the noun, which has -*ṭa* attached; or they may themselves be used with -*ṭa* as pronouns: *eṭa,* "this, these"; *eṭar,* "of this, of these," etc.

ADJECTIVES are invariable and precede the noun: *bhalo chele,* "good boy"; *boṛo baṛi,* "big house."

As predicate, an adjective needs no verb "is" or "are": *Baṛiṭa boṛo,* "The house is big."

For a comparative, put *aro,* "more," before the adjective: *Tini aro lomba,* "He/She is taller." For "than," put *chee* after the possessive, and place this phrase first: *Amar chee tini aro lomba,* "He/She is taller than I."

For a superlative, put *śob chee,* "than all," before the adjective: *Tini śob chee lomba,* "He/She is tallest."

VERBS The verb comes at the end of the sentence.

The vocabulary gives, for each verb, (1) the first person present tense, in -*i,* and (2) the polite second or third person present, in -*en* (or -*n*), which may have a modified base vowel. Thus *kōri/koren,* "do," forms *ami kōri,* "I do," *apni koren,* "you do," *tini koren,* "he/she does."

For ordinary third person with *śe,* change the -*en* or -*n* ending to -*e*: *śe kore,* "he/she/it does."

Plural is always the same as singular: *amra kōri,* "we do," *apnara koren,* "you (plural) do," etc.

For past tense, change the first present -*i* to -*lum, -len, -lo* (for first, polite, and ordinary third respectively): *ami kōrlum,* "I did"; *apnara kōrlen,* "you (plural) did," etc.

For future, similarly use the endings -*bo, -ben, -be*: *ami kōrbo,* "I shall do."

Among other verb-forms note: (1) a present continuous in -*chi, -chen, -che*; (2) the infinitive in -*te,* used with auxiliary verbs.

There are a very few irregular verbs. Note that *jai/jan,* "go," has past tense *gelum, -len, -lo* and infinitive *gete.*

The verb "be" in the sense of "exist" is *achi/achen.* Hence "There is" or "There are" with things is *ache.*

For "I have," use the possessive *amar* with *ache: Amar boiṭa ache,* "I have the book."

For a negative, add *na* after the verb: *ami kōrlum na,* "I did not do." The negative of *ache,* in the sense "There is," is *nei,* "There is not." For "am not, are not (etc.)" between nouns or with noun and adjective, use *nōi/non: Oṭa amar boi noe,* "That is not my book."

BENGALI

QUESTIONS For a yes/no question, put *ki* at the end of the corresponding statement: *Apnar boiṭa aćhe ki?*, "Have you got the book?" The word *ki* can also be earlier in the sentence but may then be ambiguous since it can also mean "what?"

The interrogative pronoun *ke*, "who?," has possessive and plural forms *kar, kara, kader* like other pronouns: *O boiṭa kar?*, "Whose is that book?"

IMPERATIVES For a polite imperative, alter the present ending *-en* to *-un* (a plain *-n* ending is unaltered): *Aśun*, "(Please) come." But in the case of an action to be carried out at some future time, use the polite future with ending *-ben*: *Kalke aśben*, "Come tomorrow."

The most reliable way of forming a negative imperative is to use the *-ben* form followed by *na*: *Jaben na*, "Don't go."

In place of "Let's," generally use a question of the form "Will you . . . ?": *Amar śongge ki jaben?*, "Will you go with me?" for "Let's go."

NUMERALS The forms of the numerals up to ninety-nine are very irregular, and it is reluctantly recommended that the beginner confine himself to those listed, calling other numbers figure by figure.

In counting human beings, attach *-jon* to the numeral: *dujon ćhele*, "two boys." In counting other things (except money), attach *-ṭa*: *dośṭa boi*, "ten books" — but the numbers "two," "three" and "four" take the special forms *duṭo, tinṭo, ćarṭe*.

CURRENCY 1 *ṭaka* ("rupee") = 100 *poeśa*: same names in India and Bangladesh, but Indians would often prefer the word *rupi*.

FORMS OF ADDRESS "Sir" and "Madam" are *mośai* and *mohaśoe*.

Before a name, "Mr" is *Sri*; "Mrs" or "Miss" *Srimoti*; for younger men, sometimes *Sriman*; for older men or women, the respectful *Srijukto*.

Various other terms of address are in use. An older term for "Mr" is *Babu* after the name.

KIN TERMS The commonest are

baba, "father"	*ma*, "mother"
dada, "elder brother"	*didi*, "elder sister"
bhai, "younger brother"	*bōn*, "younger sister"
śami, "husband"	*bou*, "wife"

For "son" and "daughter," use just *ćhele*, "boy," and *mee*, "girl." The word *bhai*, besides meaning "younger brother," is used freely as a term of address among young people of both sexes.

NAME OF LANGUAGE
Bengali is *Bangla*.

SINHALESE

Sinhalese is the official language of Sri Lanka and the prevailing language among its inhabitants except for a small Tamil-speaking region in the north. It is written in its own alphabet. Romanisation is straightforward.

PRONUNCIATION Vowels:

Long vowels Ā, Ē, II, Ō, Ū are pronounced *ah, eh, ee, oh, oo.*
Á, E, I, O, U are the same sounds shorter.
Unaccented A is the neutral sound in English unstressed syllables, for example, the *a* in "alone."
Ǎ is the short *a* in English "hat," and ǍǍ is the same sound long.

Consonants:
T and D are pronounced with the tongue forward in the position for English *th.*
Ṭ and Ḍ have the tongue back against the roof of the mouth.
Ñ indicates nasalisation of the preceding vowel.
ÑG, ÑD, ÑḌ and M̃B should be regarded as single consonants and consist of G, D, Ḍ and B pronounced so that, when the air stream is stopped preparatory to making the consonant, the nasal passage is kept open. They are distinct from the true double consonants NG, ND, NḌ, MB, which have full N or M sounds. R is slightly trilled.
W and Y are always consonants; W tends to be voiced so that it sounds like *v.*

Stress is more even than in English.

NOUNS The direct form of the noun serves as subject or object, other functions being indicated by endings. The definite article "the" is understood: *minihā,* "the man"; *gǎǎni,* "the woman"; *mála,* "the flower."

For an indefinite article, attach *-ek* to nouns denoting living things, but *-ek* or *-ák* in the case of females; *-ák* always with inanimates. Insert *y* if the noun ends in *e* or *i,* otherwise drop a final vowel: *minihek,* "a man"; *gǎǎniyek* or *gǎǎniyák,* "a woman"; *málák,* "a flower."

Plurals are formed in various ways and are shown in parentheses in the vocabulary. There is no distinction between definite and indefinite: *minissu,* "men" or "the men"; *gǎǎnu,* "women" or "the women"; *mál,* "flowers" or "the flowers."

For indirect object, add *-ṭa* in the singular, *-nṭa* (animate) or *-wálaṭa* (inanimate) in the plural: *minihāṭa,* "to or for the man"; *minissunṭa,* "to or for (the) men"; *málwálaṭa,* "to (the) flowers."

For a possessive, add *-gē* to the singular of an animate noun, *-nge* to the plural; in the case of an inanimate, change the final vowel to *e* in the singular, add *-wála* in the plural: *gǎǎnigē,* "of the woman"; *málwála,* "of (the) flowers."

The singular endings can also be added to the indefinite form: *minihekgē,* "of a man" — but *-ák* becomes *-akaṭa* for indirect object and *-aka* for possessive.

For a form of noun denoting "from" or "by means of," alter the final *-ē* or *-e* of the possessive to *-en,* or in the plural inanimate alter *-wála* to *-wálin.*

For other prepositions, a word is placed after the direct form of the noun: *gedara ǎtulē,* "inside the house."

ADJECTIVES are invariable and precede the noun: *loku minihā,* "the big man"; *táruna gǎǎniyek,* "a young woman."

As predicate, an adjective requires no verb "is" or "are" but comes at the end of the sentence with suffix *-y* (*-uy* after consonants): *Minihā lokuy,* "The man is big"; *Gǎǎni tárunay,* "The woman is young."

13

For a comparative, put *wáḍā*, "more," before the adjective: *hoṅda*, "good," *wáḍā hoṅda*, "better." The object of comparison takes the indirect object ending: *Gǟni minihāṭa wáḍā lokuy*, "The woman is bigger than the man."

For a superlative, place *wáḍāma*, "most," before the adjective or *ma* after it: *wáḍāma loku lámayā*, or *loku ma lámayā*, "the biggest boy."

ADVERBS can be formed from adjectives by adding -*ṭa* or -*in*. (Insert *y* or delete a vowel on the same principles as with noun endings.) Comparatives and superlatives are as for adjectives.

PRONOUNS First person pronouns are *máma* or *máñ*, "I", and *ápi*, "we."

For "you," the simplest forms are *oba* (singular), *obalā* (plural); but second person pronouns are often replaced by personal names or forms of address such as *máháttayā* (to a man), *nōnā* or *nōnā máháttayā* (to a woman).

In the third person use *eyā*, "he, she," *eyālā*, "they," for people; and *ēka*, "it," *ēwā*, "they," for things. There are also special forms *ū* for male animals, *ǟ* for female animals, with common plural *un*.

These third person forms strictly mean "that person," "that thing," . . . and there are parallel forms with prefixed *m*- meaning "this person," "this thing": *meyā*, *mēka*, . . .

All pronouns take endings -*ṭa*, -*gē* in the same way as singular nouns: *eyāṭa*, "to him/her"; *eyālāgē pota*, "their book," etc. There are a few contractions: *máma* (or *máñ*) forms *máṭa*, *mágē*; *ápi* has possessive *ápē*; *ēka* and *mēka* have possessives *ēke* and *mēke*.

Note that "this, these" before nouns is just *mē*, and "that, those" is *ē*; both are invariable.

VERBS The verb comes at the end of the sentence and does not change in form for person or number.

The present tense ends in -*nawā*: *Máma minihā balunawā*, "I see the man"; *Lámayā pān gēnawā*, "The boy is bringing bread."

The direct form of the noun is used even after a verb of motion, when the destination is non-particular: *Gǟni gedara yánawā*, "The woman is going home."

Past tense of each verb is given in parentheses in the vocabulary: *Máma ē minihā bǎluwā*, "I saw that man."

For the future tense, use the present. In the first person only, a future tense indicating intention can be formed by replacing the present tense -*nawā* by -*nnám*: *Ápi gedara yánnám*, "We shall go home."

For a negative verb, place *nǟ*, "not," after the form of the verb obtained by changing the present tense ending -*nawā* to -*nne*, or the past tense -*ā* to -*ē*: *Eyā yánne nǟ*, "He/She is not going"; *Máma ē minihā bǎluwē nǟ*, "I did not see that man."

The verb "be" in the sense of "exist" is *innawā* with animate nouns, *tiyenawā* with inanimate: *Eyā bás innawā*, "He/She is in the bus"; *Poták putuwa tiyenawā*, "There is a book on the chair." (Both have irregular past tenses, *hiṭiyā* and *tibunā* respectively.)

For "has" or "have," use "There is" with the English subject in the indirect object form: *Poták máṭa tiyenawā*, "I have a book." For negative "is not" or "are not," use *ǟtte nǟ* or just *nǟ*: *Máṭa sálli ǟtte nǟ* or *Máṭa sálli nǟ*, "I have no money"; *Máháttayā metana nǟ*, "The man is/was not here" or "You were not here," etc.

The infinitive ends in *-nna* and can indicate purpose, "in order to." For a present participle (English "-ing"), simply drop *-wā* from the present ending *-nawā*: this may translate a relative clause, as *geḍi wikunana gǟni,* "fruit-selling woman," "woman who is selling fruit."

QUESTIONS For a yes/no question, put *da* at the end of the sentence following the verb: *Máháttaya enawā da?,* "Are you coming?" Rarely, *da* alternatively follows a word earlier in the sentence to emphasise it.

An interrogative word such as *káwuda,* "Who?," *mokāda,* "What (animal)?," *mokákda,* "What (thing)?," *kohēda,* "Where?" is usually placed last in the sentence with *da* incorporated as shown; and the verb, if any, has the *-nne* ending: *Eyā yánne kawadāda?,* "When is he going?"

IMPERATIVES For a polite imperative, use the infinitive ending *-nna*: *Ápi ekka enna,* "(Please) come with us."

For a negative, place *epā* after the verb: *Yánna epā,* "Don't go."

For "Let's," use the ending *-mu*: *Geḍi gamu,* "Let's buy some fruit."

NUMERALS The forms given first in the table are those used when a numeral stands alone as in counting or in giving telephone numbers.

In specifying numbers of objects, use the form in parentheses (if any), and add *-denek* in the case of living things, *-ák* for non-living. In the case of living things, "one" and "two" take the special forms *ekkenek, dennek.*

The numeral is placed after the plural form of the noun, even in the case of "one": *minissu ekkenek,* "one man"; *gǟnu dennek,* "two women"; *pot tunák,* "three books." (If in doubt, revert to the simple forms of the numerals, but use them in this way following the plural noun.)

CURRENCY 1 *rupiyál* ("rupees") = 100 *sáta* ("cents"). (These are both plurals in Sinhalese.)

FORMS OF ADDRESS The terms *máháttayā* and *nōnā* (or *nōnā máháttayā*) are used for "sir" and "madam," and are more frequent than their English counterparts.

For "Mr," "Mrs," "Miss," the same terms follow the name; but in this position *máháttayā* is often abbreviated to *máhátá.*

KIN TERMS The commonest (with plurals in parentheses) are:

Tāttā (tāttalā), "father"
ámmā (ámmālā), "mother"
áyyā (áyyalā), "older brother"
ákkā (ákkālā), "older sister"
málli (mállilā), "younger brother"
nángi (nángilā), "younger sister"
putā (puttu), "son"
dū or *duwa (dūlā),* "daughter"
sǎmiyā (sǎmiyō), "husband"
biriňda (biriňdu), "wife"

NAME OF LANGUAGE

The Sinhalese language is *Siňhala*; the country is *Sri Lánkāwa.*

Tamil is the most widely spoken of the Southern Indian languages, with forty million speakers in the state of Tamil Nadu (Madras and south) and three million in Sri Lanka. It is one of the four official languages of Sinagpore and has a significant number of speakers in Fiji.

Tamil is written in its own alphabet. Both pronunciation and grammar have some regional variations, and we use a compromise romanisation.

PRONUNCIATION Vowels:

A, E, I, O are like *ah, eh, ee, aw,* but shorter: U is a rather neutral *er* or *uh* sound with lip-spread. Generally, spread the lips more than in English.

AA, Ē, II, Ō, UU are the same sounds lengthened.

Diphthong AI ordinarily as *igh,* but as short *e* at the end of a word or when unstressed in rapid speech. AU as *ow.*

Consonants:

T, D, N, L are pronounced with the tongue forward against the top teeth.

Ṭ, Ḍ, Ṇ, Ḷ have the tongue curled back against the roof of the mouth.

NG has a following *g* sound as in "finger".

V is between *v* and *w.*

Ẓ has a special sound: curl the tongue well back and intone as for a pure but breathy *rr.* (Some books transcribe this "Ṛ" or "Ḻ".)

Voiced consonants D, Ḍ, G, B in the middle of a word are very lightly pronounced without quite closing the air-stream: D, in particular (with tongue forward), nearly like *th.*

Stress the first syllable of each word: other stresses are fairly even.

Note the following variant pronunciations: (1) (in Indian Tamil only) final M, N, Ṇ may be dropped, with nasalisation of the vowel; (2) final Ḷ is often dropped, particularly from the plural ending *-gaḷ;* (3) S and CH may be both pronounced *s,* or both *ch;* (4) in Sri Lanka, Ẓ becomes like Ḷ, R is between T and Ṭ, and B, D, Ḍ, J, G are unvoiced, that is, like P, T, Ṭ, CH, K.

NOUNS denoting humans are divided into masculine and feminine; all others are neuter. More detailed grammatical distinctions are made in the case of nouns denoting humans than in the case of neuter nouns.

Nouns denoting humans

1. form plurals in *-gaḷ* (or *-kaḷ: -m* changes to *-n-* to give *-ngaḷ*): *paiyan,* "boy," *paiyangaḷ,* "boys";
2. add endings to singular or plural to indicate grammatical function as follows: *-ai* for direct object; *-ku* or *-uku* for indirect object; *-udaiya* for a possessive: *paiyanai,* "boy" (object); *paiyanuku,* "to the boy"; *paiyanudaiya pustagam,* "the boy's book."

The rules of euphony in adding endings are: if the word ends in *e, i* or *ai,* insert *y* before the ending; if it ends in another vowel, insert *v.* (Only *-u* is sometimes dropped.) These rules are quite general in Tamil.

Nouns in *-am* change this to *-at-* before adding endings.

Neuter nouns sometimes take these various endings, particularly when reference is made to a specific thing. However,

1. It is usual to use the same form for plural of a neuter noun as for singular: *viiḍu,* "house" or "houses" — and for object as well as for subject.

2. In place of a possessive, the plain form of the noun (or, in the case of a noun in *-am*, its inflexional base *-atu*) is usual: *viiḍu kadavu*, "door of the house"; *maratu kilai*, "branch of a tree."

3. The ending *-ku* or *-uku* denotes motion towards: *maratuku*, "to the tree."

Other noun-endings include: *-il*, "at, in"; *-irundu*, "from"; *-aal*, "by means of." There are no articles "the" or "a"; but *indu*, "this, these," and *andu*, "that, those," can be used (both invariable); similarly *oru*, "one", "a certain": *indu arai*, "this room"; *andu kaar*, "that car"; *oru mēsai*, "one table," "a (particular) table."

PRONOUNS take endings in the same way as nouns. The following list gives subject form, with object and possessive forms in parentheses. Attach other endings in the same way as for the object form.

"I" ("me," "my")	*naan (yennai, yen)*
"we," etc.	(addressee included) *nam (nammai, nammaḷ)*
	(addressee excluded) *naangaḷ (yengaḷai, yengaḷ)*
"you," etc.	(respectful form for both singular and plural) *niingaḷ (ungaḷai, ungaḷ)*
"he," etc.	*avan (avanai, avan)*
"she," etc.	*avaḷ (avaḷai, avaḷ)*
"it," etc.	*adu (adai, aduku)*
"they," etc.	(humans) *avargaḷ (avargaḷai, avargaḷ)*
	(non-humans) *avaigaḷ (avaigaḷai, avaigaḷuku)*

The forms given for third person, beginning in *a-*, have the meaning of "that man," "that woman," ... and there are corresponding forms in *i-* with the meaning of "this man," ...

Possessives precede the noun: *yen viiḍu*, "my house."

ADJECTIVES are invariable and precede the noun as in English: *periya uur*, "large town."

Applied to a noun, an adjective needs no verb "is" or "are": *Uur periya*, "The town is large."

There is no comparative. For "That is better," simply say *Adu nalla*, "That is good," or *Adu konjam nalla*, "That is rather good." A compared object comes first in indirect object form: *Iduku adu nalla*, "That is better than this."

For an approximation to a superlative, use *romba*, "very": *Adu romba nalla*, "That is very good," "That is the best."

ADVERBS precede the verb.

In the case of adjectives formed from an abstract noun with suffix *-aana* or *-uḷḷa*, an adverb can be formed from the same noun with *-aay*: *aẓagu*, "beauty"; *aẓagaana*, "beautiful"; *aẓagaay*, "beautifully."

VERBS The verb comes at the end of the sentence.

A vocabulary entry such as "*paartu (paarki-)*" for "to see" means that *paartu* is the participle form "seeing" and *paarki-* is the present tense stem, used to form "I see," etc.

(The participle form is used in subordinate clauses but has quite a general sense and might be used, in need, for all purposes.)

For a correct present tense, add endings *-rēn*, etc., to the present stem as in the following example:

"I see", *paarkirēn*   "we see," *paarkirōm*
"you see," *paarkiringaḷ*   "they see" (humans), *paarkiraangaḷ* ·
"he sees," *paarkiraan*   "it sees," "they see" (non-humans), *paarkiradu* or
"she sees", *paarkiraaḷ*   just *paarku*

Note specially the simple forms for all non-humans.

For past tense, delete -*u* from the participle (or add -*n* if it ends in -*i*) and then add endings -*ēn*, etc., as for present tense (omitting *r*): *paartēn*, "I saw", *paartadu*, "it saw," etc.

Form a negative in the present tense by adding -*radillai* to the present stem; the same for all persons and numbers: *paarkiradillai*, "do not see," "does not see."

For a negative participle, replace -*ki* or -*gi* of the present stem with -*aamal* (inserting *y* or *v* if necessary): *paaraamal*, "not seeing."

The infinitive is used with auxiliary verbs or in the sense "in order to." To form it, replace -*ki* by -*ga* (-*ka* after a hard consonant) or -*gi* by -*a*, perhaps inserting *y* or *v*: *paarka*, "to see." (Exception: "to go," present stem *pōgi*-, infinitive *pōga*.)

For a past tense negative, add -*villai* (invariable) to the infinitive: *paarkavillai*, "did not see."

There is a large range of other verb forms, but these will serve simple purposes.

Note the frequent use of impersonal verbs such as *vēṇḍum*, "it is necessary." To translate "I must," put the subject in indirect object form: *Yenaku paarka vēṇḍum*, "I must see."

For senses of the verb "be" other than with adjectives or between nouns, use the verb *irundu (iruki-)*: *Avan viiḍil irukiraan*, "He is in the house." Similarly for "There is": *Bas iruku*, "There is a bus."

For "have," use "There is" with the English subject as indirect object: *Kaapi yenaku iruku*, "I have some coffee."

QUESTIONS For a yes/no question, add -*aa* to the key word in the corresponding statement: *Avan aasiriyar*, "He is a teacher"; *Avan aasiriyaraa?*, "Is he a teacher?" (Insert *y* or *v* if necessary.)

Questions using interrogative words such as *yenge*, "where?", have the same word order as the corresponding statements.

IMPERATIVES For a polite imperative, replace -*ki* or -*gi* of the present stem of the verb with -*ungaḷ*: *Varungaḷ*, "(Please) come." The word "Please" needs no separate translation.

For a polite negative imperative, use -*aadēyungaḷ* instead of -*ungaḷ*: *Pōvaadēyungaḷ*, "(Please) don't go."

For "Let's," use the first person plural future tense of the verb, formed by replacing -*ki*, -*gi* or -*ngi* of the present by -*pōm*, -*vōm* or -*mbōm*: *Pōvōm*, "Let's go."

NUMERALS Use the singular form of the noun after a numeral.

Of the alternative forms for "one," *oru* is used before a noun, *oṇṇu* for other purposes.

Western numerals are general in writing.

CURRENCY In India, 1 *ruubaay* ("rupee") = 100 *paysaa*. In Sri Lanka, 1 *ruubiyal* = 100 *sata*.

FORMS OF ADDRESS The vocative ending -*ē* is common when a noun is used to address a hearer.

TAMIL

There are no regular words for "Mr," "Mrs" and "Miss," but the Hindi *Srii* (or *Sriimaan*), *Sriimati* and *Kumaari* are in increasing use in India. The words *Aiyaa*, "father," and *Ammaa*, "mother," are in common use as "Sir" and "Madam."

Note the use of the particle *ngaḷ* at the end of a sentence or after a key word to indicate respect to an older person or superior.

KIN TERMS

"father," *aiyaa* or *apaa*   "mother," *ammaa*
"older brother," *aṇṇan*   "older sister," *akaa*
"younger brother," *tambi*   "younger sister," *tangai* or *tangachi*
"son," *magan*   "daughter," *magaḷ*
"husband," *kaṇavan*   "wife," *manaivi*

The terms *tambi* and *tangachi* are used as friendly terms of address to children.

NAME OF LANGUAGE
The "l" of "Tamil" is the sound we transcribe ẓ: thus *Tamiẓ*.

EVERYDAY PHRASES

ENGLISH	PERSIAN	HINDI [URDU]
Yes	Bale *Balleh*	Jii hã *Jee hahñ*
No	Na *Nah*	Jii nahĩ *Jee na-heeñ*
Please	Khāhesh mikonam *Kho-hesh mikko-nam*	Mehrbaanii *Meh-hehr-bahnee*
Thank you	Tashakkor mikonam *Tasha-kor mikko-nam*	Śukria *Shookree-a*
Thank you very much	Kheili motashakker *Khaylee mota-sha-kair*	Bahut śukria *Ba-hott shookree-a*
Don't mention it	Chizi nist *Cheezi neest*	Koii baat nahĩ *Koee bahtt na-heeñ*
Excuse me, but . . .	Bebakhshid, . . . *Beybakh-sheed*	Suniye, . . . *Soonyeh*
Excuse me (I'm sorry)	Bebakhshid *Behbakh-sheed*	Maaf kiijiye *Mahf keejyeh*
Excuse me (Do you mind?)	Bebakhshid *Behbakh-sheed*	Maaf kiijiye *Mahf keejyeh*
Pardon? (What did you say?)	Bale? *Balleh?*	Kyaa kahaa? *Kyah ka-hah?*
Wait a moment	Yek daghighe sabr konid *Yehk dahghee-gheh shahb kohneed*	Zaraa ṭhahriye *Za-rrah t'harri-yeh*
Hurry up!	Ajale konid! *Ahjah-leh kohneed!*	Jaldii karo! *Jahldee ka-roh!*
Slowly!	Kond! *Kohnd!*	Dhiire! *D'heereh!*
Stop!	Be'istid! *Beh-iss-teed!*	Roknaa! *Rrok-nah!*
Look out!	Movāzeb bashid! *Mohvaw-zehb bawsheed!*	Dekho! *Dehk-hoh!*
Look!	Negāh konid! *Ne-gawhh kohneed!*	Dekho! *Dehk-hoh!*
How much?	Chand ast? *Chandast?*	Kitnaa? *Kittnah?*
Never mind	Eb nadārad *Ehb nahdo-rad*	Koii baat nahĩ *Koee bahtt na-heeñ*
Come in	Vāred beshavid *Vaw-rehd behsha-veed*	Andar aaiye *Ahnderr igh-yeh*
Come with me	Bā man beya *Baw mun beeya*	Mere saath aaiye *Merreh sahtt igh-yeh*
Good morning	Salām *Sah-lom*	Namaste [Salaam] *Na-mahssteh [Sa-lahm]*
Good afternoon	Salām *Sah-lom*	Namaste [Salaam] *Na-mahssteh [Sa-lahm]*
Good evening	Salām *Sah-lom*	Namaste [Salaam] *Na-mahssteh [Sa-lahm]*
Good-bye (leaving)	Khodā hāfez *Khoda hawfez*	Namaste [Khuda haafiz] *Na-mahssteh [Khooda hahfiz]*
Good-bye (staying)	Khodā hāfez *Khoda hawfez*	Namaste [Khuda haafiz] *Na-mahssteh [Khooda hahfiz]*
Good night	Shab bekher *Shahb be-khair*	Namaste [Khuda haafiz] *Na-massteh [Khooda hahfiz]*
Do you understand?	Moltafet shodid? *Molta-feht shohdeed?*	Kyaa aap samajh gayai? *Kyahp sahmahj ga-yeh?*

EVERYDAY PHRASES

BENGALI	SINHALESE	TAMIL
Hã *Hahñ*	Owu *Oh-oo*	Aamaa *Ahmah*
Na *Nah*	Nǎǎ *Naah*	Illai *Illa*
Anugroho *Onnu-gro-ho*	Kárunākara *Kahrroo-nahka-rra*	Dayavu seydu
		Dahya-voo sehdoo
Dhonnobad *D'honno-bud*	Istutiy *Issttoo-tee*	Nandri *Nahndri*
Bohu dhonnobad	Bohoma istutiy	Romba tanks
Bo-hoo d'honno-bud	*Bo-hohma issttoo-tee*	*Romba ttanks*
Ō kotha bõlben na	Máták karánna epã	Adu paravaayilla
Oh kott'ha bolben nah	*Mahttak ka-ranna eh-pah*	*Ahduh prra-vahyil-la*
Map korben, . . . *Mahp koorrben*	Áwasarai námut, . . .	Mannitukongal, . . .
	Ahwa-sarrigh nah-moot	*Manni-too-kongga*
Ami dukhito *Ahmee dook'heeto*	Sámāwánna kánagātui	Manniyangal
	Sa-mah-wanna	*Mannee-yangga*
	kahna-gah-tooee	
Jadi kichu mone na koren	Sámāwánna *Sa-mah-wanna*	Mannitukongal
Jahddi kee-choo monneh na		*Manni-too-kongga*
korren		
Ki bollen? *Kee Bohlen?*	Nǎwata kiyánna?	Yenna sonningal?
	Na-wahta kee-yanna?	*Yenna son-neengga?*
Ek muhurto dāṛan	Páddák inna *Pah-dahk in-nah*	Oru nimishamirungal
Ehk moohrrto da-rrahn		*Awruh nimi-shañ-roongga*
Taṛataṛi! *Tahra-tahri!*	Ikmán karǎnna!	Avasaram! *Ahva-sa-rahñ!*
	Ikkman ka-rranna!	
Dhire dhire! *D'heereh d'heereh!*	Hemihita! *Hehmee-heetta!*	Meduvaa! *Medduh-vah!*
Thamun! *Ttahmoon!*	Náwatinna! *Nawah-tin-nah!*	Nillu! *Nilluh!*
Dekhō! *Dehk-ho!*	Bálāgenai! *Ba-lahgeh-nigh!*	Anga paaru!
		Ahngga pahruh!
Dekhō! *Dehk-ho!*	Ára bálánna! *Ahra ba-lannah!*	Paaru! *Pahruh!*
Koto dam? *Kottoh dahm?*	Kiiyada? *Keeya-da?*	Yevlavu? *Yevva-la-vuh?*
Jak gie *Jaggeh*	Kámák nǎǎ *Kahmahk naah*	Aagaṭum *Ahga-tooñ*
Aśun *Ah-shoon*	Ǎtul wenna *Ah-tool wen-nah*	Ulle vaangal
		Oolleh vahngga
Amar śathe ćolun	Mát ekka enna *Maht ekka enna*	Yennōda vaangal
Ahmarr shahtteh tjohlun		*Yen-nohda vahngga*
Nomośkar/Salām	Áyubōwan *Ahyoo-bo-wahn*	Guḍ marning
Nomosh-karr/ Sahlam		*Good mawning*
Nomośkar/Salām	Áyubōwan *Ahyoo-bo-wahn*	Guḍ aftarnun
Nomosh-karr/Sahlam		*Good ahftarr-noon*
Nomośkar/Salām	Áyubōwan *Ahyoo-bo-wahn*	Guḍ iivning
Nomosh-karr/Sahlam		*Good eevning*
Aśi, nomośkar/Aśi, khoda hafej	Áyubōwan gehillā ennám	Pōyiṭu varēn
Ahshee, nomosh-karr/Ahshee,	*Ahyoo-bo-wahn geh-hil-la*	*Poyit-oowa-rehñ*
k'hohda hahfez	*ehn-nam*	
Aśun, nomośkar/Aśun, khoda hafej	Áyubōwan *Ahyoo-bo-wahn*	Pōyiṭu vaangal
Ahshoon, nomosh-karr/Ahshoon,		*Poyit-oo vahngga*
k'hohda hahfez		
Nomośkar/Khoda hafej	Áyubōwan *Ahyoo-bo-wahn*	Guḍ naiṭ *Good night*
Nomosh-karr/K'hohda hahfez		
Bōjhen ki? *Bohj'hen kee?*	Tērenawā da?	Puriyudaa?
	Tehrreh-na-wah da?	*Poorriyu-dah?*

21

ENGLISH	PERSIAN	HINDI [URDU]
I understand	Man mifahmam	Maĩ samajh gayaa
	Mun meefahh-mam	*Mañ sahmahj ga-yah*
I don't understand	Man nemifahmam	Maĩ nahĩ samajhaa
	Mun nehmee-fahh-mam	*Mañ na-heeñ sahmj-hah*
All right (I'll do it)	Besyār khub *Bess-yawrr khoob*	Bahut aćchaa *Ba-hotta-chah*
It's all right	Khub ast *Khoobasst*	Thiik hai *T'heek heh*

NUMERALS

zero	٠ sefr *seffrr*	٠ sifr *siffrr*
one	١ yek *yehk*	١ ek *ehk*
two	٢ do *doh*	٢ do *doh*
three	٣ se *seh*	٣ tiin *tteen*
four	٤ chahār *cha-hawrr*	٤ ćaar *tjahr*
five	٥ panj *pun-ch*	٥ pãć *pahñch*
six	٦ shesh *shesh*	٦ che *cheh*
seven	٧ haft *hahft*	٧ saat *sahtt*
eight	٨ hasht *hahsht*	٨ aath *aht*
nine	٩ noh *nohh*	٩ nau *naw*
ten	١٠ dah *da-hh*	١٠ das *dahss*
eleven	yāzdah *yozzda-hh*	gyaarah *gyahra*
twelve	davāzdah *doh-vozzda-hh*	baarah *bahra*
thirteen	sizdah *seezda-hh*	terah *ttehra*
fourteen	chahārdah *cha-hawrrda-hh*	ćaudrah *tjawdra*
fifteen	pānzdah *ponzda-hh*	pandrah *pahndrra*
sixteen	shānzdah *shonzda-hh*	solah *sawla*
seventeen	hevdah *hehvda-hh*	satrah *sahttrra*
eighteen	hejdah *hehzhda-hh*	athaarah *a-tahra*
nineteen	nuzdah *noozda-hh*	unniis *oon-neess*
twenty	bist *bist*	biis *beess*
twenty-one	bist o yek *bisto yehk*	ikkiis *ik'kiss*
thirty	si *see*	tiis *tteess*
forty	chehel *cheh-hl*	ćaaliis *tjahliss*
fifty	panjāh *panjohh*	paćaas *pa-tjahss*
sixty	shast *shahst*	saath *saht-hh*
seventy	haftād *hufftawd*	sattar *suttrr*

EVERYDAY PHRASES

BENGALI	SINHALESE	TAMIL
Bōjhi *Bohj'hee*	Máta těrenawā *Mahta tehrreh-na-wah*	Puriyudu *Poorriyu-duh*
Bōjhi na *Bohj'hee nah*	Máta těrenne nǎǎ *Mahta tehrreh-neh naah*	Puriyillai *Poorri-yilla*
Aćcha *Aht-chah*	Hā *Hah*	Ō *Oh*
Thik aćhe *T'heek a-cheh*	Ēka okkoma hári *Ehka awkko-ma hahrree*	Sari *Sarree*

NUMERALS

০ śunno *shoonoh*	binduwa *Been-dooa*	sunnam *soon-num*
১ ek *ehk*	eka *ehka*	onnu, oru *awn-nuh, awruh*
২ dui *dooee*	deka *dekka*	rendu *rrenduh*
৩ tin *tteen*	tuna (tun) *ttoona (ttoon)*	muunu *moonuh*
৪ ćar *tjahrr*	hátara *hahtta-ra*	naalu *nahluh*
৫ pāć *pahñch*	páhá (pás) *pah-ha (pahss)*	anju *anjuh*
৬ ćhoe *choh-eh*	háya *hahya*	aaru *ahrruh*
৭ śat *shahtt*	háta (hát) *hahtta (hahtt)*	yezu *yezhruh*
৮ at *aht*	áta *ahta*	yetu *yettuh*
৯ noe *naw-eh*	náwaya (náwa) *nahwa-ya (nahwa)*	ombadu *oomba-duh*
১০ doś *dosh*	dáháya *da-hahya*	patu *pattuh*
egarō *egga-rroh*	ekolahá (ekolos) *eh-kohla-ha (ehko-loss)*	padinonnu *padda-nonnuh*
barō *bahrro*	dolahá (dolos) *dohla-ha (dohloss)*	pannandu *pa-nanduh*
terō *ttehrro*	dáhátuna (dáhátun) *dahh-ttoona (dahh-ttoon)*	padimuunu *padda-moonuh*
ćōddo *tjoddo*	dáháhátara *dahh-hahtta-ra*	padinaalu *padda-nahluh*
ponerō *ponneh-ro*	páhálowa (páhálos) *pa-hahlo-wa (pa-hahloss)*	padinanju *padda-nanjuh*
śolo *shohlo*	dáhásaya *dahh-sahya*	padinaaru *padda-nahruh*
śoterō *shotta-roh*	dáháháta (dáhá hát) *dahh-hahtta (dahh haht)*	padinezu *padda-nezhruh*
atharō *aht-a-roh*	dáhá áta *dahh-ahta*	padinetu *padda-nehtuh*
uniś *oon-neesh*	dáhá náwaya (dáhánawa) *dahh nahwa-ya (dahh-nahwa)*	patombadu *pat-tom-bawduh*
kuri *koorih*	wissa *veessa*	irubadu *irra-baduh*
ekuś *ehkoosh*	wisi eka *veessi ehka*	irubatonnu *irra-ba-ttonnuh*
triś *tteereesh*	tiha (tis) *ttee-ha (tteess)*	mupadu *moopa-duh*
ćolliś *tjolleesh*	hátaliha (hátalis) *hah-ttahli-ha (hahtta-leess)*	naapadu *nahpa-duh*
ponćaś *pon-tjahsh*	pánáhá (pánás) *pahna-ha (pahnahss)*	ambadu *ahmba-duh*
śat *shaht*	háta *hat-ta*	arubadu *arra-b'duh*
śottor *shottoorr*	hắttǎǎwa (hắttǎ) *hat-ttaa-wa (hat-ttaa)*	yezubadu *yezhru-b'duh*

23

NUMERALS

ENGLISH	PERSIAN	HINDI [URDU]
eighty	hashtād *hushtawd*	assii *a-ssee*
ninety	navad *nahvad*	navve *nuvveh*
a hundred	sad *sahd*	sau *saw*
a hundred and one	sad o yek *sahdo yehk*	ek sau ek *ehk saw ehk*
a hundred and ten	sad o dah *sahdo da-hh*	ek sau das *ehk saw dahss*
two hundred	devist *deh-veest*	do sau *doh saw*
a thousand	hezār *heh-zawr*	ek hazaar *ehk ha-zahr*
ten thousand	dah hezār *dahheh-zawr*	das hazaar *dahss ha-zahr*
a hundred thousand	sad hezār *sahd heh-zawr*	ek laakh *ehk lahkh*
a million	melyun *mehlyoon*	das laakh *dahss lahkh*
ten million	dah melyun *da-hh mehlyoon*	ek karoṛ *ehk ka-roorr*
a half	nesf *nehssf*	aadhaa *ahd'hah*
... point *(decimal)*ʹ...	... momaiyez ... *mohmigh-yez*	... daśmalav *... dahshma-lahv*

DAYS OF THE WEEK

Sunday	yek shambe *yehk shahmbeh*	ravivaar [itvaar] *rrahvee-vahr [ittvahr]*
Monday	do shambe *doh shahmbeh*	somvaar [piir] *som-vahr [peerr]*
Tuesday	se shambe *seh shahmbeh*	mangalvaar [mangal] *mahnggal-vahr [mahnggal]*
Wednesday	chahār shambe *cha-hawrr shahmbeh*	budhvaar [buddh] *boodd-hvahr [boodd-hh]*
Thursday	panj shambe *pun-ch shahmbeh*	viirvaar [jumeraat] *veerr-vahr [jooma-raht]*
Friday	jom'e, ādine *johm-'eh, awdee-neh*	śukravaar [jumaa] *shookra-vahr [joo-mah]*
Saturday	shambe *shahmbeh*	śanivaar (hafta) *shahnee-vahr [huffta]*

MONTHS

January	zhānviye *zhahnvee-yeh*	janvarii *janva-rree*
February	fevriye *fehvree-yeh*	farvarii *farrva-rree*
March	mārs *morrss*	maarć *mahrtj*

24

NUMERALS

BENGALI	SINHALESE	TAMIL
aśi *ahshee*	ásūwa (ásū) *ah-soowa (ah-soo)*	yembadu *yemba-duh*
nobboi *nobboy*	ánūwa (ánū) *ah-noowa (ah-noo)*	tonnuuru *tton-oorruh*
ek śo, ek śato *ehk sho, ehk shahto*	eka siiya *ehka seeyah*	nuuru *noorruh*
ek śo ek, ek śato ek	eka siiya eka *ehka seeya ehka*	nuuti onnu *nootti awn-nuh*
ehk sho ehk, ehk shahto ehk		
ek śo doś, ek śato doś	eka siiya dáháya	nuuti patu *nootti pattuh*
ehk sho dosh, ehk shahto dosh	ehka seeya da-hahya	
dui śo, dui śato	desiiya *dess-seeyah*	irunuuru *irra-noorruh*
doosho, dooee shahto		
ek hajar *ehk hahjar*	ekdāhá (dās) *ehk da-hah (dahss)*	aayiram *ahy'rram*
doś hajar *dosh hahjar*	dáhá dāhá *da-hah da-hah*	pataayiram *patt-ahy'rram*
ek lakh, ek lokkho	eka láksaya *ehka lahk-sehya*	lacham *latcham*
ehk lahk, ehk lokk'hoh		
doś lakh, doś lokkho	dáha láksaya *dah-ha lahk-sehya*	pati lacham *patti-latcham*
dosh lahk, dosh lokk'hoh		
ek kōṭi, ek krōr	kōtiya *koh-tteeya*	kōḍi *kawdee*
ehk kohti, ehk kroorr		
adh *ahd'h*	bágaya *bah-geya*	arai *ahreh*
... dośomik ... *dosho-mik*	... dásama ... *dahssa-ma*	... puḷḷi ... *pool-lee*

DAYS OF THE WEEK

Robibar *Rohbi-barr*	Iridā *Eeree-dah*	nyaayitukizamai *nyahy'tuh kizhra-ma*
Śōmbar *Shom-barr*	Sañdudā *Sandoo-dah*	tingatkizamai *ttingga'kizhra-ma*
Mongolbar *Mongul-barr*	Añgaharuwādā *Ahngga-hahroo-ah-dah*	sevvaaykizamai *sev-vigh kizhra-ma*
Budhbar *Bood'h-barr*	Badādā *Bahd-dah-dah*	budangizamai *boo-ddahng-gizhra-ma*
Brihośpotibar *Breehosh-potti-barr*	Braháspatindā *Bra-ahsspa-tteen-dah*	viyaazakizamai *v'yazhr kizhra-ma*
Śukrobar *Shookrro-barr*	Sikurādā *Sikkoo-rah-dah*	vellikizamai *verli kizhra-ma*
Śonibar *Shonni-barr*	Senasurādā *Senna-soo-rah-dah*	sanikizamai *sahni kizhra-ma*

MONTHS

Januari *Jannoo-ari*	Janawāri *Janna-wahree*	Januvari *Jannoo-w'ree*
Phebruari *Ffebrroo-ari*	Pebarawāri *Pebba-ra-wahree*	Februvari *Febboo-w'ree*
Maċ *Mahch*	Mārtu *Mahr-ttoo*	Maarchu *Mahrch*

25

MONTHS

ENGLISH	PERSIAN	HINDI [URDU]
April	avril *ah-vreel*	aprail *a-prehl*
May	mai *may*	maii *migh-ee*
June	zhu'n *zhoo-ann*	juun *joon*
July	zhuiye *zhooi-yeh*	julaaii *ju-ligh-ee*
August	ut *oot*	agast *a-gahst*
September	septámbr *sep-tahmbrr*	sitambar *si-ttambarr*
October	oktobr *ok-tawbrr*	aktuubar *a-ttoobarr*
November	novámbr *no-vahmbrr*	navambar *na-vambarr*
December	desámbr *dess-ahmbrr*	disambar *di-sambarr*

SENTENCES

1. Is there someone here who speaks English, please? A little. I speak only a little _____.

1. Khähesh mikonam äyä injä shakhsi hast ke Englisi sohbat konad? Kami. Man faghat kami _____ sohbat mikonam. *Kho-hesh mikko-nam awyaw in-jaw shucksi hahst keh eng-glissy soh-butt kohnad? Kummy. Man fa-ghutt kummy _____ soh-butt mikko-nam.*

1. Suniye, kyaa yahĩ koii Angrezii bolnevaalaa hai? Zaraa-sii. Maĩ zaraa-sii _____ boltaa/-tii hũ. *Soonyeh, kyah ya-heeñ koee Ahng-grehzee bolneh-vahla heh? Zrrah-see. Mañ zrrah-see _____ bolltta/-ttee hooñ.*

2. I want to go to _____. Is there a bus (an aeroplane, a taxi)? Yes, there is. No, there is not.

2. Meil däram beravam be _____. Äyä otobus (haväpeimä, täksi) hast? Bale, hast. Na, nist. *Mehl daw-rum behra-vam beh _____. Awyaw awtaw-booss (havaw-paymaw, tawksi) hast? Baleh, hast. Nah, neest.*

2. Maĩ _____ jaanaa ćaahtaa/-tii hũ. Kyaa koii bas (havaaii jahaaz, taiksii) hai? Jii hã, hai. Nahĩ, nahĩ hai. *Mañ _____ jahna tjah-htta/-httee hooñ. Kyah koee bahss (ha-vigh ja-hahz, takksee) heh? Jee hahñ, heh. Na-heeñ, na-heeñ heh.*

3. Where is the bus (the railway station, the ticket office)? It is here (there, over there).

3. Otobus (Istgähe ghatär, Gisheye belit forushi) kojäst? Injä (Änjä, Dar änjä) ast. *Awtaw-booss (Eest-gawheh ghat-awr, Ghee-shehyeh be-leet fooroo-shee) ko-jawst? In-jaw (Awn-jaw, Da-rawn-jaw) asst.*

3. Bas (Gaarika stešan, Tikat ghar) kahä hai? Yahã (Vahã, Vahã) hai. *Bahss (Gahrika stehshan, Tikkat g'harr) ka-hahñ heh? Ya-hahñ (Va-hahñ, Va-hahñ) heh.*

26

MONTHS

BENGALI	SINHALESE	TAMIL
Epril *Ehpreel*	Apriyel *Ahp-reel*	Epral *Ehprahl*
Me *Meh*	Mǎyi *Meigh*	Mè *Meh*
Jun *Joon*	Jūni *Joonee*	Juun *Joon*
Julai *Joo-ligh*	Jūli *Joolee*	Juuḷai *Joo-leh*
Ogaṣṭ *Oggast*	Agōsto *A-gawsstoh*	Ogaṣṭ *Awgast*
Septembor *Sep-temboorr*	Sǎptǎmbara *Sap-tambrra*	Siṭambar *Set-ṭembarr*
Oktobor *Ok-tohboorr*	Oktōbara *Awk-tohbrra*	Akṭōbar *Ahk-tohbarr*
Nobhembor *Noh-b'hemboorr*	Novǎmbara *No-vambrra*	Navambar *Na-vembarr*
Ḍiśembor *Dis-emboorr*	Desǎmbara *Dee-sambrra*	Disambar *Di-sembarr*

SENTENCES

1. Map korben, ekhane Ingraji bolte pare, emon keu aćhe? Ektu ektu. Ami ektu ——— adhtu bolte pari.
Mahp koorrben, ek'hahneh ing-grahjee bollteh pahreh, emmon kyoo a-cheh? Ehktoo-ehktoo. Ahmee ehktoo ——— ahd'ttoo bollteh pahree.

1. Kárunākara, Ingirisi kátā karánna kenek metana innawā da? Ṭikák puluwán. Máṭa ṭikák witara ——— kátā karánna puluwán.
Kahrroo-nahka-rra, Inggrissi ka-tahkarr-na kennek mehtta-na inna-wah da? Tikkahk pooloo-wahn. Mahta tikkahk witta-ra ——— ka-tahkarra-na pooloo-wahn.

1. Inge yaarukaavadu Inglish pēsa teriyumaa? Konjam. Konjam ——— taan yenaku teriyum.
Inga yahra-kahva-duh Ingglish pehsa terri-yoo-mah? Konjoñ. Konjoñ ——— tahñ yenna-kuh terri-yuñ.

2. Ami ——— e jete ćai. Baş (Urōjahaj,Ṭaksi) aćhe ki? Hã, aćhe. Na, nei.
Ahmee ——— eh jetteh tjigh. Bahss (Ooro-ja-hahz, Takksi) a-cheh kee? Hahñ, a-cheh. Nah, neigh.

2. Máṭa ——— -ṭa yánna ōnǎǎ. Bás-ekàk (Áhásiyántrāwák, Táksiyák) tiyenawā da? Owu, tiyenawā. Nǎǎ, metana nǎǎ.
Mahta ——— -ta yanna oh-naah. Bahss-ehkak (Ah-ahsee-yantrr-ahwak, Takksee-ak) tee-yenna-wah da? Oh-oo, te-yenna-wah. Naah, metta-na naah.

2. Naan ——— -uku pōga vēnḍum. Inda idatuku baş (yerōplen, ṭaaksi) pōgumaa? Aamaa. Illai.
Nahn ——— -u-kuh pawga vehnduñ. Inda idda-tu-kuh bahss (yehro-plen, taaksi) pawgoo-mah? Ahmah. Illa.

3. Baş (Rel estiśon,Ṭikeṭ ghor) kothai? Eṭa ekhane (okhane, oikhane).
Bahss (Rehl ee-stehshon, Tikket g'horr) kot'high? Ehta ehk'hahneh (ohk'hahneh, oyk'hahneh).

3. Bás-eka (Dumriya pola, Bálapátra (kántōruwa) kohēda? Eka metana (átana, áháre) tiyenawā.
Bahss-ehka (Doomre-ya pohla, bahla-pahtrra kahn-tohroo-wa) ko-hehdah? Ehka metta-na tee-yenna-wah.

3. Baş (Ṭreyin stēshan,Ṭikaṭ aafis) yenge? Inge (Ange, Ange) iruku.
Bahss (Treh-in stehshahn, Tikkat ahfis) yengga? Ingga (Ahngga, Ahngga) irruh-kuh.

27

SENTENCES

ENGLISH	PERSIAN	HINDI [URDU]
4. How do I get to the airport (to the town)? Go that way. Go straight on (to the left, to the right).	4. Chetour man mitavānam be forudgāh (be shahr) beresam? Be ān taraf beravid. Mostaghim (Be tarafe chap, Be tarafe rāst) beravid. *Che-toor man meeta-vawnam beh for-oodgawhh (beh shawhrr) behreh-sam? Beh awn ta-ruff berra-veed. Moss-tughhim (Beh ta-ruffeh chup, Beh ta-ruffeh rawsst) berra-veed.*	4. Maĩ erodrom (śahar) kaise jaa saktaa/-tii hũ? Aap us taraf jaaiye. Aap siidhe (baayĩ taraf, daayĩ taraf) jaaiye. *Mañ ehrro-drrohm (sha-harr) kasseh jah saktta/-ttee hooñ? Ahp ooss tarrff (ba-eeñ tarrff, da-eeñ tarrff) jigh-yeh.*
5. Would you take my baggage to the bus, please. There is just one bag. There are two bags and that bundle.	5. Momken ast khāhesh konam shomā asbābhāye man rā dar otobus begozārid. Faghat yek kif ast. Do kif ast va ān baste. *Mom-kennast kho-hesh kawnam sho-maw assbawb-hawyeh man raw darr awtaw-booss beggaw-zawreed. Fa-ghutt yehk keefasst. Doh keefasst va awn bassteh.*	5. Mere saamaan ko bas mẽ rak diijiye. Sirf ek baks hai. Do bakse aur voh poṭlii haĩ. *Merreh sahmahn ko bahss meñ rahk deejyeh. Sirrf ehk bahks heh. Doh bahksseh awr vo pot-lee hehñ.*
6. When does the bus go? Show me, please. The bus is late. The bus has already gone.	6. Otobus kei miravad? Khāhesh mikonam be man neshān bedehid. Otobus ta'khir dārad. Otobus ghablan rafte ast. *Awtaw-booss keh meera-vad? Kho-hesh mikko-nam beh man ne-shon behda-heed. Awtaw-booss tah-kheer dawrad. Awtaw-booss ghab-lann roffteh asst.*	6. Bas kab jaaegii? Dikhaaiye. Bas ko der ho gayii hai. Bas ćalii gayii hai. *Bahss kahb jah-eh-ghee? Dee-kigh-yeh. Bahss ko dehrr ho ga-yee heh. Bahss tjalee ga-yee heh.*
7. A ticket for one person (for two persons) to ———, please. Two adults and one child. First class. Tourist class.	7. Khāhesh mikonam belit barāye yek nafar (barāye do nofar) be ———. Do nafar bozorg va yek bache. Daraje yek. Daraje do. *Kho-hesh mikko-nam beh-leet ba-rawyeh yehk naffahr (ba-rawyeh doh naffahr) beh ———. Doh naffahr bo-zorrg va yehk bah-cheh. Darra-jeh yehk. Darra-jeh doh.*	7. Ek ṭikaṭ (Do ṭikaṭ) ——— ke liye de diijiye. Do puure aur ek baććaa. Farsṭ klas. Ṭuriṣṭ klas. *Ehk tikkat (Doh tikkat) ——— keh-lyeh deh-deejyeh. Doh pooreh awr ehk ba-chah. Farst klahss. Toorrist klahss.*
8. Excuse me, what time is it? Two o'clock. Ten past two. Half past two. Ten to three.	8. Bebakhshid, sā'at chand ast? Sā'ate do. Dah daghighe ba'd az do. Do va nim. Dah daghighe be se. *Behbakh-sheed saw'aht chandast? Saw-atteh doh. Dahh dagheh-gheh ba'ud azz doh. Dohvah neem. Dahh dahgheh-gheh beh seh.*	8. Suniye, kyaa vakt hai? Do baje. Do baj ke das minaṭ. Saarhe do baje. Tiin baj ne me das minaṭ. *Soonyeh, kyah vahktt heh? Doh bahjeh. Doh bahdj keh dahss minnat. Sahrrheh doh bahjeh. Tteen bahdj neh meh dahss minnat.*

SENTENCES

BENGALI	SINHALESE	TAMIL

4. Ami ki kore biman bondore (śohore) jai? Oi pothe jan. Ek bare śōja (bā dike, dan dike) jan. Ahmee kee korreh beemahn bon-dorreh (sho-horreh) jigh? Aw-ee pott'heh jahn. Ehk bahreh shohjah (bahñ dikkeh, dahn dikkeh) jahn.

4. Máma kohomada guwán totupolata (nagarayata) yánne? Ara disáwen yánna. Kelin (Wámata hári, Dákunata hári) yánna. Mahma koh-ohma-da goo-wahn tohtoo-pohla-ta (nahga-rrahya-ta) yan-neh? Ahrra dee-sahwen yan-nah. Kehleen (Vahma-ta harree, Dahkna-ta harree) yan-na.

4. Yepadi vērpōrtuku (nagaratuku) pōga mudiyum? Apadi pōngal. Nēre (Idadu, Valadu) pōngal. Yeppa-ddi yairr-pawrrtuh-kuh (nagga-rratuh-kuh) pawga mooddi-yuñ? Ahpa-ddi pawngga. Nehrra (Idda-duh, Vahla-duh) pawngga.

5. Anugroho kore amar malpotrogulo base nie jaben ki? Śudhu matro ekti beg. Duto matro beg ar oi bandil-ta. Onnu-gro-ho korreh ahmarr mahl-pottrru-gooloh bahsseh nee-eh jahben kee? Shood'hoo mahttro ehktee beg. Ddoottoh mahttro beg ahr aw-ee bahn-dilta.

5. Kárunákara, mágē bádu bás-ekata árán yánna. Eka bǎg-ekai tiyenne. Bǎg dekai, ára bádumitiyai tiyenne. Kahrroo-nahka-rra, mahgeh bahdoo bahss-ehka-ta ahran yan-na. Ehka bag-ekigh tee-yen-neh. Bag dekigh, ahrra bahdoo-meeti-yigh tee-yen-neh.

5. Yen saamaanai basuku yeditu pōngal. Oru payi taan iruku. Rendu payi, anda katai iruku. Yen sahman-a bahssu-kuh yeddi-too pongga. Awruh pahyee ttahn irruh-kuh. Rrenduh pahyee, ahnda kahtta irruh-kuh.

6. Bas kokhon charbe? Anugroho kore dekhie din. Bas jete deri hobe. Bas itimodhe charle geche. Bahss kok'hon charrbeh? Onnu-gro-ho korreh ddek'hee-eh ddin. Bahss jetteh dehree hobbeh. Bahss itti-modd'heh charleh gehcheh.

6. Kiiyata da bás-eka yánne? Kárunákara máta penánna. Bás-eka párákkui. Bás-eka gihillá. Keeya-ta da bahss-ehka-ta ttee-yen-neh? Kahrroo-nahka-rra mahta peh-nahn-nah. Bahss-ehka pahrra-kwee. Bahss-ehka ghee-eel-lah.

6. Bas yepo ingērundu kilambum? Niingal yenaku kaatungal. Bas pindi varugiradu. Bas munnādiye pōyidutu. Bahss yehpo ingga-roonduh killañ-booñ? Neengga yenna-kuh kahtung-ga. Bahss pindee vahru-girra-duh. Bahss moon-nahdi-yeh poy-iddu-tuh.

7. Anugroho kore —— porjonto ek khana (du khana) tiket din to? Duta phul ar ekta haph. Prothom sreni. Porjōtok sreni. Onnu-gro-ho korreh —— porr-jontoh ehk k'hahnah (doo k'hahnah) tikket dintoh? Doota ffool ahr ehkta hahff. Prot'hom srennih. Porr-jottok srennih.

7. Kárunákara, ——-ta ekke-nakuta (dedenákuta) bálapátra denna. Wedihiti dedenek sáhá lámayek. Pálaweni pántiya. Sánchāraka pántiya. Kahrroo-nahka-rra, ——-ta ehk-keh-nahkoo-ta (dehdeh-nahkoo-ta) balla-pahtrra den-na. Veddi-heetee dehdeh-nek sa-hah lahma-yek. Palla-wehnee pahn-tteeya. Sahn-chahrra-ka pahn-tteeya.

7. Oru tikat (Rendu tikat) —— -uku kōdungal. Rendu ful tikat, oru haaf tikat. Fast kilaas. Tuurist kilaas. Awruh tikkat (Rrenduh tikkat) ——-u-kuh ko-ddungga. Rrenduh fool tikkat, awruh hahf tikkat. Farst ki-lahss. Toorist ki-lahss.

8. Map korben, ekhon śomoe koto? Duta baje. Duta beje doś minit. Arai-ta. Tinta bajte doś minit baki. Mahp koorrben, ehk'hon shommoi kottoh? Doota bahjeh. Doota bejjeh dosh minnit. A-righta. Ttinta bazhteh dosh minnit bahki.

8. Áwasarai, welāwa kiyada? Dekai. Dekai winádi dáháyai. Dekai winádi tihai. Tunata winádi dáháyai. Ahwa-sa-reigh, veh-lahva keeya-da? Deh-kigh. Deh-kigh vee-nahdi daha-yigh. Deh-kigh vee-nahdi ttee-high. Ttoona-ta vee-nahdi daha-yigh.

8. Taim yenna, aagudungal? Rendu mani. Rendu patu. Rendu mupadu. Rendu ambadu. Tighm ye-nah ahgoo-doongga? Rrenduh ma-nee. Rrenduh pahttuh. Rrenduh moo-pooduh. Rrend'ahmba-duh.

SENTENCES

ENGLISH	PERSIAN	HINDI [URDU]
9. Take me to a hotel (to the ——— Hotel). Is this (that) the hotel? How far is it?	9. Man rā be yek hotel (be Hotele ———) bebarid. Ayā in (ān) hotel ast? Che ghadr dur ast? *Man raw beh yehk ho-tell (beh ho-telleh ———) behba-reed. Awyaw een (awn) ho-tell asst? Che ghahdrr doorasst?*	9. Aap mujhe ek hotal (——— hotal) le jaaiye. Kyaa yeh (voh) hotal hai? Kitne duur hai? *Ahp moojeh ehk hohtal (——— hohtal) leh jigh-yeh. Kyah yehh (vohh) hohtal heh? Kittneh doorr heh?*
10. Have you a single room (a double room)? May I see the room? I don't like that room. I like this room.	10. Āyā shomā otāghe yek nafare (otāghe do nafare) dārid? Momken ast man otāgh rā bebinam? Man ān otāgh rā dust nadāram. Man in otāgh rā dust dāram. *Awyaw she-maw oh-tawgheh yehk na-fahreh (oh-tawgheh doh na-fahreh) dawreed? Momkennast man oh-tawgh raw behbee-nam? Man on oh-tawgh raw doost nahdaw-ram. Man in oh-tawgh doost dawram.*	10. Kyaa aap ke paas singil kamraa (dabal kamraa) hai? Kyaa maĩ kamraa dekh saktaa/-tii hū? Voh kamraa mujhe pasand nahī. Yeh kamraa pasand hai. *Kyah ahp keh pahss singgil kamrrah (dahbal kamrrah) heh? Kyah mañ kamrrah dehkh saktta/-ttee hooñ? Vohh kamrrah moojeh pasahnd na-heeñ. Yehh kamrrah pasahnd heh.*
11. Could I have the key of my room, please? Are there any letters for me (for us)?	11. Khāhesh mikonam, momken ast kelide otāgham rā begiram? Barāye man (Barāye mā) hich nāme hast? *Kho-hesh mikko-nam, mom-kennast keh-leedeh oh-tawgham raw behgee-ram? Ba-rawyeh man (Ba-rawyeh maw) heech nawmeh hast?*	11. Mere kamre ke ćaabii de diijiye. Kyaa mere liye (hamare liye) koii khat haī? *Mehreh kamrreh keh tjahbee deh-deejyeh. Kyah mehreh lee-yeh (ha-mahreh lee-yeh) koee khahtt hehñ?*
12. Could I speak to ———, please? It has to do with ———. It is very important.	12. Khāhesh mikonam mitavānam bā ——— sohbat konam? Marbut be ——— ast. Kheili mohemm ast. *Kho-hesh mikko-nam, meeta-vawnam baw ——— soh-butt kohnam? Marrboot beh ——— asst. Khaylee mo-hemmast.*	12. Kyaa maĩ ——— se baat kar saktaa/-tii hū? ——— ke baabat hai. Bahut zaruurii hai. *Kyah mañ ——— seh bahtt kahr saktta/-ttee hooñ? ——— keh bahbatt heh. Ba-hott za-rrooree heh.*
13. How much is this? I would like to buy this, please. That is too dear. I don't want it.	13. Gheimate in chand ast? Khāhesh mikonam man māyelam inrā bekharam. Ān kheili gerān ast. Man anrā nemikhāham. *Gheh-matteh een chandast? Kho-hesh mikko-nam man maw-yellam inraw bekha-ram. Awn khaylee ghe-rawn ast. Man awnraw nemmi-khawham.*	13. Yeh kitnaa ka hai? Maĩ isko khariidnaa ćaahtaa/-tii hū. Voh zyaadaa mahãgaa hai. Maĩ yeh nahī ćaahtaa/-tii hū. *Yehh kittnah kah heh? Mañ issko kha-rreednaa tjah-htta/-httee hooñ. Vohh zyahda ma-hañga heh. Mañ yehh na-heeñ tjah-htta/-httee hooñ.*

SENTENCES

BENGALI	SINHALESE	TAMIL

9. Amake ekta hotele (——
Hotele) nie jan. Etai ki (śei) hotel?
Ekhan theke koto dure?
Ahma-keh ehkta hoh-telleh
(—— Hoh-telleh) nee-eh jahn.
Eh-teigh kee (sheigh) hoh-tell?
Ehk'hahn ttehkeh kottoh
ddoorreh?

9. Máwa hótalēkata (——
Hótalēta) geniyánna. Mēkada
(Ára) hótalē? Ēka kopamana
durada?
Mahva hohtal-ehka-ta (——
Hohtal-ehta) gehnee-ann-na.
Mehka-da (Arra) hohtal-eh?
Ehka kohpa-ma-na ddoorra-da?

9. Hótaluku (—— Hótaluku)
azitu pōngat. Idu (Adu) anda
hótallaa? Yevlavu dōram?
Hohta-luhkuh (——
Hohta-luhkuh) azhri-ttuh
pongga. Idduh (Ahdduh) ahnda
hohta-lah? Yevva-lahvuh
dawrañ?

10. Ekjoner (Dujoner) kamra
ache? Kamrata dekhte ćai. Oi
kamrata ami poćhondo kōri na.
Ami ei kamra poćhondo kōri.
Ehk-jonnehr (Doo-jonnehr)
kamrra a-cheh? Kamrra-ta
dehk'hteh tjigh. Aw-ee
kamrra-ta ahmee po-chondoh
kohree nah. Ahmee eigh kamrra
po-chondoh kohree.

10. Táni kámarayák (Dedenākuta
sudusu kámarayák) tiyenawá da?
Máta kámare bäliyahäkida?
Máma kámareta ákämäti. Máma
kámareta kämäti.
Ttahni kahma-ra-yahk
(Ddehdeh-na-kootta soodoo-soo
kahma-ra-yahk) tteeya-na-
wahda? Mahta kahma-reh
ballee-ya-hakki-da? Mahma
kahma-reh-ta ahka-ma-tee.
Mahma kahma-reh-ta
kamma-tee.

10. Singil ruum (Dabil ruum)
irukaa? Naan ruum pakalaamaa?
Anda ruum pidikalai. Inda ruum
pidikudu.
Singgil rroom (Dahbil rroom)
irruh-kah? Nahn rroom
pahka-la-mah? Ahnda rroom
pi-dikka-leh. Inda rroom
pi-dikkuh-duh.

11. Anugroho kore amar rumer
ćabita deben ki? Amar (Amader)
kōno ćithi potro ache ki?
Onnu-gro-ho korreh ahmar
roomerr tjahbee-ta ddehben kee?
Ahmarr (Ah-mahderr) kohnoh
tjeet'hee pohtrro a-cheh kee?

11. Kárunākara, mágē kámare
yátura máta gáta häkida? Máta
(Ápita) liyum tiyenawá da?
Kahrroo-nahka-rra, mahgeh
kahma-reh yahttoo-ra mahta
gahtta hakki-da? Mahta
(Ah-peeta) lyoom
tteeya-na-wahda?

11. Yen ruum saavi tara
mudiyumaa? Yenaku (Yengaluku)
kadidam yedaavadu irukaa?
Yen rroom sahvee ttarra
moodee-yoo-mah? Yenna-kuh
(Yengga-luh-kuh) kahdi-ddahm
yeh-ddahvad'irruh-kah?

12. —— er śongge kotha bolte
ćai. —— śommóndhe. Eta
khub jōruri.
—— ehr shonggeh kott'ha
bollteh tjigh. ——
shom-monndeh. Ehtah k'hoob
jo-roorrih.

12. Kárunākara, ——-ta
kátá karánna puluwán da? ——
kárane gena. Ēka wädagát
káranayák.
Kahrroo-nahka-rra, ——-ta
kah-ttah ka-ranna pooloo-wahn-
dda? —— kahra-neh ghenna.
Ehka vadda-gaht kahra-na-yahk.

12. Naan —— avarōda
pēsanum. —— pati. Adu
romba mukiyam.
Nahn —— ahva-rawda
pehssa-nuhñ. —— pahttee.
Ahdduh romba mookee-yahñ.

13. Etar koto dam? Ami eta
kinte ćai. Boro beśi dam.
Ami eta ćai na.
Ehtarr kottoh dahm? Ahmee
ehta keetteh tjigh. Borro behshee
dahm. Ahmee ehta tjigh nah.

13. Mēke mila kiiyada? Máma
mēka milata gánna kämäti.
Mēke mila wedi. Máta mēka epá.
Mehkeh milla keeya-da? Mahma
mehka milla-tta gahna
kamma-tee. Mehkeh milla
veddee. Mahta mehka eh-pah.

13. Idu yevlavu? Idu vaanga
pōrēn. Adu vilai romba adigam.
Yenaku idu vēndaam.
Idduh yevv-lahvuh? Idduh
vahngga pawrreñ. Ahdduh
villeh romba ahddee-gahñ.
Yenna-kuh idduh vehn-dahñ.

31

SENTENCES

ENGLISH	PERSIAN	HINDI [URDU]
14. May I wash my hands? I would like a bath. I need some soap (a towel, hot water).	14. Momken ast man dasthāyam rā beshuyam? Man māyelam hamām konam. Man sābun (yek hole, ābe garm) lāzem dāram. *Mom-kennast man dahst-hawyam raw behshoo-yam? Man maw-yellam ha-mawm kohnam. Man sawboon (yehk hohlay, awbeh garrm) lawzehm dawram.*	14. Maĩ hath dhonaa ćaahtaa/-tii hū. Maĩ nahaanaa ćaahtaa/-tii hū. Mujhe saabun (ţauliyaa, garm paanii) ćaahiye. *Mañ hahtt-h d'hohnah tjah-htta/-httee hooñ. Mañ na-hahnah tjah-htta/-httee hooñ. Moojeh sahbun (tolliyah, garrm pahnee) tjahee-yeh.*

| 15. Is the restaurant open (closed)? Could I see the menu? I would like ——. The bill, please. | 15. Āyā rasturan bāz (baste) ast? Mitavānam liste khorāk rā bebīnam? Man —— mil dāram. Surate hesāb, khāhesh mikonam. *Awyaw rassto-ron bahz (bassteh) asst? Meeta-vawnam leesteh kho-rawk raw behbee-nam? Man —— meel dawram. Soo-ratteh heh-sawb, kho-hesh mikko-nam.* | 15. Kyaa restarent kholaa huaa (band) hai? Menyuu dikhaaiye. Maĩ —— ćaahtaa/-tii hū. Bil laaiye. *Kyah resta-ront kollah hooah (bahndd) heh? Menyoo di-khigh-yeh. Mañ —— tjah-htta/-httee hooñ. Bill ligh-yeh.* |

| 16. I would like to make a telephone call. Would you call —— for me? There is no answer. I have been cut off. | 16. Man mikhāham yek telefun bezānam. Momken ast —— rā barāye man sedā konid? Javāb nemidehad. Ghat' shode ast. *Man mee-khawham yekh tehleh-fon bezzaw-nam. Mom-kennast —— raw ba-rawyeh man se-daw kohneed? Ja-vawb neh-meedeh-had. Ghaht shoodeh ast.* | 16. Telefon karnaa ćaahtaa/-tii hū. Aap —— ko fon kar diijiye. Koii javaab nahĩ hai. Layin ko kaatdiye. *Telleh-fohn karrnah tjah-htta/-httee hooñ. Ahp —— ko fohn karr deejyeh. Koee ja-vahb na-heeñ heh. Ligh-yin ko kahtt-dyeh.* |

| 17. Could I have some notepaper (some air mail paper, some envelopes)? Where can I buy stamps? How much altogether? | 17. Momken ast meghdāri kāghaze yaddasht (meghdāri kāghaze poste havāi, meghdāri pākat) be man bedehid? Kojā man mitavānam tambr bekhāram? Ruye ham rafte chand? *Mom-kennast megh-dawree kaw-ghazzeh ya-dasht (megh-dawree kaw-ghazzeh possteh ha-vawyee, megh-dawree pawkat) beh man behda-heed? Ko-jaw man meeta-vawnam tammbrr bekhaw-ram? Rrooyeh ham raffteh chand?* | 17. Kaagaz (Halkaa kaagaz, Kūch lifaafe) de diijiye. Ţikaţ kahã khariid saktaa/-tii hū? Kitnaa hua? *Kahghaz (Hahlka kahghaz, Kooch li-fahfeh) deh-deejyeh. Tikkat ka-hahñ kha-reed saktta/-ttee hooñ? Kittnah hooa?* |

SENTENCES

14. Hat dhute ćai. Gosol korle bhalo hoto. Şabaner (Ekṭa ṭoaler, Gorom panier) dorkar. *Hahtt d'hooteh tjigh. Gossol krrleh b'hahlo hohíto. Shabahnehr (Ehkta toh-ahlehr, Gorrom pahnee-ehr) dorrkarr.*

14. Mágë atai-páya sōdā gáttā hăkida. Máma nänna kămăti. Máṭa sábán (tuwāyák, unu wátura) önăă. *Mahgeh ahta-pahya soh-dah gahtta hakki-dda. Mahma nanna kamma-tee. Mahta sahbahn (too-vahyahk, oonoo vahtoo-rra) oh-naah.*

14. Naan kayi kaẓuvanum. Naan kuḷikanum. Yenaku sóp (tunḍu, suḍu tanṇi) vēṇḍum. *Nahn ka-yee kazhroo-va-noon. Nahn koolee-ka-noon. Yenna-kuh sohp (ttoonduh, suhduh ttahnee) vehndoon.*

---

15. Resteraṭa ki khola (bondho)? Ajker menu-ṭa dekhi to. Amake ———dao. Bil-ṭa nie aśo to. *Rehss-terrah ta kee k'hoh-lah (bon-d'hoh)? Ahj-k'hehr mennyoo-ta ddehk'hee toh. Ahmah-keh ——— dow. Bill-ta nee-eh ahsho toh.*

15. Bōjana sālāwa äralā da (wáhálā da)? Máṭa kăăma laistuwa băliyahăkida? Máṭa genenna———. Kárunākara, bila genenna. *Bohja-na sah-lahva arra-lahda (vaha-lahda)? Mahta kaahma ligh-stoova balli-ya-hakki-dda? Mahta geh-nennah ———. Kahrroo-nahka-rra, billa geh-nennah.*

15. Hōṭal ṭirandu (muudi) irukaa? Menu paarkalaamaa? Yenaku ——— vēṇum. Yenaku bil vēnum. *Hohtahl tuhrran-duh (moodee) irruh-kah? Mennyoo pahrrka-la-mah? Yenna-kuh ——— vennoon. Yenna-kuh bil vennoon.*

---

16. Ami phòn korte ćai. Apni amar jonno ——— phòne ḍakben ki? Kōno uttor nai. Lain keṭe gaećhe. *Ahmee ffohn korrtteh tjigh. Ahpnee ahmarr jonnoh ——— ffohneh dahkben kee? Kohnoh oottor nigh. Lighn kehteh gighcheh.*

16. Máṭa ṭălifōn karánna önăă. Máma wenuwen ———ṭa ṭălifōn kála hăkida? Uṭṭarayák năṭa. Mágë ṭălifōnaya áwahirawună. *Mahta telli-fohn ka-rranna oh-naah. Mahma vennoo-ven ———ta telli-fohn kahla hakki-dda? Oott-tara-yak natt-ta. Mahgeh telli-fohna-ya ahva-heerra voo-na.*

16. Naan ṭelafōn paṇna vēṇum. Niingaḷ ——— kuupíḍa mudiyumaa? Badil illai. Fōn kaṭ ayudetu. *Nahn tella-fon pahna vennoon. Neengga ——— koopi-da mooddi-yoo-mah? Bahddil illeh. Fohn kaht ahyoo-d'ttuh.*

---

17. Kićhu ćiṭhi lekhar kagoj (biman daker kagoj, kham) dite paren ki? Dak ṭikeṭ kena jabe kotheke? Śobśuddho koto dam? *Keechoo tjeet'hee lehk'harr kahgohj (beemahn dahkerr kahgohj, k'hahm) ddeeteh pahrehn kee? Dahk tikket kehna jahbeh kohtt'hekkeh? Shob-shood'ho kottoh dahm?*

17. Liyum liyana kádadāsi (guwán tăpál kádadāsi, liyum káwara) ṭikák dunnahăkida? Máṭa muddara gánna puluwán kohinda? Okkōma kiiyada? *Lyoom lyahna kahda-dah-see (goo-wahn tappal kahda-dah-see, lyoom kahva-ra) tikkak doona-hakki-da? Mahta moodda-rra ganna pooloo-vahn ko-heendda? Ok-kohma keeya-dda?*

17. Yenaku nōṭpēpar (yēr meyil pēpar, kavar) vēṇum. Sṭampu yenge vaangalaam? Motum yevḷavu? *Yenna-kuh noht-pehpahrr (yehr meh-il pehpahrr, kahverr) vennoon. Stahmp' yenggeh vaangga-lahñ? Mohttuñ yevv-lahvuh?*

33

SENTENCES

ENGLISH	PERSIAN	HINDI [URDU]
18. I am ill. Where can I see a doctor? Please get a good doctor. Could I have some water?	18. Man mariz hastam. Kojā mitavānam yek doktor rā bebinam? Khāhesh mikonam doktore khub beyāvarid. Momken ast be man āb bedehid? *Man ma-rreez hasstam. Ko-jaw meeta-vawnam yehk doktorr raw behbee-nam? Kho-hesh mikko-nam dok-torreh khoob behyaw-vareed. Mom-kennast beh man awb behda-heed?*	18. Maĩ biimaar hū. Maĩ ek ḍaakṭar kahā dekh saktaa/-tii hū? Aap ek aćchaa ḍaakṭar bulaaiye. Mujhe paanii de diijiye. *Mañ bee-mahrr hooñ. Mañ ehk dahktrr ka-hahñ dehkh saktta/-ttee hooñ? Ahp ehk a-chah dahktrr boo-ligh-yeh. Moojeh pahnee deh-deejyeh.*
19. May I introduce ———. I am pleased to meet you. My name is ———.	19. Momken ast ——— rā mo'arrefi konam? Az molāghāte shomā khoshvaghtam. Esme man ——— ast. *Mom-kennast ——— raw mo'ahrreh-fee kohnam? Azz mo-lawghaw-teh sho-maw khohsh-vahghtahm. Ehssmeh man ——— asst.*	19. ——— se miliye. Aap se milke bahut khuśii hui. Meraa naam ——— hai. *——— seh-meelyeh. Ahp seh meelkeh ba-hott khooshee hooee. Mehra nahm ——— heh.*
20. Who are you? A friend. I come from ———. Go away!	20. Shomā ki hastid? Yek dust. Man az ——— miāyam. Rad shou! *Sho-maw kee hassteed? Yehk doost. Man azz ——— meeaw-yam. Raddshoh!*	20. Aap kaun haĩ? Dost. Maĩ ——— se aayaa/aaii hū. Ćale jaõ! *Ahp konn hehñ? Doostt. Mañ ——— seh-ahyah/ahee hooñ. Tjaleh jow!*
21. What is this called? What is this place called? It is called ———.	21. Be in che miguyand? Esme in mahall chist? ——— nāmideh mishavad. *Beh een cheh meegoo-yand? Ehssmeh een ma-halcheest? ——— naw-meedeh meesha-vad.*	21. Yeh ćiiz kyaa kahlaate hai? Yeh jaghaa kyaa kahlaataa hai? Yeh ——— kahlaataa/-tii hai. *Yehk tjeez kyah ka-hlahtteh heh? Yehk ja-gah kyah ka-hlahtta heh? Yehk ——— ka-hlahtta/-ttee heh.*
22. What is the matter? Don't worry. I am sorry (glad). I shall give you this.	22. Nārahati chist? Nārahat nabashid. Man mota'assef (khoshhal) hastam. Man bāyad inrā be shomā bedeham. *Nawra-hatti cheest? Nawra-hat nabbaw-sheed. Man mota-assehf (khosh-hawl) hasstam. Man bawyad in-raw beh sho-maw behda-ham.*	22. Kyaa baat hai? Fikr na karai. Mujhe afsos hua (khuśii hui). Maĩ aapko yeh de dūgaa/dūgii. *Kyah bahtt heh? Fikrr nah ka-reh. Moojeh ahfsohss hooah (khooshee hooee). Mañ ahpko yehk deh-dooñga/dooñgee.*

SENTENCES

BENGALI	SINHALESE	TAMIL

BENGALI

18. Ami ośustho. Ami kothae
daktarer śonge poramorśo korte
parbo? Ekjon bhalo ḍakṭar ḍeke
anan. Ekṭu pani ante paren ki?
*Ahmee o-shoostt'ho. Ahmee
kot'high dahk-tarrehr shonggeh
porra-moorsho korrteh parrboh?
Ehk-jon b'hahlo dahk-tarr
dehkeh ahn-ahn. Ehktoo pahnee
ahnteh pahrehn kee?*

SINHALESE

18. Máṭa sánepa náá. Máṭa
dostara kenek munagesenna
pulu-wán kohéda? Kárunákara,
dáksa dostara kenek genénna.
Máṭa wátura ṭikák lábá gáta
hákida.
*Mahta sahneh-pa naah.
Mahta doostta-rra ken-nek
moona-geh-senna pooloo-
vahn ko-heh-da?
Kahrroo-nahka-rra, dahksa
doostta-rra ken-nek
geh-nen-na. Mahta
vahtoo-rra tikkak la-bah gahta
hakki-da.*

TAMIL

18. Yenaku vudambu sari-illai.
Daakṭar yenge paarka mudiyum?
Nalla ḍaakṭar kuupidungaḷ. Konjam
taṇni tara mudiyumaa?
*Yenna-kuh voo-ddahmbuh
sahri-illeh. Dahkter yenggeh
pahrrka mooddi-yooñ? Nahlla
dahkter koopi-ddoongga.
Konjahñ tahnnee tahrra
mooddi-yoo-mah?*

19. ——— er śathe poriċoe
korie diċċhi. Apnar śathe poriċita
hoe khuśi holam. Amar
nam ———.
*——— ehr shahtteh
pohri-tjo-eh kohree-eh deetchih.
Ahpnarr shahtteh pohri-tjeetta
hweh k'hooshi ho-lahm.
Ahmarr nahm ———.*

19. Áwasarai, ándunágánna
———. Máṭa obawa hámba
wenna sántosai. Mágé náma
———.
*Ahwa-s'rra,
ahndoo-nah-gan-na ———.
Mahta ohba-wa
hahmba-venna sahn-tohsigh.
Mahgeh namma ———.*

19. Naan ——— arimuga padu-
taṭamaa? Naan ungaḷai sanditadil
sandósham. Yen peyar ———.
*Nahn ——— ahree-mooga
pahddoo-ttahta-mah? Nahn
oongga-leh sahndi-tt'dil
sahn-dohshañ. Yen pehy'rr
———.*

20. Apni ke? Bondhu. Ami ———
theke aśċhi. Jao!
*Ahpnee keh? Bond'hoo. Ahmee
——— t'hehkeh ahsh-chih.
Jow!*

20. Oba káwuda? Máma
yáháluwek. Máma enné
——— siṭa. Yánawa áhákaṭa!
*Ohba kahvoo-da? Mahma
ya-hahloo-vek. Mahma
en-neh ——— seeta.
Yanna-wa a-hahka-ta!*

20. Niingaḷ yaaru? Oru nanbar.
Naan ———-indu varén. Póngaḷ!
*Neengga yahruh? Awruh
nahnb'rr. Nahn ———-induh
vah-rehñ. Pawngga!*

21. Eke ki bole? E jaegaṭake
ki bole? ——— bole.
*Ehkeh kee bolleh? Eh jigh-
gahta-keh kee bolleh? ———
bolleh.*

21. Méke náma mokádda?
Metanaṭa kiyana náma
mokádda? Méke náma ———.
*Mehkeh namma
mo-kahd-dda? Mehtta-na-ta
kee-yanna namma
mo-kahd-dda? Mehkeh
namma ———.*

21. Iduku yenna péru? Inda
idatuku yenna péru? Idu ———.
*Idduh-kuh yenna pehruh?
Inda idda-tuh-kuh yenna
pehruh? Idduh ———.*

22. Bepar ki? Ċinta koro na. Ami
dukkhito (khuśi). Ami tomake
eṭa debo.
*Bepparr kee? Tjintta korroh nah.
Ahmee dook'heettoh (k'hooshi).
Ahmee toh-mahkeh ehta debboh.*

22. Mokádda káradaraya?
Káradara wenna epá. Máma
kánugátui (sántosai). Máma
obata méka dennám.
*Mo-kahd-dda
kahrra-da-rehya?
Kahrra-da-ra ven-na eh-pah.
Mahma kannoo-gahttooi
(sahn-ttohsigh). Mahma
ohba-ta mehka dennahm.*

22. Yenna tondaravu? Kavalai
paḍaadingaḷ. Yenaku romba dukam
(romba sandósham). Naan idu
ungaḷuku tarén.
*Yenna ttonda-ra-vuh? Kavva-leh
pahda-ddingga. Yenna-kuh
romba ddookahñ (romba
sahn-dohshañ). Nahn idduh
oongga-luh-kuh ttahrehñ.*

35

SENTENCES

ENGLISH	PERSIAN	HINDI [URDU]
23. What do you want? Please sit down. I have to leave. You must go now.	23. Shomā che mikhāhid? Khāhesh mikonam beneshinid. Man bāyad morakhas shavam. Hālā shomā bāyad beravid. *Sho-maw cheh mikhaw-heed? Kho-hesh mikko-nam behneh-sheeneed. Man bawyad morra-khass shahvam. Haw-law sho-maw bawyad berra-veed.*	23. Aapko kyaa ćaahiye? Baiṭhiye. Mujhe ab jaanaa hai. Aap ab ćale jaaiye. - *Ahpko kyah tjah-hyeh? Bat'heeyeh. Moojeh ab jahna heh. Ahp ab tjaleh jigh-yeh.*
24. I need help. I am in trouble. Please give this message to ——. As soon as possible.	24. Man komak lāzem dāram. Man dar zahmat hastam. Khāhesh mikonam in peighām rā be —— bedehid. Har che zudtar. *Man ko-makk lawzem dawram. Man dahrr zahh-matt hasstam. Kho-hesh mikko-nam in pay-ghawm raw beh —— behda-heed. Hahrrcheh zood-tahrr.*	24. Mujhe madad ćaahiye. Maĩ musiibatmā hũ. Yeh paigaam —— ko de diijiye. Jaldii se jaldii. *Moojeh maddadd tjah-hyeh. Mañ moossee-bahttmañ hooñ. Yehh peh-gahm —— ko deh-deejyeh. Jahldee seh jahldee.*
25. That is very nice (marvellous). That is bad (terrible). I have enjoyed myself very much.	25. Ān kheili khub (ā'āli) ast. Ān bad (vahshatnāk) ast. Be man kheili khosh gozasht. *On khaylee khoob (aw'awlee) asst. On badd (vahshat-nawk) asst. Beh man khaylee khosh gozasht.*	25. Voh bahut aćchaa (bahut khuub) hai. Voh buraa (bahut kharaab) hai. Mujhe bahut mazaa aya. *Vohh ba-hotta-chah (ba-hott khoob) heh. Vohh boo-rah (ba-hott kha-rrahb) heh. Moojeh ba-hottma-zah ahya.*

SENTENCES

BENGALI	SINHALESE	TAMIL

23. Ki kaje eśećen? Bośun. Amar
jabar dorkar aćhe. Apnake ekhon
jetei hobe.
*Kee kahjeh esheh-tjen? Boshoon.
Ahmarr jahbarr dorrkarr a-cheh.
Ahpnah-keh ehk'hon jetteh
hobbeh.*

23. Obaṭa mánawada ōnǟǟ?
Kárunākara wāḍi wenna.
Máma dǎn yánna ōnǟǟ. Oba
dǎn yánna ōnǟǟ.
*Ohba-ta mahna-vahda
oh-naah?
Kahrroo-nahka-rra vahddee
vennah. Mahma dann
yahnna oh-naah. Ohba dann
yahnna oh-naah.*

23. Yenna vēṇum? Utkaarungaḷ.
Naan pōga vēṇḍum. Niingaḷ uḍanē
pōga vēṇḍum.
*Yenna vennooñ? Oott-kahrung-
ga. Nahn pawga vehnduhñ.
Neengga oodd-neh pawga vehnduhñ.*

24. Apnar śahajjo dorkar. Ami
bipodgrosto. Anugroho kore ei
khoborṭa ——— ke pōućhe deben.
Jata taratari śombhob.
*Ahpnarr sha-hahjjo dorrkarr.
Ahmee beepodd-grosttoh. Onnu-
gro-ho korreh eigh k'hobborr-ta
——— keh pohñcheh debben.
Jahtta tahra-tahri shom-b'hob.*

24. Máṭa udáwwák ōnǟǟ.
Máma káradarayaka weṭilā.
Kárunākara me pániwudaya
——— -ṭa denna. Hǎki táram
ikmanin denna.
*Mahta oodd-dahwak
oh-naah. Mahma
kahrra-da-rehya-ka
vehtee-lah.
Kahrroo-nahka-rra meh
pahnee-voo-deya ——— -ta
den-na. Hakkee tahram
ikman-nin den-na.*

24. Yenaku udavi vēṇum. Naan
tondaravil irukēn. Dayavu seydu,
inda sangadiyai ——— -uku
kōdungaḷ. Uḍanē.
*Yenna-kuh oo-dahvee vennooñ.
Nahn ttonda-rrahvil irruh-kehñ.
Dahya-voo sehdoo, inda sahng-
gahddi-yeh ——— -uh-kuh
kohddoong-ga. Oodda-neh.*

25. Khub bhalo (Ćomotkar)
hoećhe. Baje (Bhiśon baje) hoećhe.
Amar khub bhalo legećhe.
*K'hoob b'hahlo (Tjomot-karr)
hweh-cheh. Bahjeh (B'heeshon
bahjeh) hweh-cheh. Ahmarr
k'hoob b'hahlo lehgeh-cheh.*

25. Ēka itā hoñdáy (itā
ápúruy). Ēka nárakáy (itā
nárakáy). Máma itā hoñdaṭa
priiti winda.
*Ehka ittah hon-digh (ittah
ahpoo-rrooi). Ehka
nahrra-kigh (ittah
nahrra-kigh). Mahma
ittah honda-ta prreettee
vinndah.*

25. Adu romba nannaa
(pramaadama) iruku. Adu mōsam
(romba mōsamaa) iruku. Yenaku
romba sandōsham.
*Ahdduh romba nahn-nah (pra-
mahda-ma) irruh-kuh. Ahdduh
mawssahñ (romba mawssahñ)
irruh-kuh. Yenna-kuh romba
sahn-dohshañ.*

37

VOCABULARY

ENGLISH	PERSIAN	HINDI [URDU]
above	bālā	... ke uupar
accident, the	hādese	durghaṭnaa (f.) [haadisaa (m.)]
address, the	neshāni	pataa (m.)
adult, the	bālegh	baalig (m., f.)
advertisement, the	āgahi	vigyapan (m.) [istihaar (m.)]
aerogramme, the	nāmeye havāi	havaaii patr (m.)
afraid	tarsān	dartaa
after	pas az	... ke baad
afternoon, the	ba'd az zohr	dopahar (f.)
again	dobāre	phir
against	khelāf	khilaaf
agree, to	movāfeghat kardan (mikonad)	maannaa
air, the	havā	havaa (f.)
air conditioner, the	dasgāhe tahniye havā	vaatnaanukuul (m.) [er kondiṣnar (m.)]
air mail, the	poste havāi	havaaii daak (f.)
airplane, the	havāpeimā	havaaii jahaaz (m.)
airport, the	forudgāh	havaaii addaa (m.) [erodrom (m.)]
alive	zende	zindaa
all	hame	sab
all right	besyār khub	thiik
almost	taghriban	kariib
alone	tanhā	akelaa
already	ghablan	pahle hii
also	ham	bhii
although	agarche	haalāki [agarći]
always	hamishe	hameśaa
among	miān	mẽ
and (between nouns)	va	aur
angry	ghazabnāk	gusse
animal, the	heivān	jaanvar (m.)
another one (different)	yeki digar	duusraa
another one (more)	yeki bishtar	ek aur
answer, to	javāb dādan (midehad)	javaab denaa
antiseptic, the	zede opuni	roganurodhak (m.) [jarasiim kuś (m.)]
apartment, the	. aparteman	makaan (m.)
apple, the	sib	seb (m.)
approximately	taghriban	takriiban
arm, the	bāzu	baazu (f.)
army, the	artesh	fauj (f.)
around	pirāmun	gird [har taraf]
arrive, to	vāred shodan (mishavad)	pahũćnaa
art, the	honar	kalaa (f.)
art gallery, the	muzeye honar	kalaabhavan (m.) [tasviir khaanaa (m.)]
artificial	masnu'i	naklii
ask (inquire), to	porsidan (miporsad)	puućhnaa

38

VOCABULARY

BENGALI	SINHALESE	TAMIL
upore	... ihála	... mēlē
durghotona	ăksidánt-eka (-dánt)	vibati
thikana	lipinaya (-na)	mugavari
praptō baoiskō	wáyas piruna ekenā	vayaduvandavar
biggapon	welenda dănwēma (-wēm)	viḷambaram
erogram	guwán liyuma (-yum)	yērogram
bhito	báya	bayam
... pore	... pásse	... piḷ
bikelbela	páswaruwa (-ru)	pagal
abar	năwata	tirumba
biruddhe	... wiruddawa	yedirē
raji hōi/hoen	ekanga wenawā (unā)	otukoṇḍu (otukoḷḷigi-)
bataś	wátaya	kaatru
śitatop-niontronkari jontro	wáyu sámekaranaya (-na)	kaaṭrikaṭupaadu
biman dak	guwán tăpál	vimaan anjal
urojahaj	áhásiyántrāwa (-wál)	vimaanam
biman bondor	guwán toṭupala	yērporṭ
jento	jiiwátwanawa	uyiruḍaḷ
śokole	okkōma	yellaam
aćcha	okkōma hári	sari
prae	... ma	perumbaalum
eka	táni	ṭaniyaay
itimoddhe	kálin	munnăḍiye
ar ...	... -t	um
jodio	... wunáti	pōdilum
śob śomoe	nitarama	yepōdum
... moddhe	... átare	uḷ
ar	há	um ... um ...
ragannito	tárāhá	kōbamaana
pośu	sátā (sáttu)	mirugam
onno ekṭi	táwa ekák	aḍuvēra
ar ekṭi	wena ekák	innuru
uttor dii/den	uttara denawā (dunnā)	badil solli (sollugi-)
poćhon rodhkari	wisabēga násaka (-kawál)	nachari
kokhō	kámaraya (-ra)	tani arai
apel	ăpal-eka (ăpál)	aapiḷ
pral	... witara	sumaar
bahu	bāhuwa (bāhu)	mētkai
śenadol	yuddasēnāwa (-nă)	sēnai
aśe-paśe	... wátēṭa	sutri
pōućhai/pōúchan	páminenawā (pámināwā)	vandu (varugi-)
kola	kálāsilpa	kalai
arṭ galari	kálā báwana (-nawál)	kalai kāṭchi
krittim	krutēma	seyatkaiyaana
ćai/ćan	áhánawā (áhuwā)	kēṭu (kēṭki-)

VOCABULARY

ENGLISH	PERSIAN	HINDI [URDU]
at	dar	... par
attempt, to	sai kardan (mikonad)	... kii kośiś karnaa
awake	bidār	jaagaa huaa
baby, the	bache	baććaa/baććii
back (rear), the	aghab	piićhaa (m.)
back (again)	baz	vaapas
backwards	aghab	piićhe ke taraf
bad	bad	kharaab
bag, the	kif	thailaa (m.)
baggage, the	asbāb	saamaan (m.)
ballpoint, the	noke khodkar	bolpoinṭ (m.)
bamboo shoots, the	neiye hendi	bās kii tehniyā (f. pl.)
banana, the	mouz	kelaa (m.)
bank (money), the	bānk	baink (m.)
bathe, to	shostoshu kardan (mikonad)	nahaanaa
bathroom, the	hammam	gusal khaanaa (m.)
battery, the	bātri	baiṭrii (f.)
beach, the	sāhel	samandar kaa kinaaraa (m.)
beans, the	lubiā	phaliiyā (f. pl.)
beard, the	rish	ḍaaṛhii (f.)
beautiful	ghashang	khuubsuurat
because	zirā	kyõki
because of	az jehate	... ke kaaran
become, to	shodan (mishavad)	ho jaanaa
bed, the	tākhte khāb	palang (m.)
beef, the	gushte gāv	gaaii kaa gośt (m.)
beer, the	ābe jou	biyar (m.) [ju ke saraab (f.)]
before (time)	pish	... ke pahile
behind	poshte sar	... ke piićhe
believe, to	bāvar kardan (mikonad)	yakiin karnaa
bell, the	zang	ghanṭaa (m.)
best	behtarin	behtariin
better	behtar	behtar
beyond	mā fough	... ke pare
bicycle, the	docharkhe	baaisikal (f.)
big	bozorg	baraa
bill, the	surate hesāb	bil (m.)
binoculars, the	durbin	duurbiin (f.)
bird, the	parande	pakśii (m.) [parindaa (m.)]
biscuit, the	biskuit	biskuṭ (m.)
black	siāh	kaalaa
blanket, the	patu	kambal (m.)
blood, the	ghun	khuun (m.)
blue	ābi	niilaa
boat, the	ghāyagh	kiśtii (f.)
body, the	badan	badan (m.)

VOCABULARY

BENGALI	SINHALESE	TAMIL
... e	... siti	... -il
ćeśṭa kŏri/koren	utsāhá karanawā (kalā)	pirayaasapaṭu (-paḍuki-)
jagriṭo hoa	áwadiwā	viẓi
śiśu	bábā (bábu)	kuẓandai
pićhon dik	piṭa pắtta	pinnāḍi
phire	ápahu	tirumbi
pićhone	pássaṭa	pinnēki
kharap	náraka	keṭa
tholi	băg-eka (băg)	payi
malpotro	bádu	saamaan
bol poinṭ	bállpoint pắắna (pắắn)	baal poinṭ
băśer ćara	bámboo pắla	pirambu
kola	keselgeḍiya (-ḍi)	vaaẓai paẓam
benk	bắnkuwa (-ku)	bank
gośol kŏri/koren	nănawā (nắắwā)	kuḷitu (kuḷigi-)
gośol khana	năna kămaraya (-ra)	kuḷikum arai
batari	bắtariya (-ri)	batri
śoikot	mūduwerala (-lawál)	biich
śim	bŏnche	biins
daṛi	răwula (-wul)	daaḍi
śundor	lássana	aẓagaana
karon	hinda	yēnendraal
dorun	hinda	adu naal
hŏi/hoen	wenawā (unā)	aadi (aadugi-)
bićhana	ằnda (ằndán)	paḍikai
gŏmangśo	hárákmás	maaṭikari
bhaluk	biira	biir
... age	issara	... munnē
... pićhon dhare	... piṭipássa	... pinnē
mone hŏi/hoen	piligánnawā (-gáttā)	nambi (nambugi-)
ghonṭa	siinuwa (-nu)	maṇi
śreśṭho	uttama	romba nalla
uttom	wáḍā hoṅda	taavilai
dure	... ehă	marubakatil
saikel	sáykalē (-kál)	saikiḷ
boṛo	loku	periya
bil	bila (bil)	billu
durbin	dūra dársakaya	bainakulas
pakhi	kurullā (-llo)	paravai
biskuṭ	wiskŏṭṭuwa (-ṭṭu)	biskaṭ
kalo	kálu	karupu
kombol	blănkeṭṭuwa (-ṭṭu)	pŏrvai
rokto	lē	ratam
nil	nil paṭa	niilam
nouko	oruwa (oru)	bŏṭu
śorir	ằṅga (ằṅgawál)	uḍambu

41

VOCABULARY

ENGLISH	PERSIAN	HINDI [URDU]
boiled	jushānde	ubla huaa
book, the	ketāb	kitaab (f.)
boot, the	chakme	juutii (f.)
born	motavalled	pedaa
both	har do	donõ
bottle, the	shishe	botal (m.)
bottle opener, the	shishe bāz kon	botal kholnevaalaa (m.)
bottom, the	tah	talaa (m.)
box, the	ja'be	baks (m.)
boy, the	pesar	larkaa (m.)
bra, the	sineband	ćolii (f.)
brake, the	tormoz	brek (m.)
brave	bibāk	bahaadur
bread, the	nān	roṭii (f.)
break, to	shekastan (mishekanad)	toṛnaa
breakfast, the	sobhāne	naaśtaa (m.)
bridge, the	pol	pul (m.)
bring, to	āvardan (miāvarad)	laanaa
brooch, the	sanjāgh	jaṛaauu pin (f.)
brown	ghahvei	bhuraa
brush, the	boros	braś (m.)
bundle, the	baste	poṭlii (f.)
bus, the	otobus	bas (f.)
businessman, the	tājer	vyopaarii (m.) [tejartii (m.)]
busy	māshgul	masruuf
but	ammā	par
butter, the	kare	makkhan (m.)
button, the	dogme	baṭan (m.)
buy, to	kharidan (mikharad)	khariidnaa
cabbage, the	kalam	pat gobhii (f.)
cake, the	kek	kek (f.)
call (telephone), the	telefun	fon kaul (m.)
called, is	namide mishavad	kahlaataa hai
call out, to	bāng zadan (mizanad)	bulaanaa
camera, the	durbine akkāsi	kaimraa (m.)
candle, the	sham'	mom battii (f.)
captain (of ship), the	nākhodā	kaptaan (m.)
car, the	otomobil	gaaṛii (f.)
carefully	bā deghat	hośiyaarii-se
cargo, the	bār	jahaaz kaa saamaan (m.)
carpet, the	farsh	kaaliin (m.)
carrot, the	havij	gaajar (f.)
carry, to	bordan (mibarad)	uthaake lejaanaa
cat, the	gorbe	billii (f.)
centimetre, the	santimetr	senṭiimiiṭar (m.)
century, the	gharn	sadii (f.)
certainly	yaghinan	zaruur

VOCABULARY

BENGALI	SINHALESE	TAMIL
phutonto	támbāpu	kodika vaita
boi	póta (pót)	pustagam
buṭ juta	us sápáttuwa (-ttu)	ḍiki
jonmo hoa	upan	piranda
duṭoi	dekama	iruvarum
bōṭol	bōṭalē (-la)	baṭil
bōṭol khulibar jontro	bōṭál árina yátura	baṭil tirakiradu
tola	áḍiya (áḍi)	aḍi
bakśo	peṭṭiya (-ṭṭi)	peṭi
balok	pirimi lámayā (-máy)	paiyan
bokho bondoni	tánapaṭa (-ṭawál)	baaḍi
brek	brēk-eka (brēk)	brēk
śahośi	nirbiita	dairiyam
ruṭi	pän	roṭi
bhangi/bhangen	káḍanawā (kǎḍuwā)	uḍaitu (uḍaiki-)
nasta	udē kǎäma	kaalaiyuṇḍi
śetu	pálama (-lám)	paalam
ani/anen	gēnawā (genāwā)	koṇḍuvandu (-varugi-)
brōć	häricchiya (-cchi)	aṇiyuuku
badami	duṁburu	kaavi niramaan
tuli	kossa (-ssu)	kuruṇgaadu
bandil	miṭiya (-ṭi)	katai
bas	bás-eka (bás)	bas
babśai	mudaláli (-lilā)	viyaabarigaḷ
besto	káḍisara	surusurupaa
kintu	námut	aanal
makhon	weṅḍaru	venṇey
bōtam	bottáma (-ttám)	baṭan
kini/kenen	gánnawā (gáttā)	vaangi (vaangugi-)
bādhakopi	gōwāgeḍiya (-ḍi)	kōs
piṭha	kēk-eka (kēk)	kēk
ṭelephōn	tǎlifōn pániwudaya (-da)	ṭelafōn
ḍak poṛen	ámatalā	peyar . . .
ćitkar kōri/koren	áṅdagasanawā (-gǎsuwā)	kuupiḍu (kuupiḍigi-)
kamera	kǎmarāwa (-rä)	kēmara
mōmbati	itipándama (-dám)	mezagu vati
kapṭan	káppittā (-ttán)	kēpṭan
gaṛi	kār-eka (kār)	kaar
śabdhane	párissamen	kavanamaay
poinno śamogri	bádu	saraku
karpeṭ	kárpet-eka (kárpet)	jamakaaḷam
gajor	kǎrát álaya (-la)	kēraṭu
bohon kōri/koren	ussāgena yánawā (giyā)	tuuki (tuukugi-)
beṛal	bálalā (bálállu)	puunai
senṭimiṭar	senṭimiiṭaraya (-ra)	senṭimiiṭar
śatabdi	sátawárse (-sa)	nuutru
niśćoi	ättenma	nichayam

43

VOCABULARY

ENGLISH	PERSIAN	HINDI [URDU]
chair, the	sandali	kursii (f.)
change (small money), the	pule khord	chuttaa (m.)
change (money), to	pul khord kardan (mikonad)	badalnaa
change (transport), to	avaz kardan (mikonad)	badalnaa
cheap	arzān	sastaa
cheese, the	panir	paniir (m.)
cherry, the	gilās	aaluu baaduu (m.)
chicken, the	juje	murgii (f.)
chief, the	ra'is	sardaar (m.)
child, the	bache	baććaa/baććii
chocolate, the	shokolāt	ćauklet (m.)
choose, to	bar gozidan (migozinad)	ćunnaa
chopsticks, the	ghashoghe chini	ćiinii kāte (m. pl.)
church, the	kalisā	girjaa (m.)
cigar, the	sigār	sigaar (m.)
cigarette, the	sigār	sigret (m.)
cinema, the	sinema	sinemaa (m.)
city, the	shahr	śahar (m.)
clean	pāk	saaf
clean, to	pāk kardan (mikonad)	saaf karnaa
clerk, the	kārmand	baabuu (m.)
clock, the	sā'at	gharii (f.)
close, to	bastan (mibandad)	band karnaa
closed	baste	band
cloth, the	pārche	kapraa (m.)
clothes, the	lebās	kapre (m. pl.)
coast, the	sāhel	samudra tat (m.)
coat, the	kot	kot (m.)
coffee, the	ghahve	kaafii (f.)
coin, the	sekke	sikkaa (m.)
cold	sard	thandaa
cold season (winter), the	zamestān	jaaraa (m.)
colour, the	rang	rang (m.)
comb, the	shāne	kanghaa (m.)
come, to	āmadan (miāyad)	aanaa
comfortable	rāhat	aaraamdeh
commercial	tejārati	vyaapaarik [tejartii]
company (firm), the	sherkat	kampanii (f.)
complain, to	shekāyat kardan (mikonad)	śikaayat karnaa
completely	be kolli	bilkul
conceal, to	panhān kardan (mikonad)	ćhipaanaa
concert, the	konesert	sāgiit samaaroh (m.)
consul, the	konsol	kaunsul (m., f.)
contain, to	shāmel budan (ast)	samaanaa
continue, to	edāme dādan (midehad)	jaarii rahnaa
convenient	monāseb	aaraamdeh
conversation, the	goftugu	baatćiit (f.)

44

VOCABULARY

BENGALI	SINHALESE	TAMIL
ćear	puṭuwa (-ṭu)	naatkaali
khućrō	podi sálli	sillarai
bhangai/bhangan	sálli māru karanawā (kalā)	maatri (maatrigi-)
bōdlai/bodlan	gámán māru karanawā (kalā)	maatri (maatrigi-)
śosta	lāba	malivaana
ponir	kēju	uraibalēdu
ćeri	cherigeḍiya (-ḍi)	cheri
murgi	kukulā (kukullu)	kōẓi
prodhan	pradānayā (-na)	talaivar
śiśu	lámayā (-máy)	kuẓandai
ćokōleṭ	chokaláṭ	chaaklaṭ
poćhondo kōri/koren	tōrā gánnawā (gáttā)	tērndeḍi (tērndeḍugi-)
khabar kaṭhi	chopsṭik jōduwák	chapsṭiks
girja	pálliya (-lli)	maadaa kōyil
ćuruṭ	suruṭṭuwa (-ṭṭu)	suruṭu
sigareṭ	sigarāṭ-eka (-rāṭ)	sigareṭu
sinema	sinimāwa (-mā)	sinimaa
śohor	nuwara (-rawál)	nagaram
poriśkar	páwitra	suddam
poriśkar kōri/koren	sudda karanawā (kalā)	suddam seydu (seygi-)
kerani	lipikaruwā (-wán)	kumastaa
ghori	oralōsuwa (-su)	kaḍigaaram
bondho kōri/koren	wáhánawā (wǎhuwā)	aḍaindu (aḍaigi-)
bondho	wáhála	aḍaita
kapoṛ	redda (redi)	tuṇi
kapoṛ ćopor	ǎndum	aadaigaḷ
upokul	werala	kaḍatkarai
kōṭ	kábāya (-bā)	uḍupu
kophi	kōpi	kaapi
mudra	kāsiya (-si)	tambaḍi
thanḍa	siitala	kuḷirnda
śit kal	siita srátuwa	kuḷirgaalam
rong	pāta	niram
ćiruni	pánāwa (-nā)	sippu
aśi/aśen	enawā (āwā)	vandu (varugi-)
aramprodo	sǎpapahásu	sōriyaama
banijo śomporkio	welenda	viyabaramaaga
kompani	kompǎniya (-ni)	kampani
naliś kōri/koren	páminili karanawā (kalā)	muraiyiṭu (-yiḍugi-)
śompurnobhabe	sámpurnayen	puura
gopon kōri/koren	sáṅgawánawā (sǎṅgǎwwā)	maraitu (maraiki-)
śomobetho bajna	wirida prasáṅgaya (-ga)	kachēri
konsal	tānāpati tǎna (tānāpatiwaru)	ayalida naatupēraalar
dhoron kōri/koren	dáranawā (dǎruwā)	piḍitu (piḍiki-)
ćalie jai/jan	karagena yánawā (giyā)	toḍandu (toḍanḍugi-)
śubidhajonok	sudusu	vasaḍi
bakkalap	sánwādaya (-da)	uraiyaaḍal

45

VOCABULARY

ENGLISH	PERSIAN	HINDI [URDU]
cook, to	pokhtan (mipazad)	pakaanaa
cookie, the	biskuit	biskuṭ (m.)
corkscrew, the	botri bāz kon	kork pēi (m.)
corner (of room), the	gushe	konaa (m.)
corner (street), the	pich	konaa (m.)
corridor, the	dālān	galiyaaraa (m.)
costs, (it)	gheimat	kiimat . . . hai
cotton, the	pambe	kapaas (m.)
cotton-wool, the	pambe	kapaas-uun (m.)
count, to	shomordan (shomārad)	ginnaa
country (nation), the	keshvar	deś (m.) [mulk (m.)]
countryside, the	hume	dehaat (m.)
course, of!	albatte!	beśak!
courtyard, the	hayāt	sahn (m.)
cover, to	pushidan (mipushad)	ḍhāknaa
crab, the	kharchang	kekṛaa (m.)
cream, the	khāme	malaaii (f.)
cross, to	obur kardan (mikonad)	paar karnaa
crowd, the	ezdehām	bhiiṛ (f.)
cup, the	fenjān	pyaalaa (m.)
curry, the	khoresht	tarkaarii (f.)
cushion, the	bālesh	gaddii (f.)
custom (way), the	rasm	dastuur (m.)
customs, the	gomrok	kasṭam (m.)
cut, to	boridan (miborad)	kaaṭnaa
dance, to	raghs kardan (mikonad)	naaćnaa
dangerous	khatarnāk	khatarnaak
dark (colour)	porang	gahraa
dark (no light)	tārik	andheraa
day, the	ruz	din (m.)
daytime, the	ruz	din (m.)
dead	morde	murdaa
dear (expensive)	gerān	mahāgaa
decide, to	tasmin gereftan (migirad)	faisalaa karnaa
deep	goud	gahraa
demand, to	taghāzā kardan (mikonad)	māgnaa
dentist, the	dandān pezeshk	dātō kaa ḍaakṭaar (m., f.)
desert, the	biābān	registaan (m.)
diamond, the	almās	hiiraa (m.)
dictionary, the	loghat nāme	śabd koś (m.) [kamus (m.)]
die, to	mordan (mimārad)	marnaa
different	mokhtalef	bhinna [muktalif]
difficult	moshkel	muśkil
dinner, the	shām	śaam kaa khaanaa (m.)
direction, the	masir	diśaa (f.) [taraf (f.)]
dirty	kasif	mailaa

46

VOCABULARY

BENGALI	SINHALESE	TAMIL
ranna kŏri/koren	uyanawā (iyuwā)	sametu (samaiki-)
kukis biskuṭ	wiskŏṭṭuwa (-ṭṭu)	biskaṭ
ćipi khulibar jontro	káskuruppuwá (-ppu)	takaivaangi
ghorer kona	mulla (mulu)	muulai
rastar mor	hándiya (-di)	munai
koriḍor	pila (pil)	nadai
dam...	mila	piḍikiradu
tulo	kápu	kaṭan
pośmi tulo	kápu pulun	panju
guni/gŏnen	gáninawā (gǎnnā)	yenni (yennugi-)
deś	ráta (-ṭawál)	naaḍu
gram onćol	gámbada	tēsam
obośoi!	sǎbǎwinma!	taan!
dorbar	midula (-dul)	mutram
ćhai/ćhan	wásanawá (wǎsuwā)	muudi (muudugi-)
kǎk	kákuluwā (-wŏ)	naṇḍu
śor	yodaya	aaḍai
paṛi dii/den	máruwánawa (mǎǎriwwā)	kadaṇḍu (kadaki-)
jonota	senaga	kuuṭam
peala	kŏppaya (-ppa)	kap
torkari	káriya (-ri)	kari
godi	koṭṭaya (-ṭṭa)	kushan
dhara	sirita (-rit)	vazakam
ritiniti	tiiruwa	kasṭams
kaṭi/kaṭen	kápanawā (kǎpuwā)	veṭi (veṭugi-)
naći/naćen	nátanawā (nǎṭuwā)	aaḍi (aaḍugi-)
bipodjonok	ánaturudayaka	iḍaruḍaiya
garo	táda pāta	iruṇḍa
andhokar	káluwara	iruḷ
din	dáwasa (-wás)	naaḷ
diner bela	dáwál kālaya	pagal
mrito	ántarāwana	seta
dami	álāba	kiraaki
ṭhik kŏri/koren	ádahás karanawā (kalā)	mudivu seydu (seygi-)
gobhir	gǎmburu	aazam
ćai/ćan	illá siṭinawá (siṭṭā)	keṭu (keḍigi-)
donto ćikitśok	dát dostara (-rawaru)	paḷ ḍaakṭar
morubhumi	kántāraya (-ra)	paalaivanam
hirok	diyamántiya (-ti)	vairam
abhidhan	ákārādiya (-di)	sotkalanjiyam
mŏri/moren	ántarā wenawā (unā)	irandu (iraki-)
onno rokom	wenás	vēru
śokto	ámāru	kashtam
noiśo bhoj	rǎǎ kǎǎma	virundu
dik	disáwa (-sā)	vazi
nŏngra	ápirisidu	azukaḍainda

47

VOCABULARY

ENGLISH	PERSIAN	HINDI [URDU]
do, to	kardan (mikonad)	karnaa
doctor, the	doktor	daakṭaar (m., f.)
dog, the	sag	kuttaa (m.)
don't!	nakonid!	na karo!
door, the	dar	darvaazaa (m.)
doubt, the	shak	śak (m.)
down	pāin	niiće
dress (woman's), the	lebās	pahnaavaa (m.) [libaas (m.)]
drink, the	mashrub	pey (m.) [ḍirink (m.)]
drink, to	āshāmidan (miāshāmad)	piinaa
drive (car), to	rāndan (mirānad)	ćalaanaa
driver, the	rānande	ćalaanevaalaa/-ii
dry	khoshk	suukhaa (inv.)
duck, the	ordak	batakh (f.)
during	dar zarfe	... ke dauraan
dusty	khāki	dhuulbharaa
duty (obligation), the	vazife	farz (m.)
each	har yaki	har
each other	yak digar	ek duusre kii
early (before time)	zud	jaldii
earrings, the	gushvāre	kante (m.) [kan ke baali (f.)]
east	mashregh	puurvii [maśrik]
easy	āsān	aasaan
eat, to	khordan (mikhārad)	khaanaa
egg, the	tokhme morgh	anḍaa (m.)
either ... or	yā ... yā	yaa ... yaa
electric	barghi	bijlii kii
elevator, the	āsānsor	lift (f.)
embassy, the	sefārat	duutaavaas (m.) [embasii (f.)]
empty	khāli	khalii
enemy, the	doshman	duśman (m., f.)
engine (car), the	motor	enjan (m.)
enjoy, to	lezzat bordan (mibarad)	mazaa lenaa [lutf uṭaanaa]
enormous	azim	bahut baraa
enough	bas	kaafii
enter, to	vāred shodan (mishavad)	andar aanaa
entrance, the	vorud	darvaazaa (m.)
envelope, the	pākat	lifaafaa (m.)
equal	barābar	baraabar
evening, the	ghorub	śaam (f.)
everybody	hame kas	har koii
everything	har chiz	sab kuch
everywhere	harjā	ćaarõ taraf
exactly	einan	bilkul ṭhiik
example, for	barāye mesāl	maslan
except	bejoz	sivaa

VOCABULARY

BENGALI	SINHALESE	TAMIL
kŏri/koren	karanawā (kalā)	seydu (seygi-)
ḍakṭar	dostara (-rawaru)	ḍaakṭar
kukur	bállā (-llŏ)	naay
...-ben na!	... epā!	seyyaadē!
dorja	dora (-rawál)	kadavu
śondeho	áwwiswāsaya (-sa)	sanḍēgam
niće	páhála	kiiẕe
mohilader pośak	gehenu ănduma	aaḍai
panio	biima (biim)	ḍirink
pan kŏri/koren	bonawā (biwwā)	kuḍitu (kuḍiki-)
ćalai/ćalan	elawánawā (elewwā)	ōṭi (ōṭugi-)
ćalok	dráywar (-warlā)	ōṭubavar
śuknŏ	wiyali	varaṇḍa
hăś	tārāwa (-wo)	vaatu
dhoria	... kálhi	nēratinidaiyē
dhulimoi	dūwili sáhita	duusi
kortobbo	káṭayutta	kaḍamai
prottek	eka eka	ovvoru
protteke	ekinetā	oruvarōdoruvar
purbe	káltiyā	mundi
kaner dul	kárābu kuṭṭám	kaataṇi
purbo	nagenahira	kiẕaku
śohoj	lēsi	sulabam
khai/khan	kánawā (kăăwā)	saapiṭu (saapiḍugi-)
ḍim	bittaraya (-ra)	muṭai
othoba ... ba	... wāt ... wāt	onḍru ... alladu
boiddutik	widuli	elekṭrik
lipht	lifṭ-eka (lift)	lifṭ
dutabaś	tānāpati káryālaya (-la)	embasi
khali	his	kaali
śatru	sáturā	yediri
enjin	ănjima (-jim)	injin
anondo kŏri/koren	priiti wiňdinawā (windā)	anubavitu (-viki-)
proćur	átiwisāla	mikaperiya
jotheśṭo	ăti tárám	pŏdum
ḍhuki/dhŏken	átul wenawā (unā)	pugundu (pugugi-)
probeś poth	doraṭuwa (-ṭu)	vaasal
kham	liyum káwaraya (-wár)	kavar
śoman	sáma	samam
śondhe	sáwasa	saayangaalam
śokole	hămoma	yellaarum
śobkićhu	siyálla	yellaam
śobkhane	hăma tănama	yengum
thikbhabe	háriyata	korrekta
jemon	udāháranayák wásyen	udaaranam
... ćhara	... hăra	tavira

49

VOCABULARY

ENGLISH	PERSIAN	HINDI [URDU]
exhibition, the	namâyeh gâh	numaaiś (f.)
exit, the	khoruj	darvaazaa (m.)
expect, to	entezâr dâshtan (dârad)	ummed karnaa
explain, to	tozih dâdan (midehad)	samjhaanaa
eye, the	chashm	ãkh (f.)
face, the	surat	ćehraa (m.)
fact, in	dar naghe	asal mẽ
fail, to	movaffagh nashodan (namishavad)	nakarnyaab honaa
fair (just)	monsef	nyaay [insaaf]
fall, to	soghut kardan (mikonad)	girnaa
family, the	khânevâde	khaandaan (m.)
famous	ma'ruf	maśuur
fan, the	bâd bezan	pankhaa (m.)
far	dur	duur
farmer, the	dehghân	kisaan (m.)
fast	tond	tez
fasten, to	mohkam kardan (mikonad)	baandhnaa
festival, the	jashn	melaa (m.)
fetch, to	âvardan (miâvarad)	laanaa
few, a	chand	thore
field, the	keshtzâr	khet (m.)
fight, to	jang kardan (mikonad)	larnaa
fill, to	por kardan (mikonad)	bharnaa
film (for camera), the	film	film (f.)
film (movie show), the	film	ćal ćitr (m.) [film (f.)]
finally	dar khâteme	aakhir
find, to	peidâ kardan (mikonad)	paanaa
finish, to	tamâm kardan (mikonad)	khatam karnaa
fire, the	âtesh	aag (f.)
first	avval	pahilaa
fish, the	mâhi	machlii (f.)
flat	hamvâr	ćaptaa
flat (tyre), the	panchar	ćaptaa taayar (m.)
floor, the	zamin	farś (m.)
flower, the	gol	phuul (m.)
fly, the	magas	makkhii (f.)
fly, to	parvâz kardan (mikonad)	urnaa
follow, to	peirovi kardan (mikonad)	piiche aanaa
food, the	khorâk	khaanaa (m.)
foot, the	pa	paaõ (m.)
football (game), the	futbal	futbaal (m.)
for	barâye	... ke liye
forbidden	mamnu'	manaa
foreign	khâreji	videśii
forest, the	jangal	jangal (m.)
forget, to	farâmush kardan (mikonad)	bhuulnaa
fork, the	changâl	kâtaa (m.)

VOCABULARY

BENGALI	SINHALESE	TAMIL
prodorśoni	pradársanaya (-na)	kaatchi
bahir hoar poth	piṭawiime doraṭuwa (-ṭu)	veḷḷi vaẓi
aśa kŏri/koren	báláporottu wenawá (uná)	yetïrbaartu (-baarki-)
bujhie dii/den	tŏranawá (tĕruwá)	vivari
ćokh	ăhă (ăs)	kaṇ
mukh	mūna (-nu)	mugam
prokrito pokkhe	káranayák wásayen	meyyaakavĕ
okritokarjo hŏi/hoen	ásamárta wenawá (uná)	tavari (tavarugi-)
najjo	sámádana	niyaayam
pŏri/poren	wăṭenawá (wăṭuná)	viẓundu (viẓugi-)
śongśar	páwula (-wul)	kuḍumbam
bikhato	prasidda	pukaẓbetra
pakha	páwána (-wán)	visiri
dure	dura	tuuratil
ćaśi	gowiyá (-yŏ)	uẓavan
taṛatari	ikmán	vĕgam
badhi/badhen	táda karanawá (kalá)	kaṭi (kaṭugi-)
utśob	utsawaya (-wa)	viẓaa
ani/anen	soyá gĕnawá (genáwá)	aẓaitu (aẓaiki-)
kićhu	siiwálpa	konjam
math	kuṁbura (-ru)	vayal
maramari kŏri/koren	gáhá gánnawá (gáttá)	saṇḍaipŏda
bhŏri/bhoren	purawanawá (piráwwá)	nirapu (nirapigi-)
philm	film-eka (film)	pilim
sinema	chitra pátiya (-ti)	sinimaa
obośeśe	áwasána wásayen	kaḍaisiyaa
pai/paen	soyá gánnawá (gáttá)	kaṇḍubiḍitu (-biḍiki-)
śeś kŏri/koren	hámára karanawá (kalá)	muḍindu (muḍigi-)
agun	giṅdara	nerupu
prothom	pálamuweni	mudal
maćh	máluwá (-lu)	miin
śomotol	sámatalá	teṭai
ćaka ćhidro hoa	huláng giya táyaraya	taṭaiyaana
mejhe	tattuwa (-ṭṭu)	tarai
phul	mála (mál)	puu
maćhi	măssá (-ssŏ)	ii
uṛi/ŏṛen	igilenawá (igiluná)	parandu (paraki-)
anuśoron kŏri/koren	pilipádinawá (-páddá)	toḍaṇḍu (toḍaṇḍugi-)
khabar	kăăma (kăăm)	saapaaḍu
pa	ádiya (ádi)	kaal
fuṭbol	pá pánduwa	kaatpandaatam
... jonno	... -ṭa	... aaka
niśiddo	táhánám tárana láda	kuuḍaadu
bideś	widĕsiiya	ayalnaaṭukuriya
jongol	kăláăwá (-láă)	kaaḍu
bhŏli/bholen	ámataka wenawá (uná)	marandu (maraki-)
kăṭa	găăráppuwa (-ppu)	fŏk

51

VOCABULARY

ENGLISH	PERSIAN	HINDI [URDU]
former	sābegh	aglaa
forwards	jelou	aage
free (vacant)	āzād	khalii
fresh	tāze	taazaa
fried	sorkh karde	talaa huaa
fried rice, the	berenge bereshte	tale hue ćaaval (m. pl.)
friend, the	dust	dost (m., f.)
from	az	... se lekar
front of, in	jeloue	... ke saamne
frontier, the	sarhadd	sarhad (f.)
frozen	yakh zade	jamaa huaa
fruit, the	mive	phal (m.)
full	por	puuraa
garden, the	bāgh	baag (m.)
gasoline (petrol), the	benzin	petrol (m.)
girl, the	dokhtar	laṛkii (f.)
give, to	dādan (midehad)	denaa
glad	shād	khuś
glass (drinking), the	livān	gilaas (m.)
glass (substance), the	shishe	śiiśaa (m.)
glove, the	dastkesh	dastaanaa (m.)
go, to	raftan (miravad)	jaanaa
go down, to	pāin raftan (miravad)	niiće jaanaa
go up, to	bālā raftan (miravad)	ćaṛhnaa
god, the	khodā	devtaa (m.) [khuda (m.)]
gold, the	talā	sonaa (m.)
good	khub	aććhaa
goods, the	māl	maal (m.)
government, the	hokumat	sarkaar (f.)
gram, the	gram	graam (m.)
grapes, the	angur	anguur
grass, the	alaf chaman	ghaas (f.)
green	sabz	haraa
grey	khākestori	surmaaii
ground, the	zamin	zamiin (f.)
guard, to	hefāzat kardan (mikonad)	hifaazat karnaa
guest, the	mehmān	mehmaan (m., f.)
guide, the	rāhnamā	gaaiḍ (m., f.)
guidebook, the	ketābe rāhnamā	gaaiḍ (m.)
gun, the	tofang	banduuk (f.)
hair, the	mu	baal (m.)
haircut, the	eslāh	hajjaamat (f.)
hairdresser, the	salmāni	naaii (m., f.)
ham, the	gushte khuke sard	suuar kaa gośt (m.)
handbag, the	kife dasti	haindbaig (m.)
handkerchief, the	dastmāl	ruumaal (m.)
harbour, the	bandar	bandargaah (m.)

52

VOCABULARY

BENGALI	SINHALESE	TAMIL
purber	issarahā eka	mundiya
agaia	idiriyaṭa	munnaadi
khali	his	summaa
tatka	álut	putiy
bhaja	bádina láda	porita
phraiḍ rais	fráyd ráys	varuta saadam
bondhu	yāluwā (-wō)	nanbar
... theke	... iṅdalā	... mudal
... śamne	... issarahā	... munnaal
śimanto	dēsasiimāwa (-mā)	ōram
himaito	midunu	aisaana
phol	geḍiya (-ḍi)	paẓam
purno	pirunu	niraiya
bagan	wátta (wátu)	tōṭam
peṭrol	peṭrol	peṭrōl
balika	genu lámayā (-máy)	peṇ
dii/den	denawā (dunnā)	koḍutu (koḍuki-)
khuśi	sátuṭu	sandōsham
gelaś	widuruwa (-ru)	gilaas
kāć	widuru	kaṇṇaaḍi
bhugolok	átwăsma (-wăsum)	kaiyurai
jai/jan	yánawā (giyā)	pōyi (pōgi-)
neme jai/jan	báhinawā (băssā)	irangi (irangugi-)
upore jai/jan	náginawā (năggā)	yēri (yērugi-)
bhogoban/Allah	dewiyā (-yō)	kadavuḷ
śōna	rátrán	pon
bhalo	hoṅda	nalla
jiniś potro	báḍu	saamaan
śorkar	āṅḍuwa	arasaangam
gram	grăm-eka (grăm)	giraam
angur	mudrika pálaya (-la)	daraachai
ghaś	tánakola	pul
śobuj	kolapăṭa	pachai
pāśute	álupăṭa	saambal kalar
maṭi	bima	tarai
pahara dii/den	āráksa karanawā (kalā)	kaaval seydu (seygi-)
otithi	ámuttā (-tto)	virundinar
porićalok	márgadēsakayā (-yō)	vaẓigaaṭi
nirdeśok boi	márgawistaraya pōta (pōt)	vaẓigaaṭi pustagam
bonduk	tuwákkuwa (-kku)	tupaaki
ćul	konda	muḍi
ćul kaṭa	konde kápánna	muḍi veṭudal
napit	bábár (bábárlā)	muḍi tirutuvan
śukorer mangśo	lunudápu urumás	pandriyiraichi
hatbag	át pásumbiya (-bi)	payi
rumal	át lēnsuwa (-su)	kaikutai
bondor	wáráya (-yawál)	turaimugam

VOCABULARY

ENGLISH	PERSIAN	HINDI [URDU]
hard (firm)	sākht	sakht
hat, the	kolāh	ṭopii (f.)
have, to	dāshtan (dārad)	rakhnaa
he	u	vah
head, the	sar	sir (m.)
headache, the	sar dard	sardard (m.)
hear, to	shenidan (mishenavad)	sunnaa
heart, the	del	dil (m.)
heavy	sangin	bhaarii
height, the	ertefa'	ũćaaii (f.)
help, to	komak kardan (mikonad)	madad denaa
her (adj.)	-esh	iskaa
here	injā	yahā
high	boland	ũćaa
hill, the	tappe	pahaarii (f.)
his	-esh	iskaa
hold, to	negāh dāshtan (dārad)	pakarnaa
holy	moghaddas	pavitra [paak]
home, at	manzel	ghar par
honest	amin	iimaandaar
hope, to	omid dādan (midehad)	ummed karnaa
horse, the	asb	ghoṛaa (m.)
hospital, the	marizkhāne	aspataal (m.)
host, the	mizbān	mezbaan (m.)
hot (weather)	dāgh	garm
hot (heated food, etc.)	dāgh	garm
hot season (summer), the	tābestān	garmii (f.)
hotel, the	mehmānkhāne	hoṭal (m.)
hour, the	sā'at	ghanṭaa (m.)
house, the	manzel	ghar (m.)
how?	chegune?	kaise?
how many?	chand?	kitne?
however (conj.)	bāri	par
hut, the	kolbe	jhopṛii (f.)
I	man	maĩ
ice, the	yakh	barf (f.)
ice cream, the	bastani	aaiskriim (f.)
if	agar	agar
ill	mariz	biimaar
immediately	fouran	abhii
important	mohemm	zaruurii
impossible	mohāl	na mumkin
in	dar	... mẽ
information, the	ettelā'at	khabar (f.)
inside	dākhel	... ke andar
instead of	avaze	... ke baajaae

VOCABULARY

BENGALI	SINHALESE	TAMIL
mojbut	táda	geṭi
ṭupi	toppiya (-ppi)	topi
... -r aćhe	tiyenawā (tiuwā)	irundu (iruki-)
tini	ohu	avan
matha	hisa (his)	talai
matha betha	isaradaya (-da)	talaivali
śuni/śōnen	āhenawā (ăhunā)	kēṭu (kēṭki-)
hridoe	hárdaya (-da)	idayam
bhari	bára	ganamaana
uććhota	usa	uyaram
śahajjo kōri/koren	udaw karanawā (kalā)	udavi (udavigi-)
tār	ăyagē	avaḷ
ekhane	metana	inge
ŭću	us	uyarnda
pahaṛ	kánda (káňdu)	kundru
tār	ohugē	avan
dhōri/dhoren	állanawā (ălluwā)	piḍitu (piḍiki-)
śuddho	pūjaniir	parisuta
baṛite	gedara	viiṭil
śot	áwánka	nērmayaana
aśa kōri/koren	báláporottu wenawā (unā)	nambi (nambugi-)
ghōṛa	áswayā (-yō)	kudirai
hāśpaṭal	ispirítālē (-la)	aaspatiri
appaionkari	tānāyám kāru (-ruwo)	virundaḷipavar
gorom	griime	veyyil
gorom	unu	suuḍaana
gorom kal	griisma srátuwa	kōḍaigaalam
hoṭel	hōṭalē (-la)	hōṭal
ghonṭa	păya (păă)	maṇi
baṛi	gē (gewál)	viiḍu
ki kōre?	kohomada?	yepadi?
koeṭa?	kiidenāda?	yetanai?
kintu	námut	yendraalum
kure ghor	păla (păl)	kuḍisai
ami	máma	naan
boroph	áys	panikaṭi
ais krim	áyskriim	aiskiriim
jodi	... nán	apadi
ośuśtho	ásaniipa	nōypata
ekhuni	dănmama	uḍanē
joruri	wădagát	mukiyam
aśombhob	băă	muḍiyaadadu
... mōddhe	ătula	... il
khōj-khobor	toratura (-ru)	takaval
... bhitore	... ătula	... uḷḷē
... bodole	... wenuwaṭa	badilaaga

VOCABULARY

ENGLISH	PERSIAN	HINDI [URDU]
interesting	jälebe tavajjoh	dilċasp
interpreter, the	motarjem	dubhaaśiyaa/dubhaaśii
		[tarjuman (m., f.)]
iron (metal), the	āhan	lohaa (m.)
is	ast	hai
island, the	jazire	dviip (m.) [jaziiraa (m.)]
isn't it?	intour nist?	nahī kaya?
it	ān	vah
jewellery, the	jouhar ālāt	gahne (m.) [zewaraat (m.)]
journey, the	safar	safar (m.)
jump, to	paridan (miparad)	kuudnaa
jungle, the	jangal	jangal (m.)
key, the	kelid	ċaabii (f.)
kill, to	koshtan (mikoshad)	maarnaa
kilogram, the	kilo	kilograam (m.)
kilometre, the	kilometr	kilomiiṭar (m.)
kind (friendly)	mehrabān	mehrbaan
king, the	shāh	raajaa (m.)
kiss, to	busidan (mibusad)	ċuumnaa
kitchen, the	matbakh	rasoii (f.) [baavarċi khaanaa (m.)]
knife, the	kārd	ċhuurii (f.)
know, to	dānestan (midānad)	jaannaa
label, the	barchasb	lebal (m.)
lake, the	daryāche	jhiil (f.)
lamb, the	barre	memnaa (m.) [bheṛ kaa baċċaa (m.)]
lamp, the	cherāgh	battii (f.)
last	ākherin	aakhrii
late (behind time)	dir	der
later on	ba'd az ān	der-se
laugh, to	khandidan (mikhandad)	hãsnaa
laundry (clothes), the	rakhtshukhāne	dhule kapṛe (m., pl.)
law, the	ghānun	kaanuun (m.)
lawyer, the	vakil	vakiil (m., f.)
lead, to	hedāyat kardan (mikonad)	aguaaii karnaa [rahnumai karnaa]
learn, to	āmukhtan (miāmuzad)	siikhnaa
least, at	aghallan	kam-se kam
leave (place), to	vedā' kardan (mikonad)	choṛnaa
leave behind, to	tark kardan (mikonad)	choṛnaa
left (hand)	chap	baayã
leg, the	sāgh	ṭãg (f.)
lemon, the	limu	niimbuu (m.)
lemonade, the	limunād	lemaned (m.)
letter (note), the	nāme	ċiṭṭhii (f.)
letter (character), the	harf	akśar (m.) [harf (m.)]
lettuce, the	kāhu	kaahuu (m.)
lie, the	dorugh	jhuuṭh (m.)

VOCABULARY

BENGALI	SINHALESE	TAMIL
mojar	sitgánnä	swarasyamaana
torjomakari	tõlkayä (-yõ)	moẓibeyarpaaḷar
louho	yákaḍa	irumbu
aćhe	innawä	uṇḍu
dip	diwayina (-yin)	tiivu
tai noi ki?	nëda?	illaiyaa?
iha	ëka	adu
juelari	äbárana	aṇimaṇikogudi
brhomon	gámana (-mán)	pirayaaṇam
laphai/laphan	páninawä (pännä)	gudi (gudiki-)
jongol	kälääwa	kaaḍu
ćabi	yátura (-ru)	saavi
mere pheli/phelen	máranawä (märuwä)	kondru (kollugi-)
kilogram	kilográm-eka (-grám)	kilagiraam
kilomiṭar	kilomiiṭar-eka (-ṭár)	kilamiiṭar
doialu	karuwánánta	anbaana
raja	rájjuruwo (rájawaru)	raajaa
ćumbon kõri/koren	imbinawä (imbä)	mutangoḍutu (-ḍuki-)
ranna ghor	kussiya (-ssi)	samayalarai
ćhuri	pihiye (-hi)	kati
jani/janen	dánnawä (däna gáttä)	arindu (arigi-)
lebel	lëbal-eka (-bál)	lëbal
rõd	wila (wil)	yëri
bheṟa	bäṭalu páṭiyä (päṭä)	aatukari
proḍip	páhána (-hán)	viḷaku
ontim	ántëma	kaḍaisi
deri kore	párákku	pindi
pore	pásse	piragu
haśi/haśen	sinäsenawä (sinäsunä)	siritu (siriki-)
londri	londariya	salavai
ain	niitiya	saṭam
ukil	ädwagát (-gátwaru)	vakiil
poth dekhai/dekhan	närgaya pennanawä (pennuwä)	munnal põyi (põgi-)
śekhai/śekhan	igenagánnawä (-gáttä)	paḍitu (paḍiki-)
antoto	yáṭát piriseyin	adaiyaavaḍu
ćhaṟi/ćhaṟen	iwatata yánawä (giyä)	viṭu (viḍugi-)
ćhaṟi/ćhaṟen	tábä yánawä (giyä)	vitupõyi (vitupõgi-)
bä	wáma	iḍaḍu
pa	kákula (-kul)	kaal
lebu	dehigeḍiya (-ḍi)	yelumicham paẓam
lebur śorbot	dehi ponsä	lemonëḍ
ćiṭhi	liyuma (-yum)	kaḍidam
akkhor	ákura (-ru)	yeẓutu
leṭis	sáláda kola	kiirai vagai
mittha	boruwa (-ru)	poyi

57

VOCABULARY

ENGLISH	PERSIAN	HINDI [URDU]
lie down, to	daraz kashidan (mikashad)	letnaa
lift, to	bar dashtan (midarad)	uthaanaa
light (colour)	roushan	halkaa
light (weight)	sabok	halkaa
lighter (cigarette), the	fandak	sigret laaitr (m.)
like (prep.)	chun	. . . usi tarah
lipstick, the	matik	surkhii (f.)
litre, the	litr	liitr (m.)
little, a	kam	zaraa
live (reside), to	sokunat kardan (mikonad)	rahnaa
lock, the	ghofl	taalaa (m.)
long (size)	deraz	lambaa
long (time)	tulani	lambaa
long ago	vaght pish	bahut din hue
look at, to	negah kardan (mikonad)	dekhnaa
look for, to	aghab gashtan (migardad)	dhudhnaa
lose (mislay), to	gom kardan (mikonad)	khonaa
lose (race, etc.), to	bakhtan (mibazad)	haarnaa
loud	boland	ucaa
love, to	mohabbat dadan (midehad)	muhabbat karnaa
low	past	niicaa
lunch, the	nahar	dopahar kaa khaanaa (m.)
machine, the	mashinalat	masiin (f.)
magazine, the	majalle	risalaa (m.)
make, to	kardan (mikonad)	banaanaa
malaria, the	tab o noube	maleriyaa (m.)
man, the	mard	aadmii (m.)
manager, the	modir	mainejar (m.)
mango, the	'anbe	aam (m.)
many	besyar	bahut
map, the	naghshe	naksaa (m.)
market, the	bazar	baazaar (m.)
married	mota'ahhel	saadii sudaa
matches, the	kebritha	maacise (f. pl.)
means, (it)	bein ma'nist	matlab . . . hai
measure, to	andaze gereftan (migirad)	naapnaa
meat, the	gusht	gost (m.)
mechanic, the	mikanik	mistrii (m.)
medicine, the	daru	davaaii (f.)
meet, to	molaghat kardan (mikonad)	milnaa
melon, the	kharbuze	tarbuuz (m.)
menu, the	liste khorak	menyuu (m.)
message, the	peigham	paigaam (m.)
metre, the	metr	miitar (m.)
middle, the	markaz	biic (m.)
midnight	nesfe shab	aadii raat (f.)
milk, the	shir	duudh (m.)

58

VOCABULARY

BENGALI	SINHALESE	TAMIL
śui/śōen	hänsi wenawā (unä)	paḍutu (paḍuki-)
ōthai/ōthan	ussanawā (issuwā)	tuuki (tuukugi-)
phike	lā pāṭa	veḷuta
halka	sāhällu	mélliya
laiṭar	láytaraya (-ra)	laiṭar
moto	. . . wágē	. . . pōl
lipsṭik	lipsṭikeka (-sṭik)	lipsṭik
liṭar	liiṭaraya (-ra)	liṭar
ekṭu	ṭikák	lésaa
thaki/thaken	jiiwát wenawā (unā)	kudiyiru (kudiyiruki-)
tala	águla (águl)	puuṭu
dirgho	diga	neḍiya
onekkhon	dērga kālayák	nēram
onek din age	ādi kālayehi	romba munnadi
takai/takan	bálanawā (bǎluwā)	paartu (paarki-)
khūji/khōjen	soyanawā (seywā)	tēdi (tēdigi-)
harai/haran	nāti karanawā (kalā)	kaanaamarpōṭu (-pōḍugi-)
porajito hōi/hoen	páradinawā (-dunnā)	tolvi (tolvigi-)
jōre	sádda wedi	uraka
bhalobaśi/bhalobaśen	ālaya karanawā (kalā)	nēsitu (nēsiki-)
niću	páhát	kiiẓa
moddhanno bhoj	dáwál kǎǎma	lansh
kol	yántraya (-tra)	iyandiram
magajin	sáṅgarāwa (-rā)	pustagam
toiar kōri/koren	hádanawā (hǎduwā)	paṇṇi (paṇṇugi-)
maleria	mǎlēriyā-una	muraikaaychal
manuś	minihā (minissu)	manidan
menejar	pālakayā (-ka)	mēlaaḷar
am	ámbageḍiya (-ḍi)	maangaay
onek	huṅgák	pal
manćitro	sitiyama (-yam)	naaṭupaḍam
bajar	márkeṭ-eka (-keṭ)	angaadi
bibahito	wiwāhā wū	kalyaanamaana
deślai	ginikūru	tiikuchi
bōjha	. . . ēke tēruma	yenna artam yendral
mapi/mapen	máninawā (mǎnnā)	aḷavu (aḷaki-)
mangśo	más	iraichi
miśtri	bāsunnǎhe (bāsla)	kammiyar
ōśudh	bēta	marundu
dekha kōri/koren	hámba wenawā (unā)	sanditu (sandigi-)
phuti	kǎkirigeḍiya (-ḍi)	mulaambaẓam
menu	laistuwa (-tu)	menu
barta	pániwudaya (-da)	sangadi
miṭar	miiṭar-eka (-ṭár)	miiṭar
majhkhan	mǎda	madi
modho ratri	máhárǎǎ	naḍuratri
dudh	kiri	paal

59

VOCABULARY

ENGLISH	PERSIAN	HINDI [URDU]
millimetre, the	milimetr	milimiiṭar (m.)
minute, the	daghighe	minaṭ (m.)
mirror, the	āine	śiiśaa (m.)
mistake, the	eshtebāh	galtii (f.)
moment, the	lahze	pal (m.) [lamhaa (m.)]
monastery, the	deir	math (m.) [dharam śalaa (f.)]
money, the	pul	paise (m. pl.)
month, the	māh	mahiinaa (m.)
monument, the	yādegār	yaadgaar (f.)
moon, the	māh	ćād (m.)
more	bish	aur
morning, the	sobh	subah (f.)
mosque, the	masjed	masjid (f.)
mosquito, the	pashe	maććhar (m.)
most	bishtar	sab se zyaadaa
motor-bike, the	motor siklet	moṭarsaaikil (f.)
mountain, the	kuh	pahaaṛ (m.)
mouth, the	dahān	mũh (m.)
movie camera, the	durbine film	ćal ćitr kaimraa (m.) [film kaimraa (m.)]
much	besyār	bahut
museum, the	muze	ajaayab ghar (m.)
mushroom, the	gharch	khuumii (f.)
music, the	musighi	sāgiit (m.) [baajaa (m.)]
must	bāyad	... zaruur ...
mustard, the	khardel	sarsõ (f.)
my	-am	meraa
name, the	nām	naam (m.)
napkin, the	dastmāl	naipkin (m.)
narrow	tang	tang
natural	tabi'i	kudratii
near (not far)	nazdik	... ke paas
near to	nazdik	nazdiik
need, to	hājat dādan (midehad)	zaruurat honaa
needle, the	suzan	suii (f.)
never	hargez	kabhii nahĩ
new	nou	nayaa
newspaper, the	ruznāme	akhbaar (m.)
next (after)	digar	aglaa
night, the	shab	raat (f.)
no (adj.)	hich	nahĩ
nobody	hich kas	koii nahĩ
noise, the	sedā	śor (m.)
noodles, the	vermishel	nuuḍals (m. pl.)
noon	zohr	dopahar
north	shamāl	uttar [sumaal]

VOCABULARY

BENGALI	SINHALESE	TAMIL
milimiṭar	milimiiṭar-eka (-ṭár)	millimiiṭar
miniṭ	miniṭṭuwa (-ṭṭu)	nimisham
aina	kánnaḍiya (-ḍi)	kaṇṇaaḍi
bhul	wárada (-dawál)	tapu
muhurto	mohota (-tawál)	kshaṇam
śonnaśir astana	tápasárámaya (-ma)	maḍam
ṭaka	sálli	kaasu
mas	máse (mása)	maasam
sritiśoudho	smárakaya (-ka)	ninaivuchinnam
čād	háňda (-ňdawál)	nilaa
arō	wáḍá	innum
śokal	udē	kaalai
mośjid	muslim pálliya (-lli)	palḷivaasal
mośa	máduruwá (-wō)	kosu
śorbadhik	itáma	migapala
moṭor saikel	moṭár sikalaya (-la)	mōṭarbaik
porbot	kánda (káňdu)	malai
mukh	káṭa (-ṭawál)	vaay
mubhi kamera	chitra páta kǎmaráwa (-rá)	sinimaa kēmara
beśi	hungák	romba
jadughor	kautukágáraya	poruṭkaatchichaalai
banger chata	bimm haṭṭa (-ṭṭu)	kaaḷan
sōnggit	sángiitaya	isai
... -ke ... hoe	... ōnǎá	vēṇḍum
śoriśa	ába	kaḍugu
amar	mágē	yen
nam	náma (nám)	peyar
gamcha	nǎpkima (-kin)	tuḍaipukiṭai
śoru	páṭu	oḍukamaana
prakritik	swabáwika	iyarkai
nikoṭ	lánga	kiṭa
... kaćhe	... lángaṭa	... kiṭa
lagi/lagen	... áwásyaya	vēṇḍum
śuć	indikaṭuwa (-tu)	uusi
kokhono na	káwadáwát nǎta	orugaalum
notun	álut	pudiya
khoborer kagoj	páttaraya (-ra)	patirigai
agami	lábana	aḍutu
ratri	rǎá (rǎǎ)	iravu
na	nǎǎ	... illai
kehoi	káwuruwát nǎta	yaarumillai
śobdo	gōsáwa (-sáwál)	saptam
śemai	núdl káma	sēmiyaa
dupurbela	máddahánaya	matiyam
uttor	utura	vaḍaku

61

VOCABULARY

ENGLISH	PERSIAN	HINDI [URDU]
not	na-	nahī̃
not at all	abadan	bilkul nahī̃
notepaper, the	kāghaze yāddāsht	kaagaz (m.)
nothing	hich	kuć nahī̃
notice, the	e'lan	noṭis (m.)
now	aknun	abhii
number, the	shomāre	nambar (m.)
nurse, the	parastār	nars (f.)
nuts, the	äjil	giriyā (f. pl.)
obtain, to	hāsel kardan (mikonad)	paanaa
occupied	mashghul	bharaa huaa
offer, to	taghdim kardan (mikonad)	peś karnaa
office, the	edāre	daftar (m.)
officer (army), the	afsar	afsar (m.)
often	bārhā	aksar
oil, the	naft	tel (m.)
old (persons)	pir	buḍḍhaa
old (things)	kohne	puraanaa
olives, the	zeitunhā	jaituun (m. pl.)
on	bar ruye	... par
once	yek daf'e	ek baar
onion, the	piāz	pyaaz (m.)
only	faghat	sirf
open	bāz	kholaa
open, to	bāz kardan (mikonad)	kholnaa
opera, the	opera	opraa (m.)
opposite	ruberu	saamne kaa
or	yā	yaa
orange, the	portoghāl	naarāgii (f.)
ordered	seforesh shode	māgaataa
ordinary	ma'muli	aam
our	-emān	hamaaraa
outside	birun	baahar
overcoat, the	pāltou	baraa koṭ (m.)
owe, to	bedehkār budan (ast)	karzdar honaa
oyster, the	sadaf	śuvit (f.) [sadfaa (m.)]
pack, to	bastan (mibandad)	bādhnaa
pain, the	dard	dard (m.)
paint, the	rang	rãg (m.)
pair, the	joft	joṛaa (m.)
palace, the	ghasr	mahal (m.)
paper, the	kāghaz	kaagaz (m.)
parcel, the	baste	paarsal (m.)
park, the	bāgh	paark (m.)
park (car), to	tanaghof kardan (mikonad)	kharii karnaa
passport, the	gozarnāme	paasporṭ (m.)

VOCABULARY

BENGALI	SINHALESE	TAMIL
... na	năă	illai
ekebare na	kohomát ... năă	apudiyellam illai
ćithi lekhar kagoj	liyum liyana kádadásiya	nótpépar
kićhui noe	mokákwát năta	vondrumillai
notiś	dănwima (-wim)	vilambaram
ekhon	dăn	ipódu
śongkha	nombaraya (-ra)	yen
narś	sáttu séwikáwa (-ka)	taadi
badam	nát-eka (nát)	parupu
pai/paen	lábágánnawá (-gáttá)	adaindu (adaigi-)
dokhole	sitinawá	ullé aal irukiradu
dite ćai/ćan	pújá karanawá (kalá)	padaiyal seydu (seygi-)
ophiś	kántóruwa (-ru)	aafis
śenanaiok	yuda pálakaya (-ka)	adigaari
prae	nitara nitara	adikadi
tel	tel	yenney
briddho	wáyás pirunu	vayadaana
puraton	párana	pazaiya
jolpai	ráta weralugediya (-di)	aaliv
... upore	... uda	... mélé
ekbar	ekawárák	oru dara
peaj	lúnugediya (-di)	vengaayam
kebol	witara	matum
khóla	ăránu	tiranda
khuli/khólen	árinawá (áriyá)	tirandu (tiraki-)
gitinato	sángiita nátataya (-ta)	isainadagam
... biporit	wirudda	... yedir
ba	nohot	alladu
komola lebu	dodámgediya (-di)	aaranju
nirdeśito	ánakaruwa	órdar kódukiradu
śadharon	sámánya	saadaaranam
amader	ápé	yengal
... baire	eliya	... veliyé
óbharkot	uda kábáya (-bá)	mélangi
rini hói/hoen	náya geti	kadan vaangu (vaangi-)
jhinuk	bellá	mutuchipi
gátie pheli/phelen	áskaranna	kati (katigi-)
bedona	ridiima	nóvu
rong	tinta	saayam
jóra	jóduwa (jódu)	inai
praśad	máligawa (-ga)	aranmanai
kagoj	káradásiga	pépar
parsol	pársále (-sál)	paarsal
park	málluyana (-nawál)	puungaa
park kóri/koren	năwatá tiyánna	paark seydu (seygi-)
ćharpotro	widósa gámán bálapátraya (-ra)	pasport

63

VOCABULARY

ENGLISH	PERSIAN	HINDI [URDU]
pastry, the	khamir	pestrii (f.)
pay, to	pardākhtan (mipardāzad)	paise denaa
peace, the	solh	śaanti (f.) [aman (m.)]
peach, the	holu	aaruu (m.)
pearl, the	morvārid	motii (f.)
peas, the	nokhode farangi	matar (m. pl.)
pen, the	ghalam	kalam (f.)
pencil, the	medād	pensil (f.)
pepper, the	felfel	kalii mirć (f.)
perfume, the	atr	itar (m.)
perhaps	shāyad	śaayad
permit, to	ejāze dādan (midehad)	ijaazat denaa
person, the	shakhs	bādaa (m., f.) [śakhs (m., f.)]
petrol (gasoline), the	benzin	petrol (m.)
pharmacy, the	davākhāne	davaa khaanaa (m.)
photograph, the	aks	foto (m.)
picture, the	tasvir	tasviir (f.)
piece, the	tekke	tukraa (m.)
pillow, the	bālesh	takiyaa (m.)
pin, the	sanjāgh	pin (f.)
pineapple, the	ānānās	anannaas (m.)
pink	surati	gulaabii
place, the	mahall	jagah (f.)
plate, the	poshghāb	rakaabii (f.)
platform (railway), the	saku	plaitfarm (m.)
pleasant	pasandide	suhaavnaa [kuśgavaar]
plum, the	ālu	aaluućaa (m.)
point out, to	neshān dādan (midehad)	dikhlaanaa
police station, the	kalāntari	thaanaa (m.)
policeman, the	pāsbān	sipaahii (m.)
poor (needy)	faghir	gariib
pork, the	gushte khuk	suuar kaa gośt (m.)
porter, the	bārbar	kulii (m.)
possible	momken	mumkin
post-box, the	sandughe post	daak baks (m.)
postcard, the	kartpostāl	post kaard (m.)
post-office, the	postkhāne	daakkhaanaa (m.)
potatoes, the	sibe zamini	aaluu (m. pl.)
practise, to	mashgh kardan (mikonad)	abhyaas karnaa [maśk karnaa]
prawn, the	meigu ·	jhingaa (m.)
present (gift), the	tohfe	tohfaa (m.)
president, the	ra'is	raaśtrapati (m., f.)
press (clothes), to	otu kardan (mikonad)	istrii karnaa
pretty	khoshgel	khuubsurat
price, the	gheimat	daam (m.)
priest, the	kashish	pujaarii (m.)
prison, the	zendān	kaidkhaanaa (m.)

64

VOCABULARY

BENGALI	SINHALESE	TAMIL
peṣṭri	ánāpu piṭi	kĕk
dam dii/den	gewanawā (gewwā)	vilaigoḍutu (-goḍuki-)
śanti	sámādāna	samaadaanam
pić	piichgeḍiya (-ḍi)	piich
mukta	mutu āṭaya (āṭa)	mutu
motorśuti	piis	payaru
kolom	pă̄na (pă̄n)	pēnaa
pensil	pănsalaya (-la)	pensil
golmorić	gám miris	miḷagu
śugondhi	suwáṅda	seṇṭ
hoeto	sámahára wiṭa	oruvēlai
anumoti dii/den	iḍa denawā (dunnā)	anumadi koḍutu (koḍuki-)
lok	ekenā (iya)	aaḷ
peṭrol	peṭrol	peṭrōl
ouśodhaloi	bēt sáppuwa (-ppu)	parmasi
ćhobi	jāyārūpaya (-pa)	fōtōs
ćhobi	pinture (-tur)	paḍam
ongśo	kālla (kāli)	tuṇḍu
baliś	koṭṭaya (-ṭṭa)	talaiyanai
alpin	álpenettiya (-tti)	kuṇḍusi
anaroś	ánnāsigeḍiya (-ḍi)	annaasi
golapi	rōsa	rōs kalar
jaega	tăna (tăn)	iḍam
pleṭ	bigāna (-gān)	taṭu
plaṭphorm	wēdikawa (-ka)	piḷaaṭpaaram
anondo prodo	priya	magizvaḷikira
plam	plámgeḍiya (-ḍi)	plam
dekhie dii/den	pennā denawā (dunnā)	kuritu (kuriki-)
thana	polisiya (-si)	kaaval nilaiyam
puliś	polis bátayā (-ta)	pōliisman
gorib	duppát	yēẓai
śukorer mangśo	ūru más	pandriyiraichi
kuli	doraṭu pālayā (-la)	pōrṭar
śombhob	puluwani	orukakuuḍiya
ḍakbakśo	tăpál peṭṭiya (-ṭṭi)	pōsṭbaaks
posṭkarḍ	tăpál páta (pát)	kaarḍ
dakghor	tăpál kántōruwa (-ru)	tabaal aafis
aluguli	ártāpál álaya (ála)	uruḷaikiẓangu
obbhaś kōri/koren	purudu wenawā (unā)	paẓaki (paẓakugi-)
ćingṛi máć	issā (issō)	iraal miin
upohar	tăăgga (-ggi)	nangoḍai
rastropoti	sábāpati (-tiwaru)	janaadibadi
ćepi/ćapen	mádinawā (măddā)	istri pōṭu (pōḍigi-)
śundor	lássana	aẓagu
dam	milagānana (-gánán)	vilai
purohit	pujakayā (-yō)	puusaari
karagar	hiragē (-gewál)	kaaval

65

VOCABULARY

ENGLISH	PERSIAN	HINDI [URDU]
private	khosusi	nijii [raaz kaa]
promise, to	va'de dādan (midehad)	vaadaa karnaa
province, the	ostān	prades (m.)
public	omumi	aam
pull, to	kashidan (mikashad)	khĭcnaa
puncture, the	panchar	ced (m.)
pure	pāk	aslii
purple	arghavāni	jaamunii
put, to	gozāshtan (migozārad)	daalnaa
quantity, the	ghadr	maatraa (f.) [mikdaar (f.)]
queen, the	maleke	raanii (f.)
question, the	so'āl	savaal (m.)
quick	tond	jaldii
quiet	sāket	cup
race (contest), the	mosābeghe	daur (f.)
radio, the	bisim	rediyo (m.)
railway, the	rāhe āhan	rel (f.)
raincoat, the	bārāni	barsaatii (f.)
raining, it is	bārān miāyad	baaris ho rahi hai
razor, the	tigh	ustaraa (m.)
read, to	khāndan (mikhānad)	parhnaa
ready	hāzer	taiyaar
receive, to	gereftan (migirad)	paanaa
record (gramophone), the	safhe	rekaard (m.)
red	ghermez	laal
register (letter), to	sant kardan (mikonad)	rajistar karnaa
religion, the	din	dharm (m.) [mazhab (m.)]
remember, to	bekhāter āvardan (miāvarad)	yaad rakhnaa
repair, to	ta'mir kardan (mikonad)	... kii maranimat karnaa
repeat, to	tekrār kardan (mikonad)	dohraanaa
reply, to	pāsokh dādan (midehad)	javaab denaa
rest, to	rāhat kardan (mikonad)	aaraam karnaa
restaurant, the	rasturān	restarent (f.)
result, the	natije	natiijaa (m.)
rice (cooked), the	berenj	caaval (m.)
rich	servatmand	amiir
right (correct)	sahih	sahii
right (hand)	rāst	daayā
ring, the	angoshtar	anguutii (f.)
ripe	raside	pakkaa
river, the	rudkhāne	nadii (f.)
road, the	rāh	sarak (f.)
roast	beriān shode	bhuunaa huaa
room, the	otāgh	kamraa (m.)
run, to	davidan (midavad)	daurnaa
sad	deltang	udaas

VOCABULARY

BENGALI	SINHALESE	TAMIL
bektigoto	pudgalika	tanimuraiyaana
protigga kŏri/koren	porondu wenawā (unā)	vaakukoḍutu (-koḍuki-)
prodeś	pálāta (-lāt)	maanilam
jonośadharon	máhájana	ṭodu
ṭani/ṭanen	ádinawā (āddā)	iẓutu (iẓuki-)
ćaka ćhidro hoa	sidura (-ru)	potal
khāṭi	pirisidu	tuuy
beguni	dám páta	uuda kalar
rakhi/rakhen	dānawa (dămma)	vaitu (vaiki-)
poriman	pramānaya (-na)	aḷavu
rani	máhárajina (-jiniyŏ)	raani
prośno	prásnaya (-na)	këlvi
taraṭari	ikmán	vëgam
śanto	nischala	nisabtam
protijogita	rēs tárangaya (-ňga)	pandayam
reḍio	rēḍiyŏ-eka (-yŏ)	rēḍiyŏ
relpoth	dumriya pára	rëlwë
borśati	wăhi kábáya (-bā)	rēnkŏṭ
briśti poṛe	wáhinawā	maẓai peyidu
khur	dălipihiya (-hi)	rēsar
pŏri/poṛen	kiyawanawā (kiyewwā)	paḍitu (paḍiki-)
toiri	lăăsti	reḍi
pai/paen	piligánnawā (-gáttā)	vaangi (vaangugi-)
koler gan	grămafŏn táṭiya (-ṭi)	rekarḍ
lal	rátu	sivapu
rejisṭri kŏri/koren	rejisṭár karanawā (kalā)	rejisṭar seydu (seygi-)
dhormo	āgama (āgam)	matam
mone rakhi/rakhen	máták wenawā (unā)	ninaivuvaitukoṇḍu (-koḷḷugi-)
meramot kŏri/koren	repeyār karanawā (kalā)	repeyar seydu (seygi-)
punorai kŏri/koren	năwata karanawā (kalā)	tirupi (tirupigi-)
uttor dii/den	uttara denawā (dunnā)	badil solli (solligi-)
bissram kŏri/koren	nischalawa siṭinawa (siṭṭā)	ilaipaari (iḷaipaarugi-)
restera	resṭoránṭ-eka (-ránṭ)	hŏṭal
phol	wipākaya (-ka)	payan
bhat	bát	saatam
dhoni	pohosát	panakara
ṭhik	hári	sari
ḍan	dákuna	valadu
angṭi	mudda (mudu)	mŏdiram
paka	idunu	mudirnda
nodi	gáňga (-ňgawál)	aaru
rasta	pára (-rawál)	saalai
bhaja	bădapu	vadakiya
ghor	kámare (-ra)	arai
ćhuṭi/ćhŏṭen	duwanawā (diwwā)	ŏdi (ŏdugi-)
dukkhito	kánagātu	tukam

VOCABULARY

ENGLISH	PERSIAN	HINDI [URDU]
safe	amn	surkśit [mehfuuz]
sailor, the	malanān	naavik (m.) [kaśti baan (m.)]
salt, the	namak	namak (m.)
same	yaksān	vahii
sandals, the	gine	ćappal (m.)
sandwich, the	sānduich	saindvić (m.)
sauce, the	sos	ćatnii (f.)
say, to	goftan (miguyad)	kahnaa
school, the	madrase	skuul (f.)
science, the	elm	vigyaan (m.) [saains (f.)]
scissors, the	gheichi	kainćii (f.)
sea, the	daryā	samudra (m.) [samandar (m.)]
seat, the	neshiman	siiṭ (f.)
second	dovvom	duusraa
second (of time), the	sāniye	sekand (m.)
secretary, the	monshi	sekreṭrii (m., f.)
see, to	didan (mibinad)	dekhnaa
seems, (it)	benazar miāyad	maaluum hotaa hai
seldom	benodrat	kabhii kabhaar
sell, to	forukhtan (miforushad)	bećnaa
send (thing), to	ferestādan (miferestāyad)	bhejnaa
separate	jodā	alag
servant, the	pishkhedmat	naukar/naukaraanii
service station, the	ta'mirgāh	peṭrol sṭeśan (m.)
several	chandin	kaii
sew, to	dukhtan (miduzad)	siinaa
shallow	shelāl	uthlaa
shampoo, the	shāmpo	śampuu (m.)
shave, to	eslāh kardan (mikonad)	hajjaamat karnaa
she	u	vah
sheet, the	malāfe	ćaadar (f.)
shelter, the	panāhgah	panaah (f.)
ship, the	kashti	paanii kaa jahaaz (m.)
shirt, the	pirāhan	kamiiz (m.)
shoe, the	kafsh	juutaa (m.)
shop, the	dokkān	dukaan (f.)
short	kutāh	ćhoṭaa
show, to	neshān dādan (midehad)	dikhaanaa
shower, the	dush	phuhaaraa snaan (m.)
side, the	pahlu	taraf (f.)
sign, to	emzā kardan (mikonad)	dastkhat karnaa
silk, the	abrishom	resam (m.)
silver, the	noghre	ćādii (f.)
since (time)	tā	jab se
sing, to	āvāz khāndan (mikhānad)	gaanaa
sit, to	neshastan (mineshinad)	baiṭhnaa

VOCABULARY

BENGALI	SINHALESE	TAMIL
nirapod	párissám	batiramaa
nabik	năwiyă (-yô)	kaḍalôḍi
lobon	lunu	upu
eki	ema	adē
ćappol	sereppuwa kuṭṭám	midiyaḍi
sanḍuić	săṇḍwich-eka (-wich)	sanḍwich
ćaṭni	săs	kuzambu
bôli/bolen	kiyanawă (kiyuwă)	solli (sollugi-)
iskul	pásala (-sál)	paḷḷikuuḍam
biggan	widayăwa	vinnyaanam
kăći	kátura	katari
śomudro	mŭda (-du)	kaḍal
aśon	ăsanaya (-na)	maṇai
ditio	deweni	renḍaavadu
sekend	tápparaya (-ra)	noḍi
śoćib	lekám (-kámwaru)	seyalaalar
dekhi/dekhen	pēnawă (penună)	paartu (paarki-)
mone hoe	. . . -lu	tôndrugiradu
kodaćit	kálăturakin	yepôdaavadu
beći/bećen	wikunanawă (wikinuwă)	vitru (vitki-)
paṭhai/paṭhan	árinawă (ăriyă)	anupi (anupugi-)
alada	wenwŭ	tuṇḍikapaṭa
ćakor	wádakărayă (-yô)	vēlaiyaaḷ
peṭrol pamp	peṭrol stăshion-eka (-shion)	petrôl sṭeshan
kićhu	kiipe	pala
śelai kôri/koren	máhánawă (măsuwă)	taitu (taiki-)
agobhir	nogăṁburu	aazamillaada
śampu	isa săădima	shampu
daṛi kamai/kaman	ráwula kápanawă (kepuwă)	shēv seydu (seygi-)
tini	ăya	avaḷ
path	ătirilla (-lli)	paḍukai viripu
assroe	ăwaranaya (-na)	sheḍ
jahaj	năwa (năw)	kapal
jama	kámisaya (-sa)	shaṭai
juta	sápáttuwa (-ttu)	shuu
dôkan	sáppuwa (-ppu)	kaḍai
bēṭe	keṭi	chinna
dekhai/dekhan	pennanawă (pennuwă)	kaaṭi (kaaṭugi-)
phoara	sháwar-eka (-wár)	shawar
dik	păṭṭa (păṭi)	pakam
śoi kôri/koren	átsán karanawă (kală)	kayi yezetu pôtu (pôdugi-)
silk	páta	paṭu
rupa	riḍii	veḷḷi
. . . theke	ewēle sita	apo irundu
gai/gan	gáyanawă (găyuwă)	paaḍi (paaḍugi-)
bôśi/bośen	wăḍi wenawă (ună)	uṭkaarndu (uṭkaarugi-)

VOCABULARY

ENGLISH	PERSIAN	HINDI [URDU]
skirt, the	dāman	ghaaghrii (f.)
sky, the	āsman	aasmaan (m.)
sleep, to	khābidan (mikhābad)	sonaa
slow	kond	dhiire
small	kuchek	ćhoṭaa
smoke, to	dud kardan (mikonad)	sigreṭ piinaa
snow, the	barf	barf (m.)
soap, the	sābun	saabun (m.)
socks, the	jurābhā	moze (m. pl.)
soda water, the	sodā	soḍaa (m.)
soft	narm	naram
soldier, the	sarbāz	sipaahii (m.)
some	ba'zi	kućh
somebody	kasi	koii
something	chizi	kućh
sometimes	gāhi	kabhii kabhaar
somewhere	jāi	kahĩ
soon	zud	jaldii
sorry	mota'assef	afsos
soup, the	ābgusht	śorbaa (m.)
sour	torsh	khaṭṭa
south	jonub	dakśin [janub]
soy sauce, the	sose chini	soyaa ćaṭnii (f.)
space, the	fāsele	jagah (f.)
speak, to	harf zadan (mizanad)	bolnaa
spectacles, the	einak	ćaśmaa (m.)
spoon, the	ghāshogh	ćamćaa (m.)
sport, the	varzesh	khel (m.)
square (place), the	meidān	ćauk (m.)
stairs, the	pellekān	siiṛii (f. sing.)
stamp (postage), the	tambr	ḍaak ṭikaṭ (m.)
stand, to	istādan (mi-istad)	khaṛaa honaa
star, the	setāre	sitaara (m.)
start, to	shoru' kardan (mikonad)	śuruu karnaa
station (railway), the	istgāh	sṭeśan (f.)
stay, to	māndan (mimānad)	rahnaa
steak, the	gushte kabābi	ṭikkaa (m.)
steep	sarāshib	ḍhaalvan
steering, the	roul	sṭiring (m.)
stick, the	chub	ćhaṛii (f.)
still (adv.)	hanuz	ab tak
stockings, the	jurābe boland	juuraabẽ (f. pl.)
stone, the	sang	patthar (m.)
storey (floor), the	tabaghe	manzil (f.)
straight on	mostaghim	siidhe
strap, the	tasme	paṭṭii (f.)
street, the	kuche	saṛak (f.)

VOCABULARY

BENGALI	SINHALESE	TAMIL
jama	sāya	paavaadai
akaś	áhása	vaanam
ghumai/ghuman	nidāgánnawā (-gáttā)	tuungi (tuungugi-)
aste	hemihin	meduvaana
chŏṭo	kuḍā	chinna
sigaret khai/khan	sigarăṭ bonawā (biwwā)	pugaitu (pugaiki-)
tuśar	hima	pani
śaban	sábán	sōp
mŏja	koṭa mēs kuṭṭám	soks
sŏḍa ōaṭar	sŏḍā wátura	sŏda
norom	murdu	menmaiyaana
śoinno	bátayā (-yŏ)	paḍaiviiran
kichu	ṭikák	sila
keu	káwudo	yaarŏ
kichu	mokákdo	yennavŏ
kokhono kokhono	sámahárawiṭa	yepŏdŏ
kŏthao	kohēdŏ	yengēyŏ
śiggir	ikmanin	siikiram
dukkhito	kánagātui	varutam
jhŏl	sup hodda	vaḍisaaru
ṭok	ămbul	puḷipaana
dokkhin	dákuna	tetku
soier cáṭni	soi sās	soi sos
jaega	iḍa	iḍaiveli
bŏli/bolen	kátā karanawā (kalā)	pēsi (pēsugi-)
caśma	kánnādikuṭṭam	kannaaḍi
camoć	hănda (hă̆ḍi)	karaṇḍi
kheladhula	kriidāwa	viḷaiyaaṭu
courasta	cháturáswaya (-wa)	sadukam
śĩṛi	páḍi pela	paḍi
ḍak ṭikeṭ	muddaraya (-ra)	sṭampu
dāṛai/dāṛan	nágiṭi siṭinawā (siṭṭā)	nindru (nitki-)
tara	táruwa (-ru)	veḷḷi
śuru kŏri/koren	pátán gánnawā (gáttā)	kiḷambi (kiḷambugi-)
iśṭiśan	dumriya pola	nilaiyam
thaki/thaken	náwatinawā (năwatunā)	tangi (tangugi-)
mangśor caka	máskuṭṭiya (-ṭṭi)	maṭu iraichi
ḍhalu	pállama sáhita	sengutu
sṭiring	sukkănám karanawā (kalā)	sṭiiring
laṭhi	koṭuwa (-tu)	kuchi
ekhonŏ	tāma	innum
mŏja	diga mēs kuṭṭám	kaalurai
pathor	gála (gál)	kal
tola .	máhála (-hál)	maaḍi
śŏja śuji	kelinma	nēre
lomba śoru camṛa	pátiya (-ti)	vaar
rasta	wiitiya (-ti)	teru

VOCABULARY

ENGLISH	PERSIAN	HINDI [URDU]
streetcar (tram), the	trāmvai	traam (f.)
string, the	rismān	larii (f.)
strong	nirumand	mazbuut
student, the	dāneshāmuz	ćhaatr/ćhaatraa
		[talibe ilm (m., f.)]
study, to	motāle'e kardan (mikonad)	parhnaa
substance, the	mādde	padaartha (m.)
suddenly	nāgāhān	aćaarnak
sugar, the	shekar	ćiinii (f.)
suitcase, the	chamedān	suutkes (m.)
summit, the	sar	ćotii (f.)
sun, the	khorshid	suuraj (m.)
sweet	shirin	miithaa
swim, to	shenā kardan (mikonad)	tairnaa
table, the	miz	mez (f.)
tailor, the	khayyāt	darzii (m.)
take, to	gereftan (migirad)	lenaa
tall	bolandghadd	lambaa
tap, the	shire āb	nal (m.)
tape (recording), the	navār	fiitaa (m.) [tep (m.)]
tape recorder, the	zabte sot	fiitaa abhilekhitra (m.)
		[teprekaardar (m.)]
taste, to	chashidan (michashad)	ćakhnaa
tax, the	māliyāt	kar (m.) [mahsuul (m.)]
taxi, the	tāksi	taiksii (f.)
tea (to drink), the	chai	ćaay (f.)
teach, to	ta'lim dādan (midehad)	sikhaanaa
teacher, the	mo'allem	ustaad/ustaanii
telegram, the	telegrāf	taar (m.)
telephone, the	telefun	fon (m.)
television, the	televizion	teliivijan (m.)
temperature, the	daraje harārat	temparećar (m.)
temple, the	ma'bad	mandir (m.)
than	az	... se
that	ān	vah
theatre, the	teātr	thietar (m.)
their	-eshān	unkaa
then (at that time)	pas	tab
there	ānjā	vahā
there is	hast	hai
they	ishān	ve
thick	koloft	motaa
thin	nazok	patlaa
thing, the	chiz	ćiiz (f.)
think, to	fekr kardan (mikonad)	soćnaa
third	sevvom	tisraa
thirsty	teshne	pyaasaa

VOCABULARY

BENGALI	SINHALESE	TAMIL
tram	trăm-eka (trăm)	tiraam
dori	lánuwa	kayiru
jōralo	sáttimát	balamaana
chatro	sisyayă (-yŏ)	maaṇavan
pŏri/poṛen	igenagánnawā (-gáttā)	paḍitu (paḍiki-)
jiniś	dáwayaya (dáwa)	poruḷ
hothat	hádisiye	uḍanaiḍiyaaga
ćini	siini	chakarai
suṭkes	sūṭkǎǎs-eka (-kǎǎs)	kaipeṭi
ūću	káňḍu muduna (-dun)	koḍumuḍi
śurjo	ira (irawál)	suuriyan
modhur	mihiri	iniya
śātar kaṭi/kaṭen	piinanawā (piinuwā)	niindi (niindugi-)
ṭebil	měse (-sa)	měsai
dorji	tělár (-lárlā)	taiyatkaarar
nei/nin	gena yánawā (giyā)	konḍubŏyi (koṇḍubōgi-)
lomba	usa	nětai
panir kol	paippe (-ppa)	kuẓai
tep	ṭěp-eka (ṭěp)	ṭěp
tep rekodar	ṭěprekŏḍar-eka (-ḍár)	ṭěp rekŏrḍar
ćekhe dekhi/dekhen	rása bálanawā (bǎluwā)	suvaibaartu (-baarki-)
kor	bádda (-ddu)	vari
ṭaksi	ṭāksiya (-si)	ṭaaksi
ća	tě wátura	ṭii
śekhai/śekhan	ugánnanawā (igǎnnuwā)	kadrukoḍutu (-ḍuki-)
śikkhok	guruwarayā (-waru)	aasiriyar
tarbarta	widule pániwudaya (-da)	tandi
phŏn	ṭālifŏn-eka (-fŏn)	ṭelafŏn
ṭelebhiśon	ṭeliwison-eka (-son)	ṭelavishan
tapmatra	usnátwaya	ṭemparachar
mŏndir	pánsala (-sál)	kŏyil
ćaite	wáda	adai vida
ŏ	ěka	adu
thieṭar	nátaya sālāwa (-wál)	tiyěṭar
tāder	owunge	avargaḷ
tokhon	etakoṭa	piragu
śekhane	etana	ange
aćhe	tiyenawā	iruku
tāra	ouhu	avargaḷ
puru	gána	keṭiyaana
śoru	tunii	melliisa
jiniś	dě (děwál)	poruḷ
ćinta kŏri/koren	kálpanā karanawā (kalā)	ninaitu (ninaiki-)
tritio	tunweni	muuṇaavadu
pipaśarto	tibahá	taagama

VOCABULARY

ENGLISH	PERSIAN	HINDI [URDU]
this	in	yah
thread, the	nakh	dhaagaa (m.)
through	az miăn	... mẽ se
throw, to	andăkhtan (miandăzad)	phẽknaa
ticket, the	belit	ṭikaṭ (m.)
ticket-office, the	baje	ṭikaṭ ghar (m.)
tie, the	krăvăt	ṭaaii (f.)
time, the	vaght	vakt (m.)
timetable, the	barnăme	ṭaaimṭebal (m.)
tin opener, the	halab băz kon	ṭiin kholnevaalaa (m.)
tip (money), the	en'ăm	bakhśiś (f.)
tired	khaste	thakaa
to	be	... ko
tobacco, the	tambăku	tambaakuu (m.)
today	emruz	aaj
together	bă ham	ek saath
toilet (men), the	mostarăh	mardaanaa pekhaanaa (m.)
toilet (women), the	mostarăh	zanaanaa pekhaanaa (m.)
toilet paper, the	kăghaze mostarăh	pekhaanekaa kaagaz (m.)
tomato, the	gouje farangi	ṭamaaṭar (m.)
tomb, the	ăramghah	makbaraa (m.)
tomorrow	fardă	kal
tonight	emshab	aaj raat
too (much)	ziăd	zyaadaa
toothbrush, the	mesvăk	dătõ kaa braś (m.)
toothpaste, the	khamire dandăn	manjan (m.)
touch, to	dast zadan (mizanad)	ćhuunaa
tourist, the	jahăngard	paryaṭak (m., f.) [salaanii (m., f.)]
towards	su	... kii taraf
towel, the	houle	tauliyaa (m.)
tower, the	borj	miinaar (f.)
town, the	shahr	śahar (m.)
town hall, the	salone shahrdari	ṭaaun haal (m.)
train, the	ghatăr	rel gaaṛii (f.)
tram, the	trămvai	ṭraam (f.)
translate, to	tarjome kardan (mikonad)	tarjumaa karnaa
travel, to	safar kardan (mikonad)	safar karnaa
tree, the	darakht	darakht (m.)
trouble, the	zahmat	takliif (f.)
trousers, the	shalvăr	patluun (m.)
true	răst	saććaa
try on, to	emtahan kardan (mikonad)	pahan ke dekhnaa
turn, in	ba'd az digari	baarii-baarii se
twice	do băr	do dafaa
typewriter, the	mashin tahrir	ṭaaipraaiṭar (m.)
typist, the	mashinnevis	ṭaaipisṭ (m., f.)

74

VOCABULARY

BENGALI	SINHALESE	TAMIL
e	mēka	idu
śuta	nūla	nuul
moddhome	... láwā	... muulamaay
pheli/phelen	wiisi karanawā (kalā)	yerindu (yerigi-)
ṭikeṭ	bálapátraya (-ra)	ṭikaṭ
ṭikeṭ ophiś	bálapátra (kántōruwa (-ru)	ṭikaṭ aafis
bondhon	táy-eka (táy)	ṭai
śomoe	welāwa (-wál)	pōẕdu
śomoetalika	kālasaṭahána	kaala atavaṇai
ṭin khulibar jontro	ṭin árina yátura	ṭin ōpanar
bokśiś	kunu godagáhána tāna	ṭips
klanto	wehesunu	kaḷaipu
... proti	... -ṭa	... -uku
tamak	dumkola	pugaiyilai
aj	áda	indraiku
ekśongge	ekaṭa	kuuḍa
paekhana	pirimi wăsikiliya	kakuus
paekhana	gehehu wăsikiliya	kakuus
paekhanai beborito kagoj	ṭoileṭ kádadāsi	kakuus pēpar
ṭomaṭō	tákkáligeḍiya (-ḍi)	takaaḷi
minar	miniiwala (-lawál)	kallarai
agami kal	heṭa	naaḷaiku
aj rattre	áda răă	indriravil
beśi	wăḍi	miga adigam
ṭuthbraś	dát burusuwa (-su)	ṭuud birash
ṭuthpeṣṭ	tūt păst	ṭuud pēst
sporśo kōri/koren	átagánawā (átagăwwā)	toṭu (toḍugi-)
porjotok	sánchārakaya (-ka)	ṭuuriṣṭ
dike	... desaṭa	tisaiyaaga
ṭōale	tuwāya (-wā)	tuṇḍu
śtombho	bálakoṭuwa (-ṭu)	kōburam
śohor	ṭáwuma (-wum)	nagaram
ṭaun hol	nágara sálāwa	nagaramaṇḍabam
relgari	dumriya (-ri)	ṭreyin
ṭram	ṭrăm-eka (trăm)	ṭiraam
torjoma kōri/koren	páriwártana karanawā (kalā)	moẕi peyarpu seydu (seygi-)
bhromon kōri/koren	gámán karanawā (kalā)	piriyaanam seydu (seygi-)
gách	gáhá (gás)	maram
muśkil	káradaraya	kashṭam
paijama	kálisama	paṇṭ
śotti	hăbă	uṇmaiyaana
ceṣṭa kōri/koren	ăṇḍa bálanawa (băluwă)	pōtupaartu (-paarki-)
por-por	hărănawa	muraiyaaga
dubar	dewárák	reṇḍu taravai
ṭaipraiṭar	yáturu liyánn yántraya (-tara)	ṭaipraiṭar
ṭaipiṣṭ	yáturu liyánnā (-nnō)	ṭaipiṣṭ

75

VOCABULARY

ENGLISH	PERSIAN	HINDI [URDU]
tyre, the	lastike charkh	ṭaayar (m.)
ugly	zesht	bad śakal
umbrella, the	chatr	ćhatrii (f.)
under	zir	... ke niiće
understand, to	fahmidan (mifahmad)	samajhnaa
unfortunately	badbakhtäne	badkismatii se
university, the	däneshgäh	viśvavidyaalaya (m.)
		[yuunivarsiṭii (f.)]
until	tä	jab tak
upstairs	tabagheye bälä	uupar
urgently	fouri	zaruurii
usually	ma'mulan	aksar
valley, the	darre	ghaaṭii (f.)
valuable	geränbahä	kiimtii
veal, the	gushte gusäle	baćhre kaa gośt (m.)
vegetables, the	sabzijat	sabziiyä (f. pl.)
very	kheili	bahut
view (outlook), the	manzare	nazaaraa (m.)
village, the	deh	gaõ (m.)
visit, to	ziärat kardan (mikonad)	aanaa
voyage, the	safare daryä	samudra yaatraa (f.)
		[samandar safar (m.)]
wait for, to	montazer shodan (mishavad)	... kaa intazaar karnaa
waiter, the	pishkhedmat	bairaa (m.)
walk, to	räh raftan (miravad)	ghuumnaa
wall (of room), the	divär	diivaar (f.)
wall (garden, etc.), the	divär	diivaar (f.)
want, to	khästan (mikhähad)	ćaahnaa
war, the	jang	laraaii (f.)
wash, to	shostan (mishuyad)	dhonaa
washbasin, the	dastshui	vaaśbesan (m.)
watch, the	sä'st	gharii (f.)
watch, to	moväzeb budan (ast)	dekhnaa
water, the	äb	paanii (m.)
we	mä	ham
weather, the	havä	mausam (m.)
week, the	hafte	haftaa (m.)
weight, the	vazn	vazan (m.)
well (adv.)	khub	ṭhiik
well (health)	tandorost	aććhaa
west	maghreb	paśćim [magreb]
wet	tar	giilaa
wet season, the	fasle bäräni	barsaat (f.)
wharf, the	langargäh	jahaaz ghaat (m.)
what?	che?	kyaa?
wheel, the	charkh	pahiyaa (m.)
when?	kei?	kab?

76

VOCABULARY

BENGALI	SINHALESE	TAMIL
ćaka	ṭáyaraya (-ra)	ṭayar
kutśit	kắta	azagillai
ćhata	kudaya (-da)	kuḍai
... tolae	... yáṭa	... kiiz
bujhi/bōjhen	tērenawā (tērunā)	purindu kondu (kollugi-)
durbhaggobośoto	kánagātu dáyaka	durdrishtamaaga
biśśobiddaloe	wiswa widyālaya (-la)	palgalaikazagam
jotokhon	kán	aduvarai
uportola	soldora	mēlmaadi
joruri bhabe	hádisi	avasaramaaga
praei	sámānien	vazakamaaga
upattoka	miṭiyāwata (-wát)	paḷḷataaku
dami	wáṭinā	madipuḷḷa
baćhurer mangśo	wáhu más	maaṭu iraichi
śakśobji	elawalu	kaaygari
khub	bohoma	romba
driśśo	dắkuma	kaṭchi
gā	gáma (gám)	kiraamam
ghure jai/jan	muna gehenna yánawā (giyā)	paartu (paarki-)
śomudro jatra	duta gámana (-mán)	payaṇam
... jonno opekkha kōri/koren	bálán innawā (sitiyā)	kartirundu (kartiruki-)
beara	sáwaka	wēṭar
hāti/hāten	ăwidinawā (ăwiddā)	naḍandu (naḍaki-)
deoal	bittiya (-tti)	suvar
praćir	tāppaya (-ppa)	suvar
ćai/ćan	... ōnăă	vēnum
juddho	yuddaya (-dda)	yudam
dhui/dhōen	sōdanawā (sēduwā)	kazuvi (kazuvugi-)
dhoar beśin	mūna sōdanabēsama (-sán)	washbēsan
ghoṛi	át oralōsuwa (-su)	kaḍigaaram
dekhi/dekhen	bálanawā (băluwā)	gavanitu (gavaniki-)
pani	wáṭura	taṇṇi
amra	ápi	naangaḷ
abhawa	dēsagunē	vaanilai
śoptaho	sumāne (-na)	vaaram
ōjon	bára	yeḍai
bhalo kōre	hoñdaṭa	nandraay
bhalo	săpa sánipa	sugam
pośćim	básnāhira	mētku
bhije	teta	nanainda
borśa kal	wársā srátuwa	mazaigaalam
jeti	toṭupala (-lawál)	kapal nirkum idam
ki?	mokádda?	yenna?
ćaka	rōdaya (-da)	chakaram
kokhon?	káwadāda?	yepo?

VOCABULARY

ENGLISH	PERSIAN	HINDI [URDU]
where (is it)?	kojā?	kahā?
where (to)?	kojā?	kahā ko?
which?	kodām?	kaunsaa?
white	sefid	safed
who?	ki?	kaun?
whose?	māle ki?	kiskaa?
why?	cherā?	kyŏ?
wide	pahnāvar	ćauṛaa
wild	vahshi	janglii
win, to	bordan (mibarad)	jiitnaa
wind, the	bād	havaa (f.)
window, the	panjare	khiṛkii (f.)
wine, the	sharāb	śaraab (f.)
wise	kheradmand	samaaj dar
with	bā	... ke saath
without	bi	... ke binaa
woman, the	zan	aurat (f.)
wonder, to	ta'ajjob kardan (mikonad)	haraanii honaa
wonderful	fogholāde	aaśćaryajanak [umdaa]
wood (timber), the	chub	lakrii (f.)
wool, the	pashm	uun (f.)
word, the	kaleme	śabd (m.) [alfaaz (f.)]
work, the	kār	kaam (m.)
workman, the	kārgar	mazduur (m.)
world, the	jahān	duniyaa (f.)
worse	badtar	badtar
worst	badtarin	sabse badtar
worth, to be	arzidan (miarzad)	... kaa honaa
write, to	nevestan (minevisad)	likhnaa
wrong	eshtebāh	galat
year, the	sāl	saal (m.)
yellow	zard	piilaa
yesterday	diruz	kal
you	shomā	aap
young	javān	javaan
your	-etān	aap kaa

VOCABULARY

BENGALI	SINHALESE	TAMIL
kothae?	kohēda?	yenge?
kothae?	kohēṭada?	yenge?
kōn?	koikada?	yenda?
śada	sudu	veḷḷai
ke?	káwuda?	yaar?
kar?	kägeda?	yaar?
keno?	mokada?	yēn?
ćoōṛa	pálala	agala
bonno	wánawara	kaṭutanam
jiti/jeten	dinanawā (dinuwā)	vetribetru (-berugi-)
haōa	hulaṅga (-lán)	kaatru
janala	jánēlaya (-la)	jannal
mod	weyn	madu
gāni	nuwanăti	gaṇyamaana
. . . śongge	. . . ekka	. . . ōḍu
betito	. . . nătuwa	. . . illaamal
nari	gāhăniya (-nu)	maadar
janite utśuk hōi/hoen	áhemahe áwwidinawā (ăwwiddā)	aachariyam
ćomotkar	āschárya	romba nanna
kaṭh	lii	maram
bonat	lom	kambaḷi
kotha	wáchane (-na)	vaartai
kaj	wăḍē (-ḍa)	vēlai
śromik	kámkaruwa (-ru)	vēlaikaaran
dunia	lōkaya (-ka)	ulagu
mondotor	waḍā náraka	mēlum mōsamaana
mondotomo	itā náraka	mōsamaana
joggo hōi/hoen	wátinta	madipu
lekhi/lekhen	liyanawā (liyuwā)	yeẓudi (yeẓudugi-)
bhul	wăradi	tapu
boćhor	áwurudda (-rudu)	varusham
holde	káhá	manjal
goto kal	iiye	nētru
apni	oba	niingaḷ
koći	táruna	iḷamaiyaana
apnar	obagē	ungaḷ

79

PART II

BURMESE
THAI
LAO
KAMPUCHEAN
VIETNAMESE

BURMESE

Burmese is the official language of Burma, spoken by at least two-thirds of the population of this linguistically complex country.

It is written in its own alphabet. There is no standard romanisation and this book uses its own.

PRONUNCIATION Vowels:

A, E, I, O, U are like *ah, eh, ee, oh, oo.*
Ă is like the unstressed English *a* in "alone."
Diphthongs AI, AU, EI, OU are like *igh, ow, eigh, owe.*
N following a vowel is often pronounced merely as a nasalisation of the vowel (part of the air escaping through the nose).

Consonants involve some special distinctions:

K, T, P, CH are more strongly aspirated (more rush of air) than in English.
GK, DT, BP, TJ are similar sounds, but with no aspiration; more like unvoiced G, D, B, J.
G, D, B, J themselves are as in English.
HS, HM, HN, HNG are breathy, unvoiced sounds otherwise resembling S, M, N, NG.
NG is as in "singer," never as in "finger," and may occur at the beginning of a word.
HY is like *sh* in the roof of the mouth.
TH is between *t* and the *th* in "thin."
DH is as *th* in "then."
Y is always a consonant, as in "yes."
' indicates a glottal stop (as in the Cockney pronunciation of "bottle" as "bo'l").

A syllable may have any one of four tones:

1. normal pitch, long — no special mark
2. high pitch, long — marked ˉ over the vowel
3. short, sharply falling — marked ˋ over the vowel
4. short and high, ending in a glottal stop ' — otherwise no special mark

Syllables of the first three tones always end in a vowel or N.

Tones affect meaning: *ka, kā, kà* and *ka'* are different words.

In compound words a glottal stop merges with a following consonant to make a double consonant: *hmou'lā,* "Isn't that so?," is pronounced *hmoul-lā.*

Note that unvoiced consonants become voiced in compounds following a syllable other than fourth tone: K and GK become G (and are so written), TH becomes DH, and so on. Hence the verb particle *-dte,* for example, often becomes *-de.*

NOUNS

The plural is not often indicated but can be formed by adding *-dtei* (becoming *-dei* after tones 1-3): *'ein,* "house" (or "houses"), *'ein-dei,* "houses."

There is no definite or indefinite article. If necessary, use *di,* "this," or *hou,* "that": *di bpyi'si,* "this bag."

The suffix *-mà* indicates feminine: *hsaya,* "teacher" (either sex), *hsayamà,* "woman teacher."

Possession is shown by placing the possessor first, changing the tone of the last syllable, if it is tone 1 or 2, to the short falling tone 3: *yau'tjā,* "man," *yau'tjà 'ein,* "the man's house."

Particles are attached to fulfil the function of prepositions: *-gkou,* "to," giving

BURMESE

for example *'ein-gou*, "to the house"; similarly *-gkà*, "from"; *-ma*, "at." The object of the verb may also take *-gkou*.

PRONOUNS In the first and second person there are different forms depending on the sex of the speaker: "I, me," *tjano* (man), *tjamà* (woman); "you" (singular), *kamyà* (man speaking), *hyin* (woman speaking).
In the third person *thu* is "he," "she" or "it," but is often omitted.
For plurals, add *-dòu* to any of these forms: "we, us," *tjanodòu* (man speaking), etc.
Grammatically, pronouns are exactly like nouns. Note, in particular, possession: *tjanò 'ein*, "my house" (man speaking).

VERBS The verb comes at the end of the sentence, and consists of a stem such as *thwā-*, "go," followed by one or more particles.
The present tense particle is *-dte* (or *-de*) as shown in the vocabulary: *Yau'tjā thwā-de*, "The man is going."
For completed action in the past, use the particle *-bpi* (*-bi*): *Mēinmà thwā-bi*, "The woman went."
For future or to indicate possibility, use *-me: Tjano/Tjamà 'ein-gou thwā-me*, "I shall (or may) go to the house."
The politeness-word *-ba-* is very frequently inserted between verb stem and particle: *Ba'sa-gkā la-bade*, "(Excuse me,) the bus is coming."
Auxiliary verbs also come between verb stem and particle, before *-ba-* if this is used. Note particularly *-chin-* (*-jin*), "want to"; *-ya-*, "have to"; *-hnain-*, "can": *Tjano thwā-jinbade*, "I would like to go."
Verb combinations are common: *thwā-tjì*, "go see"; *sà-thwā*, "begin go"; *māun-thwā*, "drive go" (= "drive away"); *yu-la*, "take come" (= "bring"). Particles follow the compound.
To form a negative in the present or future tense, prefix *mă-* to the verb and replace the tense particle by *-pū* (*-bū*): *măthwā-bū*, "is not going" or "will not go." The past tense particle is treated like an auxiliary and takes the negative itself: *thwā mă-bpībū*, "did not go," "has not gone."
The verb "be" in the sense of "exist" or "occupy a place" is *hyi: Gkā lān-ma hyi-de*, "The car is in the street"; *Leiyinbyan māhyi-bū*, "There is no plane."

ADJECTIVES In the vocabulary, adjectives are shown with present-tense particles *-dte* or *-de*, like verbs. They may, however, be used following nouns without any particle: *tjī-de*, "big," *'ein tjī*, "big house"; *gkāun-de*, "good," *gkā gkāun*, "good car."
As predicate, an adjective is treated directly as a verb and takes a tense particle: *Gkā gkāun-de*, "The car is good"; *'Ein mătjī-bū*, "The house is not big."
Note the alternative construction in which an adjective, followed by particle *-tè* (or *-dè*), may precede the noun instead of following it: *tjī-dè 'ein*, "big house," "house that is big." A whole verb phrase may also be used in this way: *Gkā māun-dè yau'tjā*, "the car-driving man," "the man driving the car."
For a comparative, put *bpou*, "more," before the adjective: *'Ein bpou tjī-de*, "The house is bigger." For "than," use *-te* (or *-de'*) after the noun: *Yau'tjā-ha mēinmà-de' bpou tjī-de*, "The man is bigger than the woman." (The particle *-ha*, "as for," here marks the subject.)
Qualifying a noun, a comparative should precede it: *bpou gkāun-dè gkā*, "a better car."

For a superlative, use *'ǎ-* before the adjective and *-hsǎn* (or *-zǎn*) after it, without necessarily any tense particle: *nge-de,* "small," *gkǎ 'ǎ-nge-zǎn,* "the smallest car."

ADVERBS can be formed from nouns, adjectives or verbs by attaching *-lou,* "in the manner of." They precede the verb.

An adverb of time such as *'A-gù,* "now," or *Di ganèi,* "today," is placed first in the sentence.

QUESTIONS For a yes/no question, attach *-lā* to the end of the corresponding statement, but replace *-te* or *-de* with *-thalā* or *-dhalā,* and similarly change the vowel of *-me* or *-bpi* (or *-bi*) to *a: Ba'sa-gkā la-dhalā?,* "Is the bus coming?"; *Thu thwā-malā?,* "Will he go?"

The most reliable way to answer a yes/no question is by repeating the verb, with or without a negative: *Thwā-me,* "Yes (he will go)"; *Māthwā-bū,* "No (he will not go)."

In questions formed with interrogative words such as *bathu,* "who?," or *be-ma,* "where?," the sentence order is as for statements, but *-lē* is placed at the end, with the same changes to particles as in the case of *-lā: Zēi be-ma hyi-dhalē?* (or just *Zēi be-ma-lē?*), "Where is the market?"

IMPERATIVES For an imperative, use the plain verb stem, adding *-bpa* (*-ba*) for politeness: *Tain-ba,* "Please sit down." For special emphasis, add *bpò.*

For a negative, prefix *mǎ-* and add *-nè; Mǎ-tain-nè,* "Don't sit down."

For "Let's," add *-jàzòu* to the stem: *Gkā-gou thwā-jàzòu,* "Let's go to the car."

NUMERALS A numeral is usually followed by a classifier characteristic of the kind of thing being counted. The order is noun-numeral-classifier: *yau'tjā thōun yau',* "three men," where *yau'* is the classifier for people. There are about twenty classifiers in common use.

A general classifier for ordinary objects is *kù.* If in doubt, repeat the noun: *'ein dta 'ein* is good grammar for "one house."

Classifiers are not needed with time and money expressions.

CURRENCY A single unit, the *tja'* ("kyat").

FORMS OF ADDRESS Burmese do not use greetings like "Good morning." *Min-gǎ-la-ba* is the nearest equivalent, but it would be more usual simply to smile.

For "sir" or "madam," generally use the same terms as for second person pronoun, *Kamyǎ* (man speaking), *Hyin* (woman speaking). Address older men as *'Ūjī.*

As the equivalent of "Mr," "Mrs," "Miss," use *'Ū* and *Do* to older men and women respectively, *Gkou* to men of one's own status, *Maun* and *Mà* to younger men and women respectively, in all cases prefixed to full name. There are no family names: women do not change their name at marriage.

KIN TERMS The commonest are:

'a-pei, "father"	*'amei,* "mother"
'a-kou, "older brother"	*'amà,* "older sister"
nyi, "younger brother (of man)"	*hnamà,* "younger sister (of man)"
maun, "younger brother (of woman)"	*nyamà,* "younger sister (of woman)"
thā, "son"	*thamī,* "daughter"

The words *yau'tjā,* "man," *mēinmà,* "woman," serve for "husband" and "wife."

BURMESE

NAME OF LANGUAGE

The Burmese language is *Bama zăgă*. To speak Burmese is to speak *bama-lou*, "in the Burmese fashion."

THAI

Thai is the national language of Thailand and the most widely spoken member of a family of languages that includes Lao and some minority languages of South China and North Burma. The Bangkok dialect is understood throughout Thailand, though there are local variations.

The language has its own alphabet. Romanisation involves compromise since there is more than the usual number of distinct sounds.

PRONUNCIATION There are nine vowel sounds:

A, E, I, O, U are like *ah, eh, ee, oh, oo,* but short.
AW has its English sound as in "raw."
AA is like short *a* in "ran."
EU is approximately English *er* (with no *r* sound), but said with the teeth nearly closed.
UH is the neutral *e* in "the" before a consonant, for example, in "the man."

Vowels may be short or long:

AH, EH, IH, OH, EUH are long vowels corresponding with A, E, I, O, EU.
UU is long U.
AW and AA are always fairly long except when followed by a glottal stop (closing of the back of the throat), that is, when written AW', AA'.

Diphthongs are pronounced like sequences of the component vowels:

AI, AHI, EHU, AAU, . . . are pronounced with I or U preceding or following other vowels.
OI is like AW plus I.
EUA, EUAI are like EU plus A, AI.

In pronouncing vowels, the main things to remember are that AA, AW, EU and UH have special sounds, and that H is not to be sounded in diphthongs such as AHI and EHU.

Consonants are as in English, except that:

DT and BP represent unvoiced D and B respectively (but with no rush of air like that after T and P).
NG is always as in "singer," never as in "finger," and may occur at the start of a syllable.
' is the glottal stop (as in the Cockney pronunciation of "bottle" as "bo'l").
K, T, P and ' at the end of a syllable represent a very perfunctory closing off of the air stream without re-opening.

Words should be pronounced as if broken into well-defined syllables.

A syllable may have any of five tones:
"Rising" and "falling" tones are indicated by ´, ` over the vowel.
"High, level" and "low, level" are indicated by ¯, ˉ.
"Mid, level" is unmarked.

Tones affect meaning: *káu, kàu* and *kău* are different words. In practice, the tune of a sentence depends on tones of key words.

NOUNS are invariable and have no plural forms.
There are no articles "a" or "the" and a noun may stand alone; but demonstratives *níh,* "this," and *nôhn,* "that," may be placed after nouns, and these

have plural forms *lǎunǐh,* "these," *lǎunōhn,* "those": *kon nǐh,* "this person"; *kon lǎunǐh,* "these persons"; *túng nōhn,* "that bag"; *rōt lǎunōhn,* "those cars."

Place the possessor after the thing possessed: *rōt kon,* "the man's car"; or insert *káwng,* "belonging to": *rōt káwng kon.*

Prepositions precede the noun as in English: *jǎhk rōt,* "from the car" — but they are often omitted when the sense is clear.

PRONOUNS Thais use various pronouns with subtle social distinctions, but the foreigner may approximate.

For "I, me," a man should say *póm* and a woman *chán*; or, if formalities have been dropped, either sex says *chán.*

For "you," say *kun* except to such people as waiters and taxi-drivers, to whom *tàhn* is less patronising.

For "he, him," "she, her," "they, them," *káu*; for "we, us," *rau.*

For "it," use *nìh,* "this," or *nòhn,* "that," or repeat the noun.

Personal names or occupation terms such as *kon-kǎp-rōt,* "driver," often replace second or third person pronouns.

Possession is the same as with nouns: *túng kun,* or *túng káwng kun,* "your bag."

ADJECTIVES follow the noun: *bàhn,* "house, houses," *bàhn yǎi,* "big house, big houses." Since no verb "is" or "are" is used with adjectives, the same construction can mean "The house is big," or "The houses are big."

For a comparative, put *gwǎh,* "more," after the adjective. This also serves to translate "than": *Nìh yǎi gwǎh,* "This is bigger"; *Nìh yǎi gwǎh nòhn,* "This is bigger than that."

For a superlative, follow the adjective with *tìhsǔt,* "most": *Bàhn yǎi tìhsǔt,* "The house is the biggest."

ADVERBS Adjectives may be used without change of form as adverbs, usually at the end of the sentence.

VERBS The verb "is" or "are" between nouns or pronouns is *bpen: Nìh bpen túng káwng kun,* "This is your bag." To indicate location it is *yǔu,* "is at": *Túng yǔu bàhn,* "The bag is in the house."

For "There is," use *mih,* which also means "have": *Mih jōtmáhi,* "There is a letter"; *Póm mih rōt,* "I (man) have a car."

Verbs do not change for person or number. Tense is also often not indicated: *Prùng-nǐh mih jōtmáhi,* "Tomorrow there will be a letter."

Auxiliaries *jǎ'* for future, *dài* for past, may be included if necessary: *Káu jǎ' kían,* "He will write"; *Káu dài kían,* "He wrote." The word *lǎau* ("already") at the end of the sentence indicates completed action: *Rau dài kían lǎau,* "We have already written."

The auxiliary *dtàwng* means "must," so that *jǎ' dtàwng* means "will need to" and *dài dtàwng* means "had to." Among other auxiliaries, note *yǎhk jǎ',* "want to"; *kuan jǎ',* "ought to."

For a negative, put *mài,* "not," before the verb: *Póm mài dài kìan,* "I (man) did not write."

If the auxiliary *dài* is placed after the verb instead of before it, it means "can": *Káu mah dài,* "He (etc.) can come"; *Káu mah mài dài,* "He (etc.) cannot come." Under the same circumstances, *bpen* means "can" in the sense of "know how to": *pùut 'ang-grìt bpen,* "can speak English."

Note the use of *mah,* "come," *bpai,* "go," in compounds such as *'au mah,* "bring," and *'au bpai,* "take away" (where *'au* alone is "take"); and in doing duty for prepositions as in *'au nángséuh mah bàhn,* "Bring the book to the house." Similarly, with other verbs such as *hài,* "give," as in *sŏng nguhn bpai hài káu,* "Give the money to him."

QUESTIONS A yes/no question is formed from an affirmative statement by adding *mái* (note different tone from *mài,* "not"): *Kun mah meuang mái?,* "Are you coming to the town?" After a negative statement, add *chài mái: Kun mài mah chài mái,* "Aren't you coming?"

The safest way to answer a yes/no question is to repeat the verb, alone or negated: *Mah,* "Yes (I'm coming)"; *Mài mah,* "No (I'm not coming)." (Other methods may be ambiguous in the case of negative questions.)

Questions of all kinds have the same word order as the corresponding statements.

IMPERATIVES For an imperative, use the plain verb, softened by being preceded by *Chuhn,* "Invite," or *Chùai,* "Help," or when asking to be given something *Káw,* "Please": *Chuhn mah,* "Do come." Additionally, *tih* (or one of several other particles) may be placed at the end of the sentence.

For a negative imperative, precede the verb with *yàh,* "don't": *Yàh bpai,* "Don't go."

For "Let's," attach *gan,* "with one another," to the verb: *Bpai gan,* "Let's go."

NUMERALS A numeral should be followed by a classifier appropriate to the kind of thing being counted, the whole being placed after the noun: *pùu-yíng sáwng kon,* "two women," where *kon* is the classifier for persons.

There are some fifty classifiers in use. A Thai would generally rather repeat a noun as its own classifier than not use one: *rót sáwng rót* is better for "two cars" than just *sáwng rót,* though the correct expression would be *rót sáwng kan.*

A classifier applicable to almost any kind of small object is *'an: bpàhk-gah sáwng 'an,* "two pens."

Classifiers should strictly also be used with singular demonstratives, in which case the order is noun-classifier-demonstrative: *bpàhk-gah 'an níh,* "this pen." They are not required in the case of time or money expressions.

The form *toh,* for "two," is used in place of *sáwng* when calling figures, as in a telephone number.

CURRENCY 1 *bàht* ("baht" or "tical") = 100 *sà-dtahng* ("satang"), but prices are often quoted in *sàléung* or quarter-bahts.

FORMS OF ADDRESS In polite conversation you must say *kráp,* if you are a man, or *ka',* if you are a woman, at the end of virtually every sentence you utter. These words are used independently of the sex of the person addressed, and have no translatable meaning; except that, used alone, they may mean "Yes," or "I agree."

To address or refer to a Thai by name, use *Kun* followed by given (first) name, adding the family name only if necessary for identification. (Although a married woman takes her husband's family name, it is still not used in ordinary conversation.)

For "sir" or "madam," use *Kun* alone.

KIN TERMS often have "polite" and "common" alternatives. The following are "polite" forms:

THAI

bī'dah and *mahndah*, "father" and "mother"
pìh chahi, pìh sáhu, "older brother, sister"
nāwng chahi, nawng sáhu, "younger brother, sister"
sáhmih, panra'yah, "husband," "wife"
bŭt chahi, bŭt sáhu, "son," "daughter"

NAME OF LANGUAGE
The Thai language is *Pahsáh Tai*. The country is *Bpra'tèht Tai.*

LAO

Lao is the national language of Laos, increasingly the language of communication among speakers of local languages throughout the country, spoken also by minorities in Thailand (whose principal language Thai it closely resembles) and Kampuchea.

Its alphabet is similar to that of Thai, and we use a conforming romanisation.

PRONUNCIATION There are nine vowels:

A, E, I, O, U are like *ah, eh, ee, oh, oo,* but short.
AW has its English sound as in "raw."
AA is like short *a* in "ran."
EU is approximately English *er* (with no *r* sound), but with lips spread in a smile.
UH is the neutral *e* sound in "the" before a consonant, for example, in "the man."

Vowels may be short or long:

AH, EH, IH, OH, AAH, EUH are long vowels corresponding with A, E, I, O, AA, EU.
UU is long U.
AW is always fairly long except when followed by a glottal stop (closing of the back of the throat), that is, when written AW'.

Diphthongs are pronounced like sequences of the component vowels:

IA, AU, AHI, UUI, AAU, . . . are pronounced with I or U preceding or following the other vowels.
UHI is like UH plus I.
OI is like AW plus I.
EUA, EUAI are like EU plus A, AI.
AII is a characteristic Laotian sound that consists approximately of A followed by EU.

In pronouncing vowels the main things to remember are that AA, AW, EU, UH and AII have special sounds, and that H is not to be sounded in diphthongs such as AHI and AHU.

Consonants are as in English, except that:

DT and BP represent unvoiced D and B (but with no rush of breath like that after T and P).
G and J are more or less unvoiced.
NG is always as in "singer," never as in "finger," and may occur at the start of a syllable.
' is the glottal stop (as in the Cockney pronunciation of "bottle" as "bo'l").
K, T, P and ' at the end of a syllable represent a very perfunctory closing off of the air stream without re-opening.

Words should be pronounced as if broken into well-defined syllables.

A syllable may have any of six tones, indicated by marks over vowels:

¯ and ̿ represent "medium high, level" and "low, level" respectively.
"Normal, level" is unmarked.
` represents "high falling."
ˆ represents a falling tone from middle to low.
ˇ represents a down-up glide.

These descriptions are for Vientiane dialect. Among differences in Luang Prabang dialect the main one is that syllables marked ¯ are pronounced fairly low and "scooped."

Tones affect meaning: *màh, māh, mǎh* and *mah* are different words. In practice, the tune of a sentence depends on the tones of key words.

NOUNS are invariable and have no plural forms.

There are no articles "a" or "the" and a noun may stand alone; but *nìh,* "this," and *nàn,* "that," may follow nouns, and these have plural forms *launìh,* "these," *launàn,* "those": *kōn nìh,* "this person"; *kōn launìh,* "these persons"; *tǒng nàn,* "that bag"; *lot launàn,* "those cars."

Place the possessor after the thing possessed, perhaps with intervening *kǎwng,* "belonging to": *tǒng kōn* or *tǒng kǎwng kōn,* "the man's bag."

Prepositions precede the noun as in English: *dtaah lot,* "from the car" — but they are often omitted when the sense is clear.

PRONOUNS Choice of pronoun may indicate an attitude towards the addressee. In the following list the forms in parentheses are formal or polite ones used on first meeting or to show special respect:

kôi (kâ'nòi), "I, me"
jàu, "you" (singular or plural)
hāu, "we, us"
lāhu (puhhn), "he, him, she, her"
kǎujàu (puhhn), "they, them" (people)
mān, "it, they, them" (animals)

For inanimate things, use the demonstratives *nìh, nàn,* or their plurals.

Personal names or occupation terms such as *kōn-kāp,* "driver," often replace second person pronouns.

A foreigner is likely to be addressed and referred to as *tahn.*

Form possessives as for nouns: *tǒng kôi* or *tǒng kǎwng kôi,* "my bag."

ADJECTIVES follow the noun: *hēuan,* "house, houses," *hēuan nyaii,* "big house, big houses." Since no verb "is" or "are" is used with adjectives, the same construction can mean "The house is big," "The houses are big."

For a comparative, put *gwah,* "more," after the adjective. This also serves to translate "than": *Nìh nyaii gwah,* "This is bigger"; *Nìh nyaii gwah nàn,* "This is bigger than that."

For a superlative, put *tihsūt,* "most," after the adjective: *Hēuan nyaii tihsūt,* "The house is the biggest."

ADVERBS Adjectives may be used without change of form as adverbs, usually at the end of the sentence.

VERBS The verb "is" or "are" between nouns or pronouns is *maahn* or *bpěn*: *Nìh maahn jōtmahi,* "This is the letter." To indicate location, it is *yuu,* "is at": *Hēuan yuu hân,* "The house is over there."

For "There is" or "There are", use *mīh,* which also means "have": *Mīh hēuan,* "There is a house"; *Kôi mīh bpèuhm,* "I have a book".

Verbs are invariable and do not indicate person or number. Tense is indicated when necessary by auxiliaries: for future, *jā',* "will," or *gǎmlāng,* "is about to," both before the main verb; for completed action in the past, or for an emphatic present, *làahu,* "already," at the end of the sentence: *Lāhu jā bpǎi,* "He/She will go"; *Kôi gǎmlāng bpǎi,* "I am about to go"; *Kǎujàu bpǎi làahu,* "They have already gone"; *Jàu yuu tihnìh làahu,* "You are here (already)!"

Note the use of *bpěn* at the end of a sentence as an auxiliary, meaning "knows how to."

For a negative, put *baw,* "not," before the verb.

Note the use of *māh,* "come," and *bpǎi,* "go," in compounds such as *'ǎu māh,* "take come," namely "bring"; and to do duty for prepositions as in *'ǎu nǎngsěuh māh hēuan,* "bring the book to the house": similarly *hâii,* "give," in *fǎhk ngūhn bpǎi hâii lāhu,* "send the money to him."

QUESTIONS A yes/no question is formed by adding *baw* at the end of the corresponding statement: *Lāhu yuu tihnìh baw?,* "Is he here?" Answer by repeating the verb; in this case, with *Yuu* or *Baw yuu.*

In the case of a question formed with a word such as *sǎii,* "where?", preserve the word order of the corresponding statement: *Hōhng-hāahm yuu sǎii?,* "Where is the hotel?"

IMPERATIVES For a simple imperative, use the plain verb; but for politeness, it can be preceded by *Kǎw,* "Ask," or *Sūhn,* "Invite," or have the polite particle *daah* at the end of the sentence, or both. A common formulation is *Jàu yâhk . . . baw?,* "Would you like to . . .?"

For an emphatic negative, "Don't," use *yah: Yah bpǎi,* "Don't go."

For "Let's," put *gǎn,* "with one another", after the verb, or again use the question form: *Hāu jā' . . . baw?,* "Shall we . . .?"

NUMERALS In specifying numbers of objects, a classifier appropriate to the kind of thing being counted is required, the order of the words being noun-numeral-classifier: *pûu-nyīng sǎhm kōn,* "three women," where *kōn* is the classifier for people. (But *neung,* "one," follows the classifier instead of preceding it: *pûu-nyīng kōn neung,* "one woman.")

There are some fifty classifiers in common use. Rather than omit the classifier entirely, repeat the noun; thus *lot sǎwng lot* is better for "two cars" than just *sǎwng lot* or *lot sǎwng,* though the correct expression would be *lot sǎwng kǎn.*

A classifier of fairly general application to small objects is *'ǎn.* No classifier is needed in time and money expressions.

CURRENCY A single unit, the *gîhp* (or *mǎn*).

FORMS OF ADDRESS In formal language, and especially in greetings, the word *kâ'nòi* is commonly attached to a sentence, or *Jàu* may introduce it. Alone, either of these words may mean "Yes" or "I agree". (They are the same as the polite pronouns "I", "you", respectively.)

"Mr", "Mrs" and "Miss" are *Nāhi, Nāhng* and *Nāhngsǎhu,* placed before given (first) name. This is the normal mode of address — even for a married woman, and the family name is used only for identification.

Note that a wide range of other terms of address may be encountered.

KIN TERMS The commonest kin terms are:

bītdǎh and *māhndǎh,* "father" and "mother"
(or less formally *paw, maah*)
'àhi, 'èuai, "older brother, sister"
nàwngsāhi, nàwngsǎhu, "younger brother, sister"

lùuksāhi, lùuksǎhu, "son", "daughter"
sǎhmīh and *pānla-nyāh,* "husband" and "wife"
   (less formally *pǔa* and *mīa*)

NAME OF LANGUAGE
Laos is *Bpā-tèht Lāhu:* its language is *Pāhsǎh Lāhu.*

KAMPUCHEAN

Kampuchean, also called Khmer, is the language of Kampuchea and of minorities in Thailand and Vietnam.

It is written in its own alphabet. There is no standard romanisation and this book uses its own.

PRONUNCIATION Vowels:

Long vowels AA, Ē, II, Ō, Ū are like *ah, eh, ee, oh, oo.*

A, I, O, U are short vowels like the corresponding long ones.

E is a neutral sound as in English "the" before a consonant, for example, in "the man."

Ĕ, Ŏ are the short vowels in "let" and "lot."

Ĭ is a short vowel with considerably more lip-spread than the English *i*, so that it is like a short version of some people's pronunciation of "Ugh!"

Ó is a prolonged Ŏ; ĚĔ and ĬĬ are prolonged Ĕ and Ĭ.

AW, EU are pure vowels as English *aw* and *er* (with no *r* sound).

Diphthongs ĂA, ÉA, ÍA, ÓA, ÚA have stress on the first syllable as indicated by the accent; hence:

ĂA is like the two vowels in "matter," run together with the *tt* omitted.

ÉA and ÍA are like English "air" and "ear" (but with no *r* sound).

ĂE (the only other difficult diphthong) is like the vowels in "adept" (with *d* omitted).

Consonants are as in English, except that:

G and J are unvoiced (like K and CH but without any puff of breath).

BP and DT are like unvoiced B and D.

P, T and K at the end of a word represent a closing of the air stream without re-opening.

Ñ is like the *ny* in "canyon."

NG is as in "singer" (no *g* sound).

' is the glottal stop (as in the Cockney pronunciation of "bottle" as "bo'l") and counts as a consonant.

H is always sounded, but with a hiss through the teeth so that it tends to be interchangeable with S.

In the case of double consonants, sound both components clearly: there are no "silent" consonants.

The tune of a Kampuchean sentence is distinctive, consisting (in short sentences) of a steady fall. In the case of a question, there is a sharp rise on the last syllable only.

Words of more than one syllable are stressed on the last one, and the second last is either equally stressed, or else, if it has an E or Ŏ vowel, is very light and neutral.

NOUNS have no separate plural, and there is no article "a" or "the"; but *nih,* "this, these," *nuh,* "that, those", or *múay,* "one," is placed after the noun if required: *ptéah,* "a house, the house, houses"; *ptéah nih,* "this house, these houses"; *ptéah múay,* "a house"; similarly *ptéah glah,* "some houses."

For a definite singular or plural, use a double demonstrative: *ptéah múay nih,* "this (one) house"; *ptéah glah nuh,* "those houses."

Place the possessor after the thing possessed: *dvía ptéah,* "door of the house";

or place the word *rebos,* "thing," between them: *ptéah srey* or *ptéah rebos srey,* "the woman's house."

PRONOUNS In polite conversation between adults the commonest pronouns are:

kñom, "I, me, we, us"
lōk (to a man or men), or *lōk-srey* (to a woman or women), "you." Less formally say *néak* to either sex.
góat, "he, she, him, her, they, them" (people)
vía, "it, they, them" (animals; sometimes children)

For inanimate objects, use *nih* or *nuh,* or a noun such as *rebos.*

Possession is expressed in the same way as with nouns: *laan kñom,* "my (or our) car"; *dvía ptéah néak,* "door of your house."

ADJECTIVES follow the noun: *ptéah tom,* "big house" (or "big houses"). As predicate, an adjective requires no verb "is" or "are," and so the same construction can mean "The house is big," or "The houses are big."

For a comparative, place *jíang* after the adjective: *laan-chnúal tom jíang,* "bigger bus" or "The bus is bigger." "Than" needs no translation: *Néak tom jíang kñom,* "You are bigger than I."

For a superlative add *gē,* "any," after *jíang: Laan-chnúal nih tom jíang gē,* "This bus is bigger than any," "This bus is the biggest."

VERBS The verb "is" or "are" between nouns or pronouns is *gĩĩ* or *gĩĩ jía: Nuh gĩĩ jía síav-pĭu,* "That is a book." (But to give someone's profession, as "is a doctor," one would use *tveu,* "works as.")

"There is" or "There are" is *mían,* which also means "have": *Mían síav-pĭu,* "There is a book," "There are books"; *Kñom mían síav-pĭu,* "I have the book" (or "books").

Verbs are invariable and do not indicate tense: *dtĭu* may mean "goes," "is going," "will go," "have gone." If necessary, put *baan* before the verb to indicate completed action, or *nĭng* to indicate future: *baan dtĭu,* "has gone"; *nĭng dtĭu,* "will go." There is a large range of similar particles.

Note that if *baan* is placed after the main verb instead of before, it means "is able to"; *Kñom dtĭu baan,* "I can go."

For a negative, place *mĭn* before the verb and *dtē* at the end of the sentence: *Góat mĭn dtĭu dtē,* "He is not going."

All verb constructions are also available with adjectives:
Ptéah mĭn tom dtē, "The house is not big."

Compound verbs are common, for example, *dtĭu meul,* "go (and) look." A second verb often serves the function of an English preposition; thus *Srey băak laan,* "The woman drives the car," can be followed by *dtĭu krong,* "goes (to the) town", to mean "The woman drives the car to the town". Similarly *mawk,* "come," for "to" in the case of motion towards the speaker; *'aoy,* "give," for "to" or "for"; *nĭu,* "stays," for "at" or "on"; sometimes *dtaam,* "follow," for "with."

Note, however, that "from" is the preposition *bpii: mawk bpii krong,* "comes from the town."

QUESTIONS For a yes/no question add *dtē* to the end of the corresponding statement, pronounced with a rising intonation. (With a falling intonation it would merely add emphasis.) To form a question from a negative statement with the *mĭn ... dtē* construction, simply give *dtē* a rising intonation: *Néak mawk dtē?,* "Are you coming?"; *Néak mĭn mawk dtē?*, "Aren't you coming?"

In answer to a question a man says *Baat* for "Yes," *Baat dtē* for "No," and a woman *Jaah* or *Jaah dtē*; but if the question is a negative one, both forms mean "No," and to give a "Yes" answer it is necessary to restate some part of the sentence; for example, *Mawk*, "(I am) coming."

In the case of an interrogative word such as *'ăe-naa*, "where (is it)?", continue to use the word order appropriate to a statement: *Haang nĭu 'ăe-naa?* "Where is the shop?"

IMPERATIVES For an imperative, use the plain verb, or, less abruptly, precede it by a term of address such as *lōk* or *lōk-srey*, or by *sōm*, "please," or both: *Sōm lōk 'ŏng-kuy nĭu 'ăe-nih*, "Sit here, sir, please."

For "Don't," use *Gom*, with or without *'ey* at the end of the sentence: *Gom prúay 'ey*, "Don't worry."

For "Let's," optionally use *Mawk*, "Come on and . . .": *Mawk dtĭu*, "Let's go."

NUMERALS In expressing numbers of objects, the numeral follows the noun: *ptéah bey*, "three houses" — but with many classes of nouns it is usual to add a classifier after the numeral. The classifier for people is *néak*, giving *srey bey néak*, "three women"; *gruu búan néak*, "four teachers."

Classifiers are also used with some words besides actual numbers: *gŏn jrăan néak*, "many children," where *jrăan* is "many."

The same construction is used with measure and container words: *skó múay gkilō* (contracted to *skó megkilō*), "one kilo of sugar." Measure words, and also words for time and money, are treated as classifiers wherever they occur, and numerals precede them.

CURRENCY 1 *rĭal* ("rial") = 100 *sēn*.

FORMS OF ADDRESS *Lōk* and *Lōk-srey* are the normal terms for "Mr," "Mrs and Miss," preceding the surname; or they can be used alone for "sir," "madam." But Kampucheans commonly replace all forms of address or pronouns with titles, kin terms in great profusion, or personal names.

KIN TERMS often do not denote precise blood-relationship so much as relative age or status in a family or community; but with this caution the following may be listed:

'evbpuk, "father"
mdaay or *néak-mdaay*, "mother"
bóng, "older brother or sister," subdivisible into
    bóng-bros, "older brother," *bóng-srey*, "older sister"
b'ŏn, "younger brother or sister," similarly subdivisible into *b'ŏn-bros* and *b'ŏn-srey*
gŏn, "son or daughter" (but also often just "child"),
    similarly subdivisible into *gŏn-bros* and *gŏn-srey*
bdey, "husband" (but a wife will address her husband as *bóng*); *brebúan*, "wife"

NAME OF LANGUAGE
The country is *Gambpujjía* or *Srok Gmăe*; the language is *Píasaa Gmăe*.

VIETNAMESE

Vietnamese is spoken throughout Vietnam except for the central highlands; and, by minorities, in Kampuchea and Laos.

A system of romanisation was designed in the seventeenth century and has become standard, replacing the older Chinese characters. It uses certain special letters and vowel-marks.

PRONUNCIATION Hanoi pronunciation, here described, differs in some details from that of the centre and south.

Vowels:

A, Ê, I, Ô, U are like *ah, eh, ee, oh, oo.*

Y is always equivalent to I.

E and O are the vowels in "man" and "law," respectively.

Â is the vowel in "sun."

Ă, Ơ, Ư are like short versions of A, Ô, U, but with the lips spread in a smile; Ư is as in some people's pronunciation of "Ugh!"

In diphthongs a second vowel A or Ê is a neutral sound like the *e* in "the" before a consonant; for example, IA is much like the English word "ear." A third vowel, if any, is fully sounded.

Before NG or C the vowels Ô, O and U are followed by a *w* sound due to closing of the mouth as the consonant is uttered.

Consonants:

D and R are like *z.*

The separate letter Đ (đ) has the sound of English *d.*

GI is like *zy*, otherwise G (also GH) is guttural as in "Ugh!"

T is like unvoiced *d* (no puff of breath).

TH is like a *t* with puff of breath as in English (but stronger).

C and K are both like unvoiced *g.*

CH and TR are both like unvoiced *j.*

NH and KH are as in "canyon" and the *ch* in "loch" respectively.

NG (or NGH) is as in "singer" (no *g* sound), and may occur at the beginning of a word.

PH is like *f.*

S and X are both like *ss.*

At the end of a word CH is like *k*, NH like *ng*, and final *p*, *t* and *k* sounds represent a shutting off of the air stream without re-opening.

The principal differences in southern pronunciation are that D and GI become like *y*, R like English *r*, S like *sh.*

A syllable may be pronounced in any of six tones, indicated by vowel-marks. Note that marks ˆ, ˘ and the lip-spread mark on Ơ and Ư represent differences in vowel quality, and that tone-marks are additional.

A vowel without any tone-mark is pronounced "mid-level";
　′ indicates "high rising";
　` indicates "low falling";
　′ indicates "low rising," starting fairly low with a slight fall followed by a rise;
　˜ indicates "high rising broken," rising from mid-level with a constriction of the throat to give it a strained quality;
A dot under the vowel indicates "low constricted," very short, cut off by closing of the throat in a glottal stop.

Tones affect meaning: *đinh, dình, đỉnh, dĩnh* and *định* are different words. In practice, only key words in a sentence get their full tonal value.

In the remainder of these notes a pronunciation guide is incorporated uniform with that in the phrases; indicating medium and high pitch by different sizes of capitals, rises and falls by question and exclamation marks, and constriction of the throat by a raised comma '.

NOUNS are invariable and have no distinction of singular or plural. A noun may stand on its own without any article "a" or "the": *ông* [OHWNG], "the man," "a man," "men."

A noun representing a person or thing is usually preceded by its classifier: *cái buồng* [GKIGH? bwohwng!], "the room," "a room," "rooms," where *buồng* alone is the word for "room" and *cái* is its classifier. In the vocabulary most nouns are shown in this way preceded by their classifiers. They need seldom be used without them.

The commonest classifier for inanimate objects is *cái* [GKIGH?]; that for persons is *người* [ngwooee!], but some very common words such as *ông* [OHWNG], "man," and *bà* [bah!], "woman," are used without classifiers.

For an indefinite article if needed, use *một* [moht'], "one," before the classifier (if any): *một cái buồng* [moht' GKIGH? bwohwng!], "a room." Similarly, for an indefinite plural, use *mấy* [MIGH?], "some, a few."

The words *này* [nigh!], "this, these," and *ấy* [EIGH?], "that, those," are placed after classifier-plus-noun: *cái buồng này* [GKIGH? bwohwng! nigh!], "this room," "these rooms"; *mấy cái buồng ấy* [MIGH? GKIGH? bwohwng! EIGH?], "those few rooms."

PRONOUNS First person pronouns are:

tôi [DTOY], "I, me"
chúng ta [TYOOWNG? DTAH], "we, us, including you"
chúng tôi [TYOOWNG? DTOY], "we, us, not you"

Second and third person pronouns indicate respect and social status. For "you," say *ông* [OHWNG] to a man, *bà* [bah!] to an older or married woman, *cô* [GKOH] to a young woman, *em* [AM] to a child.

For "you," plural, put *các* [GKAHK?] before any of these forms: *các ông* [GKAHK? OHWNG], "you (men)," etc.

For third person, add *ấy*, "that, those," to the forms given for the second person: *ông ấy* [OHWNG EIGH?], "that man," for "he, him"; *các em ấy* [GKAHK? AM EIGH?] for "they (those children)," etc.

Other pronouns are:

nó [NAW?], "it" (child or animal)
họ [haw'], "they, them" (persons)

For non-living things, use *cái ấy* [GKIGH? EIGH?], "that thing, those things." Indicate possession with *của* [gkooa?], "belonging to": *đồ của tôi* [doh! gkooa? DTOY], "my baggage." Or omit *của*, and say just *đồ tôi* [doh! DTOY].

ADJECTIVES follow the noun, but precede a demonstrative, if any: *cái hiệu* [GKIGH? hye'oo], "shop," *cái hiệu lớn* [GKIGH? hye'oo LERN?], "big shop(s)," *cái hiệu lớn ấy* [GKIGH? hye'oo LERN? EIGH?], "that big shop, those big shops."

No verb "is" or "are" is needed in applying an adjective to a noun, and so *Cái hiệu lớn* can mean "The shop is big," "The shops are big."

For a comparative, put *hơn*, "more," after the adjective: *lớn hơn* [LERN? HERN], "bigger." The word "than" needs no translation: *Cái hiệu này lớn hơn cái ấy* [GKIGH? hye'oo nigh! LERN? HERN GKIGH? EIGH?], "This shop is bigger than that one."

For a superlative, add *hơn hết* to the adjective: *Cái buồng này lớn hơn hết* [GKIGH? bwohwng! nigh! LERN? HERN HEHT?], "This room is the biggest."

ADVERBS Adjectives can be used without change of form as adverbs, and follow what they modify.

VERBS The verb "is" or "are" between nouns or pronouns is *là* [lah!]: *Ông ấy là bạn tôi* [OHWNG EIGH? lah! bahn' DTOY], "That man is my friend"; *Đồ này là đồ tôi* [doh! nigh! lah! doh! DTOY], "This baggage is my baggage," "This baggage is mine."

In specifying location or place of residence, "is" or "are" is *ở* [uh?]: *Cái hiệu ở đây* [GKIGH? hye'oo uh? DEIGH], "The shop is here."

"There is" or "There are" is *có* [GKAW?], which also means "have": *Có một cuốn sách* [GKAW? moht' GKWOHN? SAHK?], "There is a book"; *Tôi có một cuốn sách* [DTOY GKAW? moht' GKWOHN? SAHK?], "I have a book."

Verbs do not normally indicate tense, but *vừa* [VOOA?] may be placed before the verb to indicate completed action in the recent past; *đã* [DA'A?] for an ordinary past tense; *sẽ* [SA'A?] for future: *vừa đi* [VOOA? DEE], "has just gone"; *đã đi* [DA'A? DEE], "went"; *sẽ đi* [SA'A? DEE], "will go."

Note the use of verbs of motion as prepositions; for example, *Cô ấy sẽ đem cuốn sách ấy* [GKOH EIGH? SA'A? DAM GKWOHN? SAHK? EIGH?], "She (that young woman) will carry that book," can be followed by *lại khách-sạn* [ligh' KHAHK? sahn'], "comes (to the) hotel," to mean "She will bring that book to the hotel." Similarly *đi* for "to" in the case of motion away from the speaker, and *cho* [TYAW], "give," for "to" or "for."

For a negative, put *không* [KHOHWNG] or *chẳng* [tyang?], "not," before the main verb: *Ông ấy không đi* [OHWNG EIGH? KHOHWNG DEE], "He is not going."

QUESTIONS For a yes/no question, put *không* [KHOHWNG] at the end of the corresponding statement: *Cô ấy có ở kia* [GKOH EIGH? GKAW? uh? KEEA], "She is over there," *Cô ấy có ở kia không* [GKOH EIGH? GKAW? uh? KEEA KHOHWNG], "Is she over there?"

For an affirmative answer, repeat the verb or say *Đúng* [DOONG?], "Correct," and for a negative answer say *Không*. (But both of these mean "No" in answer to a negative question; for an affirmative here, repeat the verb and add emphatic *chứ* [TYUH?].)

In questions that use a special question-word such as *đâu* [DOW], "where?," generally use the same word order as in the case of a statement. Put *bao giờ* [BOW zyer!], "when?," at the end of the sentence when referring to the past, and at the beginning when referring to the future.

IMPERATIVES For an imperative, use the plain verb, or precede it with *ông* or another second person pronoun, or with *Xin* [SEEN], "Please," or *Mời* [muhee!] ("invite"): *Xin ông lại* [SEEN OHWNG ligh'], "Please come (sir)."

For emphasis, put *đi* [DEE] at the end of the sentence. For a milder command, use *nên* [NEHN], "should," as an auxiliary verb.

For "Don't," put *đừng* [duhng!] before the main verb: *Đừng đi* [duhng! DEE],

"Don't go."

For "Let's," begin the sentence with *Ta* [DTAH] and use *nên* [NEHN] before the verb: *Ta nên đi* [DTAH NEHN DEE], "Let's go."

NUMERALS In specifying numbers of objects, the numeral is placed before the classifier (if any) and noun: *hai cái buồng* [HIGH GKIGH? bwohwng!], "two rooms."

The form *tư* [TER] is optional for "four" — either alone or in its compounds; similarly, the forms *lăm* [LAM] and *nhăm* [NYAM] for "five," except that *mười lăm* [mwooee! LAM] is always used for "fifteen."

CURRENCY 1 *đồng* [dohwng!] = 10 *hào* [how!] = 100 *xu* [SOO]. In the south, the term *cắc* [GKAK?] replaces *hào*.

FORMS OF ADDRESS *Ông, Bà* and *Cô* function as "Mr," "Mrs" and "Miss" before Vietnamese surnames (first names).

KIN TERMS (used also in a family as pronouns) are:

cha [TYAH], "father"
anh [AHNG], "older brother"
em giai [AM ZYIGH], "younger brother"
con giai [GKAWN ZYIGH], "son"
chồng [tyohwng!], "husband"

mẹ [maa'], "mother"
chị [tyee'], "older sister"
em gái [AM GHIGH?], "younger sister"
con gái [GKAWN GHIGH?], "daughter"
vợ [ver'], "wife"

These are the ordinary words for "husband" and "wife," but a husband and wife will refer to one another as *nhà tôi* [nyah! DTOY], literally "my house"; and the polite terms of reference by others are *ông nhà* [OHWNG nyah!] and *bà nhà* [bah! nyah!].

NAME OF LANGUAGE
The Vietnamese language is *Tiếng Việt* [DTEEANG? veeat'].

EVERYDAY PHRASES

ENGLISH	BURMESE	THAI
Yes	Hou'bpade *HOHPbah-deh*	Krăp/Ka' *KRAHP*/KAHK
No	Măhou'bpabŭ *MaHOHPbah-boo*	Bplằhu krăp/ka' *Blow KRAHP*/KAHK
Please	Tjĕizŭ-bpyùbpi *TJEIGHZOO-BYOO!bee*	Ga'ru'nah GA-ROONAH
Thank you	Tjĕizŭ-babĕ *TJEIGHZOObah-beh*	Kåwp-kun krăp/ka' *Kawp*KOON *KRAHP*/KAHK
Thank you very much	Ămyājĭ tjĕizŭ-din-bade *A-MYAHJEE TJEIGHZOOdimbah-deh*	Kåwp-kun màhk krăp/ka' *Kawp*KOON*MAHK! KRAHP*/KAHK
Don't mention it	Kei'sà măhyì-babŭ *KEIGHSSAH! ma-shhee! bah-boo*	Mài bpen rai krăp/ka' *MIGH!pen-righ KRAHP*/KAHK
Excuse me, but . . .	Kwïn bpyùba, . . . *KWIM!pyoo!-bah*	Kăw tòht krăp/ka' . . . KAW?*TOHT! KRAHP*/KAHK
Excuse me (I'm sorry)	Dtäun-ban-bade *DTOWMbahmbah-deh*	Sĭa jăi dùai krăp/ka' SEEA? *jigh DOOEH! KRAHP*/KAHK
Excuse me (Do you mind?)	Kwìn hlwu'bpa *Kwiñ!hloop!bah*	Kun ja' rang-gĭat mái? KOON JAHRANG *geeat migh?*
Pardon? (What did you say?)	Ba bpyö-dhalĕ? *Bah BYOHtha-leh?*	'A'rai-na' krăp/ka'? A-RIGHNA *KRAHP*/KAHK
Wait a moment	Kanà sàun ba *KaNA! sowm!bah*	Dĭau-diau DEEOW?DEEOW
Hurry up!	Myan-myan! *Myañ-myañ*	Rĕhu-rĕhu kàu! *REIGHOO-REIGHOO KOW!*
Slowly!	Pyĕi-pyĕi! *PYEIGH-PYEIGH*	Chăh-chăh! *CHAH-CHAH*
Stop!	Ya' bpa! *YAHPbah*	Yŭt! *Yoot*
Look out!	Thadì pyù-ba! *TtaTHEE! PYOObah*	Ra'wang! RAH-WAHNG
Look!	Tjì-ba! *TJEE!bah*	Duu nòhn sï'! DOO *NOHN!* SEE
How much?	Balau'lĕ? *Ba-LOWLleh*	Rahkah tàurăi krăp/ka'? RAHKAH *TOW!righ KRAHP*/KAHK
Never mind	Kei'sà mahyì-babŭ *KEIGHSSA! ma-shhee!bah-boo*	Mài bpen rai *MIGH!pen-righ*
Come in	Win la-ba *Wiñlah-bah*	Kàu mah *KOW! mah*
Come with me	Tjăno-nè/Tjămà-nè lai' kè-ba *Tja-nohNEH!/TjaMAH!NEH! LIGHK-KEH!bah*	Mah-dùai gon MAH*DUH!* GAHN
Good morning	Min-gă-la-ba *Mingga-lah-bah*	Sa'watdih krăp/ka' SAWT-DEE *KRAHP*/KAHK
Good afternoon	Min-gă-la-ba *Mingga-lah-bah*	Sa'watdih krăp/ka' SAWT-DEE *KRAHP*/KAHK
Good evening	Min-gă-la-ba *Mingga-lah-bah*	Sa'watdih krăp/ka' SAWT-DEE *KRAHP*/KAHK
Good-bye (leaving)	Thwā-ba-ōun-me *TTWAHbah ohm-meh*	Lah gåwn krăp/ka' LAH*gawn KRAHP*/KAHK
Good-bye (staying)	Thwā-ba-dò *TTWAHbah DOH!*	Sa'watdih krăp/ka' SAWT-DEE *KRAHP*/KAHK

LAO	KAMPUCHEAN	VIETNAMESE
Jàu *JOW!*	Baat/Jaah *Bat/Jah*	Vâng VAHNG
Baw BAW	Baat, dte/Jaah, dte *Bat dteh/Jah dteh*	Không KHOHWNG
Gã'lu'nãh GAHLOO-NAH	Sõm *Sohm*	Xin vui lòng SEEN VOO *lowng!*
Kâwpjãii *Kawp!jigh?*	'Ó-gun *'Aw-goon*	Cám ơn ông/bà *GKAHM?* ON OHWNG/*ba!*
Kâwpjãii lãhi lãhi *Kawp!ja-la-ligh?*	'Ó-gun jrãan *'Aw-goon jwa-an*	Xin cám ơn ông/bà lắm lắm SEEN *GKAHM?* ON OHWNG/*ba! LAHM?LAHM?*
Baw bpẽn nyãng BAWP*ben nyahng?*	Mĩn 'ey dtē *M'n 'eh dteh*	Không dám KHOWNG *ZYAHM?*
Kãw tòht daah, . . . *Kaw?TOHT!* DAA	Sõm-dtõh, . . . *Sohm-dtoh*	Xin lỗi ông/bà, nhưng . . . SEEN LO'EE? OHWNG/*ba!*, NYERNG
Kãw tòht *Kaw?TOHT!*	Sõm-dtõh *Sohm-dtoh*	Xin lỗi ông/bà SEEN LO'EE? OHWNG/*ba!*
Kãw tòht *Kaw?TOHT!*	Sõm-dtõh *Sohm-dtoh*	Xin lỗi ông/bà SEEN LO'EE? OHWNG/*ba!*
Kãw tòht, jàu wàu nyãng nãw? *Kaw?TOHT!, JOWWOW! nyahng naw?*	Néak tã met? *Neeak tahmeht?*	Ông/Bà nói gì? OHWNG/*ba! NOY? ghee!*
Tãh nòi neung TAH! *noy* NERNG	Jam bõndtet *Jahm b'n-dteht*	Xin chờ một chút SEEN *tyer! mot TYOOT?*
Wãi wãi! WIGH-WIGH	Chap-chap lãang! *Chahp-chahp la-ang*	Mau lên! MOW LEHN
Sàh sàh! *SAH-SAH!*	Múay-múay! *Mooeh-mooeh!*	Đi chậm lại! DEE *chu'm li'gh*
Yũt! YOOT	Chup! *Choop!*	Đừng lại! *DUHNG? li'gh*
La'wãng! LA-WAHNG	Bróyóat! *Bro-yoaht!*	Coi chừng! GKOY *tyoong!*
Beung hân! *Berng hahn!*	Meul noa! *Merl noah!*	Nhìn kia! *Nyeen! gkeea!*
Lãhkãh taudãii? LAHKAH *tow-digh?*	Tlay bponmaan? *T'ligh bp'n-mahn?*	Bao nhiêu tiền? BOW NYEEO *dteean!*
Baw bpẽn nyãng BAWP*ben nyahng?*	Min 'ey dtē *M'n 'eh dteh*	Dừng bận tâm *Duhng! ban DTAHM*
Sũhn kâu mãh dãi SUN *kow!mah digh!*	'Õñjeuñ jol mawk *'Ng-jerng johl mawk*	Mời ông/bà vào *Moy!* OHWNG/*ba! vow!*
Sũhn mãh nãhm kôi SUN MAH-NAHM *koy!*	'Õñjeuñ mawk dtaan kñom *'Ng-jerng mawk dtahn k'yom*	Đi theo tôi DEE TTOW DTOY
Sã'bãhi-dĩh *Sa-bigh-dee?*	Jumríap-súa *Joomreeap sooa*	Chào ông/bà *Chow!* OHWNG/*ba!*
Sã'bãhi-dĩh *Sa-bigh-dee?*	Jumríap-súa *Joomreeap sooa*	Chào ông/bà *Chow!* OHWNG/*ba!*
Sã'bãhi-dĩh *Sa-bigh-dee?*	Jumríap-súa *Joomreeap sooa*	Chào ông/bà *Chow!* OHWNG/*ba!*
Lãhgawn LAHKGAWN	Jumríap-lia *Joomreeap leea*	Chào ông/bà tôi đi *Chow!* OHWNG/*ba!* DTOY DEE
Lãhgawn LAHKGAWN	Jumríap-lía *Joomreeap leea*	Chào ông/bà *Chow!* OHWNG/*ba!*

ENGLISH	BURMESE	THAI
Good night	Min-gǎ-la-ba *Mingga-lah-bah*	Sa'watdih krāp/ka' SAWT-DEE *KRAHP*/KAHK
Do you understand?	Nǎ le-dhala? *NAH lehtha-lah*	Kun kàujai mái krāp/ka'? KOON *KOW!*JIGH MIGH? *KRAHP*/KAHK
I understand	Nǎ le-bade *NAH lehbah-deh*	Pǫm/Chán kàujai krāp/ka' *Pom?/Chahn? KOW!*JIGH *KRAHP*/KAHK
I don't understand	Nǎ mǎle-babū *NAHma lehbah-boo*	Póm/Chán mài kàujai krāp/ka' *Pom?/Chahn?* MIGH *KOW!jigh KRAHP*/KAHK
All right (I'll do it)	Gkǎun-babi *GKOWMbah-bee*	Dtǒklong krāp/ka' *Dtok*LONG *KRAHP*/KAHK
It's all right	Da-gkǎun-bade *Dah GKOWMbah/deh*	Chaidai krāp/ka' CHIGHDIGH *KRAHP*/KAHK

NUMERALS

zero	O thoun-nyà *ttohnNYAH!*	O súun *soon?*
one	၁ dti' *DTIH!*	ၑ nĕung *nerng*
two	J hni' *HNIH!*	ၾ sáwng, toh SAWNG?, TOH
three	၃ thŏun *TTOHŇ*	ၮ sáhm *SAHM?*
four	၄ lēi *LEIGH*	ၸ sĭh *see*
five	၅ ngǎ *NGAH*	ၷ hàh *HAH!*
six	၆ chau' *CHOW*	ၹ hŏk *hohk*
seven	၇ kun-hni' *konHNIH!*	ၺ jĕt *jet*
eight	၈ hyi' *SHHEE!*	ၻ bpǎat *bpat*
nine	၉ gkòu *GKOH*	ၼ gàu *GOW!*
ten	၁၀ dtǎ-hse *d'hseh*	ၵၐ sĭp *sip*
eleven	hsè dti' *hseh! DTIHK*	sĭp'eht *sip*-ET
twelve	hsè hni' *hseh! HNIHK*	sĭpsáwng *sip* SAWNG?
thirteen	hsè thŏun *hseh! TTOHŇ*	sĭpsáhm *sip* SAHM?
fourteen	hsè lēi *hseh! LEIGH*	sĭpsĭh *sip see*
fifteen	hsè ngǎ *hseh! NGAH*	sĭp-hàh *sip HAH!*
sixteen	hsè chau' *hseh! CHOWK*	sĭp-hŏk *sip hohk*
seventeen	hsè kun *hseh! kohň*	sĭpjĕt *sip jet*
eighteen	hsè hyi' *hseh! SHHEEK*	sĭp-bpǎat *sip bpat*
nineteen	hsè gkòu *hseh! GKOH*	sĭpgàu *sip GOW!*
twenty	hnà-hse *HNAH!hseh*	yìhsĭp *YEE!sip*
twenty-one	hnà-hsè dti' *hnah! HSEH! DTIHK*	yìhsĭp'eht *YEE!sip*-ET
thirty	thŏunze *TTOHŇzeh*	sáhmsĭp *SAHM?* sip
forty	lēize *LEIGHzeh*	sĭhsĭp *see sip*
fifty	ngǎze *NGAHzeh*	hàhsĭp *HAH! sip*

104

EVERYDAY PHRASES

LAO	KAMPUCHEAN	VIETNAMESE
Lāhgawn LAHKGAWN	Jumrĭap-lia *Joomreeap leea*	Chào ông/bà *Chow!* OHWNG/*ba!*
Jàu kâujăii bǎw? *JOW! kow!jigh* BAW?	Néak yúal dtē? *Neeak jooal dteh?*	Ông/Bà hiểu không? OHWNG/*ba!* *hyeoo?* KHOHWNG
Kôi kâujăii *Koy! kow!jigh*	Kñom yúal hăay *K'yom jooal high*	Tôi hiểu DTOY *hyeoo?*
Kôi baw kâujăii *Koy!* BAW *kow!jigh*	Kñom min yúal dtē *K'yom m'n jooal dteh*	Tôi không hiểu DTOY KHOHWNG *hyeoo?*
Jàu *JOW!*	Nĭng hăay *N'ng high*	Vâng VAHNG
Baw bpěn nyǎng BAWP*ben nyahng?*	Drem drŏv hăay *D'rum d'ruv high*	Tốt DTOHT?

NUMERALS

O sǔun *soon?*	O sŏn *sohn*	zê-rô, không ZEHROH, KHOHWNG
໑ neung NERNG	໑ múay, me- *mooeh, m'*	một *mot*
໒ sǎwng *sawng?*	໒ bpii *bpee*	hai HIGH
໓ sǎhm *sahm?*	໣ bey *bay*	ba BAH
໔ sih SEE	໤ búan *booan*	bốn, tư *BOHN?,* DTUH
໕ hâh *hah!*	໥ bram *bram*	năm, lăm, nhăm NAHM, LAHM, NYAHM
໖ hŏk HOHK	໦ brammúay *bram-mooeh*	sáu *SOW?*
໗ jĕt JEHT	໧ brampĭl *bram-bpee*	bảy *ba'ee?*
໘ bpâaht *bpat!*	໨ brambey *bram-bay*	tám *DTAHM?*
໙ gàu *GOW!*	໩ brambúan *bram-booan*	chín *TYEEN?*
໑໐ sĭp SIP	໑໐ dŏp *dup*	mười *mwooee!*
sip'ĕt SIP-EHT	dŏp-múay *dup-mooeh*	mười một *mwooee! mot*
sipsǎwng SIP *sawng?*	dŏp-bpii *dup-bpee*	mười hai *mwooee!* HIGH
sisǎhm SIP *sahm?*	dŏp-bey *dup-bay*	mười ba *mwooee!* BAH
sipsih SIPSEE	dŏp-búan *dup-booan*	mười bốn *mwooee! BOHN?*
sip-hâh SIP-*hah!*	dŏp-bram *dup-bram*	mười lăm *mwooee! lahm*
sip-hŏk SIP-HOHK	dŏp-brammúay *dupbram-mooeh*	mười sáu *mwooee! SOW?*
sipjĕt SIP-JEHT	dŏp-brambpĭl *dupbram-bpee*	mười bảy *mwooee! ba'ee?*
sip-bpâaht SIP-*bpat!*	dŏp-brambey *dupbram-bay*	mười tám *mwooee! DTAHM?*
sipgàu SIP*GOW!*	dŏp-brambúan *dupbram-booan*	mười chín *mwooee! TYEEN?*
sǎahu SOW	mpey *m'pay*	hai mươi, hăm HIGH MWOOEE, HAHM
sǎahu-'ĕt SOW-EHT	mpey-múay *m'pay-mooeh*	hai mươi mốt HIGH MWOOEE MOHT?
sǎhmsĭp *sahm*SIP	saamsep *sahmsup*	ba mươi, băm BAH MWOOEE, BAHM
sihsĭp see-sip	sǎesep *sighsup*	bốn mươi *BOHN?* MWOOEE
hâhsĭp *hah!*SIP	haasep *hahsup*	năm mươi NAHM MWOOEE

105

NUMERALS

ENGLISH	BURMESE	THAI
sixty	chau'hse *CHOWSSseh*	hŏksĭp *hohk sip*
seventy	kunnà-hse *konNA!-hseh*	jĕtsĭp *jet sip*
eighty	hyi'hse *SHHEESSseh*	bpăatsĭp *bpat sip*
ninety	gkôuze *GKOHzeh*	gàusĭp *GOW! sip*
a hundred	dtă ya *dta-yah*	nĕung rôi *nerng ROY*
a hundred and one	dtă yà dti' *d'YAH! DTIHK*	nĕung rôi 'eht *nerng ROY*-ET
a hundred and ten	dtă yà dtă-hse *d'YAH! d'hseh*	nĕung rôi sĭp *nerng ROY sip*
two hundred	hnaya *hna-yah*	săwng rôi SAWNG? *ROY*
a thousand	dtă taun *d'towñ*	nĕung pan *nerng PAHN*
ten thousand	dtă thăun *d'TTOWÑ*	nĕung mĕuhn *nerng mern*
a hundred thousand	dtă thêin *d'TTEIGHÑ*	nĕung săan *nerng SAN?*
a million	dtă thăn *d'TTAHÑ*	nĕung lăhn *nerng LAHN*
ten million	dtă gadei *d'g'deigh*	sĭp lăhn *sip LAHN*
a half	dtă we' *d'WEHK*	krèung nĕung *KRERNG! nerng*
. . . point (decimal) . . .	. . . dăthàma . . . *dahtta-ma*	. . . jŭt . . . *joot*

DAYS OF THE WEEK

Sunday	Dta-nin-ga-nwei *D'NINGga-nweigh*	Wan'ah-tĭt WAHNNA-TIT
Monday	Dta-ninla *D'NIÑlah*	Wanjan WAHN JAHN
Tuesday	'In-ga *'Inggah*	Wan'ang-kahn WAHNNANG KAHN
Wednesday	Bou'da-hŭ *BOHTda-HOO*	Wan-pŭt WAHN *POOT*
Thursday	Tja-dhàbadĕi *Tjah-THAH!ba-DEIGH*	Wan-pă'rĕu-hăt WAHN *PARRER haht*
Friday	Thau'tja *TTOWTjah*	Wansŭk WAHN *sook*
Saturday	Sănei *Sa-neigh*	Wansáu WAHN SOW?

MONTHS

January	Zan-nawa-yi *Janna-wahyee*	Mok-grah-kom MOHK GRAH KOHM
February	Pei-pawa-yi *Pehpa-wahyee*	Gum-pah-pan GOOM PAH PAHN
March	Ma' *MAHK*	Mihnah-kom MEE NAH KOHM
April	Ei-pyi *Eigh-pyeh*	Mehsăh-yon MEH SAH? YON

NUMERALS

LAO	KAMPUCHEAN	VIETNAMESE
hŏksĭp HOHKSIP	hoksep *hoksup*	sáu mươi *SOW?* MWOOEE
jĕtsĭp JETSIP	jetsep *jetsup*	bảy mươi *ba'ee?* MWOOEE
bpăahtsĭp *bpat!*SIP	bpăetsep *bpightsup*	tám mươi *DTAHM?* MWOOEE
găusĭp *GOW!sip*	gausep *gowsup*	chín mươi *TYEEN?* MWOOEE
hŏi *HOY!*	múay-rawy, merawy *mooeh roy, m'roy*	một trăm *mot* TYAHM
hŏi neung *HOY!*NERNG	merawy múay *m'roy mooeh*	một trăm lẻ một *mot* TYAHM *laa? mot*
hŏi sĭp *HOY!sip*	merawy dŏp *m'roy dup*	một trăm mươi *mot* TYAHM *mwooee!*
săwng hŏi *sawng HOY!*	bpii-rawy *bpee roy*	hai trăm HIGH TYAHM
păn PAHN	múay-bpóan, mebpóan *mooeh bpoahn, m'bpoahn*	một nghìn, một ngàn *mot ngeen!, mot ngahn!*
mĕuhn MERN	múay-meun, memeun *mooeh mern, ma-mern*	mười nghìn *mwooee! ngeen!*
săahn *san?*	múay-săen, mesăen *mooeh sighn, ma-sighn*	một trăm ngàn *mot* TYAHM *ngahn!*
làhn *LAHN!*	múay-lían, melian *mooeh leean, m'leean*	mộ triệu *mot tye'oo*
sĭp làhn SIP*LAHN!*	múay-gaot, megaot *mooeh gowt, m'gowt*	mười triệu *mwooee! tye'oo*
kuhng K'NG	genlah *g'n-lah*	một nửa *mot noo'a?*
. . . jŭt . . . JOOT	. . . gbías . . . *g'beeass*	. . . điểm . . . *dee'am?*

DAYS OF THE WEEK

Wăn'ăh-tit WAHNa-*tit*	Tngay-'aadtĭt *T'ng-igh aht-t't*	chúa nhật *TYOOA? nya't*
Wănjăn WAHN *jahn*	Tngay-jan *T'ng-igh junn*	thứ hai *TTUH?* HIGH
Wăn'ăng-kăhn WAHN*nang* KAHN	Tngay-'ŏnggia *T'ng-igh 'ung-keea*	thứ ba *TTUH?* BAH
Wăn-put WAHN-POOT	Tngay-bput *T'ng-igh bpoot*	thứ tư *TTUH?* DTUH
Wănbpă-hăt WAHNPA-HAHT	Tngay-brehóas *T'ng-igh bra-hoahss*	thứ năm *TTUH?* NAHM
Wănsŭk WAHN SOOK	Tngay-sok *T'ng-igh sok*	thứ sáu *TTUH? SOW?*
Wănsău WAHN *sow?*	Tngay-sau *T'ng-igh sow*	thứ bảy *TTUH? ba'ee?*

MONTHS

Mokgālāh MOHKGA-LAH	Méa'geraa *Mahk-g'rah*	tháng giêng *TTAHNG?* ZEEANG
Gŭumpăh *Goom-*PAH	Gam-péa *Gahm-pehah*	tháng hai *TTAHNG?* HIGH
Mĭhnăh MEE-NAH	Minaa *Meen-neea*	tháng ba *TTAHNG?* BAH
Mĕhsăh MEH*sah?*	Mēsaa *Meh-sah*	tháng tư *TTAHNG?* DTUH

MONTHS

ENGLISH	BURMESE	THAI
May	Mei *Meigh*	Ptsa'pah-kom P'TSAH PAH KOHM
June	Zun *Zuhñ*	Mit-tu'nah-yon *MIT*TOO *nah* YON
July	Zulain *Zoolighñ*	Gräk-gdah-kom
		*GRAHK*GA DAH KOHM
August	'Ōgou' *'AwGOHK*	Sing-háh-kom SING? HAH? *kohm*
September	Se'dtinba *SETdimbah*	Gan-yah-yon GHAN YAH YON
October	'Au'dtôuba *'OWT-DOHbah*	Dtu'lah-kom DTOO LAH KOHM
November	Nouwinba *Noh-wimbah*	Ptsa'jï'gah-yon P'TS*jee* GAH *yon*
December	Dizinba *Dee-zimbah*	Tanwah-kom TAHN WAH KOHM

SENTENCES

1. Is there someone here who speaks English, please? A little. I speak only a little ———— .

1. 'Ĭn-galei' zăgă dta'tè thu hyi-badhală? Nēnē. ———— nēnē dò tjano/tjamà bpyō-da'bpade.
   'INGgaLEIGHK saGAH DTATdeh! ttoo shhee-bahtha-lah? NEH-NEH. ———— NEH-NEH DOH! tja-noh/tjaMAH! BYOH-DAHP!bah-deh.

1. Tihnih mih krai pùut pahsáh Anggrüht dài bàhn krǎp/ka'? Nĭt nŏi. Póm/Chán pùut dài ———— nit nŏi krǎp/ka'.
   TEE!NEE! MEE KRIGH POOT! PAH-SAH? ANGgr't DIGH! BAHN! KRAHP/KAHK. NITnoy POHM?/CHAHN? POOT! DIGH! ———— NITnoy KRAHP/KAHK.

2. I want to go to ———— . Is there a bus (an aeroplane, a taxi)? Yes, there is. No, there is not.

2. ———— -gou thwā-jin-de. Ba'sa-gkă (Leiyinbyan, Ta'si) hyi-dhală? Hyi-bade. Mă-hyi-babŭ.
   ———— -goh TTWAHjin-deh. BAHSS!aKAH (Leigh-yin-byahñ, Taksee) shheetha-lah? Shheebah-deh.Ma-shheebah-boo.

2. Póm/Chán dtàwng gahn bpai ———— . Mih rŏtmeh (krèuangbin, tǎaksìh) bpai mái?. Mih krǎp/ka'. Mài mih krǎp/ka'.
   POHM?/CHAHN? DTAWNG!GAHN bpigh ———— . MEE ROHTMEH (KROONG!BIN, TAKSEE!) BPIGH MIGH? MEE KRAHP/KAHK. MIGHMEE KRAHP/KAHK.

3. Where is the bus (the railway station, the ticket office)? It is here (there, over there).

3. Ba'sa-gkă (Bu-dtăyoun, Le'hma'yăundè neiya) be-hma hyi-badhăle. Di-hma (Hou-hma, Hau-ho-be'hma) hyi-bade.
   BAHSSaKAH (BooTAH-yohñ, LEM-HAHyowñ-deh! neighyah) beh-mah shhee-bahtha-leh. Dee-hmah (Hoh-hmah, How-ho-BEMmah) shheebah-deh.

3. Rŏtmeh (Sa'táhnihrŏtfai, Tih-káhi-dtúa) yŭu tih nái krǎp/ka'? Yŭu dtrong nih (tìhnàn, tìhnòhn) krǎp/ka'.
   ROHT MEH (STAH? NEE-ROHTFIGH, TEE!KIGH? DOOA?) yooTEE!NIGH? KRAHP/KAHK. Yoo DWONG NEE! (TEE! NAHN!, TEE!NOHN!) KRAHP/KAHK.

MONTHS

LAO	KAMPUCHEAN	VIETNAMESE
Peutsă'păh PERTSA-PAH	'Ose-pía 'Ohss-peea	tháng năm TTAHNG? NAHM
Mĭh-tŭnăh MEEtoo-nah	Mi-tonaa Meet-toh-nah	tháng sáu TTAHNG? SOW?
Găwlagadăh GawLA-KAdah?	Ka'gedaa Kak-g'dah	tháng bảy TTAHNG? ba'ee?
S͂'nghăh Sing!hah?	Seyhaa Say-hah	tháng tám TTAHNG? DTAHM?
Găn-nyăh GahnNYAH	Gaññaa Gahn-nyah	tháng chín TTAHNG? TYEEN?
Dtŭlăh DtooLAH	Dtolaa Dtohl-lah	tháng mười TTAHNG? mwooee!
Peutsăjĭgah Pertsa-JEE-gah?	Vijjegaa Vijja-gah	tháng mười một TTAHNG? mwooee! mot
Tănwăh TAHN WAH	Tnŭ T'noo	tháng chạp, tháng mười hai TTAHNG? tyap, TTAHNG? mwooee! HIGH

SENTENCES

1. Mĭh pûudăi yuu nĭh wàu pähsăh 'Ănggit dài daah baw? Dài nòi neung. Kôi wàu ——— dài nòi dĭau.

    MEE poo!digh yoo NEE! WOW! PAHsah? ahngGEET DIGH! da BAW? DIGH! NOY! NERNG. Koy! WOW! ——— DIGH! NOY! deeow?

2. Kôi yâhk bpăi ———. Mĭh lotbpă'jămtăhng (hĕuabĭn, lot dŏisăhn) baw? Jàu, mĭh. Baw, baw mĭh.

    Koy! YAHK? bpigh ———. MEE LOHTBA-jahm-TAHNG (HERbin, LOHT doy-sahn?) BAW? JOW!, MEE? BAW, BAW MEE?

3. Lotbpă'jămtăhng (Să'-tăhnĭh lotfái, Bawn-kăhibpĭh) yuu săi? Yuu nĭh (hân, tĭhnàn).

    LOHTBA-jahm-TAHNG (SAtah?NEE LOHT-FIGH, BAWNkigh?BPEE!) YOO sigh? YOO NEE! (hahn!, TEENAHN!)

---

1. Dtiinih mian néak jĕh niyiay 'ŏngglĕ dtĕ? Bŏndtet-bŏndtúat. K̃om jĕh niyiay ——— bŏndtet-bŏndtúat dtĕ.

    Dteeneehh meean neeak jehh nee-jyeigh 'onggleh dteh? B'n-teht b'n-dtooeht. K'yom jehh nee-jyeigh ——— b'n-dteht b'n-dtooeht dteh.

2. K̃om jŏng dtŭu ———. Mian laan-chnúal (gebpal-hŏh, dtaksii) dtĕ? Baat/Jaah, mian. Baat/Jaah, dtĕ; mĭn mian dtĕ.

    K'yom jung dteoo ———. Meean lahn-ch'nooal (gap-bahl-hohh, dtaksee) dteh? Bat/Jah, meean. Bat/Jah dteh, m'n meean dteh.

3. Laan-chnúal (Jŏmnót redtih-pleung, Gŏnlăeng-lŏk-sŏmbot) nĭu 'ăe-naa? Nĭu 'ăe-nih ('ăe-nuh, kaang-nuh).

    Lahn-ch'nooal (J'm-noht r't-dehplerng, G'n-lighng l'k-s'm-boht) neoo 'igh-nah? Neoo 'igh-neehh ('igh-noohh, kahng-noohh).

---

1. Xin lỗi, ở đây có ai nói tiếng Anh không? Một chút ít. Tôi nói được một chút ít thôi ———.

    SEEN LO'EE?, o DAY GKAW? igh NOY? DTEEANG? IGHNG KHOHWNG. Mot TYOOT? EET? DTOY NOY? DOOAK mot TYOOT? EET? TTOY ———.

2. Tôi muốn đi tới ———. Ở đây có xe buýt (có máy bay, có tắc-xi) không? Có, ở đây có. Không, ở đây không có.

    DTOY MOOAN? DEE DTOY? ———. O DAY GKAW? SA BWOOT? (GKAW? MIGH? BIGH, GKAW? DTAHK?SEE) KHOHWNG. GKAW?, o DAY GKAW? KHOHWNG, o DAY KHOHWNG GKAW?

3. Xe buýt (Nhà ga xe lửa, Phòng bán vé) ở đâu? Ở đây (đằng kia, trên kia).

    SA BWOOT? (Nyah! GAH SA loo'a?, Fowng BAHN? VEH-A?) o DOW. O DAY (dahng! GKEEA, TYEHN GKEEA).

SENTENCES

ENGLISH	BURMESE	THAI

4. How do I get to the airport (to the town)? Go that way. Go straight on (to the left, to the right).

4. Be-be'gkà leiyinbyan-gwin-gou (myòu-gou) thwà-malè? Hou-làn 'atàin thwà-ba. Hyèi-gou dtè-dè (Be-be'gkou, Nya-be'gkou) thwà-ba.
Beh-BEHKgah! leighyin-byahñ-GWIÑgoh (MYOH!goh) TTWAHmah-leh? HohLAHÑ 'a-tañ TTWAHbah. SHHEIGH!-goh DTEH!deh! (BehBEHKgoh, Nyah-BEHKgoh) TTWAHbah.

4. Póm/Chán jã' bpai sa'náhm bin (nai meuang) dài yàng 'ai kràp/ka'? Bpai tahng nãn kràp/ka'. Bpai trong-trong (lìau sàhi, lìau kwáh). POHM?/CHAHN? *JAHP*BAI SA-NAHM?BIN (NIGH *mooang*) DIGH! *yang!igh KRAHP*/KAHK. BPIGH TAHNG*NAHN KRAHP*/KAHK. BPIGH TWONG-TWONG *(LEEOW SIGH, LEEOW* KWAH?).

5. Would you take my baggage to the bus, please. There is just one bag. There are two bags and that bundle.

5. Tjanò/Tjamà bpyi'sì-dei-gou ba'sa-gkã-gou yu-ba. 'Ei' dta-lõunde hyi-bade. 'Ei' hnã-lòun-nè 'ãtou' dta-tou' hyi-bade. *TjaNOH!/TjaMAH! PYEES-SEEdeh-goh BAHSSaKAH-goh yoobah. 'EIGHTda-LOHNdeh shheebah-deh. 'EIGHNna-LOHNneh! aTOHT-daTOHK shheebah-deh.*

5. Kun chùai hiu gra'bpáu káwng póm/chán bpai tìh rõtmeh nòi kràp/ka'. Mìh gra'bpáu bai diau tàu nãn. Mìh gra'bpáu sáwng bai gàp hãw nãn. KOON *CHOOIGH!* HEEOO GRAHP-BOW? KAWNG? POHM?/ CHAHN? *bpigh TEE! ROHT*MEH *noy KRAHP*/KAHK. MEE GRAHP-BOW? SAWNG?BIGH *gahp-haw-NAHN.*

6. When does the bus go? Show me, please. The bus is late. The bus has already gone.

6. Ba'sa-gkã be 'achein twe'malè? Dta-hsei' pyà-ba. Ba'sa-gkã nau'tjà-de. Ba'sa-gkã twe'thwà-bi. *BAHSSaKAH beh a-cheighn teem!ma-leh? D'HSEIGHPpyah!bah. BAHSSa-KAH NOWTjah!deh. BAHSSaKAH TWETttwah-bee.*

6. Rõtmeh àawk mèua rãi kràp/ka'? Ga'ru'nah chùai bãwk nòi kràp/ka'. Rõtmeh mah chãh. Rõtmeh bpai làau. *ROHT*MEH *awk MER!righ KRAHP*/KAHK. GA-ROONAH *CHOOIGH! bawk noy KRAHP*/KAHK. *ROHT*MEH MAH CHAH. *ROHT*MEH *bpigh LAAOO!*

7. A ticket for one person (for two persons) to ———, please. Two adults and one child. First class. Tourist class.

7. ——— -gou le'hma' dãzaun (hna-zaun) pēi-ba. Lùji hna-yau' nè kalèi dtã-yau'. Pãtãma-dãn. Yòu-yòu dãn. ——— -goh LEM-HAHT da-zoñ (hna-zoñ) PEIGHbah. LooJEE hnaYOWN neh kaLEIGH d'YOWK. P't'mah-dahñ. YOU-YOU dahñ.

7. Dtúa sámràp kon diau (sámràp sáwng kon) bpai ——— kràp/ka'. Dtúa púu-yãi sáwng dtúa dèk nèung. Chãn nèung. Chãn tama'dah. DTOOA? SAHM?*rap* KOHNDI-OW (SAHM?-*rap* SAWNG? KOHN) *bpigh* ——— *KRAHP*/KAHK. DTOOA? POO?*yigh* SAWNG?, DTOOA? *dek-nerng. Chahn-nerng. Chahn tahma-dah.*

8. Excuse me, what time is it? Two o'clock. Ten past two. Half past two. Ten to three.

8. Kwin bpyù-ba, be hnana-yi hyi-balè? Hnã-che' tòu bi. Hnã-che' nè hse-mãni'. Hna-che' kwè. Thòun-nayi tòubòu hse-mãni'. *KWIM!pyoo!bah, behnna-nahyee shhee!bah-leh? Hna-CHEHT*

8. Káw tòht krãp/ka', wehlah tàurai kràp/ka'? Sáwng mohng. Sáwng mohng sĩp nahtih. Sáwng mohng krèung. 'Ĩhk sĩp nahtih sáhm mohng. KAW?*TOHT! KRAHP*/KAHK,

110

SENTENCES

LAO	KAMPUCHEAN	VIETNAMESE

LAO

4. Kôi jă' bpǎi <u>duhn-nyón</u>
(naii mēuang) dài jangdǎii?
Bpǎi tăhng nàn. Bpǎi <u>tăhng
nâh</u> (tăhng sǎhi, tăhng kǔa).
Koy! JAP*bigh* DERN-NYOHN
(NIGH MER-YANG) *DIGH!*
JANG*digh. Bpigh* TAHNG
NAHN! Bpigh TAHNG NAH!
(TAHNG *SIGH!,* TAHNG
kooah?).

5. Gǎ'lu'nǎh 'ǎu gǎ'bpǎu
dĕun tăhng kǎwng kòi sǎi
lot hǎi daah. Mǐh tǎah tǒng 'ǎn
dīau. Mǐh sǎwng tǒng laa'
pûuk 'ǎn nàn.
GAHLOO-NAH *ow* GAP*bow
dern* TAHNG *kawng koy!
sighloht HIGH! DAA?* MEE
TAA-*tohng ahn deeow?* MEE
sawng tohng LAA *pook!
ahn NAHN!*

6. Dǒn bpǎhn dǎi lotbpǎ'jǎmtǎhng
jeung jă' 'ǎwk? Gǎ'lu'nǎh
naa'nám kôi daah. Lot mah sǎh.
Lot 'ǎwk bpǎi làau.
Dohn bpahn digh LOHTBA-
*jahm-*TAHNG *JERNG* JA-*awk.*
GAHLOO-NAH NAA-NAHM
koy! DAA. LOHT MAH *SAH!*
LOHT *awk bpigh LAAO!*

7. Kǎw sèuh bpih <u>sǎmlǎp</u>
pûu neung (sǎmlǎp sǎwng kón)
bpǎi ———— daah. Pûu-nyai
sǎwng kón laa' dekpûu neung.
Sàn tih-neung. Sàn tǎhmmǎ'dǎh.
*Kaw? SERP!BEE!
sahm*LAHP POO!NERNG
*(sahm*LAHP *sawng?* KOHN*)
bpigh* ——— DAA.
*Poo!*NYIGH *sawng?* KOHN
LAA DEK*poo!* NERNG. *SAHN!
tee-nerng. SAHN!* TAHMMAH
dah?

8. Kǎw tòht daah, jǎk mõhng
làau? Sǎwng mõhng. Sǎwng
mõhng sip nǎhtǐh. Sǎwng mõhng
kuhng. Sǎhm mõhng nyáng sip
nǎhtǐh.
Kaw? TOHT! DAA, JAHK

KAMPUCHEAN

4. Kñom <u>dtǔu</u> jõmnót yúan-hŏh
(dtǔu dtii-grong) dtaam rawbiap-
naa? Dtǔu kaang-nuh. Dtǔu
<u>kaang-muk</u> (kaang-chvēng-day,
kaang-sdam-day).
*K'yom dteoo j'm-noht yooan-hohh
(dteoo dtee-grohng) dtahm raw-
beeap-nah? Dteoo kahng-noohh.
Dteoo kahng-mook (kahng
ch'vehng-digh, kahng s'dahm-
digh).*

5. Sŏm néak yawk hep-'eyvan
kñom dak laan-chnúal póng. Mían
dtǎe múay hep dtē. Mían bpii hep
nĭng gõñjŏp nuh.
*Sohm neeak yawk h'p-eighvahn
k'yom dukk lahn-ch'nooal pohng.
Meean dtigh mooeh h'p dteh.
Meean bpee h'p n'ng g'n-jop
noohh.*

6. Laan-chnúal jēñ maong
bponmaan? Sŏm néak bõnghaañ
kñom póng. Laan-chnúal yĭit.
Laan-chnúal jēñ hǎay.
*Lahn-ch'nooal jehng mowng
bp'n-mahn? Sohm neeak b'ng-
hahn k'yom pohng. Lahn-
ch'nooal joot. Lahn-ch'nooal
jehng high.*

7. Som sŏmbot múay <u>sŏmrap
menéak</u> (sŏmrap bpii néak) dtǔu
———— . Menus jas bpii néak nĭng
gmēng menéak. Tnak dtii múay.
Tnak sŏmrap dtēssejó.
*Som s'm-boht mooeh s'm-rahp
m'neeak (s'm-rahp bpee neeak)
dteoo* ——— . *M'nooss jahss
bpèe neeak n'ng g'mehng
m'neeak. T'nahk dtee mooeh.
T'nahk s'm-rahp dtehss-joh.*

8. Sŏm-dtŏh, maong bponmaan?
Maong bpii hǎay. Maong bpii dŏp
níadtii. Maong bpii genlah. Maong
bey gvak dŏp níadtii.
*Sohm-dtoh, mowng bp'n-mahn?
Mowng bpee high. Mowng bpee*

VIETNAMESE

4. Tôi đi lối nào <u>để tới</u>
<u>phi-trường</u> (để tới phổ)? Đi
lối kia. Đi <u>thẳng</u> (về
phía bên trái, về phía bên phải).
DTOY DEE *LOY? now! deh?
DTOY?* FEE-*tyooang! (deh?
DTOY? FOH?).* DEE *LOY?*
KEEA. *Dee ttah'ng? (veh! FEEA?*
BEHN *TYIGH?, veh! FEEA?*
BEHN*fa'ee?).*

5. Xin ông/bà vui lòng mang
hành-lý của tôi tới xe buýt.
Chỉ có một va-li thôi. Có hai
va-li và một cái đồng kia.
SEEN OHWNG/*ba!* VOO *lowng!*
MAHNG *highng!LEE? gkoo'a?*
DTOY *DTOY? SA BWOOT?
Tyee? GKAW? mot VAH-LEE*
TTOY. *GKAW?* HIGH VAH-LEE
vah! mot GKIGH? DOHWNG?
GKEEA.

6. Khi nào xe buýt chạy? Xin
ông/bà vui lòng chỉ tôi. Xe buýt
trễ rồi. Xe buýt đã chạy
rồi.
KHEE *now! SA BWOOT? tya'ee.*
SEEN OHWNG/*ba!* VOO *lowng!
tyee? DTOY. SA BWOOT?
TYE'EH? zroy! SA BWOOT?
DA'A? tya'ee zroy!*

7. Xin ông/bà vui lòng bán cho
tôi một vé <u>cho một người</u> (cho hai
người) để đi tới ——— . Hai người
lớn và một đứa nhỏ. Hạng nhất.
Hạng dành cho du-khách.
SEEN OHWNG/*ba!* VOO *lowng!
BAHN? TYAW mot ngwooee!
(TYAW* HIGH *ngwooee!) deh?*
DEE *DTOY?* ——— . HIGH
*ngwooee! LON? vah! mot
DOOA? nyo'o? Hang NYAHT?
Hang zyighng!* TYAW ZYOO-
KHIGHK?

8. Xin lỗi ông/bà, mấy giờ rồi? Hai
giờ đúng. Hai giờ mười. Hai giờ
rưỡi. Ba giờ kém mười.
SEEN LO'EE? OHWNG/*ba!, MAY?
yer! zroy!* HIGH *yer! DOONG?*
HIGH *yer! mwooee!* HIGH *yer!*

111

SENTENCES

ENGLISH	BURMESE	THAI
	TOHbee. Hna-CHEHNneh! *hsehma-nik. Hna-CHEHK* *KWEH. TTOHNnahyee* *TOHboh! hsehma-nik.*	WEHLAH *TOW!*RIGH *KRAHP/* KAHK. SAWING? MOHNG. SAWNG?MOHNG *sip*NAH-TEE. SAWNG? MOHNG *KWERNG! Eek* *sip*NAH-TEE SAHM?*mohng.*
9. Take me to a hotel (to the ——— Hotel). Is this (that) the hotel? How far is it?	9. Hodte-gou (——— hodte-gou) ko-thwă-ba. Di-ha (Hou-ha) hodte lă? Be-lau' wĕi-dhălĕ? *Hoh-dteh-goh (——— hoh-dteh-goh) kohTTWAHbah. Dee-hah (Hoh-hah) hoh-dteh LAH?* *B'LOW WEIGHtha-leh.*	9. Pah póm/chán bpai tih rohng-raam (bpai tih rohng-raam ———) dùai krăp/ka'. Nih (Nòhn) chài rohng-raam mái krăp/ka'? Yŭu glai kăa năi krăp/ka'? PAH POHM?/CHAHN? BPIGH *TEE!* ROHNG-RAM (BPIGH *TEE!* ROHNG-RAM ———) *DOOEH!* *KRAHP/*KAHK. *NEE! (NOHN!)* *CHIGH!* ROHNG-RAM MIGH? *KRAHP/*KAHK. *Yoo* GLICH *KAA* NIGH *KRAHP/*KAHK.
10. Have you a single room (a double room)? May I see the room? I don't like that room. I like this room.	10. Dtă-yau' kăn (Hna-yau' kăn) hyi-badhălă? Akăn-gou tyi-băyăzei? Hou 'ăkăn mă-tjai'bpŭ. Di 'ăkăn tjai'dte. *D'YOWK KAHÑ (HnaYOWK* *KAHÑ) shhee-bahtha-lah?* *A-KAHÑgoh TYEE!ba-yah-zeigh? Hoh-aKAHÑ* *maTJEIGHPboo? Dee-aKAHÑ* *TJEHT-deh.*	10. Kun mih hàwng dĭau (hàwng kùu) mái krăp/ka'? Póm/Chán kăw duu hàwng nŏi krăp/ka'. Póm/Chán mài chòp hàwng năn krăp/ka'. Póm/Chán chòp hàwng nih krăp/ka'. KOON MEE *HAWNG!deeow* *(HAWNG!KOO!)* MIGH? *KRAHP/*KAHK. POHM?/CHAHN? KAW? DOO *HAWNG! noy* *KRAHP/*KAHK. POHM?/CHAHN? MIGH! *CHOHP HAWNG* *NAHN KRAHP/*KAHK. POHM?/ CHAHN? *CHOHP! HAWNG* *NEE KRAHP/*KAHK.
11. Could I have the key of my room, please? Are there any letters for me (for us)?	11. Tjănò/Tjămà ăkăn thò yà-hnai-badhălă? Tjănò-bòu/ Tjămà-bòu (Tjănò-dòu-bòu/ Tjămă-dòu-bòu) sadei yau'nei-badhălă? *TjaNOH!/TjaMAH! aKAHÑ* *ttoh! YAH!hneh-bahtha-lah?* *TjaNOH!boh!/TjaMAH!boh!* *(TjaNOH!doh!boh!/* *TjaMAH!doh!boh!)* sahdeigh *YOWN-neigh-bahtha-lah?*	11. Póm/Chán kăw gunjaa kàu hàwng póm/chán nŏi krăp/ka'. Mih jŏtmáhi sámrăp póm/chán (sámrăp rau) mái krăpka'? POHM?/CHAHN? KAW? GOONJAA *KOW! HAWNG!* POHM?/CHAHN? *noy KRAHP/*KAHK. MEE *jot*MIGH? SAHM?*rahp* POHM?/CHAHN? (SAHM?*rahp* ROW) MIGH? *KRAHP/*KAHK.
12. Could I speak to ———, please? It has to do with ———. It is very important.	12. ———-gou zăgă bpyō-băyă-zei? ———-nè bpa'the'lòuba. Thei' ăyĕi-tji-bade. ———-goh zaGAH BYOHba-ya-zeigh? ———-NEH! *BPAHTttel-loh!bah. TTEIGHK* *aYEIGH-TJEEbah-deh.*	12. Póm/Chán kăw pùut gŭp ——— nŏi krăp/ka'. Dtawng tam dùai ———. Săm-kan màhk krăp/ka'. POHM?/CHAHN? KAW? *POOT!* gup ——— *noy KRAHP/*KAHK. *DTAWNG!* TAHM *DOOEH!* ———. SAHM?KAHN *MAHK!* *KRAHP/*KAHK.

112

SENTENCES

LAO	KAMPUCHEAN	VIETNAMESE

LAO

MOHNG *LAAO! Sawng?*
MOHNG. *Sawng?* MOHNG
SIPNAH-TEE. *Sawng?* MOHNG
k'ng. Sahm? MOHNG NYAHNG
SIPNAH-TEE.

KAMPUCHEAN

*dup neea-dtee. Mowng bpee
g'n-lahh. Mowng bay g'vahk
dup neea-dtee.*

VIETNAMESE

ZROO'EE? BAH *yer! KAM?
mwooee!*

). Bpăi song kôi yuu
hôhnghăahm (yuu Hôhnghăahm
———) daah. Nih (Nàn)
naahn hôhnghăahm baw?
Tàng yuu găibpăhndăii?
Bpigh SOHNG *koy!* YOO
HOHNG-HAM (YOO HOHNG-
HAM ———) DAA. *NEE!*
(NAHN!) MAN HOHNG-HAM
BAW? *TAHNG!* YOO *gigh-
bpahn-digh.*

9. Sŏm nóam kñom dtĭu
ptèah-sŏmnak (dtĭu ptèah-
sŏmnak ———). Dtăa nih (nuh)
jia ptèah-sŏmnak rĭĭ? Nĭu
dŏl naa?
*Sohm noahm k'yom dteoo
p'teea-s'm-nahk (dteoo
p'teea-s'm-nahk ———).
Dtah neehh (noohh) jeea
p'teea-s'm-nahk ruh? Neoo
dull nah?*

9. Chở tôi tới khách-sạn (tới
——— khách-sạn). Phải khách-sạn
này (kia) không? Độ bao xa?
Tyer! DTOY *DTOY?*
KHIGHK?san' (DTOY? ———
KHIGHK?san'). Fa'ee?
KHIGHK?san' nigh! (GKEEA)
KHOHWNG. *Do'* BOW SAH.

---

0. Mĭh hâwng wahng sămlăp
kôn dĭau (hâwng wahng
sămlăp săwng kôn) daah baw?
Kôi kăw buhng hâwng daah
dài baw? Kôi baw mak hâwng
nàn. Kôi mak hâwng nih.
MEE HAWNG! WAHNG
*sahm?*LAHP KOHN *deeoh?*
(HAWNG! WAHNG *sahm?*LAHP
sawng? KOHN) DAA BAW?
Koy! kaw? B'NG HAWNG!
DAA *DIGH!* BAW? *Koy!*
BAW MAHK HAWNG! *NAHN!*
Koy! MAHK *hawng! NEE!*

10. Mian bŏndtup dăel mian
grĕĕ múay (bŏndtup dăel mian
grĕĕ bpĭi) dtĕ? Kñom som meul
bŏndtup baan dtĕ? Kñom mĭn
srólañ bŏndtup nuh dtĕ. Kñom
srólañ bŏndtup nih.
*Meean b'n-dtoop dighl meean
greh mooeh (b'n-dtoop dighl
meean greh bpee) dteh? K'yom
som merl b'n-dtoop bahn dteh?
K'yom m'n s'roh-lahng b'n-dtoop
noohh dteh. K'yom s'roh-lahng
b'n-dtoop neehh.*

10. Ông/Bà có phòng cho một
người (phòng cho hai người)
không? Tôi có thể xem xét căn
phòng không? Tôi không thích
căn phòng ấy. Tôi thích căn
phòng này.
OHWNG/*Ba!* GKAW? *fowng!*
TYAW *mot ngwooee! (fowng!*
TYAW HIGH *ngwooee!)* KHOHWNG.
DTOY *GKAW?* tte'e? SEHM
SEHT? GKAHN *fowng!* KHOHWNG.
DTOY KHOHWNG TTIK?
GKAHN *fowng! EIGH?* DTOY TTIK?
GKAHN *fowng! nigh!*

---

1. Kôi kăw gă'jăah sămlăp
hâwng kăwng kôi daah. Mĭh
ŏtmăhi sămlăp kôi (sămlăp
ŭak kôi) daah baw?
KOY! *kaw?* GAT*jaa
sahm?*LAHP *hawng! kawng?
koy!* DAA. MEE JOHT*migh?
sahm?*LAHP KOY!
*(sahm?*LAHP *POOAK!*
KOY!) DAA BAW?

11. Sŏm gkŏn sao bŏndtup
kñom mawk. Mian sŏmbot mawk
kñom (mawk bpúak-yeung) dtĕ?
*Sohm gkohn sow b'n-dtoop k'yom
mawk. Meean s'm-boht mawk
k'yom (mawk bpooak-yerng)
dteh?*

11. Ông/Bà có thể đưa cho tôi chìa
khóa căn phòng không? Có lá thư
nào cho tôi (cho chúng tôi)
không?
OHWNG/*Ba!* GKAW? *tte?* DOOA
TYAW DTOY *tyeea!* KHWA?
GKAHN *fowng!* KHOHWNG.
GKAW? LAH? TTUH *now!*
TYAW DTOY (TYAW *TYOONG?*
DTOY) KHOHWNG.

---

12. Kôi kăw wàu nãhm
——— daah. Mĭh leuang giau
găp ———. Sămkăn lãhi
*t*ihsŭt.
KOY! *kaw? WOW!* NAHM
——— DAA. MEE LERNG
GEEOW! GAHP ———.
*Sahm?*KAHN *ligh?* TEE-
SOOT?

12. Kñom som niyíay jia-múay
nĭng ——— baan dtĕ? Mian
riang dtèak-dtong nĭng ———.
Riang nih sŏm-kan nas.
*K'yom som nee-jyeigh jeea-mooeh
n'ng ——— bahn dteh? Meean
rerng dteeak-dtohng n'ng
———. Rerng neehh s'm-kahn
nass.*

12. Tôi có thể nói với ———
không? Tôi cần phải nói với
———. Việc này cần-thiết lắm.
DTOY *GKAW? tte?* NOY? VOY?
——— KHOHWNG. DTOY *gkahn!
fa'ee?* NOY? VOY? ———.
Vyek nigh! gkahn! TTEEAT?
LAHM?

SENTENCES

ENGLISH	BURMESE	THAI

13. How much is this? I would like to buy this, please. That is too dear. I don't want it.

13. Di-ha balau'lē? Tjano/Tjamà di-ha-gou we-jin-bade. Zēi thei' tji-de. Mǎlou-jin-bū. *Dee-hah baLOWLleh? Tja-noh/ TjaMAH! dee-hahgoh wehjim-bahdeh. ZEIGH TTEIGHT-JEEdeh. Ma-lohjin-boo.*

13. Rahkah tàurai krāp/ka'? Póm/Chán káw sěuh 'an-nīh krāp/ka'. 'An-nīh paang pai krāp/ka'. Póm/Chán mài 'au krāp/ka'. RAHKAH *TOW!*RIGH *KRAHP/* KAHK. POHM?/CHAHN? KAW? *SEOO* AHN*NEE KRAHP/*KAHK. AHN*NEE* PANG PIGH *KRAHP/* KAHK. POHM?/CHAHN? *MIGH!* OW *KRAHP/*KAHK.

14. May I wash my hands? I would like a bath. I need some soap (a towel, hot water).

14. Le'hsēi-bǎyǎzei. Tjano/Tjamà yei chōu-jin-bade. Hsa'bpya gē (Mye'hnǎ-thou' bpǎwa, Yei nwēi) lou-jin-bade. *LEHSS-SEIGHba-ya zeigh. Tja-noh/TjaMAH! yeigh CHOHjimbah-deh. HSAHPbyah GEH (Myehnna-TTOHPba-wah, YeighNWEIGH) lohjim-bahdeh.*

14. Póm/Chán káw lǎhng meuh nŏi krāp/ka'. Póm/Chán yǎkjǎ' 'ǎhpnǎm. Póm/Chán káw sa'bǔu (pàh-chèt dtua, nǎm rāwn) dùai krāp/ka'. POHM?/CHAHN? KAW? *LAHNG* MER *noy KRAHP/*KAHK. POHM?/ CHAHN? *yahkja ahpNAHM.* POHM?/CHAHN? KAW? SAHP*boo (PAH!CHAHT* DOOA, *NAHM RAWN) DOOEH! KRAHP/*KAHK.

15. Is the restaurant open (closed)? Could I see the menu? I would like ———— The bill, please.

15. Sǎ-thau' hsai bpwin-badhǎlā (bpei'bpadhǎlā)? Hīnsǎyin tji-bǎyǎzei? ———— -gou lou-jin-de. Ngwei-sǎyin yu-laba. *SAH-TTOWSSsa PWIM!bahtha-lah (PEIGHPbahtha-lah)? HINsa-YIN TJEE!ba-ya-zeigh? ———— -goh lohjin-deh. Ngweighsa-YIN yoolah-bah.*

15. Rǎhn 'ah-hǎhn bpǔht (bpīt) mái krāp/ka'? Káw rahi-gahn 'ah-hǎhn nŏi krāp/ka'. Póm/Chán káw ———— dùai krāp/ka'. Kit nguhn dùai krāp/ka'. *RAHN*A-HAHN? *bput (bpeet)* MIGH? *KRAHP/*KAHK. KAW? RIGH-GAHNA-HAHN? *noy KRAHP/*KAHK. POHM?/CHAHN? KAW? ———— *DOOEH! KRAHP/*KAHK. KEET ngern DOOEH! *KRAHP/*KAHK.

16. I would like to make a telephone call. Would you call ———— for me? There is no answer. I have been cut off.

16. Telipoun' bpyō-jin-bade. ———— -gou ko-bpēi-ba. Bpyan mǎ-tū bū. Pya' lai'bpi. *TelliPOHM BYOHjim-bahdeh. ———— -goh kohBPEIbah. Byahn maTOO BOO. PYAHLlehpbee.*

16. Póm/Chán dtàwng gahn tohra'sǎp nŏi krāp/ka'. ga'ru'nah tǎw sǎhi nŏi krāp/ka'. Mài mih kon ráp sǎhi krāp/ka'. Sǎhi kǎht krāp/ka'. POHM?/CHAHN? *DTAWNG!* GAHN TOH-A*sap noy KRAHP/* KAHK. ———— *ga-roonah taw* SIGH? *noy KRAHP/*KAHK. MIGH?MEE KOHN *RAHP* SIGH? *KRAHP/*KAHK. SIGH?-*kaht KRAHP/*KAHK.

SENTENCES

13. Nih lãhkãh taudãii?
Kôi kãw sèuh nih daah. Nàn
pãahng pòht. Kôi baw yâhk
dài làau.
NEE! LAHKAH TOW*digh.*
KOY! *kaw? SER! NEE!*
DAA. *NAHN!* PANG *POHT!*
KOY! BAW YAHK! *DIGH!*
LAAO!

13. Rebõs nih tlay bponmaan?
Kñom jõng dtíñ rebõs nih. Rebõs
nuh tlay bpêk. Kñom mĩn jõng
baan dtê.
R'buss neehh t'ligh bp'n-mahn?
K'yom jung dt'ng r'buss neehh.
R'buss noohh t'ligh bpehk.
K'yom m'n jung bahn dteh.

13. Cái này giá bao nhiêu tiền?
Tôi muốn mua cái này. Cái đó
đắt quá. Tôi không muốn cái đó.
GKIGH? nigh! ZYAH? BOW
NYEEOO *dteean!* DTOY
MOOAN? MOOA *GKIGH?*
nigh! GKA? DAW? DAHT?
KWAH? DTOY KHOHWNG
MOOAN? GKIGH? DAW?

14. Kôi kãw làhng mēuh daah
dài baw? Kôi dtàwnggãhn jã'
'âhpnàm. Kôi yâhk dài
sã'buu 'âhpnàm (pâhset-dtôh,
nàm hãwn).
KOY! *kaw? LAHNG!* MER
DAA *DIGH!* BAW? KOY!
*DTAWNG!gahn JA
ahp!NAHM!* KOY! *yahk!
DIGH!* SAPBOO *ahp!NAHM!
(pah!*SET-*dtoh?, NAHM!
HAWN!).*

14. Kñom liang day baan dtê?
Kñom jõng ngũt dtĩk. Kñom
drõv-gaa <u>sabũ</u> (gõnsãeng-jũt-
glúan, dtĩk gdau).
K'yom leeang digh bahn dteh?
*K'yom jung-ngoot dt'k. K'yom
d'ruv-gah sap-boo (g'n-sighng
joot-glooan, dt'k g'dow).*

14. Tôi có thể rửa tay không?
Tôi muốn tắm. Tôi cần <u>xà-bông</u>
(một cái khăn, nước nóng).
DTOY *GKAW? tte? zroo'a?*
DTIGH KHOHWNG. DTOY
MOOAN? DTAHM? DTOY
gkun! sah! BOHWNG *(mot
GKIGH? KHAHN, NOOAK?
NOWNG?).*

15. Hàhn'ãh-hãhn bpûht
(bpit) làau baw? Kôi kãw
buhng lãhi-gãhn 'ãh-hãhn daah.
Kôi dtàwnggãhn ————.
Kôi kãw bãiigêp-ngũhn daah.
HAHN!a-hahn? BPERT!
(BPIT) *LAAO!* BAW? KOY!
kaw? B'NG LIGH*gahn a-hahn?*
DAA. KOY! *DTAWNG!gahn*
————. KOY! *kaw? bigh-*
GEP-G'N *daa.*

15. Dtãa põjeníataan bãak (bet)
dtê? Kñom som meul bañjii muk
mhõb baan dtê? Kñom jõng baan
————. Sõm git luy.
*Dtah pohja-neea-tahn bahk
(butt) dteh? K'yom som merl
bahng-chee mook m'hohb bahn
dteh? K'yom jung bahn* ————.
Sohm g't looi.

15. Tiệm ăn <u>có mở</u> (có đóng)
không? Tôi có thể xem thực-đơn
không? Tôi muốn ————.
Xin cho tôi phiếu tính tiền.
Dtim AHN *GKAW? mo'o?
(GKAW? DOWNG?)* KHOHWNG.
DTOY *GKAW? tte?* SEHM
*ttook-*DON KHOHWNG. DTOY
MOOAN? ————. SEEN TYAW
DTOY *FYEOO? DTING?
dteean!*

16. Kôi dtàwnggãhn jã' dtĩh
tohla'sãp. Gã'lu'nãh mũn
———— hãii kôi daah. Baw
mĩh pûudãi dtãwp. Sãhi têuhk
wahng hũu làau.
KOY! *DTAWNG!gahn*
JAT-*dee* TOHLA-SAHP.
GAHLOO-NAH *moon* ————
high! KOY! DAA. BAW MEE
POO!*digh* DTAWP! *Sigh?*
TEOOK! WAHNG *hoo LAAO!*

16. Kñom jõng brãa dtũresap.
Sõm néak hau ———— 'aoy kñom
baan dtê. 'Et mían jõmlãay dtê.
Kñom drõv gê gat.
*K'yom jung brah dtoora-sahp.
Sohm neeak how* ———— *'owee
k'yom bahn dteh? 'At meean
j'm-ligh dteh. K'yom d'ruv geh
gaht.*

16. Tôi muốn gọi điện-thoại.
Ông/Bà gọi ———— dùm tôi
được không? Không có ai trả
lời. Tôi bị cắt đường dây.
DTOY *MOOAN? goy din-ttwigh.*
OHWNG/Ba! *goy* ———— *zyoom!*
DTOY *dook* KHOHWNG.
KHOHWNG *GKAW? IGH tya'a?
loy!* DTOY *bi' GKAHT? dooang!
zyay.*

SENTENCES

ENGLISH	BURMESE	THAI

17. Could I have some notepaper (some air mail paper, some envelopes)? Where can I buy stamps? How much altogether?

17. Hma'sù-saywe'dtăkyòu (Leiyin-saywe'dtăkyòu, Sa-'ei'dtăkyòu) ya-hnain-badhălă? Dazei'găun be-ma we-ya-badhălē? 'Alōun-bāun balau'lē?
HMASsoo!sa-YEHTda-chyoh! (Leigh-yin-saYEHTda-chyoh!, Sa-eightda-chyoh!) yahn-hehñ-bahtha-lah? D'ZEIGHG-GOWÑ be-mah wehyah-bahtha-leh? AH-LOHÑ-BOWÑ ba-lowlleh?

17. Póm/Chán káw gra'dăht bun teuk (gra'dăht kian jōtmáhi, sawng) nŏi krăp/ka'. Sēuh sa'dtaam dài tih nái krăp/ka'? Tăngmŏt rahkah tàurăi krăp/ka'?
POHM?/CHAHN? KAW? *gw'daht* BOON TEEOK *(gw'daht* KEEAN? *jot*MIGH?, SAWNG) *noy KRAHP/*KAHK. *SER* S'TAAM *DIGH! TEE!*NIGH? *KRAHP/* KAHK. *TAHNGmoht* RAHKAH *TOW!*RIGH *KRAHP/*KAHK.

18. I am ill. Where can I see a doctor? Please get a good doctor. Could I have some water?

18. Tjano/Tjamà pyā-bade. Be-ma hsayawun-gou twèilòu-yà-badhălē? Gkāun-dè hsayawun-gou ko-ba. Yei yu-la-ba.
Tja-noh/TjaMAH! PYAHbah-deh. Be-mah hsahya-wooñ-goh tee!loh!-yah!bahtha-leh? GKOWNdeh! hsahya-wooñ-goh kohbah. Yeigh yoo lahbah.

18. Póm/Chán mài sa'bahi krăp/ka'. Póm/Chán jă' pai háh máw dài tih nái krăp/ka'? Ga'ru'nah năa'nam máw gēhng-gēhng. Káw năm dĕuhm nŏi krăp/ka'.
POHM?/CHAHN? *MIGH!*SA-BIGH *KRAHP/*KAHK. POHM?/ CHAHN? *jah*PIGH HAH? *DIGH! TEE!nigh KRAHP/*KAHK. GA-ROONAH *naa*-NAHM MAW? *geng*-geng. KAW?*NAHM derm noy KRAHP/*KAHK.

19. May I introduce ———. I am pleased to meet you. My name is ———.

19. ——— -nè mei'hse'bpèi-băyăzei. Twèi-yàda wün-tha-bade. Tjănò/Tjămă na-me ——— ba.
——— *-neh! MEIGHSSsep-BEIGHba-ya-zeigh. TWEE!yah!dah WOONttahbah-deh. TjaNOH!/TjaMAH! nah-meh* ——— *bah.*

19. Póm/Chán káw năa'nam ———. Póm/Chán yindih tih dài rûu jăk kun. Póm/Chán chèuh ——— krăp/ka'.
POHM?CHAHN? KAW? *naa*-NAHM ———. POHM?/CHAHN? YEENDEE *TEE! DIGH! ROO jahk* KOON. POHM?/CHAHN? *CHEOO!*———*KRAHP/*KAHK.

20. Who are you? A friend. I come from ———. Go away!

20. Kamyā/Hsin badhu-lē? Mei'hswei-ba. Tjano/Tjamà ——— -gà la-bade. Thwā-lai'!
KaMYAH/Hsin bathoo-leh? MEIGHSS-weigh-bah. Tja-noh/ TjaMAH! ——— *-gah! lahbah-deh. TTWAH lighk!*

20. Kun bpen kai? Pèuan. Póm/Chán mah jăk ———. Bpai hai pon!
KOON BPEN KIGH. *PYOOAN!* POHM?/CHAHN? MAH *jahk* ———. BPIGH HIGH POHN !

21. What is this called? What is this place called? It is called ———.

21. Di-ha belou ko-dhalē? Di nēiya belou ko-dhalē? ——— -lòu ko-bade.
Dee-hah be-loh kohtha-leh? Dee neighyah be-loh kohtha-leh? ——— *-loh! kohbah-deh.*

21. Nìh rìak wàh 'a'rai krăp/ka'? Tihnìh rìak wàh 'a'rai krăp/ka'? Riak wàh ——— krăp/ka'.
NEE! REEAK! WAH! A-RIGH *KRAHP/*KAHK. *TEE!NEE! REEAK! WAH!* A-RIGH *KRAHP/*KAHK. *REEAK! WAH!* ——— *KRAHP/*KAHK.

SENTENCES

LAO

17. Kôi kăw sèuh jia kĭan jôtmãhi (jia kĭan jôtmãhi bpãisã'nĭh tãhng 'ãhgâht, sãwng jôtmãhi) daah. Kôi jã' sèuh sã'tãahm dài yuu sãi? Hũam-tãngmôt lãhkãh taudãii?
KOY! *kaw?* SER!
JEEA!keean? JOT*migh?*
(*JEEA!keean?* JOT*migh?*
bpigh-SAHNNEE TAHNG *a*-GAHT!, SAWNG JOT*migh?*)
DAA. KOY! JAS-*SER!*
SAT-*tam DIGH!* YOO *sigh?*
WHAHM TAHNG-MOHT LAHKAH TOW*digh.*

18. Kôi baw sã'bãhi. Kôi jã' bpãi gûat nãhm tahnmãw dài yuu sãi? Gã'lu'nãh hãh tahnmãw tih mĭh kwãhm-sãhmnãhn hãii daah. Kôi kãw deuhm nãm daah.
KOY! BAW SAP*bigh?* KOY!
JA *bpigh?* gooat! NAHM *tahn-maw? DIGH!* YOO *sigh?* GAHLOO-NAH *hah?*
TAHN *maw?* TEE MEE KWAHM-SAHM-NAHN *high!* DAA. KOY!
kaw? DEOOM *NAHM!* DAA.

19. Kôi kãw naa'nãhm hãii hùu jăk ———. Kôi mĭh kwãhm nyĭndĭh tih dài hùu jăk jàu. Kôi seuh wah ———.
KOY! *kaw?* NAA-NAHM HIGH!
HOO! JAHK ———. KOY!
MEE KWAHM NYIN*dee* TEE *DIGH! HOO!* JAHK *JOW!*
KOY! *seoo wah* ———.

20. Jàu maahn pãi? Peuan kãwng jàu. Kôi mãh dtaah ———. Nĭh bpãi!
JOW! MAN *pigh?* PYOOAN *kawng? JOW!* KOY! MAH *dtaa* ———. *Nee? bpigh.*

21. Nĭh 'ùhn wah jangdãii? Sã'tãhntĭh nĭh 'ùhn wah jangdãii? 'Ùhn wah ———.
NEE! ERN! WAH JAHNG*digh.* SA*tahn?* TEE *NEE! ERN!* WAH JAHNG*digh. ERN!* WAH ———.

KAMPUCHEAN

17. Kñom som gredaas-sesë-sõmbot glah (gredaas-sdãang sõmrap sesë-sõmbot glah, sraom-sõmbot glah) baan dtë? Dtãa kñom 'aat dtëñ dtãem nĭudtii naa? Dtëang-'os tlay bponmaan?
K'yom som gr'dahss seh-seh s'm-boht glahh (gr'dahss s'dahng s'm-rahp seh-seh s'm-boht glahh, srown s'm-boht glahh) bahn dteh? Dtah k'yom 'aht dteng dtighm neoot-dee nah? Dteeang 'oss t'ligh bp'n-mahn?

18. Kñom chĩi. Dtãa kñom 'aat dtĭu júab grũ-bpëët nĭudtii naa? Sõm néak 'añjeuñ grũ-bpëët jõmnaan menéak mawk. Kñom som dtĭk bõndtet mawk baan dtë?
K'yom cher. Dtah k'yom 'aht dteoo jooap groo-bpeht neoot-dee nah? Sohm neeak 'ahng-jerng groo-bpeht j'm-nahn m'neeak mawk. K'yom som dt'k b'n-dteht mawk bahn dteh?

19. Kñom sõm lõk/lõk- srey júap ———. Kñom sapbaay dtaoy baan júap lõk/lõk-srey. Kñom chmúah ———.
K'yom sohm lohk/lohk-sreh jooap ———. *K'yom sahp-bigh dtow bahn jooap lohk/lohk-sreh. K'yom ch'mooahh* ———.

20. Néak jia nõnaa? Jía mĭt. Kñom mawk bpii ———. Dtĭu 'aoy chngaay!
Neeak jeea n'nah? Jeea mutt. K'yom mawk bpee ———. *Dteoo 'owee ch'ng-igh!*

21. Rebõs nih gë hau taa 'vey? Gõnlãeng nih gë hau taa 'vey? Gë hau taa ———.
R'buss neehh geh how tah vweigh? G'n-lighng neehh geh how tah vweigh? Geh how tah ———.

VIETNAMESE

17. Tôi có thể có vài tờ giấy nót (vài lá thư gửi máy bay, vài phong bì) không? Tôi có thể mua tem ở đâu? Tổng cộng tốn bao nhiêu tiền?
DTOY *GKAW? tte? GKAW? vigh! dto! ZYAY? NOHT?* (*vigh! LA?* TTUH *go'ee? MIGH?* BIGH, *vigh!* FOWNG *bee!*) KHOHWNG. DTOY *GKAW? tte?* MOOA DTEHM *o* DOW. *Dtoh'ng gkong DTOHN?* BOW NYEOO *dteean!*

18. Tôi bị ốm. Tôi có thể đi hỏi bác-sĩ ở đâu? Xin vui lòng chỉ tôi bác-sĩ giỏi. Xin ông/bà cho tôi ly nước.
DTOY *bi'* OHM? DTOY *GKAW? tte?* DEE *ho'ee?* BAHK?SE'E? *o* DOW. SEEN VOO *lowng! tye?* DTOY *BAHK?*-SE'E? *zyo'ee?* SEEN OHWNG/*ba!* TYAW DTOY LEE *NOOAK?*

19. Đây là ———. Tôi rất hân-hạnh được gặp ông/bà. Tên tôi là ———.
DAY *la!* ———. DTOY *ZRAHT?* HAHN-*hang doo'k gap* OHWNG/*ba!* DTEHN DTOY *la!* ———.

20. Ông/Bà là ai? Một người bạn. Tôi tới đây từ ———. Đi chỗ khác!
OHWNG/*Ba! la!* IGH. *Mot ngwooee! ba'n.* DTOY *DTOY* DAY *dtuh!* ———. DEE TYO'O? *KHAHK?*

21. Cái này gọi là gì? Chỗ này gọi là gì? Nó tên là ———.
GKIGH? nigh! goy' la! zyee! Tyaw'? nigh! goy' la! zyee! NAW? DTEHN *la!* ———.

117

SENTENCES

ENGLISH	BURMESE	THAI
22. What is the matter? Don't worry. I am <u>sorry</u> (glad). I shall give you this.	22. Ba-kei'sà hyi-badhǎlē? Mǎ-bu-banè. Tjano/Tjamà wūn nè-bade (tha-bade). Tjano/Tjamà kamyà-gou di-ha pēi-bàme. *Ba-KEIGHSSsah! shhee-bahtha-leh? Ma-boobah-neh! Tja-noh/ TjaMAH! wooñ NEHba-deh (ttahbah-deh). Tja-noh/TjaMAH! ka-MYAHgoh deehah PEIGHbah! meh.*	22. Mih rèuang 'a'rai rèuh krǎp/ka'? Mài dtòng hǔang krǎp/ka'. Póm/Chán <u>sia jai</u> (dih jai) krǎp/ka'. Póm/Chán jǎ' hài sīng nīh gǎa kun. MEE *RYOOANG!* A-RIGH RER? *KRAHP*/KAHK. *MIGH!* *DTONG!* hooang *KRAHP*/KAHK POHM?/ĆHAHN? SEEA? JIGH (DEE JIGH) *KRAHP*/KAHK. POHM?/CHAHN? *ja HIGH! sing NEE gaa* KOON.
23. What do you want? Please sit down. I have to leave. You must go now.	23. Ba lou-jin-dhalē? Tain-ba. Tjano/Tjamà thwā-yà-me. 'A-gù kamyà thwā-yà-me. *Bah lohjiñtha-leh? Tighmbah. Tja-noh/TjaMAH! TTWAHyah!meh. A-GOO! kaMYAH TTWAHyah!meh.*	23. Kun dtàwng gahn 'a'rai krǎp/ka'? Ga'ru'nah nàng loung krǎp/ka'. Póm/Chán dtàwng bpai la' krǎp/ka'. Kun dtàwng bpai díau-nih krǎp/ka'. KOON *DTAWNG!*GAHN A-RIGH *KRAHP*/KAHK. GA-ROONAH *NAHNG!*LOHNG *KRAHP*/KAHK. POHM?/CHAHN? *DTAWNG!* BPIGHLA *KRAHP*/KAHK. KOON *DTAWNG!* BPIGH DEOO?*NEE! KRAHP*/KAHK.
24. I need help. I am in trouble. Please give this message to ———. As soon as possible.	24. Tjano/Tjamà 'a'gku- 'anyi lou-bade. Tjano/Tjamà dou'kà you'nei-bade. Di-za ——— -gou pēipēi-ba. Dta'hnain-dhǎ-lau' myan-myan. *Tja-noh/TjaMAH! a-gkoo-a-nyee lohbah-deh. Tja-noh/TjaMAH! DOHKkah! YOHNneigh-bahdeh. Deezah ———-goh PEIGH-PEIGHbah. DTANhnehntha-lowm myañ-myañ*	24. Póm/Chán kǎw wahn nòi krǎp/ka'. Póm/Chán gamlang dĕuat-ràwn krǎp/ka'. Ga'ru'nah sòng kǎu nīh hài ———. Rèhu tìhsǔt tàu tìh jǎ' rèhu dài krǎp/ka'. POHM?/CHAHN? KAW? WAHN *noy KRAHP*/KAHK. POHM?/ CHAHN? G'LAHNG *dooat-RAWN KRAHP*/KAHK. GA-ROONAH *sohng kow NEE HIGH!* ———. REOO *TEE!soot TOW! TEE! ja*REOO *DIGH! KRAHP*/KAHK.
25. That is <u>very nice</u> (marvellous). That is <u>bad</u> (terrible). I have enjoyed myself very much.	25. Da thei'gkǎun-dabē (anlau'-'aun-gkaun-dabè). Da hsòu-de (thei' hsòu-de). Tjano/Tjamà thei'bpyo-gèbade. *Dah TTEIGHK-GOWÑdahbeh (ahñ-lowk owñGOWNdah-beh). Dah HSOHdeh (TTEIGHSS-SOHdeh). Tja-noh/TjaMAH! TTEIGHPbyoh-geh!bah-deh.*	25. Nàn <u>dih màhk</u> (yòt màhk) krǎp/ka'. Nàn <u>mài dih</u> (hǔai màhk). Póm/Chán sa'nuk màhk krǎp/ka'. *NAHN!* DEE *MAHK!* (*YOHT MAHK!*) *KRAHP*/KAHK. *NAHN! MIGH!*DEE (*hooeh MAHK!*). POHM?/CHAHN? *sa-nook MAHK! KRAHP*/KAHK.

SENTENCES

LAO	KAMPUCHEAN	VIETNAMESE

22. Mĭh nyăng gŭht kêun gặp jàu? Baw dtàwng gắng-wŏn. Kôi sĭajằĭi (nyĭndĭh). Kôi jă' 'àu 'ănnĭh hầii jàu.
MEE *nyahng?* G'T *k'n!* GAHP
JOW! BAW *DTAWNG!*
*gahn*WON? KOY! *seea?-jigh?*
(NYIN*dee?).* KOY! JAH-*ow*
*ahn*NEE! *high! JOW!*

22. Mían rĭang 'vey nĭng? Gom prúay 'ey. Kñom sdaay (sapbaay) nãh. Kñom nĭng 'aoy rebŏs nih dŭu néak.
Meean rerng vweigh n'ng? Gom prooeh 'eigh. K'yom s'digh (sap-bigh) nahh. K'yom n'ng 'owee r'buss neehh dteoo neeak.

22. Việcgi thê? Đừng bận tâm. Tôi xin chia buồn (vui) cùng ông/bà. Tôi sẽ cho ông/bà cái này.
V'k zyee! TTEH? Doong!
ban DTAHM. DTOY
SEEN TYEEA *booan!*
(vooi) tyoong! OHWNG/*ba!*
DTOY SE'E? TYAW OHWNG/*ba!*
GKIGH? nigh!

---

23. Jàu dtàwnggẵhn nyăng? Gắ'lu'nǎh nanglŏng. Kôi jă' bpǎi làau. Jàu jă' dtàwng bpǎi dĭaunih.
JOW! DTAWNG!gahn nyahng? GAHLOO-NAH NAHNG-LOHNG. KOY!
JAP*bigh LAAO! JOW!*
*jat*DAWNG! *bpigh deeow*NEE!

23. Néak jŏng baan 'vey? Sŏm 'ŏñĭeuñ 'ŏngkuy. Kñom drŏv dŭu vĭñ hăay. Néak drŏv dtăe dtŭu 'elŏv nĭng.
Neeak jung bahn vweigh? Sohm 'ahng-jerng 'ung-kooi. K'yom d'ruv dteoo v'ng high. Neeak d'ruv dtigh dteoo 'eh-lohv n'ng.

23. Ông/Bà muốn gì? Xin ông/bà vui lòng ngồi xuống. Tôi phải đi. Ông/Bà phải đi ngay bây giờ.
OHWNG/*Ba! MOOAN? zyee!*
SEEN OHWNG/*ba!* VOO *lowng! ngoy! SOOANG?* DTOY *fa'ee?*
DEE. OHWNG/*Ba! fa'ee?*
DEE NGIGH BAY *zyo!*

---

24. Kôi dtàwnggẵhn kwăhm suailĕua. Kôi gắhmlăng mĭh kwăhm dêuat-hàwn. Gắ'lu'nǎh song kahu nĭh hầii ———— dùaii. Wăi tau tih jă' wăi dài.
KOY! *DTAWNG!gahn*
KWAHM *sooeh-leooa?* KOY!
*gahm*LAHNG MEE KWAHM *dwat!*HAWM! GAHLOO-NAH SOHNG KOW *NEE!*
high! ———— *DOOIGH!*
WIGH TOW TEE *ja-*WIGH
DIGH!

24. Kñom drŏv gaa jumnúay. Kñom mían turéak. Sŏm néak júay yawk dŏmneng nih 'aoy ————. Jĭa bŏndtóan póng.
K'yom d'ruv gah j'm-nooeh. K'yom meean too-reeak. Sohm neeak jooeh yawk d'm-nung neehh 'owee ————. Jeea b'n-dtoahn pohng.

24. Tôi cần sự giúp-đỡ. Tôi bị rắc rối. Xin ông/bà vui lòng đưa bức điện-tín này cho ————. Càng sớm càng tốt.
DTOY *gkahn! su'*
*ZYEEOOP?*DU'UH? DTOY
bi' ZRAHK? ZROY? SEEN
OHWNG/*ba!* VOO *lowng!*
DOOA *BUHK?* DEEAN*DTEEN?*
nigh! TYAW ———— . *Gkahng!*
SERM? gkahng! DTOHT?

---

25. Nàn jŏp lăhi (wi'sêht). Nàn baw dĭh (kĭh hàhi). Kôi dài hặp kwăhm sã'nuk sã'nǎhn lăhi tihsŭt.
NAHN! JOHP ligh?
(wees-seht!). NAHN! BAW
dee? (KEE-HIGH!). KOY!
DIGH! HAHP KWAHM
SA-NOOK SA-*nahn ligh?*
*tee*SOOT.

25. Nih l'ó nas (visês-visaal). Nuh 'aagrok (gúa-'aoy-glaay). Kñom gŏmsaan sepbaay nas.
Neehh l'oh nahss (vee-sehss vee-sahl). Noohh 'ah-grok (goo'owee gligh). K'yom g'm-sahn s'p-bigh nahss.

25. Tốt lắm (Tuyệt-diệu). Tệ lắm (Tồi lắm). Tôi cảm thấy rất vui.
DTOHT? LAHM? (Dtoot-zyo').
Dte' LAHM? (Dtoy! LAHM?).
DTOY *gka'm TTAY-RAHT?*
vooi.

VOCABULARY

ENGLISH	BURMESE	THAI
above	'ă-bpo	kàhng bon
accident, the	mă-dto-dtă-hsà-ti-gai-hmu	'u'băt-hĕht
address, the	lei'sa	tih-yŭu
adult, the	lujĭ	púu-yăi
advertisement, the	tjo-nya	kòhsa'nah
aerogramme, the	leiyin-sa-ywe'	jŏtmáhi 'ahgăht
afraid	tjau'-dte	glua
after	nau'hma	láhngjăhk
afternoon, the	nyànei	wehlahbăhi
again	dtă-pan	'ĭhk
against	hsanjinbe'	dtăw sùugăp
agree, to	dhăbŏdtu-de	dtŏklong
air, the	lei	'ahgăht
air conditioner, the	lei-ĕi se'	krèuangbpŏp-'ahgăht
air mail, the	leijàun-sa	tahng-'ahgăht
airplane, the	leiyinbyan	krèuangbin
airport, the	leiyinbyan-gwĭn	sa'náhmbin
alive	'ăthe'hyin-de	mih chihwĭt
all	'ălŏun	tāngmŏt
all right	gkăun-de	sa'bahi-dih
almost	lù	gĕuap
alone	-tĕ	kondiau
already	bpĭbi	làau
also	-lĕ	dùai
although	-bpei-mè	màa-wàh
always	'ă-myĕ	sa'múh
among	jā	rā'wăhng
and (between nouns)	nè	laa'
angry	sei'hsŏu-de	grŏht
animal, the	tarei'hsan	săt
another one (different)	tă-chā	'an'ĕuhn
another one (more)	'ă-bpou	'ĭhk'an
answer, to	pyei-de	dtăwp
antiseptic, the	bpŏudhàn-hsĕiyi	bpadi-chihwa-nă'
apartment, the	'ein-gān	hàwng chàu
apple, the	bpăndhĭ	'ăap-pūhl
approximately	nĭbā	bpra'mahn
arm, the	le'	káan
army, the	sĭ'dta'	gawngtăp
around	bpa'le	ràwp
arrive, to	yau'-dte	téung
art, the	wei'za	jĭla'bpă
art gallery, the	'anubpa-nya bpyàgān	háw jĭla'bpă'
artificial	pandĭ	kóng-tiam
ask (inquire), to	mĕimyăn-de	tăhm
at	-hma	tih
attempt, to	tjŏuză-de	pa-yahyahm

120

VOCABULARY

LAO	KAMPUCHEAN	VIETNAMESE
tāhng-tūhng	leu ...	ở trên
'ū'bpā'dtī'hêht	grúas-tnak	tai-nạn
bawn-yuu	aasay-taan	địa chỉ
pûu-nyai	menus bpĕn vǐy	người lớn
gāhn-kōhsā'nāh	psaay bpíanitgam	cải quảng-cáo
jōtmǎhi bpāisā'nǐh tāhng'ǎhgâht	liket-dtaam-'aakaas	vô tuyền-điện tín
yàhn	klaat	sợ
lǎngjâhk	graoy	sau
dtǎwnbahi	resial	buổi trưa
'íhk	medóng dtíat	lại
gǎhndtaw-dtàhn	btóal	chống lại
nyin-nyàwm	yúal brawm	bằng lòng với
'ǎhgâht	kyól	không khí
keuang bpian'ǎhgâht	maasiin dtrōchéak	máy điều-hòa không khí
bpāisā'nǐh tāhng 'ǎhgâht	dtaam 'aakaas	thư máy bay
hěuabǐn	gebpal-hǒh	máy bay
duhn-nyōn	jomnót gebpal-hǒh	phi-trường
mǐhsǐhwit	rúas	sống động
tāngmōt	dtéang-'ǒs	tất cả
dàilàau	baan hǎay	dược rồi
geuap	jǐt-dǒl ...	hầu hết
pûudǐau	dtǎe 'aek	một mình
làau	rúat hǎay	rồi
kěuhgǎn	dǎe	cũng vậy
tǔhngmaahnwah	dtuah bey jía	mặc dầu
lěuailěuai	réal dóng	luôn luôn
la'wahng	jía-múay	ở giữa đám
laa'	nǐng	và
jǎii-hàhi	keng	tức giận
sat	sat	động vật
'íhk 'ǎn neung	myaang dtíat	một cái khác
dteuhm 'íhk 'ǎn neung	múay dtíat	một cái nửa
kàmdtâwp	chlǎay	trả lời
yǎh bpǎwng gǎn-pa'nyàht	sǒmraap sǒmlaap mērǒk	thuốc sát trùng
hěuansaubpěn-hâwng	ptéah bǒndtup jrǎan	một gian nhà
mâhk bpǎwm	bpom	quả táo
bpā'mǎhn	brehǎel	phòng chừng
kǎan	day	cánh tay
gǎwng-tap	dtóap	quân đội
'àwmhàwp	jumvěn	tứ phía
mǎhhàwt	dtǐu dǒl	đi tới
sǐnla'bpā'	sělbéak	nghệ-thuật
hâwng bpā'gǔat hùupdtàahm	saalaa rajjenaa	phòng triển-lãm nghệ-thuật
tiam	glǎeng glaay	nhân tạo
tǎhm	súa	hỏi
yuu	'ǎe	ở
pa'nyàh-nyàhm	law meul	thử

121

ENGLISH	BURMESE	THAI
awake	nōunei-de	dtĕuhn
baby, the	nòuzòugàlē	tahrŏk
back (rear), the	tjōbe	láng
back (again)	bpyan-...	glăp
backwards	nau'gkou	tói
bad	hsōu-de	mài dih
bag, the	'ei'	gra'bpáu
baggage, the	bpyi'sī	gra'bpáu
ballpoint, the	bō-bpin	bpahkgah lùuk lèuhn
bamboo shoots, the	hmyi'	năw măi
banana, the	hnge'bpyōdhī	glùai
bank (money), the	bandai'	ta'nah-kahn
bathe, to	yei-chōu	'ahpnăm
bathroom, the	yei-chōugăn	hàwng năm
battery, the	be'tări	tăhn faicháhi
beach, the	bpinle-gkănjei	chahi-hăht
beans, the	bpè	tŭa
beard, the	mou'hsei'	krau
beautiful	hlà-de	súai
because	jàun	prăw'wàh
because of	jàun	nèuang-jăhk
become, to	pyi'la-de	glahi-bpen
bed, the	ei'ya	dtiang
beef, the	'amēdhă	nĕua wua
beer, the	biya	bia
before (time)	'ă-yin-gà	găwn
behind	nau'hma	kàhngláhng
believe, to	youn-de	chèua
bell, the	kăunlăun	gra'dĭng
best	'ă-gkăunzōun	dih tihsùt
better	bpou-gkăun	dih gwăh
beyond	'alun-hma	guhn
bicycle, the	se'bēin	jăk-yahn
big	tjī-de	yăi
bill, the	ngweisăyin	bil
binoculars, the	hmanbyăun	glàwng săwng tahng glai
bird, the	hnge'	nŏk
biscuit, the	bisă-gku'	ka'nómbpang wăhn
black	ne'-dte	dam
blanket, the	saun	păh hŏm nawn
blood, the	thwēi	lèuat
blue	bpya-de	síhnăm-nguhn
boat, the	hlei	reua
body, the	gkou'	ràhnggahi
boiled	bpyou'bpĭdhă	dtòm
book, the	sa-'ou'	nangséuh

VOCABULARY

LAO	KAMPUCHEAN	VIETNAMESE
hùumeua-kêun	pñéak	thức tỉnh
lùuk'āwn	gòn gmēñ	dứa bé
tāhng-lăng	graoy	đằng sau
gàp kēuhn	mawk veñ	trở lại
bpăi-tāhng-lăng	drelŏp	hướng về đằng sau
sua	'aagrŏk	xấu
tŏng	hep	cái túi
gă'bpău dŭhn tāhng	hep-'eyvan	hành lý
bpâhkgăh mëuhn	slaap-bpakaa	đầu bút
naw mài	dtra-póamng	măng
mâhk gùai	jèk	quả chuối
ta'nahkăhn	bang	nhà băng
'ăhpnàm	ngūt dtĭk	tắm
hâwng'ăhpnàm	bŏndtup-dtĭk	phòng tắm
tahnfái	tmóbpil	bình điện
hâhtsăhi	móat semut	bờ biển
mâhk tua	sŏndăek	đậu
nŭat	bpuk-móat	râu
ngāhm	l'ó	đẹp
paw'wah	bprúah	bởi vì
paw'wah	bprúah mawk bpii	bởi vì
găhi-bpĕn	dtĭu jia	biến thành
dtĭangnàwn	grēĕ	cái giường
sin-ngŭa	saat-gō	thịt bò
lâubĭa	byéa	rượu bia
gawn	mun . . .	trước
tāhng-lăng	graoy	đằng sau
seua-tĕuh	jia	tin
la'kăng	gŏndteng	cái chuông
dĭhtihsùt	l'ó nas	tốt nhất
dĭhgua	grían-băa	tốt hơn
tatbpăi	húas-bpii . . .	ở bên kia
lot-tĭhp	gŏng	xe đạp
nyaii	tom	lớn
băiigèp-ngūhn	vigayban	cái phiếu
gàwngsawng-tāhnggăi	găev yit	ống nhòm
nok	sat-hăa	con chim
kă'nŏmbpăng	num	bánh bít-qui
dăm	kmau	đen
pâ-hom	púay	cái chăn
lèuat	chíam	máu
sĭhfăh	kíav	xanh
hĕua	dtŭk	cái thuyền
hahnggăhi	glúan	thân-thể
dtòm	bpuh	sôi
bpèum	síav-pĭu	cuốn sách

VOCABULARY

ENGLISH	BURMESE	THAI
boot, the	bu'pǎna'	rawng-tǎhu buut
born	mwēi-de	gǔht
both	-salòun	tǎngsáwng
bottle, the	bpalīn	kǔat
bottle opener, the	bpalīn-pwìndan	tìh-bpěuht-kǔat
bottom, the	'au'chei	gòn
box, the	thi'dta	hīhp
boy, the	lugalèi	pǔuchahi
bra, the	yinzī-'īnji	sèua-chán-nai
brake, the	banei'	brěhk
brave	yē-yin-de	glàh
bread, the	bpounmòun	ka'nómbpang
break, to	chòu-de	dtǎak
breakfast, the	màne'sa	'ah-háhn chāu
bridge, the	dǎdǎ	sa'pahn
bring, to	yula-de	'au . . . mah
brooch, the	yindōu	kém bpra'dǎp gai
brown	nyou-de	síhnǎm-dtahn
brush, the	we'hmìnbī	bpraang
bundle, the	'ǎ-tou'	hǎw
bus, the	ba'sa-gkā	rótmeh
businessman, the	sībwǎ-yēidhǎmā	nǎk-tū'rā'gīt
busy	'ǎlou'hyou'-dte	mih tū'rā'
but	dabeimè	dtǎa
butter, the	tōba'	nuhi
button, the	tjedhī	gra'dum
buy, to	we-de	sèuh
cabbage, the	gobidou'	ga'lǎm-bplih
cake, the	gkei'mòun	ka'nóm-kēk
call (telephone), the	pōun-kodhan	tohn-jǎp
called, is	ko-de	rìak
call out, to	ko-tou'-dte	ráwng
camera, the	gkinmǎra	glàwng
candle, the	pa-yǎundain	tian
captain (of ship), the	yeiyin-hmū	gapdtan-rěua
car, the	mo-dto-gkā	rót
carefully	dhadì-nè	ra'wang
cargo, the	gkoun	sín-kāh
carpet, the	gkozō	prom
carrot, the	mounlà'ùwa	húa-pak-gaht
carry, to	the-de	téuh
cat, the	gkyaun	maau
centimetre, the	sintimìdta	sendtimēt
century, the	yazù-hni'	sa'dta'wǎt
certainly	'ǎ-hman	nàa
chair, the	gkala-tain	gàu'ih

VOCABULARY

LAO	KAMPUCHEAN	VIETNAMESE
gûhp-hûm-kaang	sbăek jeung	giảy ống
dàigŭht	găat	sinh ra
tăngsăwng	dtéang-bpii	cả hai
gàau	dawp	cái chai
keuang kăigàau	brŏdtap băak dawp	đồ mở chai
pèuhn	baat	cái đáy
găp	bro'ŏp	cái hộp
dĕknòi-pûusăhi	bros	con giai
sêua nyoksŏng	aav dtrawnoap	vú
keuang hâhmlàw	vraang	cái hãm
gàhhăhn	hían	can đảm
kâujih	numbpang	bánh mì
hăk	bŏm băek	dánh gãy
'ăhhăhn sàu	baay brĭk	bữa ăn sáng
kŭa	spían	cái cầu
'ăumăh	yawk . . . mawk	mang lại
jìh-kătsêua	gŏnlah	cái trâm
sĭh-nàhmdtăhn	sukkolaa	màu nâu
bpăang	jraas	bàn chải
pûuk	gŏnjŏp	bó
lotbpă'jăm-tăhng	laan-chnúal	xe buýt
nak-tu'ra'gĭt	chmúan	thương gia
kăhwiak	revúal	bận việc
dtaa-wah	bpon dtăe	nhưng
nàmmănbŭh	boa	bơ
ga'dŭm	lèv	cái khuy
sèuh	dtĕñ	mua
ga'lahmbpĭh	spĭy-gdaop	cải bắp
kă'nŏm-kai	num	bánh ngọt
tohla'săp	hau dtūsap	cái điện-thọai
'ŭhn wah	hau taa	gọi là
hàwng	srăek hau	gọi lớn
gàwng-tahi-hùup	maasiin-tót-rūp	máy ảnh
tian-kăi	dtían	cây nến
năhi-hêua	niavía brómuk	thuyền-trưởng
lot	laan	xe hơi
la'matla'wăng	breyat	cẩn-thận
sĭn-kàhbăn-tuk	bŏndtuk	hàng hóa chở trong tầu
pâh-pŏm	bprum	cái thảm
hŭa-păkgâht-dăahng	gaarot	củ cà-rốt
tĕuh	yúa	đem
măau	chmaa	con mèo
săngtihmaat	sŏngdtiimăet	phần
săt-dtă'wăt	sattevóat	thế-kỷ
naanawn	bpit braagŏt	chắc chắn
dtang'ĭh	gau'ey	cái ghế

VOCABULARY

ENGLISH	BURMESE	THAI
change (small money), the	'ănou'	nguhn bplíhk
change (money), to	lĕ-de	làak bplĭan
change (transport), to	bpyăun-de	bplĭan
cheap	bpó-de	tùuk
cheese, the	dein-gĕ	nuhi káang
cherry, the	cheri	chuhrìh
chicken, the	tje'thă	găi
chief, the	lují	húa nàh
child, the	kălĕi	dĕk
chocolate, the	chò-kale'	chok-gohlaat
choose, to	ywĕi-de	lèuak
chopsticks, the	dtu	dta'giap
church, the	kări'yan payă-tjăun	bŏht
cigar, the	hsĕibyĭnlei'	si'gah
cigarette, the	sĭ-gkale'	bu'rĭh
cinema, the	you'hyĭn-youn	pahpa-yon
city, the	myòu	meuang
clean	thàn-hyĭn-de	sa'ăht
clean, to	hsĕi-de	tam hài
clerk, the	sa-yĕi	sa'mĭan
clock, the	na-yi	nahlì'gah
close, to	bpei'-dte	glài
closed	bpei'tă-de	bpĭt
cloth, the	'ă-te	pàh
clothes, the	'awu'ăsă	sèua-pàh
coast, the	bpinle-gkăn-na	făng ta'leh
coat, the	gkou'-'ĭnji	sèua nàwk
coffee, the	gka-pi	gahfaa
coin, the	sèi	rian
cold	ĕi-de	yen
cold season (winter), the	hsăun-dwĭn	rùh'duu náhu
colour, the	'ă-yaun	síh
comb, the	bĭ	wĭh
come, to	la-de	mah
comfortable	the'tha-de	sa'bahi
commercial	sĭbwăbyi'-dte	gahn-kăh
company (firm), the	gkoun-bpani	bawri'săt
complain, to	dtain-de	răwng tùk
completely	'ă-gkoun	srĕt
conceal, to	pwe'-dte	săwn
concert, the	gkăbwĕ	gahn-sa'daang-don-trih
consul, the	gkaunsi'wun	gongsún
contain, to	bpa-win-de	banjŭ'
continue, to	hse'lou'-dte	dtàw
convenient	'ă-hsin-bpyei-de	sa'dŭak
conversation, the	zăgă	son-ta'nah
cook, to	che'-dte	tam'ah-háhn

126

VOCABULARY

LAO	KAMPUCHEAN	VIETNAMESE
ngŭhn-nòi	luy 'ap	tiền lẻ
làahkbpian	dtō	thối tiền
dtaw	dtō	dồi xe
têuhk	taok	rẻ tiền
fŏhmàh	prŏmaat	phó mát
mâhk sŭhrĭhs	sèriis	quả hay cây anh đào
gai	móan	gà hay chim non
hŭanâh	brŏmuk	thủ-lãnh
dĕknòi	gŏn	đứa bé con
kă'nŏmsŏhgŏhlăh	sokōlaa	kẹo súc-cù-là
lèuak	reus	chọn lọc
mài-tūu	jŏngkăas	đũa
wat-kŭn-paw	wat	nhà thờ
gâwk-yăh-nyaiisĭhgăh	siigaa	điều thuốc xì gà
gâwk-yăh	barey	thuốc lá
hŏhngsĭhnĕh	rŏnggon	xi-nê
mèuang	grong	thành- thị
să'âht	s'aat	sạch
tahm-kwăhmsă'âht	sŏm'aat	lau sạch
sà'mian	smian	người thư ký
mŏhng-nyaii	nialĕgaa	đồng hồ treo
bpit	bet	đóng lại
bpit	bet	đóng
pâh	grŏnat	vải dạ
keuang nung	sŏmliak-bŏmpéak	quần áo
fang-ta'lĕh	jnĕ semut	bờ biển
sêua-nyaii	'aau	áo lông
găhfēh	gafē	cà-phê
ngŭhnlĭan	géak	tiền đồng
năhu	dtrójéak	lạnh
la'dŭu-năhu	rŏdŏv-rengia	mùa đông
sĭh	bpóa	màu sắc
wĭh	grah-set-sŏk	cái lược
màh	mawk	lại
yahngsŭksă'băhi	srúal	tiện nghi
giaugăpgăhn-kàh	jumnúañ	thuộc về buôn bán
băwli'sàt	grom-hun	công-ty
dtaw-wah	raw'ū	phàn nàn
yahng-kop-tûan	grup-sŏp	đầy đủ
bpitbăng	bang	chồn
găhnsă'dăahng dŏndtĭh	mawhaosrŏp	cuộc hòa tấu
'ŭp-bpă'tùht	gongsul	lãnh-sự
bănjū'	mian	chứa
dtăhmnŭhn dtawbpăi	dtó	tiếp tục
să'dûak	srónok srúal	tiện lợi
găhnsŏn-ta'năh	bpi-píaksaa	cuộc đàm thoại
hetgĭn	dam sló	nấu nướng

VOCABULARY

ENGLISH	BURMESE	THAI
cookie, the	tăminje'	ka'nómbpang wáhn
corkscrew, the	we'u	tìh-pŭhtjŭt-kŭat
corner (of room), the	dàun	mum
corner (street), the	dàun·	mum
corridor, the	zīnjan	rā'biang
costs, (it)	tja-de	rahkah
cotton, the	chide	fàhi
cotton-wool, the	wagŭn	sámlih
count, to	yei-dtwei'-dte	nãp
country (nation), the	pyei	bpra'tèht
countryside, the	dtōne	bàhn-nàwk
course, of!	da bpò!	nàa nawn!
courtyard, the	wīnjan	sa'náhm-yàh
cover, to	'ou'-dte	klum
crab, the	gănăn	bpuu
cream, the	mălain	krihm
cross, to	gkŭ-de	kàhm
crowd, the	luzù	fŭungchon
cup, the	kwe'	tùai
curry, the	hīn	gaang
cushion, the	hmi-'ōun	màwn
custom (way), the	dălèi	bpra'pehnih
customs, the	'ă-gkau'dto	pahsihjula'gah-gawn
cut, to	pya'-dte	dtăt
dance, to	gkà-de	dtèhnram
dangerous	'andăre-hyi-de	'andta'rahi
dark (colour)	ne'-dte	sih-găa
dark (no light)	hmaun-de	mèuht
day, the	ye'	wan
daytime, the	nèigīn	glahngwan
dead	thei-de	dtahi lāau
dear (expensive)	zēimyā-de	paang
decide, to	hsōun-pya'-dte	dtătsinjai
deep	ne'-dte	lēuk
demand, to	dtăun-de	kwahndtonggahn
dentist, the	thwā-hsăya-wun	máw fan
desert, the	thēganda-yà	ta'lehsahi
diamond, the	sein	pret
dictionary, the	'ăbidan	bpă'tahnŭ'grom
die, to	thei-de	dtahi
different	chănā-de	dtăhng
difficult	ke'kē-de	yàhk
dinner, the	nyàza	'ah-háhn-yen
direction, the	'ăya'mye'hna	tīt
dirty	nyi'bpa'-dte	sokga'bprok
do, to	lou'-dte	tam
doctor, the	hsaya-wun	máw

VOCABULARY

LAO	KAMPUCHEAN	VIETNAMESE
kǎ'nǒmbpǎng	num	bánh bít-qui
keuang kǎidǎwn'ǎtgàau	bródap-dok-chnok-dóp	cái mở nút chai
jǎah	gian	góc
jǎah	jrung	góc
hawmnǎii-hēuan	rawbiang	hành lang
bpěn ngūhn	tlay	đáng giá
fǎhi	kapbaas	bông
pǎhfǎhi-bpon-kǒnsāt	sǒmley	bông
nap	réap	đếm
bpā'tèht	srok	quốc-gia
bǎhnnàwk	srok-srǎe	miền quê
tàah làau!	'añjeng hǎay!	dĩ nhiên!
duhn	tlia	cái sân
bpǒkbpīt	grawp	phù
gā'bpǔu	gdaam	con cua bể
gā'tǐ'	krǎem	kem
kâhm	chlong	đi qua
fǔungsōn	menus jrǎan	đám đông
tûai	bpěěng	cái chén
ga'rīh	kaarii	bột cà-ri
bǎw'	bpǔk	cái gối
bpā'-pāhnǐh	dtumníam-dtumlóap	phong-tục
dahn-pǎhsǐh	geñ	thuế
dtāt	gat	cắt
dtènlām	róam	nhảy
mǐh 'ǎndtā'lāhi	brógóp daoy grúas-tnak	nguy hiểm
gaah	bpoa jah	đậm
mèuht	ngengǐt	tối
mèuh	tngay	ngày
mèuhsǔai	bpěl tngay	ban ngày
tih dtǎhi-làau	ngóap	chết
pǎahng	tlay	đắt
dtātsǐhnjǎii	sǒmróat jět	định quyết
lǔhk	jřiu	sâu
kǎw-hàwng	dtíamdtia	yêu cầu
māw-kâau	bpěět-tmǐñ	nha-sĩ
tā'lěhsāhi	búang'āem	sa mạc
pet	bpīt	kim cương
potjā'nǎhnuhgǒm	vajjenaanugrǒm	tự điển
dtǎhi	slap	chết
dtàahkdtǎhng	blǎek	khác
nyàhk	bpibaak	khó
kâulāang	bóripǒk bpěl lngíat	bữa cơm chiều
tit-tāhng	dǔh	phương hướng
bpèuan	grókvǒk	bẩn
hět	tveu	làm
tahnmǎw	grù-bpěět	bác-sĩ

VOCABULARY

ENGLISH	BURMESE	THAI
dog, the	kwēi	máh
don't!	mǎ-... nè!	yǎh...!
door, the	dagā	bpra'dtuu
doubt, the	thandhǎyà	sóngsáhi
down	'au'gkou	long
dress (woman's), the	mēinmà-'ǎ-wu'	ga'bprohng
drink, the	thau'saya	krèuang dēuhm
drink, to	thau'-dte	dēuhm
drive (car), to	māun-de	kǎp
driver, the	gkǎdhǎmā	kon-kǎprōt
dry	chau'	háang
duck, the	wānbē	bpèt
during	-dtôun	ra'wǎhng
dusty	poun-tu-de	mih fun
duty (obligation), the	dta-wun	nàhtìh
each	-si	tūk
each other	dtǎ-yau'-nè-dtǎ-yau'	sèung-gan-lǎa'gan
early (before time)	sōzō	mah-gǎwn
earrings, the	nǎdāun	dtūm-húu
east	'ǎ-hyèi	dta'wan'ǎwk
easy	lwe-de	ngàhi
eat, to	sā-de	rǎp-bpra'tahn
egg, the	'ù	kǎi
either ... or	... pyi'pyi' ... pyi'pyi'	... gàw ... gàw
electric	hlya'si'	faifáh
elevator, the	da'hleigā	lif
embassy, the	than-yōun	sa'táhn-tùut
empty	'ǎlu'	wàhng bplǎhu
enemy, the	yandhu	kahsèuhk
engine (car), the	se'	krèuang-yon
enjoy, to	dhǎbō-tja-de	sa'nǔk
enormous	tjītje-de	yǎi-toh
enough	dtodo	paw
enter, to	win-de	kàu
entrance, the	winbau'	tahng kàu
envelope, the	sa-'ei'	sawng
equal	nyi-hmyà-de	tàu
evening, the	nyànei	wehlah-yen
everybody	'ǎlōun	tūk kon
everything	'ǎlōun	tūk yǎhng
everywhere	neiyadāin	tūk hǎang
exactly	'ǎ-dtì-'ǎ-tjà	tǔuk-dtrong
example, for	ùpǎma	dtua-yǎhng
except	lwē-lòu	náwk jǎhk
exhibition, the	bpyàbwē	gahn-sa'daang
exit, the	twe'bpau'	tahng 'ǎwk

VOCABULARY

LAO	KAMPUCHEAN	VIETNAMESE
măh	chkǎe	con chó
yah!	gom!	đừng!
bpǎ'dtǔu	dvia	cánh cửa ra vào
kâwsŏngsǎi	gaasŏngsay	sự nghi ngờ
lum	joh	hạ xuống
gǎ'bpohng	rôp	quần áo
keuang deum	pēsejéak	đồ uống
deum	pek	uống
kǎp	bǎak	lái xe
kŏn-kǎp	sŏvóa	tài xế
hàahng	sngúat	khô
pēt	dtía	con vịt
la'wahng	reviang	tiong khi
bpěn fun	bpěñ dtaoy tūlii	bụi-bặm
nâh-tihgǎhn	muk-ngía	bổn phận
dtaahla'ǎn	nimúay-nimúay	mỗi
seunggǎnlaa'gǎn	dtǔu-vǐn-dtǔu-mawk	cùng nhau
dtaahsàu	munbpēl	sớm
dtùmhǔu	króvil	nhẫn đeo tai
tǎhng-tit-dtǎhwěn'âwk	kaang-gǎat	phía đông
ngahi	ngíay	dễ
gǐn	dtedtúal dtían	ǎn
kai	bpawng	quả trứng
. . . lěuh . . .	rǐi . . . rǐi	. . . hay . . .
dùaifǎifǎh	'akkiisenii	thuộc về điện
keuang nyōk	júandǎa-yōng	thang máy
sǎ'tǎhn-tùut	'ǎek 'géak rúattūt	tòa đại sứ
wahngbpau	dtawdtě	trống rỗng
sǎt-dtǔu	sadtrŏv	kẻ thù
keuangjǎk	grǐang maasiin	bộ máy
mak	gŏmsaan	thưởng thức
nyailǎhi	mawhěmía	khổng lồ
píang-pǎw	lmawm . . .	đủ
kâu	jŏl	đi vô
tǎhng-kâu	dvia jŏl	lối vô
sǎwng jōtmǎhi	sraom-sŏmbot	phong bì
tǎugǎn	smǎa	bằng nhau
nyǎhmlǎahng	lngíat	buổi tối
mŏt-tuk-kōn	grup rũp	mọi người
tuksing	dtíang'ŏs	mọi thứ
tuk-tukhaahng	grup gŏnlǎeng	mọi nơi
kaknaah	gúat	đúng y-trang
dtǔa-yahng	'o-tíahó	thí dụ
nàwkjâhk	leuk-lěěng-dtǎe	ngoại trừ
gǎhnbpǎ'gûat	gaa bŏnghaañ	cuộc triển lãm
tǎhng'âwk	dvia jěng	lối ra

131

VOCABULARY

ENGLISH	BURMESE	THAI
expect, to	hmyonei-de	kàht-wàh
explain, to	hyìn-bpyà-de	'ah-ti'bahi
eye, the	mye'sì	dtah
face, the	mye'hna	nàh
fact, in	'ǎ-hman-gàdò	kwahm-jing
fail, to	mǎ'aunmyin-bū	mài sámret
fair (just)	pyàunma'-dte	yūt-dti'tahm
fall, to	tjà-de	dtŏk
family, the	mìdhāzu	kràwp-krua
famous	tjotjā	mih chèuh-siang
fan, the	bpan-gka	pàtlom
far	wēi	glai
farmer, the	ledhǎmā	chahu-nah
fast	myan-de	rehu
fasten, to	chi-de	pǔuk
festival, the	bpwēdo	ngahn
fetch, to	yula-de	nam mah
few, a	nēnē	nŏi
field, the	le-gwīn	sa'nahm
fight, to	dtai'kai'-dte	dtǎwsùu
fill, to	pyì-de	dtuhm
film (for camera), the	pǎlin-lei'	film-tǎhi-rùu
film (movie show), the	pǎlin	pahpa-yon
finally	nau'hsōun-hma	nai-tìhsǔt
find, to	dtwèi-de	pŏp
finish, to	bpī-de	tamsēht
fire, the	mī	faimài
first	bpǎ-tǎmà	tìhnĕung
fish, the	ngā	bplah
flat	pyā-de	baan
flat (tyre), the	leiyòbī	baan
floor, the	tjàn	pèuhn
flower, the	bpān	dǎwkmāhi
fly, the	yin-gaun	ma'laang wan
fly, to	bpyan-de	bin
follow, to	lai'-dte	dtahm
food, the	'ǎsa'ǎsa	'ah-háhn
foot, the	chei	tāu
football (game), the	bòlōunbwē	futboll
for	'ǎ-pòu	sàmrǎp
forbidden	dtǎmyi-tā-dè	hàhm
foreign	nain-ganjā	dtǎhng bpra'tèht
forest, the	thi'dtŏ	bpǎh
forget, to	mèi-de	leuhm
fork, the	kayīn	sàwm
former	'ǎ-yin	gŏn

VOCABULARY

LAO	KAMPUCHEAN	VIETNAMESE
kàhtmăhi	sŏngkĭm	hy vọng
'ă'ti'băhi	bpúanyúal	giải thích
dtăh	pnĕĕk	con mắt
nâh	muk	gương mặt
dtăhmkwăhmjĭng-làau	dtaam bpit	thật ra
bawsămlèt	tlĕak	thất bại
nyu'dti'tàm	yudtĕ-toa	công bằng
dtōk	tlĕak	rớt xuống
kàwp-kūa	grúasaa	gia đình
mĭh seuhsĭang	lbey-lbaañ	nổi tiếng
patlòm	dŏnghal	cái quạt
găi	chngaay	xa
săhu-năh	néak-srăe	nông dân
wāi	lían	nhanh
mat	jóng	buộc lại
bŭn	bon	buổi tiệc
bpăi-hap	dtŭu yawk . . . mawk	mang lại
leknòi	glah-glah	mấy
tong	vĭal srăe	khu-vực
dtawsûu	chlúah	đánh nhau
hèt-hâidtĕm	bŏmbpĕñ	lấp đầy
fĭmhùup	pvil	phim
hùup-ngāu	gkon	phim
pŏnsūt-tàhi	dtii bañjōp	cuối cùng
sàwk	rawk	tìm
hetlàaulàau	bañjōp	hoàn tất
fāi	pleung	hỏa-hoạn
tihneung	dtii-múay	thứ nhất
bpah	drey	cọn cá
piang	ríap	bằng phẳng
dtĭhnlot dtâahk	kóng băek	lỗ
pèuhn	gdaa-graal	sàn nhà
dâwkmài	pgaa	hoa
māahng-wān	ruy	con ruồi
bĭn	hăa	bay
dtit-dtăhm	dtaam	đi theo
'ăhhăhn	'aahaa	thức ăn
dtĭhn	jeung	bàn chân
dtĕ'băhn	bal dtóat	bóng tròn
sămlăp	sŏmroap	cho
hăhm	haam	ngăn cấm
dtahngdàhu	bóredtēh	ngoại quốc
bpahmài	bprĭy	rừng
lĕuhm	plĭt	quên
sâwm	sawm	cái xiên
'ăhdĭht	néak mun	trước

VOCABULARY

ENGLISH	BURMESE	THAI
forwards	hyèidhòu	kàhng-nàh
free (vacant)	'ā	wàhng
fresh	la'hsa'-dte	sòt
fried	tjo-de	tàwt
fried rice, the	tămin-jo	kàhu påt
friend, the	mei'hswei	pèuan
from	-gkà	jåhk
front of, in	hyèi-hma	kàhng nàh
frontier, the	nejā	promdaan
frozen	kēne-dè	bpen năm káang
fruit, the	thi'thī	pónla'măi
full	bpyi-de	dtem
garden, the	'uyin	súan
gasoline (petrol), the	da'hsi	năm-man bensihn
girl, the	mēin-kàlēi	děk ying
give, to	bpēi-de	hǎi
glad	wăntha-de	yindih
glass (drinking), the	pan-gwe'	tùai gàau
glass (substance), the	hman	gàau
glove, the	le'ei'	túng meuh
go, to	thwā-de	bpai
go down, to	hsīn-de	long bpai
go up, to	dte'-dte	kèuhn bpai
god, the	payā	prā'jàu
gold, the	hywei	tawng
good	gkāun-de	dih
goods, the	gkounzi	sin-kāh
government, the	'āsōuyà	rát-ta'bahn
gram, the	gkǎlǎbē	gram
grapes, the	dhǎbyi'thī	'a'ngǔn
grass, the	mye'bpin	yàh
green	sēin-de	kìau
grey	mīgōuyaun	tau
ground, the	myeijī	din
guard, to	sàun-de	fau
guest, the	'èdhe	kǎak
guide, the	lānbyà	pùu nam tìau
guidebook, the	lān-hnyunsa-'ou'	sa'mǔt nam tìau
gun, the	thǎ-hna'	bpeuhn
hair, the	zǎbin	póm
haircut, the	zǎbin-hnya'	dtǎt-póm
hairdresser, the	zǎbin-hnya'thǎmā	chàhng-dtǎt-póm
ham, the	we'bpaunjau'	haam
handbag, the	le'gkain-ei'	gra'bpáu hìu
handkerchief, the	le'gkainbàwa	pàh chēt nàh
harbour, the	thinbōzei'	tàh reua
hard (firm)	kain-de	káang

134

VOCABULARY

LAO	KAMPUCHEAN	VIETNAMESE
bpǎi-tǎhngnâh	dtǔu muk	vẽ phía trước
bpau-wahng	dtumnē	trống
sōt	srǒs	tươi mát
jěuhn	liing	chiên
kâii kǔa	baay liing	cơm rang
peuan	mǐt-sǒmlañ	bạn
dtaah	bpii . . .	tử
dtawnâh	nǐu muk . . .	phía trước
kâwp-kêht-kwǎhmhùu	brum-dǎen	biên giới
saah-yěn	gók	đông lạnh
mǎhkmài	plǎe-cheu	trái cây
dtěm	bpǐñ	đầy
sǔan	súan jbaa	cái vườn
nàmmǎn'âahtsǎng	sang	dầu ga-sôn
pǔusǎhu	srey	cô gái
'ǎu-hǎii	'aoy	cho
dǐhjǎii	sapbaay	hân hạnh
jâwkgàau	gǎev	cái ly
gàau	gañjǒk	thủy tinh
tǒngmèuh	sraom day	găng tay
bpǎi	dtǔu	đi
lùtlòng	joh	đi xuống
kêunsǔung	lǎang	đi lên
těhwa'dǎh	bpréah	thần linh
kàm	mǐah	vàng
dǐh	l'ó	tốt
sǐn-kàh	dtumnǐñ	hàng hóa
lat-tǎ'bǎhn	rǒtaa-pibaal	chính phủ
gǎhm	graam	gam
mǎhk lǎahsǎahng	drǒbpéang-baay-jū	nho
nyâh	smau	cỏ
sǐh-kǐau	baydtóng	xanh lá cây
sǐh-kǐh-tau	bró-péak	xám
pèuhndǐn	dey	đất
yuu-nyǎhm	yiam	canh giữ
kâahk-pûumǎh-yǎhm	pñiav	khách
kǒnnǎm-tiau	néak nóam plǒv	người chỉ dẫn
bpèuhmnǎm-tiau	siav-piu nóam plǒv	sách chỉ dẫn
bpěuhn	gam pleung	khẩu súng
pǒm	sǒk	tóc
dtàt-pǒm	gat-sǒk	cắt tóc
sahngdtaahng-pǒm	néak gat-sǒk	thợ hớt tóc
sihn-kǎhmǔu	jǒmbong	thịt heo
gǎ'bpǎu pǔu-nyǐng	gaabǒbyúa	túi nhỏ
pǎh-pǎahmǒn	gǒnsǎeng-day	khăn tay
tahhěua	jrǒy semut	hải-cảng
nǎahnnǎh	rǐng	chắc

135

VOCABULARY

ENGLISH	BURMESE	THAI
hat, the	'ou'tou'	mŭak
have, to	hyi-de	mih
he	thu	káu
head, the	gäun	húa
headache, the	gäun-gkai'na	bpŭat húa
hear, to	tjä-de	dài yin
heart, the	hnàlōun	húajai
heavy	lēi-de	nǎk
height, the	'ǎ-myìn	kwahmsúung
help, to	gku-nyi-de	chuai
her (adj.)	thù	. . . káu
here	di-hma	tihnìh
high	myìn-de	súung
hill, the	dtaun	káu
his	thù	. . . káu
hold, to	gkain-de	tèuh
holy	myìnmya'-dte	sǎksĭt
home, at	'ein-hma	tih-bàhn
honest	pyàunma'-dte	sèuh dtrong
hope, to	hmyolìn-de	wáng
horse, the	myìn	máh
hospital, the	sēiyoun	rohng pa'yahbahn
host, the	'ein-hyin	jàu-bàhn
hot (weather)	bpu-de	rāwn
hot (heated food, etc.)	bpu-de	rāwn
hot season (summer), the	nwēi	rǔh'duu rāwn
hotel, the	ho-dte	rohng raam
hour, the	nayi	chùa mohng
house, the	'ein	bàhn
how?	be lou'lē?	yǎhng-rai?
how many?	be lou'myǎlē?	gǐh . . . ?
however (conj.)	dabeimè	yǎhng-rai
hut, the	dtē	grà'tàwm
I	tjano/tjamà	póm/chán
ice, the	yeigē	nǎm káang
ice cream, the	yeigēmòun	'aisa'krihm
if	-yin	tàh
ill	na-pyǎ-de	bpŭai
immediately	che'chìn	tan-tih
important	'ǎyēitjī	sǎm-kan
impossible	mǎ-pyi'hnain	bpen bpai mài dài
in	dwin	nai
information, the	dhǎdìn	rahi-lǎ'ĭad
inside	'ǎ-tē	kàhng nai
instead of	'ǎsǎ	taan-tih
interesting	sei'winzǎbwe-gkǎun-de	nàh són jai
interpreter, the	zǎgǎbyan	pa'nak-ngahn bplaa

VOCABULARY

LAO	KAMPUCHEAN	VIETNAMESE
mǔak	múak	cái mũ
mǐh	mían	có
lāhu	góat	ông ấy
hǔa	gbaal	cái đầu
'ǎhgǎhnjēp-hǔa	chīī gbaal	nhức đầu
dài-nyīn	līī	nghe
hǔajǎi	běhdŏng	quả tim
nāk	tngúan	nặng
kwāhmsǔung	gǒmbpúas	sức nặng
soilěua	júay	giúp đỡ
. . . lāhu	. . . góat	. . . của bà ấy
yuunih	'ǎe-nih	đây
sǔung	kbúas	cao
pǔunòi	pnum	ngọn đồi
. . . lāhu	. . . góat	. . . của ông ấy
jǎp	gan	giữ lại
tihsǎkgā'la'bǔusāh	bpréah- . . .	thánh thiện
yuu hěuan	nǐu ptěah	tại nhà
sātseuh	smŏh dtrŏng	thật-thà
wǎng	sǒngkǐm	hy vọng
màh	sěh	con ngựa
hŏhngmǎw	múandtii bpěět	nhà thương
jàu-pâhp	mjas ptěah	chủ nhà
hàwn	gdau	nóng
hàwn	gdau	nóng
la'dǔu-hàwn	rǒdòv-gdau	mùa hạ
hŏhnghǎahm	ptěah-sǒmnak	khách-sạn
sua-mǒhng	maong	giờ giấc
hěuan	ptěah	nhà
bpěn-yahngdǎii?	yaang naa?	cách nào?
lǎhi-bpǎhndǎii?	bponmaan?	bao nhiêu?
yahngdǎiigǎwdtǎhm	bpondtǎe	tuy nhiêu
dtǔup	ktawm	cái lều
kôi	kňom	tôi
nàmgàwn	dtǐk-gók	băng đá
ga'lǎahm	gaarěm	kem lạnh
tâhwah	bǎa sen jía	nếu
bpuai	chīī	ốm
tān-tǐh	plíam	tức thi
sǎm-kān	sǒm-kan	quan-trọng
bpěnbpǎibawdài	min'aat-dtveu-baan	không thể xảy ra
yuunǎi	gnong	bên trong
kahu	dǒmneng	tin tức
tǎhngnāi	kaang gnong	bên trong
tǎahn-tǐh	jumnúas	thay vì
nâhsǒnjǎii	mían bróyòt	hay
nǎhi-pǎhsǎh	néak brǎe píasaa	người thông dịch

VOCABULARY

ENGLISH	BURMESE	THAI
iron (metal), the	than	lèk
is	hyi-de	bpen
island, the	tjūn	gaw'
isn't it?	hmou'lā?	mài chài réuh?
it	thu	man
jewellery, the	le'wu'le'sā	krèuang bpra'dăp gai
journey, the	kayī	duhn-tahng
jump, to	koun-de	gra'dŏht
jungle, the	dtō	bpăh
key, the	thò	gunjaa
kill, to	tha'-dte	kàh
kilogram, the	gkilougăran	gi'lohgram
kilometre, the	gkiloumidta	gi'lohmēt
kind (friendly)	tjin-nada'-dte	jaidih
king, the	hyinbayin	ga'sàt
kiss, to	nān-de	jùup
kitchen, the	mībougān	krua
knife, the	dā	miht
know, to	thi-de	rūu
label, the	'ă-hma'dàzei'	bpàhi
lake, the	gkan	ta'lehsăhp
lamb, the	thōu	lùuk gaa'
lamp, the	mi-'ein	kohm faifāh
last	nau'sōun	sùt tāhi
late (behind time)	nau'tjà-de	chāh
later on	nau'dtò	tih láng
laugh, to	yi-de	húa rāw'
laundry (clothes), the	doubizain	rahn-sak-pah
law, the	'ùbadei	gòtmahi
lawyer, the	hyèinei	ta'nahi kwahm
lead, to	'ū-hsaun-de	nam
learn, to	thin-de	rian
least, at	'ănēzōun	yăhng nōi
leave (place), to	twe'kwa-de	jăhk bpai
leave behind, to	chan-tā-de	lā'tīng
left (hand)	bebe'	sāhi
leg, the	cheidau'	káh
lemon, the	hyau'thī	ma'nahu
lemonade, the	thanbàyayei	nām ma'nahu
letter (note), the	sa	jòtmáhi
letter (character), the	salōun	dtua
lettuce, the	tăyou'nan-nan	păkgăht háwm
lie, the	mudhāzàgā	goh-hŏk
lie down, to	hlē-de	nawn
lift, to	mà-de	yók
light (colour)	nù-de	sih-'awn

VOCABULARY

LAO	KAMPUCHEAN	VIETNAMESE
lēk	dăek	sắt
maahn	jía	là
gaw'	gŏh	hòn đảo
maahn baw?	dtē rĩĩ?	phải không?
mān	vía	cái ấy
hàn-kăhi-keuang'èh	grĩang míah-bpĭt	nữ trang
gằhndŭhn-tāhng	dŏmnăa	cuộc hành trình
gā'dôht	lōt	nhảy
dŏng	bprĩy	rừng rậm
gā'jāah	gkŏn sao	chìa khóa
kâh	sŏmlap	giết
gĭ'lòh	gilō	kilô-gam
gĭ'lòhmaat	gilŏmăet	kilô-mét
jõp	slōt	thân thiện
jàusihwīt	sdat	vua
jùup	tăap	hôn
hēuan-kūa	ptēah-baay	nhà bếp
miht	gambet	con dao
hùujāk	deng	biết
bpàhi	sañaa	dấu hiệu
ta'lēhsâhp	beng	cái hồ
lùukgāa'	jíam	con cừu
kõhmfāi	jŏnggiang	cái đèu
sūt-tàhi	jong-graay	cuối cùng
sàh	yĩit	trễ
dtawbpāi	graoy mawk dtíat	lát nữa
hũa	săat	cười
keuang 'āubpăisak	gaa-baok-'ut	phòng giặt ủi
gõtmăhi	jbap	luật lệ
ta'nāhi-kwāhm	néak jbap	luật sư
năm-păhbpāi	nóam	dẫn
hian	rían	học
yahngnòi	yíang haot nas	ít nhất
jâhk	jaak-jeñ	rời đi
bpā'wài	dtuk-jaol	để lại
tāhngsàhi	chvēng	bên trái
kăh	jeung	chân
mâhk nāhu	grŏt chmaa	quả chanh
nàm-mâhk-nāhu	dtĭk maanad	nước chanh
jõtmăhi	sŏmbot	bức thư
dtŏh năngsĕuh	dtúa 'aksó	chữ
păk sā'lat	saalat	rau diếp
gằhndtūa	bpíak gohŏk	lời nói dối
năwnlõng	dtum-rēt	nằm xuống
nyok-kêuhn	leuk	nâng lên
sĭh'awn	gjey	nhạt

139

VOCABULARY

ENGLISH	BURMESE	THAI
light (weight)	bpò-de	bau
lighter (cigarette), the	da'mìtji'	fai chāak
like (prep.)	lou	méuan gan
lipstick, the	hnà-kăn-hsôuzêi	lif-dtŭk
litre, the	li'dta	lìt
little, a	nēnē	nìt nŏi
live (reside), to	nei-de	yŭu
lock, the	thò-'ein	gunjaa
long (size)	hyei-de	yahu
long (time)	tjaja	nahn
long ago	'ăyindôun-gà	nahn mah lāau
look at, to	tji-de	duu
look for, to	hya-de	háh
lose (mislay), to	bpau'-dte	háhi
lose (race, etc.), to	hyôun-de	pāa
loud	tje-de	dang
love, to	chi'-dte	rāk
low	nèin-de	dtăm
lunch, the	nèileza	'ah-háhn glahng-wan
machine, the	se'	krèuang
magazine, the	me'gàzìn	máakga'síhn
make, to	lou'-dte	tam
malaria, the	hnge'pyā	mahleh-ria
man, the	yau'tjā	pùuchahi
manager, the	man-neija	pùu jat gahn
mango, the	thàye'thī	ma'mùang
many	myā	màhk
map, the	myeiboun	páan-tìh
market, the	zēi	dta'lăht
married	'eindaun tjà-de	dtăang ngahn
matches, the	mìtji'	măi-kĭhtfai
means, (it)	soulou-de	máhi kwahm
measure, to	dtāin-twa-de	wāt
meat, the	'amēdhā	nēua
mechanic, the	se'hsàya	chàhng-krèuang
medicine, the	hsēi	yah
meet, to	dtwèi-de	pŏp
melon, the	păyedhī	dtaang-tai
menu, the	hinsăyin	rahi-gahn 'ah-háhn
message, the	'ă-tjăuntjāza	kău
metre, the	mìdta	mēt
middle, the	'ale	glahng
midnight	thăn-gaun	tiang keuhn
milk, the	nwānòu	nom
millimetre, the	milimìdta	minlihmēt
minute, the	mini'	nahtih

VOCABULARY

LAO	KAMPUCHEAN	VIETNAMESE
bǎu	sraal	nhẹ
gāpfāilēk	dǎek gěh	đồ bật lửa
kàhi-kēuh	dót	tương tự
nàmdǎahng-tāhsǒp	grǎem líap móat	môi son
lit	liit	lít
nòi-neung	bǒndtet	một ít
'ǎhsǎiyuu	nǐu	ở
ga'jāah	sao	cái khóa
nyǎhu	věěng	dài
dǒn	yū	lâu
dǒnnǎhnlàau	yū mawk hǎay	xa xưa
buhng	meul	nhìn
sâwk-hǎh	rawk meul	tìm kiếm
sǐa	bat	làm mất
lînsǐa	jañ	thua
dǎng	glang	lớn
hak	srólañ	yêu
dtam	dtiap	thấp
'ǎhhǎhn-gǎhngwǎn	baay tngay	bữa cơm trưa
keuangjak	maasiin	bộ máy
wǎhla'sǎhn	dtúahseníavedtey	tạp chi
het	tveu	làm
pa'nyàht-kâibpah	jumngǐǐ-grun-jañ	bệnh sốt rét
pûusǎhi	menus-bros	ông
pûujǎtgǎhn	néak-jat-gaa	quản trị viên
mâhk muang	swaay	quả soài
lǎhi	jrǎan	nhiều
pǎahn-tǐh	pǎen-dtii	bản đồ
dtǎ'lâht	psaa	chợ
dtaahng-ngǎhnlàau	ríap gaa	kết hôn
gapfǎi	cheugkus	diêm quẹt
mǎhi-kwǎhmwah	mían nǐy	nghĩa là
tàahk	vóas	đo
sihn	sat	thịt
sahngbpǎahngjǎk	néak-brǎa-naasiin	thợ sửa xe
yǎh	dtnam	thuốc
pop	júap	gặp
mâhk mǒh	dtrósǒk srǒv	quả dưa bở
lǎhi-gǎhn 'ǎhhǎhn	bañjii muk mhǒp	thực đơn
kahu	dǒmneng	bức điện tín
maat	mǎet	mét
kuhnggǎhng	gǒndaal	ở giữa
tiang-kēuhn	gǒndaal yúap	nửa đêm
nàmnǒm	dtǐk-dǒh-gō	sữa
mihlǐhmaat	miiliimǎet	mili-mét
nǎhtǐh	níadtii	phút

VOCABULARY

ENGLISH	BURMESE	THAI
mirror, the	hman	gra'jŏk
mistake, the	'ă-hmā	kwahm pĭt
moment, the	kanà	ka'nă'nán
monastery, the	põunjī-tjăun	wăt
money, the	pai'hsan	nguhn
month, the	là	deuan
monument, the	tjau'dtain	'a'nu'sáhwa'rih
moon, the	là	prä'jan
more	bpou-ywèi	màhk gwăh
morning, the	màne'	chàu
mosque, the	băli	bŏht 'Ĭs-lahm
mosquito, the	chin	yung
most	'ă- . . . -hsõun	máhk tĭhsŭt
motor-bike, the	modtosain-ke	rŏt moh-tuhsai
mountain, the	dtaun	puu kái
mouth, the	băza'	bpăhk
movie camera, the	you'hyin-gkinmăra	glàwng tăhi-náng
much	myā	màhk
museum, the	bpyădai'	pĭ'pit-ta'pan
mushroom, the	hmou	hět
music, the	gidtà	dondtrih
must	-yà	dtàwng
mustard, the	moun-nyīn	năm jim mahsdtăht
my	tjănò/tjămà	. . . póm/ . . . chán
name, the	na-me	chèuh
napkin, the	le'thou'bpawa	pàh chĕt meuh
narrow	tjīn-de	kàap
natural	dhàbawàtjà	tram-chàh-dti'
near (not far)	nĭ-de	yŭu glài
near to	'ănī-hma	glài-găp
need, to	lounei-de	dtàwng gahn
needle, the	'a'	kém
never	bedò-hma	mài kuhi
new	thi'-dte	măi
newspaper, the	dhădīnza	nángséuh-pim
next (after)	nau'	kàhng-nàh
night, the	nyà	glahng-keuhn
no (adj.)	be- . . . -hma	mài
nobody	be-dhu-hma	mài mih krai
noise, the	'ăthan	siang
noodles, the	kau'hswē	gúai-dtíau
noon	mūndtè	tiang
north	myau'	tĭt néua
not	mà	mài
not at all	'ă-hlyīn măhou'	mài chài
notepaper, the	sayèise'gku	gra'dtăht bun tĕuk
nothing	bamà	mài mih 'a'rai

142

VOCABULARY

LAO	KAMPUCHEAN	VIETNAMESE
gā'jōk	gañjōk	gương để soi
kwāhm-pit	gŏmhos	lỗi lầm
la'nya'wehlāh	pliam núah	một lúc
gūt-dti'pa'	voat	tu viện
ngūhn	brak luy	tiền
dĕuan	kăe	tháng
'ā'nu'săhwa'līh	vimían	bia kỷ niệm
pa'jăn	lŏk-kăe	mặt trăng
'ĭhk	dtiat	... hơn
mèuhsàu	brĭk	buổi sáng
bôht 'Islāhm	mas	đền thờ
nyung	mūh	con muỗi
lăhi tihsūt	jiang-ge	... hơn hết
lotjāk	mŏdtŏ	xe gắn máy
pūu-kău	pnum	ngọn núi
bpâhk	móat	miệng
gàwng-tahi-hùup-ngău	maasiin tót gkon	máy quay phim
lăhi	jrăan	nhiều
hăw-pi'pit-tā'pān	saaremundtii	bảo tàng viện
hĕt	pset	nấm
dŏndtĭh	plĕng	nhạc
dtàwng	drŏv dtăe	phải
nàmmâhk-pētlĕuang	gaylaat	bột hạt cải
... kôi	... kñom	... của tôi
seuh	chmúah	tên
pâhsētmēuh	gŏnsăeng	khăn bàn
kàahp	dtòt	chật
dtăhm-tāmma'sàt	tóam jiat	thiên nhiên
gài	jĭt	gần
gàigàp	jĭt	gần
dtàwnggăhn	drŏv-gaa	cần
kĕm	mjul	cái kim
baw-kūhi	mĭn-dăel	không bao giờ
maii	tmey	mới
năngsĕuh-pīm	gaasăet	tờ báo
dtawbpăi	graoy	tiếp theo
găhng-kĕuhn	yup	ban đêm
baw mĭh	dtĕ	không
baw-mĭh-păi	kmian néak naa sŏh	không có ai
siangdăng	sŏmlĕng	tiếng động
sênmih	guy dtiav	mì
dtăwn-tiang	tngay-trŏng	buổi trưa
titnĕua	kaang-jeung	phía bắc
baw	mĭn ... dtĕ	không
baw bpĕn nyăng dâwk	mĭn ... sŏh	không ... chút nào cả
jia-kianjòtmăhi	gredaas-sesĕ-sŏmbot	giấy nót
baw-mĭh-nyăng	'et 'ey dtĕ	không có gì hết

143

VOCABULARY

ENGLISH	BURMESE	THAI
notice, the	'a-tjăuntjăza	bpra'găht
now	'agù	diau-nìh
number, the	'ayei-'a-dtwe'	lèhk
nurse, the	thu-nabyù-hsàya	nahng pa'yahbahn
nuts, the	thi'thĭma	tūa
obtain, to	yà-de	dài-ráp
occupied	yu-tă-de	mài wàhng
offer, to	pĕi-de	sa'núh
office, the	yŏun	'ăwfìt
officer (army), the	si'bou	nahi ta'háhn
often	matja-matja	bŏi
oil, the	hsi	năm-man
old (persons)	lu-'ou	găa
old (things)	hăun	gău
olives, the	than-lwindhĭ	mă'gŏk
on	-bpo	bon
once	dta-kau'	krăng nĕung
onion, the	gkye'thun-ni	húa háwm
only	-de	tàunăn
open	bpwìn-de	bpŭht
open, to	bpwìn-de	bpŭht
opera, the	bpyăza'	'ŭp-rah-gawn
opposite	dta-pe' dtache'	dtrong kàhm
or	nòu măhou'	réuh
orange, the	leinmo	sòm
ordered	'ămèin-tou'tă-de	bpen rā'biap
ordinary	thaman	tahma'dah
our	tjanodòu/tjamàdòu	. . . rau
outside	'ă-bpyin-hma	kàhng nawk
overcoat, the	'ă-bpyin'ĭnji	sèua-klum
owe, to	hsa'saya-hyi-de	bpen nìh
oyster, the	kăyù	hói nahngrom
pack, to	tou'-dte	gĕp káwng
pain, the	na-tjinjĭn	kwahm jĕp bpŭat
paint, the	thou'hsĕi	sih
pair, the	zoun	kùu
palace, the	năndo	wang
paper, the	se'gku	gra'dăht
parcel, the	bpa-hsedou'	hăw
park, the	bpănjan	súan
park (car), to	ya'tă-de	jăwt
passport, the	nain-gan-gŭle'hma'	nángséuh duhn tahng
pastry, the	mòun	pàang 'ŏpsuk
pay, to	bpĕi-de	jăhi
peace, the	nyĕinjăn-yĕi	kwahm sa'ngŏp
peach, the	thi'dtodhĭ	lùuk-tàw
pearl, the	pălĕ	kăimùk

VOCABULARY

LAO	KAMPUCHEAN	VIETNAMESE
bpā'gàht	dtaarang	thông cáo
dǐaunih	'eylōv	bây giờ
jǎmnūan	lēk	số
nǎhng-pa'nyāhbǎhn	gilíanuptaak	y tá
mâhk gaw	gróap	hạt
dàilap	baan	kiếm được
têuhk-kàwp-kāwng	rawvǒl	chiếm
nyok-hâii	jūn	dâng
hôhnggǎhn	mundtiijatgaa	văn phòng
nāhi-ta'hǎhn	niay-dtiahóan	sĩ quan
lèuailèuai	ñǐk-ñóap	thường thường
nàmmān-keuang	brēng	dầu
tâu	jah	già
gau	jah	cũ
mâhk 'ǒhlìu	'ōliiv	quả ô-liu
tāhng-tūhng	leu	ở trên
kàngneung	medóng	một lần
pǎk bua	gtǐm baaréang	hành
taunàn	gróan-dtǎe	chỉ có
bpûht	bǎak	mở
kǎi	bǎak	mở
la'kāwn-pēhng	'ōbpēraa	nhạc kịch
gǒnggǎn-kâhm	dtúal-muk	đối diện
lěuh	rīi	hay là
mâhk gìang	grōt	quả cam
têuhksāng	bañjia dtěñ	thứ tự
tāmma'dǎh	tóamdaa	tầm thường
... pùak hāu	... yeung	... của chúng tôi
tāhngnâwk	grau-bpii ...	bên ngoài
sêuagǎnnǎhu	'aav-grau	áo khoác
dtǐtnîh	jumbpéak	nơ
hǒi-nāhnglōm	ngíav	sò
jàt-keuang	vǐt	gói lại
kwāhmjēp-bpûat	gaa chīijap	cơn đau
nàmsǐh	líap	sơn
kuuneung	gǔ	một cặp
pa'làtsa'vāng	véang	cung điện
jìa	gredaas	tờ giấy
haw	gañjōp	gói đồ
sǔanbawn-yawnjǎi	súan-jbaa	công viên
jâwt	jót	đậu xe
nǎngsěuh-pahndǎahn	liket-chlóng-dǎen	sổ thông hành
kā'nǒm	num-p'ǎem	bột nhồi
jahi-hâii	bong brak	trà
kwāhmsǎ'ngop	sǒndtě-piam	sự bằng an
mâhk kāhi	bpǎes	quả đào
kaimuk	gut	ngọc trai

ENGLISH	BURMESE	THAI
peas, the	bpē	tŭa
pen, the	gkalaundan	bpåhkgah
pencil, the	kēdan	dinsáw
pepper, the	ngàyou'gkāun	prĭk-tai
perfume, the	'ă-hmwēi-'ă-tjain	nàm háwn
perhaps	. . . -gkāun	bahng tih
permit, to	kwin-bpyu-de	'a'nŭ'yàht
person, the	lu	kon
petrol (gasoline), the	da'hsi	nàm-man bensihn
pharmacy, the	hsēi-zain	rähn káhi yah
photograph, the	da'bpoun	rùup tăhi
picture, the	bpoun	rùup
piece, the	'ă-bpàin-'ăsà	chin
pillow, the	gaun'ōun	máwn
pin, the	twe-'a'	kém mŭt
pineapple, the	nàna'thī	sap-bpa'rŏt
pink	bpăn-nu	chom-puu
place, the	neiya	hăang
plate, the	baganbyā	jahn
platform (railway), the	bpăle'pàun	chahn-cha'lah
pleasant	thaya-de	sa'nŭk sa'bahi
plum, the	zĭthī	lùuk-gĕht
point out, to	hnyun-bpyà-de	chĭh
police station, the	yēsă-kàn	sa'táhnih dtamrŭat
policeman, the	bpălei'	dtamrŭat
poor (needy)	hsīn-yē-de	jon
pork, the	we'thā	nêua múu
porter, the	'ă-tăndhămā	kon-kón-kóng
possible	pyi'hnain	bpen bpai dài
post-box, the	sadai'bōun	tùu bpraisa'nih
postcard, the	bpòusă-gka'	bpraisa'nih ya'băt
post-office, the	sadai'	tih-tam-gahn bpraisa'nih
potatoes, the	'alū	man fa'răng
practise, to	lèitjin-de	hăt
prawn, the	băzun	gùng
present (gift), the	le'hsaun	káwng kwáhn
president, the	thămădà	bpra'tahnah tĭ'bawdih
press (clothes), to	mĭbu-dtai'-dte	riht
pretty	hlà-de	súai
price, the	'ă-pōu	rahkah
priest, the	kari'yan-pōunjī	prà'
prison, the	taun	kŭk
private	koubain	sŭan dtua
promise, to	gădì-pēi-de	sán-yah
province, the	kăyain	jang-wăt
public	ludù	sah-tahra'nă'

146

VOCABULARY

LAO	KAMPUCHEAN	VIETNAMESE
mâhk tua-nyat	sŏndǎek	đậu
bpâhkgǎh	slaap-bpakkaa	cây bút mực
sǎwdǎhm	gmau-day	cây bút chì
mâhk pik-tāi	mrĭt	tiêu
nàmhǎwm	dtĭk 'ŏp	nước hoa
bǎhngtĭh	brehǎel	có lẽ
'ā'nu'nyàht	'aknuññaat	cho phép
bǔk-kŏn	menus	người
nàmmǎn'âahtsāng	brèng-gaat	dầu hỏa
hàhn-kǎhi-yǎh	faamesii	hiệu thuốc
hùup-tahi	rūp-tót	bức hình
hùupdtàahm	kumnŭ	bức hình
dtawn	dom	mảnh
mǎwn	knǎay	cái gối
kěmgàt	mjul	đinh ghim
mâhk nat	mnóas	dứa
sĭh-bǔa	sii-jumbpŭ	hồng
sā'tǎhn-tĭh	gŏnlǎeng	chỗ
jǎhn	jaan	cái mâm
sǎhn	jěñjǎam plŏv redteh-pleung	trạm
tĭhhâii-kwāhm-pāwjǎii	sapbaay	vui lòng
mâhk bprŭn	bprŭn	mận
sĭhhâiibuhng	jŏng'ol	chỉ
sā'tahnĭh-dtǎmlùat	nawkawbaal-jíat	sở cảnh-sát
nāhi-dtǎmlùat	bpoliis	cảnh-sát viên
tuk-nyàhk	gró	nghèo
sĭhnmǔu	sat-jrŭk	thịt heo
gǔ'lĭh-hâp-kǎwng	chnam dtvía	người khuân vác
'àhtjā'bpěnbpǎidài	'aat-dtveu-baan	có thể
dtùu-bpǎisā'nĭh	brŏ'ŏp-sŏmbot	thùng thư
hùupbat	ban brěsney	cạc pốt-tan
hŏhnggǎhn bpǎisā'nĭh	bpos	bưu điện
mānflang	dŏmlŏng	khoai tây
fěukhàt	hat	thực tập
gùng-ta'lěh	bŏnggóng	con tôm
kǎwng-kǔan	'ŏmnaoy	quà tặng
bpā'tǎhnāh-tĭhbǎwdĭh	brŏtian	tổng thống
lĭht-pâh	'ut	đè nén
ngāhm	l'ó-l'o	đẹp
lāh-kāh	dŏmlay	giá tiền
kǔubǎh	bǒbjit	tu sĩ
kuk	ptéah-guk	nhà giam
suan-tǔa	'ǎek jun	tư nhân
sân-nyāh	sŏnyaa	hứa
kwǎahng	kǎet	tính ly
haahngsǎh-tǎhla'na'	saatiarenak	công cộng

VOCABULARY

ENGLISH	BURMESE	THAI
pull, to	hswē-ngin-de	deuhng
puncture, the	leiyòbī	rūa
pure	sintje-de	bawri'sŭt
purple	kǎyān-yaun	sìh mùang
put, to	tā-de	sǎi
quantity, the	'ǎyei-'ǎ-dtwe'	jam nuan
queen, the	bayinmà	pra'rah-chi'nih
question, the	'ǎmēi	kam táhm
quick	myan-de	rehu
quiet	ngyein-the'-dte	ngìap
race (contest), the	bpyēibwe	kǎang-kan
radio, the	reidiyou	wit-ta'yu'
railway, the	yǎ-tā	tahng ròtfai
raincoat, the	mōuga-'īnji	sèua fón
raining, it is	mōu ywa-de	fón dtŏk
razor, the	thindōundā	mìht gohn
read, to	pa'-dte	'ǎhn
ready	'athin	pràwm
receive, to	le'kan-de	ràp
record (gramophone), the	da'bpyā	pǎan síang
red	ni-de	daang
register (letter), to	hma'bpoun-tin-de	long ta'bian
religion, the	badhayèi	sǎhsa'náh
remember, to	hma'mì-de	jam dài
repair, to	bpyin-de	sàwm
repeat, to	ta'bpyō-de	sàm
reply, to	zǎgā bpyan-de	dtǎwp
rest, to	nānei-de	pàk
restaurant, the	tǎmīnzain	rahn 'ah-háhn
result, the	'a-tjou	pón
rice (cooked), the	tǎmīn	kàhu
rich	chāndha-de	ruai
right (correct)	hman	tǔuk
right (hand)	nyabe'	kwáh
ring, the	le'su'	wáan
ripe	hmè-de	sŭk
river, the	myi'	màa-nàm
road, the	lān	ta'nón
roast	gkin-de	'ŏp
room, the	'ǎkān	hàwng
run, to	bpyēi-de	wìng
sad	wūn-nē-de	sàu sŏhk
safe	lounjoun-de	bplǎwt-pai
sailor, the	thà-mbodhǎ	ta'háhn reua
salt, the	hsā	gleua
same	'ǎ-dtudu	meuan

VOCABULARY

LAO	KAMPUCHEAN	VIETNAMESE
dĕung	dtíañ	dầy lên
dtĭhnlot dtâahk	kóng băek	cái lỗ
băwli'sŭt	bórisot	thuần túy
sĭh-muang	svaay	tím
'ăusaii	dak	để vào
jăhmnŭan	jumnúan	số lượng
pa'lăhsĭhnĭh	gsadtreyaanii	nữ hoàng
kăm-tăhm	sŏmnúa	câu hỏi
wăi	chap	nhanh
mit	sngat	yên lặng
găhn-kaahng-kăn	brŏnang	cuộc đua
wit-ta'nyu'	vidtyuk	ra-dô
tăhng-lotfăi	plŏv-redtih pleung	đường xe-lửa
sêuagănfŏn	'aav plíang	áo mưa
fŏn dtōk	pliang	trời đang mưa
mĭht-tăah	gambet-gao	đồ cạo râu
'ahn	meul	đọc
păwm-làau	rúat	sẵn sàng
lap	dtedtúal	nhận
paahnsĭang	taas jŏmríang	đĩa hát
sĭh-dăahng	grehóm	đỏ
lŏng-ta'bĭan	řĭkkemŏndē	bảo-đảm
sâtsă'năh	sahsnaa	tôn giáo
jeuh	jam	nhớ
sâwmsăahm	găe-gkon	sửa chữa
tŭan-kēuhn	dtveu lăangvit	lặp lại
dtâwp	chlăay	trả lời
yŭt-pak-pawm	sŏmraak	nghỉ
hăhn'ăhhăhn	pŏjeníataan	nhà hàng
pŏn	lóat-pŏl	kết quả
kâu	baay	cơm
hangmĭh	mían	giàu
têuhk	drŏv	đúng
tăhng-kŭamēuh	sdam	bên phải
wăahn	júañjían	cái nhẫn
sŭk	dtum	chín
maah-nàm	dtúanlē	sông
tă'nŏn	plŏv	con đường
bpĭhng	gvay	nướng
hâwng	bŏndtup	buồng
laahn	rúat	chạy
sâusôhk	brúay	buồn
bpâwt-păi	rúat-klúan	an-toàn
kŏnlaahn-hēua	góng níavía	thủy thủ
gĕua	'ŏmbel	muỗi
kēuhgăn	dŏdăel	tương tự

VOCABULARY

ENGLISH	BURMESE	THAI
sandals, the	hnya'păna'	rawng-tāhu tǎa'
sandwich, the	hsăn-dwi'	saan-wĭch
sauce, the	hsò	sàws
say, to	bpyō-de	pùut-wàh
school, the	tjăun	rohng-rian
science, the	thei'bpan	wĭt-ta'yahsǎht
scissors, the	gka'tjĕi	gan-grai
sea, the	bpinle	ta'leh
seat, the	tainzăya	tĭh nàng
second	dù-tìyà	tĭh sáwng
second (of time), the	se'gkàn	wĭ'nahtih
secretary, the	'ă-dtwĭn-yĕi-hmŭ	lehkáh-nŭ'gahn
see, to	myin-de	hėn
seems, (it)	tin-yà-de	duu mĕuan
seldom	-kē-	mài bŏi
sell, to	yăun-de	káhi
send (thing), to	bpòu-de	sŏng
separate	thījă	yàak
servant, the	'aseigan	kon chăi
service station, the	da'hsizain	sa'táhnih bawri'gahn
several	ka'myămyă	láhi
sew, to	chou'-dte	yėp
shallow	dtein-de	dtèuhn
shampoo, the	găun-hyoyei	chaampuu
shave, to	mou'hsei'yei'-dte	gohn
she	thu	káu
sheet, the	'ei'yă-kĭn	pàh bpuu tĭh nawn
shelter, the	kouzăya	tĭh-ròm
ship, the	thĭnbō	reua
shirt, the	hya'-'ĭnji	sèua chŭht
shoe, the	hyŭ-pana'	rawng-tāhu
shop, the	hsain	rāhn
short	dtou-de	sàn
show, to	bpyà-de	sǎ'dáang
shower, the	yeichōujin	'ahpnăm
side, the	pe'	kàhng
sign, to	le'hma'tōu-de	sen chèuh
silk, the	bpōu	mái
silver, the	ngwei	nguhn
since (time)	-gkadēgà	dtàng-dtǎa
sing, to	thăchĭn-hsou-de	rāwng-plehng
sit, to	tain-de	nàng
skirt, the	lounji	gra'bprohng
sky, the	gkăun-gin	fáh
sleep, to	'ei'-dte	lăp
slow	hnēi-de	chăh
small	nge-de	lēk

150

VOCABULARY

LAO	KAMPUCHEAN	VIETNAMESE
gûhpsăngdàhn	sbăekjeung sŏngrăek	giày săng đan
kâujih-nyatsâi	sŏngvĭj	bánh mì san-wich
nàmjaau	dtik jrawlúak	nước sốt
wàu	taa	nói
hŏhnghĩan	selaa	trường học
wit-ta'nyăhsâht	vĭjjiasăs	khoa-học
miht-dtăt	gŏndray	cái kéo
ta'lĕh	semut	biển
bawn-nang	gŏnlăeng 'ŏng-kuy	chỗ ngồi
tihsăwng	dtii-bpii	thứ hai
wi'năh-tĩh	viniadtii	giây
să'mĩan	smían	thư ký
hĕn	keuñ	nhìn
kàhi-găpwăh	dòt-jia	hình như
nòi-teua-tihsūt	dtaoy-gŏmraw	ít khi
kăhi	lúak	bán
song	pñăa	gửi
nyàahk'âwk	bŏm-băek	phân chia
kònsàii	néak bŏmrăa	người đầy tớ
bpàhm-nàmmăn	yian-taan	trạm xăng
lăhi	jrăan	nhiều
nyîpsaau	dĕ	may
dtèuhn	réak	nông cạn
yăhsă'pŏm	tnam gŏk sŏk	nước gội đầu
tăah-nûat	gao	cạo
làhu	góat	bà ấy
pâhbpŭubawn	gŏmraal-bpŭk	mảnh
bawnsòn	jumrawk	chỗ trú ẩn
gămbpan	gebpal	cái thuyền
sêua	'aav	áo sơ-mi
gŭhp	sbăek-jeung	giày
hàhn-kăhi-kăwng	haang	hiệu
sàn	kley	ngắn
'ău-hâiibuhng	bŏnghaañ	trình bày
'âhpnàm	ngŭt-dtŭk	cơn mưa ngắn
kâhng	kaang	bên
sĕnseuh	jos hatĕlekaa	ký tên
măii	sòt	lụa
ngŭhn	brak	bạc
dtàngdtaah	dtang-bpii . . .	từ khi
hàwng-pĕhng	jriang	hát
nang	'ŏng-kuy	ngồi
gă'bpohng	sŏm-put	cái váy
fàh	mĕk	bầu trời
năwn	dĕk	ngủ
sàh	yĩit	chậm
nòi	dtòt	bé

VOCABULARY

ENGLISH	BURMESE	THAI
smoke, to	‚hseilei'thau'-dte	sŭup
snow, the	hnin	hi'mā'
soap, the	hsa'bpya	sa'bŭu
socks, the	chei-'ei'	túng-tàu
soda water, the	souda	năm sohdah
soft	pyò-de	'ăwn
soldier, the	si'thā	ta'háhn
some	dtachòu	bahng
somebody	dtăyau'yau'	bahng kon
something	dta-kùgù	bahng sĭng
sometimes	dta-ka dtalei	bahng-tih
somewhere	dtaneiyaya	săk hăang nĕung
soon	màtjami	mài chăh
sorry	wūn-nē-de	sía jăi
soup, the	hìnjou	sūp
sour	chin-de	bprìau
south	dtaun	tĭt dtài
soy sauce, the	bpē-ngan-bpyayei	sih 'ăiu
space, the	neiya	tìh-wàhng
speak, to	bpyò-de	pùut
spectacles, the	mye'hman	wàan dtah
spoon, the	zūn	chăwn
sport, the	bpyēi-koun-bpyi'bpwē	gihlah
square (place), the	lēidàunsa'sa'	sĭh yàak
stairs, the	hleigā	bandai
stamp (postage), the	dăzei'gāun	sa'dtaamp
stand, to	ya'-dte	yeuhn
star, the	tje	dahu
start, to	sà-de	rùhm
station (railway), the	bu-dtāyoun	sa'táhnih
stay, to	nei-de	yŭu
steak, the	'ăthăgin	nĕua sa'dtēhk
steep	ma'sau'-dte	chan
steering, the	să-tiyarin	puang-mahlai-rŏt
stick, the	dou'	măi
still (adv.)	-thēi	yang
stockings, the	cheizu'hyei	túng tàu yau
stone, the	tjau'kē	hĭn
storey (floor), the	'a-ta'	chăn
straight on	hyèi-dtè-dè	dtrong
strap, the	tjŏubyă	kém-kăt
street, the	làn	ta'nón
streetcar (tram), the	da'ya-tā	rŏt rahng
string, the	tjōu	chèuak
strong	tàundìn-de	káang raang
student, the	tjăundhă	năk rian
study, to	sathin-de	rian

VOCABULARY

LAO	KAMPUCHEAN	VIETNAMESE
sûup-yǎh	júak	hút thuốc
hǐ'ma'	tlěak dtǐk-gók	tuyết
sǎ'buu	sabù	xà-bông
tǒng-tàusân	sraom-jeung	vớ
nàmsóhdǎh	dtǐk sòdaa	nước sô-đa
'awn	dtúan	mềm
ta'hǎhn	dtíahian	người lính
jǎknôi	. . . glah	mấy
kǒndǎii-kôn-neung	nenaa	người
'ǎndǎii'ǎn-neung	'vey	vật
bǎhng-teua	júan-gaal	thỉnh thoảng
bawndǎii-bawn-neung	'ǎe-naa	nơi
nǎiibawsàhnih	bǒndtet-dtiat	sớm
sǐajǎii	sdaay	xin lỗi
gǎahng	sup	súp
sôm	jù	chua
tit-dtàii	kaang-tbôhng	phía nam
nàmsih'ìu	dtǐk sii'iiv	xì dầu
bawnwahng	jǒnlǒh	không gian
bpâhk	niyíay	nói
waahndtǎh	věěn-taa	cặp kính
buang	slaap-bría	cái thìa
gǐ'lǎh	geylaa	thể thao
wóng-wian	búan jrung	vuông
maah-kândǎi	júandǎa	thang lầu
sǎ'dtǎahm	dtǎem	tem
yěuhn	chaw	đứng
dǎhu	pkaay	ngôi sao
dtàngdtòn	jap-pdǎam	bắt đầu
sǎ'tǎhnǐh	staanii-redtih-pleung	nhà ga
yuu	nǐu	ở lại
sihn bpǐhng	sat-kǒ	thịt bò chiên
sàn	jaot	dốc
pǔangmǎ'lai	jǒnggòt	tay lái
mǎi	gǒmnat cheu	cây gậy
nyǎng-yuu	nǐu-dtǎe . . .	yên lặng
tǒng-tàu-nyǎhu	sraom-jeung	vớ
hǐhn	tmó	cục đá
sàn	jóan	lầu
seuh	dròng	thẳng
sǎhi-hat	ksǎe-sbǎek	giây da
tǎ'nòn	plôv	con đường
lotlǎhng	rǒt-'akkiisenii	xe chuyên chở công cộng
sèuak	ksǎe	sợi dây
kǎahnghǎahng	klang	mạnh
naksèuksǎh	gòn-ses	học sinh
sěuksǎh	rian	học

VOCABULARY

ENGLISH	BURMESE	THAI
substance, the	'ǎ-hni'hyi-bpyi'sī	sáhn
suddenly	you'kǎnē	tandai
sugar, the	dhajā	nǎm dtahn
suitcase, the	'ǎwu'thi'dta	gra'bpáu
summit, the	dtaundei'	yáwt-sǔt
sun, the	nei	prä'ahtìt
sweet	chou-de	wǎhn
swim, to	yei gkǔ-de	wàhi nǎm
table, the	zabwē	dtò'
tailor, the	se'chou'thamā	chǎhng dtǎt sèua
take, to	yu-de	'au
tall	myin-de	sǔung
tap, the	bounbain-gāun	gāwk
tape (recording), the	dtei'kwei	muan tehp
tape recorder, the	dtei're-gkoda	krèuang ban-tèuhk síang
taste, to	myī-de	chim
tax, the	'ǎ-gkau'dtogun	pahsih
taxi, the	dte'si	tǎaksìh
tea (to drink), the	la-pe'yei	nǎm chah
teach, to	thintjā-pēi-de	sáwn
teacher, the	hsàya	kruu
telegram, the	thanjōuza	tohra'lèhk
telephone, the	dteli-pōun	tohra'sǎp
television, the	you'myinthanjäse'	tohra'pàhp
temperature, the	'ǎ-bpujein	kwahm rǎwn
temple, the	kǎlǎ-pǎyǎtjǎun	wǎt
than	-de'	gwǎh
that	hou	nàn
theatre, the	you'hyin-youn	rohng lǎ'kawn
their	thudòu	. . . káu
then (at that time)	houdōun-gà	wehlah nǎn
there	hou-hma	tìhnòhn
there is	hyi-de	mih
they	thudòu	káu
thick	tu-de	náh
thin	bpà-de	bahng
thing, the	hou-ha	sǐng
think, to	sei'tin-de	kìt
third	tà-tǎyà	tìh sáhm
thirsty	yei-nga'-dte	gra'háhi-nǎm
this	di	nìh
thread, the	chi	dàhi
through	dtǎ-hsìn	pǎhn
throw, to	bpyi'-dte	kwàhng
ticket, the	le'hma'	dtúa
ticket-office, the	le'hma'yāun	tìh-káhi-dtúa

154

VOCABULARY

LAO	KAMPUCHEAN	VIETNAMESE
pǎhsa'na'	saarejǐat	phần quan trong
tǎndǎiinàn	plíam nǒh	thinh linh
nàmdtǎhn	skó	đường
hǐhpdǔhn-tǎhng	hep	va li
nyàwt-kǎu	gǒm-pūl	cực điểm
dtǎh-wēn	préah 'aadtit	mặt trời
wǎhn	p'ǎem	ngọt
lōinàm	hǎel	bơi
dtǒ'	dtok	cái bàn
sahngdtǎt-keuang	néak gat dè	thợ may
'ǎu	yawk	lấy
sǔung	kpúas	cao
gǎwknàm	jǒmpúay dtǐk	máy nước
dtèhp	gsǎe 'at	băng nhạc
keuang-bǎn-teuksǐang	maasiin tót sǒmlēng	máy hát
sǐm	plúak	nếm
pǎhsǐh	dtak	thuế
lotdǒisǎn	dtaksii	tắc-xi
nàmsāh	dtǐk-dtǎe	nước chè
sǎwn	bǒngrían	dạy
nǎhi-kūu	grū	thày giáo
tohla'lèhk	dtūrelēk	bức điện-tín
keuang tohla'sǎp	dtūresap	điện thoại
tohla'tat	dtūredtúah	tivi
'ǔnhǎ'pūum	'aagaastiat	nhiệt độ
wat	vihia	đền thờ
gua	jǐang	hơn
nàn	nuh	ấy
hōhng-la'kāwn	rōng lkaon	nhà hát
... kǎujàu	... góat	của chúng nó
nǎiiwēhlǎhnàn	dteup	lúc đó
yuu hân	'ǎe-nuh	đó
mǐh	mían	có
kǎujàu	góat	chúng nó
nǎh	graas	dày
bǎhng	sdǎang	mỏng
keuang-kǎwng	rebǒs	vật
kit	gǐt	nghĩ ngợi
tihsǎhm	dtii-bey	thứ ba
yàhknàm	srēk-dtǐk	khát
nih	nih	này
mǎi-nyīp	jēh	sợi chỉ
dǒi-pahn	dtaam ...	xuyên qua
kwahng	jaol	thầy
pih	sǒmbot	vé
bawn-kǎhi-pih	gǒnlǎeng-lǒk-sǒmbot	phòng bán vé

ENGLISH	BURMESE	THAI
tie, the	lezì	nĕk-tai
time, the	'ăchein	wehlah
timetable, the	'ăcheinsàyin	dtahrahng wehlah
tin opener, the	bù-pwindan	tìh-bpŭht-grā'póng
tip (money), the	lă-pe'yeibòu	nguhn tip
tired	mò-de	nĕuai
to	-gou	téung
tobacco, the	hsĕilei'hsĕi	yah sŭup
today	di ganèi	wan-nìh
together	'ă-dtudu	dùai gan
toilet (men), the	'eindha	hàwng năm
toilet (women), the	'eindha	hàwng năm
toilet paper, the	nau'pĕise'gku	gra'dăht chamrā'
tomato, the	kàyănjindhi	ma'kĕua-tèht
tomb, the	thinjàin-gu	lúmfáng sŏp
tomorrow	ne'pyin-ga	prùng-nìh
tonight	di-nyà	keuhn-nìh
too (much)	. . . lŭn	màhk bpai
toothbrush, the	dhăbu'dtan	bpraang sĭh fan
toothpaste, the	thwădai'hsĕi	yah sĭh fan
touch, to	tì-de	jăp
tourist, the	kăyèdhe	năk tàwng tìu
towards	thòu	bpai-tahng
towel, the	mye'hnă-thou'bpăwa	pàh chĕt dtua
tower, the	hmyozin	háw-koi
town, the	myòu	meuang
town hall, the	myòudo-kănmà	sáhlah-nă'kawn-meuang
train, the	mìya-tà	rót fai
tram, the	da'ya-tà	rót rahng
translate, to	badha-bpyan-de	bplaa
travel, to	kàyìthwà-de	duhn tahng
tree, the	thi'bpin	dtònmái
trouble, the	dou'kà	kwahm lambăhk
trousers, the	băunbi-hyei	gahnggehng
true	hman-de	jing
try on, to	tjòuzà-de	lawng
turn, in	'ă-hlèjà	sŏng
twice	hnă-ka	sáwng krăng
typewriter, the	le'hnei'se'	krèuang pim dĭht
typist, the	le'hnei'se'săyèi	pa'năk ngahn pim dĭht
tyre, the	dtain-ya	yahng rót
ugly	'ăyou'hsòu-de	nàh glìat
umbrella, the	tì	ròm
under	-'au'hma	dtài
understand, to	nă-le-de	kàujai
unfortunately	gkanmă-gkăun-lòu	chòhk-mài-dih

VOCABULARY

LAO	KAMPUCHEAN	VIETNAMESE
gǎhla'wat	jóng	cà vạt
wěhlǎh	bpěl	giờ
dtǎhdtǎ'lǎhng-wěhlǎh	taaraang jǎek bpěl velia	thời khoá biểu
keuang-kǎi-gǎ'bpǎwng	brǒdtap bǎak gǒmbong	đồ mở hộp
ngǔhnlǎhng-wǎn	gǒmray-grau	tiền trà nước
meuai	'ǒs-gǒmlang	mệt
bpǎi	'ǎe	tới
yǎhsên	tnam	thuốc lá
mèuhnih	tngay	hôm nay
nǎmgǎn	jia-múay-knía	cùng nhau
hâwngnàm	bǒnggúan-bros	phòng rửa mặt
hâwngnàm	bǒnggúan-srey	phòng rửa mặt
jia 'a'nǎhmai	gredaas-bǒnggúan	giấy vệ-sinh
mâhk den	bpěng bpǒh	cà chua
kǔmfǎngsōp	pnôl-kmaot	cái mộ
mèuh'eun	tngay-s'ǎek	ngày mai
kèuhnnih	yup-nih	tối nay
pòht	bpěk	nhiều quá
bpǎahng-tǔu-kâau	jraas-dos-dmēñ	bàn chải đánh răng
yǎh-tǔu-kâau	tnam-dos-dmēñ	kem đánh răng
bǎhi	bpóal	sờ mó
nak-tawng-tiau	dtěssejó	du khách
hǎh	dǒmrǒng	về phía
pâhset-dtôh	gǒnsǎeng-jǔt-glúan	cái khăn
hǎw-kōi	bpóm	cái tháp
mēuang	grong	tỉnh-ly
sǎ'mōhsǎwn	saalaa-grong	toà đô sảnh
lotfǎi	redtih-pleung	xe lửa
lotlǎhng	dtram	xe điện
bpǎah	bók brǎe	dịch
dǔhn-tǎhng	dtveu dǒmnǎa	đi du lịch
dtònmài	dǎam-cheu	cái cây
kwǎhmdêuat-hàwn	turéak	sư rắc rối
sông-kǎh-nyǎhu	kao	quần dài
tàah	bpit braagǒt	thật
lǎwng	law	thử
bpian-pǐan	mdóng-menéak	đến phiên
sǎwng-tēua	bpii dóng	hai lần
jǎkdtǐh-pim	daktilō	máy đánh chữ
kǒndtǐhjǎk	néak-vay-daktilō	thư ký đánh máy
dtǐhnlot	gǒng	lốp xe
kǐhdǐat	'aagrǒk	xấu xí
kǎn-hom	chat	cây dù
yuulum	graom	ở dưới
kâujǎii	yóal	hiểu
sòhkbawdǐh	'akgosól	không may

VOCABULARY

ENGLISH	BURMESE	THAI
university, the	dte'gkathou tjäun	ma'háh wīt-ta'yahlai
until	dtain'aun	jon
upstairs	'a-bpoda'	kàhng bon
urgently	'ǎ-hlyin-'ǎmyan	rihp-rèhng
usually	thaman-'ǎ-pyin	dtahm tahma'dah
valley, the	dtaunjä	hǔp-kau
valuable	'ǎ-pōu tai'-dte	mih rahkah
veal, the	nwägǎlèithä	nēua lùuk wua
vegetables, the	hindhi-hin-ywe'	pǎk
very	thei'	màhk
view (outlook), the	'ǎmyin	wiu
village, the	ywa	mǔubàhn
visit, to	thwä le-de	yiam
voyage, the	yeijäun-kǎyī	gahnduhn-tahng
wait for, to	sàun-de	koi
waiter, the	zabwēdòu	kon duhn dtô'
walk, to	län-hyau'-dte	duhn
wall (of room), the	nan-yan	fáh pa'náng
wall (garden, etc.), the	sīyōu	gampaang
want, to	lou-de	dtàwng gahn
war, the	si'	sóng-krahm
wash, to	hsēi-de	láhng
washbasin, the	zàloun	'ǎhng-láhng
watch, the	nayi	nahli'gah kàw meuh
watch, to	sàun-de	duu
water, the	yei	nām
we	tjanodòu/tjamàdòu	rau
weather, the	yadhi-'ù-dtù	'ahgǎht
week, the	ye'tha'dtàba'	'ah-tīt
weight, the	'ǎlēijein	nām nǎk
well (adv.)	gkäun-gäun	gêhng
well (health)	nei gkäun	sa'bahi-dih
west	'anau'	tīt dta'wan dtǒk
wet	sou-de	bpīak
wet season, the	mōudwin	rǔh'duu fón
wharf, the	hsei'kandǎdä	tàh
what?	ba-lē?	'a'rai?
wheel, the	bēin	läw
when?	bedò-lē?	mèua rǎi?
where (is it)?	be-hma-lē?	tìh nái?
where (to)?	begou-lē?	bpai nái?
which?	be- . . . -lē?	nái?
white	pyu-de	káu
who?	badhu-lē?	krai?
whose?	badhù . . . -lē?	. . . káwng krai?
why?	ba pyi'loù-le?	tam mai?
wide	tje-de	gwàhng

VOCABULARY

LAO	KAMPUCHEAN	VIETNAMESE
ma'hăhwit-ta'nyăhlăi	mehaa-vittyialay	đại học
jŏn-gua	dtóal-dtăe	đến khi
yuu-tŭhng	jóan kaang leu	trên lầu
yahnghihpduan	yaang bróñap	một cách khẩn cấp
dtăhm-kŭhi	jrăan-dtăe	thường thường
hawmpŭu	jrók pnum	thung lũng
mĭh-kah	mian dŏmlay	quí giá
sihn-ngŭanòi	sat-gŏn-gò	thịt bê
păk	bŏnlăe	rau
lăhi	. . . nas	rất
tĭhu-tat	dtèspíap	cành
bàhn	pŭm	làng
yăhm	dtĭu lĕng	thăm
găhndŭhn-tăhng	dŏmnăa	cuộc hành trình
kŏi-tăh	jam	chở
kŏnhăpsàinai-hàhn'ăhhăhn	baoy	người bồi
nyahng	dăa	đi bộ
făh	júañjèang	tưởng
găm-păahng	rawbóng	tường
dtàwnggăhn	jŏng	muốn
sûhksŏng-kăhm	sŏnggriam	chiến tranh
lahng	liang	rửa
'ahngsuainâh	păang	cái chậu
mŏhngsaii-kăahn	nialĕgaa	đồng hồ
buhng	bpinit	nhìn
nàm	dtĭk	nước
pùak hău	yeung	chúng tôi
'ăhgàht	tiat 'agaah	thời tiết
'ăh-tit	'aadtĭt	tuần lễ
nàmnak	dtumngúan	trọng lượng
dĭh	l'ó	tốt
kăahnghăahngdĭh	sok-sapbaay	tốt
tit-dtăhwĕndtŏk	kaang-lĭt	phía tây
bpĭak	dtedtĭk	ướt
la'dŭu-fon	rŏdŏv-bliang	mùa mưa
tahhĕua	păe	bãi đậu cho thuyền
nyăng?	'vey?	cái gì?
gŏng	gŏng	bánh xe
nyăhmdăii?	gaal-naa?	bao giờ?
bawndăii?	nĭu 'ăe-naa?	đâu?
tăhng-bawndăii?	dtĭu 'ăe-naa?	đâu?
'ăndăii?	naa múay?	cái nào?
kăhu	só	trắng
pûudăii?	nenaa?	ai?
. . . kăwng păi?	. . . nenaa?	. . . của ai?
bpĕn-nyăng?	hăet 'vey?	tại sao?
gùang	dtuliay	rộng

VOCABULARY

ENGLISH	BURMESE	THAI
wild	tjän-de	bpåh
win, to	nain-de	cha'nä'
wind, the	lei	lom
window, the	byădinbau'	nàh-dtăng
wine, the	'äye'chou	làu 'a'ngun
wise	bpà-nya hyì-de	cha'lăt
with	-nè	găp
without	mă-hsìbē	bpråhtsa'jähk
woman, the	mēinmà	pùu-yíng
wonder, to	'àn-ō-de	bplăak-jai
wonderful	'àn-ōzăya-gkăun-de	bplăak bpra'låht
wood (timber), the	thi'thă	măi
wool, the	thōumwēi	kón găa'
word, the	zăgălóun	kam
work, the	'ălou'	ngahn
workman, the	'ălou'thămă	kon ngahn
world, the	găba	lôhk
worse	bpou-hsōu-de	lehu gwăh
worst	'ă-hsōuzōun	lehu tihsŭt
worth, to be	tai'dtan-de	mih-kàh
write, to	yēi-de	kían
wrong	hmă-de	pĭt
year, the	hni'	bpih
yellow	wa-de	lêuang
yesterday	manèigà	mèua wan
you	kamyă/hyin	kun
young	nge-de	'ăwn
your	kamyà/hyin	. . . kun

VOCABULARY

LAO	KAMPUCHEAN	VIETNAMESE
bpah	gaat	mạn dã
pàah	chnéah	thắng
lóm	kyŏl	gió
bpawng'ìam	bŏng'úat	cửa sổ
làuwāahng	sraa	rượu vang
sā'làht	jĕh git	khôn ngoan
găp	jía-múay-nĭng	vời
bpăhsā'jâhk	'et mían	không có
pùu-nyīng	srey	người đàn bà
sŏngsăi	kĭt	thắc mắc
wi'sêht	brósaa	tuyệt diệu
mài	cheu	gỗ
kŏnsăt	rŏm sat	len
kwăhm	bpíak	chữ
wiak	gĕt-gaà	công việc
kŏn-ngāhn	néak-tveu-gaa	thợ
lòhk	bpi-pup lŏk	thế giới
kĭhhàhi-gwahgau	'aagrŏk chiang	tệ hơn
kĭhhàhi-tihsūt	'aagrŏk nas	tệ nhất
mīh kah	mían dtŏmlay	đáng giá
kĭan	sesē	viết
pit	kos	sai
bpīh	chnam	năm
sĭhlĕuang	lĭang	vàng
mèuhwāhn-nìh	msel-mẽñ	hôm qua
jàu	néak	ông/bà
num	gmèng	trẻ
. . . jàu	. . . néak	. . . của ông/bà

PART III

**MANDARIN
CANTONESE
HOKKIEN
JAPANESE
KOREAN**

MANDARIN

Mandarin is the national language of China, spoken as a first language by two-thirds of native Chinese (easily more people than for any other language); a language of communication throughout China, and gaining ground among Chinese abroad.

It is written in the traditional characters, with some modern simplifications; but there is a long-term plan to adopt the roman alphabet. We use the official romanisation known as Pinyin.

PRONUNCIATION Consonants:

B, D, G are very light and "unvoiced," like *p, t, k,* except that they do not have the rush of air that follows these consonants in English.

ZH, Z are like very light and unvoiced *j* and *dz* with the lips pushed forward.

P, T, K, CH and C (which is like *ts*) are all more explosive than in English.

S is always *ss,* never *z.*

J, Q, X have the special sounds of *dz, ts* and *hs* (somewhere between *s* and *sh*) pronounced in the roof of the mouth, before French-style *i* or *u* vowels (lips pursed).

R is nearly a vowel sound, the best prescription for which is to make a *zh* sound (middle of "pleasure") in the back of the mouth.

Vowels:

A, I, O, U are normally *ah, ee, aw, oo.*

I and U following J, Q, X or Y are like French *i* and *u* (lips pursed).

I has the special sound of *er* (without the *r*) when it stands alone after Z, C, S, ZH, CH or SH.

Ü is French *u.*

E is like the neutral *e* in "the" before a consonant, for example, in "the man."

Words divide into well-defined syllables each of which ends in a vowel, or N, or NG. The R occasionally found at the end of a word is a relic of an extra syllable and is pronounced as a retroflex, that is, with the tongue curled back. (It also occurs in the word *èr,* "two.")

A syllable may have any of four tones:

1. high and level
2. rising from medium to high
3. a slight fall at a low pitch, followed by a slow rise
4. sharply falling from high to low

These are pictured by accent-marks over the vowels. Tones affect meaning: *shī, shí, shǐ* and *shì* are different words (exemplifying the four tones in order).

Only key syllables get full tonal value; minor syllables are in so-called "neutral tone" (here unmarked).

When two syllables which would normally have third tone come together in a phrase, the first is pronounced with a rise like second tone (and is here so marked).

Pronunciation guides uniform with those in the phrases are inserted in the remainder of these notes. Capitals indicate high pitch, and question and exclamation marks indicate rises and falls.

NOUNS are invariable and have no distinction of singular and plural: *rén* [R'N?], "person" or "persons."

There are no articles "a" or "the," but *zhèige* [TJAY!g'], "this," and *nèige*

[NAY!g'], "that," may be used if needed: *zhèige rén* [TJAY!g r'n?], "this person"; *nèige rén* [NAY!g r'n?], "that person."

Similarly *yīge* [YEEg'], "one," for "a, an." (The word *ge* in these formulations is a classifier, and other classifiers may replace it: see below.)

The word *xiē* [SYEH], "some," can replace *ge* to give effective plurals: *zhèixie rén* [TJAY!syeh R'N?], "these people." "Some" on its own is *yīxie: yīxie háizi* [YEEsyeh HIGH?dz], "some children."

For possessive, add *de*: *nèige rén de bǐ* [NAY!g R'N?d bee?], "that person's pen."

PRONOUNS are as follows:

wǒ [waw?], "I, me"	*wǒmen* [wawMN], "we, us"
nǐ [nee?], "you" (singular)	*nǐmen* [neeMN], "you" (plural)
tā [TAH], "he, him, she, her, it"	*tāmen* [TAHmn], "they, them"

For possessives, add *de* as for nouns: *wǒde* [wawD'], "my"; *wǒmende* [wawMNd'], "our"; and similarly.

ADJECTIVES precede the noun they qualify: *dà* [DAH!], "big," *dà fēijī* [DAH! FAYJEE], "big plane."

As predicate an adjective can be treated directly as a verb and needs no verb "is" or "are"; but *hěn*, "very," is used more than in English: *Nèige fēijī hěn dà* [NAY!g FAYJEE h'n DAH!], "That plane is big."

For a comparative, put *gèng* before the adjective: *gèng dà* [G'NG DAH!], "bigger." For "than," use *bǐ*, "compares with," placing the clause before the adjective, and omit *gèng*: *Nǐ bǐ tā dà* [NEE? bee? TAH DAH!], "You are bigger than he is."

For a superlative, put *zuì* before the adjective and *de* after it: *zuì dà de rén* [DZWAY! DAH!d r'n?], "the biggest man."

Note the use of *de* after almost any word or phrase to make an adjective: *huì Yīngwén*, "knows English," *huì Yīngwén de rén* [HWAY! YINGw'n?d R'N?], "person who knows English."

VERBS The verb *shì* [SHER!], "is" or "are," may be used between nouns or pronouns or before adjectives, but is usually omitted except to give emphasis.

In indicating location, "is at" or "are at" is *zài* [DZIGH!]: *Tāmen zài wūzi* [TAHmn DZIGH! WOOdz'], "They are in the room."

For "There is" or "There are," use *yǒu* [yoh?], which also means "have": *Yǒu wūzi* [yoh? WOOdz'], "There is a room"; *Wó yǒu wūzi* [WAW? yoh? WOOdz'], "I have a room."

It is common for a sentence to have a second verb that fills out or supplements the first. For example, *Nèige nǚren názhe yīge dàizi* [NAY!g nü-r'n? NAH?tj YEEg DIGH!dz'], "That woman takes a bag," can be followed by *qù mǎi dōngxi* [TSYÜ! migh? DTAWNGsee], "goes (to) buy things," to mean "The woman takes a bag and goes shopping."

The second verb may have the force of a preposition: *zài* for "in" or "at" as in *Yǒu rén zài wūzi* [yoh R'N? DZIGH! WOOdz'], "There is someone in the room." Similarly *qù* [TSYÜ!], "go" and *lái* [LIGH?], "come," can translate "to" in the case of motion away from or towards the speaker respectively; and *gěi* [gay?], "give," can translate "to" or "for" before a noun or pronoun indicating a person.

Tense is not often indicated, but completed action can be indicated by attaching-*le* to the verb: *Tā láile* [TAH LIGH?le], "He has come." (But *le* at the end of a sentence has the slightly different sense of making a comment on a new situation: *Xiàyǔ le* [SYAH!yü le], "It's raining!")

To indicate a continuing state, put *zài* before the verb: *Tā zài kàn shū* [TAH DZIGH! KAHN! SHOO], "He is reading a book."

For "will" in the sense of "intend to," use *yào*: *Wǒ yào qù lǚguǎn* [waw? YOW! tsyü! LÜ?gwahn?], "I shall go to the hotel."

To form a negative, generally prefix *bù*, "not," to the verb or adjective; note *búshi* [BOOsher], "is not, are not" between nouns. The alternative word *méi* [MAY?] is used before the verb *yǒu* to form *méiyǒu* [MAY?yoh?], "There is not," "has not"; and this is also used in the same way as in English for the negative of a past tense: *Tā méiyǒu lái* [TAH MAY?yoh? LIGH?], "He has not come."

QUESTIONS There are two equally common ways of forming yes/no questions: (1) add *ma* to the corresponding statement, or (2) repeat the verb in the negative, either in the middle or at the end of the sentence. Hence for "Is there a car?," say (1) *Yǒu chē ma?* [yoh CHEHma], or (2) *Yǒu chē méiyǒu?* [yoh CHEH MAY?yoh?]. Similarly *Nèige fēijī dà ma?* [NAY!g FAYJEE DAH!ma] or *Nèige fēijī shì-bu-shi dà de?* [NAY!g FAYJEE SHER!bsher DAH!d'], "Is the plane a big one?"

Answer a yes/no question by repeating the verb, with or without a negative word: hence often *Shì* [SHER!], "Yes (it is)"; *Búshi* [BOOsher], "No (it is not)."

Questions using words such as *shuí* [SHWAY?], "who?," have the same word order as corresponding statements: *Tā shi shuí?* [TAHsher SHWAY?], "Who is he (she)?"

IMPERATIVES For an imperative, use the simple verb; it may be preceded by *Qǐng* [TSYING?], "Please," and perhaps also by the pronoun *nǐ* or *nǐmen*, and may have *ba* at the end of the sentence for emphasis (but this is also rather abrupt).

"Don't" is *Bùyao* [BOO!yow], or, for short, *Bié* [BYEH?]: *Bié qù* [BYEH? TSYÜ!], "Don't go."

For "Let's," use the simple verb, or prefix the pronoun *Wǒmen*, or again add *ba* at the end of the sentence, or both.

NUMERALS In indicating numbers of objects the order is numeral-classifier-noun, where the classifier is a word characteristic of the kind of thing being counted: *jiàn* [TSHYEN!] for houses and rooms, *liàng* [LYAHNG!] for vehicles, and so forth: *sān jiàn wūzi* [SAHN TSHYEN! WOOdz'], "three rooms"; *sì liàng chē* [SER! LYAHNG! CHEH], "four cars."

The word *ge*, besides being the normal classifier for people, may be used when in doubt for almost any kind of object. A respectful classifier for people is *wèi* [WAY!].

Classifiers are not needed in telling the time, or with money.

Of the alternative forms for "two," *liǎng* is preferred when used alone, *èr* when in combination with other numerals.

CURRENCY 1 *kuài* (or *yuán*) = 10 *máo* = 100 *fēn*.

FORMS OF ADDRESS In China the official form of address for all purposes is . *tóngzhì* [TAWNG?tjer!], "comrade," but older forms are still in use, particularly to foreigners: *xiānshēng* [SYENSH'NG], "Mr"; *tàitai* [TIGH!tigh], "Mrs"; *xiáojiĕ* [SYOW?jyeh?], "Miss" — all used either alone or following the family name (first name) or full name, or a description of occupation.

KIN TERMS often signify degrees of intimacy or respect, but the most usual are:

fùqin [FOO!tsyin], or more familiarly *bàba* [BAH!ba], "father"
mŭqin [mooTSYIN], or *māma* [MAHma], "mother"
gēge [GHEHg'] and *jiĕjie* [tshyeh?tshy'], "older brother, sister"
dìdi [DEE!dee] and *mèimei* [MAY!may], "younger brother, sister"
érzi [AHRR?dz'] and *nŭer* [nüAHRR], "son" and "daughter"
zhāngfu [TJAHNGfoo] and *tàitai* [TIGH!tigh], "husband" and "wife"

NAME OF LANGUAGE

China is *Zhōngguó* [TJAWNG-GWAW?]. The Chinese language generally is *zhōngwén* [TJAWNG-W'N?], and Mandarin is called the "national language," *guóyŭ* [GWAW?yü?].

CANTONESE

After Mandarin, Cantonese is the most important Chinese dialect. It is the language of Guangdong province, Hong Kong and Macau, and of a majority of Chinese abroad.

It shares a written form (in Chinese characters) with Mandarin and other dialects of Chinese. This book adopts Yale romanisation.

PRONUNCIATION Vowels:

A, E, I, O, U are like *ah, eh, ee, aw, oo*.
AA is the same as A, but longer.
"Short diphthongs" AI, AU, EI, OU, OI are approximately as English *igh, ow, eigh, owe, oy*.
AAI, AAU and UI are more clearly compound; *ah-ee, ah-oo, oo-ee*.
U before N and T becomes like French *u* (lips pursed).
EU is like French *eu* (English *er* with lips pursed), and also occurs in the diphthong EUI (*er-ee*).

Consonants are as in English, except that

B, D, G, J are unvoiced, like *p, t, k, ch*, but without any puff of air following.
NG is as in "singer" (no *g* sound).
P, T, K at the end of a syllable are pronounced with a closing of the air stream without re-opening.
H after a vowel is not pronounced, but indicates that the vowel has a low tone; similarly in the words *m̀h* and *ńgh*, in which M and NG are in effect vowels.

A syllable may have any of seven tones:

"high, level," "high rising" and "high falling" tones are indicated by marks ˉ, ´, ˋ over the vowel;
"mid, level" tone is unmarked;
"low rising" and "low falling" tones are also marked ´, ˋ, but H is written after the vowel;
"low, level" is indicated by H after an unmarked vowel.

"High, level" and "high falling" tones are rather alike.

Tones affect meaning: *sàu, sáu, sau* and *sàuh* are different words. In rapid speech only key syllables get full tonal value.

NOUNS are invariant and have no separate plural: *nàahmyán*, "man" or "men."

No definite or indefinite article is needed, but *dī*, "some, several," is often used to mean "the" in the plural: *dī nàahmyán*, "some men" or "the men."

Demonstratives *nī-go*, "this," and *gó-go*, "that," may be used either alone or before nouns. (The word *go* that occurs as the second half of each of these forms is a classifier, and may sometimes be replaced by other classifiers: see below.) The combinations *nī-dī* and *gó-dī* mean "these" and "those."

For an indefinite singular "a" or "an," use *yāt-go*, "one" (where *go* is again a classifier).

Form a possessive by placing possessor first, followed by *ge*: *gó-go nàahmyán ge ngūk*, "that man's house."

Prepositions indicating location generally follow the noun: *yahpbihn*, "inside," *ngūk yahpbihn*, "in the house."

PRONOUNS are as follows:

ngóh, "I, me" *ngóhdeih,* "we, us"
néih, "you" (singular) *néihdeih,* "you" (plural)
kéuih, "he, him, she, her" *kéuihdeih,* "they, them"

For "it," use the words for "this" or "that," or omit altogether.

Form possessives with *ge* as for nouns: *ngóh ge ngŭk,* "my house"; *kéuihdeih ge ngŭk,* "their house."

ADJECTIVES precede the noun they qualify, and also often take *ge* in the same way as a possessive: *daaih,* "big," *daaih nàahmyán* or *daaih ge nàahmyán,* "big man."

As predicate an adjective can be treated directly as a verb and takes no verb "is" or "are": *Gó-go nàahmyán daaih,* "The man is big."

For a comparative, add *gwo* to the adjective. "Than" needs no translation: *Kéuih daaih-gwo ngóh,* "He is bigger than I am."

For a superlative, use *jeui,* "the most," before the adjective: *jeui daaih,* "the biggest," *jeui daaih ge nàahmyán,* "the biggest man."

VERBS The verb "is" or "are" between nouns or pronouns is *haih: Nī-go néuihyán haih yīsāng,* "This woman is a doctor." In indicating location it is *hái: Gó-go nàahmyán hái ngŭk yahpbihn,* "The man is in the house."

"There is" or "There are" is *Yáuh,* and *hái* may also serve as a preposition: *Yáuh nàahmyán hái ngŭk yahpbihn,* "There is a man in the house" (or "There are men in the houses," etc.).

In the case of transitive verbs, the order is subject-verb-object as in English, but compound verbs are common in which the second component may be separated and serve as above as a preposition. For example, *Gó-go nàahmyán nìng syù,* "The man carries the book," may be followed by *heui poutáu,* "goes (to) the shop," to mean "The man takes the book to the shop."

Similarly *lèih,* "come," can translate "to" in the case of motion towards the speaker; and *béi,* "give," followed by a noun or pronoun indicating a person, can translate "to" or "for." For "from" use *hái.*

Tense is not often indicated, but a past tense can be indicated by attaching *-ge* to the verb; a perfect tense (indicating completed action) by attaching *-jó;* and a present continuous by attaching *-gán: lèih-ge,* "came"; *lèih-jó,* "has come"; *lèih-gán,* "is (in the process of) coming." For future, use the adverbial phrase *jahnlèih* before the verb.

To form a negative, prefix *m̀h-,* "not," to the verb: *m̀h-haih,* "is not." The verb *yáuh,* "have, there is," has the separate negative *móuh,* "have not, there is not"; and this is also used to form a past tense negative, "did not": *Kéuih móuh lèih,* "He did not come."

QUESTIONS A yes/no question can be formed by adding *ma* to the corresponding statement: *Néih haih hohksāang,* "You are a student," *Néih haih hohksāang ma?,* "Are you a student?" Alternatively, express the verb in both affirmative and negative: *Néih haih m̀h-haih hohksāang?,* "You are/are not a student?"

Answer a question by repeating the verb; hence in the above case *Haih* for "Yes," *M̀h-haih* for "No."

In the case of questions containing interrogative words such as *mātyéh,* "what?," the word order is the same as for statements: *Néih hohk mātyéh?,* "What do you study?"

IMPERATIVES For an imperative, use the simple verb; but *Néih*, "You," or its plural *Néihdeih*, often precedes the verb for emphasis.

For "Don't," put *Mh-hóu*, "It is not good to," before the verb; or, more directly, *Meih: Meih choh*, "Don't sit down."

For "Let's," simply use *Ngóhdeih*, "We"; or say *Ngóhdeih jeui hóu* . . . , "We had better . . ."

NUMERALS In expressing numbers of objects the order is numeral-classifier-noun, where the classifier is a word characteristic of the kind of object counted; for example, *léuhng-go nàahmyán*, "two men," where *-go* is the classifier for persons.

A "polite" classifier for persons is *-wái*. In the case of buildings or rooms, use *-gàan*, for vehicles *-ga*, etc: *saam-gàan poutáu*, "three shops"; *sei-ga fēigèi*, "four planes." But when in doubt, use *-go*, which is of wide application.

Classifiers are also used, as noted above, following singular demonstratives *nī*, "this," and *gó*, "that."

No classifier is needed when telling the time, or with money.

The form *léuhng* for "two" is used in specifying two objects, the form *yih* in counting or calling numbers figure by figure.

CURRENCY in Hong Kong: 1 *mān* (HK dollar) = 10 *hòuhjí* = 100 *sīn*.

FORMS OF ADDRESS In China the official term of address for all purposes is *tùhngji*, "comrade," alone or following the surname (first name). Elsewhere *sīnsàang* is used for "sir" or "Mr" (and also means "teacher"), *taaitáai* for "madam" or "Mrs," *síujé* for "Miss"; all these are used alone or following the surname, or a description of occupation.

KIN TERMS occur in various levels of formality and respect, but the most serviceable forms are:

fuhchàn or colloquially *bàhbā*, "father"
móuhchàn or *màhmā*, "mother"
    (but for special respect the addressee's father and mother will be referred to as
    lihngjyún and *lihngtóng*)
gohgō and *gājē*, "older brother, sister"
sailóu and *múi*, "younger brother, sister"
saimānjái and *néui*, "son" and "daughter"
    (or respectfully of addressee's son *lihnglóng*)
sīnsàang, "husband"; *lóuhpòu* or *taaitáai*, "wife"

NAME OF LANGUAGE
Cantonese is called *Gwóngjàuwá*. The general word for the Chinese language is *Jùngwá* or (for the written language) *Jùngmàhn*.

HOKKIEN

This important Chinese dialect has fifty million speakers in Fujian province in and around the port of Xiamen (Amoy), is widely spoken in Taiwan, and is the major language of Chinese people in Singapore and Penang.

It is more a spoken than a written language; those Hokkien speakers who know Chinese characters would usually read them in Mandarin. This book uses its own romanisation of spoken Hokkien.

PRONUNCIATION There are two ranges of vowel sounds, plain and nasal:

The plain vowels A, E, I, O, U are like *ah, eh, ee, aw, oo.*

Nasal vowels AÑ, EÑ, IÑ, OÑ, UÑ are like the plain ones pronounced with part of the air escaping through the nose. (Ñ is not separately pronounced.)

After the letters M, N, NG the vowel is also nasal, although not specially marked.

Diphthongs IA, AU, AI, . . . are blends of their component vowels: *ee-ah,* etc.

When Ñ follows, it indicates nasalisation of the whole.

M and NG sometimes occur, in effect, as vowels. A word such as *nng* is pronounced as N followed by NG.

Consonants are mainly as in English, but:

BP, GK are unvoiced, like P and K except that they do not have any following rush of air.

D is always unvoiced (similarly like T).

P, K, T are more explosive than in English.

At the end of a syllable, P, K, T and the glottal stop ' (as in the Cockney pronunciation of "bottle" as "bo'l") represent a closing of the air stream without re-opening.

A syllable may have any of five tones:

"rising," "falling" and "high, level" tones are indicated by ´, `, ¯ over the vowel; "mid, level" is unmarked;

"low, level" is indicated by writing H after the vowel or vowel combination.

The so-called "neutral tone" that occurs in unstressed syllables is not here distinguished from "mid, level."

Tones affect meaning: *tsâi, tsài, tsai* and *tsaih* are different words.

Systematic changes of tone take place in syllables preceding others in a compound word or phrase. In phrases we show tones as actually pronounced, hence sometimes differently from those of single words in the vocabulary. Where a word is shown with dots after it, for example " 'uh . . . ," this means that the tone shown is as used in combination with a following word. The tones unaffected by following syllables are those of the final syllable of a noun or pronoun subject, of an emphasised phrase, of a clause, or of a sentence (excluding final particles).

NOUNS are invariant and have no separate plurals: *láng,* "person" or "persons." When a plural must be indicated, precede the noun with *tsià' 'e* . . . , "these," or *hià' 'e* . . . , "those," or *'uh 'e* . . . , "some."

There is no article "a" or "the," but in the singular *tsît 'e* . . . , "this," or *hît 'e* . . . , "that," or *tsiht 'e* . . . (note that the tone is different from that of *tsît 'e* . . .), "one," may be used: *tsît 'e láng,* "this person"; *hît 'e dabpoláng,* "that man"; *tsiht 'e tsabōláng,* "a woman."

For possession, place the possessor first, followed by *'e* . . .: *hît 'e lang 'e chuh,* "that person's house." (But *'e* . . . is sometimes omitted.)

PRONOUNS are like nouns but have separate plural forms:

guà, "I, me"

lì, "you" (singular)
'ĭ, "he, him, she, her, it" (people and animals)

làn, "we, us, including you"
gùn, "we, us, not you"
lìn, "you" (plural)
'ĭn, "they, them" (people and animals)

There is no third person pronoun for inanimate objects and it is necessary to say *tsĭt 'e mĭ'*, "this thing," or *tsià' 'e mĭ'*, "these things."

Possession is the same as for nouns: *'in 'e chuh*, "their house."

ADJECTIVES precede the noun, but adjectives or phrases of more than one syllable must be accompanied by *'e* . . .: *duah láu*, "big building," but *tsin duah 'e láu*, "very big building."

As predicate an adjective can be treated directly as a verb and takes no verb "is" or "are": *Tsĭt 'e láu tsin dua*, "The building is very big."

For a comparative, precede the adjective with *kà'* . . . , "more": *kà' dua*, "bigger." For "than" use *bpĭ* . . . , "compares with," inserting the clause before the adjectival expression: *Tsĭt 'e láng bpĭ guà kà' dua*, "This person is bigger than I am."

For a superlative, put *deh'ĭt* . . . , "most," before the adjective: *deh'ĭt duah 'e dabpoláng*, "the biggest man."

VERBS The verb "is" or "are" between nouns or pronouns is *sih* . . . : *Tsĭt 'e tsabōláng sih 'i-siĕng*, "The woman is a doctor."

"There is" or "There are" is *'Uh* . . . : *'Uh 'i-siĕng*, "There is a doctor" (or "There are doctors"). The location words *Tsiā*, "Here," and *Hiā*, "Over there," can be treated as if they were subjects of *sih* . . . or *'uh* . . . : *Tsiā sih cheh'*, "Here is the book."

Otherwise "is at" or "is in" is *sih dih* . . . *Tsià' 'e láng sih dih chiā*, "The people are in the car." Use *dih* . . . also, in effect, as a preposition: *'Uh lang dih chuh*, "There is someone in the house" (or "There are people in the houses," etc.).

Normal order is subject-verb-object as in English, but compound verbs are common in which the second component may be separated and serve (like *dih* . . . above) as a preposition. For example, *Hĭt 'e láng teh' cheh'*, "The person takes the book," may be followed by *laih diahn*, "comes to the shop," to mean "The person brings the book to the shop." Similarly *kĭ* . . . , "go," can translate "to" in the case of motion away from the speaker; and *hoh* . . . , "give (to)," can translate "for" or "on behalf of."

Note the use of *'uh* . . . before a main verb for emphasis: *'uh kì* "does go."

Verbs have no tenses, but the future is usually indicated by one of the auxiliaries *'ueh* . . . , "may, will probably," or *bè* . . . , "intend to, is going to" (also "would like to").

For continuing action (past, present or future) use the auxiliary *dè'* . . . : *dè' tsiā'*, "is eating," "was eating," etc.

To indicate completion of an action, attach *liàu*: *tsiah' liàu*, "finish eating," "has finished eating," etc. The particle *la* at the end of a sentence indicates a completed action, or a changed or new situation: *'Ĭ kì la*, "He has gone!"

To form a negative, put *'mh* . . . , "not," before the verb: *'mh sih* . . . , "is not." The verb *'uh* . . . , in its several meanings as "have," "there is" and as emphasiser has the separate negative *bou* . . . , "have not," "there is not," or emphatic negative. (In the last case it replaces *'mh* . . .) The negative of the auxiliary *bè'* . . . , "intend to," is *'m* . . . , "not intend to" (different only in tone from *'mh* . . . , "not").

QUESTIONS A yes/no question is formed by repeating the verb in the negative at the end of the sentence, with or without *'ā . . .*, "or": *Lì sih hahksiēng, 'ā 'mh si?*, or *Lì sih hahksiēng, 'mh si?*, "Are you a student?" A common form is to use the emphatic *'uh . . .* as auxiliary verb, and its negative *bou*, sometimes very perfunctory and unaccented, at the end: *'Ī 'uh kì diahn bou?*, "Did he go to the shop?"

Answer a question by repeating the verb; hence often *'U*, "Yes," or *Bóu*, "No." *'Ā be*, "Not yet," is commonly used for "No" where relevant.

In the case of questions containing interrogative words such as *sīmmī'*, "what?," the word order is the same as for statements: *Lì 'ou' sīmmī'?*, "What do you study?"

IMPERATIVES For an imperative, use the simple verb; but *Lì*, "You," or plural *Lìn*, often precedes it for emphasis.

For "Don't," use *'Mh tang . . .* ("Must not").

For "Let's," use the inclusive pronoun *Làn*, or, in an invitation, *Làn lai . . . .*

NUMERALS In expressing numbers of objects the order is numeral-classifier-noun, where the classifier is a word characteristic of the kind of object counted: *nngh 'uih láng*, "two people," where *'uih . . .* is the "polite" classifier for persons.

The same style may be used with singular demonstratives and various measure-words: *tsīt 'uih láng*, "this person" (polite). (Note that the *'e . . .* that is used after an ordinary adjective is not a classifier and cannot be replaced in this way.)

For buildings and rooms, use the classifier *gkieng . . .*, for vehicles, *diēng . . .*: *sañ gkieng diahn*, "three shops"; *sì diēng huigkī*, "four planes." A classifier of very general application is *'e . . .*, which should be used when in doubt; it is also the ordinary classifier for persons.

No classifier is needed when telling the time, or with money.

The "literary forms" shown second in the case of the numbers 0–9 are used when giving telephone numbers (etc.) figure by figure.

CURRENCY in Singapore and Malaysia: 1 *kō* (dollar) = 10 *gkahk* = 100 *tsiām*.

FORMS OF ADDRESS In China the official term of address for all purposes is *dongtsih*, "comrade," used alone or following the surname (first name), or a term indicating occupation. Elsewhere *siansiñ* is used for "sir" or "Mr" (and also means "teacher"); *tàitaih* or *siansiñmú* for "madam" or "Mrs"; *siôu-tsià* for "Miss"; all these alone or following the surname or occupation term.

In Singapore and Malaysia local terms are also common: see under Malay.

KIN TERMS have various forms, of which the most generally useful are:

lauhbpe and *lauhbù*, "father" and mother" (but in reference to one's own father and mother, use the humble forms *gka-hu* and *gkabù*)
hiāñ and *duah-tsì*, "older brother, sister"
siôudi and *siôube*, "younger brother, sister"
siansīñ and *tàitaih*, "husband" and "wife" (but there are also the humble forms for these)
gkiàñ, "child"; *duahgkiàñ*, "eldest son"; *hauhsīñ*, "son" (polite); *tsabōgkiàñ*, "daughter"

NAME OF LANGUAGE
Hokkien is called *Hōk-gkiàn'ue*. The general word for the Chinese language is *Diong-gkōk'ue* or (for the written language) *Hànbún*.

JAPANESE

The language of eighty million in Japan, widely understood in Korea, Taiwan and elsewhere in the Pacific.

The system of writing is the world's most complicated, with Chinese characters having alternative readings in different contexts, supplemented by two phonetic syllabaries each of forty-eight letters.

Romanisation is straightforward and is taught in Japanese schools but little used.

PRONUNCIATION Vowels A, E, I, O, U as *ah, eh, ee, aw, oo,* but shorter: Ā, Ē, Ī, Ō, Ū are the same sounds twice the length.

Note, however, that short U is usually very lightly sounded, particularly at the end of a word, so that *desu,* "am, is, are," usually sounds like *"dess."*

Consonants are as in English, except that

G is like *ng* in "singer."

NG is the same sound, but longer.

R is flapped, a bit like *d.*

N at the end of a word is usually nasal (like the first part of an *ng* sound).

Double consonants must be double: *onna,* "woman," as *on-na.*

Stress is fairly even. Generally regard a sentence as made up of syllables of nearly constant length: *Ha-i so-o a-ri-ma-s(u),* "Yes, there is." Allow an extra syllable for a double consonant or for an extra N or M: *Shi-m-bu-n de-s(u),* "It's a newspaper."

NOUNS have no distinction of singular and plural, and there are no articles "a" or "the." For "this" or "these," use *kono* before the noun: *kono shimbun,* "this newspaper." For "that" or "those," use *sono* in the case of an object near the addressee, and *ano* if further away: *ano hito,* "that person (over there)."

The role of a noun in a sentence is indicated by a particle placed after it. This may be the equivalent of an English preposition:

heya ni, "in the room"

heya e, "to the room"

heya no, "of the room"

as in *heya no kii,* "key of the room." The direct object of a transitive verb is indicated by *o: heya o mimasu,* "see(s) the room."

The subject of a verb is less clearly indicated, and is often omitted altogether when the sense is clear. The particle *wa,* sometimes translated "as for," marks a noun as central to what the sentence is about: *Heya wa ōkii desu,* "As for the room, (it) is large," or just "The room is large."

The similar particle *ga* ties its noun more closely to the verb and is preferred when the subject is indefinite. For "There is" or "There are," use *ga* with the verb *arimasu: Heya ga takusan arimasu,* "There are lots of rooms."

ADJECTIVES precede nouns when they qualify them directly; or precede *desu,* "am, is, are," when this is used to connect them.

The ordinary adjective, like *ōkii,* "large," ends in *-i,* preceded by another vowel, but a common alternative is a noun followed by *na:* thus, *ko,* "child"; *kirei na ko,* "pretty child"; in this case omit *na* before *desu,* thus *Ko wa kirei desu,* "The child is pretty."

PRONOUNS "I" is *watashi* and "you" is *anata:* there are various other forms but these are adequate to simple needs. *Watashi* has the commonly used plural *watashitachi*, "we," but *anata* will serve as singular or plural.

There are no third person pronouns, but *hito*, "person(s)," or *ano hito*, "that person, those persons" can be used, and the form *hitobito* can be used when a clear plural is wanted. *Kore*, "this, these" and *sore* or *are*, "that, those" can be used for inanimate objects.

Pronouns take particles in the same way as nouns: *watashi o*, "me" (object), *watashi no heya*, "my room."

Japanese "respect" language often takes the place of pronouns. Thus for "wife," Japanese has the humble form *kanai* and the respectful *okusan*: the first of these usually means "my wife," and the second, "your wife" or "his wife."

VERBS The verb comes at the end of the sentence and is almost never omitted. The main verb of a sentence is generally put in its "polite" form, with present tense ending *-masu* as shown in the vocabulary: *Ano hito wa ikimasu*, "He/She is going."

For past tense, change *-masu* to *-mashita*: *Watashi wa heya e ikimashita*, "I went to the room." For future use present tense.

Desu, "am, is, are," is also a polite form, past tense *deshita*, "was, were."

For a negative verb in the present tense, change *-masu* to *-masen*: *Kono onna wa ikimasen*, "This woman is not going." *Desu* takes the long form *de arimasen*.

For past tense negative, add *deshita* to the present tense negative: *Uchi o mimasen deshita*, "(I, He, etc.) didn't see the house."

Japanese verbs have a wide range of forms, but these few will take the beginner a long way.

Note that many verbs are compound, consisting of a noun followed by *shimasu*, "do": *benkyō shimasu*, "study." Do not separate such compounds.

Also note the "desiderative" form, in which *-masu* is replaced by *-tai*, with *no desu* added for politeness: *mimasu*, "see"; *mitai no desu*, "would like to see."

QUESTIONS For a yes/no question, add *ka* after the verb: *Kore wa anata no pen desu ka?*, "Is this your pen?" Alternatively, add *ne*, with the force of "Isn't it so?" *Kore wa anata no pen desu ne?*, "This is your pen, isn't it?"

IMPERATIVES For an imperative (polite form) add *kudasai* to the participle of the verb: this is obtained by deleting *-masu* and adding *-te*, except that contractions commonly take place, dropping or modifying a preceding consonant: *ikimasu*, "go"; *itte kudasai*, "Please go"; *kakimasu*, "write"; *kaite kudasai*, "Please write." If in doubt, just delete *-masu*, add *o* as if the result were a noun, and add *kudasai*: you will be understood.

For "Let's," alter *-masu* to *-mashō*: *Ikimashō*, "Let's go."

For a negative imperative (polite form), form the negative participle of the verb by changing *-masu* to *-naide* (in some cases a preceding *i* changes to *a*) and add *kudasai*: *Ikanaide kudasai*, "Don't go."

NUMERALS follow the noun, with classifiers attached to them characteristic of the kind of thing being counted: *san*, "three"; *jidōsha sandai*, "three cars"; *seito sannin*, "three students"; *tegami sanmai*, "three letters."

There are about forty classifiers in common use, but the novice can conceivably be understood if he omits them. In this case he should use the long forms *hitotsu, futatsu*, . . . of the numbers from "one" to "ten."

CURRENCY A single unit, the *en* ("yen"). The word *en* combines with numerals like a classifier: *hyakuen,* "a hundred yen."

ADDRESS AND RESPECT LANGUAGE Address either sex by surname followed by *san* ("Mr," "Mrs," "Miss"). Do not attach or otherwise use given names with adults.

A teacher or doctor gets *sensei* in place of *san.*

Japanese respect language is complicated: note the use of especially polite verbs, such as *gozaimasu* for *arimasu.* The novice will have to ignore most of this.

Note however separate forms of the verb "to give": the humble *agemasu* when you give to someone else, the grateful *kudasaimasu* when someone else gives to you.

KIN TERMS The following are the commonest kin terms in their humble and polite forms; the latter to be used for relatives of the person addressed or of third persons other than those of one's own family.

	"Mine"	"Yours," etc.
father	*chichi*	*otōsan*
mother	*haha*	*okāsan*
elder brother	*ani*	*onīsan*
younger brother	*otōto*	*otōto san*
elder sister	*ane*	*onēsan*
younger sister	*imōto*	*imōto san*
brothers and sisters	*kyōdai*	*gokyōdai*
husband	*otto*	*goshujin*
wife	*kanai*	*okusan*
son	*musuko*	*botchan*
daughter	*musume*	*ojōsan*
children	*kodomo*	*okosan*

The polite prefix *o-* is regularly used to replace "your"; *okuni,* "your country": one's own country would be just *kuni.*

NAME OF LANGUAGE
The Japanese name for the Japanese language is *Nihongo.*

Korean is the language of the forty-five million inhabitants of Korea, and of some half-million in Japan. A standard language based on Seoul dialect is understood by most speakers.

Korean is written in its own phonetic alphabet, but an older style that incorporates Chinese characters is still found. North and South diverge slightly in details of spelling. There are competing systems of romanisation and this book uses a compromise.

PRONUNCIATION Vowels:

A, E, I, O, U are approximately *ah, eh, ee, aw, oo*, but for A, E and I the lips are spread as in a smile.

AA, Ŏ, Ŭ are as in "hat," "hut" and "hook" respectively, but all with the lips spread.

OE is like French *eu* (English *er* with lips pursed).

Consonants are generally as in English, but

KK, TT, PP and JJ have a characteristic Korean "tight throat" sound.

G, D, B, J are comparatively lightly sounded, unvoiced at the beginning of a word.

NG is as in "singer" (no *g* sound).

R (same letter as L in the Korean alphabet) is a light flap; often not unlike *d*.

H is always strongly sounded.

S before I is pronounced *sh*.

At the end of a word, K, T, P represent a closing of the air passage without re-opening.

Consonants change their sounds in different contexts, particularly at the end of a word when they may attach themselves to the word following. Note, in particular, that T at the end of a word may become like *ss* or *sh* when there is a vowel at the beginning of the word following.

There is no strong stress, but what there is is usually on the second last syllable.

NOUNS are invariable and do not indicate singular or plural; but plural may be shown if needed by adding *dŭl*: *saram*, "person, persons," *saram dŭl*, "persons."

There is no article "a" or "the," but *i*, "this, these," and *gŭ*, "that, those," or *jŏ*, "that, those" (more remote), are much used: *i namja*, "this man, these men"; *gŭ yŏja*, "that woman, those women."

A particle placed after a noun indicates its role in a sentence. Sometimes this is the equivalent of an English preposition: *bang e*, "to the room"; *bang ŭi*, "of the room"; *bang sŏ*, "from the room."

As a possessive, *ŭi* is frequently omitted: *gŭ yŏja ŭi so-gabang*, or just *gŭ yŏja so-gabang*, "that woman's handbag."

The subject of a verb is marked by the particle *i (ga* after a vowel) and the object by *ŭl (rŭl* after a vowel): *gŭ saram i*, "that person" (subject); *gŭ saram ŭl*, "that person" (object); *bihaang-gi ga*, "the plane" (subject); *bihaang-gi rŭl*, "the plane" (object); *Gŭ saram i bihaang-gi rŭl bomnida*, "That person sees the plane"; *Yŏja ga so-gabang ŭl gajimnida*, "The woman carries a handbag."

PRONOUNS *na*, "I," *ŭri*, "we," *dangsin*, "you" (singular or plural), behave like nouns: *ŭri ga*, "we" (subject); *dangsin ŭl*, "you" (object); *dangsin (ŭi) chaak*, "your book."

KOREAN

The pronoun "I" as subject is *naa ga,* and possessive "my" also has the special form *naa* (never with *ŭi*): *naa jim,* "my baggage."

There are no third person pronouns; use *gŭ saram,* "that person, those persons," or *gŭ gŏt,* "that thing, those things."

VERBS The verb comes at the end of the sentence.

Verbs do not indicate person or number, but take a special "honorific" form when the subject is the person addressed or an "esteemed" third person such as an older person, someone of social standing or a relative of the addressee: *gamnida* (ordinary form), "I/we are going," or in ordinary reference "He/She/It/They are going"; *gasimnida* (honorific), "You are going" or "He/She/They (esteemed) are going."

Actual pronoun subjects are regularly omitted.

The vocabulary gives the ordinary present tense of the verb followed by the base in parentheses. To form the honorific present tense add *-simnida* to the base (*-ŭsimnida* after a consonant): *anssumnida (anj-);* "sit," ordinary present *anssŭmnida,* "I (etc.) sit"; honorific *anjŭsimnida,* "You (etc.) sit."

The verb "is" or "are" between nouns or pronouns is *imnida (i-),* and the second noun needs no particle: *Naa chin-gu isimnida,* "You are my friend."

To indicate location, "is at" or "are at" is *issŭmnida (iss-),* and can also be used for "have" or "There is": *Bihaang-gi ga issŭmnida,* "There is a plane." As "have" it takes two subjects: *Yŏja i chaak i issŭmnida,* "The woman has a book"; *Chaak i issŭsimnida,* "You (etc.) have a book."

Note that a few verbs have completely different honorific forms. Thus *issŭmnida* in the sense "is at" has honorific *gyesimnida.* The ordinary word for "eat" is *meksŭmnida,* the honorific *japsusimnida.*

Note that many verbs consist of an invariant word followed by *hamnida (ha-),* "do"; for example, *sanbo hamnida,* "walk." Do not separate such compounds.

Negatives are formed by attaching *-ji* to the base and adding the auxiliary phrase *an hamnida,* "does not," or honorific *an hasimnida.* In adding *-ji,* assimilate *d, t, tt, s, ss* of the base to the *j* to make *-jji;* combine *h* with it to make *-chi.* The auxiliary verb takes all further inflections.

The verb *issŭmnida* has the special negative *ŏpsŭmnida (ŏps-),* and the verb *amnida,* "know, understand," has the negative *molŭmnida (molŭ-).* In the case of the verb *imnida,* the negative is *ani imnida.*

When two verbs are linked together in a sentence, the first takes the ending *-go* (assimilate *d, t, tt, j, ch, jj, k, kk* to give *-kko;* assimilate *h* to give *-ko*). This may occur either where in English the verbs would be joined by "and," as *gago anssŭmnida,* "goes and sits down," or where one verb modifies another, in *gago sipssŭmnida,* "wants to go." For honorific form, the ending is *-sigo* after a vowel or *-ŭsigo* after a consonant.

All the verb forms in these notes and in the phrases are in the so-called "formal style," appropriate to first acquaintance with the person addressed. These forms are adequate for the novice, but, in normal polite speech after formalities are dropped, the endings in *-mnida* are usually replaced by shorter ones, for example, present tense in *-e yo.*

ADJECTIVES precede the noun: *jŏlmŭn saram,* "young person"; *kŭn gŏnmŭl,* "big building."

As predicate an adjective takes endings like a verb: *Gŏnmŭl i kŭmnida,* "The building is big." For the ordinary form, add the ending *-mnida* to the base of the adjective shown in parentheses in the vocabulary; or, if it ends in a consonant, add *-sŭmnida* but assimilate *d, t, j, ch, r, l* or *h* to the *s* to make *ss*: *johŭn (joh-),* "good," *Chaak i jossŭmnida,* "The book is good."

Form honorifics as for verbs.

Adjectives for which no base form is shown are invariable, and take the verb *imnida* as "is" or "are."

Note that verbs can also be used as adjectives, with the participle ending *-n* or *-ŭn*: *anjŭn saram,* "sitting person."

ADVERBS can be formed from adjective or verb bases by adding *-ge,* subject to the same consonant assimilation as when adding *-go*: *nappun (nappu-),* "bad," *nappuge,* "badly"; *johŭn (joh-),* "good," *jo-ke,* "well."

QUESTIONS A yes/no question may be formed by changing the ending *-mnida* of the verb, either in ordinary or honorific form, to *-mnikka*: *Gŭ saram i Yŏngŏ rŭl hamnikka?,* "Does he (etc.) speak English?"

Use the same form of the verb with interrogative words such as *ŏdi,* "where?": *Bihaang-jang i ŏdi issŭmnikka?,* "Where is the airport?"

In answering negative questions, it is best to repeat the verb.

IMPERATIVES For a polite imperative, replace *-simnida* by *-sipsiyo* in the honorific present tense of the verb: *Anjŭsipsiyo,* "(Please) sit down."

Requests are often constructed using the infinitive of the verb (same as the base, or with *-ŏ* added) followed by *jusipsiyo,* "give": *Boyŏ jusipsiyo,* "Please show (me)."

For a negative, use *masipsiyo* following the *-ji* form of the verb: *Gaji masipsiyo,* "Don't go."

For "Let's," replace the *-sipsiyo* of the polite imperative by *-sipsida*: *Anjŭsipsida,* "Let's sit down."

NUMERALS A numeral may come before or after a noun, with or without a classifier; the simplest construction is before the noun as in English.

For general purposes in the case of numbers up to ninety-nine, use the second of the two forms listed, and immediately before the noun omit the letters shown in parentheses from the forms for one, two, three, four and twenty: *du jadongcha,* "two cars"; *sŭmul-ne saram,* "twenty-four people."

The alternative forms (Chinese-derived, listed first in the table) are used for numbers from 100 up, and also always in specifying dates or amounts of money.

CURRENCY 1 *wŏn* ("wen," Korean dollar) = 100 *chŏn.*

FORMS OF ADDRESS Korean has an intricate system of social styles that the novice will largely have to ignore. Address men and women alike as *sŏnsaang,* or, more deferentially, *sŏnsaang-nim.* For "Mr," "Mrs" or "Miss," place *sŏnsaang* (less formally sometimes *ssi*) after the name. The word *sŏnsaang* also means "teacher."

KIN TERMS The following are the commonest kin terms in their ordinary and honorific forms. The latter form is used, particularly in formal speech, in reference to relatives of the person addressed.

	"Mine," etc.	"Yours," etc.
father	*abŏji*	*abŏ-nim*
mother	*ŏmŏni*	*ŏmŏ-nim*

older brother	(of man)	*ŏnni*	*hyŏng*
	(of woman)	*oppa*	*olaboni*
older sister	(of man)	*nuna*	*nu-nim*
	(of woman)	*ŏnni*	*hyŏng*
younger brother/sister		*dongsaang*	*dongsaang*
husband		*nam-pyŏn*	*nam-pyŏn*
wife		*anaa*	*buin*
son		*adŭl*	*adŭ-nim*
daughter		*ttal*	*tta-nim*

Note also that "house," in reference to one's own house, is *jip,* and in reference to the addressee's or other esteemed person's house, *daak*; and that besides the ordinary word *saram* for "person(s)" there is an honorific word *bun.*

NAME OF LANGUAGE
Korea is called *Han-guk* in the South and *Josŏn* in the North. The language is correspondingly *Han-guk mal* or *Josŏn mal.*

EVERYDAY PHRASES

ENGLISH	MANDARIN	CANTONESE
Yes	Shì *SHER!*	Haih *High*
No	Bú shì *BOO?SHER!*	Mh-haih *Mm-high*
Please	Qǐng *Tsying?*	Mh-gòi *Mm-GOY!*
Thank you	Xièxie *SYEH!syeh*	Dòjeh *DAW!dyeh*
Thank you very much	Dōuxiè *DTOH-SYEH!*	Dòjeh dòjeh *DAW!dyeh DAW!dyeh*
Don't mention it	Méi shénme *MAY? SH'mer*	Mh-hóu haak-hei *Mm-*HOH*? *HAHK-HEIGH
Excuse me, but ...	Duìbuqǐ, ... *DER!b'tsyee*	Dēui-mh-jyuh, ... *DER-mm-dyoo*
Excuse me (I'm sorry)	Duìbuqǐ *DER!b'tsyee*	Dēui-mh-jyuh *DER-mm-dyoo*
Excuse me (Do you mind?)	Duìbuqǐ *DER!b'tsyee*	Dēui-mh-jyuh *DER-mm-dyoo*
Pardon? (What did you say?)	Qǐng zài shuō yíbiàn? *Tsying? DZIGH! SHWAW yeeBYEN!*	Mātyéh waah? *MATyeh wah?*
Wait a moment	Děng-yi-děng *D'ng YEEd'ng*	Dáng yāt-jahn *DAHNG? YATdyahn*
Hurry up!	Kuàidianr! *KWIGH! dyahnr*	Faai dī! *FIGH DEE*
Slowly!	Màndianr! *MAHN! dyahnr*	Maahn! *Mahn*
Stop!	Tíng! *TING?*	Tìhng! *Teeng!*
Look out!	Xiǎoxin! *SyowSYIN*	Síu-sàm! SYOO*?SAHM!*
Look!	Nǐ kàn! *Nee KAHN*	Tái! TIGH*?*
How much?	Duōshao qián? *DWAWshow TSYEN?*	Géido? GEIGH*?DAW*
Never mind	Méi guānxi *MAY? GWAHNsee*	Mh-gányiu *Mm-*GAHN*?YOO*
Come in	Jìnlai *TJIN!ligh*	Yàhp-léih *Yahp!leigh?*
Come with me	Gēn wǒ lái *GK'N waw ligh?*	Pùih ngóh lèih *Pooi! ngyaw? leigh!*
Good morning	Zǎo *Dzow?*	Jóu sàhn DYOH*?sahn!*
Good afternoon	Nín hǎo *NING? how?*	Ngh-ón *Ng-*AWN*?*
Good evening	Nín hǎo *NING? how?*	Ngh-ón *Ng-*AWN*?*
Good-bye (leaving)	Zàijiàn *DZIGH!JYEN!*	Joigin DYOY-GEEN
Good-bye (staying)	Zàijiàn *DZIGH!JYEN!*	Joigin DYOY-GEEN
Good night	Wǎnān *WahnAHN*	Jóu táu DYOH*?TOW?*

EVERYDAY PHRASES

HOKKIEN	JAPANESE	KOREAN
Si SEE	Hai *High*	Ne *Ne-eh*
'Mh si '*Mm* SEE	Iie *Ee-eh*	Aniyo *Ahnee-yaw*
Chiàñ *CHYAHÑ!*	Dōzo *Dawzaw*	Mian haji man
		Mee-ahn ahjee mahn
Gkāmsia *GKAHMSEEA*	Arigatō *Ahrree-gah-taw*	Gomapsŭmnida
		Gkoo-mahps'm-needah
Tsin gkāmsia lì	Dōmo arigatō gozaimasu	Daadanhi gomapsŭmnida
TSIN *GKAHMSEEA LEE!*	*Dawmaw ahrree-gah-taw*	*Daa-dannhee gkoo-mahps'm-*
	gaw-zighmahss	*needah*
Bue BWEH	Dō itashimashite	Won chŏnmaneyo
	Daw i-tahshee-mahshteh	*Wunn ch'n-mahneh-yo*
Tiènghau tsiht 'e, ...	Shitsurei desu ga, ...	Silye hamnida, ...
TENG!HOW *tsit'*EH	*Sh'tsoo-rreigh dess-nga*	*Shilye ahm-needah*
Duìbpŭttsu *DEE!BOOTTSOO*	Gomen nasai *Gaw-mehñ na-*	Mian hamnida
	sigh	*Mee-ahn ahm-needah*
Duìbpŭttsu *DEE!BOOTTSOO*	Kamaimasen ka?	Jossŭmnikka? *Chohss'm-*
	Ka-migh-ma-sengka?	*nikkah?*
Sīmmī? *SIMMI'*	Sumimasen *Soomi-ma-sehñ*	Muoragoyo? *Moorr-ahgo-yo?*
Dàn tsiht 'e *DAHN! tsit'*EH	Chotto matte kudasai	Jamkkan *Jahm-kkahn*
	Chawttaw mahtteh koodah-	
	sigh	
Gka-kuaih! GKAH*kwigh*	Isoide kudasai!	Ppalli! *Ppahllee!*
	Eesso-eedeh koodah-sigh!	
Gkaban! GKAH-BAHN	Yukkuri! *Yook-koorree!*	Chŏn-chŏn hi! *Chon-chonnee!*
Tièng! TENG?	Tomatte! *To-mahtteh!*	Chŏngji! *Chong-jee!*
Gkò-kuah! *GKAW!kwah*	Abunai! *Ahboo-nigh!*	Jo sim hasipsiyo!
		Chaw sh'm hashp-shyo!
Kuah! *Kwah*	Mite! *Meeteh!*	Bosipsiyo! *Bpaw-shipshyo!*
Luah tsueh? *Lwah tseh*	Ikura desu ka?	Ŏlma yimnikka?
	Eekoo-rra desska?	*Oylmah yim-nikkah?*
Bou yàugkin BOH	Kamaimasen *Ka-migh-ma-sehñ*	Yŏmnyŏ masipsiyo
YOW!GKIN!		*Y'm-nyo mahshp-shyo*
Dzihp laih *Dzip ligh*	Ohairi kudasai	Ŏsŏ dŭrŏ osipsiyo
	O-highrree koodah-sigh	*Aw-soo d'raw aw-shipshyo*
Lai gka guà LIGH GKAH	Kite kudasai	Iri osipsiyo
GWAH!	*Keeteh koodah-sigh*	*Eerree aw-shipshyo*
Gàutsà *GOW-TSAH!*	Ohayō gozaimasu	Annyŏnghi chumusŏtsumnikka?
	O-highyoh gaw-zighmahss	*Ahn-y'ngee ch'moosso-s'm-*
		nikkah?
'Ehbpō *'EhBPAW*	Konnichi wa *Kawn-neechi-wah*	Annyŏng hasimnikka?
		Ahn-y'ng ahshim-nikkah?
'Àmmí *'AHM!MEE?*	Komban wa *Kawm-bahñ-wah*	Annyŏng hasimnikka?
		Ahn-y'ng ahshim-nikkah?
Chiàñ *CHYAHÑ!*	Sayonara *Sighyo-nahrra*	Annyŏnghi gyesipsiyo
		Ahn-y'ngee gye-shipshyo
Chiàñ *CHYAHÑ!*	Sayonara *Sighyo-nahrra*	Annyŏnghi gasipsiyo
		Ahn-y'ngee gye-shipshyo
Chiàñ *CHYAHÑ!*	Oyasumi nasai	Annyŏnghi chumusipsiyo
	O-yah-soomi nah-sigh	*Ahn-y'ngee choomooshp-shyo*

183

EVERYDAY PHRASES

ENGLISH	MANDARIN	CANTONESE
Do you understand?	Ní dǒng ma? *NEE? dawng MA*	Néih mìhng mh-mìhngbaahk? *Neigh? ming! mm-ming!bahk*
I understand	Wǒ dǒng *WAW? dawng?*	Ngóh mìhngbaahk *Ngaw? ming!bahk*
I don't understand	Wǒ budǒng *Waw BOOdawng?*	Ngóh mh-mìhngbaahk *Ngaw? mm-ming!bahk*
All right (I'll do it)	Xíng *SYING?*	Hóu *HOH?*
It's all right	Hǎo *How?*	Seuhnleih gáai-kyut *Sern-leigh GIGH?KYOOT*

NUMERALS

	MANDARIN	CANTONESE
zero	líng *LING?*	lìhng *ling!*
one	yī *YEE*	yāt *YAT*
two	èr, liǎng *AHRR!, lyahng?*	yih, leuhng *yee, lerng*
three	sān *SAHN*	saam SAHM
four	sì *SER!*	sei SEIGH
five	wǔ *woo?*	ńgh *ng?*
six	liù *LEEOH!*	luhk *look*
seven	qī *TSYEE*	chāt *CHAT*
eight	bā *BPAH*	baat BAHT
nine	jiǔ *jyoh?*	gáu GOW?
ten	shí *SHER?*	sahp *sahp*
eleven	shíyī *sh'YEE*	sahpyāt *sahpYAT*
twelve	shíèr *shr-AHRR!*	sahpyih *sahp-yee*
thirteen	shísān *sh'SAHN*	sahpsaam *sahpSAHM*
fourteen	shísì *sh'SER!*	sahpsei *sahpSEIGH*
fifteen	shíwǔ *SH'?woo?*	sahpnǵh *sahp-ng?*
sixteen	shíliù *sh'LEEOH!*	sahpluhk *sahp-look*
seventeen	shíqī *sh'TSYEE*	sahpchāt *sahpCHAT*
eighteen	shíbā *sh'BAH*	sahpbaat *sahpBAHT*
nineteen	shíjiǔ *SH'?jeeoh?*	sahpgáu *sahpGOW?*
twenty	èrshí *AHRR!sh'*	yihsahp *yee sahp*
twenty-one	èrshíyī *AHRR!sh'YEE*	yihsahp yāt *yee sahp YAT*
thirty	sānshí *SAHNsh'*	saamsahp *SAHMsahp*

EVERYDAY PHRASES

HOKKIEN	JAPANESE	KOREAN
Tiañ 'uh bou? TYAHÑ '*oo* BOH	Wakarimasu ka? *Wah-kahrree-mahss ka?*	Asimnikka? *Ahshim-nikkah?*
Guà 'ueh hiãu tiàñ *GWAH! 'weh YOW TYAHÑ*	Wakarimasu *Wah-kahrree-mahss*	Amnida *Ahm-needah*
Guà bueh hiãu tiàñ *GWAH! bweh YOW TYAHÑ*	Wakarimasen *Wah-kahrree-mahss-ehñ*	Morŭmnida *Mawroom-needah*
'Ueh tsueh dĭt *'Weh tsweh DTIT*	Yoroshii desu *Yo-rraw-shee dess*	Johsŭmnida *Johssoom-needah*
Hòu *HOH!*	Ii desu *Ee dess*	Johsŭmnida *Johssoom-needah*

NUMERALS

liéng, kohng LENG?, *kawng*	rei *rreigh*	yong, gong *yong, gkong*
tsìt, 'iht *TSIT, 'it*	一 ichi, hitotsu *eechee, hee-tottsuh*	il, han(a) *ill, hahnah*
nng, dzi *noñ,* DZEE	二 ni, futatsu *nee, ff'tahtsuh*	i, du(l) *yee, dtool*
sañ, sàm *SAHÑ, SAHM*	三 san, mittsu *sahñ, meettsuh*	sam, se(t) *hsahm, set*
sih, suh *see, sweh*	四 shi, yottsu *shee, yottsuh*	sa, ne(t) *sah, net*
go, ngò GAW, *NGAW!*	五 go, itsutsu *gaw, ee-tsootsuh*	o, dasŏt *aw, dtahsoot*
làk, liòk *LAHK, LYAWK*	六 roku, muttsu *rrokkuh, mootsuh*	yuk, yŏsŏt *dyook, yerssoot*
chiht, chiht *chit, chit*	七 shichi, nanatsu *sheechee, na-nattsuh*	chil, ilgop *chill, irrgawp*
bpueh', bpaht *bpweh', bpet*	八 hachi, yattsu *hahchee, yahttsuh*	pal, yŏdŏl *pahll, yuddull*
gkàu, gkiù *GKOW!, GKYOO!*	九 ku, kokonotsu *kuh, kaw-kawnottsuh*	gu, ahŭp *gkoo, ha-hop*
tsàp *TSAHP*	十 jū, tō *joo, taw*	sip, yŏl *ship, yerll*
tsahp'iht *tsahp'it*	jūichi *joo-eechee*	sip-il, yŏl-han(a) *shibill, yerll-hahnah*
tsahpdzi *tsahp*DZEE	jūni *joo-nee*	sip-i, yŏl-du(l) *shib-ee, yerll-dtool*
tsahpsàñ *tsahpSAHÑ*	jūsan *joo-sahñ*	sip-sam, yŏl-se(t) *ship-sahm, yerll-set*
tsahpsih *tsahp-see*	jūshi, jūyon *joo-shee, joo-yon*	sip-sa, yŏl-ne(t) *ship-sah, yerll-let*
tsahpgo *tsahp*GAW	jūgo *joogaw*	sip-o, yŏl-dasŏt *shibbaw, yerll-dtahsoot*
tsahplàk *tsahpLAHK*	jūroku *joo-rrokkuh*	sip-yuk, yŏl-yŏsŏt *shim-nyook, yerll-yerssoot*
tsahpchiht *tsahp-chit*	jūshichi *joo-sheechee*	sip-chil, yŏl-ilgop *ship-chill, yerll-irrgawp*
tsahp-bpueh' *tsahp-bpeh'*	jūhachi *joo-hahchee*	sip-pal, yŏl-yŏdŏl *ship-pahll, yerll-yuddull*
tsahpgkàu *tsahpGKOW!*	jūku *joo-kuh*	sip-gu, yŏl-ahŭp *ship-gkoo, yer-rowp*
dzih-tsàp *dzeeTSAHP*	nijū *neejoo*	i-sip, sŭmu(l) *yee-ship, s'mool*
dzih-tsahp'iht *dzee-tsahp'it*	nijūichi *neejoo eechee*	i-sip il, sŭmul-han (a) *yeeshib-ill, s'moo-rrah-nah*
sañtsàp SAHÑ*TSAHP*	sanjū *sahñjoo*	sam-sip, sŏrŭn *hahmship, surrun*

185

NUMERALS

ENGLISH	MANDARIN	CANTONESE
forty	sìshí *SER!sh'*	seisahp SEIGHsahp
fifty	wǔshí *wooSH'*	ńghsahp *ng-sahp*
sixty	liùshí *LEEOH!sh'*	luhksahp *look sahp*
seventy	qīshí *TSYEEsh'*	chātsahp *CHATsahp*
eighty	bāshí *BPAHsh'*	baatsahp BAHT*sahp*
ninety	jiǔshí *jeeohSH'*	gáusahp GOW?*sahp*
a hundred	yìbǎi *YEE!bigh?*	baak BAHK
a hundred and one	yìbǎi líng yī *YEE!bigh LING? YEE*	baak lìhng yāt BAHK *ling! YAT*
a hundred and ten	yìbǎi yī (shí) *YEE!bigh YEE(sh')*	baak yāt BAHK *YAT*
two hundred	èrbǎi, liǎngbai *AHRR!bigh?, lyahngBIGH*	yih baak *yee* BAHK
a thousand	yìqiān *YEE!TSYEN*	yāt chìn *YAT CHEEN!*
ten thousand	yíwàn *yeeWAHN!*	yāt maahn *YAT mahn*
a hundred thousand	shíwàn *sh'WAHN!*	sahp maahn *sahp mahn*
a million	yìbǎi wàn *YEE!bigh WAHN!*	baak maahn BAHK *mahn*
ten million	yìqiān wàn *YEE!TSYEN WAHN!*	sahp yìk *sahp YEEK!*
a half	bàn *BAHN!*	yāt-bún *YAT* BOON?
... point (decimal) ...	... diǎnr ... *dyahnr?*	... dím ... DEEM?

DAYS OF THE WEEK

Sunday	xīngqīrì *SINGTSEE-RER!*	láihbaai *leigh?*BIGH
Monday	xīngqīyī *SINGTSEE-YEE*	láihbaai yāt *leigh?*BIGH *YAT*
Tuesday	xīngqīèr *SINGTSEE-AHRR!*	láihbaai yih *leigh?*BIGH *yee*
Wednesday	xīngqīsān *SINGTSEE-SAHN*	láihbaai saam *leigh?*BIGH SAHM
Thursday	xīngqīsì *SINGTSEE-SER!*	láihbaai sei *leigh?*BIGH SEIGH
Friday	xīngqīwǔ *SINGTSEE-woo?*	láihbaai ńgh *leigh?*BIGH *ng?*
Saturday	xīngqīliù *SINGTSEE-LEEOH!*	láihbaai luhk *leigh?*BIGH *look*

MONTHS

January	yīyuè *YEE WER!*	yāt yuht *YAT yoot*
February	èryuè *AHRR! WER!*	yih yuht *yee yoot*
March	sānyuè *SAHN WER!*	saam yuht SAHM *yoot*
April	sìyuè *SER! WER!*	sei yuht SEIGH *yoot*

NUMERALS

HOKKIEN	JAPANESE	KOREAN
si-tsăp *SEE!TSAHP*	shijū, yonjū *shee-joo, yonjoo*	sa-sip, mahŭn *sah-ship, mahh'n*
goh-tsăp *gawTSAHP*	gojū *gaw-joo*	o-sip, swin *awship, shoon*
lahktsăp *lahkTSAHP*	rokujū *rrokkoo-joo*	yuk-sip, yesun *yookship, yess'n*
chĭttsăp *CHIT-TSAHP*	shichijū, nanajū *sheechee-joo, nah-nahjoo*	chil-sip, irŭn *chilship, eerr'n*
bpuĕ'tsăp *BPWEH'!TSAHP*	hachijū *hahchee-joo*	pal-sip, yŏdŭn *pahllship, yerr'n*
gkău-tsăp *GKOW-TSAHP*	kyūjū, kujū *kyoojoo, kuh-joo*	gu-sip, ahŭn *gkooship, ahh'n*
tsiht bpah' *tsit bpah'*	hyaku *hyahkuh*	baak *bpek*
tsiht bpă' kòng 'iht *tsitBPAH'! KAWNG 'it*	hyaku ichi *hyahkuh eechee*	baak il *bpegill*
tsiht bpă' tsăp *tsitBPAH'! TSAHP*	hyaku jū *hyahkuh joo*	baak sip *bpekship*
nngh bpah' *noñBPAH'!*	ni hyaku *nee-hyahkuh*	i-baak *yee-bek*
tsiht chiĕng *tsitCHENG*	sen *sehñ*	chŏn *chonn*
tsahp chiĕng [tsiht ban] *tsahpCHENG [tsit*BAHN]	ichi man *eechee mahñ*	man *mahn*
tsiht bpă' chiĕng [tsahp ban] *tsitBPAH'!CHENG [tsahp*BAHN]	jū man *joo mahñ*	sip-man *shimmahn*
tsiht ban [bpă' ban] *tsit*BAHN [*BPAH'!*BAHN]	hyaku man *hyahkuh mahñ*	baak-man *bpengmahn*
tsahp ban [tsiht chieng ban] *tsahp*BAHN [*tsit*CHENG BAHN]	sen man *sehñ mahñ*	chŏn-man *chonmahn*
puahñ *pwahñ*	han *hahñ*	ban *bpahn*
... diăm ... *DYAHM*	... ten ... *tehñ*	... jŏm ... *tjom*

DAYS OF THE WEEK

lĕbpăi *LEH-BPIGH!*	nichiyōbi *neechee yawbee*	Ilyoil *Irr'yaw-ill*
bpăi 'iht *BPIGH!'it*	getsuyōbi *gettsoo yawbee*	Wŏlyoil *Awrr'yaw-ill*
bpăi dzi *BPIGH!DZEE*	kayōbi *kah yawbee*	Hwayoil *Whah-yaw-ill*
bpăi săñ *BPIGH!SAHÑ*	suiyōbi *sooi yawbee*	Suyoil *Soo-yaw-ill*
bpăi sih *BPIGH!see*	mokuyōbi *mawkoo yawbee*	Mokyoil *Mawg-yaw-ill*
bpăi goh *BPIGH!gaw*	kin-yōbi *keeñ yawbee*	Gŭmyoil *Gkom-yaw-ill*
bpăi lăk *BPIGH!LAHK*	doyōbi *daw yawbee*	Toyoil *Taw-yaw-ill*

MONTHS

tsiañ gĕ', 'it gĕ' *TSYEÑ GOY', 'IT GOY'*	ichigatsu *eechee gahtsuh*	Ilwŏl *Irr'wool*
dzih gĕ' *dzee GOY'*	nigatsu *nee gahtsuh*	Iwŏl *Yeewool*
săñ gĕ' *SAHÑ GOY'*	sangatsu *sahñ gahtsuh*	Samwŏl *Hahmwool*
sì gĕ' *SEE! GOY'*	shigatsu *shee gahtsuh*	Sawŏl *Hahwool*

187

MONTHS

ENGLISH	MANDARIN	CANTONESE
May	wǔyuè *woo WER!*	nǵh yuht *ng? yoot*
June	liùyuè *LEEOH! WER!*	luhk yuht *look yoot*
July	qīyuè *TSYEE WER!*	chāt yuht *CHAT yoot*
August	bāyuè *BPAH WER!*	baat yuht BAHT *yoot*
September	jiǔyuè *jyoh WER!*	gáu yuht GOW*? yoot*
October	shíyuè *SH'? WER!*	sahp yuht *sahp yoot*
November	shíyiyuè *sh'YEE WER!*	sahpyāt yuht *sahpYAT yoot*
December	shíèryuè *shr-AHRR! WER!*	sahpyih yuht *sahp-yee yoot*

SENTENCES

1. Is there someone here who speaks English, please? A little. I speak only a little ———.

1. Zhèli yǒu rén huì shuō Yīngwén ma? Yìdiǎnr. Wǒ zhǐ huì shuō yì diǎnr ———.
TJER! lee yoh R'N? HWAY!
SHWAW YINGw'n?! ma.
YEE!dyahnr? WAW? tjer
HWAY! SHWAW YEE!
dyahnr ———.

1. Chéng mahn nídouh yáuh móuh yàhn góng Yingmàhn? Dígamdēu jē. Ngóh wáih góng dígamdēu ———.
CHENG? mahn NEEdoh yow?
moh? yan! GOHNG?
YING!mahn.
DEEGAHMDER DYEH.
Ngaw? wigh? GOHNG?
DEEGAHMDER ———.

2. I want to go to ———. Is there a bus (an aeroplane, a taxi)? Yes, there is. No, there is not.

2. Wǒ xiǎng qù ———. Yǒu gōnggòng qìchē (fēijī, jìchéngchē) ma? Yǒu. Méiyou.
WAW? syahng? TSU!
———. Yoh GAWNG-
GAWNG! TSYEE!CHER
(FAY-JEE, TJEE-
ch'ngCHER) ma. Yoh?
MAY?you.

2. Ngóh yiu heui ———. Yáuh móuh bāsí (fēigēi, dīksí) nē? Yáuh. Móuh.
Ngaw? YOO HOY ———.
Yow? moh? BAHSEE?
(FEIGH-GEIGH!,
DEEKSEE?) NEH. Yow?
Moh?

3. Where is the bus (the railway station, the ticket office)? It is here (there, over there).

3. Gōnggòng qìchē (Huǒchezhàn, Mǎipiàode dìfang) zài nǎr? Zài zhèr (nàr, nèibian).
GAWNG-GAWNG!
TSYEE!CHER
(HwawCHER-TJAN!,
MIGH!PYOW!d'
DEE!fahng) DZIGH!
nahrr? DZIGH! TJERR!
(NAHRR!, NAY!byen).

3. Bāsí (Fóchè jaahm, Piufóng) haih binsyu? Haih nísyu (gósyu, gósyu).
BAHSEE? (FAWCHEH!
dyahm, PYOO-FONG?) high
BEEN-SYOO. High NEE-
SYOO (GAW?SYOO,
GAW?SYOO).

4. How do I get to the airport (to the town)? Go that way. Go straight on (to the left, to the right).

4. Dào fēijīchǎng (chénglǐ) zénme zǒu? Wǎng nèibian zǒu. Yìzhí zǒu (Zhuán zuǒ, Zhuán yòu).
DTOW! FAY-JEEchang?
(CH'NG?lee?) DZ'N?mer
dzoh? Wahng NAY!byen
dzoh? YEE!JER? zoh?
(TJWAHN? dzoh?, Tjwahn
YOH!).

4. Bīntiuh louh haih heui fēigēicheuhng (sèhngsíh)? Gó-bihn hàahng. Yātjihk (Jóbihn, Yauhbihn) hàahng.
BEENtyoo loh high HOY
FEIGH!-GEIGH!cherng!
(sehng!see?). GAW?been
hahng! YATdyeek
(DYAW?been, Yow-been)
hahng!

MONTHS

HOKKIEN	JAPANESE	KOREAN
goh gē' *gaw GOY'*	gogatsu *gaw gahtsuh*	Owŏl *Aw-wool*
lahk gē' *lahk GOY'*	rokugatsu *rrawkoo gahtsuh*	Yuwŏl *Yoo-wool*
chĭt gē' *CHIT GOY'*	shichigatsu *sheechee gahtsuh*	Chilwŏl *Chilwool*
bpuè' gē' *BPWEH'! GOY'*	hachigatsu *hahchee gahtsuh*	Palwŏl *Pahllwool*
gkau gē' GKOW *GOY'*	kugatsu *kuh gahtsuh*	Guwŏl *Gkoo-wool*
tsahp gē' *tsahp GOY'*	jūgatsu *joo gahtsuh*	Siwŏl *Shibwool*
tsahp'ĭt gē' *tsahp'IT GOY'*	jūichigatsu *joo-eechee gahtsuh*	Sibilwŏl *Shibbillool*
tsahpdzih gē' *tsahp-dzee GOY'*	jūnigatsu *joonee gahtsuh*	Sibiwŏl *Shibbee-wool*

SENTENCES

1. Tsiă 'uh bou lang gkŏng 'Angmo'ue? Dahmbpóu'. Guà tsi 'ueh gkŏng dahmbpouh' ———.
   TSYAH 'ooBOH LAHNG GKAWNG 'AHNGMAW'WEH. DtahmBOH'. GWAH! TSEE 'weh GKAWNG dtahmboh' ———.

1. Koko ni Eigo no dekiru hito ga imasu ka? Sukoshi dekimasu. Honno sukoshi ——— ga dekimasu.
   Hawkaw nee Eighgaw naw dehkee-rroo hheeto nga ee-mahsska? S'kawshee dehkee-mahss. Hawnnaw s'kawshee ——— nga dehkee-mahss.

1. Yŏngŏ rŭl hanŭn saram i issŭmnikka? Jogum hamnida. ——— man jogum hamnida.
   Y'ngga rrool hahnoon sahrahm ee iss'm-nikkah? Tjawgoom hahm-needah. ——— mahn tjawgoom hahm-needah.

2. Guà 'ài ki ———. 'Uh bàsi (huigkī, diēksī) bou? 'U. Bóu.
   GWAH! 'IGH! KEE! ———. 'Oo BAH!SEE (HWEEGKEE, DTEK-SEE) BOH. 'OO. BOH?

2. ——— ni ikitai no desu. Basu ga (Hikōki ga, Takushii ga) arimasu ka? Hai, arimasu. Iie, arimasen.
   ——— nee eekee-tigh naw dess. Bahss'nga (Hee-kawkee nga, Tahk'shee nga) ahrree-mahsska? High, ahrree-mahss. Ee-eh, ahrree-mahss-ehñ.

2. ——— e gago sipsumnida. Bŏsŭ ga (Bihaanggi ga, Taaksi ga) issŭmnikka? Ne, issŭmnida. Aniyo, ŏpsŭmnida.
   ——— eh gkahgaw ships'm-needah. Bpawsoo gah (Bpee-henggee gah, Takshi gah) iss'm-nikkah? Neh, iss'm-needah. Ahnee-yo, awps'm-needah.

3. Bàsi (Hēchia-tsam, Piouh-gkièk) dih dōulōu'? Dih tsitbpiéng (hăbpiéng, hă-tsihtbpiéng).
   BAH!SEE (HOYCHYAH-TSAHM, Pyoh-GKEK) dtee DTOHLOH'. Dtee TSIT-BPENG? (HAH-BPENG?, HAHtsitBPENG?).

3. Basu wa (Eki wa, Kippu-uriba wa) doko desu ka? Koko (Soko, Asoko) desu.
   Bahssoo wa (Ehkee wa, Keep-poorri-ba wa) dawkaw desska? Kawkaw (Sawkaw, A-sawkaw) dess.

3. Bŏsŭ ga (Jonggojang ga, Maapyoso ga) ŏdi issŭmnikka? Yŏgi (Gŏgi, Jŏgi) issŭmnida.
   Bawsoo gah (Tjawnggo-tjahng gah, Mah-pyawsaw gah) oodee iss'm-nikkah? Yooghee (Gkooghee, Tjoo-ghee) iss'm-needah.

4. Dui dōulōu' guà ki huigkidiú (siañchi)? Dùi hiă kih. Kì diht-dit (dòubpiéng, tsiăñbpiéng).
   DTWEE! DTOHLOH' GWAH! KEE! HWEH-GKEE-DYOW? (SAHNCHEE). DTWEE! HYAH kee. KEE! dtitDTIT (DOH!- BPENG?, TSAHÑ!BPENG?).

4. Hikōjō e (Machi no mannaka e) dō ittara ii desu ka? Achira e itte kudasai. Massugu (Hidari e, Migi e) itte kudasai.
   Hee-kawjaw eh (Mahchee naw mahn-nahkah eh) daw eet-tahrrah ee desska? Ahchee-rrah eh eet-teh koodah-sigh. Mahss-soogoo (Hi-dahrree eh, Meeghee eh) eet-teh koodah-sigh.

4. Bihaang-jang ŭro (Dosi ŭro) ŏttŏhke gamnikka? Jŏrŏ-ke gamnida. Baro ap ŭro (Oen pyŏn ŭro, Barun pyŏn ŭro) gamnida.
   Bpee-hengjahng oo-raw (Dtawshee oo-raw) oot-toohkeh gkahm-nikkah? Tjoorroo-keh gkahm-needah. Bpahraw ahp oo-raw (Wen py'n oo-raw, Bpahr'n py'n oo-raw) gkahm-needah.

SENTENCES

ENGLISH	MANDARIN	CANTONESE
5. Would you take my baggage to the bus, please. There is just one bag. There are two bags and that bundle.	5. Qǐng nǐ bǎ wǒde xíngli nádao gōnggòng qìchē shàngqu. Zhǐyǒu yíge xiāngzi. Yǒu liǎngge xiāngzi he nèige bāor. *TSYING? nee BPAH? wawD' TSING?lee NAH?dow GAWNG-GAWNG! TSYEE!CHER SHAHNGtsu. TJER?yoh YEEg SYAHNGdz her NAY!g BOWRR.*	5. Mh-gòi néih nīk ngóh-ge hàhngléih heui bāsi ma? Jauh yāt-go pèihgīp. Yáuh léuhng-go pèihgip tùhngmaaih gó-go bàau. *Mm-GOY!neigh? NIK ngaw?geh hahng!leigh?* HOY *BAH*SEE? MAH. *Dyow? YAT*GAW *peigh!GHIP. Yow? lerng?*GAW *peigh!GHIP toong!migh?* GAW?GAW *BOW!*
6. When does the bus go? Show me, please. The bus is late. The bus has already gone.	6. Gōnggòng qìchē shénme shíhour kai? Zhí gěi wǒ kàn. Gōnggòng qìchē chíle. Gōnggòng qìchē yǐjing zǒule. *GAWNG-GAWNG! TSYEE!CHER SH'mer SH'hohrr kigh. TJER? GAY? wo KAN! GAWNG-GAWNG! TSYEE!CHER CHER?la. GAWNG-GAWNG! TSYEE!CHER yeeJING dzohLA.*	6. Bāsi géi-si hōi a? Mh-gòi jíbéi ngóh tái-ha. Bāsi lèih chih jó. Bāsi yih-gíng hoi jó la. *BAH*SEE? GEIGH?SEE? *HOY* AH. *Mm-GOY!* DYEE?BEIGH? *ngaw?* TIGH?HAH? *BAH*SEE? *leigh? chee* DYAW? *BAH*SEE? *yee*GING? HOY DYAW? LA.
7. A ticket for one person (for two persons) to ——, please. Two adults and one child. First class. Tourist class.	7. Yīzhāng (Liǎngzhāng) dào —— qùde piào. Liǎng dà yī xiǎo. Tóuděng. Èrděng. *YEE!TJAHNG (LyahngTJAHNG) DTOW! —— TSU!d PYOW! Lyahng DTAH! YEE syow? TOH?d'ng. AHRR!d'ng.*	7. Mh-gòi béi yāt-jeung fei (léuhng-jeung fei) heui ——. Léuhng-go daaihyàhn tùhngmaaih yāt-go saimānjái. Tàuhdáng. Yihdáng. *Mm-GOY!* BEIGH? *YAT*DYERNG FEIGH (LERNG?DYERNG FEIGH) HOY ——. LERNG?GAW *digh-YAHN! toong!migh? YAT*GAW *sighMANJ*IIGH? *Tow!*DAHNG? *Yee*DAHNG?
8. Excuse me, what time is it? Two o'clock. Ten past two. Half past two. Ten to three.	8. Duìbuqǐ, xiànzài shì jǐ diǎnzhōng le? Liáng diǎnzhōng le. Liángdiǎn shífēn. Liángdianbàn. Sāndiǎn chà shífēn. *DER!b'tsyee, SYAN!dzigh! sh' TJEE? dyenTJAWNG ler. LYAHNG? dyenTJAWNG ler. LYAHNG?dyen? SHER?F'N. LYAHNG?dyen BAHN! SAHN dyen? CHAH! SHER?F'N.*	8. Chéng mahn, géi dímjūng la? Léuhng dímjūng. Léuhng dím léuhng-go jí. Léuhng dím bún. Léuhng dím sahp-go jí. CHEHNG? *mahn,* GEIGH? DIM?*DYOONG* LA. LERNG? DIM?*DYOONG.* LERNG? DIM? LERNG?GAW DYEE? LERNG? DIM? BOON? LERNG? DIM? *sahp*GAW DYEE?

190

SENTENCES

HOKKIEN

5. Lì 'eh sài giã' guã 'e hiēnglì ki bàsi beh'? 'Uh tsiht ka' hiēnglì. 'Uh nngh ka' hiēnglì gka hit 'e bpāu.
LEE!'eh SIGH! GYAH' GWAH'ᴇʜ HENG-LEE! KEE! BAH!ꜱᴇᴇ beh'. 'Oo tsit'ᴇʜ HENG-LEE! 'Oo noñ 'ᴇʜ HENG-LEE! GKAH HIT'ᴇʜ BPOW.

6. Tsīt 'e bàsi dihsí gkiáñ? Chiãñ hoh guã kuahñ. Tsīt 'e bàsi 'uahñ. Tsīt 'e bàsi ki liàu lo.
TSIT'ᴇʜ BAH!ꜱᴇᴇ deeꜱᴇᴇ? GKYAHÑ? CHYAHÑ haw GWAH kwahñ. TSIT'ᴇʜ BAH!ꜱᴇᴇ 'wahñ. TSIT'ᴇʜ BAH!ꜱᴇᴇ kee LYOW! ʟᴀᴡ.

7. Chiãñ tsiht 'e duãñ hoh tsiht láng (hoh nngh láng) kì ———. Nngh 'e duahláng gka' tsiht 'e gìn'à. Deh'it bpãn. Dehdzih bpãn.
CHYAHÑ tsit'ᴇʜ DWAHÑ haw tsit-ʟᴀʜɴɢ? (haw noñ ʟᴀʜɴɢ?) KEE ———. Noñ'ᴇʜ dwah-ʟᴀʜɴɢ? gkah tsit'ᴇʜ GHEEN-AH! Deh'IT BPAHN. Deh dzee BPAHN.

8. Huìsín 'e, tsīt tsun gkuī diàm? Nngh diàm. Nngh diàm nngh 'e dzi. Nngh diàm bpuahñ. Kòu' nngh 'e dzi sañ diàm.
HWEE!ꜱɪɴ?'ᴇʜ, TSIT ᴛꜱᴏᴏɴ GKWEE DYAHM! Noñ DYAHM! Noñ DYAHM noñ'ᴇʜ DZEE. Noñ DYAHM bpwahñ. KOH'! noñ'ᴇʜ ᴅᴢᴇᴇ ꜱᴀʜñ DYAHM!

JAPANESE

5. Watashi no nimotsu o basu e motte itte kudasaimasen ka? Kaban hitotsu dake desu. Kaban futatsu to ano tsutsumi desu.
Wa-tahshee naw nee-mawtsoo aw bahssoo eh mawt-teh eet-teh koodah-sighmahss-engka? Kah-bahñ hee-tawts' dahkeh dess. Kah-bahñ ff'tahtsuh taw ahnaw ts'tsoomee dess.

6. Basu wa itsu demasu ka? Misete kudasai. Basu wa osoi desu. Basu wa mõ dete imasu.
Bahssoo wa eetsoo deh-mahsska? Meesseh-teh koodah-sigh. Bahssoo wa aw-soee dess. Bahssoo wa maw dehteh ee-mahss.

7. ——— no kippu o ichimai (nimai) kudasai. Otona futari to kodomo hitori. Ittõ de. Ni-tõ de.
——— naw keep-poo aw eechee-migh (neemigh) koodah-sigh. Aw-tawnah ff'tahrree taw kaw-dawmaw hee-tawrree. Eet-taw deh. Nee-taw deh.

8. Shitsurei desu ga, nanji desu ka? Ni-ji desu. Ni-tõ de. San-ji jippun mae desu.
Sh'tsoo-rreigh dess'nga, nahnjee desska? Neejee dess. Neejee jeep-poon sooghee dess. Neejee hahñ dess. Sahnjee jeep-poon migh dess.

KOREAN

5. Naa jim ŭl bŏsŭ e gajigo gatta jusipsiyo. Ot gabang hana man issŭmnida. Ot gabang dul hago gŭ dabal i issŭmnida.
Neh tjim ull bpawsoo eh gkahtji-gaw gkat-tah tjooshp-shyo. Awt gkahbahng hahnnah mahn iss'm-needah. Awt gkahbahng dtoorr hahgaw gkuh dtahbahl ee iss'm-needah.

6. Bŏsŭ ga ŏnje ttŏnamnikka? Jom boyŏ jusipsiyo. Bŏsŭ ga nŭssŭmnida. Bŏsŭ ga bŏlssŏ ttŏnassŭmnida.
Bawsoo gah on-jeh tt'n-ahm-nikkah? Tjom bawyoo tjooshp-shyo. Bawsoo gah nerss'm-needah. Bawsoo gah b'll-ssuh tt'n-ahss'm-needah.

7. Pyo rŭl hana (dul) ——— kkaji jusipsiyo. Sung-in dul gwa ban pyo hana. Il dŭng. I dŭng.
Bpyaw rrool hahnnah (dtool) ——— kkahtjee tjooshp-shyo. Soong-een dtool gkwah bahn bpyaw hahnnah. Ill dtoong. Yee dtoong.

8. Silye hamnida, jigŭm myŏtsi imnikka? Dusi imnida. Dusi sip pun imnida. Dusi ban imnida. Sesi sip pun jŏn imnida.
Shillye ahm-needah, tj'goom myer-shee 'm-nikkah? Dtooshee 'm-needah. Dtooshee ship-poon 'm-needah. Dtooshee bahn 'm-needah. Hehshee ship-poon jern 'm-needah.

SENTENCES

ENGLISH	MANDARIN	CANTONESE
9. Take me to a hotel (to the ——— Hotel). Is this (that) the hotel? How far is it?	9. Sòng wǒ dào yìjiān lǚguǎn qu (——— Lǚguǎn). Zhèi (Nèi) jiushi lǚguǎn ma? Duō yuǎn? *SAWNG! wo DOW! YEE!jyen LU?gwahn? tsu (——— LU?gwahn?). TJAY! (NAY!) jyoo-sh' LU?gwahn MA. DWAW yooen?*	9. Dāi ngóh heui yāt-gàan jáudim (——— jáudim). Haih m̀h-haih nī-gàan (gó-gàan) jáudim? Gei yúhn a? *DIGH ngaw? HOY YAT-GAHN! DYOW?DIM (——— DYOW?DIM). High mm-high NEE-GAHN! (GAW?GAHN!) DYOW?DIM. GEIGH YOON? AH.*
10. Have you a single room (a double room)? May I see the room? I don't like that room. I like this room.	10. Nǐ yǒu dānrenfáng (shuānrenfáng) ma? Wǒ kěyi kànkan fángjiān. Wǒ bù xihuāng nèige fángjiān. Wǒ xihuāng zhèige fángjiān. *NEE? yoh? DANr'nFAHNG (SHWAHNr'n-FAHNG?) ma. WAW? ker-yee KAHN!-kahn FAHNG?JYAHN ma. Waw BOO! syeeHWAHNG NAY!g FAHNG?JYEN. Waw syeeHWAHNG TJAY!g FAHNG?jyen.*	10. Néih yáuh yāt-gàan dàan-yàhn-fóng (yāt-gàan sèung-yàhn-fóng) ma? Ngóh hó m̀h-hó yíh tái hā gàan fóng? Ngóh m̀h-júng yíh gó-gàan fóng. Ngóh júng yíh nī-gàan fóng. *Neigh? yow? YAT-GAHN! DAHN!yahn! (YAT-GAHN! SERNG!yahn!FOHNG?) MA. Ngaw? HAW? mm-HAW? yee? TIGH? HAH gahn! FOHNG? Ngaw? mm-DYOONG? yee? GAW?GAHN! FOHNG? Ngaw? DYOONG? yee? NEE-GAHN! FOHNG?*
11. Could I have the key of my room, please? Are there any letters for me (for us)?	11. Qǐng bǎ wǒ fángjiānde yàoshi gěi wǒ. Wǒ (Wǒmen) yǒu xìn ma? *TSYING? BPAH? waw FAHNG?JYENd YOW!sh GAY? waw? WAW? (WawMN) yoh SYIN ma.*	11. M̀h-gòi, béi fóng-ge sósìh ngóh. Ngóh (Ngóhdeih) yáuh móuh seun a? *Mm-GOY!, BEIGH? FOHNG?GEH SAW?see! ngaw? Ngaw? (Ngaw?deigh?) yow? moh? SERN a.*
12. Could I speak to ———, please? It has to do with ———. It is very important.	12. Qǐng nǐ zhǎo shuōhuà. Shì guānyu ——— de. Hěn zhòngyao. *TSYING? NEE? tjow? ——— SHWAW-HWAH! SHER! GWAHNyoo ——— der. H'n TJAWNG!yow.*	12. Chéng mahn ngóh hóyíh tùhng ——— góng syutwah. Haih tùhng ——— yáuh gwan. Haih hóu ganyiu a. *CHEHNG? mahn ngaw? HAW?yee? toong! ——— GAWNG? SYOOT-WAH. High toong! ——— yow? GWAHN. High HOH? GAHN-YOO a.*
13. How much is this? I would like to buy this, please. That is too dear. I don't want it.	13. Zhèige yào duōshao qián? Wǒ yào mǎi zhèige, xièxie nǐ. Tài guì le. Wǒ buyào. *TJAY!g YOW! DTAWshow TSYEN? Waw YOW! migh TJAY!g, SYER!syer nee? TIGH! GWAY! ler. Waw booYOW!*	13. Nī-gaw géidò chín a? Ngóh séung maaih nī-go, m̀h-gòi. Nī-go tāi gwai. Ngóh m̀h-séung maaih la. *NEEgaw GEIGH?DAW! CHEEN? a. Ngaw? SERNG? migh NEEgaw, mm-GOY! NEEgaw TIGH GWIGH. Ngaw? mm-SERNG? migh? LA.*

SENTENCES

HOKKIEN

9. Chiâñ lí chuah guā ki lûgkuàn (ki —— lûgkuàn). Sih 'mh sih tsit 'e (hit 'e) lûgkuàn? Tsuā huì?
CHYAHÑ LEE chwah GWAH KEE! LOO-GWAHN! (KEE! —— LOO-GWAHN!). See-mm-see TSIT'EH (HIT'EH) LOO-GWAHN! TSWAH HWEE!

10. 'Uh siek-bpáng (duah-bpáng) 'o? Guà 'eh sài kuàñ hit 'e bpáng beh'? Guà beh' 'ài hit 'e bpáng. Guà 'ài tsit 'e bpáng.
'Oo SEHK-BAHNG? (dwahBAHNG?) 'AW. GWAH! 'eh SIGH! KWAHÑ! HIT'EH BPAHNG? BEH'. GWAH! beh' 'IGH! HIT'EH BPAHNG? GWAH! 'IGH! TSIT-'EH BPAHNG?

11. 'Eh sài hoh guà guā 'e bpang 'e sōusi beh'? 'Uh pue hoh guà (hoh guā láng) bou?
'Eh SIGH! haw GWAH! GWAH'EH BPAHNG-'EH SOHSEE? beh'. 'Oo PWEH haw GWAH! (haw GWAH LAHNG?) BOH.

12. Chiâñ guà 'eh sài gkōng 'ue gka —— beh'? 'Uh su gka ——. Tsin 'iàugkin.
CHYAHÑ GWAH! 'eh SIGH! GKAWNG 'WEH GKAH —— beh'. 'Oo SOO GKAH ——. TSIN 'YOW!GKIN!

13. Tsit 'e luah tsue? Guà 'ài buē tsit 'e. Tsit 'e siuñ kuih. Guà 'maih.
TSIT'EH lwah TSWEH. GWAH! 'IGH! BWEH TSIT'EH. TSIT'EH SYOOÑ kwee. GWAH! migh.

JAPANESE

9. Hoteru e (Hoteru —— e) tsuretette kudasai. Kore wa (Are wa) hoteru desu ka? Dono gurai arimasu ka?
Haw-tehrroo eh (Haw-tehrroo —— eh) tsoorreh-tehtteh koodah-sigh. Kawrreh wa (Ahrreh wa) haw-tehrroo desska? Dawnaw goo-righ ahrree-mahsska?

10. Hitori no heya ga (Futari no heya ga) arimasu ka? Heya o misete itadakemasu ka? Ano heya wa suki ja arimasen. Kono heya ga suki desu.
Hee-tawrree naw heh-ah nga (Ff'tahrree naw heh-ah nga) ahrree-mahsska? Heh-ah aw meesseh-teh eetah-dahkee-mahsska? Ahnaw heh-ah wa ss'kee jah ahrree-mahss-ehñ. Kawnaw heh-ah nga ss'kee dess.

11. Watashi no heya no kagi o kudasai. Tegami ga watashi ni (watashitachi ni) arimasu ka?
Wa-tahshee naw heh-ah naw kahngi aw koodah-sigh. Teh-gahmee nga wa-tahshee nee (wa-tahsh'tahchee nee) ahrree-mahsska?

12. —— irasshaimasu ka? —— ni tsuite desu. Taihen jūyō desu.
—— ee-rrahss-shigh-mahsska? —— nee tsooee-teh dess. Tigh-hehñ joo-yaw dess.

13. Kore wa ikura desu ka? Kore o itadakimasu. Sore wa takasugimasu. Irimasen.
Kawrreh wa eekoo-rra desska? Kawrreh aw eetah-dahkee-mahss. Sawrreh wa tah-kah-sooghee-mahss. Eerree-mahss-ehñ.

KOREAN

9. Na rŭl yŏgwan e (yŏgwan —— e) derigo gajusipsiyo. I gŏt i (Gŭ gŏt i) gŭ yŏgwan imnikka? Ŏlmana mŏmnikka?
Nah rrool yer-gwahn eh (yer-gwahn —— eh) dtahrree-gaw gkahjooshp-shyo. Yee goosh ee (Gkoo goosh ee) gkoo yer-gwahn 'm-nikkah? Ooll-mahnah m'm-nikkah?

10. Chimdaa hana ga innŭn bang i (Chimdaa dul i innŭn bang i) issŭmnikka? Bang ŭl boyŏ jusigessŭmnikka? Gŭ bang ŭl joha haji an hamnida. I bang ŭl joha hamnida.
Chimdeh hahnnah gah in-nern bpahng ee (Chimdeh dtool ee in-nern bpahng ee) iss'm-nikkah? Bpahng ool bawyoo tjooshee-yess'm-nikkah? Gkoo bpang ool jaw-ah hahjee ahn ahm-needah. Yee bpang ool jaw-ah hahm-needah.

11. Naa bang ŭi yŏlsoe rŭl jusipsiyo. Na hante (Uri hante) pyonji ga issŭmnikka?
Neh bpang wee yerlsoo rrool tjooshp-shyo. Nah hahnteh (Oorree hahnteh) pyernjee gah iss'm-nikkah?

12. —— gwa yiyagi halsu issŭmnikka? —— e gwan haasŭ imnida. Daadan hi jungyo hamnida.
—— gkwah yee-yahghee hahlss'iss'm-nikkah? —— eh gkwahn ehss' 'm-needah- Dehdahn ee tjoong-yaw ahm-needah.

13. Ŏlma imnikka? I gŏt ŭl sagessŭmnida. Nŏmu bissamnida. An sagesŭmnida.
Oyl-mah 'm-nikkah? Yee gooss ool sah-gehss'm-needah. Nawmoo bissahm-needah. Ahn sah-gehss'm-needah.

SENTENCES

ENGLISH	MANDARIN	CANTONESE

14. May I wash my hands? I would like a bath. I need some soap (a towel, hot water).

14. Wǒ kěyǐ xǐxi shǒu ma? Wǒ xiǎng xǐge zǎo. Wǒ yào <u>féizào</u> (yìtiao máojing, rèshuǐ).
WAW? kerYEE syeeSYEE shoh MA. WAW? syahng syeeG dzow? Waw YOW! FAY?ZOW!(YEE!tyow MOW?JING, RER!shway?).

14. Ngóh hó m̀h-hó yíh sái sáu? Ngóh séung sáisàn. Ngóh sèuiyiu dī fàangáan (yāt-tìuh mòuhgān, yiht- séui).
Ngaw? HAW? mm-HAW? YEE? SIGH? SOW? Ngaw? SERNG? SIGH?SAHN! Ngaw? SER-YOO DEE FAHN!GAHN? (YATtyoo! moh!GAHN, yit SOY?).

15. Is the restaurant <u>open</u> (closed)? Could I see the menu? I would like ————. The bill, please.

15. Fànguǎn <u>kāimén</u> (guānle) ma? Wǒ kěyǐ kànkan càidān ma? Wǒ yào ————. Qǐng nǐ jiézhàng.
FAHN!gwahn? KIGH-MN? (GWAHNler) ma. WAW? kerYEE KAHN!kahn TSIGH!-DAHN ma. Waw YOW! ————. TSYING? nee JYER-JAHNG!

15. Go-gàan chāan-gún haih m̀h-haih hoimùhn (sàanmùhn) a? Ngóh hóyíh tái choidāan ma? Ngóh sèuiyiu ————. Dāan, m̀h-gòi.
GAWGAHN! CHAHNGOON? high mm-high HOYmoon! (SAHN!moon!) a. Ngaw? HAW?yee? TIGH? CHOYDAHN MA. Ngaw? SER!YOO ————. DAHN, mm-GOY!

16. I would like to make a telephone call. Would you call ———— for me? There is no answer. I have been cut off.

16. Wǒ xiǎng dǎge diànhuà. Nǐ kěyǐ tì wǒ dǎ diànhuà gěi ———— ma? Méiyou rén tīng. Yǒuren bǎ diànhuà guàduànle.
WAW? syahng dahG DYEN!HWAH!. NEE? kerYEE TEE! WAW? dtah DYEN!HWAH! gay ———— ma. MAY?yoh R'N? TING. YohR'N bpah DYEN!HWAH! GWAH!DWAHN!ler

16. Ngóh séung dádihnwá. M̀h-gòi néih bòng ngóh dádihnwá béi ————. Móuh yàhn tàng. Tìuhsìhn yihgíng tyúhm jó.
Ngaw? SERNG? DAH?deenWAH? Mm-GOY! neigh? BOHNG! ngaw? DAH?deenWAH? BEIGH? ————. Moh? yahn! TAHNG! Teeoo!seen yeeGING? tyoon? dyaw?

17. Could I have <u>some notepaper</u> (some air mail paper, some envelopes)? Where can I buy stamps? How much altogether?

17. Wǒ kěyǐ yào yìxiē <u>biàntiáo zhǐ</u> (hángkōng xìnzhǐ, xìnfēng) ma? Dào nǎr qu mǎi yóupiào? Yígòng dōshao qián?
WAW? kerYEE YOW! yeeSYER BYAHN!-TYOW! tjer! (HAHNG?KAWNG SYIN!dj, syin!F'NG) ma. DTOW! nahrr? TSU migh YOH?PYOW! YEE?GAWNG! DAWshow TSYEN?

17. Béi dī seunjí (dī hohnghūng seunjí, dī seunfūng). Bīnsyu hóyíh máaih yàuhpiu? Hahmbaahnglaahng géidò chín?
BEIGH? DEE SERN-DYEE? (DEE hohng-HOONG SERN-DYEE?, DEE sernFOONG). BEENsyoo HAW?yee? migh? yow!PYOO. Hahm-bahng-lahng GEIGH?DAW! CHEEN?

194

SENTENCES

HOKKIEN

14. Guà 'eh sài suē chiù beh'?
Guà 'ài tsang'ièk. Guà 'ài 'ieng
sāpbún (duañlàk, dzuah' tsuì).
GWAH! 'eh SIGH! SWEH
CHYOO! beh'. GWAH!
'IGH! TSAHNG*'YEHK.*
GWAH! 'IGH! 'Y'NG
*SAHP*BOON?
(DWAHÑ*LAHK!, dzah'*
TSWEE!).

15. Tsīt 'e chàigkuàn kuī
(gkuāiñ) beh'? Guà 'eh sài kuàñ
hīt 'e chàiduañ beh'? Gua 'ài
———. Chiàñ duañ.
*TSIT'*EH *CHIGH!GWAHN!*
KWEE (gkahñ) beh'.
GWAH! 'eh SIGH!
*KWAHÑ! HIT'*EH
CHIGH!DTWAHÑ! beh'.
GWAH! 'IGH! ———.
CHYAHÑ DTWAHÑ.

16. Guà 'ài pà' dian. Lì 'eh
gkiòu ——— hoh guà beh'?
Bou lang 'ihn. Guà diouh' gkuà'
kih liàu.
GWAH! 'IGH! PA'! DTYEN.
LEE! 'eh GKYOH! ———
haw GWAH! beh'. BOH
LAHNG *'een. GWAH! dtyoh'*
GKWAH' kee LYOW!

17. 'Eh sài hoh gùa
dahmbpouh' siādzih-tsuà
(dahmbpouh' huigki tsuà,
dahmbpouh' puelóng) beh'?
Guà kì dôulōu' buē 'iu-piouh?
Lōngtsòng luah tsueh?
'Eh SIGH! haw GWAH!
dtahmboh'
SYAHdzeeTSWAH!
(dtahmboh' HWEEGKEE
TSWAH!, dtahmboh' PWEH-
LAWNG?) *beh'. GWAH!*
KEE! DTOHLOH' BWEH
'YOO-*pyoh. LAWNG-*
TSAWNG lwah tseh.

JAPANESE

14. Te o aratte mo ii desu ka?
Ofuro ni hairi tai desu. Sekken
ga (Taoru ga, Oyu ga) irimasu.
Teh aw ah-rahtteh maw ee
desska? Aw-ffoorraw nee ha-
eerree tigh dess. Sek-kehñ
nga (Towrroo nga, Aw-yoo
nga) eerree-mahss.

15. Shokudō wa aite (shimatte)
imasu ka? Menyū o misete
itadakemasu ka? ——— ga
hoshii desu. Okanjō o
onegaishimasu.
Shokkoo-daw wa ah-ee-teh
(shi-mahtteh) ee-mahsska?
Mehnyoo aw meesseh-teh
eetah-dahkeh-mahsska?
——— *ga haw-shee dess. O-*
kahnjaw aw aw-nehga-
eeshee-mahss.

16. Denwa o kaketai no desu.
——— e denwa o kakete
kudasaimasen ka? Demasen.
Kirete imasu.
Dehñ-wah aw kahkeh-tigh
naw dess. ——— *eh dehñ-*
wah aw kahkeh-teh koodah-
sighmahss-engka? Deh-
mahss-ehñ. Kee-rrehteh ee-
mahss.

17. Binsen ga (kōkūbin no
binsen ga, Futō ga) hoshii desu.
Kitte wa doko de kaemasu ka?
Minna de ikura desu ka?
Beeñ-sehñ ga (Kaw-koo-beeñ
naw beeñ-sehñ ga, Ffootaw
ga) haw-shee dess. Keet-teh
wa dawkaw deh ka-eh-
mahsska? Meen-nah deh
eekoo-rra desska.

KOREAN

14. Son ŭl ssisŭdo jossŭmnikka?
Mogyok ŭl hago sipsŭmnida. Binu
rŭl (Sugŏn ŭl, Dŏun mŭl ŭl)
jusipsiyo.
Sawn ool sish'daw tjawss'm-
nikkah? Mawgyawg ool
hahgaw ships'm-needah.
Bpeenoo rrool (Soog'n ool,
Ttohn moorrool) tjooshp-
shyo.

15. Sikdang i yŭngŭp jung
(jungchi) imnikka? Menu rŭl
boyŏ jusipsiyo. ——— ŭl
jusipsiyo. Gyesan sŏ rŭl
jusipsiyo.
Sh'k-dahng ee y'ngop tjoong
(tjoongjee) 'm-nikkah?
Mehnyoo rrool bpawyoo
tjooshp-shyo. ——— *ool*
tjooshp-shyo. Gkyehsahn
s'rrool tjooshp-shyo.

16. Jŏnhwa rŭl hago sipsŭmnida.
——— rŭl gŏrŏ jusipsiyo.
Daadap i ŏpsŭmnida. Sŏni jungdan
doetsŭmnida.
Tjernah rrool hahgaw
ships'm-needah. ———
rrool gkoorroo tjooshp-shyo.
Dehdahn ee awps'm-needah.
Sernee tjoongdahn dterts'm-
needah.

17. Jong i (Han-gongji ga,
Bongtu ga) jusipsiyo. U-pyo nŭn
ŏdisŏ samnikka? Jŏnbu ŏlma
imnikka?
Tjawng ee (Hahn-gawngjee
gah, Bpawngtoo gah)
tjooshp-shyo. Oo-pyaw nunn
awdee-so sahm-nikkah?
Tjernboo oyl-mah 'm-
nikkah?

195

SENTENCES

ENGLISH	MANDARIN	CANTONESE
18. I am ill. Where can I see a doctor? Please get a good doctor. Could I have some water?	18. Wǒ bìngle. Dào nǎr qù kàn yīsheng? Qǐng nǐ chiào yíge hǎode yīsheng lai. Qǐng gěi wǒ diǎnr shuǐ hē. *Waw BPING!la. DTOW! nahrr? TSU! KAHN! YEEsh'ng. TSYING? nee CHYOW! yeeG howD YEEsh'ng ligh. TSYING? GAY? waw DYAHNR? shway HER.*	18. Ngóh yáuh behng. Bīnsyu hóyìh tái yīsāng? Mh-gòi heui giu yāt-go hóu yīsāng. Béi bùiséui ngóh, dāk ma? *Ngaw? yow? behng. BEENsyoo haw?yee? TIGH? YEE-SAHNG. Mm-GOY! HOY GYOO YATgaw HOH? YEE-SAHNG. BEIGH? BOOI!soy? ngaw?, DAHK MA.*
19. May I introduce ———. I am pleased to meet you. My name is ———.	19. Ràng wǒ gěi nǐ jièshao ———. Jiúyǎng. Wǒ jiào ———. *RAHNG! waw GAY? nee JYER!show ———. JYOO?yahng. Waw JYOW! ———.*	19. Ngóh gāi-sīu ———. Ngóh hóu hòisàm yuhgin néih. Ngóh giujouh ———. *Ngaw? GIGH-SEEOO ———. Ngaw? HOH? HOY!SAHM! yooGEEN neigh? Ngaw? GYOOdyoh ———.*
20. Who are you? A friend. I come from ———. Go away!	20. Nǐ shì shéi? Yíge péngyou. Wǒ cóng ——— lái. Zǒukāi! *NEE? SHER SHAY? YEEg P'NGyoh. Waw TSAWNG? ——— LIGH? DzohKIGH.*	20. Néih haih bīn-go? Pàhngyáuh. Ngóh haih yau ——— leih. Hàahng hòi! *Neigh? high BEENGAW. Pahng!yow? Ngaw? high YOW ——— leigh. Hahng! HOY!*
21. What is this called? What is this place called? It is called ———.	21. Zhèige jiào shénme? Zhèige dìfang jiào shénme? Jiào ———. *TJAY!g JYOW! SH'mer. TJAY!g DEEfahng JYOW! SH'mer. JYOW! ———.*	21. Nī-go giujouh mātyéh a? Nī-daat deihfòng giujouh mātyéh a? Giujouh ———. *NEEgaw GYOOdyoh MATyeh? AH. NEEDAHT deighFOHNG! GYOOdyoh MATyeh? AH. GYOOdyoh ———.*
22. What is the matter? Don't worry. I am <u>sorry</u> (glad). I shall give you this.	22. Shénme shì? Bié dānxin. Wó hěn <u>nánguò</u> (gāoxing). Zhèige gěi nǐ. *SH'mer SHER! BYER? DTAN-SYIN. WAW? h'n NAHN?GWAW! (GOW-SYING!). TJAY!g GAY? nee?*	22. Jouh mātyéh a? Mh-sái dāamsàm. <u>Dēui-mh-jyùh</u> (Hòisàm). Ngóh séung sung nī-go béi néih. *Dyoh MATyeh? AH. Mm-SIGH? DAHM-SAHM! DOY-mm-dyoo (HOY!sahm!). Ngaw? SERNG? SOONG NEEgaw BEIGH? neigh?*

196

SENTENCES

HOKKIEN	JAPANESE	KOREAN

18. Guà puàbpiñ. Guà ki
dōulōu' kuàñ lōugkūn? Chiàñ
gkiòu hōu 'e lōugkūn. 'Eh sài
hoh guà dahmbpouh' tsuì beh'?
*GWAH! PWAH!ᴮᴾᴱʜÑ.
gwah KEE! DTOHLOH'
KWAHÑ! LOH-GKOON.
CHYAHÑ GKYOH! HOH
'ᴇʜ LOH-GKOON. 'Eh
SIGH! haw GWAH!
dtahmboh' TSWEE beh'.*

18. Watashi wa guai ga warui
desu. Doko de oisha-san ni mite
moraemasu ka? Ii oisha-san o
yonde kuda-sai. Mizu o
itadakemasen ka?
*Wa-tahshee wa goo-igh nga
wa-rrooee dess. Dawkaw deh
o-eesha-sahn nee meeteh mo-
righ-mahsska? Ee o-eesha-
sahn aw yondeh koodah-sigh.
Meezoo aw eetah-dahkeh-
mahss-engka?*

18. Mom i apumnida. Ŭisa ga
ŏdi issŭmnikka? Ŭisa rŭl bulŏ
jusipsiyo. Mul jom jusipsiyo.
*Mawm ee ahpoom-needah.
Ooa-sah gah oodee iss'm-
nikkah? Ooa-sah rrool
bpooloo tjooshp-shyo. Mool
tjom tjooshp-shyo.*

19. Guà kah lī gkàisiauh
———. Guà huañhī gkāp lì.
Guà 'e miá ———.
*GWAH! kah LEE
GKIGH!syow ———.
GWAH! ʜᴡᴀʜÑHEE
GKAHP LEE! GWAH!'ᴇʜ
ᴍʏᴀʜ? ———.*

19. ——— o go-shōkai
itashimasu. O-me ni kakarete
ureshū gozaimasu. Watashi wa
——— to mōshimasu.
*——— aw gaw-shawkigh
ee-tahshee-mahss. O-meh nee
kah-kahrreh-teh oorreh-shoo
go-zigh-mahss. Wa-tahshee
wa ——— taw mawshee-
mahss.*

19. ——— rŭl sogaa hamnida.
Chŏum boepgetsumnida.
——— rago hamnida.
*——— rrool sawgeh hahm-
needah. Chaw-oom bperp-
gehts'm-needah. ———
rrahgaw hahm-needah.*

20. Lì tsih-tsui? Bpieng'iù. Guà
——— lái 'e. Tsàu!
*LEE! tseeᴛꜱᴡᴇᴇ.
ʙᴘᴇɴɢ'YOO! GWAH!
——— LIGH'? 'ᴇʜ. TSOW!*

20. Anata wa donata desu ka?
Tomodachi desu. Watashi wa
——— kara kimashita. Atchi e
itte kudasai!
*A-nahtah wa dawnah-tah
desska? Tawmaw-dahchee
dess. Wa-tahshee wa ———
kahrah kee-mahshtah. Aht-
chee eh eetteh koodah-sigh!*

20. Nugu sijiyo? Chingu
imnida. ——— sŏ wassŭmnida.
Jŏri ga!
*Noogoo sh'j'yo? Chinggoo
'm-needah. ——— ser
wahss'm-needah. Tjurree
gkah!*

21. Tsīt 'e gkiòu sīmmī'? Tsīt 'e
'ui gkiòu sīmmī'? Tsīt 'e gkiòu
*TSIT'ᴇʜ GKYOH! SIMMI'.
TSIT'ᴇʜ 'WEE GKYOH!
SIMMI'. TSIT'ᴇʜ GKYOH!
———.*

21. Kore wa nan to iimasu ka?
Koko wa nan to iimasu ka?
——— to iimasu.
*Kawrreh wa nahn taw ee-
mahsska? Kawkaw wa nahn
taw ee-mahsska? ———
taw ee-mahss.*

21. I gŏt ŭn muoraga hamnikka?
Yŏgi nŭn muoraga hamnikka?
——— rago hamnida.
*Yee gerss'n mwawrrah-gaw
hahm-nikkah? Yerghee noon
mwawrrah-gaw hahm-
nikkah? ——— tah-gaw
hahm-needah.*

22. Sīmmī' daihtsih? 'Mh-tang
huanlòu. Guà bpàng sīm (huañ-
hi). Guà hoh lì tsīt 'e.
*SIMMI' digh-tsee. Mm-
ᴛᴀʜɴɢ ʜᴡᴀʜɴLOH!
GWAH! BPAHNG! SIM
(hwahñHEE!). GWAH! haw
LEE! TSIT'ᴇʜ.*

22. Dō shimashita ka? Ki ni
shinaide kudasai. Zannen
(Ureshii) desu. Kore o anata ni
agetai no desu.
*Daw shee-mahshta ka? Kee
nee shee-nighdeh koodah-
sigh. Zahn-nehñ (Oo-resh-
shee) dess. Kawrreh aw ah-
nahtah nee ahgeh-tigh naw
dess.*

22. Woe gŭrŏsŭmnikka? Yŏmnyŏ
masipsiyo. Mian hamnida
(Daahang imnida). I gŏt ŭl
durigessŭmnida.
*Weh ghe-rrerss'm-nikkah?
Yumnyuh mahshp-shyo.
Mee-ahn ahm-needah (Dtah-
eng 'm-needah). Yee g'ss ool
dtoorree-gess'm-needah.*

197

SENTENCES

ENGLISH	MANDARIN	CANTONESE
23. What do you want? Please sit down. I have to leave. You must go now.	23. Nǐ yào shénme? Qǐng zuò. Wǒ yào chūqule. Nǐ yīdìng yào zǒu. *Nee YOW! SH'mer. Tsying DZWAW! Waw YOW! CHOOtsu-ler. Nee YEE-DING! YOW! dzoh?*	23. Néih yiu mātyéh a? Chéng chóh. Ngóh yātdihng yiu jáu. Néih yìhgá yātdihng yiu jáu. *Neigh?* YOO *MA*Tᴇʜ? ᴀʜ. ᴄʜᴇʜɴɢ? *chaw? Ngaw?* YA*Tdeeng* ʏᴏᴏ ᴅʏᴏᴡ? *Neigh?* ʏᴇᴇ!ɢᴀʜ? YA*Tdeeng* ʏᴏᴏ ᴅʏᴏᴡ?
24. I need help. I am in trouble. Please give this message to ———. As soon as possible.	24. Qǐng nǐ bāngbang máng. Wó yóu diǎnr máfàn. Qǐng ní bǎ zhèizhang tiáozi gěi ———. Yuè kuài yuè hǎo. *TSYING? nee BPAHNGbahng MAHNG? WAW? YOH? dyahnr MAH?fan. TSYING? nee bpah TJAY!jahng TYOW?dz gay ———. YOOER! KWIGH! YOOER! how?*	24. Ngóh sèuiyiu bòngjoh. Baihgàfó la. Chéng nīk ni-go syutwah béi ———. Jùhn faai. *Ngaw? SOY!*ʏᴏᴏ *BOHNG!dyaw. Bigh*GAH!ғᴀᴡ? ʟᴀ. ᴄʜᴇʜɴɢ? *NEEK NEE*ɢᴀᴡ sʏᴏᴏᴛ*wah* ʙᴇɪɢʜ? ———. *Dyoon!* ғɪɢʜ.
25. That is <u>very nice</u> (marvellous). That is <u>bad</u> (terrible). I have enjoyed myself very much.	25. Hén hǎo (Hǎo jíle). <u>Buhǎo</u> (Hěn buhǎo). Wó hěn kāixīn. *H'N? how? (How TJEE?ler). BOOhow? (H'n BOOhow?). WAW? h'n KIGH-SYIN.*	25. Nī-go <u>hóu hóu</u> (hóu dāk gāaugwàan). Nī-go <u>m̀h-hóu</u> (m̀h-hóu dāk gāaugwàan). Ngóh hóu hòisàm a. *NEE*ɢᴀᴡ ʜᴏʜ?ʜᴏʜ? (ʜᴏʜ? *DAHK GOW-GWAHN!). NEE*ɢᴀᴡ *mm*-ʜᴏʜ? (*mm*-ʜᴏʜ? *DAHK GOW-GWAHN!). Ngaw?* ʜᴏʜ? ʜᴏʏ!sᴀʜᴍ! ᴀʜ.

SENTENCES

HOKKIEN

23. Lì 'ài sìmmĭ'? Chiàñ tse. Guà diouh' sieng gkiáñ. Lì diouh' gkiañ dong-gkim.
LEE! 'IGH! SIMMI'. CHYAHÑ TSEH. *GWAH! dtyoh'* SENG GKYAHÑ? *LEE! dtyoh'* GKYAHÑ DTAWNG*GKIM.*

24. Guà 'ài gkǎp dauh. Guà 'uh kùnlán. Chiàñ tsit 'e siausit hoh ———. Gkīn-gkìn.
*GWAH! 'IGH! GKAHP dow. GWAH! 'oo KOON!*LAHN? *CHYAHÑ TSIT'*EH SYOW-SIT *haw* ———. *GKIN-GKIN!*

25. Hìt 'e tsin hòu (deh'ĭt hòu). Hìt 'e bou hòu (deh'ĭt bou hòu). Guà tsin huañ-hì.
*HIT'*EH TSIN *HOH! (deh'IT HOH!). HIT'*EH *boh HOH! (deh'IT boh HOH!). GWAH!* TSIN HWAHÑ*HEE!*

JAPANESE

23. Nani ga irimasu ka? O-kake kudasai. Watashi wa kaeranakereba narimasen. Anata wa ima kaeranakereba narimasen.
Nahnee nga eerree-mahsska? O-kahkeh koodah-sigh. Wa-tahshee wa kah-ehrrah-nahkeh-rrehbah nahrree-mahss-ehñ. A-nahtah wa eemah kah-ehrrah-nahkeh-rrehbah nahrree-mahss-ehñ.

24. Watashi wa tasuke ga irimasu. Watashi wa komatte imasu. Dōzo kono kotozuke o ——— ni shite kudasai. Naru take hayaku onegai shimasu.
Wa-tahshee wa tahss'keh nga eerree-mahss. Wa-tahshee wa kaw-mahtteh ee-mahss. Dawzaw kawnaw kawtaw-zookeh aw ——— nee sh'teh koodah-sigh. Nahroo tahkeh ha-yahkoo ohneh-gigh she-mahss.

25. Taihen ii (Subarashii) desu. Warui (Hidoi) desu. Totemo tanoshii deshita.
Tigh-hehñ ee (S'bah-rrah-shee) dess. Wah-rrooee (Hee-dawee) dess. Taw-tehmaw tahnaw-shee deshta.

KOREAN

23. Muŏt ŭl chassŭmnikka? Ŏsŏ anjŭsipsiyo. Gaya gessŭmnida. Gasyoya hamnida.
Mooass ool chahss'm-nikkah? Awsoo ahn-tjooshp-shyo. Gkahyah gkess'm-needah. Gkahshaw-ya hahm-needah.

24. Jom do-a jusipsiyo. Yil i saang gyossŭmnida. ——— ege i gŏt ŭl jŏnhaa jusipsiyo. Ppalli.
Tjawm daw-ah tjooshp-shyo. Yeerr ee seng gyerss'm-needah. ——— ehgeh yee g'ss ool jern-eh tjooshp-shyo. Ppahllee.

25. Aju jossŭmnida (hulryunghan). Goyak hamnida (Aju nappŭmnida). Jami rŭl ma-ni boassŭmnida.
A-ahjoo tjawss'm-needah (hool-yoong-ahn). Gkawyahk ahm-needah (A-ahjoo nahp-poom-needah). Tjehmee rrool mahnee bpaw-ahss'm-needah.

VOCABULARY

ENGLISH	MANDARIN	CANTONESE
above	shàngbianr	seuhngbihn
accident, the	yìwài	yi-ngoih
address, the	dìzhǐ	deihji
adult, the	dàren	daaih-yàhn
advertisement, the	guǎngào	gwónggou
aerogramme, the	hángkōng yóujiǎn	yàuhgáan
afraid	hàipà	pa
after	yǐhòu	yihhauh
afternoon, the	xiàwǔ	hahjau
again	zài	joi
against	fǎnduì	ngahk
agree, to	tóngyì	tùhngyi
air, the	kōngqì	hùnghei
air conditioner, the	lěngqìjī	láahngheigēi
air mail, the	kōngyóu	hùngyàuh
airplane, the	fēijī	fēigèi
airport, the	fēijīchǎng	fēigèichèuhng
alive	huó de	sàang
all	dōu	gogo dōu
all right	hǎo	hóuhóu
almost	chàbuduō	jāangdī
alone	yìgeren	jihgéi
already	yǐjing	yíhgìng
also	yě	yihkdōu
although	suīrán	sèuiyìhn
always	zǒngshi	sìhsìh
among	zài ... zhī zhōng	hái ... léuihbihn
and (between nouns)	hé	tùhng
angry	shēngqì	nàu
animal, the	dòngwu	duhngmaht
another one (different)	biéde	lìhng-ngoih
another one (more)	zài ... yìge	joi
answer, to	huídá	wùihdaap
antiseptic, the	fángfǔjì	siu tùkyeuhkséui
apartment, the	fángzi	wàahngdihm
apple, the	píngguǒ	pìhnggwó
approximately	dàyuē	jóyáu
arm, the	shǒubèi	sáubei
army, the	jūnduè	gwàndéui
around	zhōuwéi	jàuwàih
arrive, to	dào	dou
art, the	yìshù	méihseuht
art gallery, the	měishùguǎn	méihseuhtgún
artificial	rénzàu de	yàhnjouh ge
ask (inquire), to	wèn	mahn
at	zài	hái
attempt, to	chángshì	si

VOCABULARY

HOKKIEN	JAPANESE	KOREAN
diēngbin	ue ni	... wi e
chia-hou	jiko	sago
tsuh-tsì	jūsho	juso
duahláng	otona	ŏrŭn
gkŏng-gkouh	kōkoku	gwanggo
huigki-puē	eā-retā	hanggong yŏbsŏ
gkiāñ	kowai	kep nan (na-)
'ī'au	... ato de	... hu e
'ehbpŏ	gogo	ohu
gkòu'tsihtbpài	mata	tto
kòng ...	... ni taishite	... e ban hayŏ
tsànsiéng	shōdaku shimasu	dong-ŭi hamnida (ha-)
kongkih	kūki	gonggi
liēngkih	ea-kon	naang bang
huigki-puē	kōkūbin	hanggong u-pyŏ
huigki	hikōki	bihaanggi
huigkidiúñ	hikōjō	bihaangjang
'uā'	ikite iru	sara innŭn (iss-)
lōngtsòng	zembu	modŭn
hòu	yoroshii	johŭn (joh-)
hiam ...	hotondo	gŏŭi
gkagkih tsiht láng	hitori de	honja
'ī-gkiēng	mō	bŏlssŏ
yah ...	mata	yŏksi
suidzian ...	tatoe ... to wa ie	birok ... iljirado
bpūt-sì	itsumo	nŭl
gkidiōng	... no naka ni	... ui gaunde
gka' ...	to	wa
ki-hōng	okotta	songnan (songna-)
dohngbŭt	dōbutsu	dongmul
bpaht 'é	betsu no	darŭn
gkòu' tsiht 'é	mō hitotsu	tto hana
'ihn	kotaemasu	daadap hamnida (ha-)
'iou'tsuì	bōfūzai	bangbuje
bpáng	apāto	apatŭ
piahng-gkòu	ringo	sagwa
daih'iohk	goro	han ...
chiū	ude	pal
gkundui	guntai	yukkun
'ui ...	... no atari ni	... juwi e
gkauh	tsukimasu	dochak hamnida (ha-)
bīsùt	geijutsu	yesul
bīsuhtgkuān	garō	hwarang
gkē	jinzō no	in-gongjok
mng	tazunemasu	mussŭmnida (mur-)
dih ...	... ni	... e sŏ
chih	kokoromimasu	noryok hamnida (ha-)

VOCABULARY

ENGLISH	MANDARIN	CANTONESE
awake	xǐng de	fanséng
baby, the	yīnghái	bìhbī
back (rear), the	hòubianr	hauh
back (again)	huílai	fàanlèih
backwards	xiànghòu	fàanlèih
bad	bùhǎo	m̀h-hóu
bag, the	dàizi	doih
baggage, the	xínglǐ	hàhnglèih
ballpoint, the	yuánzibǐ	yùhnjíbāt
bamboo shoots, the	zhúsǔn	jùkséun
banana, the	xiāngjiāo	hēungjīu
bank (money), the	yínháng	ngàhnhòhng
bathe, to	xǐzǎo	sáisàn
bathroom, the	xǐzǎo fáng	sáisànfóng
battery, the	diànchí	dihnchìh
beach, the	shātān	hóipèih
beans, the	dòuzi	dáu
beard, the	húxū	sòu
beautiful	měilì	hóu
because	yīnwèi	yànwaih
because of	yīnwèi	yànwaih
become, to	biàncheng	binsèhng
bed, the	chuáng	chòhng
beef, the	niúròu	ngàuhyuhk
beer, the	píjiǔ	bējáu
before (time)	yǐqián	. . . jichìhn
behind	hòubianr	. . . hauhbihn
believe, to	xiàngxin	sèungseun
bell, the	zhōng	jùng
best	zuìhǎo de	jeui hóu ge
better	hǎo yīdiǎnr de	hóugwo
beyond	chāoguo	hái . . . góbihn
bicycle, the	zixíngchē	dāanchē
big	dà	daaih
bill, the	zhàngdān	dāan
binoculars, the	wàngyuǎnjing	mohngyúhn-geng
bird, the	niǎo	jéuk
biscuit, the	bǐnggān	bénggōn
black	hēi	hāk
blanket, the	tǎnzi	jín
blood, the	xiě	hyut
blue	lán	làahm ge
boat, the	chuán	téhng
body, the	shēntǐ	sàntái
boiled	zhǔ	gwán
book, the	shū	syù

VOCABULARY

HOKKIEN	JAPANESE	KOREAN
kùn-kui	okite iru	jamŭl kkaan (kkaa-)
'eñ'àñ	akambō	aagi
'auhbin	ushiro	dwi
touhlái	kaette	dwi
touhbpiéng	ushiro no hō	dwi e
bou hòu	warui	nappŭn (nappŭ-)
hiengli	kaban	jumŏni
hiengli	tenimotsu	jim
'iantsuhbpiht	bōru-pen	bolpen
sùn	take-no-ko	juksun
giengtsiōu	banana	ppanana
gunháng	ginkō	ŭnhaang
tsang'iĕk	furo ni hairimasu	myŏkkamsŭmnida (myŏkkam-)
'iehk-gkiĕng	furoba	mogyok sil
diahnsim	batterii	batteri
hāisuā	kaigan	haa byŏn
dau	mame	kong
hochiù	hige	suyŏm
sui	utsukushii	ippŭn (ippŭ-)
'in'uih . . .	. . . no de	. . . ttaamun e
'in'uih . . . 'e gkuanhe	. . . no tame	. . . ttaamun e
bpiahn	narimasu	doemnida (doe-)
binchńg	betto	chimdaa
gubah'	gyūniku	so gogi
bihttsiù	biiru	maakju
'ī-tsiéng	mae ni	. . . jŏn e
'auhbin	. . . no ushiro ni	. . . dwi e
siongsihn	shinjimasu	missŭmnida (mir-)
liéng	kane	jong
deh'it hòu	ichiban ii	gajang johŭn (joh-)
kà' hòu	yori ii	dŏ johŭn (joh-)
hngh-bpiéng	. . . no mukō ni	. . . ŭi jŏjjok e
kadah'chiā	jitensha	jajŏn-gŏ
dua	ōkii	kŭn (kŭ-)
duañ	kanjō	chŏnggusŏ
bpong-gkiahñ	sōgankyō	ssang-an-gyŏng
tsiàu	tori	saa
bpiàñ	bisuketto	bisŭket
'ō	kuroi	gŏmŭn (gŏm-)
tān'à	mōfu	damyo
huih'	chi	pi
lám	aoi	purŭn (purŭ-)
tsún	bōto	baa
sin-kù	karada	mom
tsù	waita	salmŭn (salm-)
cheh'	hon	chaak

203

VOCABULARY

ENGLISH	MANDARIN	CANTONESE
boot, the	chángtǒngxuē	hèu
born	chūshēng	chēutsai
both	dōu	léuhng . . . dōu
bottle, the	píng	jēun
bottle opener, the	kāiqishuǐde	dá-hòi jēun ge yéh
bottom, the	dǐ	dái
box, the	xiāngzi	háp
boy, the	nánháizi	nàahmjái
bra, the	nǎizào	hùngwai·
brake, the	zhá	jai
brave	yónggǎn	yúhnggáam
bread, the	miànbāo	mihnbāau
break, to	dǎpò	jínglaahn
breakfast, the	zǎocān	jóuchāan
bridge, the	qiáo	kiuh
bring, to	dài	ningleih
brooch, the	biézhēn	sàmhójām
brown	hésè de	jūngsīk ge
brush, the	shuāzi	cháat
bundle, the	bāor	bàau
bus, the	gōnggòng qìchē	bāsi
businessman, the	shāngrén	sèungyàhn
busy	máng	mh-dākhàahn
but	dànshi	daahnhaih
butter, the	niúyóu	ngàuhyàuh
button, the	niǔkòu	ngáu
buy, to	mǎi	máaih
cabbage, the	juǎnxīncài	yèhchoi
cake, the	dàngāo	béng
call (telephone), the	diànhuà	dihnwá
called, is	jiào	giujouh
call out, to	dàshēngjiào	giu
camera, the	zhàoxiàngjī	yíngséunggèi
candle, the	làzhú	laahpjŭk
captain (of ship), the	chuánzhǎng	syùhnjéung
car, the	chē	chè
carefully	xiǎoxīnde	siusàm
cargo, the	huò	fo
carpet, the	dìtǎn	deihjīn
carrot, the	húluóbo	hùnglòhbaak
carry, to	názhe	nìng
cat, the	māo	māau
centimetre, the	gōngfēn	gùngfān
century, the	shìjì	saigéi
certainly	yídìng	dòngyìhn
chair, the	yǐzi	yí

VOCABULARY

HOKKIEN	JAPANESE	KOREAN
duah 'ué	būtsu	janghwa
chŭt-sih	umareta	nan (na-)
nng	futatsu tomo	dul da
gkuăn	bin	byŏng
gkuăn-taudōu	sen-nuki	byŏng ttage
kăde	soko	mit
'ă'	hako	sangja
dabpō gīn'ă	otoko-no-ko	sonyŏn
laihsăñ	burajă	bra
buhtliĕk	burēki	bureki
'iŏng-gkàm	yŭkan na	yonggam han (ha-)
mihbpáu	pan	sik-ppang
puah	oremasu	kkaattŭrimnida (-ttŭri-)
tsiah'tsă-ki	asabohan	choban
gkióu	hashi	dari
tĕ'lái	motte kimasu	gajigo omnida (o-)
gkimbpái	burōchi	brotch
gkoubpisiehk	chairo	galsaak . . .
chièng	burashi	sol
bpău	tsutsumi	dabal
bàsi [gkong-gkiohng]	basu	bŏsŭ
sienglĭláng	kaisha-in	sirŏbga
bou'iéng	isogashii	bappŭn (bappŭ-)
bpŭtgkouh	keredomo	gŭraa do
gu'iŭ	bată	bŏtŏ
liŭ'à	botan	danchu
buè	kaimasu	samnida (sa-)
bpauchaih	kyabetsu	yangbaachu
bpiăñ	kēki	gwaja
diahn'ue	denwa	jŏnhwa
gkióu . . .	. . . to iimasu	. . . rago hamnida
gkiouh	yobimasu	bŭrŭmnida (bŭrŭ-)
hipsiohng-gkī	kamera	kamera
lah'tsiĕk	rōsoku	yang cho
tsun-tau	senchō	sŏnjang
chiă	kuruma	jadongcha
suèdzih . . .	chŭi-bukaku	josimsŭrŏpge
heh	funa-ni	baatjim
deh-tsiăn	jŭtan	yangdan
labpăk	ninjin	danggŭn
gkiă'	motte ikimasu	gajimnida (gaji-)
niău	neko	goyangi
gkonghŭn	senchi	sentimeta
sègki	seiki	segi
tsŭntsùn	tashika ni	bunmyŏng-hi
'ĭ	isu	ŭija

VOCABULARY

ENGLISH	MANDARIN	CANTONESE
change (small money), the	língqián	seuingán
change (money), to	huànqián	wuhn
change (transport), to	huàn	wuhn
cheap	piányi	pèhng
cheese, the	gānlè	chìsí
cherry, the	yīngtao	yìngtòuh
chicken, the	jī	gāi
chief, the	shóulíng	táu
child, the	háizi	saimānjái
chocolate, the	qiǎokelìtáng	jyūgūlēut
choose, to	xuǎn	gáan
chopsticks, the	kuàizi	faaijí
church, the	lǐbàitáng	láihbaaitòhng
cigar, the	xuějiā	léuihsungyin
cigarette, the	xiāngyān	yīnjái
cinema, the	diànyǐng	yìngheiyún
city, the	chéngli	sèhngsíh
clean	gānjing	gònjehng
clean, to	nùng gānjing	sáigònjehng
clerk, the	shūji	syùgei
clock, the	zhōng	jūng
close, to	guānshang	sàanmàaih
closed	guānle	sàanmùhn
cloth, the	bù	chòihlíu
clothes, the	yīfu	sāam
coast, the	yénhǎi de dìfang	hóibīn
coat, the	shàngyī	daaihláu
coffee, the	kāfei	gafē
coin, the	yìngbì	sáanngán
cold	lěng	láahng
cold season (winter), the	dōngtian	láangtin
colour, the	yénsè	sìkséui
comb, the	shūzi	sò
come, to	lái	lèih
comfortable	shūfu de	syufuhk
commercial	shāngyè de	sèungyíhp ge
company (firm), the	gōngsi	gūngsì
complain, to	sùkǔ	ngàhmchàhm
completely	wánquán	sèhng
conceal, to	cángqilai	bengmàaih
concert, the	yīnyuèhuì	yàmngohk-wúi
consul, the	lǐngshì	líhngsí
contain, to	bāokuò	yáuh
continue, to	jìxù	jipjyuh
convenient	fāngbian	fòngbihn
conversation, the	huìhuà	tàahmwá
cook, to	zuò	jyufaahn

VOCABULARY

HOKKIEN	JAPANESE	KOREAN
lansantsiñ	komakai kane	gǒsǔrǔm don
'uañ	kaemasu	bakkǔmnida (bakkǔ-)
'uañ	norikaemasu	bakkǔmnida (bakkǔ-)
bpan-gí	yasui	ssan (ssa-)
chìsi	chiizu	chissǔ
chēli ['Ieng-tòu]	sakurambo	bǒt
gkuē	tori	tak
tauhláng	chō	udumǒri
gin'à	kodomo	ai
Angmo-tńg	chokorēto	chokolletǔ
gkièng	erabimasu	taak hamnida (ha-)
du [di]	ohashi	jǒtgarak
lēbpàidńg	kyōkai	gyohoe
duah hun-gki	hamaki	ssiga dambaa
hun-gki	tabako	dambaa
hi-hńg	eiga	yǒnghwa-
siañchi	machi	dosi
chieng-kih	kirei na	kkaakkǔt han (ha-)
bpiàñsauh	sōji shimasu	soje hamnida (ha-)
hēgkih	jimuin	samuwǒn
tsièng	tokei	sigye
gkuàiñ	shimemasu	dassǔmnida (dad-)
gkuàiñ	shimatte iru	dadǔn (dad-)
bpoh	kire	ot gam
sañ-koh	ishō	ot
hāi-huañ	engan	haa-an
duahsāñ	kōto	oetu
gkoubpih	kōhii	kǒpi
gun'ā kiàñ	kōka	dongjǒn
gkuáñ	samui	chan (cha-)
gkuañ-tiñ	fuyu	gyǒul
siehk	iro	bikkal
sasē [luah'à]	kushi	bit
lái	kimasu	omnida (o-)
sòng	kimochi no ii	pyǒnan hamnida (ha-)
siengli	shōgyō no . . .	sangǒp-ǔi
gkongsī	kaisha	hoesa
hiám	fuhei o iimasu	bǔlpyǒng ǔl mal hamnida (ha-)
tsahp hun . . .	kanzen ni	wanjǒn hage
kngh	kakushimasu	gamchumnida (gamchu-)
gkuán	konsāto	ǔmak hoe
lièngsu	ryōji	yǒngsa
diñ	fukumimasu	poham hamnida (ha-)
gkèsiok	tsukukemasu	gyesok hamnida (ha-)
lihbpian	benri na	pyǒnri han (ha-)
gkōng'ue	kaiwa	hoehwa
tsù	ryōri shimasu	yori hamnida (ha-)

VOCABULARY

ENGLISH	MANDARIN	CANTONESE
cookie, the	bǐnggān	bénggon
corkscrew, the	jiǔzuàn	jáujyun
corner (of room), the	jiǎoluò	gok
corner (street), the	guǎiqiǎo	gok
corridor, the	zǒuláng	jáulóhng
costs, (it)	zhí	yiu
cotton, the	miánbù	mìhnfà
cotton-wool, the	miánhuā	mìhnfà
count, to	shǔ	sóu
country (nation), the	guó	gwok
countryside, the	xiāngxià	hèunghá
course, of!	dāngrán!	dòngyín!
courtyard, the	yuànzi	tìnjéng
cover, to	zhēgài	kám
crab, the	xièzi	háaih
cream, the	rǔluò	geihlìm
cross, to	guò	gwo
crowd, the	qúnzhòng	yātkwàhn yàhn
cup, the	bēi	būi
curry, the	jiālǐ	galèi
cushion, the	zuòdiàn	jín
custom (way), the	fēngsú	fùngjuhk
customs, the	shuǐguān	seui
cut, to	gē	got
dance, to	tiàowǔ	tiumóuh
dangerous	wēixiǎn de	ngaihhím
dark (colour)	shēn	sàm
dark (no light)	hēiàn de	ngam
day, the	rì	yaht
daytime, the	báitiān	yahttáu
dead	sǐ de	séi ge
dear (expensive)	guì	gwai
decide, to	juédìng	kyutdihng
deep	shēn	sàm
demand, to	yāoqiú	yìukàuh
dentist, the	yáyī	ngàhfō yìsāng
desert, the	shāmò	sà-mohk
diamond, the	zuànshí	jyunsehk
dictionary, the	zìdiǎn	chihdín
die, to	sǐ	séi
different	bùtóng de	mh-tùhng
difficult	kùnnàn de	nàahn
dinner, the	wǎncān	máahn faahn
direction, the	fāngxiàng	fōngheung
dirty	zāng de	wūjòu
do, to	zuò	jouh
doctor, the	yīsheng	yìsāng

VOCABULARY

HOKKIEN	JAPANESE	KOREAN
bpiàñ	kukkii	bisǔket
chiùtsuan	koruku-sen-nuki	byǒng ttage
gkahk	sumi	gusǒk
gkahk	kado	motungi
goh-ka-ki	rōka	bokdo
gkè-tsiñ . . .	kakarimasu	gap nagamnida
miñ	momen	som
miñ	dasshi-men	yangmo
sngh	kazoemasu	semnida (se-)
gkōk-gkā	kuni	nara
gkuaiñ	inaka	sigol
diahñdiōu'!	mochiron!	mulon!
chimtsiñ	nakaniwa	madang
kahm	kakemasu	dǒpsǔmnida (dǒp-)
tsim	kani	ge
guleng-pé	kuriimu	kǔrim
gkeh	ōdan shimasu	gǒnnumnida (gǒnnu-)
kueh'	hito-gomi	gunjung
'āu	chawan	jan
gkali	karē	kare
tsim-táu	zabuton	bangsǒk
hongsiōk	shūkan	pungsok
hāigkuán	zeikan	segwan
gkuah'	kirimasu	bemnida (be-)
diàubù	odorimasu	chumnida (chu-)
gui-hiàm	kiken na	wihǒm han (ha-)
'ōsiehk	koi	ǒdun (ǒdu-)
'ahm	kurai	ǒdun (ǒdu-)
dzit	nichi	nal
dziht-si	hiruma	nat
si	shinda	jugǔn (jug-)
gkuih	takai	bissan (bissa-)
gkuàtdieng	kimemasu	gyǒlsim hamnida (ha-)
chim	fukai	gipǔn (gip-)
'iaugkiú	yōkyǔ shimasu	yogu hamnida (ha-)
chui-ki lōugkūn	haisha-san	chigwa ǔisa
suabōk	sabaku	samak
gkimgkongtsiōu'	daiyamondo	gǔmgangsǒk
dzihdiàn	jisho	sajon
si	shinimasu	jugsǔmnida (jug-)
bou siáng	chigatte iru	darǔn (darǔ-)
gkan-kò	muzukashii	ǒryǒun (ǒryǒw-)
tsiah' 'e-hñg	bangohan	jǒnyǒk
bpiéng	hōkō	banghyang
lasám	kitanai	dǒrǒun (dǒrǒw-)
tsueh	shimasu	hamnida (ha-)
lōugkūn	oisha-san	ǔisa

VOCABULARY

ENGLISH	MANDARIN	CANTONESE
dog, the	gǒu	gáu
don't!	buyào!	m̀h-hóu!
door, the	mén	mùhn
doubt, the	huáiyí	sìyìh
down	xiàmian	lohk
dress (woman's), the	qúnzi	sāam
drink, the	hēde	yámbūn
drink, to	hē	yám
drive (car), to	kāichē	sái
driver, the	sījī	sìgēi
dry	gān de	gòn
duck, the	yāzi	ngáap
during	dāng	. . . gójahnsí
dusty	chén'āimánbù de	yìnchàhn ge
duty (obligation), the	zérèn	búnfahn
each	gè	múih
each other	hùxiāng	bēichí
early (before time)	zǎo	jóu
earrings, the	ěrhuánzi	yìhwáan
east	dōngbianr	dùng
easy	róngyi de	yùhngyìh
eat, to	chī	sihk
egg, the	jīdàn	dáan
either . . . or	háishi . . . háishi	waahkhaih . . . waahkhaih
electric	diàn de	dihn
elevator, the	diàntī	dihntài
embassy, the	dàshǐguǎn	daaihsigún
empty	kòng de	hùng
enemy, the	dírén	dihkyàhn
engine (car), the	yǐnqing	gēihei
enjoy, to	xiǎnglè	fùnhéi
enormous	jùdà de	fēisèuhngdaaih ge
enough	gòu	gau . . .
enter, to	jìnrù	yahp
entrance, the	rùkǒu	mùhnháu
envelope, the	xìnfēngr	seunfūng
equal	xiāngděng de	dángyù
evening, the	wǎnshang	ngāaimāan sihhauh
everybody	měirén	múihyàhn
everything	měijian dōngxi	múihgo
everywhere	chùchù	hái múihdaai
exactly	zhèngquèdi	ngāamngāam
example, for	pǐrú	peiyùh
except	chúle . . . yǐwài	chèuihjó
exhibition, the	zhánlǎnhuì	jínláahmwúi
exit, the	chūkǒu	chēutháu

210

VOCABULARY

HOKKIEN	JAPANESE	KOREAN
gkàu	inu	gaa
'mh tang . . .!	shinaide kudasai!	masipsiyo!
mńg	doa	mun
hiamgi	utagai	uisim
. . . lòu'	shita ni	araa e
tsabòsāñ	fujin-fuku	ūisang
tsui	nomimono	sul
līm [tsiā']	nomimasu	masimnida (masi-)
sài	doraibu shimasu	unjŏn hamnida (ha-)
sāichiā 'e	untenshu	unjŏnsu
dā	kawaite iru	marŭn (mar-)
'ah'	ahiru	ori
. . . sí	. . . no aida	. . . hanŭndongan
tō-hńg	chiri darake no	mŏnji tusŏngui
tsiëkdzim	gimu	uimu
mui . . .	ono-ono	gak
sañ . . .	o tagai ni	sŏro
tsà	hayaku	iljjik
hih-kuán	iaringu	gwigori
dangbin	higashi	dong
'ióng	yasashii	swiun (swiw-)
tsiā'	tabemasu	jabsumnida (jabsu-)
nng	tamago	al
'ā . . . 'ā . . .	ka . . . ka	na . . . na
dian	denki- . . .	jŏn-gi
diahntài	erebētā	sŭngganggi
duah-gkuán	taishikan	daasagwan
kāng	kara na	bin (bi-)
diehkdzín	teki	jŏk
gki-kih	mōtā	enjin
chit-tóu	tanoshimimasu	jŭlgimnida (jŭlgi-)
tsueh	bakudai na	gwangdaa han (ha-)
gkauh	jūbun	nŏknŏk
dzip	hairimasu	dŭssŭmnida (dur-)
mng-kàu	iriguchi	ipgu
puelóng	fūtō	bongtu
bpíñ	byōdō na	gatŭn (gat-)
'e-hñg	yūgata	jŏnyŏk
dahk láng	dare demo	modŭn saram
dahk hang	banji	modu
tsiht sigkueh	doko demo	ŏdidŭnji
tsiàñtsiahñ	chōdo	kkok
chinchiuñ	tatoeba	ye rŭl dŭl myon
du-ki . . . 'igua	. . . no hoka wa	. . . rŭl je oe hamyŏn
diūnlāmgkuán	tenrankai	jŏllam hoe
chuht-kàu	deguchi	chulgu

VOCABULARY

ENGLISH	MANDARIN	CANTONESE
expect, to	qīwàng	jíyíh
explain, to	jiěshì	gáai
eye, the	yǎnjing	ngáahn
face, the	liǎn	mihn
fact, in	shìshí	sihsahtseung
fail, to	shībài	sātbaaih
fair (just)	gōngpíng	gùngpihng
fall, to	diēxià	ditdóu
family, the	jiārén	gàtìng
famous	yǒumíng de	chèutméng
fan, the	shànzi	fùngsin
far	yuǎn	yúhn
farmer, the	nóngmín	gàangtihnlóu
fast	kuài	faai
fasten, to	bǎngqilai	bóngjyuh
festival, the	jiérì	jit
fetch, to	nálái	ló
few, a	yidiǎnr	géi-
field, the	dì	tìhn
fight, to	dǎjià	cháanchèuih
fill, to	chōngmǎn	jámmúhn
film (for camera), the	ruǎnpiàn	feilám
film (movie show), the	diànyǐng	yíngpín
finally	zhōngyú	sàumēi
find, to	fāxiàn	wándóu
finish, to	wán	jouhsèhng
fire, the	huǒ	fójùk
first	dìyī	daihyāt
fish, the	yú	yú
flat	píngtǎn de	bín
flat (tyre), the	sàqì	baau tàai
floor, the	dìbǎn	deihháh
flower, the	huā	fā
fly, the	cānyíng	wūyíng
fly, to	fēi	fèi
follow, to	gēn	gànjyuh
food, the	shíwù	sihk maht
foot, the	zú	geuk
football (game), the	zúqiú	jùkkàuh
for	gěi	bòng
forbidden	jìnzhǐ	gamjí ge
foreign	wài	ngoihgwok ge
forest, the	sēnlín	syuhlàhm
forget, to	wàng	m̀h-geidāk
fork, the	chāzi	chā
former	zàixiān de	yíhchìhn

VOCABULARY

HOKKIEN	JAPANESE	KOREAN
'uh-gkahk	kitai shimasu	baramnida (bara-)
suātbiéng	setsumei shimasu	sŏlmyŏng hamnida (ha-)
bahktsiŭ	me	nun
bin	kao	ŏlgŭl
suhsĭt	yōsuru ni	sasil un
sĭtbpai	shippai shimasu	silpaa hamnida (ha-)
gkongdou	kōhei na	gongpyŏng han (ha-)
dòu	ochimasu	ttŏrŏ jimnida (ji-)
gkegkuahn	kazoku	gajok
chŭtmiá	yūmei na	yumyŏng han (ha-)
sihñ	sensu	buchaa
hng	tōi	mŏrŭn (mŏr-)
tsièngchán 'e	hyakushō	nogbŭ
gkin	hayai	pparŭmnida (pparŭ-)
tsiahp	shimemasu	dongyŏ maamnida (maa-)
lauhdziăt	omatsuri	jŏl
tē'lái	itte motte kimasu	chajŏ omnida (o-)
tsiht gkuà	shōshō-sukoshi	yŏrŏ
diúñ	hatake	bat
pah'	tatakaimasu	ssaumnida (ssau-)
duēdiñ	tsumemasu	chaaumnida (chaau-)
nñg-pihñ	fuirumu	pillŭm
diahn'iàñ	eiga	yŏnghwa
lohbè	saigo ni	najung e
chediou'	mitsukemasu	chassŭmnida (chaj-)
liàu	owarimasu	machimnida (machi-)
hè	kaji	bŭl
deh'iht	dai-ichi	chŏt
hú	sakana	gogi
bpíñ	taira	panpan han (ha-)
lauhhōng	panku	ppangkku
to-ká	yuka	maru
huĕ	hana	kkoch
hosin	hae	pari
bpĕ	tobimasu	nassŭmnida (nar-)
deh	tsuite ikimasu	jossŭmnida (joch-)
bpng	tabemono	ŭmsik
kā	ashi	bal
ka-gkiú	futto bōru	chukku
gkah ...	... ni	... hante
gkìmtsi	kinjita	gŭm han (ha-)
guahgkŏk ...	gaikoku no	oegugui
chiuhná	shinrin	sup
bueh gkih dit	wasuremasu	issŭmnida (ij-)
chiā-mà	fōku	fok
tiĕngbpâi	zensha	jŏn

VOCABULARY

ENGLISH	MANDARIN	CANTONESE
forwards	xiàngqián	chìhnbihn
free (vacant)	kòng de	hùng
fresh	xīnxiān de	sānsin
fried	chǎo de	cháau
fried rice, the	chǎofàn	cháau faahn
friend, the	péngyou	pàhngyáuh
from	cóng	hái
front of, in	qiánbianr	hái . . . chìhnbihn
frontier, the	biānjiè	bīn-gaai
frozen	dòng de	syutchòhng
fruit, the	shuǐguǒ	sàanggwó
full	mǎn	sèhng
garden, the	huāyuán	fàyún
gasoline (petrol), the	qìyóu	dihnyàuh
girl, the	nǚháizi	néuihjái
give, to	gěi	béi
glad	gāoxìng	fùnghéi
glass (drinking), the	bēi	būi
glass (substance), the	bōlí	bōlēi
glove, the	shǒutào	sáumāt
go, to	qù	heui
go down, to	xià	lohkheui
go up, to	shàng	sèuhngheui
god, the	shén	sàhn
gold, the	jīn	gām
good	hǎo	hóu
goods, the	huòwù	fo
government, the	zhèngfǔ	jingfú
gram, the	gōngkè	gùngfān
grapes, the	pútáo	pòuhtàihjí
grass, the	cǎo	chóu
green	lǜse de	luhk ge
grey	huīsè de	fūisīk ge
ground, the	dì	deihhá
guard, to	shǒuwèi	hòn
guest, the	kèrén	yàhnhaak
guide, the	xiàngdǎo	daai
guidebook, the	zhǐnán	jí-nàahm
gun, the	qiāng	chèunghaaih
hair, the	tóufa	tàuhfaat
haircut, the	lǐfà	jíntàuhfaat
hairdresser, the	lǐfàshī	léihfaatsī
ham, the	huótuǐ	fótéui
handbag, the	shǒutídài	sáudói
handkerchief, the	shǒujuànr	sáugánjái
harbour, the	gǎngkǒu	góngháu
hard (firm)	yìng	ngaahng

VOCABULARY

HOKKIEN	JAPANESE	KOREAN
tau-tsiéng	mae no hó	ap e
kǎng	aite iru	bin (bi-)
chiñ	shinsen na	saang
chà	... -furai	twigin
cha bpng	yakimeshi	twigin bap
bpieng'iú	tomodachi	chin-gu
duì ...	... kara	... sŏ
bihntsiéng	... no mae ni	... ap e
gkaugkaih	kyōkai	gukkyŏng
gkián	reitō no	ŏrŭn (ŏr-)
gkuě-tsi	kudamono	kwail
diñ	ippai ni	gadŭk chan (cha-)
hńg	niwa	jŏngwŏn
chia'iú	gasorin	hwibaryu
tsabò	onna-no-ko	yŏja
hò	itadakimasu/agemasu	jumnida (ju-)
huañhi	ureshi	gippŭn (gipp-)
bpuě	koppu	yuri jan
bpoulé	garasu	yuri
chiǔlóng	tebukuro	janggap
gkiáñ	ikimasu	gamnida (ga-)
lóu'ki	orimasu	naarimnida (naari-)
ki-ki	agarimasu	ollimnida (olli-)
tihñ-gkòng	kami	sin
gkim	kin	gŭm
hòu	ii	johŭn (joh-)
heh	kamotsu	mulgŏn
tsièng-hù	seifu	jŏngbu
gkonghùn	guramu	gŭrem
pudóu	budō	podo
chàu	kusa	pul
chiñ	midori	purŭn (purŭ-)
hě	nezumi-iro	hoesaak
due	jimen	badak
bpòu hòu	mamorimasu	chikimnida (chiki-)
lang-keh'	okyaku-san	son nim
chuahlo 'e	gaido	annaaja
chuahlo cheh'	ryokō-annai-sho	yŏhaang annaasŏ
chiehng	jū	chong
tau-mńg	kami	mŏritŏl
gkǎ-tau-mńg	sampatsu/katto	i bal
tsiǎn-huât-sai-hu	biyōshi	i bal sa
hě-tui	hamu	haam
chiǔbiěk	hando-baggu	son-gabang
chiǔgkŭn	hankachi	sonsugŏn
gkàng	minato	hanggu
dieng	katai	dandan han (ha-)

VOCABULARY

ENGLISH	MANDARIN	CANTONESE
hat, the	màozi	móu
have, to	yǒu	yáuh
he	tā	kéuih
head, the	tóu	tàuh
headache, the	tóutèng	tàuhtung
hear, to	tīng	tènggin
heart, the	xīn	sàm
heavy	zhòng	chúhng
height, the	gāodù	gòudouh
help, to	bāngzhù	bòng
her (adj.)	tāde	kéuih ge
here	zhèr	nī-syu
high	gāo	gou
hill, the	shān	sàan
his	tāde	kéuih ge
hold, to	názhù	jà
holy	shénshèng de	sàhnsing
home, at	zài jiā	hái ngūkkéi
honest	chéngshí de	lóuhsaht
hope, to	xīwàng	hèimohng
horse, the	mǎ	máh
hospital, the	yīyuàn	yìyún
host, the	zhǔrén	jyúyán
hot (weather)	rè de	yiht
hot (heated food, etc.)	rè de	yiht
hot season (summer), the	xiàtian	hahtīn
hotel, the	lǚguǎn	jáudim
hour, the	xiǎoshí	dímjùng
house, the	fángzi	ngūk
how?	zěnme?	dím?
how many?	duōshǎo?	géidò?
however (conj.)	kěshi	m̀h-léih
hut, the	xiǎo wūzi	ngūkjái
I	wǒ	ngóh
ice, the	bīng	syut
ice cream, the	bīngqílín	syutgòu
if	yàoshi . . . jiù	yùhgwó
ill	bìng	yáuh behng
immediately	lìkè	jìkhāk
important	zhòngyào	gányiu
impossible	bùkě'néng	bāthó-nàhng
in	zài . . . lǐ	hái
information, the	zīliào	chìhngbou
inside	lǐbianr	yahpbihn
instead of	dàitì	tai
interesting	yǒuyìsi	hóu yáuhcheui
interpreter, the	fānyìyuán	fàanyìhk

216

VOCABULARY

HOKKIEN	JAPANESE	KOREAN
bóu	bóshi	moja
'u	motte imasu	issŭmnida (iss-)
'ī	kare	gŭ i
tầu	atama	mŏri
tầu-tiahñ	zutsū	du tong
tiañ-kiñ	kikoemasu	dŭssŭmnida (dŭr-)
sīm	shinzō	maŭm
dang	omoi	mugŏun (mugŏw-)
gkuaiñ-gke	takasa	nopi
bpangtsan	tetsudaimasu	dowa jumnida (ju-)
'i 'e...	kanojo no	gŭ nyŏ
tsiā	koko	yŏgi
gkuáiñ	takai	nopŭn (nop-)
sūañ	oka	ŏndŏk
'i 'e...	kare no	gŭ ŭi
gkiā'	mochimasu	dŭssŭmnida (dŭr-)
sinsiehng	shinsei na	sinsŏng han (ha-)
chuh ni	uchi ni	jip e
lầusit	shōjiki na	jŏngjik han (ha-)
'ngbang	... to ii desu	baramnida (bara-)
bè	uma	mal
lōugkunchuh	byōin	byŏngwon
tsūláng	shujin	juin
dzuā'	atsui	ttŭgŏun (ttŭgŏw-)
dzuā'	atsui	ttŭgŏun (ttŭgŏw-)
dzuah'tiñ	natsu	yŏrŭm
lūgkuàn	hoteru	yŏgwan
diàmtsiēng	jikan	sigan
chuh	uchi	jip
tsāiñ'iuñ?	dō?	ŏttŏke?
luah tsueh...?	ikutsu?	ŏlmana?
bpŭtgkouh	shikashi	yŏhagan
diàu	koya	odumak jip
guà	watashi	na
bpiēng	kōri	ŏrŭm
bpiēng	aisu-kuriimu	aisŭ-kŭrim
nah...	moshi	... imyŏn
bpiñ	byōki no	alhun (alh-)
tsièk-kièk	sugu ni	got
yầugkin	taisetsu na	jungyo han (ha-)
tsuèbuela	fukanō na	bul ganŭng han (ha-)
dih...	... ni	... e
siausiht	tsūchi	bodo
laihbin	naka ni	an e
tuè...	... no kawari ni	daasine
chùbi	omoshiroi	jaami inŭn (i-)
he'ue 'e	tsūyaku	tŏngyokja

VOCABULARY

ENGLISH	MANDARIN	CANTONESE
iron (metal), the	tiě	tit
is	shì	haih
island, the	dǎo	dóu
isn't it?	búshìma?	haih m̀h-haih?
it	tā	gó-go
jewellery, the	zhūbǎo	jyùbóu
journey, the	lǚxíng	léuihhàhng
jump, to	tiào	tiu
jungle, the	sēnlín	sàmlàhm
key, the	yàoshi	sósìh
kill, to	shā	jíngséi
kilogram, the	gōngjīn	gùnggàn
kilometre, the	gōnglǐ	gùngléih
kind (friendly)	hǎoxīn de	hóu
king, the	guówáng	gwokwòhng
kiss, to	jiēwěn	sekháh
kitchen, the	chúfáng	chyùhfóng
knife, the	dāozi	dōu
know, to	zhīdao	jīdou
label, the	biāoqiān	jìupàaihjì
lake, the	hú	wùh
lamb, the	yángròu	yèuhngmējái
lamp, the	dēng	dāng
last	zuìhòu de	jeuihauh
late (behind time)	chí	chìh
later on	yǐhòu	hāumēi
laugh, to	xiào	siu
laundry (clothes), the	zāngyīfu	sái ge sāam
law, the	fǎlü	faatleuht
lawyer, the	lùshī	johngsī
lead, to	lǐngdǎo	daai
learn, to	xuéxí	hohk
least, at	zhìshǎo	ji síu
leave (place), to	líkāi	jàu
leave behind, to	liú	làuhdài
left (hand)	zuǒbianr	jósáu
leg, the	tuǐ	geuk
lemon, the	níngméng	nìhngmūng
lemonade, the	níngméngshuǐ	nìhngmūngséui
letter (note), the	xìn	seun
letter (character), the	zìmǔ	jih
lettuce, the	wōjù	sàangchoi
lie, the	huǎnghuà	daaihwah
lie down, to	tǎngxià	fandài
lift, to	jǔqǐ	nìnghéi
light (colour)	qiǎn	chín

VOCABULARY

HOKKIEN	JAPANESE	KOREAN
tih'	tetsu	soe
sih . . .	desu	issŭmnida (iss-)
dōusu	shima	sŏm
hoñ?	sō desu ne?	gŭrŭjiyo?
mih'gkiañ	sore	gŭ gŏt
gkim-kih	hōseki	bosŏk
tsua	ryokō	yŏhaang
tiauh	tobimasu	ttwimnida (ttwi-)
bpā	janguru	sup
sōusi	kagi	yŏlsoe
pà'si	koroshimasu	jugimnida (jugi-)
gkonggkūn	kiro	killogŭrem
gkongli	kiro	killometa
'uehtsueh	shinsetsu na	chinjŏl han (ha-)
'ōng	ō	wang
tsīm	kisu shimasu	ipmatchumnida (-tchu-)
tsàu-kā	daidokoro	buŏk
dou'à	naifu	kal
tsāi	shirimasu	amnida (ar-)
piouh	fuda	sangpyo
'ó	mizu-umi	hosu
'iúñ	ramu	ŏrin yang
hè	sutando	dŭng
sua'bè	saigo no	majimak
'uahñ	osoi	nŭjŭn (nŭj-)
'auhlái	ato de	issda
chiouh	waraimasu	ussŭmnida (us-)
sañ-koh	sentakumono	ppallaa
huātlūt	hōritsu	bŏmyul
luht-sū	bengoshi	byŏnhosa
chua	sendō shimasu	indo hamnida (ha-)
'ōu'	naraimasu	baaumnida (baau-)
tsī-tsiòu	sukunaku to mo	jŏgŏdo
lih-kui	kaerimasu	ttŏnamnida (ttŏna-)
'uiliú	okiwasuremasu	namgimnida (namgi-)
dòubpiéng	hidari	oen pyŏn
ka-tui	ashi	dari
siūgkām	remon	remŏn
siūgkamtsui	remonēdo	remŏnei
puē	tegami	pyŏnji
dzi	moji	ja
siengchaih	retasu	sangchi
bpeh'chāt	uso	gŏjitmal
dòulou'	yoko ni narimasu	nupsŭmnida (nup-)
gkiā'ki	agemasu	ollimnida (olli-)
kñg	iro ga usui	yatŭn (yat-)

VOCABULARY

ENGLISH	MANDARIN	CANTONESE
light (weight)	qīng de	hèng
lighter (cigarette), the	dáhuǒjī	dáfógèi
like (prep.)	xiàng	hóuchìh
lipstick, the	kǒuhóng	háusèuhn-gōu
litre, the	gōngshēng	gùngsing
little, a	yìdiǎnr	dīgamdēu
live (reside), to	zhù	jyuh
lock, the	sǒ	só
long (size)	cháng	chéuhng
long (time)	jiǔ	nói
long ago	hén jiǔ yǐqiān	hóu noih yíhchìhr
look at, to	kàn	táigán
look for, to	xúnzhǎo	wán
lose (mislay), to	bujiàn	sàtjó
lose (race, etc.), to	shūle	syùjó
loud	dàshēngr	daaihsèng
love, to	ài	deui
low	dī	dài
lunch, the	wǔcān	ngáanjau
machine, the	jīqi	gèihei
magazine, the	zázhì	jaahpji
make, to	zuò	jouh
malaria, the	nuèjí	faatláahng
man, the	nánren	nàahmyàhn
manager, the	gīnglǐ	gingléih
mango, the	mángguǒ	mònggwó
many	duō	hóu dò
map, the	dìtú	deihtòuh
market, the	shìchǎng	sihchèuhng
married	yǐhūn de	gitjó fàn meih
matches, the	huǒchái	fócháai
means, (it)	yìyì	yisi
measure, to	cèliáng	lèuhng
meat, the	ròu	yuhk
mechanic, the	jīshī	gèiheijái
medicine, the	yàopǐn	yeuhk
meet, to	jiē	yuhgin
melon, the	guā	gwà
menu, the	càidān	choidàan
message, the	tiáozi	làuhdài syutwah
metre, the	gōngchǐ	gùngchek
middle, the	zhōngjiànr	jùnggàan
midnight	wǔyè	bunyé
milk, the	niúnǎi	náaih
millimetre, the	gōnglǐ	gùnglèih
minute, the	fēnzhōng	fàn

VOCABULARY

HOKKIEN	JAPANESE	KOREAN
kīn	karui	gabyŏun (gabyŏw-)
diămhun-gki	raită	raita
chinchiuñ	... tōri	... gachi
'iantsī	kuchibeni	ipsul yŏnji
gkongtsiuñ	rittoru	ritŏ
dahmbpōu'	sukoshi	jom
kia	sunde imasu	sassŭmnida (sar-)
sòu	jō	jamulsoe
dńg	nagai	girŭn (gir-)
gkù	nagai aida	girŭn (gir-)
tsă si	zutto mae	oraa jŏn
kuahñ	mimasu	bomnida (bo-)
che	sagashimasu	chassŭmnida (chaj-)
pàng-kiñ	nakushimasu	ilssŭmnida (ilh-)
sū	makemasu	jimnida (ji-)
duahsiañ	koe ga ōkii	yoran (yora-)
tiahñ	ai shimasu	sarang hamnida (ha-)
gke	hikui	najŭn (naj-)
tsiah'ehdauh	ohirugohan	jŏmsim
gki-kih	kikai	gigye
tsahptsih	zasshi	japji
tsueh	tsukurimasu	jissŭmnida (jis-)
liĕngdzuah'bpiñ	mararia	hakjil
lám	otoko	namja
taugkē	shihainin	jibaain
suañ'iá	mangō	manggo
tsue	takusan no	manhŭn (manh-)
dehdó	chizu	jido
bpasaht	ichiba	sijang
gkiăt-hün	kekkon shita	kyŏlhon han (ha-)
hēchá	matchi	sŏngnyangdŭl
'isuh	... o imi shimasu	ttŭt i ... imnida (i-)
niúñ	hakarimasu	jaamnida (jaa-)
bah'	niku	gogi
gki-kiláng	shūrikō	gigyegong
'iōu'	kusuri	yak
tsih'	aimasu	mannamnida (manna-)
gkuā	meron	chamoe
chàiduăñ	menyū	menu
siausit	messēji	tongsin
gkongchiouh'	mētoru	meta
diong'ńg	mannaka	jung
bpuăñmí	mayonaka	bamjung
ni	miruku	uyu
gkonglí	mirimētoru	millimeta
huntsiĕng	fun	bŭn

VOCABULARY

ENGLISH	MANDARIN	CANTONESE
mirror, the	jìngzi	geng
mistake, the	cuòwu	cho
moment, the	yihuǐr	yàtjahngāan
monastery, the	héshàngmiào	sàudouhyún
money, the	qián	chín
month, the	yuè	yuht
monument, the	jìniànwù	géihnihmbèi
moon, the	yuèliàng	yút
more	gèngduō de	juhng
morning, the	zǎochen	jiutàuhjóu
mosque, the	huíjiàotáng	wùihgaautòhng
mosquito, the	wénzi	mān
most	zuì	ji
motor-bike, the	mōduōchē	dihndāanchē
mountain, the	shān	sàan
mouth, the	kǒu	háu
movie camera, the	diànyǐngjī	dihnyínggèi
much	duō	géido
museum, the	bówùguǎn	bokmahtyún
mushroom, the	jùnzi	dūnggù
music, the	yīnyuè	yàmngohk
must	bìxū	yātdihng yiu
mustard, the	jièmò	gaailaaht
my	wǒde	ngóh ge
name, the	míngzi	méng
napkin, the	cānjīn	chāan-gān
narrow	xiázhǎi de	jaak
natural	zìrán de	tinyín ge
near (not far)	jìn	jógán
near to	jiējìn	káhnjyuh
need, to	xūyào	sèuiyiu
needle, the	zhēn	jàm
never	cónglai bù	chùhnglòihmeih
new	xīn	sàn
newspaper, the	bào	boují
next (after)	xià yige	daihyih
night, the	wǎnshang	máahn
no (adj.)	búshì de	móuh
nobody	méiyou rén	móuhyàhn
noise, the	xiǎngshēng	sèng
noodles, the	miàn	mihn
noon	zhōngwǔ	ngaanjau
north	běibianr	bāk
not	bù	m̀h
not at all	yidiǎnr yě bù	yāt dī dōu m̀h
notepaper, the	biàntiáozhǐ	séji
nothing	méi shenme	móuh yéh

222

VOCABULARY

HOKKIEN	JAPANESE	KOREAN
gkiahñ	kagami	gǒul
chouh	machigai	jalmot
kà'tiéng	shunkan	sun-gan
lêbpàidńg	sŏin	sudowǒn
tsiñ	okane	don
gē'	tsuki	dal
kiliambpíñ	kinenhi	bisǒk
gē'	tsuki	dal
gke . . .	motto	dǒ
diēngbpō	asa	achim
huegkàudńg	jiin	hoegyo sawǒn
băng'à	ka	mogi
duah bpuah	taitei no	gajang
diahndah'chiä	mōtā-baiku	otobai
suáñ	yama	san
chuih	kuchi	ip
'uah'dahng hīpsiohnggkī	eiga-kamera	charyǒngi
tsue	takusan	manhi
bpōumi'gkuàn	hakubutsukan	bakmulgwan
dang-kò	ki-no-ko	bǒsǒt
imgàk	ongaku	ŭmak
diouh' . . .	. . . -nakute wa narimasen	. . . -e ya hamnida (ha-)
gkaihluä'	karashi	geja
guä 'e . . .	watashi no	na ŭi
miá	namae	irŭm
chuìgkūn	nafukin	naapkin
'uē'	semai	jobŭn (job-)
tsuhdzián	shizen no	jayŏn (jayo-)
hùgkun	chikai	gakkaun (gakkaw-)
gkuhn . . .	. . . no chikaku ni	. . . gakkapge
diòu'	irimasu	piryo hamnida (ha-)
tsiäm	hari	banŭl
lōng bou . . .	kesshite	gyǒlko . . . ani-
sìn	atarashii	saa
bpòu-tsuà	shimbun	sinmun
'eh . . .	tsugi ni	daŭm
mí	yoru	bam
bou . . .	nai	ani
bou láng	dare mo	amudo . . . ani-
siáñ	zatsuon	sori
mi	o-udon	guksu
'eh-tauh	hiru	jŏng-o
bpahk	kita	buk
bou . . .	-masen	an
bou 'iàñ	chitto mo . . . -masen	mot
pue-tsuà	binsen	pyŏnjiji
bou hang	nani mo	amu gŏt . . . ani-

VOCABULARY

ENGLISH   MANDARIN   CANTONESE

ENGLISH	MANDARIN	CANTONESE
notice, the	tōngzhī	tùnggou
now	xiànzài	yìhgā
number, the	shùmù	soumuhk
nurse, the	hùshi	hònwuh
nuts, the	jiānguǒ	haht
obtain, to	qǔdé	dākdóu
occupied	yǒu ren de	m̀h-hùng
offer, to	gěi	chēut
office, the	bàngōngshì	séjihlàuh
officer (army), the	jūnguān	jīkyùhn
often	chángcháng	sìhsìh
oil, the	yóu	yàuh
old (persons)	lǎo	lóuh
old (things)	jiù	gauh
olives, the	gánlǎn	baahkláam
on	zài . . . shàng	hái . . . seuhngbihn
once	yícì	yāt-chi
onion, the	yángcōng	yèuhngchūng
only	zhíyǒu	ji haih
open	kāi de	hòimùhn
open, to	kāi	dáhòi
opera, the	gējù	gò-kehk
opposite	xiāngduì de	deuimihn
or	huòzhě	dihng
orange, the	chéngzi	cháang
ordered	shùnxù	ódá
ordinary	tōngcháng	pìhngsèuhng ge
our	wǒmende	ngóhdeih ge
outside	wàibianr	ngoihbihn
overcoat, the	dàyī	daaihlāu
owe, to	qiàn	him
oyster, the	háo	hòuh
pack, to	bāozhá	jāp
pain, the	tòngkǔ	tung
paint, the	yùqī	yàuhchāt
pair, the	yí duì	deui
palace, the	huánggōng	gùngdihn
paper, the	zhǐ	jí
parcel, the	bāoguǒ	bàau
park, the	gōngyuán	gùngyún
park (car), to	tíngchē	tìhng
passport, the	hùzhào	wuhjiu
pastry, the	bǐng	dímsàm
pay, to	gěiqian	béichín
peace, the	hépíng	wòhpìhng
peach, the	táozi	tóu
pearl, the	zhēnzhū	jānjyu

VOCABULARY

HOKKIEN	JAPANESE	KOREAN
tonggkouh	chūi	tongji
tsit tsun	ima	jigŭm
houhbè	bangō	su
misi	kangofu-san	ganhobŭ
dau	kinomi	gyŏngwadŭl
dihtdiou'	emasu	ossŭmnida (ot-)
mh-kāng	aite inai	jŏmyŏng han (ha-)
hohchuht	agemasu	jechul hamnida (ha-)
bpahnsuhchuh	jimusho	samusil
gkuāñ	shōkō	janggyo
siong . . .	tabi-tabi	jaju
'iŭ	abura	girŭm
lau	toshiyori	nai ga manhŭn (manh-)
gku	furui	nargŭn (narg-)
gkahn'à	oriibu	gamnamdŭl
. . . dièng	. . . no ue ni	. . . wi e
tsiht bpài	ichido	han bŏn
chang-táu	tamanegi	yangpa
tsī . . .	honno	. . . man
kuī	aite iru	yŏrŭn (yŏr-)
kuī	akemasu	yŏssŭmnida (yŏr-)
hi-gkiōk	opera	opera
duibin	hantai ni	majŭn pyŏn e
'ā . . .	ka	. . . ina
chiám	orenji	gyul
diahñtsueh	chūmon-chū	jumun han (ha-)
bpiengsióng	futsū no	botong
gūn 'e . . .	watashitachi no	uri
guahbin	. . . no soto ni	bak e
duah sāñ	ōbā	oetu
kiahm	kari ga arimasu	bijŭl jimnida (ji-)
'ó	kaki	gul
duè	nizukuri shimasu	jimŭl ssamnida (ssa-)
tiahñ	itami	apŭm
chaht	penki	pengkki
duih	. . . kumi	kyŏlle
gkong-tiāñ	kyūden	daagwŏl
tsuà	kami	jongi
bpāu	kozutsumi	sopo
gkong-hńg	kōen	gongwon
tiengchiā	chūsha shimasu	juchamnida (jucha-)
hoh-tsiouh	pasupōto	yŏ-gwŏn
bpiàñ	okashi	gwaja
gkāu	haraimasu	naamnida (naa-)
bpieng'ān	heiwa	pyŏnghwa
tou'à	momo	bogsunga
tsŭ	shinju	jinju

VOCABULARY

ENGLISH	MANDARIN	CANTONESE
peas, the	wǎndòu	dáu
pen, the	gāngbǐ	mahkséuibāt
pencil, the	qiānbǐ	yùhnbāt
pepper, the	hújiāo	wùhjiu
perfume, the	xiāngshuǐ	hèungséui
perhaps	yéxǔ	waahkjé
permit, to	xúkě	jéun
person, the	rén	yàhn
petrol (gasoline), the	qìyóu	dihnyàuh
pharmacy, the	yàofáng	yeuhkfòhng
photograph, the	zhàopiàn	séung
picture, the	huàr	wá
piece, the	yīkuài	faai
pillow, the	zhěntóu	jámtàuh
pin, the	biézhēn	jàm
pineapple, the	bōluó	bòlòh
pink	fěnhóngsè de	fánhúng ge
place, the	dìfang	deihfòng
plate, the	diézi	díp
platform (railway), the	yuètái	yuhttòih
pleasant	yúkuài de	gòu-hing
plum, the	lǐzi	léi
point out, to	zhǐshì	jíchēut
police station, the	jǐngchájú	gíngchaatgúk
policeman, the	jǐngchá	chàaiyàhn
poor (needy)	qióng	kùhng
pork, the	zhūròu	jyùyuhk
porter, the	tiāofū	gūléi
possible	kěnéng	jouhdākdou
post-box, the	xìnxiāng	seunsēung
postcard, the	míngxìnpiàn	mìhngseunpín
post-office, the	yóujú	yàuhjinggúk
potatoes, the	mǎlingshú	syùhjái
practise, to	liànxí	lihnjaahp
prawn, the	xiā	hā
present (gift), the	lǐwù	láih
president, the	zóngtǒng	júngtúng
press (clothes), to	tàng	tong
pretty	hǎokàn	hóuyéung
price, the	jiàqian	gachìhn
priest, the	shénfù	sàhnfuh
prison, the	jiānyù	gāamfòhng
private	sīrèn de	jihgéi ge
promise, to	dāyìng	yìngsihng
province, the	shěng	sáang
public	gōngzhòng de	gùngguhng

VOCABULARY

HOKKIEN	JAPANESE	KOREAN
dau	mame	wandu
bpiht	pen	pen
'ianbpiht	empitsu	yǒnpil
ho-tsiŏu	koshŏ	huchu
pangtsui	kŏsui	hyangsu
kiāmchāi . . .	tabun	ama
tsùn	kyoka shimasu	hǒrak hamnida (ha-)
láng	hito	saram
chia'iú	gasorin	hwibaryu
'iouh'diahm	kusuriya	yagjesa
siong	shashin	sajin
siong	e	gǔrim
deh	hen	han jogak
tsīm-táu	makura	byǒgaa
tsiām	pin	pin
'onglái	painappuru	painaapul
chià'áng	pinku	bunhong
dueh-hng	tokoro	got
bpuáñ	osara	jǒbsi
hēchiadái	hŏmu	sǔnggangjang
hòu	tanoshii	maǔm e dúrǔn (dǔr-)
muiñ	puramu	oyat
gki chutlai	shiteki shimasu	jijǒk hamnida (ha-)
gkièngchātgkiėk	keisatsu-sho	gyǒng-chalsǒ
gkièngchaht	omawari-san	gyǒnggwan
gkiėng	mazushii	ganan han (ha-)
dibah'	butaniku	dwaaji gogi
gkiah'hiengli láng	akabŏ	jimkkun
'uehsài	dekiru	ganǔng han (ha-)
puesiùñ	yūbimbako	uche tong
pueduáñ	hagaki	yǒbsǒ
'iu-tsiènggkièk	yūbinkyoku	u-pyǒn-guk
hantsú	jagaimo	gamjadǔl
lian	okonaimasu	yǒnsǔp hamnida (ha-)
he	ebi	saau
lēmī'	okurimono	sǒnmul
tsùsiėk	dai-tóryŏ	hoejang
'uht	airon o shimasu	darimnida (dari-)
hòu kuahñ	kirei na	ippǔn (ippǔ-)
gkè-tsíñ	nedan	gabs
biuhsū	sŏryo	sinbǔ
ka-kugkiėng	keimusho	gamok
gkòudzín	shiteki no	sasa-ui . . .
dà'iehng	yakusoku shimasu	yaksok hamnida (ha-)
tsiú	shū	do
gkonggkiong	kŏshū no	gongsǒk e so issnǔn (iss-)

VOCABULARY

ENGLISH	MANDARIN	CANTONESE
pull, to	lā	màng
puncture, the	bàotāi	lung
pure	chúncuì de	sèuhnseuih
purple	zǐsè de	jísīk ge
put, to	fàng	jài
quantity, the	shùliàng	leuhng
queen, the	nǚhuang	néuih wòhng
question, the	wèntí	mahntàih
quick	kuài	faai
quiet	ānjìng de	jihng
race (contest), the	bǐsài	béichoi
radio, the	shōuyīnjī	mòuhsindihn
railway, the	tiělù	titlouh
raincoat, the	yǔyī	yúhlāu
raining, it is	xiàyǔ	lohkyúh
razor, the	tìdāo	sòupáau
read, to	kàn	tái
ready	zhǔnbèi hǎole	yuhbeihhóu la
receive, to	shōu	sàudóu
record (gramophone), the	chàngpiàn	cheungdíp
red	hóng	hùhngsīk ge
register (letter), to	guàhào	gwa-houh
religion, the	zōngjiào	gaau
remember, to	jìzhù	geidāk
repair, to	xiūlǐ	saujíng
repeat, to	chóngfù	yauh jouh
reply, to	huídá	daap
rest, to	xiūxi	táu
restaurant, the	fànguǎn	chāan-gún
result, the	chéngji	gitgwó
rice (cooked), the	bai fàn	faahn
rich	yǒuqián	yauhchín
right (correct)	duì	ngāam
right (hand)	yòubianr	yauhsáu
ring, the	jièzhi	gaaiji
ripe	chéngshóu de	suhk
river, the	hé	hòh
road, the	lù	louh
roast	kǎo	sìu
room, the	fángjiān	fóng
run, to	pǎo	jáu
sad	bēiāi de	bai-ngai
safe	ānquán de	móuhsih
sailor, the	shuǐshǒu	séuisáu
salt, the	yén	yìhm
same	yíyàng	yùhnlòih

VOCABULARY

HOKKIEN	JAPANESE	KOREAN
tuǎ	hikimasu	kkǔssǔmnida (kkǔr-)
lauh-hóng	panku	bangkku
tsintsǐn	junsui na	sunsu han (ha-)
lam'e-nǎ	murasaki no	ja saak . . .
he –	okimasu	nossǔmnida (noh-)
tsuehtsue	bunryō	yang
tsabō'óng	jōō	yǒwang
buhnduė	shitsumon	jilmun
gkin	hayai	pparǔn (pparǔ-)
'antsieng	shizuka na	goyo han (ha-)
tau-tsàu	kyōsō	gyǒngju
siu'imgkǐ	rajio	radio
hēchiǎ	tetsudō	chǒldo
louh'hohsǎñ	rēnkōto	biot
louh' ho	ame ga futte imasu	bi ga omnida
tǐ-taudōu	kamisori	myǒndo kal
kuǎñ cheh'	yomimasu	ilgǔmnida (ilg-)
bpiañ	dekiru	junbiga doen (doe-)
siu	moraimasu	bassǔmnida (bad-)
chiùñ-pǐñ	rekōdo	rekod
'áng	akai	bǔlgǔn (bǔlg-)
dienggkih	kakitome ni shimasu	dǔnggi hamnida (ha-)
tsonggkauh	shūkyō	jonggyo
'ueh gkih dit	oboete imasu	giǒk hamnida (ha-)
siulǐ	naoshimasu	susǒn hamnida (ha-)
gkòu'tsihtbpài	kurikaeshimasu	doepuri hamnida (ha-)
'ihn	kotaemasu	daadap hamnida (ha-)
hiouh'	yasumimasu	swimnida (swi-)
chaigkuàn	shokudō	sikdang
gkiǎtgkòu	kekka	gyǒrgwa
bpng	gohan	bap
'uh tsiñ	kanemochi no	don i manhǔn (manh-)
diōu'	tadashii	barǔn (bar-)
tsiàñbpiěng	migi	barǔn pyǒn
chiù-tsì	yubiwa	banji
sièk	jukushita	igǔn (ig-)
hóu	kawa	gang
lo	dōro	gil
pu [siòu]	rōsuto-	gubǔn (gub-)
bpáng	heya	bang
tsàu	hashirimasu	dwiǒ gamnida (ga-)
chàm	kanashii	sǔlpǔn (sǔlp-)
'antsuán	anzen na	anjǒn han (ha-)
tsuǐchiù	norikumiin	sǒnwǒn
yám	oshio	sogǔm
siáng	onaji	gatǔn (gat-)

VOCABULARY

ENGLISH	MANDARIN	CANTONESE
sandals, the	liángxié	tō-háai
sandwich, the	sānwénzhì	sàammàhnjih
sauce, the	jiàng	jeung
say, to	shuō	góng
school, the	xuéxiào	hohkhaauh
science, the	kēxué	fò-hohk
scissors, the	jiǎndāo	gaaujín
sea, the	hǎi	hói
seat, the	zuòwei	wái
second	dìèr de	daihyih
second (of time), the	miǎo	míuh
secretary, the	mìshū	syùgei
see, to	kànjiàn	tái
seems, (it)	sìhū	hóuchíh . . . gám
seldom	hénshǎo	hóu síu
sell, to	mài	maaih
send (thing), to	sòng	sung
separate	fēnlí de	fānhòi
servant, the	yòngren	gùngyàhn
service station, the	qìyóuzhàn	yàuhjaahm
several	jǐ	géi-
sew, to	féng	lyùhn
shallow	qiǎn	chín
shampoo, the	xǐtóushuǐ	sáitàuhséui
shave, to	tì	tai
she	tā	kéuih
sheet, the	bèidān	péihdāan
shelter, the	zhēgàiwù	duhng
ship, the	chuán	syùhn
shirt, the	chènshān	sēutsāam
shoe, the	xié	hàaih
shop, the	shāngdiàn	poutáu
short	duǎn	dyún
show, to	biǎoshì	jíbéi . . . tái
shower, the	línyù	chùnglèuhng
side, the	biānr	bihn
sign, to	qiānmíng	chìmméng
silk, the	sī	sì
silver, the	yín	ngán
since (time)	zì . . . yǐlái	jihchùhng
sing, to	chàng gēr	cheung
sit, to	zuò	chóh
skirt, the	qúnzi	kwàhn
sky, the	tiān	tìn
sleep, to	shuì	fan
slow	màn	maahn
small	xiǎo	sai

VOCABULARY

HOKKIEN	JAPANESE	KOREAN
'e duahñ	sandaru	ssaandarŭ
samenchù	sandowitchi	ssaandŭwichwi
dauh-tsiuhñ	sōsu	ssoossŭ
gkòng	iimasu	mal hamnida (ha-)
'ouh'dńg	gakkō	hakkyo
ko-hāk	kagaku	gwahak
kadōu	hasami	gawi
hài	umi	bada
'ì	seki	jari
dehdzi	dai-ni	du jjaa
biàu	byō	cho
bpìsŭ	hisho	sŏgi
kuahñ-gkiñ	mimasu	bomnida (bo-)
chinchiuñ	... no yō ni miemasu	boimnida
tsintsiòu...	metta ni ... -masen	dŭmurge
bue	urimasu	passŭmnida (par-)
sahng	dashimasu	bonaamnida (bonaa-)
lih-kuī	betsu no	bulli doen (doe-)
gkangláng	meshitsukai	hain
'iu-tiāñ	gasorin-sutando	jŏngyuso
gkuīnah...	ikutsu ka no	yŏrō
tiñ	nuimasu	kkwe maamnida (maa-)
chiàn	asai	yŏtŭn (yŏt-)
tau-mng sāpbún	shampū	shampu
kūn	sorimasu	myŏndo hamnida (ha-)
'ī	kanojo	gŭ i
pehduāñ	shiitsu	hotibul
diáu	hinanjo	daapi so
tsún	fune	baa
huhnsām	shatsu	syassŭ
'ué	kutsu	gudu
diahm	mise	sangjŏm
dè	mijikai	jjalbŭn (jjalb-)
gki	misemasu	boemnida (boe-)
tsangtsui	shawā	syawo
bpiéng	soba	yŏp
chiam miá	shomei shimasu	sŏmyŏng hamnida (ha-)
sī	kinu	bidan
gún	gin	ŭn
'īlái	... kara	... i hu
chiuhñ	utaimasu	noraa hamnida (ha-)
tse	kakemasu	anssŭmnida (anj-)
gkún	sukāto	chima
tiñ	sora	hanŭl
kuhn	nemasu	jamnida (ja-)
ban	osoi	chŏnchŏn han (ha-)
sueh	chiisai	jagŭn (jag-)

VOCABULARY

ENGLISH	MANDARIN	CANTONESE
smoke, to	xiyēn	sihkyin
snow, the	xuě	syut
soap, the	féizào	fàan-gáan
socks, the	wàzi	maht
soda water, the	sūdáshuǐ	sōdáséui
soft	róuruǎn de	yúhn
soldier, the	bīng	gwànyàhn
some	yìxiē	dī
somebody	yǒu rén	yàuhyàhn
something	yǒujiàn dōngxi	dī-yéh
sometimes	yǒushí	yàuhsìh
somewhere	yīge dìfang	bīnsyu
soon	jíkè	yàtháh
sorry	bàoqiàn	deui-mh-jyuh
soup, the	tāng	tòng
sour	suān de	syùn
south	nánbianr	nàahm
soy sauce, the	jiàngyóu	sih-yàuh
space, the	kōngjiān	deih
speak, to	shuō	góng
spectacles, the	yěnjìng	ngáahn-géng
spoon, the	tāngchí	chìhgāng
sport, the	yùndòng	wahnduhng
square (place), the	guángchǎng	deihfòng
stairs, the	lóutī	làuhtài
stamp (postage), the	yóupiào	yàuhpiu
stand, to	zhàn	kéih
star, the	xīng	sìng
start, to	kāishǐ	héisáu
station (railway), the	huǒchēzhàn	jaahm
stay, to	liú xià	jyuh
steak, the	niúpái	ngàuhpá
steep	dǒuqiào de	che
steering, the	jiàshǐpán	táaih
stick, the	shǒuzhàng	sihdīk
still (adv.)	hái	juhng
stockings, the	chángwàzi	sì-muht
stone, the	shítou	sehk
storey (floor), the	lóu céng	láu
straight on	yìzhízǒu	yàtjihk
strap, the	pídài	daai
street, the	jiē	gāai
streetcar (tram), the	diànchē	dihnchè
string, the	shéngzi	sin
strong	yǒulì de	gaulihk
student, the	xuésheng	hohksāang
study, to	xuéxí	hohk

VOCABULARY

HOKKIEN	JAPANESE	KOREAN
tsiah' hun-gkī	tabako o suimasu	piumnida (piu-)
sè'	yuki	nun
sàpbún	sekken	binu
bē'	kutsushita	yangmal
soda-tsuì	sōdasui	soda
nǹg	yawarakai	yŏn han (ha-)
bpiēng	heitai	byŏngjŏng
gkuī ...	ikura ka	yŏrŏ
'uh láng	dare ka	nuga
'uh hang	nani ka	muŏt
'uh si ...	tokidoki	gakkŭm
bpaht 'ui	doko ka	ŏde-inji
liambpiñ	sugu	swii
bpàngsim	zannen na	sŏpsŏp han (ha-)
tǹg	sūpu	guk
sǹg	suppai	sin (si-)
lám	minami	nam
dauh'iú	oshōyu	ganjang
'ui	kankaku	saa
gkòng	hanashimasu	mal hamnida (ha-)
bahk-gkiahñ	megane	an-gyŏng
tngsi	supūn	sugal
'uhndong	supōtsu	undong
sigkahk	hiroba	gwang jang
lau-tuī	kaidan	chŭngchŭngdari
'iu-piouh	kitte	u-pyo
kiade'	tachimasu	sŭmnida (sŭ-)
chiñ	hoshi	byŏl
kī chiù	hajimemasu	sijak hamnida (ha-)
hēchia-tsam	eki	jŏnggŏjang
diahm	tomarimasu	issŭmnida (iss-)
gubah'	sutēki	sŭteik
chiá	kyū na	gaparŭn (gapar-)
sàichia'uē	handoru	ŭnjŏndaa
chá	bō	jipangi
yāu ...	mada	ajik
bē'	kutsushita	yangmaldŭl
tsiōu'	ishi	dol
tsahn	kai	chŭng
dihtdīt	massugu	gokke
peduah	kawahimo	gajukkŭn
gkuē	tōri	gil
diahnchiā	densha	jŏncha
sōu'à	himo	kkŭn
'iòng	tsuyoi	sen (se-)
hahksiēng	gakusei	haksaang
tahk cheh'	benkyō shimasu	gongbŭ hamnida (ha-)

VOCABULARY

ENGLISH	MANDARIN	CANTONESE
substance, the	wùzhí	yéh
suddenly	tūrán	fātyìhn
sugar, the	táng	tòhng
suitcase, the	xiāngzi	pèihgip
summit, the	dǐngdiǎn	jeuigōufūng
sun, the	tàiyang	yahttáu
sweet	tiánmì de	tìhm
swim, to	yóuyǒng	yàuhséui
table, the	zhuōzi	tói
tailor, the	cáifeng	chòihfúng
take, to	ná	ja
tall	gāo	gòu
tap, the	shuǐlóngtóu	séui-hàuh
tape (recording), the	lùyīndài	luhkyāmdáai
tape recorder, the	lùyīnjī	luhkyāmgèi
taste, to	chángchang	si
tax, the	shuì	seui
taxi, the	jichéngchē	dīksí
tea (to drink), the	chá	chàh
teach, to	jiāo	gaau
teacher, the	jiàoyuán	sīnsàang
telegram, the	diànbào	dihnbou
telephone, the	diànhuà	dihnwá
television, the	diànshì	dihnsih
temperature, the	wēndù	douh
temple, the	miào	míu
than	bǐ	béi
that	nèi	gó-go
theatre, the	xìyuàn	heiyún
their	tāmende	kéuihdeih ge
then (at that time)	jiù	gójahnsí
there	nàr	gósyu
there is	yǒu	yáuh
they	tāmen	kéuihdeih
thick	hòu	háuh
thin	báo	bohk
thing, the	dōngxi	yéh
think, to	yǐwéi	nám
third	dìsān de	daihsàm
thirsty	kóukě de	génghot
this	zhèi	nī-go
thread, the	xiàn	sin
through	chuānguò	gwo
throw, to	rēng	diuh
ticket, the	piào	fēi
ticket-office, the	màipiàosuǒ	piufòhng

234

VOCABULARY

HOKKIEN	JAPANESE	KOREAN
mih'gkiañ	busshitsu	silche
hūtdzian . . .	kyū ni	kkambak
tńg	osatō	sŏltang
hienglì	sūtsukēsu	gabang
suañdièng	chōjō	kkokdaagi
dziht-tàu	taiyō	haa
dīñ	amai	dan (da-)
siu tsuì	oyogimasu	heŏm chimnida (chi-)
douh'	tēburu	sang
chai-hong	yōfukuya-san	yangboksang
tē'	torimasu	gajimnida (gaji-)
louh	sei no takai	ki ga kun (ku-)
tsuì-tsuahn-táu	jaguchi	tabu
liohk'im	tēpu	nok ŏm
liohk'imgkī	tēpu-rekōdā	tepŭ rekoda
tsiah'kuahñ	ajiwaimasu	mat bomnida (bo-)
seh	zei	se
dièksī	takushii	taaksi
dè	ocha	cha
gkah	oshiemasu	garŭchimnida (garuchi-)
siansīñ	sensei	sŏnsaang
diahnbpouh	dempō	jŏnbo
diahn'ue	denwa	jŏnhwa
diahnsi	terebi	terebi
dziaht-do	ondo	ondo
biou	otera	jŏl
bpī . . .	yori mo	. . . boda
hit 'e . . .	sore	gŭ
hi-hńg	gekijō	gŭkjang
'īn 'e . . .	karera no	gŭ saram dŭl ŭi
hit tsun	sono toki	gŭ ttaa
hiā	asoko ni	gŏgi
'uh	arimasu	. . . i issŭmnida
'īn	karera	gŭ saram dŭl
gkau	atsui	dukkŏun (dukkŏw-)
sàn	usui	yalbŭn (yalb-)
mih'gkiañ	mono	gŏt
siuhn-gkòng	omoimasu	saanggak hamnida (ha-)
dehsāñ	dai-san	se jjaa
chuidā	nodo no kawaite iru	mokmarŭn (mokmarŭ-)
tsīt 'e . . .	kore	i
suahñ	ito	sil
gkienggkè . . .	o tōshite	. . . ŭl tong hayŏ
hihñ	nagemasu	naadŏnjimnida (naadŏnji-)
duañ [piouh]	kippu	pyo
duañ-tiāñ [pioù-tiāñ]	mado-guchi	maapyoso

VOCABULARY

VOCABULARY

HOKKIEN	JAPANESE	KOREAN
tai ['ahmduah]	nekutai	nektai
si-kān	toki	sigan
si-kan-piouh	jikan-hyō	sigan pyo
gkuàn-taudôu	kan-kiri	kkangtong-ttage
siūñ 'e tsíñ	chippu	tip
sian	tsukarete iru	pigon han (ha-)
ki . . .	. . . ni	. . . e
hun-gkichàu	tabako	dambaa
gkin'ādzīt	kyō	onŭl
sañ-gkahp	issho ni	gachi
lam 'e chèsò	otoko no benjo	namja hwajang sil
tsabō 'e chèsò	onna no go-fujō	yŏja hwajang sil
chèsō-tsuà	toiretto-pēpā	hwajangji
'Angmo hantsú	tomato	domado
bong	haka	nŭng
bin'ādzīt	ashita	naail
gkin mí	komban	onŭlbam
siūñ	. . . -sugimasu	nŏmu
kībin	ha-burashi	chisol
kigkōu	ha-migaki	chiyak
bōng	furemasu	manjimnida (manji-)
seh'kuan	kankōkyaku	yŏhaangja
'ng . . .	. . . no hō e	. . . jok ŭro
duañlàk	taoru	sugŏn
tā'	tō	tap
tsiu-hu	machi	gŏri
siañchih-dńg	machi-yakuba	sigonggwan
hēchiā	kisha	gicha
diahnchiā	densha	jŏncha
huan'iēk	yakushimasu	bŏnyŏk hamnida (ha-)
ki-keh'	ryokō shimasu	yŏhaang hamnida (ha-)
chiu	ki	namu
kùnlán	shimpai	sugo
koh	zubon	baji
tsīn	hontō	chamdoen (chamdoe-)
chiehng-kuahñ	kite mimasu	yibŏ bomnida (bo-)
lunliú	mata	jada
nngh bpài	nido	du baaro
pà'dzihgkī	taipuraitā	taipuraita
pà'dzih'uán	taipisuto	tajasu
lián-tāi	taiya	taiya
paiñ-kuahñ	minikui	chuak han (ha-)
hohsuahñ	kasa	usan
'eh-duè	. . . no shita ni	. . . arae e
'ueh hiàu	wakarimasu	amnida (ar-)
kōusiouh'	ainiku	bŭlhaang hage

VOCABULARY

ENGLISH	MANDARIN	CANTONESE
university, the	dàxué	daaihhohk
until	zhídào	yātjihk ... dou
upstairs	lóushàng	làuhseuhng
urgently	jǐnjí de	gán-gāp
usually	píngcháng	pihngsèuhng
valley, the	shāngǔ	sàanngaau
valuable	guìzhòng de	gwaijuhng ge
veal, the	xiǎoniúròu	ngàuhjáiyuhk
vegetables, the	cài	choi
very	hěn	hóu
view (outlook), the	fēngjǐng	fùnggíng
village, the	cūnzi	chyūn
visit, to	bàifǎng	taam
voyage, the	hǎichéng	léuihhàhng
wait for, to	děng	dánggán
waiter, the	huǒji	fógéi
walk, to	zǒulù	hàahng
wall (of room), the	qiángbì	chèuhng
wall (garden, etc.), the	wéiqiang	chèuhng
want, to	yào	yiu
war, the	zhànzhēng	jinjàng
wash, to	xǐ	sái
washbasin, the	xǐshǒupén	mihnpún
watch, the	shóubiǎo	bīu
watch, to	kànzhe	táijyuh
water, the	shuǐ	séui
we	wǒmen	ngóhdeih
weather, the	tiānqi	tìnhei
week, the	xingqi	láihbaai
weight, the	zhòngliàng	juhngleuhng
well (adv.)	hǎo	hóu
well (health)	hǎo	hóu
west	xībianr	sài
wet	shī	sāp
wet season, the	yǔchì	yúhgwai
wharf, the	mǎtóu	máhtàuh
what?	shénme?	mātyéh?
wheel, the	lúnzi	chēlūk
when?	shénme shíhour?	géiśí?
where (is it)?	zài nǎr?	bīnsyu?
where (to)?	xiàng nǎr?	heui bīnsyu?
which?	něi?	bīn-?
white	bái	baahk
who?	shéi?	bīn-go?
whose?	shéide?	bīn-go ge?
why?	wèi shénme?	jouh mātyéh?
wide	kuò de	fut

VOCABULARY

HOKKIEN	JAPANESE	KOREAN
duah'ou'	daigaku	daahakkyo
tièng-hauh . . .	. . . made	. . . gaji
laudièng	nikai ni	wi chǔng
gkin-gkip	kinkyū ni	gin-gǔp hage
po-tong . . .	tsune ni	botong
suañ-gkòk	tani	goljjagi
daht-tsiñ	kichō na	kwi han (ha-)
gugkiañbah'	ko-ushi no niku	song-aji gogi
chiñchaih	yasai	chaaso
tsin . . .	taihen	daadan hi
hong-gkièng	keshiki	gyŏngchi
gkuè	mura	maǔl
kuahñ	hōmon shimasu	simbang hamnida (ha-)
gkiañtsún	koko	hanghaa
tièng-hau	machimasu	gidarimnida (gidari-)
hègkih	kyūji	weita
gkiáñ	arikimasu	sanbo hamnida (ha-)
bpiah'	kabe	byŏk
chiúñ	nei	tam
beh'	irimasu	wŏn hamnida (ha-)
tsiahn	sensō	jŏnjaang
suè	araimasu	sesu hamnida (ha-)
bihn-tàng	semmendai	sesu daaya
bpiou'à	tokei	sigye
dziäga	nagamemasu	gugyŏng hamnida (ha-)
tsui	mizu	mul
gùn	watashitachi	uri
tiñ-kih	otenki	nalssi
lèbpaih	shūkan	jugan
dang	mekata	muge
hòu . . .	yoku	jal
hòu	kenkō na	pyŏngan han (ha-)
sài	nishi	sŏ
dám	nureta	jŏjǔn (jŏj-)
hoh-tiñ	tsuyu	jangma
bè-táu	hatoba	budu
sìmmī'?	nani?	muŏt?
lún	wa	ba-kwi
dihsi?	itsu?	ŏnje?
dôulôu'?	doko ni?	ŏdi?
dih dôulôu'?	doko e?	ŏdi?
dôulôu' tsiht 'e?	dochira no . . .?	ŏnǔ . . .?
bpè'	shiroi	hǔin (hǔi-)
tsih-tsui?	dare?	nugu?
tsih-tsui 'e . . .?	dare no . . .?	nugu-ǔi?
sìmmī' daih-tsì . . .?	dō shite?	waa?
kuah'	hiroi	nŏlbǔn (nŏlb-)

VOCABULARY

ENGLISH	MANDARIN	CANTONESE
wild	yě de	yéh
win, to	yíng	yèhng
wind, the	fēng	fùng
window, the	chuānghu	chēungmún
wine, the	jiǔ	jáu
wise	cōngmíng de	chùngmihng
with	gēn	tùhng
without	méiyou	móuh
woman, the	nǚrén	néuih-yán
wonder, to	bù míngbái	mh-jìdímgáai
wonderful	hǎojíle	kèihjit ge
wood (timber), the	mù	muhk
wool, the	yángmáo	yèuhngmòuh
word, the	zìr	jih
work, the	gōngzuò	jouhsih
workman, the	gōngren	gùng-yàhn
world, the	shìjiè	saigaai
worse	gènghuài de	juhng
worst	zuìhuài de	jeui-yáih
worth, to be	zhí	jihk
write, to	xiě	sé
wrong	cuò	cho
year, the	nián	nihn
yellow	huáng	wòhng
yesterday	zuótiān	kahmyaht
you	nǐ	néih
young	niánqīng	hauhsàang
your	nǐde	néih-ge

VOCABULARY

HOKKIEN	JAPANESE	KOREAN
'iá	yasei no	yaasang-ŭi . . .
'iáñ	kachimasu	igimnida (igi-)
hōng	kaze	baram
tang'ä-mńg	mado	chang
tsiù	budōshu	sul
kiahng	kashikoi	hyŏnmyŏng han (ha-)
gkäp . . .	. . . to	. . . hago
bou . . .	. . . nashi de	. . . ŏpsŭn
tsabóláng	onna no hito	yŏja
'mh tsäi	. . . ka to omoimasu	mussŭmnida (mut-)
tsin hòu	subarashii	sintong han (ha-)
chiuhdóng	mokuzai	namu
'iuñ-mńg	yōmō	yangtŏl
'ue	kotoba	dan-ŏ
gkäng	shigoto	nodong
gkangláng	rōdōsha	nodongja
sègkaih	sekai	segye
kà' bou-hòu	yori warui	dŏ nappŭn (nappŭ-)
deh'ït bou-hòu	mottomo warui	gajang nappŭn (nappŭ-)
dät	kachi ga arimasu	gapsi issŭmnida (iss-)
sià	kakimasu	ssŭmnida (ssŭ-)
'mh diouh'	warui	nappŭn (nappŭ-)
ní	toshi	haa
'ńg	kiiroi	nurŭm (nurŭ-)
tsadzït	kinō	ŏje
lì	anata	dangsin
siàulián	wakai	jŏlmŭn (jŏlm-)
lì 'e . . .	anata no	dangsin

PART IV

MALAY AND INDONESIAN
TAGALOG
SPANISH
PORTUGUESE
FRENCH

PART IV

Malay and Indonesian are the same language, except that Indonesian is a little simpler and there are some vocabulary preferences. With minor variations, the language is spoken not only throughout Malaysia, Singapore and Indonesia, but also in parts of Thailand and Kampuchea.

The roman alphabet is normal, though in Malaysia a modified Arabic script is in occasional use as an alternative. Malaysia and Indonesia adopted a common spelling, previously divergent, in 1972. In the phrases and vocabulary Indonesian variants are in square brackets [ ].

PRONUNCIATION Vowels:

A, I, O, U are like *ah, ee, aw, oo,* but short.
Accented É is like short *eh.*
Unaccented E is the neutral *e* in English "the" before a consonant; for example, in "the man."
Diphthongs AI, AU, UA are like double syllables *ah-ee, ah-oo, oo-ah.*

Consonants are as in English, except that
Ć is pronounced like a *ch* forward in the mouth.
H is always strongly sounded.
R is slightly trilled.
S is always *ss,* never *z.*
NG is as in "singer" (no *g* sound).
NGG has the extra *g* sound as in "finger."

In combinations such as NY and SY, always sound Y as a consonant.

Syllables are clearly and evenly enunciated, with accent on the second last unless this is unaccented E, in which case on the last. (But for this purpose added syllables do not count; for example, the accented *ma-* in *makan,* "eat," is retained in *makanan,* "food.")

Note that in normal writing Ć is just C, and É and E are not distinguished.

NOUNS are invariable and have no distinction of singular and plural, except that a few nouns can be doubled: *orang,* "man, person"; *orang-orang,* "people, mankind."

There is no article "a" or "the," but demonstratives *ini,* "this, these," and *itu,* "that, those," are freely used, placed after the noun: *orang ini,* "this man, these men."

Place the possessor after the thing possessed: *rumah orang itu,* "that man's house."

The prepositions *ke,* "to," and *dari,* "from," become *kepada* and *daripada* before words for people: *ke rumah,* "to the house"; *kepada perempuan itu,* "to that woman."

PRONOUNS in common use are:

saya, "I, me"
kita, "we, us, including you"
kami, "we, us, not you"
dia, "he, him, she, her, it, they, them"

For second person "you" (singular or plural): in Malaysia, *inćik* (to males), *ćik* (to females, but familiarly also to males); in Indonesia, *engkau* (to either sex). But second person pronouns are frequently avoided in favour of a term of address such as *saudara* (see below).

The possessor follows the thing possessed, as for nouns: *nama saya,* "my name" — but *dia* becomes *-nya* attached to the noun: *namanya,* "his (etc.) name."

ADJECTIVES follow the noun: *hotél besar,* "large hotel." Since no verb "is" or "are" is needed in applying an adjective to a noun, the same construction can mean "The hotel is large."

When there are two adjectives, the second is predicative, as *Hotél besar baik,* "The large hotel is good"; otherwise the relative pronoun *yang,* "which, who," would be inserted: *kamar besar yang terang,* "Large room, which (is) bright," "large bright room."

When *ini* or *itu* is placed first, what follows is predicative: *Ini kamar,* "This is the room"; *Ini murah,* "This is cheap."

For a comparative, use *lebih,* "more," or *kurang,* "less," before the adjective; "than" is *daripada*: *lebih besar daripada hotél,* "bigger than the hotel."

For a superlative, put *sekali,* "uniquely," after the adjective: *baik sekali,* "the best."

ADVERBS Adjectives may be used without change of form as adverbs.

VERBS do not indicate person, number or tense. If necessary, use the auxiliary *sudah* to indicate a completed action in the past, *nanti* similarly for the future: *Saya sudah makan,* "I have eaten"; *Saya nanti lihat dia,* "I shall see him."

Other common auxiliaries are: *boléh,* "can" (in Indonesia generally *bisa*); *hendak,* "intend to" (shortened by Malaysians to *nak*); *suka,* "like to"; *ingin* or *mau,* "want to"; *tahu,* "know how to": *Saya suka makan nasi,* "I like eating" (literally "eating rice"); *Orang itu hendak pergi rumah,* "That man is going to go home."

To indicate location, "is" or "are" is *ada*: *Saya ada disini,* "I am here." Use *Ada* also for "There is" or "There are": *Ada kedai di hotél,* "There is a shop in the hotel."

For a negative, put *tidak* (or *tak*), or, more emphatically, *bukan,* before the verb: *Dia tidak ada disini,* "He (etc.) isn't here."

The suffix *-kan* is causative, turning any part of speech into a transitive verb; for example, *murahkan,* "to cheapen," from *murah,* "cheap."

The prefix *di-* forms the passive: *beri,* "give," *diberi oléh,* "is given by."

QUESTIONS Yes/no questions may be indicated simply by tone of voice, or by attaching *-kah* to the principal word being questioned: *Anak itu laparkah?,* "Is the child hungry?" In Indonesia a common alternative is to begin the sentence with *Apa* (normally "what?"): *Apa anak itu lapar?*

The answers *Ya,* "Yes," and *Tidak,* "No," are considered abrupt, and it is usually better to repeat part of the sentence with or without a negative: *Lapar,* "Yes, hungry," or *Tidak lapar,* "No, not hungry." Note also the common use of *Belum,* "Not yet."

Interrogative words such as *dimana,* "where?," may be placed first in the sentence, but equally often the order is the same as for a statement: *Hotél dimana?,* "Where is the hotel?"

IMPERATIVES For an imperative, use the plain verb, generally preceded by one of the courtesy words *Baik,* "It would be a good idea to"; *Boléhkah,* "Can you" (in Indonesia *Bisakah*); or *Minta*, "Help by," "Please" (in Indonesia more often *Silakan*).

"Let's" is *Mari kita*, where *Mari* is a special imperative word meaning "Come": *Mari kita duduk*, "Let's sit down."

For a negative imperative, use *Jangan*, "Don't," or *Tak usah*, "There is no need to": *Jangan pergi*, "Don't go."

NUMERALS A numeral is followed by a classifier characteristic of the thing being counted, for example, by *orang* in the case of human beings: *dua orang perempuan*, "two women."

For animals, the classifier is *ékor* ("tails"); for most objects, *buah* (which as a noun means "fruit"): *dua buah buku*, "two books"; *sebuah rumah*, "one house," "a house." For small objects, use *biji* ("seed") instead of *buah*; oddly, *biji* is also used with fruits, thus we even find *dua biji buah*, "two pieces of fruit." There are some thirty other classifiers, but these serve most purposes.

The word *berapa*, "how many?," takes a classifier in the same way as numerals. No classifier is needed with time and money expressions.

CURRENCY In Malaysia, 1 *ringgit* = 100 *sén*, and in some areas 10 *sén* is called 1 *kupang*.

In Singapore, 1 *dolar* = 100 *sén*.

In Indonesia, 1 *rupiah* = 100 *sén*, but the word *ringgit* is used for $2\frac{1}{2}$ *rupiah*.

FORMS OF ADDRESS The commonest greeting is *Apa kabar?*, "What news?"; the reply is *Kabar baik*, "The news is good." (Even if it isn't.)

In Malaysia, titles are common and forms of address elaborate, but the foreigner may simplify them. Use *Inćik* for "sir" or before a surname for Mr, and *Ćik* similarly for "madam," "Mrs" or "Miss." (But *Ćik* is also used less formally for "sir" or "Mr.") Among friends and family the terms *saudara* (when speaking to men), *saudari* (when speaking to women; also sometimes *saudara*), are commonest. Use any of these terms also as second person pronouns.

In Indonesia, *saudara* ("brother, sister, friend") is a democratic possibility when speaking to any age and sex, but *Bapak* is most common for "sir" or "Mr," *Nyonya* for "madam" or "Mrs," *Nona* for "Miss." In writing, *Tuan* is commonest when addressing men. The word *engkau* is a general second person pronoun, but in polite address it would be usual to substitute one of the terms of address.

KIN TERMS The following are common to Malaysia and Indonesia:

bapak or *ayah*, "father"; *ibu*, "mother"
suami, "husband"; *bini* or *isteri*, "wife"
saudara, "brother or sister"
abang or *kakak*, "older brother or sister"
adik, "younger brother or sister"
anak, "son, daughter, child"

When necessary, add *laki-laki* for males, *perempuan* for females: *saudara laki-laki*, "brother"; *anak perempuan*, "daughter."

NAME OF LANGUAGE

The name of the language is, according to choice, *Bahasa Melayu* (or *Malaysia*) or *Bahasa Indonésia*.

TAGALOG

Tagalog is the most widely spoken of some 100 languages of the Philippines. It is understood by about half the population of forty million, mainly in the island of Luzon, but is spreading elsewhere as a language of communication. A standardised Tagalog, called Pilipino, is the official language, together with English.

The roman alphabet is used.

PRONUNCIATION Vowels:

A, E, I, O, U are like *ah, eh, ee, aw, oo*, but short.

In the combinations AW, IW, pronounce W as a consonant; approximately *ah-oo, ee-oo*, but with the mouth nearly closed on the final sound.

OY, AY, EY, UY are approximately *oy, igh, eigh, oo-ee*, but the Y is also more like a consonant than a vowel.

In all other cases, vowels in sequence should be separated by a slight pause or glottal stop (closing of the back of the throat, as in the Cockney pronunciation of "bottle" as "bo'l"): for example, *saan* as *sa'an*.

Consonants:

P, T, K are pronounced without the puff of breath that usually follows them in English.

NG is as in "singer," never as in "finger," and may occur at the beginning of a word.

H is always sounded.

R is slightly trilled, with the tongue behind the top teeth.

Accent marks have the following meanings:

´ indicates stress (on syllables other than second last).

` indicates a "closed" vowel, that is, with a following glottal stop.

^ is a combination of ´ and `.

Stress is on the second last syllable unless otherwise marked (with ´ or ^). Tone is even, and stress consists in the lengthening of a vowel rather than a rise in pitch.

NOUNS do not change in form. Plural need not be indicated, but may be formed if required by placing *mga* (pronounced *m'ng-ah*) before the noun: *bahay*, "house, houses," *mga bahay*, "houses."

There is no definite article. The role of a noun in a sentence is indicated by a word placed before it: *ang* for a subject; *ng* (pronounced *n'ng*) for object or possessive; *sa* for a preposition, "to, from, for, in, at": *ang bahay*, "a house" or "the house" (subject); *ang mga bahay*, "houses" or "the houses" (subject); *na bahay*, "a house" or "the house" (object), or "of the house"; *sa bahay*, "to the house," "at home," etc.

Before a personal name use *si* instead of *ang*: *si Carlos*, "Carlos" (subject).

A sentence can equate two nouns by putting them together, each preceded by *ang* (or *si*): *lalaki*, "man"; *Ang lalaki ang tsupér*, "The man is the driver"; *Si Carlos ang tsupér ng kotse*, "Carlos is the driver of the car."

An indefinite noun is placed first, without *ang*: *Tsupér ang lalaki*, "The man is a driver."

ADJECTIVES An adjective normally precedes its noun, but may follow it. In either case the link-word *na* is placed between them, becoming -*ng* attached to the preceding word if this ends in a vowel: *mahusay na tsupér*, "good driver" (or

248

tsupér na mahusay); *malakíng kotse,* "big car" (or *kotseng malakí*).

In a sentence in which an adjective is applied to a noun the adjective comes first, without the use of "is" or "are": *Malakí ang kotse,* "The car is big."

An adjective may be used alone as a noun: *ang malakí,* "the big one."

Adjectives that begin with *ma-* (the vast majority) can be made plural by reduplicating the consonant and vowel (or just vowel) following *ma-*: *ang malalakí,* "the big ones."

For a comparative, put *mas,* "more," before the adjective; and "than" is *kaysa sa* (*kaysa kay* before a personal name): *Mas malakí ang lalaki kaysa sa babae,* "The man is bigger than the woman." *Mas* may sometimes be omitted.

For a superlative, attach *pinaka-* to the beginning of the adjective: *pinakamalakí,* "the biggest."

VERBS are shown in the vocabulary with certain letters in parentheses, for example *p(um)ú(pu)ntá,* "go." Read the whole word for the present or past imperfect tense: *pumúpuntá,* "goes," "is going" or "was going."

In a normal sentence the verb comes first: *Pumúpuntá ang babae sa bahay,* "The woman is (was) going to the house"; *Naglílinis ang tsupér ng kotse,* "The driver is (was) cleaning the car."

For a verb form indicating completed action, delete the second parenthesis; hence from *p(um)ú(pu)ntá* get *pumuntá,* "went," "has gone"; or from *(nag)(li)linis* get *naglinis,* "cleaned."

For future or contemplated action, if the first parenthesis is *(um),* delete it; if it is *(na), (nag)* or *(nang),* retain it but change initial *n* to *m*: *pupuntá,* "will go"; *maglílinis,* "will clean." In deleting a stressed syllable, shift the stress to the preceding one.

Certain verbs which have *(in)* in place of *(um)* are like passives in that it is their subject that is marked with *ng* and their object with *ang* (or *si*). A verb with first parenthesis *(in)* forms its tenses in the same way as one with *(um),* except that, when *(in)* is deleted, it is added at the end (or *-hin* following a vowel): *h(in)í(hi)ntáy,* "wait for"; *híhintayín,* "will wait for"; *Híhintayín ng babae ang batà,* "The woman will wait for the child." (But if a verb in *(in)* begins with *i-* or ends with *-an,* its tenses are just like those of *(um)* verbs.)

To form a negative, place *Hindî,* "not," before the verb at the start of the sentence.

There is no verb "is," "are." For "There is" or "There are," use the invariable *Mayroón* (for short *May*), which also means "have" when used with a subject. It has the special negative *Walâ,* "has not" or "There is not," etc.

The invariable verb *Gustó,* which takes a subject introduced by *ng,* means "wants," "would like." It is followed by an infinitive (same form as for completed action, except that initial *n* becomes *m,* and *in* is transferred to the end): *Gustó ng batà pumuntá sa bahay,* "The child wants to go home."

Gustó also has a special negative *Ayaw,* "does not want."

PRONOUNS have three forms, subject, object-possessive, and prepositional, as follows:

akó, ko, sa akin, "I, me"
ka, mo, sa iyó, "you" (singular)
siyá, niyá, sa kaniyá, "he, him, she, her, it" (people and animals)
tayo, natin, sa atin, "we, us, including you"

kamí, namin, sa amin, "we, us, not you"
kayó, ninyó, sa inyó, "you" (plural)
silá, nilá, sa kanilá, "they, them" (people and animals)

The subject and object-possessive forms are used in the same way as nouns with *ang* or nouns with *ng,* respectively.

The second person singular *ka* has the longer form *ikáw* when it occurs at the beginning of the sentence.

For inanimates use;

itó, nitó, sa ditó, "this"
iyón, niyón, sa diyón, "that"

A pronoun as subject or object immediately follows the verb, or follows *Hindî* when this comes first: *Púpuntá akó,* "I shall go"; *Hindî akó púpuntá,* "I shall not go".

A possessive follows the noun in the same way as for a *ng* phrase: *bahay ko,* "my house."

QUESTIONS To turn a statement into a question, insert *ba* after the verb, or after *Hindî* if this is the first word: *Púpuntá siyá,* "He/She will go"; *Púpuntá ba siyá?,* "Will he/she go?"; *Hindî ba siyá púpuntá?,* "Won't he/she go?" (But put *ka* before *ba* if this is the subject: *Púpuntá ka ba?,* "Will you go?")

In answer to a negative question the word *'O'o,* normally "Yes," counts as negative; hence make sure by repeating part of the sentence.

Question words such as *Anó,* "What?," *Sino,* "Who?" (plural *Sinu-sino*), *Kailán,* "When?," are placed first in the sentence. For "What?," as object in a sentence such as "What did you see?," form a noun out of the verb by preceding it with *ang: Anó ang nakitá ko?*

IMPERATIVES For a plain imperative, use the infinitive of the verb followed by the second person subject: *Pumuntá ka,* "Go," plural *Pumuntá kayó.*

For a polite request, prefix *Paki-* to the base of the verb, with *mo* after it, and use *ang* before the object: *Pakilinis mo ang kotse,* "Please clean the car."

For "Let's," use the inclusive subject *tayo* following the infinitive: *Pumuntá tayo,* "Let's go."

For "Don't," use *Huwág,* with the subject immediately following: *Huwág ka pumuntá,* "Don't go."

NUMERALS A numeral is linked to a noun with *na* or *-ng* in the same way as an adjective: *dalawáng babae,* "two women."

In money and (especially) time expressions the Spanish numerals, shown second in the table, are more common than the native ones.

CURRENCY 1 *piso* ("peso") = 100 *pera* (or *séntimos,* "centavos").

FORMS OF ADDRESS The politeness word *pô* (sometimes *hô*) is very frequently inserted following the first word or phrase of a sentence, translatable approximately as "sir" or "madam."

"Mr," "Mrs" and "Miss" preceding names are *Ginoóng, Gináng* and *Binibining.*

KIN TERMS The commonest kin terms are:

amá, or colloquially *tatay,* "father"
iná, or colloquially *nanay,* "mother"

kapatíd na lalaki, "brother"; *kapatíd na babae,* "sister"
kuya, "oldest brother"; *ate,* "oldest sister" (or any older sister)
anák na lalaki, "son"; *anák na babae,* "daughter"
asawa, "husband or wife" (but popularly "husband" *tao,* "wife" *maybahay*)

NAME OF LANGUAGE

Pronounce *Tagalog* with the stress on the second syllable. The country is *Pilipinas.*

SPANISH

Although Spanish is now little spoken in Asia or the Pacific, it is assured of
continuing influence in the area as the language of the majority of Latin America.

This account deals mainly with American Spanish; but this has its own regional
variations as well as differing to some extent from the language of Spain. Some
alternatives, local or European, are given in square brackets [ ].

PRONUNCIATION Vowels:

A, E, I, O, U are like *ah, eh, ee, aw, oo.*

Y at the end of a word has the same sound as I.

Compound vowels AY, UI, IE, . . . are like sequences of their components: *ah-ee,
oo-ee, ee-eh,* . . .

Consonants are as in English, with the following exceptions:

D is pronounced with tongue forward against the teeth, and between vowels
becomes like *th* in "this."

J is like guttural *ch* in "loch."

G before E or I is like guttural *ch* in "loch," otherwise hard as in English.

C before E or I is like *ss,* otherwise like *k.*

H is silent, except in the combination CH, which is as in English.

LL is like *ly* or just *y.*

Ñ is like *ny.*

QU is always as *k.*

R is trilled when at the beginning of a word, or when double.

S and Z are both always like *ss.*

B and V are alike, like *b* with the lips not quite closed.

The accent ´ indicates stress. If not indicated, stress is on the second last
syllable if the word ends in a vowel, or a vowel plus S or N; or on the last if it ends
in another consonant.

Among regional variants in South America, note: LL becoming *zh* or *dzh;*
tendency to drop D between vowels; J becoming simple *h;* final S also weakening
to *h.*

The principal difference in Castilian Spanish (the preferred norm of Spain) is
that Z always, and C when it is before E or I, are pronounced like soft *th* in "thin."

NOUNS There are two genders, masculine and feminine, distinguished in the
vocabulary by prefixing the definite article *el* or *la: el hombre,* "the man"; *la casa,*
"the house."

Form plurals by adding *-s* after vowels, *-es* after consonants. Words ending in
-z form plural in *-ces.* The definite article has masculine plural *los,* feminine *las:
los hombres,* "the men"; *las casas,* "the houses."

The indefinite article "a, an" (also "one") is *un* or *una;* plurals ("some") *unos,
unas: una casa,* "a house"; *unas casas,* "houses."

The prepositions *de,* "of, from," and *a,* "to, at," combine with the article *el* to
give *del* and *al* respectively: *del hombre,* "of the man."

ADJECTIVES generally follow the noun, but a few common ones precede it.
They agree with the noun in gender and number.

Adjectives ending in *-o* have feminine *-a,* adding *-s* in either case for the plural.
Adjectives ending in *-e* or a consonant are generally the same in masculine and
feminine, and add *-s* or *-es* (respectively) for the plural: *hombre alto,* "tall man";
señoras altas, "tall women"; *casa azul,* "blue house."

For a comparative, put *más* before the adjective; "than" is *que*: *más alto que una casa*, "taller than a house." There are a few special comparatives: *bueno* (or *buen*), "good," *mejor*, "better."

For a superlative, use the definite article with *más*: *el más alto*, "the tallest" — but when a noun is qualified, the definite article remains in front of the noun: *el hombre más alto*, "the tallest man."

PRONOUNS have separate subject and object forms, and, in the case of "we," "they" and "them," separate masculine and feminine:

yo, "I"	*me*, "me"
nosotros/nosotras, "we"	*nos*, "us"
él, "he"	*lo*, "him"
ella, "she"	*la*, "her"
ellos/ellas, "they"	*los/las*, "them"

For "it," use the form appropriate to the gender of the noun; but in the case of abstract things, use *lo* as object form for either gender.

For "you," the polite form is *usted* (singular, pronounced *OOSTeh*) or *ustedes* (plural); these are strictly nouns and are treated as third person.

The forms *le*, *les* with verbs mean "to him (etc.)" and "to them (etc.)."

There is a third person reflexive pronoun *se*, "himself, themselves (etc.)"; it is sometimes used as the indefinite subject, "one," "people," or to replace *le* or *les*.

After a preposition, use *mí* for "me"; in other cases, use the subject forms: *para él*, "for him."

Possessive pronouns *mi*, *mis*, "my," and *su*, *sus*, "his, her, its, your, their," agree in number with their nouns; and *nuestro/-a/-os/-as*, "our," must also agree in gender. Note the possible addition of *de él, de ella, de usted* or their plurals to phrases containing *su* or *sus*, to discriminate the various meanings: *su libro de usted*, "your book."

VERBS Verb endings change for person, number and tense. For each tense we distinguish in order first and third singular, first and third plural.

There are two different verbs "to be," *ser* (present *soy, es, somos, son*; past *fui, fue, fuimos, fueron*) and *estar* (present *estoy, está, estamos, están*; past *estuve, -vo, -vimos, -vieron*). The difference between them is that *ser* indicates a permanent or intrinsic state and *estar* a temporary or accidental one. For example, *Es barato* means "It is cheap (an inexpensive commodity)"; and *Está barato* means "It is cheap (low in price at the moment)."

"There is" or "There are" is *Hay*.

Regular verbs in *-ar* form the present tense *-o, -a, -amos, -an*; the past, *-é, -ó, -amos, -aron*. Regular verbs in *-er* or *-ir* form the present tense *-o, -e, -emos* (or *-imos*), *-en*; the past, *-í, -ió, -imos, -ieron*.

Many verbs change the final vowel of the root when it is stressed, and this change is shown in the vocabulary. For example, *pensar* (*-ie-*), "think," has as present tense *pienso, piensa, pensamos, piensan*.

Among irregular verbs, note: *tener*, "have" (present *tengo, tiene, tenemos, tienen*; past *tuve, tuvo, tuvimos, tuvieron*); *venir*, "come" (present *vengo, viene*, etc.; past *vine, vino*, etc.); *ir*, "go" (present *voy, vas, vamos, van*; past, the same as for *ser*).

For the future tense, in virtually all cases add *-é, -á, -emos, -án* to the infinitive. There are various other verb forms, but these will serve simple purposes.

Pronoun subjects are generally omitted. Pronoun objects generally precede the verb, and an indirect object precedes a direct one: *Me lo dio,* "(He) gave it to me."

For a negative, place *no,* "not," before the verb (and before object pronouns): *No voy,* "I'm not going." Use this even when there is another negative in the sentence.

QUESTIONS are formed by changing the word order in the same way as in English; but in the case of an unexpressed pronoun subject there will be no difference: *Puedo entrar?,* "May I come in?"

IMPERATIVES A polite imperative in the case of an *-ar* verb has the ending *-e* (singular), *-en* (plural); in the case of an *-er* or *-ir* verb, *-a* (singular), *-an* (plural). Generally put *usted* or *ustedes* after the verb: *Hable usted más despacio,* "Speak more slowly."

For a negative, precede with *No.*

For "Let's," use *Vamos a* with the infinitive: *Vamos a comer,* "Let's eat." (*Vamos* alone means "Let's go.")

In the case of an affirmative imperative, direct or indirect object pronouns follow and are attached to the verb, instead of preceding it: *Muestreme,* "Show me."

NUMERALS For "one" use *uno* or *una,* agreeing with the noun. Other numerals are invariable.

CURRENCY In Mexico, Cuba, Argentina, Uruguay, Chile, Colombia, 1 *peso* = 100 *centavos* (Uruguay *centésimos*). Other Latin American countries have different names for the major unit. In Spain, 1 *peseta* = 100 *céntimos.*

FORMS OF ADDRESS "Mr" is *El señor,* "Mrs" is *La señora* and "Miss" is *La señorita* (or very commonly also *La señora*). Omit *El* or *La* when actually addressing someone by name.

Use the same terms for "sir" or "madam."

KIN TERMS

padre, "father"	*madre,* "mother"
hijo, "son"	*hija,* "daughter"
hermano, "brother"	*hermana,* "sister"
marido or *esposo,* "husband"	*mujer* or (particularly of addressee's wife) *esposa* or *señora,* "wife"

NAME OF LANGUAGE

The language is *español.*

PORTUGUESE

Formerly very influential in Asia, Portuguese is now spoken only in Macau, and, to a small extent, in former Portuguese colonies such as Goa and Timor. It is, however, assured of permanence as the language of Brazil.

This account deals mainly with Brazilian Portuguese, which differs in some details from that of Portugal and its colonies. Some European Portuguese alternatives are given in square brackets [ ].

PRONUNCIATION Stressed and unstressed vowels are differently pronounced:

A, E, I, O, U, when stressed, are pronounced *ah, eh, ee, aw, oo.*
Ã and Õ, when stressed, are nasal equivalents of A and O (part of the air escaping through the nose).
Any vowel is nasal when followed by M or N.
Unstressed A is like English *er,* unstressed E like short *ee.*
Unstressed O is like short *oo* in "took."
Compound vowels are generally as sequences of their components.

Consonants are as in English, with the following exceptions:

QU and GU before E or I are like plain *k* and *g,* otherwise like *kw* and *gw.*
C and G before E or I are soft (*ss* and *zh*), otherwise hard.
Ç is always like soft *ss.*
LH and NH are like *ly* and *ny.*
CH is like *sh.*
H is otherwise silent.
J is like *zh.*
R is generally strongly vibrated, with a rush of air, when at the beginning of a word, or when double.
S is like *z* between vowels and before voiced consonants, otherwise *ss.*
X is like *sh,* becoming *ss* or *z* before a consonant or in EX- at the start of a word.
D and T are pronounced with the tongue forward; DI and TI are like *dj* and *tj.*

Accents ´, ^, ` indicate stress, and are sometimes used to distinguish words otherwise spelt alike. When no stress is indicated, stress the second last syllable of a word ending in A, E or O or in one of these vowels with M or S, and the last syllable of other words.

The principal difference in European pronunciation (also heard in Rio) is that S and Z, before consonants or at the end of a word, are pronounced *sh* or *zh.*

NOUNS There are two genders, masculine and feminine, indicated in the vocabulary by definite articles *o* and *a*: *o homem* [oo awmerñ: in these pronunciation guides we indicate nasalisation by a following ñ], "the man"; *a mulher* [er mool-yehrr], "the woman."

For plurals, add *-s* after vowels, generally *-es* after consonants, but change *-m* to *-ns, -l* to *-is,* and leave words ending in *-s* unchanged; there are a very few exceptions, noted in the vocabulary. The definite article becomes *os, as*: *os homens* [ooss awmerñss], "the men"; *as mulheres* [erss mool-yehrrerss], "the women."

The indefinite article "a, an" (also "one") is *um* or *uma*; plurals ("some"), *uns* and *umas* (but these are normally omitted): *um jornal* [ooñ zhoorr-nahl], "a newspaper"; *uma casa* [oomer kahzer], "a house."

Note the tendency of prepositions to combine with the definite article; *de,* "of, from," gives *do/da/dos/das,* "of the, from the"; *a,* "to," gives *ao/à/aos/às; em,* "in, on, at," gives *no/na/nos/nas.*

255

ADJECTIVES generally follow the noun, but a few common ones precede it. They agree with the noun in gender and number.

Adjectives ending in -*o* have feminine -*a*; those in -*ão* drop the -*o*; those ending in a consonant or -*e* remain unchanged (exceptions noted in the vocabulary). Plurals are formed from singulars in the same way as for nouns: *homem alto* [awmerñ ahltoo], "tall man"; *casas grandes* [kahzerss grahnderss], "big houses."

For a comparative, put *mais* [mighss], "more," before the adjective; "than" is *que*: *mais alto que uma casa* [mighss ahltoo keh oomer kahzer], "taller than a house." There are a few special comparatives such as *maior* [mighoor], "bigger"; *melhor* [merl-yawrr], "better."

For a superlative, use the definite article before the comparative, or before the noun with comparative: *o mais alto* [oo mighss ahltoo], "the tallest"; *o homem mais alto* [oo awmerñ mighss ahltoo], "the tallest man."

PRONOUNS The principal pronouns are:

eu, "I"; *me*, "me"
êle, "he, him"; *ela*, "she, her"
nós, "we, us"
êles and *elas*, "they, them" (masculine and feminine)

For second person "you," it is usual to use a name or title, or the forms *o senhor, a senhora*; more familiarly, *você*, plural *vocês*.

The reflexive pronoun *se* is used for "himself, herself, themselves"; also for "yourself, yourselves."

The forms *lhe, lhes* with verbs mean "him, to him (etc.)" and "them, to them," respectively.

European Portguese uses *o, a, os, as* as direct object forms in the third person and has a variety of compound direct-indirect object forms such as *mo*, "it to me."

Possessive pronouns agree in gender and number with the noun following. The forms (masculine/feminine) are:

meu/minha, "my"
seu/sua, "his, her, their, your"
nosso/nossa, "our"

For plurals add -*s*. They are sometimes preceded by the definite article: *o meu quarto* [oo mehoo kwahrrtoo], "my room."

VERBS Verb endings change for person, number and tense, but second person forms are not required; in what follows we give first and third persons, plus plurals.

There are two different verbs "to be": *ser* (present *sou, é, somos, são*; past *fui, foi, fomos, foram*) and *estar* (present *estou, está, estamos, estão*; past *estive, -ve, -vemos, -veram*). The difference between them is that *ser* indicates a permanent or intrinsic state and *estar* a temporary or accidental one; for example, *É barato* means "It is cheap (an inexpensive commodity)," and *Está barato* means "It is cheap (low in price at the moment)."

"There is" or "There are" is *Tem*.

Regular verbs in -*ar* form the present tense -*o, -a, -amos, -am*; the past tense, -*ei, -ou, -ámos, -aram*. Regular verbs in -*er* form the present tense -*o, -e, -emos, -em*; the past, -*i, -eu, -emos, -eram*. Regular verbs in -*ir* form the present tense -*o, -e, -imos, -em*; the past, -*i, -iu, -imos, -iram*.

Among irregular verbs, note: *ter*, "have" (present *tenho, tem, temos, têm*; past *tive, teve, tivemos, tiveram*); *vir*, "come" (present *venho, vem*, ...); *ir*, "go" (present *vou, vai, vamos, vão*; past, the same as for *ser*).

For future tense, almost without exception add *-ei, -á, -emos, -ão* to the infinitive. There are various other verb forms but these will serve simple purposes.

Subject pronouns are regularly omitted. Direct or indirect object pronouns may either follow (and may be attached to) the verb, or may precede it, though they do not usually start the sentence: *O homem olha-me* [oo awmerñ awlyer-meh] or *O homem me olha*, "The man is looking at me."

For a negative, place *não*, "not," before the verb (and before the object pronoun if it precedes the verb): *Não vou* [nowñ voh], "I'm not going." Use this even when there is another negative in the sentence.

QUESTIONS are formed from statements by changing the word order in the same way as in English; but in the case of an unexpressed pronoun subject, there will be no difference: *Posso entrar?* [pawssoo ehn-trahrr], "May I come in?"

IMPERATIVES An imperative has the ending *-e*, plural *-em*, in the case of an *-ar* verb, and *-a*, plural *-am*, in the case of an *-er* or *-ir* verb. A subject such as *o senhor* is sometimes placed after the verb: *Fale mais devagar*, or *Fale o senhor mais devagar* [fahlee oo ser-nyawrr mighss derva-gahrr], "Speak more slowly."

For a negative, precede the verb with *Não*.

For "Let's," use the ending *-emos* with an *-ar* verb, *-amos* with the others: *Vamos* [vahmooss], "Let's go." Or use *Vamos* with the infinitive: *Vamos comer* [vahmooss koo-mehrr], "Let's eat."

In the case of affirmative imperatives, direct or indirect object pronouns follow and are attached to the verb instead of preceding it: *Mostre-me* [mawsstrer-meh], "Show me."

NUMERALS Note that *um, uma* and *dois, duas* have alternative masculine and feminine forms: the others are invariable.

CURRENCY In Brazil: 1 *cruzeiro* = 100 *centavos*. In Macau: 1 *pataca* = 100 *avos*. In Portugal: 1 *escudo* = 100 *centavos*.

FORMS OF ADDRESS "Mr" is *o Senhor*, "Mrs" is *a Senhora* and "Miss" is *a Senhorita* (or very commonly *a Senhora*; the term *Senhorita* is not used at all in Portugal). Omit *o* and *a* when actually addressing someone by name.

Use the same terms for "sir," "madam."

KIN TERMS

pai, "father"	*mãe*, "mother"
irmão, "brother"	*irmã*, "sister"
filho, "son"	*filha*, "daughter"
marido, "husband"	*mulher*, "wife"

NAME OF LANGUAGE

The language is sometimes *Brasileiro*, usually *Português*.

FRENCH

French is the only European language apart from English that is much spoken in Asia and the Pacific; it is the official language of New Caledonia and French Polynesia (Tahiti), and is a second language in Kampuchea and Laos. On the American continent it is spoken in French Guiana, and, beside English, in Quebec and Ontario in Canada.

PRONUNCIATION French vowels are characteristic:

A is between English short and long *a* in "cat" and "cart."

E is generally like neutral *e* in "the" before a consonant; but the final -E or -ES of a word of more than one syllable is not sounded.

É is like the short sound in "get," but with the lips spread.

È and Ê are as in English "they" (but a pure vowel).

I and Y are as in "machine."

O is between *oh* and *aw*.

U is like *oo* pronounced very high in the roof of the mouth.

Double vowels are generally pure vowels, not diphthongs:

AI and EI are like the *e* in "get," but longer.

AU and EAU as *oh*.

OU as *oo*.

EU and OEU as *er*, but in the roof of the mouth.

OI as *wah*.

A vowel followed by a single M or N is nasal (pronounced so that part of the air escapes through the nose); but

IN, AIN and EIN (or the same combinations with M) are like a nasal short *a* (nasal version of the *a* in "cat").

UN (or UM) is like a nasal version of the short *u* (in "cut").

Consonants are generally as in English, but

H is silent.

J has the soft sound in the middle of "pleasure."

G also has this sound when it precedes E, I or Y; otherwise it is hard, as in "go."

QU is always like *k*.

CH is as in "machine."

GN is like *ny*.

LL is like the consonant *y*.

Ç is like *ss*.

R is strongly trilled or guttural.

A final consonant is seldom pronounced unless it is C, F, L or R.

Stress is fairly evenly distributed on all syllables of a word.

NOUNS There are two genders, masculine and feminine, normally indicated in the vocabulary by writing the definite article *le* [ler] or *la* [lah] (respectively) before the noun: *la maison* [lah meyzoñ], "the house," feminine.

Nouns beginning in a vowel (including mute *h*) abbreviate the article to *l*': *l'homme* [lom], "the man" — and in these cases gender is separately shown.

The plural is formed by adding *-s* (sometimes *-x*), unless the noun already ends in *-s*, *-z* or *-x*; but the ending is in any case not pronounced. The plural definite article is *les* (both genders; the *s* is pronounced if a vowel follows): *les maisons* [ley meyzoñ], "the houses"; *les hommes* [ley zom], "the men." Nouns ending in

258

-al change this to *-aux*; *l'animal* [lahneemahl], "the animal"; *les animaux* [ley zahneemoh], "the animals."

The indefinite article is *un*, feminine *une*. Before a vowel the *n* of *un* is pronounced with the following word: *un homme* [er nom], "a man"; but *un train* [erñ trañ], "a train."

Note that the prepositions *de*, "of," and *à*, "to," combine with the definite article *le* to give *du, au*; and with *les* to give *des, aux*; and that *de* becomes *d'* before a vowel.

Note also the use of *de* with the definite article to mean "some": *des hommes* [dey zom], "some men" (as well as "of the men"); *du café* [du kahfeh], "some coffee" (as well as "of the coffee").

ADJECTIVES generally follow the noun, but a few common ones precede it. They agree with the noun in gender and number.

Generally add *-e* for feminine, possibly doubling a final consonant; change *-x* to *-se*; leave final *-e* unaltered. Form the plural from the singular in both genders as for nouns; endings are not pronounced, but adding *-e* may cause a preceding consonant to be pronounced: *petit* [p'tee], "small," feminine *petite* [p'teet].

Form the comparative by putting *plus* [plü], "more," before the adjective: *plus grand* [plü grahñ], "bigger." "Than" is *que*: *plus grand que la maison* [plü grahñ ker lah meyzoñ], "bigger than the house."

Form the superlative by prefixing the definite article to the comparative.

The adjective *bon* [boñ], "good," has the comparative *meilleur* [mey-yerr], and the superlative *le mieux* [ler myer].

ADVERBS are generally formed from adjectives by adding *-ment* to the feminine singular: *lentement* [lahñt-mahñ], "slowly."

PRONOUNS The second person pronoun *tu* is used in addressing relatives and close friends. Other pronouns, with their object forms, are:

je [zher], "I"	*me* [mer], "me"
il [eel], "he"	*le* [ler], "him"
elle [el], "she"	*la* [lah], "her"
nous [noo], "we"	*nous* [noo], "us"
vous [voo], "you"	*vous* [voo], "you"
ils/elles [eel/el], "they"	*les* [ley], "them"

In the third person only there are special indirect-object forms *lui* [lwee, "to him, to her"; *leur* [ler-rr], "to them."

Note also the forms *y* [ee], "there, to there" and *en* [ahñ], "of it, of them, some," which may be placed with object pronouns before verbs.

Certain pronouns have special forms when used with prepositions: *moi* [mwah], "me"; *elle*, "her"; *eux* [er] (masculine) and *elles* [el] (feminine), "them." In other cases use indirect object forms.

Possessive adjectives agree with nouns in gender and number; thus *mon* [moñ], "my," feminine *ma* (*mon* before a vowel), plural *mes* [mey]; similarly *ce* [ser], "this, that" (*cet* [set] before a vowel), feminine *cette* [set], plural *ces* [sey].

VERBS change their endings for person and number. We give first and third persons singular, first, second and third persons plural.

The majority of verbs have the infinitive in *-er* and form the present tense *-e, -e, -ons, -ez, -ent*; the ending *-ent* of verbs is never pronounced. Other regular verbs

FRENCH

comprise those in *-ir* (present *-is, -it, -issons, -issez, -issent*) and a few in *-re* and *-evoir*.

Among irregular presents, note those of *être* [eytrr], "be" (*suis* [swee], *est* [eh], *sommes* [som], *êtes* [eyt], *sont* [soñ]); *avoir* [ahvwahrr], "have" (*ai* [ey], *a, avons, avez, ont* [oñ]); and *aller* [aleh], "go" (*vais, va, allons, allez, vont*).

For a past tense, use the perfect form, namely, the auxiliary verb *avoir* with the past participle. The past participles of *-er, -ir, -re* and *-evoir* verbs are in *-é, -i, -u, -u*, respectively: from *parler*, "speak," we get *il a parlé* [eelah parrleh], "he has spoken," "he spoke." Verbs of motion and reflexive verbs (with object *se*, etc.) use *être* instead of *avoir*: *je suis allé* [zher sweez aleh], "I went."

For a future tense, add the endings *-ai, -a, -ons, -ez, -ont* to the infinitive of the verb; but drop the *-e* of an *-re* infinitive and abbreviate *-evoir* to *-evr.*

For a negative, place *ne* before the verb and *pas* after it (or in the perfect tense, after the auxiliary): *Il ne parle pas* [eel ner parrl pah], "He is not speaking"; *Nous n'avons pas parlé*, [noo nahvoñ pah parrleh], "We didn't speak." Words such as *rien* [reeahñ], "nothing" and *jamais* [zhahmay], "never," replace *pas*, but the verb retains *ne*: *Nous n'avons rien vu* [noo nahvoñ reeahñ vu], "We saw nothing."

Pronoun objects precede the verb, the indirect object before the direct: *Il m'a donné la valise* [eel mah donneh lah vahleez], "He gave me the suitcase"; *Il me la donne* [eel mer lah donn], "He is giving it to me." In a negative, *ne* precedes the pronouns.

There are various other verb forms, but these will serve most purposes.

"There is" or "There are" is the special phrase *Il y a* [eel ee ah]: *Il y a des autos* [eel ee ah dey zohtoh], "There are some cars."

QUESTIONS For a yes/no question, interchange the order of subject and verb as in English; but in the case of a noun subject it is usual to state the subject first, then ask the question using a pronoun: *L'auto est-elle ici?* [lohtoh ehtel ee-see], "Is the car here?" Note that the *t* of the verb ending is pronounced before *il, elle, ils* or *elles*, and that *t* is inserted when it is not already there: *Parle-t-il?* [parrl teel], "Is he speaking?"; *Y a-t-il . . . ?* [ee ahteel], "Is there . . . ?"

IMPERATIVES For an imperative, use the second person of the verb: *Parlez* [parrleh], "Speak." In this case, place the pronouns after the verb, the direct before the indirect; and use the form *moi* in the first person: *Donnez-le-moi* [donneh-ler mwah], "Give it to me."

For a negative imperative, use *Ne . . . pas* as with indicatives, but put the pronouns before the verb again: *Ne me le donnez pas* [ner mer ler donneh pah], "Don't give it to me."

For "Let's," use the first person plural: *Allons* [ahloñ], "Let's go."

NUMERALS The number "one" has separate masculine and feminine forms *un, une*; others are invariable.

CURRENCY (the same name, though not value, in all French territories): 1 *franc* [frrahñ] = 100 *centimes* [sahñteem].

FORMS OF ADDRESS "Mr" is *Monsieur* [m'syer], "Mrs" is *Madame* [m'dahm], and "Miss" is *Mademoiselle* [m'mzel]. Use these also (more particularly the first two) alone as the equivalents of "sir," "madam." They are used more than these terms are used in English.

FRENCH

KIN TERMS

père [pairr], "father"
fils [feess], "son"
frère [frrairr], "brother"
mari [mahrree], "husband"

mère [mairr], "mother"
fille [fee-y'], "daughter"
soeur [ser-rr], "sister"
femme [fum], "wife"

NAME OF LANGUAGE

French is *français* [frrahñssay].

EVERYDAY PHRASES

ENGLISH	MALAY [INDONESIAN]	TAGALOG
Yes	Ya *Yah*	'O'o *'Aw'aw*
No	Tidak *Teedah'*	Hindî *Hindi'*
Please	Minta [Silakan] *Minta [Seelakahn]*	Paki- . . . *Pa-kee*
Thank you	Terima kasih *T'rreema kasseehh*	Salamat sa iyó *Sa-lahmat sa-yo*
Thank you very much	Banyak terima kasih *Bahnyah' t'rreema kasseehh*	Maraming salamat sa iyó *Ma-rahming sa-laahmat sa-yo*
Don't mention it	Terima kasih kembali *T'rreema kasseehh k'm-bahlee*	Waláng anumán *Wahlahng ahnoo-mahn*
Excuse me, but . . .	Maafkan, . . . *Ma'ahf-kahn*	Ipagpaumanhín, . . . *Eepahk-pawman-hin*
Excuse me (I'm sorry)	Minta maafkan *Minta ma'ahf-kahn*	Ipagpaumanhín *Eepahk-pawman-hin*
Excuse me (Do you mind?)	Permisi *Prr-missee*	Ipagpaumanhín *Eepahk-pawman-hin*
Pardon? (What did you say?)	Maaf? *Ma'ahf?*	Anó 'ka mo? *Ahno kah mo?*
Wait a moment	Tunggu sebentar *Toonggoo s'b'ntahrr*	Sandalî lang *Sahnd-lee lahng*
Hurry up!	Lekaslah! *L'kahss-lahh!*	Madalî ka! *Mahdda-lee kahng!*
Slowly!	Perlahan-lahan! *Prr-lahhan-lahhan!*	Dahan-dahan! *Da-han-da-hahn!*
Stop!	Berhenti! *Brr-h'ntee!*	Para! *Pahrah!*
Look out!	Jaga baik-baik! [Hati-hati!] *Jahga bighk-bighk! [Hahtee-hahtee!]*	Ingat! *Eeng-aht!*
Look!	Lihat! *Leehaht!*	Tingnán mo! *Ting-n'n maw!*
How much?	Berapa harganya? *Brr-ahpa hahrrga-nya?*	Magkano? *M'k-kahnaw?*
Never mind	Tidak apa *Teedah' ahpa*	Hindî bali *Hindi bahlee*
Come in	Mari masuk *Mahrree mahsoo'*	Tulóy kayó *Tooloo kah'yaw*
Come with me	Datanglah dengan saya *Dahtahng-lah d'ng-ahn sahya*	Sumama ka sa akin *Soo-mahma kah sah-kin*
Good morning	Selamat pagi *S'lahmaht pahghee*	Magandáng umaga *Mahg'ndahng oo-mahga*
Good afternoon	Selamat tengah hari [Selamat sore] *S'lahmaht t'ng-ah hahrree [S'lahmaht sawrreh]*	Magandang hapon *Mahg'ndahng hahpon*
Good evening	Selamat petang [Selamat malam] *S'lahmaht p'tahng [S'lahmaht mahlahm]*	Magandang gabí *Mahg'ndahng ga-bee*
Good-bye (leaving)	Selamat tinggal *S'lahmaht teenggal*	Paálam na pô *Pa'ahlm na paw*
Good-bye (staying)	Selamat jalan *S'lahmaht jahlahn*	Adyos pô *A-dyooss paw*
Good night	Selamat malam *S'lahmaht mahlahm*	Magandang gabí *Mahg'ndahng ga-bee*
Do you understand?	Mengertikah? [Apa engkau mengerti?] *M'ng-rr-tee-kahh? [Ahpa 'ng-kow m'ng-rr-tee?]*	Náintindihán mo ba? *Na-in-tindi-hahn maw bah?*

EVERYDAY PHRASES

SPANISH	PORTUGUESE	FRENCH
Sí *See*	Sim *Siñ*	Oui *Wee*
No *Naw*	Não *Nowñ*	Non *Noñ*
Por favor *Pawrr fa-vawrr*	Por favor *Poorr fa-vawrr*	S'il vous plaît *Silvoo play*
Gracias *Grahssyass*	Obrigado/-a *Awbrree-gahdoo/-a*	Merci *Mehrrsee*
Muchas gracias *Moocha-grahssyass*	Muito obrigado/-a *Moot'awbrree-gahdoo/-a*	Merci beaucoup *Mehrrsee baw-koo*
No hay de que *Naw eh da keh*	De nada *Dee nahda*	De rien *Der-ree-eñ*
Dispénseme, ... *Deess-pehnsseh-meh*	Com licença, ... *Koñ lee-sensa*	Pardon monsieur/madame, ... *Parr-dawñ m'syer/ma-dahm*
Dispénseme *Deess-pehnsseh-meh*	'Desculpe *Dess-koolpee*	Excusez-moi *Ehk-skyoozeh mwa*
Perdóneme *Pehrr-dawneh-meh*	Com licença *Koñ lee-sensa*	S'il vous plaît *Silvoo play*
¿Perdóneme? *Pehrr-dawneh-meh?*	Como? *Kawmoo?*	Pardon? *Parr-doñ?*
Espere un momento *Ehss-pehrr' oon maw-mehntaw*	Espere um momento *'Spehrr oo maw-mehntoo*	Attendez un moment *At-tahñdeh un mo-mahñ*
¡Dése prisa! *Desseh preessa!*	Depressa! *Dee-prrehssa!*	Dépêchez-vous! *Deh-paysheh-voo!*
¡Despacio! *Dehss-pahssyo!*	Devagar! *Dee-vah-gahrr!*	Doucement! *Dooss'moñ!*
¡Deténganse! *Deh-tehnga-seh!*	Pare! *Pahrree!*	Arrêtez-vous! *A-rrayteh-voo!*
¡Cuidado! *Kwee-thahthaw!*	Cuidado! *Kwee-dahdoo!*	Attention! *At-toñ-syoñ!*
¡Mire usted! *Meerreh ooss-ted!*	Olhe! *Awlee!*	Regardez! *Rer-gahrr-deh!*
¿Cuánto es? *Kwahntaw ehss?*	Quanto? *Kwahntoo?*	C'est combien? *Seh kooñ-byeñ?*
No importa *Neem-pawrrta*	Não se preocupe *Nowñ see pree-awkoo-pee*	Ça ne fait rien *San' fay rryeñ*
Pase [Adelante] *Pahsseh [Ahdeh-lannteh]*	Entre *Ehntrree*	Entrez *Ahñ-trreh*
Venga conmigo *Venggah kon-meegaw*	Venha comigo *Vehña kaw-meego*	Venez avec moi *Verneh za-vek mwa*
Buenos días *Bwehnoss deeahss*	Bom dia *Bawñ deea*	Bonjour *Boñ-zhoorr*
Buenas tardes *Bwehnass tahrrdess*	Boa tarde *Bwa tahrrdee*	Bonjour *Boñ-zhoorr*
Buenas tardes *Bwehnass tahrrdess*	Boa noite *Bwa noyt'*	Bonsoir *Boñ-swahrr*
Adiós *Ahdee-oss*	Até logo *'Teh lawgo*	Au revoir *Orr-vwahrr*
Adiós *Ahdee-oss*	Até logo *'Teh lawgo*	Au revoir *Orr-vwahrr*
Buenas noches *Bwehnass nawchess*	Boa noite *Bwa noyt'*	Bonsoir *Boñ-swahrr*
¿Comprende usted? *Kawm-prehnd' ooss-teh?*	Você compreende? *Vawseh kawm-prrehndee?*	Comprenez-vous? *Koñ-prerneh-voo?*

EVERYDAY PHRASES

ENGLISH	MALAY [INDONESIAN]	TAGALOG
I understand	Saya mengerti *Sahya m'ng-rr-tee*	Náintindihán ko *Na-in-tindi-hahn kaw*
I don't understand	Saya tidak mengerti *Sahya teedah' m'ng-rr-tee*	Hindî ko náintindihán *Hindi kaw na-in-tindi-hahn*
All right (I'll do it)	Baiklah *Bigh'lahh*	O sige *O seeggeh*
It's all right	Baik *Bigh'*	Tamà na *Tah-mahna*

NUMERALS

zero	kosong [nol] *kawsawng [nol]*	walâ *wa-la'*
one	satu, se- *sahtoo, s'-*	isá, uno *ee-sa, oono*
two	dua *dooa*	dalawá, dos *dulla-wa, dawss*
three	tiga *teega*	tatló, tres *taht-lo, trrehss*
four	empat *'m-paht*	apat, kuwatro *ah-pat, kwahtrroh*
five	lima *leema*	limá, singko *lee-ma, singkoh*
six	enam *'nnahm*	anim, seis *ah-nim, seh-eess*
seven	tujuh *toojoohh*	pitó, siyete *peet-to, s'yehteh*
eight	lapan [delapan] *lahpahn [d'lahpahn]*	waló, otso *wah-lo, awtsoh*
nine	sembilan *s'm-beelahn*	siyám, nuwebe *s'yahm, n'wehbeh*
ten	sepuluh *s'pooloohh*	sampû, diyés *sahmpo', d'yehss*
eleven	sebelas *s'b'lahss*	labíng-isá, onse *la-bing ee-sa, onnsseh*
twelve	duabelas *dooa-b'lahss*	labíndalawá, dose *la-bin-dulla-wa, dawsseh*
thirteen	tigabelas *teega-b'lahss*	labíntatló, trese *la-bin-taht-lo, trrehsseh*
fourteen	empat belas *'mpaht b'lahss*	labíng-apát, katorse *la-bing-ah-pat, ka-tawrrsseh*
fifteen	lima belas *leema b'lahss*	labínlimá, kinse *la-bin-lee-ma, kinsseh*
sixteen	enam belas *'nnahm b'lahss*	labíng-anim, disiseis *la-bing-ah-nim, dissi-seh-eess*
seventeen	tujuhbelas *toojooh-b'lahss*	labímpitó, disisiyete *la-bim-peet-to, dissi-s'yehteh*
eighteen	lapan belas [delapan belas] *lahpahn b'lahss [d'lahpahn b'lahss]*	labíngwaló, disiotso *la-bing-wah-lo, dissi-awtsoh*
nineteen	sembilan belas *s'm-beelahn b'lahss*	labínsiyám, disinuwebe *la-bin-s'yahm, dissi-n'wehbeh*
twenty	duapuluh *dooa-pooloohh*	dalawampû, beynte *dulla-wahmpo', beighnteh*
twenty-one	duapuluh satu *dooa-pooloohh sahtoo*	dalawampút isá, beyntiuno *dulla-wahm-poot-ee-sa, beighnti-oonoh*
thirty	tigapuluh *teega-pooloohh*	tatlumpû, treynta *tahtloom-po', trreighnta*

EVERYDAY PHRASES

SPANISH	PORTUGUESE	FRENCH
Comprendo *Kawm-prehndo*	Eu compreendo *Yo kawm-prrehndoo*	Je comprends *Zher koñ-proñ*
No comprendo *Naw kawm-prehndo*	Eu não compreendo *Yo nowñ kawm-prrehndoo*	Je ne comprends pas *Zhern' koñ-proñ pa*
Bueno *Bwehnaw*	'Ta bem *Tah behñ*	D'accord *Dahk-korr*
Está bien *Ehss-tah vyehn*	'Tá tudo certo *Tah tood sehrrt'*	Ça va *Sa va*

NUMERALS

cero *sehrro*	zero *zairroo*	zéro *zehrraw*
uno/una *oonaw/oona*	um/uma *ooñ/ooma*	un/une *uñ/oon*
dos *dawss*	dois/duas *doyss/dooass*	deux *der*
tres *trehss*	três *trehss*	trois *trrwa*
cuatro *kwahtraw*	quatro *kwahtrroo*	quatre *kattrr*
cinco *seengkaw*	cinco *seengkoo*	cinq *sañk*
seis *sehss*	seis *seighss*	six *seess*
siete *syehteh*	sete *sehtee*	sept *set*
ocho *awchaw*	oito *oytoo*	huit *weet*
nueve *nwehveh*	nove *nawvee*	neuf *nerf*
diez *dee-ess*	dez *deighss*	dix *deess*
once *awnsseh*	onze *awnzee*	onze *oñz*
doce *dawsseh*	doze *dawzee*	douze *dooz*
trece *trehsseh*	treze *trrehzee*	treize *trrayz*
catorce *ka-tawrrseh*	quatorze [catorze] *ka-tawrrzee*	quatorze *kat-torrz*
quince *keensseh*	quinze *keenzee*	quinze *kañz*
dieciséis *dee-ehssee-sehss*	dezesseis *dzeh-seighss*	seize *sayz*
diecisiete *dee-ehssee-syehteh*	dezessete *dzeh-sehtee*	dix-sept *deess-set*
dieciocho *dee-ehssee-awchaw*	dezoito *dehz-oytoo*	dix-huit *deez-weet*
diecinueve *dee-ehssee-nwehveh*	dezenove *dzeh-nawvee*	dix-neuf *deez-nerf*
veinte *veighnteh*	vinte *veentee*	vingt *vañ*
veintiuno/-a *veighntee-oonaw/-oona*	vinte e um/uma *veent'ee ooñ/ooma*	vingt et un/une *vañteh uñ/oon*
treinta *trreighnta*	trinta *trreenta*	trente *trrahñt*

265

NUMERALS

ENGLISH	MALAY [INDONESIAN]	TAGALOG
forty	empat puluh *'mpaht pooloohh*	ápatnapû, kuwarenta *ah-pahtna-po', kwah-rrenta*
fifty	lima puluh *leema pooloohh*	limampû, singkuwenta *leemam-po', singkoo-enta*
sixty	enampuluh *'nnahm-pooloohh*	ánimnapû, sesenta *ahnim-na-po', sess-enta*
seventy	tujuhpuluh *toojooh-pooloohh*	pitumpû, setenta *pittoom-po', seh-tenta*
eighty	lapan puluh [delapan puluh] *lahpahn pooloohh [d'lahpahn pooloohh]*	walumpû, otsenta *wahloom-po', awt-senta*
ninety	sembilan puluh *s'm-beelahn pooloohh*	siyámnapû, nobenta *s'yahmna-po', naw-benta*
a hundred	seratus *s'rrahtooss*	isáng daán, siyento *ee-sahng da-ahn, s'yento*
a hundred and one	seratus satu *s'rrahtooss sahtoo*	isáng daán at isá, siyentouno *ee-sahng da'ahn at ee-sa, s'yento oono*
a hundred and ten	seratus sepuluh *s'rrahtooss s'pooloohh*	isáng daán at sampû, siyento diyés *ee-sahng da-ahn at sahm-po', s'yento d'yehss*
two hundred	dua ratus *dooa rrahtooss*	dalawáng daán, dosiyentos *dulla-wahng da'ahn, dossi-enntoss*
a thousand	seribu *s'rreeboo*	isáng libo, mil *ee-sahng leebo, meel*
ten thousand	sepuluh ribu *s'poolooh rreeboo*	sampúng libo, diyés mil *sahm-poong leebo, dyess meel*
a hundred thousand	seratus ribu *s'rrahtooss rreeboo*	isáng yutà, siyén mil *ee-sahng yootah, s'yen meel*
a million	semilion, sejuta *s'-milli-awn, s'jootah*	isáng angaw, milyón *ee-sahng ahng-ow, meel-yawn*
ten million	sepuluh milion, sepuluh juta *s'pooloohh milli-awn, s'pooloohh jootah*	sampúng angaw, diyés milyón *sahm-poong ahng-ow, dyess meel-yawn*
a half	separuh, setengah *s'pahrroohh, s't'ngahh*	kalahati *kulla-hahtee*
... point (decimal) ...	... perpulohan ... [... koma ...] *prr-poolo-hahn [kommah]*	.... punto ... *poontoh*

DAYS OF THE WEEK

Sunday	Ahad, Minggu *Ahhad, Meenggoo*	Linggó *Ling-gaw*
Monday	Isnen [Senin, Senén] *Eessnen [S'-nin, S'-nen]*	Lunes *Looness*
Tuesday	Selasa *S'lahssah*	Martés *Marrtess*
Wednesday	Rabu *Rrahboo*	Miyérkolés *M'yehrrko-less*

NUMERALS

SPANISH	PORTUGUESE	FRENCH
cuarenta *kwah-rrehnta*	quarenta *kwa-rrehnta*	quarante *ka-rrahñt*
cincuenta *sing-kwehnta*	cinquenta *sing-kwehnta*	cinquante *sañ-kahñt*
sesenta *sess-enta*	sessenta *seh-sehnta*	soixante *swa-sahñt*
setenta *set-enta*	setenta *set-tehnta*	soixante-dix *swa-sahñt-deess*
ochenta *aw-chenta*	oitenta *oy-tehnta*	quatre-vingts *kattrr-vañ*
noventa *naw-venta*	noventa *naw-vehnta*	quatre-vingt dix *kattrr-vañ-deess*
ciento, cien *syentaw, syen*	cem *sehñ*	cent *soñ*
ciento uno/-a *syentaw oonaw/-oona*	cento e um/uma *seht'ee ooñ/ooma*	cent un *soñ uñ*
ciento diez *syentaw the-ess*	cento e dez *seht'ee deighss*	cent dix *soñ deess*
doscientos *doss-syentoss*	duzentos *doo-zehnss*	deux cents *der soñ*
mil *meel*	mil *meeoo*	mille *meel*
diez mil *dee-ess meel*	dez mil *dehz meeo*	dix mille *dee meel*
cien mil *syen meel*	cem mil *sehñ meeo*	cent mille *soñ meel*
un millón *oon meel-yawn*	um milhão *oo meel-yowñ*	un million *uñ meel-yoñ*
diez millones *dee-ess meel-yawness*	dez milhões *dehz meel-yoiss*	dix millions *dee meel-yoñ*
medio/-a *mehthee-aw/-a*	meio/-a *mehyoo/-a*	demi/-ie *der-mee*
...punto... *poonto*	...ponto... *pawnt'*	...point... *pwahñ*

DAYS OF THE WEEK

domingo *daw-meenggo*	domingo *daw-meenggo*	dimanche *dee-moñsh*
lunes *loonehss*	segunda *seh-goonda*	lundi *lerñ-dee*
martes *mahrrtehss*	têrça *tehrrssa*	mardi *mahrr-dee*
miércoles *mee-ehrrkaw-lehss*	quarta *kwahrrta*	mercredi *mairrkrr-dee*

DAYS OF THE WEEK

ENGLISH	MALAY [INDONESIAN]	TAGALOG
Thursday	Khamis [Kamis, Kemis] *Kahmiss [Kahmiss, K'miss]*	Huwebes *H'wehbess*
Friday	Jumaat [Jumat] *Jooma'aht [Joomaht]*	Biyernes *B'yehrrness*
Saturday	Sabtu *Sahptoo*	Sábadó *Sahba-daw*

MONTHS

January	Januari *Jannoo-ahree*	Enero *En-ehraw*
February	Fébruari [Pébruari] *Febroo-ahree [Pebroo-ahree]*	Pebrero *Pe-brrehrraw*
March	Mać [Maret] *Mahch [Mahrret]*	Marso *Mahrrsaw*
April	April *Apprill*	Abríl *A-brreel*
May	Méi *Meigh*	Mayo *Mahyaw*
June	Jun [Juni] *Joon [Joonee]*	Hunyo *Hoonyaw*
July	Julai [Juli] *Jooligh [Joolee]*	Hulyo *Hoolyaw*
August	Ogos [Agustus] *Awgawss [A-goosstooss]*	Agosto *A-gawstaw*
September	Séptémber *Sep-tembrr*	Septiyembre *Sep-tyehmbrreh*
October	Oktober *Ok-tawbrr*	Oktubre *Awk-toobrreh*
November	Novémber [Nopémber] *Nawvembrr [Naw-pembrr]*	Nobyembre *Naw-byehmbrreh*
December	Disémber [Désémber] *Deesembrr [Deh-sembrr]*	Disyembre *Dees-syehmbrreh*

SENTENCES

1. Is there someone here who speaks English, please? A little. I speak only a little ———.

2. I want to go to ———. Is there a bus (an aeroplane, a taxi)? Yes, there is. No, there is not.

1. Adakah disini seseorang yang tahu berćakap [berbićara] bahasa Inggeris? Sedikit. Saya tahu berćakap [berbićara] bahasa ——— sedikit.
   Ahda-kahh dis-seenee s's'awrrahng yahng tow brr-chahkahp [brr-b'chahrra] b'hahssa Eeng-grriss? S'deekit. Sahya tow brr-chahkahp [brr-b'chahrra] b'hahssa ——— s'deekit.

2. Saya mau pergi ke ———. Adakah bas [bis] (pesawat, téksi)? Ya, ada. Tidak, tidak ada.
   Sahya mow prr-ghee ker ———. Ahda-kah bahss [biss] (p'sahwaht, tehksee)? Yah, ahda. Teedah', teedah' ahda.

1. Mayroón ba ritong nakapagsásalitá ng Inglés? Kauntí. Marunong lamang ako nang kauntí ———.
   Meh-rawn ba rreet'ng nukkah-puk-sahsah-lee-ta' n'ng Ing-glehss? Kawn-ti'. Mahroo-nong lahmahng a-kaw nahng kawn-ti' ———.

2. Ibig kong tumungo ———. May bus (eroplano, taksi) ba? 'O'o, mayroón. Walâ.
   Eebik kawng toomoong-gaw ———. Me-booss (erro-plahno, tukksee) ba? Aw'aw, mehrawn. Wa-la'.

268

DAYS OF THE WEEK

SPANISH	PORTUGUESE	FRENCH
jueves *hwehvehss*	quinta *keenta*	jeudi *zher-dee*
viernes *vyehrrnehss*	sexta *sehssta*	vendredi *voñdrr-dee*
sábado *sahba-daw*	sábado *sahba-do*	samedi *sam-dee*

MONTHS

enero *eh-nehrro*	janeiro *zhahn-eighrroo*	janvier *zhahñvee-eh*
febrero *fe-vrrehrro*	fevereiro *fehveh-rreighrroo*	février *fevrree-eh*
marzo *mahrrsso*	março *mahrrssoo*	mars *mahrrss*
abril *a-vrreel*	abril *a-brreel*	avril *ah-vrreel*
mayo *mahyo*	maio *mahyoo*	mai *may*
junio *hoonyo*	junho *zhoonyoo*	juin *zhoo-añ*
julio *hoolyo*	julho *zhoolyoo*	juillet *zhooee-yeh*
agosto *ah-gawssto*	agôsto *a-gosstoo*	août *oot*
septiembre *set-tyehmbrreh*	setembro *set-tembrroo*	septembre *sep-toñbrr*
octubre *awk-toovrreh*	outubro *oh-toobrroo*	octobre *ok-tobrr*
noviembre *naw-vyehmbrreh*	novembro *naw-vehmbrroo*	novembre *no-voñbrr*
diciembre *dee-syehmbrreh*	dezembro *deh-zembrroo*	décembre *deh-soñbrr*

SENTENCES

1. ¿ Hay alguien aquí que hable inglés, por favor? Un poco. Sólo hablo un poco de ———.
Igh algyen a-kee keh avleh eeng-glehss, pawrr fa-vawrr? Oom pawkaw. Sawlaw ahvlaw oom pawkaw deh ———.

1. Tem aqui alguém que fale inglês, por favor? Um pouco. Eu falo muito pouco ———.
Tehñ a-kee algheeñ k' fahl' eeng-glehss, poo fa-vawrr? Ooñ pawkoo. Yo fahloo mooeetoo pawkoo ———.

1. S'il vous plaît, monsieur/ madame, y a-t-il quelqu'un ici qui parle anglais? Un peu. Je parle seulement un peu de ———.
Silvoo play, m'syer/madahm, ee ah-teel kelkuñ eessee kee pahrrl oñ-glay? Uñ per. Zher pahrrl serlmoñ uñ per der ———.

2. Quiero ir a ———. ¿ Hay un autobús (un avión, un taxi)? Sí, hay. No, no hay.
Kyehrro eer ah ———. Igh oon owtoh-booss (oon ahveeonn, oon takksee)? See, igh. Naw, naw igh.

2. Eu quero ir para ———. Tem um ônibus (um avião, um táxi)? Sim, tem. Não, não tem.
Yo kehrroo eer pahrra ———. Tehñ ooñ awneebooss (ooñ ahvee-owñ, ooñ tahksee)? Siñ, tehñ. Nowñ, nowñ tehñ.

2. Je veux me rendre à ———. Y a-t-il un bus (un avion, un taxi)? Oui. Non, il n'y en a pas.
Zher ver m' rahñdrr ah ———. Ee ahteel uñ booss (un a-vyoñ, uñ tahksee)? Wee. Noñ, eel nyonnah pa.

269

SENTENCES

ENGLISH	MALAY [INDONESIAN]	TAGALOG
3. Where is the bus (the railway station, the ticket office)? It is here (there, over there).	3. Dimanakah bas [bis] (perhentian [setasiun] keréta api, tempat penjualan tékét [karćis])? Disini (Disana, Disebelah sana).	3. Násaán ang bus (ang estasyón ng tren, ang tanggapang bílihan ng tiket)? Nárito (Náriyán, Nároón).
	Dee-mahna-kahh bahss [biss] (prr-h'ntee-ahn [s'tahsy'n] k'rrehta ahpee, t'mpaht p'n-jwahlahn tehkeht [kahrrchiss])? Dee-seenee (Dee-sahna, Deess'b'lahh sahna).	*Na-sahn ahng booss (ahng essta-syawn n'ng trren, ahng tahng-gah-pahng beelee-han n'ng teekeht)? Nahrree-taw (Nahrree-yan, Nahrraw-awn).*
4. How do I get to the airport (to the town)? Go that way. Go straight on (to the left, to the right).	4. Bagaimana saya bisa ke lapangan terbang (ke kota)? Pergilah ke arah itu. Pergi terus saja (kekiri, kekanan).	4. Paano akó makatútungo sa lápagan ng eroplano (sa bayan)? Tumungo ka sa daáng iyón. Tuwirín mo ang daáng iyán (Kumaliwâ ka, Kumanan ka).
	Bahgigh-mahna sahya bissa k'la-pahng-an trr-bahng (k' kawta)? Prrghee-lahh ke'ahrrahh eetoo. Prrghee t'rrooss sahjja (k'keerree, k'kahnahn).	*Pa-ahno ahko mahka-tootoo-ngaw sa lahpahng-gahn n'ng ehro-plahno (sa bahyahn)? Toomoo-ngaw ka sa d'ahng ee-yawn. Toowi-reen maw ahng d'ahng ee-yahn (Kooma-leewa ka, Koo-mahnahn ka).*
5. Would you take my baggage to the bus, please. There is just one bag. There are two bags and that bundle.	5. Tolong bawa barang saya ke bas [bis]. Hanya ada sebuah tas. Ada dua buah tas dan bungkusan itu.	5. Pakidalá mo ang maleta ko sa bus. Íisá lamang ang maleta. May delawáng maleta at ang balutang iyón.
	Tawlawng bahwa bahrrahng sahya k' bahss [biss]. Hahnya ahda s'bwahh tahss. Ahda dooa bwahh tahss dahn boong-koossahn eetoo.	*Pahkee-da-la maw ahng ma-lehta kaw sa booss. Ee-sah la-mahng ahng ma-lehta. Meh dulla-wahng ma-lehta at ahng ba-lootahng ee-yawn.*
6. When does the bus go? Show me, please. The bus is late. The bus has already gone.	6. Bila bas [bis] berangkat? Tolong tunjokkan kepada saya. Bas [Bis] terlambat. Bas [Bis] sudah pergi.	6. Kailán áalís ang bus? Iturò mo ngâ sa akin. Náhulí ang bus. Nakaalís na ang bus.
	Beela bahss [biss] brr-ahngkaht? Tawlawng toon-jawkkahn k'pahda sahya. Bahss [Biss] trr-lahmbaht. Bahss [Biss] soodahh prr-ghee.	*Keh-lan a'ah-leess ahng booss? Eetoo-ro maw nga' sah ahkin. Nahoo-lee ahng booss. Nahka-ahleess n'ahng booss.*

SENTENCES

SPANISH	PORTUGUESE	FRENCH

3. ¿Dónde está el autobús (la estación de ferrocarril, la boletería)? Está aquí (allí, allá).
Dond'ehsst' el owtoh-booss (l'essta-syonn deh ferro-karreel, la volleh-teh-rreeya)? Esst' ah-kee (a-yee, a-yah).

3. Onde fica o ponto do ônibus (a estação de trem, o guichê)? Fica aqui (la, mais pra la).
Awndee feeka oo pawntoo dee awnee-booss (a ehss-tasowñ dee trrehñ, aw gheesheh)? Feek' ah-kee (lah, mighss prra lah).

3. Où est le bus (la gare, le guichet)? C'est ici (là, la-bas).
Oo eh ler booss (la gahrr, ler gheesheh)? Seh tee-see (la, la-ba).

---

4. ¿Cómo llego al aeropuerto (a la ciudad)? Vaya por ahí. Siga derecho (Vaya a la izquierda, Vaya a la derecha).
Kawmaw yehgaw 'l ehrropwawrrtoh (ah la syoothahdh)? Vahya pawrr eighyee. Seega deh-rehchoh (Vahya'l' eess-kyehrrda, Vahya'la deh-rehcha).

4. Como posso ir para o aeroporto (para a cidade)? Va por ali. Va reto (a esquerda, a direita).
Kawmoo possoo eerr pahrra oo a-ehrroo-pawrrtoo (pahrr' ah see-dahdeh)? Vah poorr ah-lee. Vah rrehtoo (ah eesskehrrda, ah dee-reighta).

4. Comment va-t-on à l'aéroport (à la ville)? Allez par là. Allez tout droit (à gauche, à droite).
Kommoñ va-toñ ah la-ehrroporr (ah la veel)? Alleh parr la. Alleh too drrwa (ah gohsh, ah drrwaht).

---

5. ¿Podría llevar mi equipaje al autobús, por favor? Hay sólo una maleta. Hay dos maletas y ese lío.
Po-threea yeh-vahrr mee ehkee-pahh' al owtoh-booss, pawrr fa-vawrr? Igh sawlaw oona ma-lehta. Igh dos malehtahss ee ehseh leeoh.

5. O senhor poderia levar a minha bagagem para o ônibus, por favor? Tem so uma bôlsa. Tem duas bôlsas e esse embrulho.
Oo see-yawrr pawd'rreea lehvahrr ah meeya ba-gahzhehñ pahrra oo awnee-booss, poorr fa-vawrr? Tehñ saw ooma bawlssa. Tehñ dooahz bawlssahz eh ehss' ehmbrrool-yoo.

5. Veuillez porter mes bagages au bus, s'il vous plaît. Il n'y a qu'une seule valise. Il y a deux valises et ce paquet-là.
Ver-yeh porrteh meh bagahzh oh booss, silvoo play. Eel nya kooñ serl va-leez. Eel ya der va-leez eh ser pakkeh la.

---

6. ¿Cuándo parte el autobús? Muéstreme, por favor. El autobús está atrasado. El autobús ya se ha ido.
Kwahndo pahrrt' el owtohbooss? Moysstreh-meh, pawrr fa-vawrr. El owtohbooss esst' ahtrahss-ahthoh. El owtoh-booss eea s' ah eethoh.

6. Quando parte o ônibus? Mostre-me, por favor. O ônibus 'tá atrasado. O ônibus ja partiu.
Kwahndoo pahrrteh oo awnee-booss? Mosstree-mee, poorr fa-vawrr. Oo awneebooss t'ahtrra-sahdoo. Oo awnee-booss jah pahrr-teeoo.

6. À quelle heure part le bus? Veuillez me l'indiquer. Le bus est en retard. Le bus est déjà parti.
Ah kel err pahrr ler booss? Ver-yeh mer lañ-deekeh. Ler booss eh-toñ rr'tahrr. Ler booss eh dehzhah parr-tee.

SENTENCES

7. A ticket for one person (for two persons) to ——, please. Two adults and one child. First class. Tourist class.

7. Karćis untuk seorang (dua orang) ke ——. Dua orang dewasa dan seorang anak. Kelas satu. Kelas ekonomi.
Kahrrchiss oontoo' se'awrrahng (dooa awrrahng) ker ——. Dooa awrrahng d'wahssa dahn se'awrrahng ahnahk. K'lahss sahtoo. K'lahss eh-konno-mee.

7. Tiket ngâ pará sa isáng tao (pará sa dalawáng tao) sa ——. Dalawá pará sa matandâ at isá sa batà. Pará sa primera klase. Pará sa turista.
Tikeht nga pa-rah sa ee-sahng tah-oh (pa-rah sa dulla-wahng tah-oh) sa ——. Dulla-wah pa-rah sa mahtahn- da' at ee-sah sa ba-tah. Pa-rah sa pree-mehrra klahsseh. Pa-rah sa too-rreesta.

8. Excuse me, what time is it? Two o'clock. Ten past two. Half past two. Ten to three.

8. Maaf, pukul berapakah sekarang? Pukul dua. Pukul dua léwat sepuluh minit. Pukul dua setengah [Pukul setengah tiga]. Kurang sepuluh minit pukul tiga [Pukul tiga kurang sepuluh minit.].
Ma'ahf, pookool brr-ahpa-kahh s'kahrrahng? Pookool dooa. Pookool dooa lehwaht s'pooloohh minnit. Pookool dooa s't'ngahh [Pookool s't'ngahh teega]. Koorrahng s'pooloohh minnit pookool teega [Pookool teega koorrahng s'pooloohh minnit].

8. Ipagpaumanhin, anong oras na ba? Alás dos na. Sampúng minuto makalampás ang alás dos. Treynta minutos makalampás ang alás dos. Sampúng minuto bago mag-alás tres.
Eepahk-pawman-hin, ahnong awrass na ba? A-lahss dawss nah. Sahm-poong mee-nooto mahka-lahm-pahss ahng a-lahss dawss. Trreighnta mee-nootoss mahka-lahm-pahss ahng a-lahss dawss. Sahm-poong mee-nooto bahgo m'g-a-lahss trehss.

9. Take me to a hotel (to the —— Hotel). Is this (that) the hotel? How far is it?

9. Bawalah saya ke sebuah hotél (ke Hotél ——). Apakah ini (itu) hotél tersebut? Berapa jauhkah hotél itu?
Bahwa-lahh sahya k's'bwahh haw-tell (k' Haw-tell ——). Ahpa-kahh eenee (eetoo) haw-tell trr-s'boot? Brr-ahpa jowhh-kahh haw-tell eetoo?

9. Ihatíd mo ngâ akó sa otél (sa —— Otél). Itó (Iyón) ba ang otél? Gaano ang layó nitó?
Eeha-tid maw nga a-kaw sa aw-tehl (sa —— Aw-tehl). Ee-taw (Ee-yawn) bahng aw-tehl? Gahnaw ahng lahyaw nee-to?

10. Have you a single room (a double room)? May I see the room? I don't like that room. I like this room.

10. Apakah ada kamar tunggal (kamar untuk dua orang)? Boléhkah saya lihat kamar itu? Saya tidak suka kamar itu. Saya suka kamar ini.
Ahpa-kahh ahda kahmarr toonggahl (kahmarr oontook dooa awrrahng)? Bawleh-kahh sahya leehaht kahmarr eetoo? Sahya teedah' sooka kahmarr eetoo. Sahya sooka kahmarr eenee.

10. Mayroón ba kayóng kuwartong pang-isahan (kuwartong pandalawahan)? Maáari bang mákita ko ang kuwarto? Hindî ko gustó ang kuwartong iyón. Itó ang kuwartong gustó ko.
Meh-rawn ba ka-yawng k'wahrrtawng pahng-ee-sahan (k'wahrrtawng pahn-dahla-wahan)? Mah-ahri bahng mah-keeta kaw ahng k'wahrrto? Hindi kaw gooss-taw ahng k'wahrrtawng ee-yawn. Ee-taw ahng k'wahrrtawng gooss-taw kaw.

SPANISH

7. Un pasaje para una persona (para dos personas) a ——, por favor. Dos adultos y un niño. Primera clase. Clase turista.

Oom pahssa-heh pahrra oona pehrr-sonna (pahrra doss pehrr-sonnahss) ah ——, pawrr fa-vawrr. Doss a-thooltoss ee oon neenyoh. Pree-mehrra klahsseh. Klahsseh too-rreessta.

8. Dispénseme, ¿ qué hora es? Las dos. Las dos diez. Las dos y media. Diez para las tres.

Deess-pehnsseh-meh, ky'awrra ehss? Lahss doss. Lahss doss dee-ess. Lahss doss ee mehtheea. Dee-ess pahrra lahh trrehss.

PORTUGUESE

7. Uma passagem para uma pessoa (para duas pessoas) para ——, por favor. Dois adultos e uma criança. Primeira classe. Classe turística.

Ooma pah-sahzhehñ pahrr' ooma pess-aw-a (pahrra dooahss pess-awss) pahrra ——, poorr fa-vawrr. Doyz a-dooltss eh ooma kree-ahnssa. Pree-mehrra klahss. Klahss too-reessti-ka.

8. Desculpe, que horas são? Duas horas. Duas e dez. Duas e meia. Dez para as três.

Dehss-koolpeh, kee awrrahss sowñ? Dooaz awraz. Dooaz eh deighss. Dooaz eh mehya. Dehz pahrr'ss treighss.

FRENCH

7. Un billet pour une personne (pour deux personnes) pour ——, s'il vous plaît. Deux adultes et un enfant. Première classe. Classe touriste.

Un beeyeh poorr oon pehrr-sonn (poorr der pehrr-sonn) poorr ——, silvoo play. Der-za-doolt eh un oñ-foñ. Prer-myairr klahss. Klahss too-rreest.

8. Pardon monsieur/madame, quelle heure est-il? Deux heures. Deux heures dix. Deux heures et demi. Trois heures moins dix.

Parr-doñ m'syer/ma-dahm, kel err eh-teel? Der-zerr. Der-zerr deess. Der-zerr eh d'mee. Trrwa-zerr mwahñ deess.

---

9. Lléveme a un hotel (al Hotel ——). ¿ Es éste (aquél) el hotel? ¿Cuán lejos está?

Yehveh-meh a' oon aw-tehl (al Aw-tehl ——). Ehss essteh (ah-kel) el aw-tehl? Kwahn leh-hoss ess-tah?

10. ¿ Tiene usted una habitación sencilla (una habitación doble)? ¿ Puedo ver la habitación? No me gusta esa habitación. Me gusta esta habitación.

Tyehn' ooss-teh oon' ahbee-ta-syonn sehn-seeya (oon' ahbee-ta-syonn dohvleh)? Pwehtho vairr la'ahbee-ta-syonn? Naw meh goossta ehss' ahbee-ta-syonn. Meh goossta ehss' ahbee-ta- syonn.

9. Leve-me para um hotel (para o Hotel ——). Ésse (Àquèle) é o hotel? Qual é a distância daqui?

Lehvee-mee pahrr' ooñ aw-tell (pahrr' oo Aw-tell ——). Ehssee (A kehlee) eh oo aw-tell? Kwah eh ah deess-tahnseea dah-kee?

10. O senhor/A senhora tem um apartamento para um (um apartamento para dois)? Poderia ver o apartamento? Não gosto daquêle apartamento. Eu gosto dêsse apartamento.

Oo see-yawrr/Ah see-yawrra tehñ ooñ a-pahrrteh-mehntoo pahrra ooñ (ooñ a-pahrrteh-mehntoo pahrra doyss)? Pood'rreea vehrr oo a-pahrrteh-mehnt'? Nowñ gawsst' da-kehl' a-pahrrteh-mehnt'. Yo gawsstoo dehss' a-pahrrteh-mehnt'.

9. Conduisez-moi à un hôtel (à l'Hôtel ——). Ceci (Cela), est ce l'hôtel? Quelle est la distance d'ici?

Koñ-dweezeh-mwa ah un ot-tel (ah lot-tel ——). Ser-see (S'la), ehsser lot-tel? Kel eh la deess-tahñss dee-ssee?

10. Avez-vous une chambre à un lit (une chambre à deux lits)? Puis-je voir la chambre? Je n'aime pas cette chambre-là. J'aime mieux cette chambre.

Ahveh-voo oon shahñbrrr ah uñ lee (oon shahñbrr ah der lee)? Pweezh' vwahrr la shahñbrr? Zher naym pa set shahñbrr-la. Zhaym myer set shahñbrr.

SENTENCES

ENGLISH	MALAY [INDONESIAN]	TAGALOG

11. Could I have the key of my room, please? Are there any letters <u>for me</u> (for us)?

11. Boléhkah saya minta kunći kamar saya. Apakah ada surat <u>untuk saya</u> (untuk kita)?
Bawleh-kahh sahya minta koonchee kahmarr sahya. Ahpa-kahh ahda soorraht oontoo' sahya (oontoo' keeta)?

11. Ibigáy mo ngâ sa akin ang susì. May mga sulat ba <u>pará sa akin</u> (pará sa amin)?
Ībbi-geh maw nga sa ahkin ahng so-osi. Meh m'gah soolat ba pa-rah sa ahkin (pa-rah sa ahmin)?

12. Could I speak to ———, please? It has to do with ———. It is very important.

12. Boléhkah saya berćakap [Bisa saya berbićara] dengan ———. Ini berhubungan dengan ———. Ini sangat penting.
Bawleh-kahh sahya brr-chahkahp [Bissa sahya brr-b'chahrra] d'ng-ahn ———. Eenee brr-hoo-boong-an d'ng-ahn ———. Eenee sahng-at p'nting.

12. Maáari bang mákausap ko si ———. Tungkól ito sa ———. Isáng bagay na importante.
Mah-ahrri bahng mahkaw-sahp kaw see ———. Toong-kawl eeto sa ———. Ee-sang bahgeh na eempawrr-tahnteh.

13. How much is this? I would like to buy this, please. That is too dear. I don't want it.

13. Berapakah hargánya ini? Saya ingin membeli ini. Itu sangat mahal. Saya tidak mau itu.
Brr-ahpa-kahh hahrrga-nya eenee? Sahya eeng-een m'mb'lee eenee. Eetoo sahng-at mahhal. Sahya teedah' mow eetoo.

13. Magkano itó? Itó ang gustó kong bilhín. Mahál namán. Ayaw ko na.
Mahk-kahn' ee-to? Ee-to ahng gooss-taw kawng beel-hin. Ma-hahl na-mahn. Ahyaw kaw na.

14. May I wash my hands? I would like a bath. I need <u>some soap</u> (a towel, <u>hot water</u>).

14. Boléhkah saya menćući tangan saya? Saya ingin mandi. Saya perlu <u>sabun</u> (anduk, air panas).
Bawleh-kahh sahya m'n-choochee tahng-an sahya? Sahya eeng-een mahndee. Sahya prr-loo sahboon (ahndoo', ighrr pahnahss).

14. Maáari bang maghugas ng kamáy? Gustó kong maligò. Kailangan ko ng sabón (ng tuwalya, ng tubig na mainit).
Mah-ahrree bahng mahg-hoogahss n'ng ka-meh? Gooss-taw kawng ma-lee-gaw. Keh-lahng'n kaw n'ng sa-bawn (n'ng too-wahlya, n'na toobig na ma-ee nit).

15. Is the restaurant <u>open</u> (closed)? Could I see <u>the menu</u>? I would like ———. The bill, please.

15. Apakah réstoran itu <u>buka</u> (tutup)? Boléhkah [Bisakah] saya lihat daftar makanannya? Saya ingin ———. Tolong beri bil [rékening] saya.
Ahpa-kahh rrehssto-rrahn eetoo bookah (tootoop)? Bawleh-kahh [Bissa-kahh] sahya leehaht dahftarr ma-kahnahn-nya? Sahya eeng-een ———. Tawlawng brr-ee bil [rrehk'ning] sahya.

15. <u>Bukás</u> (Sarado) ba ang restawrán? Maáari bang mákita ang menú? Ang gustó ko ay ———. Ibigáy mo ngâ sa akin ang bill.
Boo-kahss (Sa-rahdo) bahng resstow-ran? Mah-ahrree bahng mahkeet'ahng meh-noo? Ahng gooss-taw kaw igh ———. Ibbi-geh maw nga sa ahkin ahng beel.

SENTENCES

SPANISH

11. ¿Me podría dar la llave de mi habitación, por favor? ¿Hay alguna carta para mí (para nosotros)?

Meh paw-thrreea dahrr la yahveh deh mee ahbee-ta-syonn, pawrr fa-vawrr? Igh ahl-goonah karrtah pahrra mee (pahrra naw-sawtrross)?

12. ¿Podría hablar con ————, por favor? Tiene que ver con ————. Es muy importante.

Paw-thrree' ah-vlahrr kawn ————, pawrr fa-vawrr? Teenah keh vairr kawn ————. Ehss moy eempawrr-tahnteh.

13. ¿Cuánto vale esto? Me gustaría comprar esto, por favor. Eso es muy caro. No lo quiero.

Kwahntoh vahl' ehssto? Meh goossta-rreea kawm-prrahrr ehssto, pawrr fa-vawrr. Ehsso ehss mwee kahrro. Naw law kyehrro.

14. ¿Puedo lavarme las manos? Me gustaría tomar un baño. Necesito jabón (una toalla, agua caliente).

Pwehtho lah-vahrrmeh lahss mahnoss? Meh goossta-rreea tohmahrr oom vahnyo. Nehsseh-seeto hah-vonn (oona toh-ahlya, ahgwah kahl-yehnteh).

15. ¿Está abierto (cerrado) el restaurante? ¿Podría ver la carta [el menú]? Me gustaría ————. La cuenta, por favor.

Ehsst' ah-vyeerrtoh (seh-rrahtho) el rrehssto-rrahhnteh? Paw-thrreea vairr la kahrrta [el meh-noo]? Meh goossta-rreea ————. La kwehnta, pawrr fa-vawrr.

PORTUGUESE

11. O senhor/A senhora poderia me dar a chave do meu apartamento, por favor? Tem correspondência para mim (para nós)?

Oo see-yawrr/Ah see-yawrra pood'-rreea mee dahrr ah chahvee doo meeoo a-pahrrteh-mehnt', poorr fa-vawrr? Tehñ kawrress-pawñ-dehnsya pahrra miñ (pahrra nawss)?

12. Poderia falar con ————, por favor? E sôbre ————. E muito importante.

Pood'rreea fuhluhrr kawñ ————, poorr fa-vawrr? Eh sawbrree ————. Eh mooeet' eempoorr-tahntee.

13. Quanto custa isso? Eu gostaria de comprar isso, por favor. Aquilo e muito caro. Não quero levar.

Yo goossta-rreea dee kooñ-prrahrr eessoo, poorr fa-vawrr. A-keeloo' mooeetoo kahrroo. Nowñ kehrroo leh-vahrr.

14. Posso lavar as mãos? Eu gostaria de tomar um banho. Eu preciso de sabonete (uma toalha, água quente).

Pawss' lah-vahrr 'z mownñz? Yo goossta-rreea dee too-mahrr ooñ bahyoo. Yo prree-seezoo dee sahb'nehteh (ooma too-ahlya, ahgwah kehntee).

15. O restaurante 'tá aberto (fechado)? Poderia ver o cardápio? Eu gostaria de ————. A conta, por favor.

Oo rehssta-ranntee tah 'behrrtoo (feh-shahdoo)? Pood'rreea vehrr oo kahrr-dahpyoo? Yo goossta-rreea deh ————. A konntah, poorr fa-vawrr.

FRENCH

11. Veuillez me donner la clef de ma chambre. Y a-t-il des lettres pour moi (pour nous)?

Ver-yeh mer donneh la kleh d'ma shahñbrr. Ee ahteel deh lettrr poorr mwa (poorr noo)?

12. Est-il possible de parler avec ————, s'il vous plaît? Cela concerne ————. C'est très important.

Ehteel poss-seebl' der pahrrleh a-vek ————, silvoo play? S'la koñ-sehrrn ————. Seh trrayz añ-porr-tahñ.

13. C'est combien? Je voudrais acheter ceci, s'il vous plaît. C'est trop cher. Je n'en veux pas.

Seh koñ-byeñ? Zher voodrray ahshteh ser-see, silvoo play. Seh trro shehrr. Zher nahñ ver pa.

14. Puis-je me laver les mains? Je voudrais prendre un bain. J'ai besoin de savon (d'une serviette, d'eau chaude).

Pweezh' mer lahveh leh mañ? Zher voodrray prrahhñdrr uñ bañ. Zhay ber-zwahñ der sa-voñ (doon sehrr-vyet, doh shohd).

15. Le restaurant est-il ouvert (fermé)? Puis-je regarder le menu? Je désire ————. L'addition, s'il vous plaît.

Ler ressto-rrahñ eh-teel oo-vairr (fairrmeh)? Pweezh' r'gahrrdeh ler mer-nu? Zher deh-zeerr ————. La-dissyoñ, silvoo play.

SENTENCES

ENGLISH	MALAY [INDONESIAN]	TAGALOG

16. I would like to make a telephone call. Would you call ——— for me? There is no answer. I have been cut off.

16. Saya hendak menalipon [menélpon]. Boléhkah saudara/-i menalipon [Bisakah engkau télpon] ——— untuk saya. Tidak ada jawapan. Saluran saya telah diputuskan.
Sahya h'ndah' m'n-ahlee-pon [m'n-ehlpon]. Bawleh-kahh sow-darra/-ee m'n-ahlee-pon [Bissa-kahh 'ng-kow tellpon] ——— oontoo' sahya. Teedah' ahda ja-wahpahn. Sa-loorrahn sahya t'lahh deepoo-toosskahn.

16. Ibig kong tumeléponó. Tawagan mo ngâ si ——— pará sa akin? Waláng sumásagót. Nawalâ ang koneksiyón.
Ibbig kawng toomeh-lehpaw-naw. Ta-wahgan maw nga see ——— pa-rah sa ahkin? Wa-lahng soo-mahssa-gawt. Nawah-lah'ng kaw-nek-syawn.

17. Could I have <u>some notepaper</u> (some air mail paper, some envelopes)? Where can I buy stamps? How much altogether?

17. Boléhkah saya mendapatkan <u>beberapa keping [lembar] kertas ćatatan</u> (beberapa keping [lembar] kertas udara, beberapa keping [lembar] sampul)? Dimana boléh saya beli setém [perangko]? Berapa kesemuanya?
Bawleh-kahh sahya m'n-dahpaht-kahn b'brr-ahpa k'ping [l'm-barr] krr-tahss cha-tahtahn (b'brr-ahpa k'ping [l'm-barr] krr-tahss oo-darra, b'brr-ahpa k'ping [l'm-barr] sahmpool)? Dee-mahna bawlehh sahya b'lee s'tehm [prr-ahngko]? Brr-ahpa k's'mooa-nya?

17. Bigyán mo ngâ akó ng papél na masúsulatan (papél pang-air mail, sobre)? Saán akó makabíbili ng selyo? Magkano ang magiging halagá ng lahát?
Bee-gyahn maw ahng nga a-kaw n'ng pa-pehl na ma-soosoo-lahtahn (pa-pehl pahng ehrr-mehl, sawbrreh)? Sahn a-kaw mahka-beebee-lee n'ng sehlyaw? M'g-kahnaw ahng mahghee-gheeng hahla-gah n'ng la-haht?

18. I am ill. Where can I see a doctor? Please get a good doctor. Could I have some water?

18. Saya sakit. Dimanakah boléh saya berjumpa doktor [Dimana saya bisa mendapatkan dokter]? Tolong ćari doktor [dokter] yang baik. Boléhkah saya mendapat sedikit air?
Sahya sahkit. Dee-mahna-kahh bawlehh sahya brr-joompah doktorr [Dee-mahna sahya bissa m'n-dahpaht-kahn dokt'rr]? Tawlawng chahrree doktorr [dokt'rr] yahng bighk. Bawleh-kahh sahya m'n-dahpaht s'deekit ighrr?

18. Akó ay may sakit. Saán akó maáaring kumunsulta sa doktór? Tumawag ka ngâ ng mabuting doktór. Bigyán mo ngâ ako ng inumin.
Ah-kaw eh meh sa-kit. Sahn a-kaw mah-ahring koomoon-soolta sa dawk-tawrr? Too-mahwahg ka nga n'ng ma-booting dawk-tawrr. Bee-gyahn maw nga ahkaw n'ng eenoo-meen.

SENTENCES

SPANISH

16. Me gustaría hacer una llamada telefónica. Podría llamar a ——— para mí? No contestan. Me han cortado.
Meh goossta-rree' ah-thairr oona ya-mahda tehleh-fawnee-ka. Paw-threea ya-mahrr ah ——— pahrra mee? Naw kawn-tehsstahn. Meh ahn kawrr-tahtho.

17. ¿Me podría dar una esquela (papel aéreo, unos sobres)? ¿Dónde puedo comprar estampillas? ¿Cuánto es todo?
Meh paw-threea dahrr oona ehss-kehla (pahpehl a-ehrreh-o, oonoss sawbrrehss)? Dawntheh pwehtho kawm-prrahrr ehsstahm-peeyahss? Kwahnto ehss tawthaw?

18. Estoy enfermo/-a. ¿Dónde puedo ver doctor? Por favor, traiga un buen doctor. ¿Me podría dar agua?
Ehss-toy ehn-fehrrmo/-a. Dawntheh pwehtho vairr dawktawrr? Pawrr fa-vawrr, trrighga oom bwehn dawktawrr. Meh paw-threea dahrr ahgwa?

PORTUGUESE

16. Eu gostaria de fazer uma chamada telefónica. O senhor/A senhora poderia chamar ——— para mim? Não atende. A ligação foi cortada.
Yo goossta-rreea dee fah-zehrr ooma shah-mahda tehleh-fawnee-ka. Oo see-yawrr/Ah see-yawrra poodeh-rreea shah-mahrr ——— pahrra miñ? Nowñ a-tehndee. Ah leega-sowñ foy kawrr-tahda.

17. O senhor/A senhora poderia me dar um pedaço de papel (papel aéreo, alguns envelopes)? Onde posso comprar sêlos? Quanto é tudo?
Oo see-yawrr/Ah see-yawrra pood'-rreea mee dahrr ooñ peh-dahss' dee pah-pell (pah-pell a-ehrreh-oo, al-goonz ehñv'loppeess)? Awndee poss' kooñ-prrahrr sehlooss? Kwahnt' eh toodoo?

18. Estou doente. Onde posso encontrar um médico? Por favor, consiga-me um bom médico. O senhor/A senhora poderia me dar um pouco de água?
Ehss-toh doo-ehnteh. Awndee poss' ehnkoon-trrahrr oo mehdee-ko? Poorr fa-vawrr, kawñ-seega-mee ooñ bawñ mehdee-ko. Oo see-yawrr/Ah see-yawrra poodeh-rreea mee dahrr ooñ pawkoo dee ahgwah?

FRENCH

16. Je voudrais téléphoner. Veuillez appeler ——— pour moi. Il n'y a pas de réponse. Mon appel a été interrompu.
Zher voodrray telleh-fohn-neh. Ver-yeh ahp'leh ——— poorr mwa. Eel nya pa d'rreh-poñss. Mon ahp-pel ah ehteh añ-teh- rroñ-pü.

17. Je désire du papier à lettres (du papier avion, des enveloppes). Où puis-je acheter des timbres? C'est combien en tout?
Zher deh-zeerr du pa-pyeh ah lettrr (du pa-pyeh ah-vyoñ, deh-zahñ-v'lop). Oo pweez' ahshteh deh tañbrr? Seh kon-byeñ ahñ too?

18. Je suis malade. Où puis-je consulter un médecin? S'il vous plaît, faîtes venir un bon médecin. Veuillez m'apporter de l'eau fraîche.
Zher swee m'lahd. Oo pweez' koñ-soolteh uñ med-sañ? Silvoo play, fert v'neerr uñ boñ med-sañ. Ver-yeh mahp-porrteh der loh frraysh.

ENGLISH	MALAY [INDONESIAN]	TAGALOG

19. May I introduce
———. I am pleased to
meet you. My name
is ———.

19. Ingin saya perkenalkan
———. Gembira bertemu
dengan saudara/-i [engkau].
Nama saya adalah ———.
*Eeng-een sahya prr-k'n-
ahlkahn ———. G'm-birra
brr-t'moo d'ng-ahn sow-
darra/-ee ['ng-kow]. Nahma
sahya ahda-lahh ———.*

19. Ipinakikilala ko sa iyó si
———. Ikinagágalák kong
mákilala ka. Ang ngalan ko ay
———.
*Eepee-nah-keekee-lahla kaw
sa ee-yaw see ———. Ee-
keenah-gahgah-lahk kawng
mahkee-lahla ka. Ahng
ngahlahn kaw igh ———.*

20. Who are you? A friend.
I come from ———.
Go away!

20. Siapakah saudara/-i
[engkau]? Seorang teman. Saya
datang dari ———. Pergi
sana!
*Syahpa-kahh sow-darra/-ee
['ng-kow]? Se'awrrahng
t'mahn. Sahya dahtahng
dahrree ———. Prr-ghee
sahnah!*

20. Sino ka? Isáng kaibigan.
Akó ay galing sa ———.
Umalís ka!
*Seenaw ka? Ee-sahng ka-ee
beegahn. Ah-kaw eh gahling
sa ———. Ooma-leess-ka!*

21. What is this called?
What is this place called?
It is called ———.

21. Apakah namanya ini?
Apakah namanya tempat ini?
Namanya adalah ———.
*Ahpa-kahh nahma-nya
eenee? Ahpa-kahh nahma-
nya t'm-paht eenee? Nahma-
nya ahda-lahh ———.*

21. Anó ang tawag dito? Anó
ang tawag sa lugár na itó? Itó
ay tinátawag na ———.
*A-naw ahng tahwahg
deetaw? A-naw ahng
tahwahg sa loogahrr na ee-
taw? Ee-taw eh tee-nah-
tahwahg na ———.*

22. What is the matter?
Don't worry. I am <u>sorry</u>
(glad). I shall give you this.

22. Ada apa? Jangan kawatir.
Saya <u>menyesal</u> (senang). Saya
akan <u>memberi</u> saudara/-i
[engkau] ini.
*Ahda ahpa? Jahng-ahn
k'wahteerr. Sahya m'n-y'sahl
(s'nahng). Sahya ahkahn
m'mbrree sow-darra/-ee
['ng-kow] eenee.*

22. Anó ang nangyari? Huwág
kang mag-alalá. <u>Ikinalúlungkót</u>
(Ikinagágalák) ko. Ibíbigáy ko
sa iyó itó.
*A-naw 'ng nahng-yahree?
Hoo-wahg kahng m'g-ahla-
lah. Eekee-na-loo-loong-kawt
(Eekee-na-gahga-lahk) kaw.
Ee-beebee-geh kaw sa ee-yaw
ee-taw.*

23. What do you want?
Please sit down. I have to
leave. You must go now.

23. Apa yang saudara/-i
[engkau] inginkan? Silakan
duduk. Saya harus pergi.
Saudara/-i [Engkau] harus
pergi sekarang.
*Ahpa yahng sow-darra/-ee
['ng-kow] eeng-een-kahn?
Seela-kahn doodoo'. Sahya
hahrrooss prr-ghee. Sow-
darra/-ee ['Ng-kow]
hahrrooss prr-ghee
s'kahrrahng.*

23. Anó ang gustó mo? Maupô
ka. Kailangan kong umalís.
Makaáalis ka na.
*A-naw 'ng gooss-taw maw?
Mawpo ka. Keh-lahng'n
kawng ooma-leess. Mahka-
ahleess ka na.*

SENTENCES

SPANISH

19. ¿Puedo presentarle
———— ? Encantado de
conocerlo. Mi nombre es
————.
Pwehtho prehssen-tahrrleh
———— ? Ehn-kahn-tahdo
deh kawnaw-sehrrlo. Mee
nawmbrreh ehss ————.

20. ¿Quién es usted? Un
amigo. Vengo de ————.
¡Váyase!
Kehn' ehss oosstehd? Oon a-
meegoh. Vehnggoh deh
————. Vahyah-seh!

21. ¿Cómo se llama ésto?
¿Cómo se llama este lugar? Se
llama ————.
Kawmaw seh yahma ehssto?
Kawmaw seh yahma ehssteh
loogahrr? Seh yahmah
————.

22. ¿Qué pasa? No se
preocupe. Lo siento (Estoy
contento/-a). Le daré ésto.
Keh pahssa? Naw seh prraw-
koopeh. Law syehnto (Ehss-
toy kawn-tehnto/-a). Leh
dah-rreh ehssto.

23. ¿Qué quiere? Por favor,
siéntese. Debo irme. Usted debe
irse.
Keh kyehrreh? Pawrr fa-
vawrr, syehnteh-seh. Dehbo
eerrmeh. Oossteh dehbeh
eerrseh.

PORTUGUESE

19. Posso apresentar-lhe
———— ? Muito prazer em
conhecê-lo/-la. O meu nome é
————.
Poss' awpree-zen-tahrrlee
———— ? Mooeet' pra-zehrr
ehñ kawñeh-sehloo/-la. Oo
meeoo nawmee eh ————.

20. Quem é o senhor/a
senhora? Um amigo/Uma
amiga. Eu venho de ————.
Va embora!
Kehñ 'oo see-yawrr/'ah see-
yawrra? Ooñ a-meegoo/Oom'
a-meega. Yo vehñyoo dee
————. Vah'ñbawrra!

21. Como se chama isso?
Como se chama êsse lugar?
Chama-se ————.
Kawmoo see shahmah
eessoo? Kawmoo see
shahmah ehssee loo-gahrr?
Shahmah-see ————.

22. Qual é o problema? Não se
preocupe. Sinto muito (Eu estou
contente). Eu vou lhe dar isso.
Kah'eh oo praw-blehma?
Nowñ see proh-koopee.
Sintoo mooeetoo (Yo ahsstoh
koon-tehnt'). Yo voh lee
dahrr eessoo.

23. Que é que o senhor/a
senhora deseja? Por favor,
sente-se. Eu tenho que sair. O
senhor/A senhora tem que ir-se
agora.
Kee eh kee oo see-yawrr/ah
see-yawrra deh-sehzha?
Poorr fa-vawrr, sehntee-see.
Yo tehñ' kee sa-eerr. Oo see-
yawrr/Ah see-yawrra tehñ
kee eerr-seh 'gwahrra.

FRENCH

19. Puis-je présenter ————?
Enchanté de faire votre
connaisance. Je m'appelle
————.
Pweezh' prreh-zahñteh
———— ? Ahñ-shahñteh d'
fairr vottrr konnay-sahñss.
Zher map-pel ————.

20. Qui êtes-vous? Un ami. Je
suis venu de ————. Allez-
vous-en!
Kee ayt-voo? Un ah-mee.
Zher swee v'nü der ————.
Alleh-voo-zahñ!

21. Comment appelez-vous
cela? Comment s'appelle cet
endroit? Il/Elle s'appelle
————.
Kommoñ ap-p'leh-voo s'la?
Kommoñ sap-pel settahñ-
drrwa? Eel/El sap-pel
————.

22. Qu'est-ce qu'il y a? Ne
vous inquietez pas. Je suis peiné
(heureux/-se). Je voudrais vous
donner ceci.
Kehss keel ya? Ner vooz añ-
kyeh-teh pa. Zher swee
payneh (er-rrer/er-rrerz).
Zher voodrray voo donneh
ser-see.

23. Que voulez-vous? Veuillez
vous asseoir. Je dois partir. Il
est nécessaire que vous vous en
alliez maintenant.
Ker vooleh-voo? Ver-yeh
voos-ass-wahrr. Zher dwa
pahrr-teerr. Eel eh nesseh-
sairr ker voo vooz-on al-yeh
mañ-t'nahñ.

SENTENCES

ENGLISH	MALAY [INDONESIAN]	TAGALOG
24. I need help. I am in trouble. Please give this message to ———. As soon as possible.	24. Saya perlu pertolongan. Saya sedang dalam kesusahan. Tolong sampaikan pesan ini kepada ———. Secepat mungkin. *Sahya prr-loo prr-taw-lawng-an. Sahya s'dahng dahlahm k'soo-sahhahn. Tawlawng sahm-pighkahn p'sahn eenee k'pahdah ———. S'ch'paht moongkeen.*	24. Kailangan ko ang tulong. Nasa magulóng pangyayari akó. Pakidalá mo ngâ ang mensaheng itó sa ———. Sa lalong madalíng panahón. *Keh-lahng'n kawng toolong. Nahsa m'g-oo-lawng pahng-ya-yahrree a-kaw. Pahkee-de-la maw nga'ng men-saheng ee-taw sa ———. Sa lahlawng mudda-leeng pahna-hawn.*
25. That is very nice (marvellous). That is <u>bad</u> (terrible). I have enjoyed myself very much.	25. <u>Baik sekali</u> (Bagus sekali). <u>Tidak baik</u> (Buruk sekali). Saya sangat puas hati [Saya sangat senang]. *Bighk s'kahlee (Bahgooss s'kahlee). Teedah' bigh' (Boorrook s'kahlee). Sahya sahng-aht pwahss hahtee [Sahya sahng-aht s'nahng].*	25. Iyán <u>ang mainam</u> (kahanga-hangá). <u>Masamá</u> (Terible) iyán. Akó ay labís na nasiyahán. *Ee-yahn ahng ma-eenam (ka-hahnga-hahnga). Mahssa-ma (Te-rreebleh) ee-yahn. A-kaw eh lahbeess na na-seeya-hahn.*

SENTENCES

SPANISH

24. Necesito ayuda. Estoy en dificultades. Por favor, déle este recado a ———. Lo más pronto posible.
Nehsseh-seeto a yoodah. Ehsstoy ehn deefee-kooltahthess. Pawrr fa-vawrr, dehl' ehssteh reh-kahdo ah ———. Law mahss prrawnto paw-sseevleh.

25. Eso es <u>muy bonito</u> (maravilloso). Eso está <u>mal</u> (terrible). Lo he pasado muy bien.
Ehsso ehss moy vaw-neeto (mahrra-vee-yawsso). Ehsso 'sstah mahl (teh-rreevleh). Law eh pa-sahdo moy vyehn.

PORTUGUESE

24. Eu preciso de ajuda. Eu estou em dificuldades. Por favor, dê êsse recado a ———. Quanto mais cedo possível.
Yo pree-seez' dee a-zhoodah. Yo ehsstoh eeñ diffkooldahdeez. Poorr fa-vawrr, deh ehssee ree-kahdoo ah ———. Kwahntoo mighss sehdoo poss-eevel.

25. Isso é <u>muito agradável</u> (maravilhoso). Isso é <u>mau</u> (terrível). Eu me diverti muito.
Eessoo eh mooeet' agrahdahvehl (mahrr'veel-yawzoo). Eessoo eh maw-oo (teh-rreevehl). Yo m' dee-vehrrtee mooeetoo.

FRENCH

24. J'ai besoin de secours. J'ai des difficultés. Veuillez donner ce message à ———. Aussi vite que possible.
Zhay b'zwahñ d' s'koorr. Zhay deh diffi-kool-teh. Ver-yeh donneh ser mehss-ahzh ah ———. Ohssee veet ker poss-seebl'.

25. C'est très joli (merveilleux). C'est <u>mauvais</u> (terrible). Je me suis beaucoup amusé.
Seh tray zhol-lee (mairr-vay-yer). Seh moh-vay (teh-rreebl'). Zher mer swee bohkoo-pa-mü-zeh.

VOCABULARY

ENGLISH	MALAY [INDONESIAN]	TAGALOG
above	diatas	sa itaás
accident, the	kećelakaan	sakunâ
address, the	alamat	tirahan
adult, the	orang dewasa	may gulang
advertisement, the	iklan	anunsiyó
aerogramme, the	surat udara [warkatpos udara]	erograma
afraid	takut	takót
after	setelah	pagkalipas
afternoon, the	petang	hapon
again	semula [sekali lagi]	mulî
against	lawan	laban sa
agree, to	menyetujui	s(um)á(sa)ngayon
air, the	udara	hangin
air conditioner, the	air conditioner [a.c. *(AHseh)*]	air con
air mail, the	pos udara	air mail
airplane, the	kapal terbang	eroplano
airport, the	lapangan udara	lápagan ng eroplano
alive	hidup	buháy
all	segala	lahát
all right	baiklah	mabuti
almost	hampir	halos
alone	sendiri	nag-iisá
already	telah	handâ na
also	... pun	din
although	walaupun	kahit na
always	selalu	lagi
among	diantara	kasama ng
and (between nouns)	dan	at
angry	marah	galít
animal, the	haiwan [binatang]	hayop
another one (different)	lain	ibá
another one (more)	satu lagi	ibá pa
answer, to	jawab	s(um)á(sa)gót
antiseptic, the	antiseptik	antiséptikó
apartment, the	bilék	apartment
apple, the	buah épal [apel]	mansanas
approximately	kira-kira	halos
arm, the	lengan	bisig
army, the	angkatan darat	hukbó
around	sekeliling	sa paligid
arrive, to	tiba	d(um)á(ra) ting
art, the	kesenian	sining
art gallery, the	musium kesenian	galeryá ng sining
artificial	buatan	artipisyál
ask (inquire), to	bertanya	(nag)(tá)tanóng
at	di-	sa
attempt, to	menćuba	(nag)(tá)tangkâ

VOCABULARY

SPANISH	PORTUGUESE	FRENCH
sobre	acima de	au-dessus
el accidente	o acidente	l'accident (m.)
la dirección	o endereço	l'adresse (f.)
el adulto/la adulta	o adulto/a adulta	l'adulte (m., f.)
el aviso	o anúncio	l'annonce (f.)
el aerograma	o aerograma	l'aérogramme (f.)
asustado	com mêdo	effrayé
después	depois de	après
la tarde	a tarde	l'après-midi (m.)
otra vez	de nôvo	encore
contra	contra	contre
estar de acuerdo	concordar	être d'accord
el aire	o ar	l'air (m.)
el aire acondicionado	o ar condicionado	le climatiseur
el correo aéreo	o correio aéreo	le courrier avion
el avión	o avião (-ões)	l'avion (m.)
el aeropuerto	o aeroporto	l'aéroport (m.)
vivo	vivo	vivant
todo	todo	tout
muy bien	bem	bien
casi	quase	presque
solo	sòzinho	seul
ya	já	déjà
también	tambëm	aussi
aunque	embora	bien que
siempre	sempre	toujours
entre	entre	entre
y	e	et
enojado	bravo	fâché
el animal	o animal	l'animal (m.)
otro/-a	outro/-a	un/une autre
otro/-a	mais um/uma	encore un/une
contestar	responder	répondre
el antiséptico	o antiséptico	l'antiseptique (m.)
el apartamento [el departamento]	o apartamento	l'appartement (m.)
la manzana	a maçã	la pomme
casi	aproximadamente	à peu près
el brazo	o braço	le bras
el ejército	o exército	l'armée (f.)
alrededor de	em volta de	autour de
llegar	chegar	arriver
el arte	a arte	l'art (m.)
la galería de arte	a galeria de arte	le musée de peinture
artificial	artificial	artificiel
preguntar	perguntar	demander
a	em	à
intentar	tentar	essayer

VOCABULARY

ENGLISH	MALAY [INDONESIAN]	TAGALOG
awake	jaga	gising
baby, the	bayi	sanggól
back (rear), the	belakang	likód
back (again)	balék	bumalík
backwards	terkebelakang	pauróng
bad	jahat	masamâ
bag, the	bég [tas]	bag
baggage, the	barang-barang	bagahe
ballpoint, the	péna bolpoin	bolpoint
bamboo shoots, the	rebung	usbóng ng kawayan
banana, the	pisang	saging
bank (money), the	bank	bangko
bathe, to	mandi	(na)(li)ligò
bathroom, the	bilék mandi [kamar mandi]	banyo
battery, the	béteri [aki]	bateryá
beach, the	pantai	aplaya
beans, the	kaćang	sitaw
beard, the	janggut	balbás
beautiful	indah	magandá
because	sebab	sapagká't
because of	disebabkan oléh	dahil sa
become, to	menjadi	(nag)(i)ing
bed, the	tempat tidur	kama
beef, the	daging lembu [daging sapi]	karné ng baka
beer, the	bir	serbesa
before (time)	sebelum	bago
behind	dibelakang	sa likód ng
believe, to	perćaya	(na)(ni)niwalà
bell, the	lonćéng	kampanà
best	yang terbaik	pinakámabuti
better	lebih baik	lalong mabuti
beyond	melebihi	sa kabilâ ng
bicycle, the	beskal [sepéda]	bisikleta
big	besar	malakí
bill, the	bil [rékening]	kuwenta
binoculars, the	teropong	largabista
bird, the	burung	ibon
biscuit, the	biskut [biskwit]	bískuwit
black	hitam	itím
blanket, the	selimut	kumot
blood, the	darah	dugô
blue	biru	bugháw
boat, the	perahu	bangkâ
body, the	badan	katawán
boiled	rebus	kulô

284

VOCABULARY

SPANISH	PORTUGUESE	FRENCH
despierto	acordado	éveillé
el bebé	o bebê [o neném]	le bébé
el fondo	o fundo	l'arrière (m.)
de vuelta	de volta	retourné
hacia atrás	para trás	en arrière
malo	mau	mauvais
la bolsa	a bôlsa	la valise
el equipaje	a bagagem	les bagages (m.)
el bolígrafo	a esferográfica	le stylo à bille
los tallos de bambú	os brôtos de bambú	les pousses de bambou (f.)
el plátano	a banana	la banane
el banco	o banco	la banque
bañarse	tomar banho	prendre un bain
el cuarto de baño	o banheiro [a casa de banho]	la salle de bain
la batería [la pila]	a pilha	la pile
la playa	a praia	la plage
os frejoles	a vagem [o feijão verde]	les haricots verts (m.)
la barba	a barba	la barbe
hermoso	bonito	beau/belle
porque	porque	parce que
a causa de	por causa de	à cause de
hacerse	tornar-se	devenir
la cama	a cama	le lit
la carne de vaca	a carne de vaca	le boeuf
la cerveza	a cerveja	la bière
antes	antes de	avant
detrás de	atrás de	derrière
creer	acreditar	croire
la campana	o sino	la sonnette
el/la mejor	o/a melhor	mieux
mejor	melhor	meilleur
más allá de	além de	au delà
la bicicleta	a bicicleta	la bicyclette
grande	grande	grand
la cuenta	a conta [a factura]	l'addition (f.)
los binoculares	o binóculo	les binoculaires (m.)
el pájaro	a ave	l'oiseau (m.)
la galleta	o biscoito	le biscuit
negro	prêto	noir
la frazada [la manta]	o cobertor	la couverture
la sangre	o sangue	le sang
azul	azul	bleu
el bote	o barco	le bateau
el cuerpo	o corpo	le corps
cocido	cozido	bouilli

VOCABULARY

ENGLISH	MALAY [INDONESIAN]	TAGALOG
book, the	buku	aklát
boot, the	sepatu tinggi	bota
born	dilahirkan	ipinanganák
both	berdua	kapwâ
bottle, the	botol	botelya
bottle opener, the	pembuka botol	pambukás ng bote
bottom, the	dasar	ilalim
box, the	kotak	kahón
boy, the	anak laki-laki	batang lalaki
bra, the	ćoli [béha]	bra
brake, the	brék [rém]	preno
brave	berani	matapang
bread, the	roti	tinapay
break, to	memećahkan	s(um)i(si)rà
breakfast, the	makan pagi	almusál
bridge, the	jambatan	tuláy
bring, to	membawa	(nag)(dá)dalá
brooch, the	bros	brotse
brown	pérang [ćoklat]	kayumanggî
brush, the	berus [sikat]	sipilyo
bundle, the	bungkusan	balutan
bus, the	keréta bas [bis]	bus
businessman, the	pengusaha	mángangalakál
busy	asyék [sibuk]	abalá
but	tetapi	nguni't
butter, the	mentéga	mantekilya
button, the	kanćing	butones
buy, to	membeli	b(um)i(bi)lí
cabbage, the	kobis [kubis]	repolyo
cake, the	kuéh	keik
call (telephone), the	panggilan	tmeleponó
called, is	dipanggil	tinátawag
call out, to	menyebut	t(um)á(ta)wag
camera, the	kaméra	kámerá
candle, the	dian [lilin]	kandilà
captain (of ship), the	juragan	kapitán
car, the	keréta	awto
carefully	berhati-hati [hati-hati]	nang maingat
cargo, the	muatan	kargada
carpet, the	permadani	alpombra
carrot, the	lobak mérah [bortel]	karot
carry, to	membawa	d(in)á(da)lá
cat, the	kućing	pusà
centimetre, the	séntiméter	sentimetró

VOCABULARY

SPANISH	PORTUGUESE	FRENCH
el libro	o livro	le livre
la bota	a bota	la botte
nacido	nascido	né
ambos/-as	ambos/-as	tous les deux
la botella	a garrafa	la bouteille
el destapador de botellas	o abridor de garrafas	l'ouvre-bouteilles (m.)
	[o abre garrafas]	
el fondo	o fundo	le bas
la caja	a caixa	la boîte
el niño	o rapaz	le garçon
el sostén [el brassiere]	o soutien	le soutien-gorge
el freno	o breque [o travão (-ões)]	le frein
valiente	corajoso	courageux
el pan	o pão	le pain
romper	quebrar	casser
el desayuno	o café da manhã	le petit déjeuner
	[o pequeno almoço]	
el puente	a ponte	le pont
traer	trazer	apporter
el prendedor	o broche	la broche
café	marrom/-one [castanho]	brun
el cepillo	a escôva	la brosse
el lío	o embrulho	le paquet
el autobús	o ônibus [o autocarro]	l'autobus (m.)
el hombre de negocios	o homem de negócios	l'homme d'affaires (m.)
ocupado	ocupado	occupé
pero	mas	mais
la mantequilla	a manteiga	le beurre
el botón	o botão (-ões)	le bouton
comprar	comprar	acheter
el repollo [la col]	a couve	le chou
el pastel [la torta]	o bôlo	le gâteau
la llamada	o telefonema	l'appel (m.)
se llama	chama-se	s'appelle
gritar	gritar	crier
la cámara	a máquina fotográfica	l'appareil photographique (m.)
[la máquina fotográfica]		
la vela	a vela	la chandelle
el capitán	o capitão (-ões)	le capitaine
el coche [el carro]	o carro	l'auto (f.)
con cuidado	cuidadosamente	soigneusement
la carga	a carga	la cargaison
la alfômbra	o tâpete [o carpete]	le tapis
la zanahoria	a cenoura	la carotte
llevar	carregar	porter
el gato	o gato	le chat
el centímetro	o centímetro	le centimètre

VOCABULARY

ENGLISH	MALAY [INDONESIAN]	TAGALOG
century, the	abad	dantaón
certainly	mémang	tiyák
chair, the	kerusi [kursi]	silya
change (small money), the	uang kembali	baryá
change (money), to	menukarkan	(nag)(pá)palít
change (transport), to	berganti	l(um)i(lí)pat
cheap	murah	mura
cheese, the	kéju	keso
cherry, the	buah céri	ceresa
chicken, the	ayam	manók
chief, the	ketua [kepala]	punò
child, the	anak	anák
chocolate, the	coklat	tsokolate
choose, to	memilih	p(um)i(pi)li
chopsticks, the	supit	mga sipit
church, the	geréja	simbahan
cigar, the	cerutu	tabako
cigarette, the	rokok	sigarilyo
cinema, the	wayang gambar [bioskop]	sine
city, the	bandar raya [kota besar]	siyudád
clean	bersih	malinis
clean, to	membersihkan	(nag)(lí)linis
clerk, the	kerani	kawani
clock, the	jam	relós
close, to	menutup	(nag)(sá)sará
closed	tutup	sarado
cloth, the	kain	tela
clothes, the	pakaian	mga damít
coast, the	pantai	baybayin
coat, the	baju [jas]	amerikana
coffee, the	kopi	kapé
coin, the	mata uang	sinsilyo
cold	dingin	malamíg
cold season (winter), the	musim dingin	taglamíg
colour, the	warna	kulay
comb, the	sikat [sisir]	suklay
come, to	datang	d(um)á(ra)tíng
comfortable	nikmat	maginhawa
commercial	perdagangan	pangkalakal
company (firm), the	syarikat [perusahaan]	kompanyá
complain, to	mengadukan	(nag)(sú)sumbóng
completely	genap	nang ganáp
conceal, to	bersembunyi	(nag)(ta)tagò
concert, the	konsér	konsiyerto
consul, the	konsol	konsúl
contain, to	berisi	(ma)(pá)pagkasya

VOCABULARY

SPANISH	PORTUGUESE	FRENCH
el siglo	o século	le siècle
ciertamente	certamente	certainement
la silla	a cadeira	la chaise
el vuelto [el cambio]	o trôco	la petite monnaie
cambiar	trocar	changer
cambiar	mudar	changer de
barato	barato	à bon marché
el queso	o queijo	le fromage
la cereza	a cereja	la cerise
el pollo	a galinha	le poulet
el jefe	o chefe	le chef
el niño/la niña	a criança	l'enfant (m., f.)
el chocolate	o chocolate	le chocolat
elegir (-i-)	escolher	choisir
los palillos	os pauzinhos	les bâtonnets (m.)
la iglesia	a igreja	l'église (f.)
el cigarro [el tabaco]	o charuto	le cigare
el cigarrillo	o cigarro	la cigarette
el cine	o cinema	le cinéma
la ciudad	a cidade	la grande ville
limpio	limpo	propre
limpiar	limpar	nettoyer
el/la oficinista	o funcionário/a funcionária	l'employé/-ée de bureau
el reloj	o relógio	l'horloge (f.)
cerrar	fechar	fermer
cerrado	fechado	fermé
la tela	o pano	le drap
la ropa	a roupa	les vêtements (m.)
la costa	a costa	la côte
el abrigo [la chaqueta]	o casaco	l'habit (m.)
el café	o café	le café
la moneda	a moeda	la pièce de monnaie
frio	frio	froid
el invierno	o inverno	l'hiver (m.)
el color	a côr	la couleur
el peine	o pente	le peigne
venir (-ie-)	vir	venir
cómodo	confortável	confortable
comercial	comercial	commercial
la compañia	a companhia	la compagnie
quejarse	queixar-se	se plaindre
completamente	inteiramente	complètement
esconder	esconder	cacher
el concierto	o concêrto	le concert
el cónsul	o cônsul	le consul
contener (-ie-)	conter	contenir

VOCABULARY

ENGLISH	MALAY [INDONESIAN]	TAGALOG
continue, to	meneruskan	(nag)(pá)patuloy
convenient	sesuai [baik sekali]	maginhawa
conversation, the	perćakapan	úsapan
cook, to	memasak	(nag)(lú)lutò
cookie, the	kuéh	biskuwít
corkscrew, the	koterék	tribusón
corner (of room), the	sudut	sulok
corner (street), the	sudut	pánulukan
corridor, the	balai	koridór
costs, (it)	harganya	magkahalagá
cotton, the	kapas [katun]	bulak
cotton-wool, the	kapas [katun]	haluáng bulak at lana
count, to	membilang [menghitung]	b(um)i(bi)lang
country (nation), the	negeri	bayan
countryside, the	daérah pedalaman	lalawigan
course, of!	mémang! [tentu saja!]	talagá!
courtyard, the	halaman	patyo
cover, to	tutup	(nag)(tá)takip
crab, the	ketam [kepiting]	alimasag
cream, the	kepala susu	krema
cross, to	menyeberang	t(um)á(ta)wid
crowd, the	orang banyak	pulutóng ng tao
cup, the	ćawan [mangkok]	tasa
curry, the	gulai [kari]	kari
cushion, the	bantal alas	almuhadón
custom (way), the	adat kebiasaan	kustumbre
customs, the	kastam [béa-ćukai]	pag-uugali
cut, to	memotong	g(um)ú(gu)pít
dance, to	menari	s(um)á(sa)yáw
dangerous	merbahaya [berbahaya]	mapanganib
dark (colour)	berwarna tua	maitím
dark (no light)	gelap	madilím
day, the	hari	araw
daytime, the	siang [pagi hari]	araw
dead	mati	patáy
dear (expensive)	mahal	mahál
decide, to	memutuskan	(nag)(pá)pasiyá
deep	dalam	malalim
demand, to	meminta	h(in)i(hi)ngî
dentist, the	doktor gigi [dokter gigi]	dentista
desert, the	padang pasir	disyerto
diamond, the	intan	brilyante
dictionary, the	kamus	diksiyunaryo
die, to	mati	(na)(má)matáy
different	lain	magkaibá
difficult	sukar	mahirap

VOCABULARY

SPANISH	PORTUGUESE	FRENCH
continuar	continuar	continuer
cómodo	conveniente	commode
la conversación	a conversa	la conversation
cocinar	cozinhar	cuire
la galleta	o biscoito	le biscuit
el tirabuzón [el sacacorchos]	o saca-rôlhas	le tire-bouchon
el rincón	o canto	le coin
la esquina	a esquina	le coin
el corredor	o corredor	le couloir
cuesta	custa	coûte
el algodón	o algodão	le coton
el algodón	o algodão	l'ouate (f.)
contar (-ue-)	contar	compter
el país	o país	le pays
el campo	o interior	la campagne
¡claro!	naturalmente!	naturellement!
el patio	o pátio	la cour
cubrir	cobrir	couvrir
el cangrejo	o carangueio	le crabe
la crema	o crème	la crème
cruzar	atravessar	traverser
la multitud	a multidão	la foule
la taza	a xícara [a chávena]	la tasse
el curry	o curry	le curry
el cojín	a almofada	le coussin
la costumbre	o costume	l'usage (m.)
la aduana	a alfândega	la douane
cortar	cortar	couper
bailar	dançar	danser
peligroso	perigoso	dangereux
oscuro	escuro	foncé
oscuro	escuro	obscur
el día	o dia	le jour
el día	o dia	le jour
muerto	morto	mort
caro	caro	cher
decidir	decidir	se décider
hondo	fundo	profond
exigir	exigir	demander
el dentista	o dentista	le dentiste
el desierto	o deserto	le désert
el diamante	o diamante	le diamant
el diccionario	o dicionário	le dictionnaire
morir (-ue-)	morrer	mourir
diferente	diferente	différent
difícil	difícil	difficile

VOCABULARY

ENGLISH	MALAY [INDONESIAN]	TAGALOG
dinner, the	makan malam	hapunan
direction, the	arah	direksiyón
dirty	kotor	marumí
do, to	buat	g(um)á(ga)wâ
doctor, the	doktor [dokter]	doktór
dog, the	anjing	aso
don't!	jangan!	huwág mong . . . !
door, the	pintu	pintô
doubt, the	kebimbangan	pag-aálinlangan
down	bawah	ibabâ
dress (woman's), the	pakaian perempuan	bestido
drink, the	minuman	inumín
drink, to	minum	(um)i(i)nóm
drive (car), to	memandu [menyetir]	(nag)(má)maneho
driver, the	pemandu [supir]	tsupér
dry	kering	tuyô
duck, the	itik	pato
during	sedang	habang
dusty	berdebu	maalikabók
duty (obligation), the	kewajiban	tungkulin
each	tiap-tiap satu	bawa't isá
each other	masing-masing	bawa't isá
early (before time)	awal [ćepat]	maága
earrings, the	anting-anting	mga hikaw
east	timur	silangan
easy	mudah	maalwán
eat, to	makan	k(um)á(ka)in
egg, the	telur	itlóg
either . . . or	sama ada . . . atau [atau . . . atau]	. . . o kayá'y . . .
electric	léterék [listrik]	eléktrika
elevator, the	lift	élebeytor
embassy, the	kedutaan	embahada
empty	kosong	waláng lamán
enemy, the	musuh	kalaban
engine (car), the	motor	motór
enjoy, to	menyukai [menikmati]	(na)(sí)siyahán
enormous	sangat besar	lubháng malakí
enough	ćukup	sapát
enter, to	masuk	p(um)á(pa)sok
entrance, the	pintu masuk	pasukán
envelope, the	sampul	sobre
equal	sama	magkatulad
evening, the	malam	gabí
everybody	semua orang	bawa't isá
everything	segala sesuatu	bawa't bagay
everywhere	dimana-mana	saanmán

VOCABULARY

SPANISH	PORTUGUESE	FRENCH
la cena	o jantar	le dîner
la dirección	a direção	la direction
sucio	sujo	sale
hacer	fazer	faire
el médico	o médico	le médécin
el perro	o cachorro [o cão (os cães)]	le chien
¡ no . . . !	não!	ne . . . pas!
la puerta	a porta	la porte
la duda	a dúvida	le doute
abajo	em baixo	en bas
el vestido	o vestido	la robe
la bebida	a bebida	la boisson
tomar	beber	boire
manejar	guiar	conduire
el chofer	o/a motorista	le conducteur
seco	sêco	sec/sèche
el pato	o pato	le caneton
durante	durante	pendant
polvoriento	empoeirado	poussiéreux
el deber	o dever	le devoir
cada	cada	chaque
se . . . el uno al otro	um com o outro	l'un l'autre
temprano	cêdo	de bonne heure
los pendientes	os brincos	les boucles d'oreille (f.)
este	leste	est
fácil	fácil	facile
comer	comer	manger
el huevo	o ôvo	l'oeuf (m.)
o . . . o	ou . . . ou	ou . . . ou
electrico	elétrico	électrique
el ascensor	o elevador	l'ascenseur (m.)
la embajada	a embaixada	l'ambassade (f.)
vacio	vazio	vide
el enemigo	o inimigo/a inimiga	l'ennemi (m.)
el motor	o motor	le moteur
gozar de	divertir-se	prendre plaisir à
enorme	enorme	énorme
bastante	bastante	assez
entrar en	entrar em	entrer
la entrada	a entrada	l'entrée (f.)
el sobre	o envelope	l'enveloppe (f.)
igual	igual	égal
la tarde	a tarde	le soir
todo el mundo	todo mundo	tout le monde
todo	tudo	tout
en todas partes	em todo lugar	partout

VOCABULARY

ENGLISH	MALAY [INDONESIAN]	TAGALOG
exactly	betul	tamang-tamà
example, for	misalnya	halimbawà
except	selain	máliban sa
exhibition, the	paméran	tanghalan
exit, the	pintu keluar	lábasan
expect, to	mengharap	(um)á(a)sa
explain, to	menjelaskan	(nag)(pá)paliwanag
eye, the	mata	matá
face, the	muka	mukhâ
fact, in	sebenarnya	sa katótohánan
fail, to	tidak dapat	(na)(bí)bigô
fair (just)	adil	makatárungan
fall, to	jatuh	(na)(hú)hulog
family, the	keluarga	mag-anak
famous	termasyhur	tanyág
fan, the	kipas	abaniko
far	jauh	malayò
farmer, the	orang tani	magsasaká
fast	ćepat	matulin
fasten, to	mengikat	(nag)(ká)kabít
festival, the	perayaan	piyesta
fetch, to	mengambil	k(um)ú(ku)ha
few, a	beberapa	kauntî
field, the	lapangan	bukid
fight, to	bertengkar	l(um)á(la)ban
fill, to	mengisi	(nag)(pú)punô
film (for camera), the	filem [pilem]	pelíkulá
film (movie show), the	filem [gambar hidup]	pelíkulá
finally	akhirnya	sa wakás
find, to	dapat [menemukan]	(na)(ká)kakita
finish, to	habiskan	(na)(yá)yari
fire, the	api	apóy
first	yang pertama	una
fish, the	ikan	isdâ
flat	rata	patag
flat (tyre), the	panćet [ban kempés]	gomang hupâ
floor, the	lantai	suwelo
flower, the	bunga	bulaklák
fly, the	lalat	langaw
fly, to	terbang	l(um)i(li)pád
follow, to	mengikut	s(um)ú(su)nód
food, the	makanan	pagkain
foot, the	kaki	paá
football (game), the	bola [sepakbola]	putból
for	untuk	pará sa

VOCABULARY

SPANISH	PORTUGUESE	FRENCH
exactamente	exatamente	exactement
por ejemplo	por exemplo	par exemple
excepto	exceto	excepté
la exhibición	a exposição (-ões)	l'exposition (f.)
la salida	a saída	la sortie
esperar	esperar	attendre
explicar	explicar	expliquer
el ojo	o ôlho	l'oeil (m.)
la cara	o rôsto [a cara]	le visage
en realidad	de fato	en effet
fracasar	faltar	manquer
justo	justo	juste
caer	cair	tomber
la familia	a família	la famille
famoso	famoso	célèbre
el ventilador	o ventilador [a ventoinha]	l'éventail (m.)
lejos	longe	loin
el labrador	o fazendeiro	le fermier
rápido	depressa	vite
amarrar	apertar	fixer
la fiesta	o festival	la fête
traer	ir buscar	aller chercher
unos pocos	poucos	quelques
el campo [el terreno]	o campo	le champ
pelear	lutar	se battre
llenar	encher	remplir
el rollo [la película]	o filme [o rôlo]	le film
la película	o filme	le film
finalmente	finalmente	finalement
encontrar (-ue-)	achar	trouver
terminar	acabar	finir
el fuego	o fôgo [o lume]	le feu
primero	primeiro	premier
el pescado	o peixe	le poisson
plano	plano	plat
el pinchazo	o pneu furado	le pneu à plat
el piso	o chão	le plancher
la flor	a flôr	la fleur
la mosca	a môsca	la mouche
volar (-ue-)	voar	voler
seguir (-i-)	seguir	suivre
la comida	a comida	la nourriture
el pie	o pé	le pied
el partido de fútbol	o jôgo de futebol [o desafio de futebol]	le football
para	para	pour

295

VOCABULARY

ENGLISH	MALAY [INDONESIAN]	TAGALOG
forbidden	pantang [terlarang]	ipinagbábawal
foreign	luar [asing]	dayuhan
forest, the	hutan	gubat
forget, to	lupa	l(um)i(li)mot
fork, the	garpu	tinidór
former	dahulu	dati
forwards	kedepan	pasulóng
free (vacant)	kosong	bakante
fresh	baru	sariwà
fried	goréng	pinirito
fried rice, the	nasi goréng	piniritong kanin
friend, the	kawan	kaibigan
from	dari	buhat sa
front of, in	dimuka	sa haráp ng
frontier, the	batas	hangganan
frozen	membeku	ilado
fruit, the	buah	prutas
full	penuh	punô
garden, the	kebun	hálamanán
gasoline (petrol), the	minyak bénsin	gasolina
girl, the	budak perempuan [gadis]	batang babae
give, to	memberi	(nag)(bi)bigáy
glad	suka hati [senang]	masayá
glass (drinking), the	alat gelas	baso
glass (substance), the	kaća	salamín
glove, the	sarung tangan	guwantes
go, to	pergi	t(um)ú(tu)ngo
go down, to	turun	b(um)á(ba)bâ
go up, to	naik	(um)á(a)kyát
god, the	tuhan	diyós
gold, the	emas	gintô
good	baik	mabuti
goods, the	barang	mga bagay
government, the	pemerentah	gobyerno
gram, the	gram	gramo
grapes, the	buah anggur	mga ubas
grass, the	rumput	damó
green	hijau	lungtian
grey	kelabu	abuhín
ground, the	bumi	lupà
guard, to	menjaga	(nag)(bá)bantáy
guest, the	tamu	bisita
guide, the	pembimbing	patnubay
guidebook, the	buku pedoman	aklat-patnubay
gun, the	senapan	baril
hair, the	rambut	buhók
haircut, the	potong rambut	gupit

VOCABULARY

SPANISH	PORTUGUESE	FRENCH
prohibido	proïbido	défendu
extranjero	estrangeiro	étranger
el bosque	a floresta	la forêt
olvidar	esquecer de	oublier
el tenedor	o garfo	la fourchette
antiguo	anterior	antérieur
hacia adelante	para frente	en avant
libre	vago	libre
fresco	fresco	frais/fraîche
frito [estrellado]	frito	frit
el arroz frito	o arroz frito	le riz frit
el amigo/la amiga	o amigo/a amiga	l'ami/l'amie
desde	de	de
delante de	diante de	devant
la frontera	a fronteira	la frontière
helado	gelado [congelado]	gelé
la fruta	a fruta	les fruits (m.)
lleno	cheio	plein
el jardín	o jardim	le jardin
la gasolina	a gasolina	l'essence (f.)
la niña	a moça [a menina]	la fille
dar	dar	donner
feliz	feliz	heureux
el vaso	o copo	le verre
el vidrio	o vidro	le verre
el guante	a luva	le gant
ir	ir	aller
bajar	descer	descendre
subir	subir	monter
el dios	o deus	le dieu
el oro	o ouro	l'or (m.)
bueno	bom/boa	bon
las mercancías	as mercadorias	les biens (m.)
el gobierno	o govêrno	le gouvernement
el gramo	a grama	le gramme
las uvas	as uvas	les raisins (m.)
la hierba	a grama [a relva]	l'herbe (f.)
verde	verde	vert
gris	cinzento	gris
la tierra	o chão	la terre
vigilar a	guardar	garder
el huésped	o/a hóspede	l'invité/-ée
el/la guía	o/a guia	le guide
la guía	o guia	le guide
el fusil	a arma de fogo	le fusil
el cabello	o cabêlo	les cheveux (m.)
el corte de pelo	o corte de cabêlo	la coupe de cheveux

VOCABULARY

ENGLISH	MALAY [INDONESIAN]	TAGALOG
hairdresser, the	penata rambut	mángungulót
ham, the	daging paha babi	hamón
handbag, the	tas tangan	bag
handkerchief, the	sapu tangan	panyô
harbour, the	pelabohan	kublihan
hard (firm)	keras	matigás
hat, the	topi	sumbrero
have, to	mempunyai	(nag)(ká)karoón
he	dia	siyá
head, the	kepala	ulo
headache, the	sakit kepala	sakít ng ulo
hear, to	mendengar	(na)(rí)rinig
heart, the	jantong	pusò
heavy	berat	mabigát
height, the	tinggi	taás
help, to	menolong	t(um)ú(tu)long
her (adj.)	-nya	kaniyâ
here	disini	dito
high	tinggi	mataás
hill, the	bukit	buról
his	-nya	kaniyâ
hold, to	pegang	h(um)á(ha)wak
holy	kudus	sagrado
home, at	di rumah	sa bahay
honest	lurus [jujur]	matapát
hope, to	mengharap	(um)á(a)sa
horse, the	kuda	kabayo
hospital, the	rumah sakit	ospitál
host, the	tuan rumah	maybisita
hot (weather)	panas	mainit
hot (heated food, etc.)	panas	mainit
hot season (summer), the	musim panas	tag-init
hotel, the	hotél	otél
hour, the	jam	oras
house, the	rumah	bahay
how?	bagaimana?	paáno?
how many?	berapa?	ilán?
however (conj.)	akan tetapi	gayón man
hut, the	pondok	kubo
I	saya	akó
ice, the	air batu [és]	yelo
ice cream, the	éskrim	sorbetes
if	jikalau	kung
ill	sakit	may sakít
immediately	sekarang [segera]	kaagád
important	penting	mahalagá
impossible	tidak mungkin	di-mangyáyari

VOCABULARY

SPANISH	PORTUGUESE	FRENCH
el peluquero	o cabeleireiro/a cabeleireira	le coiffeur
el jamón	o presunto	le jambon
la cartera	a bôlsa [a mala de mão]	le sac à main
el pañuelo	o lenço	le mouchoir
el puerto	o pôrto	le port
duro	duro	dur
el sombrero	o chapéu	le chapeau
tener (-ie-)	ter	avoir
él	êle	il
la cabeza	a cabeça	la tête
el dolor de cabeza	a dor de cabeça	le mal de tête
oir	ouvir	entendre
el corazón	a coração (-ões)	le coeur
pesado	pesado	lourd
la altura	a altura	la hauteur
ayudar	ajudar	aider
su	seu/sua	son/sa/ses
aquí	aqui	ici
alto	alto	haut
la colina	a colina	la colline
su	seu/sua	son/sa/ses
tener (-ie-)	segurar	tenir
sagrado	santo	sacré
en casa	em casa	à la maison
honrado	honesto	honnête
esperar	esperar	espérer
el caballo	o cavalo	le cheval
el hospital	o hospital	l'hôpital (m.)
el dueño de casa	o anfitrião (-ões)	l'hôte (m.)
caliente	quente	chaud
caliente	quente	chaud
el verano	o verão (-ões)	l'été (m.)
el hotel	o hotel	l'hôtel (m.)
la hora	a hora	l'heure (f.)
la casa	a casa	la maison
¿cómo?	como?	comment?
¿cuántos/-as?	quantos/-as?	combien?
sin embargo	porém	cependant
el bohío [la choza]	a cabana	la cabane
yo	eu	je
el hielo	o gêlo	la glace
el helado	o sorvete [o gelado]	la glace
si	se	si
enfermo	doente	malade
inmediatamente	imediatamente	tout de suite
importante	importante	important
imposible	impossível	impossible

VOCABULARY

ENGLISH	MALAY [INDONESIAN]	TAGALOG
in	dalam	sa
information, the	maklumat [keterangan]	impormasyón
inside	didalam	sa loób
instead of	pengganti	sa halíp
interesting	menarék	kawili-wili
interpreter, the	juru bahasa	intérprete
iron (metal), the	besi	bakal
is	adalah	-ay
island, the	pulau	pulô
isn't it?	bukan?	hindî ba?
it	dia	siyá
jewellery, the	permata	alahas
journey, the	perjalanan	paglálakbáy
jump, to	lompat	l(um)ú(lu)ksó
jungle, the	rimba	kagubatan
key, the	kunći	susi
kill, to	membunuh	p(um)á(pa)táy
kilogram, the	kilo	kilo
kilometre, the	kilométer	kilómetró
kind (friendly)	ramah-tamah	mabaít
king, the	raja	hari
kiss, to	menćium	h(um)á(ha)lik
kitchen, the	dapur	kusina
knife, the	pisau	lanseta
know, to	tahu	(ná)(la)laman
label, the	lébal [étikét]	etiketa
lake, the	tasék [danau]	lawà
lamb, the	anak kambing	tupa
lamp, the	lampu	lampará
last	yang terakhir	hulí
late (behind time)	terlambat	tanghali
later on	kemudian	mámayâ
laugh, to	tertawa	t(um)á(ta)wa
laundry (clothes), the	pakaian menćući	lálabháng damít
law, the	undang-undang	batás
lawyer, the	peguam [pengaćara]	mánananggól
lead, to	pimpin	(um)á(a)kay
learn, to	belajar	(ná)(tu)tuto
least, at	sekurang-kurangnya	man lamang
leave (place), to	keluar	l(um)i(li)san
leave behind, to	meninggalkan	(in)i(i)wan
left (hand)	sebelah kiri	kaliwâ
leg, the	kaki	bintî
lemon, the	limau [jeruk limun]	kalamansî
lemonade, the	air limau [limun]	limonada
letter (note), the	surat	liham

VOCABULARY

SPANISH	PORTUGUESE	FRENCH
en	em	dans
la información	uma informação	les renseignements (m.)
dentro	dentro	dans
en vez de	em vez de	au lieu de
interesante	interessante	intéressant
el/la intérprete	o/a intérprete	l'interprète (m., f.)
el hierro	o ferro	le fer
es	é	est
la isla	a ilha	l'île (f.)
¿verdad?	não é?	n'est-ce pas?
lo	êle/ela	il/elle
las joyas	a joalheria	la bijouterie
el viaje	a viajem	le voyage
saltar	saltar	sauter
la selva	a selva	la jungle
la llave	a chave	le clef
matar	matar	tuer
el kilo	o quilo	le kilo
el kilómetro	o quilômetro	le kilomètre
amable	gentil	gentil
el rey	o rei	le roi
besar	beijar	baiser
la cocina	a cozinha	la cuisine
el cuchillo	a faca	le couteau
saber	saber	savoir
el rótulo	a etiquêta	l'etiquette (f.)
el lago	o lago	le lac
el cordero	o cordeiro	l'agneau (m.)
la luz	a lâmpada [o candieiro]	la lampe
último	último	dernier
tarde	atrasado	en retard
después	mais tarde	plus tard
reirse (-i-)	rir	rire
la ropa	a roupa	la blanchisserie
la ley	a lei	la loi
el abogado	o advogado	l'avocat (m.)
llevar	conduzir	conduire
aprender	aprender	apprendre
por lo menos	pelo menos	au moins
salir	partir [abalar]	partir
dejar	deixar	laisser
izquierdo	esquerdo	gauche
la pierna	a perna	la jambe
el limón	o limão (-ões)	le citron
la limonada	a limonada	la limonade
la carta	a carta	la lettre

VOCABULARY

ENGLISH	MALAY [INDONESIAN]	TAGALOG
letter (character), the	huruf	letra
lettuce, the	daun selada	litsugas
lie, the	bohong	kasinungalingan
lie down, to	berbaring	h(um)i(hi)gâ
lift, to	mengangkat	b(um)ú(bu)hat
light (colour)	warna muda	maputî
light (weight)	ringan	magaán
lighter (cigarette), the	gerétan	lighter
like (prep.)	saperti	kamukhâ
lipstick, the	ginću	lipstik
litre, the	liter	litro
little, a	sedikit	kauntî
live (reside), to	berdiam	t(um)i(ti)rá
lock, the	kunći	kandado
long (size)	panjang	mahabà
long (time)	lama	malaon
long ago	dahulu	noóng unang panahón
look at, to	melihat	t(um)i(ti)ngin
look for, to	menćari	h(um)á(ha)nap
lose (mislay), to	kehilangan	(na)(wá)walán
lose (race, etc.), to	kalah	(na)(tá)talo
loud	keras	malakás
love, to	kasih [ćinta]	(um)i(i)big
low	rendah	mababà
lunch, the	makan siang	tanghalian
machine, the	mesin	mákiná
magazine, the	majalah	mágasin
make, to	membuat	g(um)á(ga)wâ
malaria, the	malaria	malarya
man, the	orang laki-laki	lalaki
manager, the	pengurus [pemimpin]	mánedyér
mango, the	mangga	manggá
many	banyak	marami
map, the	peta	mapa
market, the	pasar	pámilihan
married	kawin [menikah]	may-asawa
matches, the	manćis api [korék api]	mga pósporó
means, (it)	bererti	nangángahulugán
measure, to	ukuran	s(um)ú(su)kat
meat, the	daging	karné
mechanic, the	ahli mesin	mekánikó
medicine, the	ubat	gamót
meet, to	bertemu	s(um)á(sa)lubong
melon, the	semangka	milón
menu, the	daftar makanan	menú
message, the	pesan	mensahe

VOCABULARY

SPANISH	PORTUGUESE	FRENCH
la letra	a letra	la lettre
la lechuga	alface	la laitue
la mentira	a mentira [a peta]	le mensonge
acostarse (-ue-)	deitar-se	se coucher
levantar	levantar	soulever
claro	claro	clair
liviano	leve	léger
el encendedor	o isqueiro	le briquet
como	como	comme
el lápiz de labios	o batom	le rouge à lèvres
el litro	o litro	le litre
un poco	pouco	un peu
vivir	morar	demeurer
la cerradura	a fechadura	la serrure
largo	comprido	long
largo	longo	long
hace tiempo	faz muito tempo	il y a longtemps
mirar	olhar	regarder
buscar	procurar	chercher
perder (-ie-)	perder	perdre
perder (-ie-)	perder	perdre
fuerte	alto	bruyant
querer (-ie-)	amar	aimer
bajo	baixo	bas
el almuerzo	o almôço	le déjeuner
la máquina	a máquina	la machine
la revista	a revista	le magazine
hacer	fazer	faire
el paludismo	a malária	le paludisme
el hombre	o homem	l'homme (m.)
el gerente [el encargado]	o gerente	le directeur
el mango	a manga	la mangue
muchos/-as	muitos/-as	beaucoup de
el mapa	o mapa	la carte
el mercado	o mercado [a praça]	le marché
casado	casado	marié
las cerillas [los fósforos]	os fósforos	les allumettes (f.)
significa	quer dizer	veut dire
medir (-i-)	medir	mesurer
la carne	a carne	la viande
el mecánico	o mecânico	le mécanicien
la medicina	o remédio	le médicament
encontrarse (-ue-)	encontrar	rencontrer
el melón	a melão (-ões)	le melon
el menú	o cardápio [a ementa]	le menu
el recado	a mensagem	le message

303

VOCABULARY

ENGLISH	MALAY [INDONESIAN]	TAGALOG
metre, the	méter	metro
middle, the	tengah	gitnâ
midnight	tengah malam	hátinggabí
milk, the	susu	gatas
millimetre, the	miliméter	milímetró
minute, the	minit	minuto
mirror, the	ćermin	salamín
mistake, the	salah	malî
moment, the	saat	saglít
monastery, the	tempat orang rahib [biara]	monasteryo
money, the	uang	kuwarta
month, the	bulan	buwán
monument, the	tanda peringatan	monumento
moon, the	bulan	buwán
more	lebih	lalò
morning, the	pagi hari	umaga
mosque, the	mesjid	meskita
mosquito, the	nyamuk	lamók
most	terbanyak·	pinaká
motor-bike, the	motosikal [sepéda motor]	motorsiklo
mountain, the	gunung	bundók
mouth, the	mulut	bungangà
movie camera, the	kamera hidup	sineng kámerá
much	banyak	marami
museum, the	muzium [musium]	museo
mushroom, the	ćendawan	kabuté
music, the	muzik [musik]	músiká
must	harus	dapat
mustard, the	mostar	mustasa
my	... saya	akin
name, the	nama	pangalan
napkin, the	tuala [serbét]	serbilyeta
narrow	sempit	makitid
natural	biasa	likás
near (not far)	dekat	malapit
near to	dekat	malapit sa
need, to	perlu	(na)(ngá)ngailangan
needle, the	jarum	karayom
never	belum pernah	hindî kailanmán
new	baru	bago
newspaper, the	surat khabar	páhayagán
next (after)	berikutnya	sa susunód
night, the	malam	gabí
no (adj.)	tidak ...	walâ
nobody	tidak siapa-siapa	waláng sinuman
noise, the	gaduh	ingay
noodles, the	mi	mike

VOCABULARY

SPANISH	PORTUGUESE	FRENCH
el metro	o metro	le mètre
el centro	o meio	le centre
media noche	meia noite	minuit
la leche	o leite	le lait
el milímetro	o milimetro	le millimètre
el minuto	o minuto	la minute
el espejo	o espêlho	le miroir
el error	o êrro	l'erreur (m.)
el momento	o momento	le moment
el monasterio	o mosteiro	le monastère
el dinero [la plata]	o dinheiro	l'argent (m.)
el mes	o mês	le mois
el monumento	o monumento	le monument
la luna	a lua	la lune
más	mais	plus
la mañana	a manhã	le matin
la mezquita	a mesquita	la mosquée
el mosquito	o mosquito	le moustique
lo máximo	o/a mais	le/la plus
la motocicleta	a motocicleta [a motorizada]	la moto
la montaña	a montanha	la montagne
la boca	a bôca	la bouche
la filmadora	a máquina de filmar	la caméra
mucho	muito	beaucoup
el museo	o museu	le musée
el champiñón [el hongo]	o cogumelo	le champignon
la música	a música	la musique
tener que	dever	doit
la mostaza	a mostarda	la moutarde
mi	meu/minha	mon/ma/mes
el nombre	o nome	le nom
la servilleta	o guardanapo	la serviette
angosto	estreito	étroit
natural	natural	naturel
cerca	perto	proche
cerca de	perto de	près de
necesitar	precisar de	avoir besoin de
la aguja	a agulha	l'aiguille (f.)
nunca	nunca	jamais
neuvo	nôvo	nouveau/nouvelle
el periódico [el diario]	o jornal	le journal
después	próximo	prochain
la noche	a noite	la nuit
nada de	nenhum	aucun
nadie	nunguém	personne
el ruido	o barulho	le bruit
los fideos	o macarrão	les nouilles (f.)

VOCABULARY

ENGLISH	MALAY [INDONESIAN]	TAGALOG
noon	tengah hari	tanghali
north	utara	hilagà
not	tidak	hindî
not at all	sekali-kali tidak	waláng anumán
notepaper, the	kertas ćatatan	sulatáng papél
nothing	tidak ada apa-apa	waláng-walâ
notice, the	pemberitahuan	paunawà
now	sekarang	ngayón
number, the	angka	númeró
nurse, the	jururawat	nars
nuts, the	buah berkulit keras	niyóg
obtain, to	mendapat	(na)(ká)kakuha
occupied	diduduki	okupado
offer, to	menawarkan	(nag)(há)handóg
office, the	pejabat [kantor]	tanggapan
officer (army), the	pegawan [opsir]	pinunò
often	kerapkali	madalás
oil, the	minyak	langís
old (persons)	tua	matandâ
old (things)	lama	lumà
olives, the	buah zaitun	oliba
on	diatas	sa ibabaw
once	sekali	minsán
onion, the	bawang	sibuyas
only	. . . sahaja [hanya]	lamang
open	buka	bukás
open, to	membuka	(nag)(bú)bukás
opera, the	opera	operá
opposite	bertentangan	kasalungát
or	atau	o
orange, the	jeruk manis	dalanghita
ordered	telah dipesan	nag-utos
ordinary	biasa	karaniwan
our	. . . kita	amin
outside	diluar	sa labás
overcoat, the	baju luar [mantel]	gabán
owe, to	berhutang	(um)ú(u)tang
oyster, the	tiram	talabá
pack, to	membungkus	(nag)(i)impake
pain, the	sakit	kirót
paint, the	ćat	pintura
pair, the	sepasang	pares
palace, the	istana	palasyo
paper, the	kertas	papél
parcel, the	bungkusan	pakete
park, the	taman	liwasan

VOCABULARY

SPANISH	PORTUGUESE	FRENCH
mediodía	meio dia	midi
norte	norte	nord
no	não	pas
no . . . nada	de modo algum	pas du tout
la esquela	o papel de carta	le papier à lettres
nada	nada	rien
el aviso	o aviso	l'avis (m.)
ahora	agora	maintenant
el número	o número	le numéro
la enfermera	a enfermeira	le/la garde-malade
las nueces	as nozes	les noix (f.)
obtener (-ie-)	obter	obtenir
ocupado	ocupado	occupé
ofrecer (-ezc-)	oferecer	offrir
la oficina	o escritório	le bureau
el oficial	o oficial	l'officier (m.)
a menudo	muitas vêzes	souvent
el aceite	o óleo	l'huile (f.)
viejo	velho	vieux/vieille
viejo	velho	vieux/vieille
las aceitunas	as azeitonas	les olives (f.)
sobre	em	sur
una vez	uma vez	une fois
la cebolla	a cebola	l'oignon (m.)
solamente	sòmente	seulement
abierto	aberto	ouvert
abrir	abrir	ouvrir
la ópera	a ópera	l'opéra (m.)
enfrente	em frente	en face
o	ou	ou
la naranja	a laranja	l'orange (f.)
pedido	encomendado	commandé
ordinario	ordinário	ordinaire
nuestro	nosso/-a	notre/nos
afuera	lá fora	en dehors
el abrigo [el tapado]	a capa	le pardessus
deber	dever	devoir
el ostión [la ostra]	a ostra	l'huître (f.)
empaquetar	fazer a mala	emballer
el dolor	a dor	la douleur
la pintura	a tinta	la peinture
el par	o par	la paire
el palacio	o palácio	le palais
el papel	o papel	le papier
el paquete	o pacote	le paquet
el parque	o parque	le parc

ENGLISH	MALAY [INDONESIAN]	TAGALOG
park (car), to	menempatkan [memarkir]	p(um)á(pa)rada
passport, the	paspot	pasport
pastry, the	kuéh	pastél
pay, to	bayar	(nag)(bá)bayad
peace, the	damai	kapayapaán
peach, the	buah persik	melokotón
pearl, the	mutiara	perlas
peas, the	kaćang hijau	mga gisantes
pen, the	péna	pluma
pencil, the	pénsel	lapis
pepper, the	lada	pamintá
perfume, the	minyak wangi	pabangó
perhaps	barangkali	marahil
permit, to	idzin	(nag)(pá)pahintulot
person, the	orang	tao
petrol (gasoline), the	minyak bénsin	gasolina
pharmacy, the	rumah ubat	botika
photograph, the	foto [poto]	retrato
picture, the	gambar	larawan
piece, the	sepotong	piraso
pillow, the	bantal	unan
pin, the	peniti	ispilí
pineapple, the	buah nenas	pinyá
pink	mérah muda	kulay rosas
place, the	tempat	lugár
plate, the	piring	plato
platform (railway), the	péron	plataporma
pleasant	sedap	nakalúlugód
plum, the	buah plum	siruwelas
point out, to	menunjukkan	it(in)ú(tu)rò
police station, the	balai polis [kantor polisi]	himpilan ng pulisyá
policeman, the	mata-mata [polisi]	pulis
poor (needy)	miskin	mahirap
pork, the	daging babi	karnéng baboy
porter, the	pemikul barang	portero
possible	mungkin	maáari
post-box, the	peti surat [kotakpos]	busón
postcard, the	pos kad [kartupos]	poskard
post-office, the	pejabat pos [kantor pos]	post opis
potatoes, the	ubi kentang	patatas
practise, to	melatih	(nag)(sa)sanay
prawn, the	udang	ulán̄g
present (gift), the	pemberian [hadiah]	rigalo
president, the	présidén	pangulo

VOCABULARY

SPANISH	PORTUGUESE	FRENCH
estacionar	estacionar	garer
el pasaporte	o passaporte	le passeport
el pastel	o doce	la pâtisserie
pagar	pagar	payer
la paz	a paz	la paix
el durazno [el melocotón]	o pessêgo	la pêche
la perla	a pérola	la perle
los chícharos [las arvejas]	as ervilhas	les petits pois (m.)
la pluma	a caneta	la plume
el lápiz	o lápis	le crayon
el pimiento	a pimenta	le poivre
el perfume	o perfume	le parfum
tal vez	talvez	peut-être
permitir	permitir	permettre
la persona	a pessoa	la personne
la gasolina	a gasolina	l'essence (f.)
la farmacia	a farmácia	la pharmacie
la fotografía	a fotografia	la photographie
el cuadro	o quadro	l'image (f.)
el pedazo	o pedaço	le morceau
la almohada	o travesseiro [a travesseira]	l'oreiller (m.)
el alfiler	o alfinête	l'épingle (f.)
la piña	o abacaxi [o ananás]	l'ananas (m.)
rosado	côr de rosa	rose
el lugar	o lugar	la place
el plato	o prato	l'assiette (f.)
el andén	a plataforma	le quai
agradable	agradável	agréable
la ciruela	a ameixa	la prune
indicar	mostrar	indiquer
la estación de policía [la comisaría]	a delegacia [o posto da polícia]	le commissariat de police
el agente de policía	o guarda [o polícia]	l'agent de police (m.)
pobre	pobre	pauvre
la carne de cerdo	o porco	le porc
el cargador [el mozo]	o carregador [o descarregador]	le porteur
posible	possível	possible
el buzón	a caixa postal	la boîte aux lettres
la tarjeta postal	o cartão postal [o bilhete postal]	la carte postale
la oficina de correos	a agência do correio [a estação dos correios]	le bureau de poste
las patatas [las papas]	as batatas	les pommes de terre (f.)
hacer ejercicios de	praticar	s'exercer
el langostino [la gamba]	o camarão (-ões)	la crevette
el regalo	o presente	le cadeau
el/la presidente	o/a presidente	le président

VOCABULARY

| --- | --- | --- |
press (clothes), to	menyeterika	(nag)(pa)plantsa
pretty	canték	magandá
price, the	harga	halagá
priest, the	paderi [pendeta]	pari
prison, the	penjara	bilangguan
private	pribadi	pansarili
promise, to	janji	(na)(ngá)ngakò
province, the	daérah [propinsi]	probinsiyá
public	umum	pampúblikó
pull, to	menarék	h(um)i(hi)la
puncture, the	bocor	butas
pure	murni	dalisay
purple	ungu	biyoleta
put, to	menaruh	(nag)(lá)lagáy
quantity, the	jumlah	dami
queen, the	ratu	reyna
question, the	pertanyaan	tanóng
quick	cepat	madalî
quiet	diam	tahimik
race (contest), the	perlumbaan	karera
radio, the	radio	radyo
railway, the	jalan keréta api	daáng-bakal
raincoat, the	jas hujan	kapote
raining, it is	turun hujan	umúulán
razor, the	pisau cukur	pang-ahit
read, to	membaca	b(um)á(ba)sa
ready	siap	handâ
receive, to	menerima	t(um)á(ta)nggáp
record (gramophone), the	piringan hitam	plaka
red	mérah	pulá
register (letter), to	mendaftar	ip(in)a(ré)rehístro
religion, the	ugama [agama]	relihiyón
remember, to	ingat	(na)(tá)tandaán
repair, to	memperbaiki	(nag)(kú)kumpuné
repeat, to	mengulangi	(in)ú(u)lít
reply, to	jawab	s(um)á(sa)gót
rest, to	beristirahat	(nag)(pá)pahingá
restaurant, the	réstoran	restawrán
result, the	akibat	kinálabasán
rice (cooked), the	nasi	kanin
rich	kaya	mayaman
right (correct)	tepat	wastô
right (hand)	sebelah kanan	kanan
ring, the	cincin	singsing
ripe	masak	hinóg

VOCABULARY

SPANISH	PORTUGUESE	FRENCH
planchar	passar	repasser
bonito	lindo	joli
el precio	o preço	le prix
el sacerdote	o padre	le prêtre
la cárcel [la prisión]	a prisão (-ões)	la prison
privado	particular	privé
prometer	prometer	promettre
la provincia	a província [o estado]	la province
público	público	publique
tirar de	puxar	tirer
el pinchazo	o furo	la crevaison
puro	puro	pur
morado	roxo	pourpre
poner	pôr	mettre
la cantidad	a quantidade	la quantité
la reina	a rainha	la reine
la pregunta	a pergunta	la question
rápido	rápido	vite
tranquilo	tranquilo	tranquille
la carrera	a corrida	la course
el radio	o rádio [a telefonia]	la radio
el ferrocarril	a estrada de ferro [o caminho de ferro]	le chemin de fer
el impermeable [la gabardina]	o impermeável	l'imperméable (m.)
llueve	está chovendo	il pleut
la máquina de afeitar	a navalha	le rasoir
leer	ler	lire
preparado	pronto	prêt
recibir	receber	recevoir
el disco	o disco	le disque
rojo	vermêlho [encarnado]	rouge
certificar	registrar [registar]	enregistrer
la religión	a religião (-ões)	la religion
acordarse (-ue-)	lembrar-se de	se souvenir de
componer	consertar [reparar]	réparer
repetir (-i-)	repetir	répéter
contestar	responder	répondre
descansar	descansar	se reposer
el restaurante	o restaurante	le restaurant
el resultado	o resultado	le résultat
el arroz	o arroz	le riz
rico	rico	riche
correcto	certo	correct
derecho	direito	droit
el anillo	o anel	la bague
maduro	maduro	mûr

VOCABULARY

ENGLISH	MALAY [INDONESIAN]	TAGALOG
river, the	sungai	ilog
road, the	jalan	lansangan
roast	panggang	mag-ihaw
room, the	kamar	kuwarto
run, to	lari	t(um)á(ta)kbó
sad	susah hati [sedih]	malungkót
safe	aman	ligtás
sailor, the	anak kapal [pelaut]	magdaragát
salt, the	garam	asín
same	sama	pareho
sandals, the	sandal	mga sandalyas
sandwich, the	sandwich [sa-suap dengan roti]	sanwits
sauce, the	kićap [saus]	sarsa
say, to	kata	(nag)(sá)sabi
school, the	sekolah	eskuwelahán
science, the	ilmu sain	siyensiyá
scissors, the	gunting	gunting
sea, the	laut	dagat
seat, the	kerusi [tempat duduk]	úpúan
second	yang kedua	ikalawá
second (of time), the	saat	segundo
secretary, the	setiausaha [sekretaris]	kalihim
see, to	lihat	t(in)i(ti)ngnán
seems, (it)	rupanya	tila
seldom	jarang	bihirà
sell, to	menjual	(nag)(bi)bilí
send (thing), to	mengirim	(nag)(pá)padalá
separate	terpisah	hiwaláy
servant, the	orang gaji [pelayan]	utusán
service station, the	pompa bensin	himpilan
several	beberapa	ilán
sew, to	menjahit	t(um)à(ta)hî
shallow	dangkal	mababaw
shampoo, the	langir	panggugò
shave, to	berćukur	(nag)(á)ahit
she	dia	siyá
sheet, the	seperei	kumot
shelter, the	perlindungan	kanlungan
ship, the	kapal	barkó
shirt, the	keméja	kamisadentro
shoe, the	sepatu	sapatos
shop, the	kedai	tindahan
short	péndek	maiklî
show, to	memperlihatkan	(nag)(pa)pakita
shower, the	panćuran	dutsa

VOCABULARY

SPANISH	PORTUGUESE	FRENCH
el río	o rio	le fleuve
la carretera	a estrada	la route
asado	assado	rôti
la habitación	o quarto	la salle
correr	correr	courir
triste	triste	triste
seguro	seguro	en sûreté
el marinero	o marinheiro	le marin
la sal	o sal	le sel
mismo	mesmo	même
las sandalias	as sandálias	les sandales (f.)
el sandwich	o sanduíche [o sande]	le sandwich
la salsa	o môlho	la sauce
decir (-i-)	dizer	dire
la escuela	a escola	l'école (f)
la ciencia	a ciência	la science
las tijeras	a tesoura	les ciseaux (m.)
el mar	o mar	la mer
el asiento	o lugar	la place
segundo	segundo	deuxième
el segundo	o segundo	le second
el secretario/la secretaria	o secretário/a secretária	le/la secrétaire
ver	ver	voir
parece	parece	paraît
rara vez	raramente	rarement
vender	vender	vendre
mandar	mandar	expédier
separado	separado	séparé
el criado/la criada	o empregado/a empregada	le/la domestique
el puesto de gasolina	o pôsto de gasolina [a estação de serviço]	la station-service
varios/-as	vários/-as	plusieurs
coser	costurar	coudre
poco profundo	pouco profundo	peu profond
el champú	o shampú [o champô]	le shampooing
afeitar	fazer a barba	se raser
ella	ela	elle
la sábana	o lençol	le drap
el refugio	o abrigo	l'abri (m.)
el barco	o navio	le navire
la camisa	a camisa	la chemise
el zapato	o sapato	la chaussure
la tienda	a loja	le magasin
corto	curto	court
indicar	mostrar	montrer
la ducha	o chuveiro	la douche

VOCABULARY

ENGLISH	MALAY [INDONESIAN]	TAGALOG
side, the	sebelah	gilid
sign, to	menandatangani	(ni)(lá)lagdaán
silk, the	sutera	sutlâ
silver, the	pérak	pilak
since (time)	dari	mulâ
sing, to	menyanyi	k(um)á(ka)ntá
sit, to	duduk	(um)ú(u)pô
skirt, the	kain sarung [rok]	palda
sky, the	langit	langit
sleep, to	tidur	(na)(tú)tulog
slow	lambat	mabagal
small	kećil	maliít
smoke, to	merokok	h(um)i(hi)tít
snow, the	thalji [salju]	niyebe
soap, the	sabun	sabón
socks, the	sarung kaki [kaus kaki]	medyas
soda water, the	air belanda	soda
soft	lembék [lunak]	malambót
soldier, the	soldadu [serdadu]	kawal
some	beberapa	mga ilán
somebody	seseorang	may tao
something	sesuatu	may bagay
sometimes	kadang-kadang	kung minsán
somewhere	sesuatu tempat	sa kung saán
soon	segera	agád
sorry	sesal	nagdáramdám
soup, the	sup	sopas
sour	masam	maasim
south	selatan	timog
soy sauce, the	tauyu [kećap]	toyò
space, the	angkasa	kalawakan
speak, to	berćakap [berbićara]	(nag) (sá)salitâ
spectacles, the	ćermin mata [kaćamata]	salamin
spoon, the	sendok	kutsara
sport, the	olahraga	isport
square (place), the	lapangan	plasa
stairs, the	tangga rumah	hagdán
stamp (postage), the	setém [perangko]	selyo
stand, to	berdiri	t(um)á(ta)yô
star, the	bintang	bituin
start, to	memulai	(nag)(si)simulâ
station (railway), the	setésén [setasiun]	estasyón
stay, to	tinggal	(na)(ná)natili
steak, the	bistik	bisték
steep	ćuram [terjal]	matarík
steering, the	setir	manibela
stick, the	tongkat	kawayan

314

VOCABULARY

SPANISH	PORTUGUESE	FRENCH
el lado	o lado	le côté
firmar	assinar	signer
la seda	a sêda	la soie
la plata	a prata	l'argent (m.)
desde	desde	depuis
cantar	cantar	chanter
sentarse (-ie-)	sentar-se	s'asseoir
la falda [la pollera]	a saia	la jupe
el cielo	o céu	le ciel
dormir (-ue-)	dormir	dormir
lento	devagar	lent
pequeño	pequeno	petit
fumar	fumar	fumer
la nieve	a neve	la neige
el jabón	o sabonete	le savon
los calcetines	as meias [os peúgos]	les chaussettes (f.)
la soda	a soda [a água de sifão]	le soda
blando	mole	mou
el soldado	o soldado	le soldat
unos/unas	algum/-uma	quelque
alguien	alguém	quelqu'un
algo	qualquer coisa	quelque chose
a veces	algumas vêzes	quelquefois
alguna parte	em algum lugar	quelque part
pronto	em breve	bientôt
siento	sentido	peiné
la sopa	a sopa	la soupe
agrio	azêdo	aigre
sur	sul	sud
la salsa de soya	o môlho de soja	la sauce de soya
el espacio	o espaço	l'espace (m.)
hablar	falar	parler
las gafas	os óculos	les lunettes (f.)
la cuchara	a colher	la cuillère
el deporte	o esporto [o desporto]	le sport
la plaza	a praça	la place
la escalera	a escada	l'escalier (m.)
la estampilla	o sêlo de correio	le timbre
levantarse [pararse]	ficar de pé	être debout
la estrella	a estrêla	l'étoile (f.)
comenzar (-ie-)	começar	commencer
la estación del ferrocarril	a estação de trem	la gare
permanecer (-ezc-)	ficar	rester
el bistec [el filete]	o bife	la tranche
escarpado	ingreme	escarpé
el volante	o volante	la direction
el palo	a bengala	le bâton

VOCABULARY

ENGLISH	MALAY [INDONESIAN]	TAGALOG
still (adv.)	masih	hanggáng ngayón
stockings, the	sarung kaki [kaus kaki]	medyas
stone, the	batu	bató
storey (floor), the	tingkat	palapág
straight on	maju	diretso
strap, the	tali kulit	tali
street, the	jalan	kalye
streetcar (tram), the	keréta trém [trém]	trambiyá
string, the	tali	sinulid
strong	kuat	malakás
student, the	pelajar	mag-aarál
study, to	belajar	(nag)(á)aral
substance, the	benda [zat]	sustánsiyá
suddenly	tiba-tiba	kapagdaka
sugar, the	gula	asukal
suitcase, the	bég pakaian [kopor]	maleta
summit, the	puncak	tuktók
sun, the	matahari	araw
sweet	manis	matamís
swim, to	berenang	l(um)á(la)ngóy
table, the	méja	mesa
tailor, the	tukang jahit	sastre
take, to	mengambil	k(um)ú(ku)ha
tall	tinggi	matangkád
tap, the	pili [keran]	tapík
tape (recording), the	tép	pagkikintál-tinig
tape recorder, the	téprekorder	nagkikintál-tinig
taste, to	mengecap	t(um)i(ti)kím
tax, the	cukai [pajak]	buwís
taxi, the	téksi [taksi]	taksi
tea (to drink), the	téh	tsa
teach, to	mengajar	(nag)(tú)turó
teacher, the	guru	guró
telegram, the	kawat taligeram [télgram]	telegrama
telephone, the	talipon [télpon]	telépónó
television, the	talivésyen [télévisi]	telebisyón
temperature, the	suhu	temperatura
temple, the	kuil	templo
than	daripada	kaysa
that	itu	iyón
theatre, the	panggung	tanghalan
their	... meréka	kanilá
then (at that time)	pada waktu itu	noón
there	disana	doón
there is	ada	may

VOCABULARY

SPANISH	PORTUGUESE	FRENCH
todavía	ainda	encore
las medias	as meias [as compridas]	les bas (m.)
la piedra	a pedra	la pierre
el piso	o andar	l'étage (m.)
derecho	reto	tout droit
la correa	a correia	la courroie
la calle	a rua	la rue
el tranvía	o bonde [o elétrico]	le tramway
la cuerda [el cordón]	o barbante [o cordel]	la ficelle
fuerte	forte	fort
el/la estudiante	o aluno/a aluna	l'étudiant/-ante
estudiar	estudar	étudier
la sustancia	a substância	la substance
de repente	de repente	soudainement
el azúcar	o açúcar	le sucre
la maleta	a mala	la valise
la cima	o pico	le sommet
el sol	o sol	le soleil
dulce	dôce	doux
nadar	nadar	nager
la mesa	o mesa	la table
el sastre	o alfaiate	le trailleur
llevar	pegar	prendre
alto	alto	grand
el grifo [la llave del agua]	a torneira	le robinet
la cinta magnética	a fita	la bande
la grabadora	o gravador	le magnétophone
probar	sentir o gôsto de	goûter
el impuesto	o impôsto	l'impôt (m.)
el taxi	o táxi	le taxi
el té	o chá	le thé
enseñar	ensinar	enseigner
el maestro	o professor	le professeur
el telegrama	o telegrama	le télégramme
el teléfono	o telefone	le téléphone
la televisión	a televisão	la télévision
la temperatura	a temperatura	la température
el templo	o templo	le temple
que	que	que
ese	aquilo	cela
el teatro	o teatro	le théâtre
su	seu/sua	leur/leurs
entonces	naquela vez	en ce temps-là
allí	lá	là
hay	tem	il y a

VOCABULARY

ENGLISH	MALAY [INDONESIAN]	TAGALOG
they	meréka	silá
thick	tebal	makapál
thin	tipis	payát
thing, the	benda	bagay
think, to	berfikir	(nag)(i)isíp
third	yang ketiga	ikatló
thirsty	haus	uháw
this	ini	iré
thread, the	benang	sinulid
through	terus	sa
throw, to	melémparkan	p(um)ú(pu)kól
ticket, the	tékét [karćis]	tiket
ticket-office, the	tempat penjualan tékét [tempat penjualan karćis]	takilya
tie, the	tali léhér [dasi]	kurbata
time, the	waktu	panahón
timetable, the	jadwal	taláorasán
tin opener, the	pembuka blék	abre-lata
tip (money), the	hadiah	pabuyà
tired	letih	pagód
to	ke-	sa
tobacco, the	tembakau	tabako
today	hari ini	ngayón
together	bersama-sama	magkasama
toilet (men), the	jamban	kasilyas
toilet (women), the	jamban	kasilyas
toilet paper, the	kertas jamban	pamandewang
tomato, the	buah tomato [tomat]	kamatis
tomb, the	kubur [kuburan]	puntód
tomorrow	bésok	bukas
tonight	malam ini	mámayáng gabí
too (much)	terlampau	labis
toothbrush, the	berus gigi [sikat gigi]	sipilyo ng ngipin
toothpaste, the	ubat gigi [pasta-gigi]	kolgeit
touch, to	menyentuh	h(um)í(hi)pò
tourist, the	pelanćong	turista
towards	ke arah	patungo ukol sa
towel, the	tuala [anduk]	tuwalya
tower, the	menara	tore
town, the	bandar [kota]	bayan
town hall, the	déwan bandaran [balaikota]	munisipyo
train, the	keréta api	tren

VOCABULARY

SPANISH	PORTUGUESE	FRENCH
ellos/-as	êles/elas	ils/elles
grueso	grosso	épais
delgado	magro	mince
la cosa	a coisa	la chose
creer	pensar	penser
tercio	terceiro	troisième
con sed	com sêde	assoiffé
esto	isso	ceci
el hilo	a linha	le fil
a través	através	à travers
tirar	jogar	jeter
el billete	a passagem [o bilhete]	le billet
la taquilla [la boletería]	o guichê	le guichet
la corbata	a gravata	la cravate
la hora	o tempo	le temps
la guía [el horario]	o horário	l'horaire (f.)
el abrelatas	o abridor de latas [o abrelatas]	l'ouvre-boîte (m.)
la propina	a gorjeta	le pourboire
cansado	cansado	fatigué
a	para	à
el tabaco	o fumo [o tabaco]	le tabac
hoy	hoje	aujourd'hui
juntos/-as	juntos/-as	ensemble
el baño de caballeros	o banheiro dos homens [o retrete dos homens]	la toilette des messieurs
el baño de señoras	o banheiro das senhoras [o retrete das senhoras]	la toilette des dames
el papel higiénico	o papel higiènico	le papier hygiénique
el tomate	o tomate	la tomate
la tumba	a tumba	la tombe
mañana	amanhã	demain
esta noche	esta noite	ce soir
demasiado	demais	trop
el cepillo de dientes	a escôva de dentes	la brosse à dents
la pasta de dientes	a pasta de dentes	la pâte dentifrice
tocar	tocar	toucher
el/la turista	o/a turista	le/la touriste
hacia	para	vers
la toalla	a toalha [o lençol]	la serviette
la torre	a tôrre	la tour
el pueblo	a cidade	la ville
el ayuntamiento	a prefeitura [a câmara Municipal]	l'hôtel de ville (m.)
el tren	o trem [o comboio]	le train

VOCABULARY

ENGLISH	MALAY [INDONESIAN]	TAGALOG
tram, the	kerĕta trém [trém]	trambiyá
translate, to	menterjemahkan	(nag)(sá)salin
travel, to	berjalan [bepergian]	(nag)(lá)lakbáy
tree, the	pokok [pohon]	punungkahoy
trouble, the	kesukaran	ligalig
trousers, the	seluar [ćelana]	salawál
true	benar	totoó
try on, to	menćoba	(nag)(sú)sukat
turn, in	bergilir	turnúhan
twice	dua kali	makálawá
typewriter, the	mesin taip [mesin tik]	makinílya
typist, the	juru taip [juru tik]	taypis
tyre, the	tayar [ban]	gulóng na goma
ugly	buruk [jelék]	pangit
umbrella, the	payung	payong
under	dibawah	sa ilalim ng
understand, to	mengerti	(um)i(i)ntindí
unfortunately	malangnya [sayang]	sa kasamaáng-palad
university, the	unibersity [universitas]	pámantasan
until	sampai	hanggáng
upstairs	diatas	sa itaás
urgently	sangat segera	kailangang-kailangan
usually	biasanya	karaniwan
valley, the	jurang [lembah]	lambák
valuable	berharga	mahalagá
veal, the	daging anak lembu	karné ng guyà
vegetables, the	sayor-sayoran	mga gulay
very	sangat	lubhâ
view (outlook), the	pemandangan	palagáy tánawin
village, the	dĕsa	nayon
visit, to	mengunjongi	d(um)á(da)law
voyage, the	pelayaran	paglálayág
wait for, to	menanti	(nag)(hí)hintáy
waiter, the	pelayan	serbidór
walk, to	jalan kaki	(nag)(lá)lakád
wall (of room), the	dinding	dingding
wall (garden, etc.), the	tĕmbok	padér
want, to	mahu [mau]	gustó
war, the	perang	digmaan
wash, to	membasuh [menćući]	(nag)(hú)hugás
washbasin, the	tempat basuh tangan [waskom]	lababo
watch, the	jam tangan [arloji]	relós
watch, to	memperhatikan	(nag)(má)masid
water, the	air	tubig
we	kami	kami
weather, the	ćuaća [hawa]	panahón
week, the	minggu	linggó

VOCABULARY

SPANISH	PORTUGUESE	FRENCH
el tranvia	o bonde [o elétrico]	le tramway
traducir (-uzc-) ·	traduzir	traduire
viajar	viajar	voyager
el árbol	a árvore	l'arbre (m.)
el apuro	a dificuldade	la peine
los pantalones	as calças	le pantalon
verdadero	verdade	vrai
probarse	provar	essayer
por turno	em ordem	tour à tour
dos veces	duas vêzes	deux fois
la máquina de escribir	a máquina de escrever	la machine à ecrire
el dactilógrafo/la dactilógrafa	o datilógrafo/a datilógrafa	le/la dactylo
la llanta [el neumático]	o pneu	le pneu
feo	feio	laid
el paraguas	o guarda-chuva	le parapluie
debajo de	debaixo de	sous
comprender	compreender	comprendre
desgraciadamente	infelizmente	malheureusement
la universidad	a universidade	l'université (f.)
hasta	até	jusqu'à
arriba	em cima	en haut
urgentemente	urgente	d'urgence
normalmente	geralmente	d'habitude
el valle	o vale	la vallée
valioso	valioso	précieux
la ternera	a carne de vitela	le veau
las legumbres	os legumes	les légumes (m.)
muy	muito	très
la vista	a vista	la vue
el pueblo	a aldeia	le village
visitar	visitar	visiter
el viaje	a viagem	le voyage
esperar	esperar	attendre
el camarero [el mozo]	o garçom [o criado de mesa]	le garçon
andar	ir a pé	marcher
la pared	a parede	le mur
la tapia	o muro	le mur
querer (-ie-)	querer	désirer
la guerra	a guerra	la guerre
lavar	lavar	laver
el lavatorio	a pia [o lavatório]	le lavabo
el reloj	o relógio	la montre
observar	olhar	garder
el agua	a água	l'eau (f.)
nosotros/-as	nós	nous
el tiempo	o tempo	le temps
la semana	a semana	la semaine

VOCABULARY

ENGLISH	MALAY [INDONESIAN]	TAGALOG
weight, the	berat	timbáng
well (adv.)	dengan baik	nang mabuti
well (health)	sihat	malusóg
west	barat	kanluran
wet	basah	basâ
wet season, the	musim hujan	tag-ulán
wharf, the	pengkalan	dáungan
what?	apa?	anó?
wheel, the	roda	gulóng
when?	bila?	kailán?
where (is it)?	dimana?	násaán?
where (to)?	kemana?	saán?
which?	yang mana?	alín?
white	putih	putî
who?	siapa?	sino?
whose?	... siapa punya?	kanino?
why?	mengapa?	bakit?
wide	lébar	maluwáng
wild	liar	mabangís
win, to	menang	(na)(nà)nalo
wind, the	angin	hangin
window, the	jendéla	dúrungawan
wine, the	air anggur [anggur]	alak
wise	arif	matalino
with	dengan	na may
without	tanpa	na walâ
woman, the	perempuan	babae
wonder, to	ingin tahu	(nag)(tá)taká
wonderful	ajaib	kahanga-hangà
wood (timber), the	kayu	kahoy
wool, the	kain wol	lana
word, the	kata	salitâ
work, the	pekerjaan	gáwain
workman, the	pekerja	manggagawà
world, the	dunia	mundó
worse	lebih burok	lalong masamâ
worst	yang terburok	pinakámasamâ
worth, to be	berharga	(nag)(ká)ka halagá
write, to	menulis	s(um)ú(su)lat
wrong	salah	malî
year, the	tahun	taón
yellow	kuning	diláw
yesterday	kemarin	kahapon
you	awak	ikáw
young	muda	batà
your	... awak	iyó

VOCABULARY

SPANISH	PORTUGUESE	FRENCH
el peso	o pêso	le poids
bien	bem	bien
sano	bem	en bonne santé
oeste	oeste	ouest
mojado	molhado	mouillé
la estación de lluvia	a estação chuvosa	la saison pluvieuse
muelle	o cais	le quai
¿qué?	quê?	que?
la rueda	a roda	la roue
¿cuando?	quando?	quand?
¿dónde?	onde?	où?
¿dónde?	para onde?	où?
¿cuál?	qual?	quel?
blanco	branco	blanc/blanche
¿quién?	quem?	qui?
¿de quién?	de quem?	de qui?
¿por qué?	por quê?	pourquoi?
ancho	largo	large
salvaje	selvagem	sauvage
ganar	ganhar	gagner
el viento	o vento	le vent
la ventana	a janela	la fenêtre
el vino	o vinho	le vin
sensato	sábio	sage
con	com	avec
sin	sem	sans
la señora	a mulher	la femme
preguntarse	querer saber	se demander
maravilloso	maravilhoso	merveilleux
la madera	a madeira	le bois
la lana	a lã	la laine
la palabra	a palavra	le mot
el trabajo	o trabalho	le travail
el trabajador	o operário	l'ouvrier (m.)
el mundo	o mundo	le monde
peor	pior	pire
el/la peor	o/a pior	le/la pire
valer	valer	valoir
escribir	escrever	écrire
incorrecto	errado	mauvais
el año	o ano	l'an (m.)
amarillo	amarelo	jaune
ayer	ontem	hier
usted	o senhor/a senhora	vous
joven	nôvo	jeune
su	. . . do senhor/ . . . da senhora	votre/vos

PART V

NEW GUINEA PIDGIN
FIJIAN
TONGAN
SAMOAN
TAHITIAN

NEW GUINEA PIDGIN

Sometimes called Neo-Melanesian. This is the officially recognised common language of Papua New Guinea, where it is spreading even in areas previously dominated by English or Police Motu. It is spoken with variations in the Solomons and Vanuatu (New Hebrides) and resembles the Pidgin that was once widespread in the Pacific, Southeast Asia and Australia.

It is written phonetically in the roman alphabet. Although vocabulary is mainly of English origin, the language needs to be learned as a foreign one.

PRONUNCIATION Vowels A, E, I, O, U are like *ah, eh, ee, oh, oo,* but generally fairly short.

Diphthongs AI, AU as *igh, ow.*

Consonants as in English, except that P is somewhere between *p* and *f*; S is always as *ss,* never *z.*

Stress is broadly as in the English source-words, but less emphatic.
Pronunciation is sometimes closer to standard English than the spelling suggests.

NOUNS, ARTICLES Nouns have no separate plural form, but the distinction between singular and plural is made with the use of articles:

dispela man, "the man," "this man," "that man"
wanpela man, "a man"
ol man, "the men," "men"
sampela man, "some men"

The word for "all" is *olgeta*; *olgeta meri,* "all women," "all the women"

PRONOUNS The singular pronouns are *mi,* "I"; *yu,* "you"; *em,* "he, she, it."

In the first person plural a distinction is made between *yumi,* for "we, us" in the sense of "you and I," and *mipela* for "we, not you." (Also *yumipela* for "you and we.") The other plural pronouns are *yupela,* "you" (plural), and *ol,* "they."

Numerals *tu, tri,* are frequently incorporated in the plural pronouns; for example, *yumitupela,* "the two of us, you and I"; *mitupela* "the two of us, not you"; *yutripela,* "the three of you"; *oltripela,* "the three of them."

Pronouns are invariable, except that *em* becomes *en* in object position or after a preposition, when it refers back to a thing (not person) previously mentioned: *Mi gat en,* "I have it"; *dua bilongen,* "its door."

ADJECTIVES There are three different styles:

1. Monosyllables preceding the noun, with *-pela* attached: *bikpela man,* "big man"; *naispela meri,* "pretty woman." (Some of these have *-pela* wherever they occur, and are so shown in the vocabulary.)

2. Adjectives of two or more syllables, following the noun: *man nogut,* "bad man"; *maunten antap,* "high mountain." Note the exception *liklik,* which precedes: *liklik pikinini,* "small child."

3. Relative clauses following the noun: *klos i bruk,* "torn clothes"; *man i gat moni,* "rich man."

Comparatives are formed with *moa,* and "than" is *long* or *olsem*: thus *moa bikpela long* or *moa bikpela olsem,* "bigger than."

For superlatives, follow the adjective with *moa, olgeta, tru* or *tumas,* or precede it with *nambawan*: thus *nambawan bikpela diwai,* "the biggest tree."

Nouns qualifying other nouns follow them: *haus pos,* "post office."

327

ADVERBS are like the corresponding adjectives, but without *-pela*.

PREPOSITIONS *Bilong* indicates possession, as in *bek bilong mi*, "my bag," and sometimes purpose, as *gut bilong kaikai*, "good to eat."

For all other prepositions, use *long*, if necessary with a qualifying adverb: *bihain long*, "behind," "after"; *klostu long*, "near."

Note the use of *i go* and *i kam* before *long*: *i kam long ples*, "(coming) to or from the village."

"With" is usually *wantaim long*, sometimes just *wantaim*.

VERBS Verbs are introduced by *i*, except when the subject is *mi* or *yu*: *Mi go*, "I am going" (or "went," etc.); *Yu go*, "You are going"; but *Em i go*, "He (etc.) is going"; *Mipela i go*, "We are going."

A pronoun is often inserted after a noun subject, thus *Dispela man em i go*, "This man is going."

Transitive verbs with minor exceptions end in *-im*: *givim*, "give"; *kisim*, "get." Verbs are otherwise invariable.

Tense need not be indicated, but *bai* or *baimbai* before the verb or at the beginning of the sentence indicates future; and *bin* before the verb, or *pinis* after it or at the end of the sentence, indicates the past: *Bai em i kam*, "He (She, It) will come"; *Ol bin go* or *Ol go pinis*, "They went." (Note, however, that *i dai pinis* means "is dead," whereas *i dai* alone means "lie down" or "go to sleep"; similarly *pinis* changes the meaning of one or two other verbs.)

Common auxiliary verbs are *laik*, "want to"; *save*, "know how to"; *ken*, "is likely to," "will possibly."

For a negative, precede the verb with *no*.

To apply an adjective to a noun, use *i* alone: *San i hat*, "the sun is hot." In other cases, the verb "to be" is *stap*: thus *Mi stap long ples bung*, "I am in the market-place." Following another verb, *i stap* indicates a continuing state or action: *Ol i ron i stap*, "They are running."

"There is" or "There are" is *I gat*.

QUESTIONS Yes/no questions are indicated by tone of voice alone, or by adding *no nogat*, "or not." The usual care is necessary in interpreting answers to questions framed in the negative.

Word order in questions is strictly the same as in statements: *Yu stap we?*, "Where are you?"

IMPERATIVES For imperatives, use plain sentence-forms with *Yu* or *Yupela* (omitting *i*): *Yu go* (singular) or *Yupela go* (plural), "Go."

For "Let's," use *Yumi* in the case of two people, *Yumipela* if more than two: *Yumi go*, "Let's go (you and I)."

In the negative, put *no* before the verb; or, alternatively, prefix *Nogut* to the whole statement: *Yu no go* or *Nogut yu go*, "Don't go," "You mustn't go."

NUMERALS Add *-pela* to a numeral preceding a noun, except in the case of the larger units (*handet* and up); thus *sikispela man na meri*, "six people."

CURRENCY 1 *kina* = 100 *toea* (pronounced "toy-a").

FORMS OF ADDRESS The terms *man* and *meri* have generally been used of natives, and *masta* and *missis* of Europeans, but this distinction is naturally breaking down.

Conventions regarding forms of address are not firm, but suggestions are:

mista to most men
meri to women and girls
boi to labourers and junior servants
manki to young boys
lapun or *tumbuna* for respect to the elderly of either sex

KIN TERMS "Father" and "mother" are *papa* and *mama*, but kin terms generally refer to extended families and are applied broadly to distant relatives or unrelated friends.

Brata means a relative of similar age and the same sex as oneself, and *susa*, similarly, one of different sex: thus a girl's sisters and female cousins are *brata* and her brothers and male cousins *susa*.

"Son" and "daughter" are just *pikinini man* and *pikinini meri*, and "husband" and "wife" are just *man* and *meri* (or sometimes *kuk*).

The word *tambu*, "forbidden," is also a kin term denoting a man's sister-in-law or a woman's brother-in-law.

NAME OF LANGUAGE
Pidgin's name for itself is *Tok pisin*.

FIJIAN

The language known as Fijian was originally the dialect of the small island of Bau, but has become the language of communication throughout the Fijian islands.

It is written in the roman alphabet. We follow modern practice in dropping accent marks.

PRONUNCIATION Vowels A, E, I, O, U are pronounced as *ah, eh, ee, oh, oo.*

In combinations, pronounce each vowel separately: AI, AU, EI approximately as *igh, ow, eigh.*

Consonants are as in English, except that

B is pronounced *mb.*
D is pronounced *nd.*
G is pronounced as *ng* in "singer" (no *g* sound).
Q is pronounced as *ng* in "finger" (*ng* followed by *g* sound).
C is pronounced as hard *th* in "then."
DR is pronounced as *n* followed by rolled *r.*
K is slightly guttural (like *gh* in "Ugh!").

Stress is nearly always on the second-last syllable.

NOUNS are generally the same in singular and plural: *na tagane,* "the man," "the men"; *na yalewa,* "the woman," "the women."

The article *na* almost invariably precedes a common noun. The marker *i* that appears in many nouns is written as a separate word but is effectively part of the noun: *na i vola,* "the book," "the books."

A very few nouns have separate plural forms: note only *na vale,* "the house," *na veivale,* "the houses"; *na ka,* "the thing," *na veika,* "the things."

Proper names (and certain pronouns) are preceded by the article *o* (sometimes *ko*): *o Viti,* "Fiji." (Standing alone, this means "It is Fiji.")

ARTICLES *Na,* alone, means "the." For "a" or "an," put *e dua* before *na*: *e dua na vale,* "a house"; *e dua na gone,* "a child." (The same formulations can mean "There is a house," "There is a child.")

For "some," substitute *so* for *dua*: *e so na gone,* "some children" (or "There are some children").

For "this" or "these," use *na* before the noun and *oqo* after it: *na vale oqo,* "this house"; *na veivale oqo,* "these houses."

For "that" or "those," use *na* before the noun and *oqori* (for things near the addressee) or *ko ya* (for things further away) after it: *na tagane ko ya,* "that man" or "those men."

ADJECTIVES An adjective follows its noun: *na vale levu,* "the big house"; *na tagane vinaka,* "the good man"; *na sala balavu,* "the long road."

A number of common adjectives have plural forms in which the first syllable is reduplicated; note: *na veivale lelevu,* "the big houses"; *na tagane vivinaka,* "the good men."

To predicate an adjective of a noun, place it first, following *e*: *E levu na vale,* "The house is big."

Comparison can be expressed by contrast: *E levu na tagane, e lailai na yalewa* (literally "The man is big, the woman is small") for "The man is bigger than the woman"; and this can be said even when either component alone would be inappropriate. Alternatively, use *e* as a preposition to mean "in comparison with": *E levu na tagane e na yalewa.*

330

For a superlative, use *i matai ni*, "first of," before the qualified noun: *na i matai ni yalewa balavu*, "the tallest woman."

ADVERBS The usual way to form an adverb from an adjective is to prefix *vaka-*: *vinaka*, "good"; *vakavinaka*, "well."

VERBS When the subject is a noun, the verb usually precedes it, introduced by particle *e* (or emphatic *sa*) for present tense, *a* for past tense and *na* for future:

E lako na waqavuka, "The plane is going";
A lako na waqavuka, "The plane went";
Na lako na waqavuka, "The plane will go."

In the past and future tense *e* or *sa* is sometimes included as well, preceding the other particle.

The verb "be" in the sense "exist" is *tiko*, and *E tiko* is the usual translation of "There is," as in *E tiko e dua na motoka*, "There is a car." (But *E tiko* may be omitted as indicated earlier.)

A present continuous, for a state-verb such as *moce*, "sleep," can be formed by placing *tiko* after the verb: *E moce tiko na yalewa*, "The woman is sleeping."

The word *rawa* following the verb indicates possibility: *E vosa rawa na gone*, "The child can speak."

A pronoun subject such as *au*, "I," precedes the verb: *Au na lako*, "I shall go"; but the third person pronoun *o koya*, "he, she," follows it like a noun.

A transitive verb always has a suffix ending in *a*, either a single syllable *-a, -ca, -ga, . . .* or a double syllable *-caka, -kaka, . . .* and is immediately followed by its direct object: *Au a raica na rumu*, "I saw the room"; *Au na wilika na i vola*, "I shall read the book."

When the object of the verb is a proper name or a pronoun that normally takes *o, o* is omitted, but the *-a* of the verb changes to *-i: Au a raici koya*, "I saw him/her."

For a negative, put *sega ni* between prefix and verb: *A sega ni lako na waqavuka*, "The plane did not go"; *Au na sega ni wilika na i vola*, "I shall not read the book." For "There is not," say *E sega ni tiko*: as, for example, *E sega ni tiko e dua na motoka*, "There is no car."

PRONOUNS can be singular (for one person); dual (for just two); trial (for three or a few, up to about ten); or plural (for large numbers). For "we" and "us," there are also alternative forms depending on whether the person or persons addressed are included:

au (or *u*)		*iko*	*o koya*
"I, me"		"you" (singular)	"he, him, she, her"
daru	*keirau*	*o drau*	*rau*
"the two of us, you and I"	"the two of us, not you"	"the two of you"	"the two of them"
datou	*keitou*	*o dou*	*ratou*
"we few, including you"	"we few, not you"	"you few"	"the few of them"
da	*keimami*	*o ni*	*ra*
"we many, including you"	"we many, not you"	"you many"	"they many"

Some pronouns have variant forms, mainly with extra initial *k*, or vowel, or both.

A pronoun subject or object is frequently omitted if the sense is clear.

There are no pronouns for inanimate objects and it is necessary to say *na ka,* "the thing," or *na veika,* "the things."

POSSESSION Before a noun, "of the" is *ni*: *na yaca ni gone,* "the name of the child"; *na dela ni vale,* "the top of the house."

Before proper names there are different words for "of"; *nei* is used for ordinary possessions, as in *na i vola nei Tomasi,* "Thomas's book"; and *i* for parts of the possessor's body, or for his relatives: *na uli i Tomasi,* "Thomas's head"; *na taci i Tomasi,* "Thomas's sister."

The same distinction is made in the case of possessive pronouns. The ordinary possessives in the singular are

na noqu	*na nonu*	*na nona*
"my"	"your"	"his, her"

but in the case of parts of the body and relatives, the possessives are *-qu, -mu* and *-na* attached to the noun (which is still preceded by *na*):

na noqu i vola, "my book," but
na uluqu, "my head"
na nona vale, "his/her house," but
na tacina, "his/her sister"

(Note also: *na yacaqu,* "my name.")

There is a full range of dual, trial and plural forms, but the novice will be understood (though not strictly grammatical) if he treats pronouns in the same way as proper names and uses *nei* or *i*.

Note that Fijians make a further distinction by using *kei* when the possession is a food and *mei* when it is a drink (with a range of corresponding pronoun forms).

QUESTIONS Yes/no questions are distinguished from statements only by their intonation: *E levu na tauni?,* "The town is big?," "Is the town big?"

In polite questions the word *beka,* "perhaps," often follows the verb.

Questions with interrogative words such as *vei,* "where," usually have the same word order as statements.

IMPERATIVES For an imperative, use the plain verb form, or soften it by adding *mada*: *Lako,* or *Lako mada,* "Go." In the case of a compound verb the *mada* goes between: *Lako mada mai,* "Come."

For "Let's," put the appropriate inclusive pronoun before the verb; for example: *Daru lako,* "Let's go (the two of us)."

For a negative, precede the verb in any of these cases with *Kua ni*: *Kua ni lako mada,* "Don't go."

NUMERALS The numeral, preceded by *e,* is normally placed before the definite article: *e tolu na i vola,* "three books" (or "There are three books"). The noun always retains its singular form.

In reference to persons the word *lewe* is placed before the numeral: *e lewe rua na gone,* "two children" (or "There are two children").

When the sense of the definite article must be preserved, the numeral expression follows the noun: *na i vola e tolu,* "the three books"; *na koro e lima oqo,* "these five villages."

The same constructions are used with numerical adjectives such as *vuqa,* "many," and *vica,* "how many?": *E lewe vica na tamata?,* "How many people are there?"

FIJIAN

CURRENCY 1 *dola* = 100 *sede*.

FORMS OF ADDRESS No special terms are in common use. *Saka* is a polite word meaning "sir" or "madam." In addressing someone of high rank the formal plural pronoun *kemuni* is preferred to the singular *iko*.

KIN TERMS nearly always carry one of the suffixed possessive pronouns such as *-qu*, "my." The commonest ones, here listed with *-na*, "his/her," are:

tamana, "father"
tinana, "mother"
luvena, "offspring" (of either sex)
tuakana, "elder brother/sister"
tacina, "younger brother/sister"
ganena, "brother/sister" (general)
watina, "husband/wife"

Optionally, add *tagane* for "male" or *yalewa* for "female": *tacina yalewa*, "(his/her) younger sister."

In referring to relatives of the person addressed or a third person the use of the article *o* instead of *na* implies acquaintance: *o watimu*, "your husband/wife (whom I have met)."

NAME OF LANGUAGE
The Fijian language is *na vosa vaka-Viti*; more precisely, *na vosa vaka-Bau*.

TONGAN

Tongan is the language of the independent kingdom of Tonga, or the Friendly Islands.
It is written in a reduced roman alphabet.

PRONUNCIATION Vowels:

A, E, I, O, U are like *ah, eh, ee, oh, oo*, but shorter; and E is pronounced with lips spread, making it like French *é*.
Long vowels Ā, Ē, Ī, Ō, Ū are twice the length of short. They are sometimes written AA, EE, II, OO, UU.
Vowels in sequence should be pronounced individually; for example, EUA as a quick *eh-oo-ah*.

Consonants are as in English, except that

K, P and T are more like unvoiced G, B and D, that is, with no following puff of air.
NG is as in "singer," never as in "finger."
H is always strongly pronounced.
Between short vowels the glottal stop, written ', is as in the Cockney pronunciation of "bottle" as "bo'l." Elsewhere it is often very weakly pronounced.

Normal stress is on the last vowel if it is long, otherwise on the second last. It may move to the last syllable of a noun-phrase to emphasise it, and it sometimes moves when two words are read as one. We use an accent ´ to mark any unusual stresses.

NOUNS are usually invariable.
For plurals, put *kau* before the noun for adult persons, *koe* for children, *fanga* for birds or animals, *ngaahi* or *'ū* for things. The definite article "the" is *e* or *he: e tangata*, "the man"; *e kau tangata*, "the men"; *e fale*, "the house"; *e ngaahi fale*, "the houses."
A very few nouns have special plural forms — note *tamasi'i*, "child," plural *tamaiki* — but the plural marker is used as well: *e koe tamaiki*, "the children."
The indefinite article "a, an" is *ha: ha fefine*, "a woman"; *ha vaka*, "a ship." In the plural it means "some": *ha kau tangata*, "some men."
Prepositions commonly combine with articles: *kihe*, "to the"; *kiha*, "to a"; *ihe*, "in the."
Note that it is usual to place the word *ko* before a noun-phrase standing alone and not part of a sentence, for example, in an exclamation or in answer to a question: *Koe pasi*, "The bus!", "It's the bus"; *Ko Sione*, "It's John."

ADJECTIVES follow the noun, and a very few have special plural forms; note *si'i*, "small," plural *iiki*; *lahi*, "large, many," plural *lalahi: ha vakapuna lahi*, "a big plane"; *ha 'ū vakapuna lalahi*, "big planes."
To form a comparative, put *ange* after the adjective; "than" is *'i: lahi ange 'ihe fale*, "bigger than the house."
For a superlative, put *taha* after the adjective: *lahi taha*, "biggest."

ADVERBS Adjectives can be used directly as adverbs.

VERBS Tense is indicated by a prefix; hence with *'alu,* "go":

'oku 'alu, "is going";
na'e 'alu, "went";
kuo 'alu, "has gone";
'e 'alu, "will go."

In the case of a noun subject the verb usually comes first and subject and object follow in either order, the subject introduced by *'e* and the object by *'a*; but *'a* combines with the definite article *e* to give *'ae* (and may be omitted before *ha*): *lau,* "read"; *'Oku lau 'e he tangata 'ae tohi,* "The man is reading the book."

If there is a subject but no object, *'a* is preferred and the sense shows whether it is subject or object: *'Oku 'alu 'ae vakapuna,* "The plane is going"; *Na'e lea 'ae tangata,* "The man spoke."

The verb "is" or "are" between nouns is omitted, and each noun is introduced by *ko*: *Ko e fefine ko hono uaifi,* "The woman is his wife."

Tense indicators are used before adjectives as the equivalent of "is," "are," etc: *'Oku lahi 'ae vaka,* "The ship is big"; *Na'e lōloa 'ae hala,* "The road was long."

"There is" or "There are" is *'Oku 'iai,* and a following noun requires no prefix: *'Oku 'iai ha fale,* "There is a house."

For a negative, use *'ikai ke* (*'ikai te* when a pronoun subject follows) as an auxiliary verb, and put the tense particle before it: *'Oku 'ikai ke 'alu 'ae tangata,* "The man is not going."

"There is not" is just *'Oku 'ikai*: *'Oku 'ikai ha pasi,* "There is no bus."

Note the common use of *atu,* "away from me," and *mai,* "towards me," with verbs of motion: *fua atu,* "carry away"; *fua mai,* "bring."

QUESTIONS A yes-no question has the same form as the corresponding statement: *'Oku lahi 'ae vaka?,* "Is the ship big?"

For "Where is . . . ?" say *'Oku 'i fē . . . ?* In the case of words such as *'afe,* "when?", it is not necessary to alter the sentence order: *'E alu 'ae motokā 'afe?,* "When will the car go?"

IMPERATIVES For an imperative, use the plain verb, preceded as appropriate by *Fakamolemole 'o* or *Kataki 'o* when making a request.

For "Don't," put *'Oua 'e* before the verb: *'Oua 'e 'alu atu,* "Don't go away."

For "Let's," use the pronoun *Ta* before the verb if there are two people, *Tau* if there are three or more: *Ta 'alu,* "Let's go (you and I)."

PRONOUNS A pronoun subject comes between tense indicator and verb: *ne,* "he, she"; *'Oku ne lea,* "He/She is speaking." (*Na'e* becomes *Na'a.*)

Pronoun objects follow the verb.

There are separate pronoun forms for subject and object position; also for singular, dual and plural, of which dual must be used for just two people, plural for three or more; and for addressee-inclusive and addressee-exclusive first person dual and plural. In the following list the object forms are in parentheses:

Singular
ou, ku, u (au), "I, me"
ke (koe), "you" (singular)
ne (ia), "he, him, she, her, it"

Dual	Plural (three or more)
ma (kimaua), "we two, you and I"	mau (kimautolu), "we, incl. you"
ta (kitaua), "we two, not you"	tau (kitautolu), "we, not you"
mo (kimoua), "you two"	mou (kimoutolu), "you"
na (kinaua), "the two of them"	nau (kinautolu), "they, them"

Examples: *Kuo ma lau 'ae tohi*, "You and I have read the book"; *'Oku ou 'o'ange ha tohi kia kinautolu*, "I am giving a book to them (three or more)."

In the case of inanimate things *ne* and *ia* are commonly used for dual and plural as well as for singular.

POSSESSION The word "of," when it denotes possession of things that can be described as the owner's property, is *'a*; it combines with the definite article to give *'ae*: *e pa'anga 'ae tangata*, "the man's money"; *e tohi 'ae ta'ahine*, "the girl's book."

In other cases, such as in reference to body parts, relatives, one's house or country and other such "intrinsic" possessions, the word is *'o*, becoming *'oe*: *e 'ulu 'oe tamasi'i*, "the child's head"; *e fale 'oe fefine*, "the woman's house."

There are two parallel sets of possessive pronouns making the same distinctions: *'eku kato*, "my suitcase"; *hoku fonua*, "my country"; *ho'o tohi*, "your book"; *ho fale*, "your house"; *'ene tikite*, "his/her ticket"; *hono mali*, "his/her spouse." For forms other than these, the beginner may, in need, use *'a* and *'o* with the object forms of personal pronouns.

NUMERALS follow the noun, preceded by *'e*, and the noun need carry no plural marker: *ha tohi 'e ua*, "two books." In reference to persons the numeral carries the prefix *toko-*: *ha fefine 'e tokotolu*, "three women." (The word *toko-* is also prefixed to some other words indicating number: *ha fefine 'e tokolahi*, "many women.")

CURRENCY 1 *pa'anga* equals 100 *seniti*.

FORMS OF ADDRESS The beginner will be excused the graded courtesies of Tongan society. To call to someone whose name you do not know, say *Me'a!* More respectful vocatives are *Tangata'eiki*, "sir," and *Fine'eiki*, "madam," but they have limited use.

KIN TERMS The commonest kin terms are:

tamai, "father"; *fa'ē*, "mother"
tokoua, "brother or sister"
ta'okete, "older brother or sister of the same sex"
tehina, "younger brother or sister of the same sex"
tuonga'ane, "brother" (of a woman)
tuofefine, "sister" (of a man)
foha, "son" (of a man); *'ofefine*, "daughter" (of a man)
tama, "son" (of a woman); *tama fefine*, "daughter" (of a woman)
'alo, "son or daughter"
mali, "spouse."

The words for "brother" and "sister" extend broadly to cousins.

TONGAN

NAME OF LANGUAGE
The Tongan name for Tongan is *e lea faka-Tonga.*

SAMOAN

Samoan is the language of the independent state of Western Samoa, extending also throughout American Samoa and spoken by some two hundred thousand people.

It is written in a reduced roman alphabet.

PRONUNCIATION Vowels:

A, E, I, O, U, are like *ah, eh, ee, oh, oo*, but short.
Long vowels Ā, Ē, Ī, Ō, Ū, are the same sounds pronounced longer.
In the case of vowels in sequence, pronounce all components in rapid succession; for example *'Ioe,* "Yes," as *ee-oh-eh.*

Consonants are as in English, except that G is like the *ng* in "singer." It may occur at the beginning of a word.

The glottal stop ' between vowels is clearly sounded (as in the Cockney pronunciation of "bottle" as "bo'l"). In other positions it is relatively weak.

Long vowels always receive stress, otherwise the stress is on the second last syllable.

Note that in written Samoan long vowels and the glottal stop are not always consistently shown.

NOUNS A handful of nouns have separate plural forms, but most nouns are invariable.

The definite article "the" is *le* in the singular and is omitted in the plural: *le fale,* "the house": *fale,* "the houses."

The indefinite article "a" or "an" is *se,* and plural "some" is *ni: se fale,* "a house"; *ni fale,* "some houses," "houses."

The particle *'o* is placed before a noun-phrase when it stands alone not as part of a sentence, for example, in an exclamation or in answer to a question; or when (atypically) it precedes the verb as its subject: *'O le ta'avale,* "The car!", "It's the car."

VERBS The tense of a verb is indicated by a prefix; for example, in the case of *alu,* "go":

E alu le va'a, "The ship is going"
Sa (or *Na*) *alu le va'a,* "The ship went"
Ua alu le va'a, "The ship has gone"
O le ā alu le va'a, "The ship will go."

Present continuous in the case of a state-verb such as *moe,* "sleep," has the prefix *O lo'o: O lo'o moe le fafine,* "The woman is sleeping."

Note that *ua* is more commonly used than *e* in the case of a present state that continues from some past time: *Ua timu,* "It is raining."

The noun is sometimes placed first for emphasis: *'O le va'a e alu,* "The ship is going."

A pronoun subject is placed first in the case of present tense, and *e* becomes *te: 'Ou te alu,* "I am going." In any other case the pronoun comes between prefix and verb: *Sa 'ou alu,* "I went."

Many verbs have separate plural forms, but modern usage is tending to drop them. Note the especially irregular forms of *alu,* "go," plural *o*; and *sau,* "come," plural *o mai*. In other cases, a plural may be recognised by a reduplicated syllable or by the prefix *fe-*: *alofa*, "love," plural *alolofa*; *inu*, "drink," plural *feinu*. Hence *E o mai va'a*, "The ships have come"; *Ua o ni fafine*, "Some women have gone."

For a negative, put *lē* before the verb itself: *Ua lē sau le fafine*, "The woman has not come."

Between nouns, the verb "is" or "are" is omitted, but both nouns are preceded by *'o*: *'O le tagata 'o le foma'i*, "The man is the doctor."

For "There is," "There was," etc, use *i ai* with a tense prefix: *E i ai se va'a*, "There is a ship"; *Sa i ai ni tamaiti*, "There were some children." "There is not" is *E leai*: *E leai se ta'avale*, "There is no car."

ADJECTIVES An adjective follows the noun: *le tamāloa malosi*, "the strong man"; *le fafine umi*, "the tall woman."

Adjectives have plurals formed by reduplicating the stressed syllable, or by lengthening it if it is a vowel alone: *tamāloa malolosi*, "the strong men"; *ni fafine ūmi*, "some tall women."

To predicate an adjective of a noun, treat the adjective directly as a verb and use the appropriate prefix, often *ua* for present tense: *E* (or *Ua*) *umi le tamāloa*, "The man is tall."

A comparative such as "The man is taller than the woman" is usually expressed in the form "The man is tall, the woman is not tall," *E umi le tamāloa, e lē umi le fafine*; say this even where it would be inappropriate to say on its own *E lē umi le fafine*.

Alternatively, use *sili ona* for "more" and *i* for "than": *E sili ona umi le tamāloa i le fafine*.

For a superlative, use *sili ona* for "most": *E sili ona umi le fafine*, "The woman is tallest"; or use *tele*, "very": *E umi tele le fafine*.

QUESTIONS A yes-no question is often indicated merely by tone of voice, but may be formed by prefixing *Pe* or *Po*, or by placing *'ea* at the end. *Pe e tele le va'a?*, "Is the ship big?"; alternatively, *'O le va'a e tele 'ea?* etc.

Po is also sometimes used at the beginning of a sentence that has an interrogative word, for example, *'o ai*, "who?": *Po 'o ai le 'aveta'avale?*, "Who is the driver?"

IMPERATIVES For an imperative, use the verbal particle *Ia*, or more politely *Se'i*: *Se'i sau*, "Come." *Ia* sometimes follows the verb: *Fo'ai ia!*, "Give (it to me)!"

A negative imperative is formed by *'Aua*, "Don't," generally with the additional *lē*: *'Aua lē alu*, "Don't go."

For "Let's," use *Se'i* with the inclusive pronoun *ta* (two people) or *tatou* (more than two) before the verb: *Se'i ta alu*, "Let's go (you and I)."

PRONOUNS have singular, dual and plural forms, of which the dual must be used when the reference is to just two people, the plural only in the case of three or more. There is also a distinction between "inclusive" and "exclusive" first person dual and plural. In the following list the forms in parentheses are used in object position or with prepositions:

Singular
'ou (a'u), "I, me";

e ('oe), "you";
na (ia), "he, him, she, her";

Dual	Plural (three or more)
ta (tāua), "we two, you and I";	*tatou (tatou),* "we, incl. you";
ma (māua), "we two, not you";	*matou (matou),* "we, not you";
lua (oulua), "you two";	*tou (outou),* "you";
la (laua), "the two of them"	*latou (latou),* "they, them."

Note that there are no pronouns for inanimate objects; for these, use *le mea,* "the thing," and *mea,* "the things."

For pronouns standing alone, use *'o* before the object forms. Always use *'o* before *ia.*

POSSESSION The preposition "of," in reference to things that can be described as property of their owners, is *a: le naifi a le tagata,* "the man's knife"; *le tusi a le teine,* "the girl's book."

In the case of more intrinsic possessions such as the body and its parts, relatives, and one's country or town, the pronoun is *o: le lima o le tagata,* "the man's hand"; *le nu'u o le teine,* "the girl's village." Generally, food, language and conduct are in the *a* category, but houses and boats, or clothing actually worn, are in the *o* category.

Possessive pronouns also have alternative forms. With things in the *a* category these are:

Singular: *la'u,* "my"; *lau,* "your"; *lana,* "his, her."
Dual: *la ta,* "our" (incl.); *la ma,* "our" (excl.); *la oulua,* "your"; *la la,* "their."
Plural: *la tatou,* "our" (incl.); *la matou,* "our" (excl.); *la outou,* "your"; *la latou,* "their."

For the *o* category, change the first *la* to *lo* in each case. Examples: *la'u ta'avale,* "my car"; *lo'u tamā,* "my father"; *la latou mea'ai,* "their food"; *lo latou atunu'u,* "their country."

The initial *l* in these forms represents the definite article and is dropped in the plural: *o matou fale,* "our houses."

NUMERALS usually follow the noun, preceded by *e,* but may precede, as in English: *fale e lua,* "two houses," sometimes *lua fale.*

Applied to persons, numerals take the prefix *to'a-: teine e to'alua* (or *to'alua teine*), "two girls"; *tama e to'atolu,* "three boys," etc. The same prefix is used with *tele,* "many," and *itiiti,* "few": *tagata e to'atele,* "many people."

CURRENCY 1 *tālā* ("dollar") equals 100 *sene.* (The same names are used in Western and in American Samoa.)

FORMS OF ADDRESS Samoan "chiefly" language has elaborate forms and conventions, but there are few other forms of address in common use. The word *ali'i* is sometimes used for "sir."

Certain words have alternative "respectful" and "ordinary" forms, the latter for use when referring to oneself. Pronouns are then often omitted; hence *fale,* the humble word for "house," comes to mean "my house." The honorific forms are used mainly to those of high rank, but sometimes more widely.

A few common pairs of ordinary/respectful words are: *'ai/taumafa*, "eat"; *inu/taumafa*, "drink"; *'ioe/o lea lava*, "yes"; *iloa/silafia*, "know"; *oti/maliu*, "die"; *fafine/tama'ita'i*, "woman"; *va'ai/silasila*, "see"; *tōfā/soifua*, "goodbye"; *sau/afio*, "come"; *āvā/faletua*, "wife"; *atali'i/alo*, "son"; *afafine/alo* (or *alo tama'ita'i*), "daughter."

KIN TERMS other than those in the preceding paragraph have one form only. The commonest are:

tamā, "father"; *tinā*, "mother";
tāne, "husband";
uso, "brother/sister of the same sex";
tuagane, "brother" (of a woman);
tuafafine, "sister" (of a man).

NAME OF LANGUAGE
The Samoan language is *le gagana Sāmoa*.

TAHITIAN

Tahitian is the native language of Tahiti in the Society Islands, and a language of communication throughout French Polynesia.
It is written in a reduced roman alphabet.

PRONUNCIATION Vowels:
A, E, I, O U are like *ah, eh, ee, oh, oo,* but short; and E is pronounced with lips spread so that it sounds like French *é*.
Long vowels A, Ē, Ī, Ō, Ū are the same sounds long.
Vowels in sequence are separately sounded in quick succession; for example, *'Eiaha,* "Don't," has four syllables *'E-i-a-ha.*

Consonants are as in English, except that:

H between vowels may be like guttural *ch* in "loch."
R is slightly trilled or flapped.
The glottal stop ' counts as a consonant and is strongly sounded (as in the Cockney pronunciation of "bottle" as "bo'l"), especially between vowels.

Stress is not strongly marked, but tends to be on long vowels or on the first vowel of a sequence, otherwise on the second last syllable.
In written Tahitian long vowels and the glottal stop are not always consistently shown.

NOUNS themselves do not vary in form, but articles indicate singular, dual or plural number. "Dual," in fact, overlaps with plural and may be used for objects in groups up to about ten.
The definite article "the" is *te* (singular), *nā* (dual) or *te mau* (plural): *te fare,* "the house"; *nā tā'ata,* "the persons" (two or a few); *te mau ta'ata,* "the people" (many); *nā metua,* "the parents" (father and mother).
The indefinite article "a" or "an" is *te hō'ē,* and the indefinite plural "some" is *te hō'ē mau: te hō'ē fare,* "a house"; *te hō'ē mau fare,* "some houses."
The particle *'o* is used in front of any of these forms when they stand alone and not as part of a sentence, and similarly with proper names or pronouns; it may roughly be translated "It is," as in *'O Tahiti,* "It is Tahiti"; *'O te vahine,* "It is the woman"; *'O vau,* "it is I."
The particle *e* has the same function with a common noun and no article: *E vahine,* "It is a woman."

VERBS The verb is preceded by a tense particle, *tē* for present, *'ua* for normal past or perfect or for a present state that continues from the past, and *e* for future. When *tē* is used, the words *nei* or *ra* (or *maira*) must come after the verb, *nei* indicating closeness to the speaker, *ra* distance away:

tē parua nei, "is speaking (here)";
tē inu nei, "is drinking (here)";
tē tāmā'a maira, "is eating (over there)";
'ua haere, "has gone";
e haere, "will go."

The verb normally comes first in the sentence, followed by its subject, and its object is introduced by *i* (*iā* for a proper noun): *'Ua inu te vahine i te ū*, "The woman drank the milk"; *E fa'ahoro te ta'ata i te pereo'o i te 'oire*, "The man will drive the car to the town."

The combination *i . . . na* indicates recent past: *I haere na vau i te mātete*, "I went to the market."

For "There is," "There are," etc., use *E*, negative *'Aita e*: *E fare*, "There are houses"; *'Aita e fare*, "There are no houses."

In the case of negative sentences, the normal order is for the subject to precede the verb, the sentence starting with the negative word *'Aita*, or, in the future tense, *E'ita*; and the *tē* of the present tense becomes *e*: *'Aita te vahine e inu nei*, "The woman is not drinking"; *E'ita te tamāroa e haere i te mātete*, "The boy will not go to the market."

ADJECTIVES follow the noun: *te fare rahi*, "the big house"; *te hō'ē ta'ata 'ite*, "a wise man."

A few adjectives reduplicate one or more syllables in the dual or plural or both: *te mau fare rarahi*, "the big houses (plural)."

The comparative is formed by placing *a'e* after the adjective: *rahi a'e*, "bigger." For "is bigger than," say "is a bigger thing than," where "than" is *i* and "thing" is *mea*: *E mea rahi a'e te tamāroa i te teine*, "The boy is bigger than the girl."

For a superlative, place *roa a'e* after the adjective: *te tamāroa iti roa a'e*, "the smallest boy."

When an adjective is predicated of a noun, an extra noun must be inserted to carry it: *E mea rahi te fare*, "The house is big"; *E teine 'ite te teine*, "The girl is clever."

PRONOUNS may be singular, dual or plural, and in the first person dual and plural they may include or exclude the addressee. As with nouns, "dual" means "two or a few." The list is:

Singular

vau (after *-a, -o* or *-u*) ⎫
au (after *-e* or *-i*) ⎬ "I";
⎭
'oe, "you";
'oia, "he, she."

Dual	Plural
tāua, "we few, incl. you";	*tātou*, "we many, incl. you";
māua, "we few, not you";	*mātou*, "we many, not you";
'ōrua, "you few";	*'outou*, "you many";
rāua, "they few."	*rātou*, "they many."

"He, she" can also be *'ōna*, with the sense of "that one already mentioned."

As object of the verb, "me" has the special form *iā'u*, and "him, her", *iāna*. In other cases, place the object marker *ia* in front of the ordinary form: *ia 'oe*, "you" (singular), etc.

There are no pronouns for inanimate objects; for these, use *te mea*, "the thing," and *nā mea* (dual) or *te mau mea* (plural), "the things."

QUESTIONS For a yes-no question, place *ānei* after the verb: *'Ua haere mai ānei 'oia?*, "Did he come?" In the case of a negative question, *ānei* follows the negative particle: *'Aita ānei 'ua 'ite 'oe,* "Didn't you understand?" (Be careful with "yes" and "no" answers.)

Questions with "who?" and "what?" begin with *'O vai* and *E aha* (respectively), and a following verb has the particle *tē* for the present or future tense, and *tei* for the past: *'O vai tē haere mai?,* "Who is coming?"; *'O vai tei 'ite i te puta?,* "Who has seen the book?" There are various more complicated constructions, but they may be avoided.

IMPERATIVES For an imperative, precede the verb with *'A* (very abrupt), *E* (less so) or *'Ia* (gentle exhortation): *'Ia haere mai,* "(Please) come." A subject may be placed after the verb as usual if required.

"Don't" is *'Eiaha e* (strong prohibition) or *'Eiaha* (gentle): *'Eiaha pārahi,* "Don't sit down."

For "Let's," use the same forms but attach inclusive subject *tāua* (dual) or *tātou* (plural): *'Ia pārahi tāua,* "Could we sit down (we few)?"

POSSESSION The simplest way of indicating possession is to put the possessor first, preceded by *ta*: *ta te teine puta,* "the girl's book." However, it is usual to distinguish between possession of things that are describable as property — in which case use *tā* (with long *ā*) — and more intrinsic possessions such as parts of the body, relatives and one's country or town or house — in which case use *tō*; hence *tā te teine puta,* "the girl's book"; *tō te teine rima,* "the girl's hand"; *tō nā metua fare,* "the parents' house."

Alternatively, put the possessor after the thing possessed, connected by *a* or *o*: *te tamāhine o te ta'ata,* "the man's daughter"; *te 'ohipa a te tamāroa,* "the boy's work."

Use the first-mentioned construction with pronouns: *ta* (or *tā*) *'oe puta,* "your book"; *ta* (or *tō*) *'oe rima,* "your hand." "My" has the contracted form *ta'u* (or *tā'u* or *tō'u*), and "his, her" the form *tana* (or *tāna* or *tōna*): *tō'u fenua,* "my country."

NUMERALS may either precede or follow the noun, and are preceded by *e*: *e piti nā ta'ata,* or *nā ta'ata e piti,* "two people." The first of these forms can also mean "there are two people."

In the case of the numbers from ten to nineteen, *e* is omitted; and *nā* is not used with numbers above ten: *hō'ē 'ahuru mā piti ta'ata,* "twelve people," or "there are twelve people."

In the case of small numbers of persons, *to'o-* is sometimes prefixed to the numeral: *nā fafine e to'omaha,* "four women."

CURRENCY 1 *toata* or *farāne* (equals French Pacific franc) equals 100 *tenetimi*; and 5 *toata* is called a *tārā.*

FORMS OF ADDRESS There are virtually no compulsory forms of address. For "Mr" or "Mrs," place *tāne* or *vahine* after the proper name.

KIN TERMS The commonest are:

metua tāne or *pāpā,* "father"; *metua vahine* or *māmā,* "mother"
taea'e, "brother/sister of the same sex"

tua'ana, "older brother/sister of the same sex"
teina, "younger brother/sister of the same sex"
tu'āne, "brother" (of a woman); *tuahine*, "sister" (of a man)
tamaiti, "son"; *tamāhine*, "daughter, girl"
tāne, "husband"; *vahine*, explicitly *vahine fa'aipoipo*, "wife"

The words for "brother," "sister," "son," "daughter" are used broadly for cousins, nephews and nieces.

NAME OF LANGUAGE
The Tahitian language is *te reo Tahiti*.

EVERYDAY PHRASES

ENGLISH	NEW GUINEA PIDGIN	FIJIAN
Yes	Yes *Yess*	Io *Eeoh*
No	Nogat *Nohgaht*	Sega *Seng-a*
Please	Plis *Pleess*	Yalo vinaka *Yallo v'nahka*
Thank you	Tenkyu *Tenkyoo*	Vinaka *V'nahka*
Thank you very much	Tenkyu tumas *Tenkyoo too-mahss*	Vinaka vakalevu *V'na' v'lehvoo*
Don't mention it	Maski *Mahsskee*	Mo guilecava *Mo ngweeleh-thahva*
Excuse me, but . . .	Plis, . . . *Pleess*	Vosoti au, . . . *V'sottee ow*
Excuse me (I'm sorry)	Sori *Sorree*	Vosoti au *V'sottee ow*
Excuse me (Do you mind?)	Sori *Sorree*	Vosoti au *V'sottee ow*
Pardon? (What did you say?)	Yu tok wanem samting? *Yoo tawk wahnehm sahmting?*	Kaya tale mada? *Kahya tahleh mahnda?*
Wait a moment	Yu wet liklik *Yoo weht liklik*	Wawa vakalailai *Wahwah vong-a-laylay*
Hurry up!	Hariap! *Hahree-ahp*	Vakatotolo! *Vong-a-to-tohloh*
Slowly!	Isi isi! *Eessee eessee*	Vakamalua! *Vo' mah-looa*
Stop!	Holim! *Hollim*	Tu vakadua! *Too va'ndooa*
Look out!	Lukaut! *Look-kowt*	Qaraura! *Gah-rrowrr'*
Look!	Lukim! *Lookim*	Raica! *Rraytha*
How much?	Haumas? *Howmahss?*	E vica na kena i sau? *Eh vitha na ken' ee sow?*
Never mind	Maski *Mahsski*	Veitalia *Vay-ta-leea*
Come in	Kam insait *Kahm in-sight*	Curu mai *Thoorroo migh*
Come with me	Yu kam wantaim long mi *Yoo kahm wahnt'm long mee*	Muri au mai *Moorree oh migh*
Good morning	Gude *Good-deh*	Sa yadra *Sa yahndrra*
Good afternoon	'Apinun *Ahpee-noon*	Sa bula *Sa mboolla*
Good evening	'Apinun *Ahpee-noon*	Sa bogi *Sa mbohng-ee*
Good-bye (leaving)	Gut bai *Goot bigh*	Sa moce *Sa motheh*
Good-bye (staying)	Gut bai *Goot bigh*	Sa moce *Sa motheh*
Good night	Gut nait *Good night*	Sa moce *Sa motheh*
Do you understand?	Yu save? *Yoo savveh?*	E sa macala? *Eh sa ma-thahla?*
I understand	Mi save *Mee savveh*	E sa macala vei au *Eh sa ma-thahla vee ow*
I don't understand	Mi no save *Mee no savveh*	E sega ni macala vei au *Eh seng-a nee ma-thahla vee ow*
All right (I'll do it)	Orait *Aw-right*	Sa vinaka *Sa v'nahka*
It's all right	Em i orait *Em ee aw-right*	Sa vinaka *Sa v'nahka*

346

EVERYDAY PHRASES

TONGAN	SAMOAN	TAHITIAN
'Io *Eeoh*	'Ioe *Ee-oy*	'Ē *'Eh*
'Ikai *Ee-kigh*	Leai *Leh-igh*	'Aita *'Ighta*
Fakamolemole	Fa'amolemole	'Ia ti'a ia 'oe *'Eea tee'a eea 'oy*
Fah-mohleh-mohleh	*Fah-mohleh-mohleh*	
Mālō *Mah-loh*	Fa'afetai *Fahf-tigh*	Māuruuru ia 'oe
		Mow-rooroo eea 'oy
Mālō 'aupito *Mahlo ow-peeto*	Fa'afetai tele lava	Māuruuru roa
	Fahf-tigh telleh lahva	*Mow-rooroo roh-a*
'Oua teke lea ki ai	'Aua le ta'ua *Ow-al' ta-ooa*	'Aita pe'ape'a
Oh-a tehg' leh' ghee igh		*'Ighta peh'a-peh'a*
Kātaki mu'a, ...	Ia malie, ... *Eea m'lee-eh*	E hoa, ... *Eh hoh-a*
Ka-tahkee moo-ah		
Kātaki *Ka-tahkee*	Ia e malie *Eea eh m'lee-eh*	'Ē'ē, auē ho'i ē
		'Eh'eh, ow-eh ho'ee eh
Tulou *Too-low*	Fa'amolemole	'Ia ti'a ia 'oe *'Eea tee'a eea 'oy*
	Fah-mohleh-mohleh	
Ae ha? *Igh hah?*	O le ā? *Ohleh ah?*	E aha? *Eh ha?*
Tatali si'i *Ta-tahlee see*	Fa'atali la'itiiti lava	He'erū ma'a taime iti
	Fah-tahlee la'titti lahva	*Heh'ehroo mah tighmeh tee*
Vave! *Vahveh*	Vave! *Vahveh*	Ha'avitiviti! *Ha'veetee-veetee*
Māmālie! *Mah-mah-leea*	Fai fai lemū! *Figh figh l'moo*	Tāere! *Tigh-reh*
Tu'u! *Too'*	Taofi! *Ta-offi*	Fa'aea! *Fa'igh-a*
Tokanga! *Toh-kahng-a*	Va'ai ane 'oe! *Va'igh ahneh oy*	Hi'o maita'i! *Hee'o migh-t'ay*
Sio! *Seeoh*	Va'ai! *Va'igh*	'A hi'o! *'Ah hee'o*
'Oku fiha? *Ohg' feea?*	Pe fia? *Peh feea?*	E hia moni? *Eh heea mohnee?*
Tuku ai pē ā *Too' igh beh ah*	E le āfaina *Eh leh ahfa-eena*	'Aita pe'ape'a
		'Ighta peh'a-peh'a
Hū mai *Hoo migh*	Sau i totonu *Sow eet'tohnoo*	'A haere mai *'Ah highreh may*
Ha'u mo au *Ha'oo moo ow*	Sau ta ō *Sow tah oh*	Haere mai 'ē o vau
		Highreh may 'eh oh vow
Malo e lelei *Mahlo leh-lay*	Talofa *Tah-loffa*	'Ia ora na *'Yaw-rahna*
Malo e lelei *Mahlo leh-lay*	Talofa *Tah-loffa*	'Ia ora na *'Yaw-rahna*
Malo e lelei *Mahlo leh-lay*	Talofa *Tah-loffa*	'Ia ora na *'Yaw-rahna*
Nofo ā *Nohfoh igh*	Tōfā *Toh-fah*	Pārahi 'oe *Pahrr-hee 'oy*
'Alu ā *Ahloo igh*	Tōfā *Toh-fah*	Pārahi 'oe *Pahrr-hee 'oy*
Mohe ā *Mo-eh igh*	Tōfā *Toh-fah*	Pārahi 'oe *Pahrr-hee 'oy*
'Oku mahino kia koe?	Ua e mālamalama?	'Ua ta'a ia 'oe?
Ohg' ma-heeno gheea goy?	*Oo-eh mahlma-lahma?*	*'Ooa ta'ah eea 'oy?*
'Oku mahino kiate au	Ua 'ou mālamalama	'Ua ta'a iā'u *'Ooa ta'ah yah'oo*
Ohg' ma-heeno ghee-ahteh ow	*Oo'oh mahlma-lahma*	
'Oku 'ikai mahino kiate au	'Ou te lē mālamalama	'Aita i ta'a iā'u
Oh'gigh ma-heeno	*Oh t' leh mahlma-lahma*	*'Ighta ee t'ah yah'oo*
ghee-ahteh ow		
Tuku pē ia kiate au	Ua lelei *Ooa l'leigh*	E na rira ia vau
Toogoo beh eea ghee-ahteh ow		*Eh na reerra eea vow*
'Oku sai pē ia	Ua lelei *Ooa l'leigh*	E mea 'āfaro
Ohg' sigh beh eea		*Eh meh-a 'a-fahrro*

347

ENGLISH	NEW GUINEA PIDGIN	FIJIAN
zero	nating *nahting*	saiva *sayva*
one	wan *wahn*	dua *ndooa*
two	tu *too*	rua *rrooa*
three	tri *tree*	tolu *tolloo*
four	foa *foh-a*	va *vah*
five	faiv *fighv*	lima *leema*
six	sikis *sikkis*	ono *onno*
seven	seven *sevven*	vitu *veetoo*
eight	et *eight*	walu *wahloo*
nine	nain *nighn*	ciwa *theewa*
ten	ten *ten*	tini *teenee*
eleven	wanpela ten wan *wahnp'la ten wahn*	tini ka dua *teenee ka ndooa*
twelve	wanpela ten tu *wahnp'la ten too*	tini ka rua *teenee ka rrooa*
thirteen	wanpela ten tri *wahnp'la ten tree*	tini ka tolu *teenee ka tolloo*
fourteen	wanpela ten foa *wahnp'la ten foh-a*	tini ka va *teenee ka vah*
fifteen	wanpela ten faiv *wahnp'la ten fighv*	tini ka lima *teenee ka leema*
sixteen	wanpela ten sikis *wahnp'la ten sikkis*	tini ka ono *teenee ka onno*
seventeen	wanpela ten seven *wahnp'la ten sevven*	tini ka vitu *teenee ka veetoo*
eighteen	wanpela ten et *wahnp'la ten eight*	tini ka walu *teenee ka wahloo*
nineteen	wanpela ten nain *wahnp'la ten nighn*	tini ka ciwa *teenee ka theewa*
twenty	tupela ten *toop'la ten*	ruasagavulu *rrooa-sa-ng'vooloo*
twenty-one	tupela ten wan *toop'la ten wahn*	ruasagavulu ka dua *rrooa-sa-ng'vooloo ka ndooa*
thirty	tripela ten *treep'la ten*	tolusagavulu *tolloo-sa-ng'vooloo*
forty	fopela ten *fawp'la ten*	vasagavulu *vah-sa-ng'vooloo*
fifty	faipela ten *fighp'la ten*	limasagavulu *leema-sa-ng'vooloo*
sixty	sikispela ten *sikkis-p'la ten*	onosagavulu *onno-sa-ng'vooloo*
seventy	sevenpela ten *sevven-p'la ten*	vitusagavulu *veet'sa-ng'vooloo*
eighty	etpela ten *eightp'la ten*	walusagavulu *wahloo-sa-ng'vooloo*
ninety	nainti, nainpela ten *nighntee, nighnp'la ten*	ciwasagavulu *theewa-sa-ng'vooloo*
a hundred	wan handet *wahn hahnd't*	dua na drau *ndooa na ndrow*
a hundred and one	wan handet wan *wahn hahnd't wahn*	dua na drau ka dua *ndooa na ndrow ka ndooa*
a hundred and ten	wan handet ten *wahn hahnd't ten*	dua na drau ka tini *ndooa na ndrow ka teenee*
two hundred	tupela handet *toop'la hahnd't*	rua na drau *rrooa na ndrow*

NUMERALS

TONGAN	SAMOAN	TAHITIAN
noa *noh-a*	selo *sehlo*	'aore *'owreh*
taha *ta-hh*	tasi *tahssi*	hō'ē, tahi *hoh'eh, tahhee*
ua *ooa*	lua *looa*	piti *pittee*
tolu *tolloo*	tolu *tohloo*	toru *tohroo*
fā *fah*	fa *fah*	maha *mah-ha*
nima *neema*	lima *leema*	pae *pay*
ono *onno*	ono *onno*	ono *onno*
fitu *fittoo*	fitu *feetoo*	hitu *heetoo*
valu *vahloo*	valu *vahloo*	va'u *vah'oo*
hiva *heeva*	iva *eeva*	iva *eeva*
hongofulu *hong-o-fooloo*	sefulu *s'fooloo*	hō'ē 'ahuru *hoh'eh 'a-hooroo*
hongofulu mā taha	sefulu tasi *s'fooloo tahssi*	hō'ē 'ahuru mā hō'ē
hong-o-fooloo ma ta-hh		*hoh'eh 'a-hooroo mah hoh'eh*
hongofulu mā ua	sefulu lua *s'fooloo looa*	hō'ē 'ahuru mā piti
hong-o-fooloo ma ooa		*hoh'eh 'a-hooroo mah pittee*
hongofulu mā tolu	sefulu tolu *s'fooloo tohloo*	hō'ē 'ahuru mā toru
hong-o-fooloo ma tolloo		*hoh'eh 'a-hooroo mah tohroo*
hongofulu mā fā	sefulu fa *s'fooloo fah*	hō'ē 'ahuru mā maha
hong-o-fooloo ma fah		*hoh'eh 'a-hooroo mahm-hah*
hongofulu mā nima	sefulu lima *s'fooloo leema*	hō'ē 'ahuru mā pae
hong-o-fooloo ma neema		*hoh'eh 'a-hooroo mah pay*
hongofulu mā ono	sefulu ono *s'fooloo onno*	hō'ē 'ahuru mā ono
hong-o-fooloo ma onno		*hoh'eh 'a-hooroo mah onno*
hongofulu mā fitu	sefulu fitu *s'fooloo feetoo*	hō'ē 'ahuru mā hitu
hong-o-fooloo ma fittoo		*hoh'eh 'a-hooroo mah heetoo*
hongofulu mā valu	sefulu valu *s'fooloo vahloo*	hō'ē 'ahuru mā va'u
hong-o-fooloo ma vahloo		*hoh'eh 'a-hooroo mah vah'oo*
hongofulu mā hiva	sefulu iva *s'fooloo eeva*	hō'ē 'ahuru mā iva
hong-o-fooloo ma heeva		*hoh'eh 'a-hooroo mah eeva*
uofulu *ooa-fooloo*	luasefulu *looa-s'fooloo*	piti 'ahuru *pittee 'a-hooroo*
uofulu mā taha	luasefulu tasi	piti 'ahuru mā hō'ē
ooa-fooloo ma ta-hh	*looa-s'fooloo tahssi*	*pittee 'a-hooroo mah ho'eh*
tolungofulu *tolloo-ngo-fooloo*	tolusefulu *tohloo-s'fooloo*	toru 'ahuru *tohroo 'a-hooroo*
fāngofulu *fah-ngo-fooloo*	fasefulu *fahss-fooloo*	maha 'ahuru *mah-ha 'a-hooroo*
nimangofulu *neema-ngo-fooloo*	limasefulu *leema-s'fooloo*	pae 'ahuru *pay 'a-hooroo*
onongofulu *onno-ngo-fooloo*	onosefulu *onss-fooloo*	ono 'ahuru *onno 'a-hooroo*
fitungofulu *fittoo-ngo-fooloo*	fitusefulu *feets-fooloo*	hitu 'ahuru *heetoo 'a-hooroo*
valungofulu *vahloo-ngo-fooloo*	valusefulu *vahloo-s'fooloo*	va'u 'ahuru *vah'oo 'a-hooroo*
hivangofulu *heeva-ngo-fooloo*	ivasefulu *eeva-s'fooloo*	iva 'ahuru *eeva 'a-hooroo*
teau *teh-ow*	selau *s'low*	hō'ē hānere *hoh'eh hah-nehreh*
teau mā taha	selau ma le tasi	hō'ē hānere e hō'ē
teh-ow ma ta-hh	*s'low ma leh tahssi*	*hoh'eh hah-nehreh eh hoh'eh*
teau mā hongofulu	selau sefulu *s'low s'fooloo*	hō'ē hānere e hō'ē 'ahuru
teh-ow ma hong-o-fooloo		*hoh'eh hah-nehreh eh hoh'eh*
		'a-hooroo
uangeau *ooa-ngeh-ow*	lua selau *looa s'low*	piti hānere *pittee hah-nehreh*

NUMERALS

ENGLISH	NEW GUINEA PIDGIN	FIJIAN
a thousand	tausen *towz'n*	dua na udolu *ndooa na oo-ndolloo*
ten thousand	tenpela tausen *tenp'la towz'n*	tini na udolu *teenee na oo-ndolloo*
a hundred thousand	handetpela tausen *hahnd't-p'la towz'n*	dua na drau na udolu *ndooa na ndrow na oo-ndolloo*
a million	wan milian *wahn milly'n*	dua na milioni *ndooa na meelee-ohnee*
ten million	tenpela milian *tenp'la milly'n*	tini na milioni *teenee na meelee-ohnee*
a half	hap *hahp*	veimama *vay-mahma*
... point (decimal) ...	... poin ... *poyn*	... voidi ... *voyndee*

DAYS OF THE WEEK

Sunday	Sande *Sahndeh*	Siga Tabu *Sing-a Tamboo*
Monday	Mande *Mahndeh*	Siga Monite *Sing-a Mo-neeteh*
Tuesday	Tunde *Toondeh*	Siga Tusite *Sing-a Too-seeteh*
Wednesday	Trinde *Treendeh*	Siga Vukelulu *Sing-a Voong-a-looloo*
Thursday	Fonde *Fawndeh*	Siga Lotulevu *Sing-a Lohtoo-lehvoo*
Friday	Fraide *Frighdeh*	Siga Vakaraubuka *Sing-a Vong-a-row-booka*
Saturday	Sarere *Sarra-reh*	Siga Vakarauwai *Sing-a Vong-a-row-way*

MONTHS

January	Janueri *Jannyoo-ahree*	Janueri *Jannoo-erry*
February	Februeri *Febbroo-ahree*	Feperueri *Fep'rroo-erry*
March	Mas *Mahss*	Maji *Mahch'*
April	Epril *Ep-rill*	Epereli *Eppa-rrelly*
May	Me *Meh*	Me *Meh*
June	Jun *Joon*	June *Chooneh*
July	Julai *Jooligh*	Julai *Choo-ligh*
August	Ogas *Awgahss*	Okosita *Okka-seeta*
September	Septemba *Sep-temba*	Seviteba *Sevvi-temba*
October	Oktoba *Awk-tohba*	Okotova *Okka-tohva*
November	Novemba *No-vemba*	Noveba *No-vemba*
December	Desemba *Dee-semba*	Tiseba *Tee-semba*

NUMERALS

TONGAN	SAMOAN	TAHITIAN
taha afe *ta-hhff*	afe *ahfeh*	hō'ē tauatini *hoh'eh tow-a-teenee*
taha mano *tah-manno*	sefulu afe *s'fooloo ahfeh*	hō'ē 'ahuru tauatini
		hoh'eh 'a-hooroo tow-a-teenee
taha kilu *tah-keeloo*	selau afe *s'low-wahfeh*	hō'ē hānere tauatini
		hoh'eh hah-nehreh tow-a-teenee
taha miliona *tah millee-ohna*	miliona *milli-ohna*	hō'ē mirioni *hoh'eh meeree-ohnee*
hongofulu miliona	sefulu miliona	hō'ē 'ahuru mirioni
hong-o-fooloo millee-ohna	*s'fooloo milli-ohna*	*hoh'eh 'a-hooroo meeree-ohnee*
vaheua *va-heh-ooa*	'o le 'afa *o leh ahfa*	'āfa *'ahfa*
... poini ... *poyn'*	... piliota ... *pilli-otta*	... tāpa'o ... *tahp'ow*

DAYS OF THE WEEK

Sāpate *Sah-pahteh*	Aso Sā *Ahsso Sah*	Tāpati *Tah-pahtee*
Mōnite *Moh-neeteh*	Aso Gafua *Ahssohng-fooa*	Monirē *Mo-neereh*
Tūsite *Too-seeteh*	Aso Lua *Ahsso Looa*	Mahana Piti *M'hahna Pittee*
Pulelulu *Pooleh-looloo*	Aso Lulu *Ahsso Looloo*	Mahana Toru *M'hahna Tohroo*
Tu'apulelulu	Aso Tofi *Ahsso Toffee*	Mahana Maha *M'hahna M'ha*
Too'a-pooleh-looloo		
Falaite *Fa-lighteh*	Aso Faraile	Mahana Pae, Farairē
	Ahsso F'righleh	*M'hahna Pay, F'rrighreh*
Tokonaki *Toggo-nahkee*	Aso To'ona'i	Mahana Mā'a *M'hahna Mah'a*
	Ahsso To'nah'	

MONTHS

Sānuali *Sannoo-ahlee*	Ianuari *Yannoo-ahree*	Tenuare *Tehnoo-ahreh*
Fēpueli *Feppoo-ehlee*	Fepuari *Feppoo-ahree*	Fepuare *Fehp-wahreh*
Ma'asi *Ma'ahssee*	Mati *Mahtee*	Māti *Mahtee*
'Epeleli *Eppa-lehlee*	'Aperila *Appeh-reela*	'Eperēra *'Ehp-rrehrra*
Mē *Meh*	Mē *Meh*	Mē *Meh*
Sune *Sooneh*	Iuni *Yoonee*	Tiunu *Tyoonoo*
Siulai *Syoo-ligh*	Iulai *Yoo-ligh*	Tiurai *Tyoo-righ*
'Akosi *Ah-kossee*	'Aukuso *Ow-koosso*	'Ātete *'Ahteh-teh*
Sēpitema *Seppi-tehma*	Setema *Set-temmah*	Tetepa *Teh-tehpa*
'Okatopa *Okka-topp'*	'Oketopa *Okkeh-toppah*	'Atopa *'Ah-tohpa*
Nōvema *No-vehma*	Novema *No-vemmah*	Novema *Noh-vehma*
Tisema *Tee-sehma*	Tesema *Teh-semmah*	Titema *Tee-tehma*

SENTENCES

ENGLISH	NEW GUINEA PIDGIN	FIJIAN

1. Is there someone here who speaks English, please? A little. I speak only a little ———.

    1. I gat man i save tok Inglis, plis? Liklik. Mi save liklik ——— tasol.
Ee gaht mahn ee savveh tawk Ing-liss, pleess? Liklik. Mee savveh liklik ——— tahssol.

    1. E tiko beka e dua eke ka rawa ni vosa vaka-Vavalagi? Vakalailai. Au kila ga vakalailai na vosa vaka- ———.
Eh teeko mbek' eh ndooa ehkeh ka raw' nee vossa vong-a-Vahva-lahng-ee? Vong-a-laylay. Ow keela nga vong-a-laylay na vossa vahka- ———.

---

2. I want to go to ———. Is there a bus (an aeroplane, a taxi)? Yes, there is. No, there is not.

    2. Mi laik go long ———. I gat bas (balus, taksi) no nogat? Yes, i gat. Nogat, i no gat.
Ee gaht bahss (bahlooss, tahksee) no nohgaht? Yess, ee gaht. Nohgaht, ee no gaht.

    2. Au via lako ki ———. E tiko beka e dua na kena basi (waqavuka, tekisi)? Io, e dua. Sega, e sega ni tiko.
Ow veea lahgo kee ———. Eh teeko mbek' eh ndooa na kenna mbahssi (wahngga-vooka, tekka-see)? Eeoh, eh ndooa. Seng-a, eh seng-a nee teeko.

---

3. Where is the bus (the railway station, the ticket office)? It is here (there, over there).

    3. Stesin bilong kisim bas (Stesin bilong kisim tren, Tiket ofis) i stap we? Em i hia (long hap, long hap).
Stehssin b'long kissim bahss (Stehssin b'long kissim trehn, Tikket ofiss) ee stahp weh? Em ee heea (long hahp, long hahp).

    3. E vei beka na basi (na siteseni ni tereni, na vale ni saumi tikite)? E tiko beka eke (ekeri, e kea).
Eh vay mbekka na mbahssi (na s'tehss'nee nee t'rennee, na vahleh nee sowmee t'keeteh)? Eh teeko mbek' eh-keh (eh-kehrree, eh keh-ah).

---

4. How do I get to the airport (to the town)? Go that way. Go straight on (to the left, to the right).

    4. Mi go long ples balus (long taun) long wanem rot? Yu go long dispela rot. Yu go stret (lephan, raithan).
Mee go long pless bahlooss (long town) long wahnehm roht? Yoo go long dissp'la roht. Yoo go streht (lepphan, right-han).

    4. Evei na gaunisala ki na rara ni waqavuka (na tauni)? Muri e kea. Muri vakadodonu (ki na i mawi, ki na i matau).
Ehvay na ngownee-sahlah kee na rrahrra n'wahngga-vook' (na town')? Moorree eh keh-ah. Moorree va'ndoh-ndohnoo (kee na ee ma-wee, kee na ee ma-tow).

SENTENCES

TONGAN	SAMOAN	TAHITIAN
1. Fakamolemole mu'a pe 'oku 'i ai ha taha 'i heni 'oku lea fakapilitania? Si'i pe. 'Oku ou lava pe lea ni'ihi ——. *Fah-mohleh-mohleh mooa, peh ohg' ee igh ah ta-ha ee hehnee ohg' leh-a fah-pilli-tah-neea? See peh. Ohg' oh lahva beh leh-a nee-hh ——.*	1. Fa'amolemole, pe i ai seisi i'inei e tautala fa'a-Peretania? E le lelei tele. E fa'a le lelei tele ——. *Fah-mohleh-mohleh, peigh igh seighsee ee'neigh eh tow-tahla fah-Perreh-ta-neea? Eh leh l'leigh telleh. Eh fah leh l'leigh telleh ——.*	1. Tē vai ra te hō'ē i 'ūnei tei parau Paratāne, 'ia ti'a ia 'oe? Ma'a vāhi iti. E mea na'ina'i roa tau e parau ——. *Teh vay ra teh hoh'eh ee 'oo-neigh teigh p'rrow P'rra-tahneh, 'eea tee'a eea 'oy? M'ah vahee eetee. Eh meh-a nah'ee-nah'ee roh-a tow eh p'rrow ——.*
2. 'Oku ou fiema'u keu alu ki ——. 'Oku 'i ai ha pasi (ha vakapuna, ha tekisi)? 'Io, 'oku 'i ai. 'Ikai, 'oku 'ikai. *Ohg' oh feea-mow gheeoo ahloo ghee ——. Ohg' ee igh hah pahssi (hah vahga-poona, hah deg-see)? Eeoh, ohg' ee igh. Ee-kigh, ohgoo ee-kigh.*	2. 'Ou te fia alu i ——. E i ai se pasi (se va'alele, se ta'avale la'u pāsese)? O lea lava. E leai. *Oh t' fee-ahloo ee ——. Eigh ay s' pahssi (s' vah-lehleh, s' tah-vahleh la'oo pah-sehseh)? Oh leh-a lahva. Eh leh-igh.*	2. Hina'aro vau i te haere i ——. E pereo'o mata'eina'a (manureva, pereo'o uira) ānei? 'Ē, tē vai ra. 'Aita, 'aita roa. *Heen'ahrro vow ee teh highreh ee ——. Eh pehreh'oh maht'ehn'ah (mahnoo-rehva, pehreh'oh weera) ahneigh? 'Eh, teh veighra. 'Ighta, 'ighta roh-a.*
3. Koe fe'ia 'ae pasi ('ae tau'anga lēlue, 'ae ōfisi tikite)? Ko'eni ia ('i hē, 'ihe feitu'u koe). *Koy feh-ee'igh pahssi (igh tow-ahng-a lehloo-eh, igh oh-fissi teekit-eh)? Ko-ehnee eea (ee eh, ee-eh fay-too goy).*	3. 'O fea le pasi (le nofoāga mo nofoāfi, le 'ōfisa fa'atau pepa)? Olea e i'inei (Olea e i'ō, Ole la e i'ō). *O feh-a l' pahssi (l' noffo-ahng-a mo noffo-ahfee,leh oh-feessa fah-tow pehpa)? Oh-leh-a eh ee'neigh (Oh-leh-a eigh'oh, Oh-leh lah eigh'oh).*	3. Tei hea roa te pereo'o mata'eina'a (te vāhi tapaera'a pereo'o auahi, te ho'ora'a titeti)? Tei 'unei (terā, terā i 'ō). *Teigh heh-a roh-a teh pehreh'oh maht'ehn'ah (t'vahee ta-pehrr'ah pehreh'oh ow-hee, teh hoh'ohrr'ah tee-tehtee)? Teigh 'oo-neigh (t'rrah, t'rrah ee 'oh).*
4. Teu 'alu 'ife kihe mala'e vakapuna (kihe kolo)? 'Alu he hala koe. 'Alu hangatonu (kihe to'ohema, kihe to'omata'u). *Teeoo ahloo ee-feh keea mahlah-eh vahga-poona (gheea kohloh)? Ahlo eh hahlah goy. Ahloo 'nga-tohnoo (gheea toh-hehma, gheea tohma-ta-ooh).*	4. E fa'apēfea ona 'ou alu i le malae va'alele (i le 'a'ai)? Alu i'ō. Alu sa'o (i le tauagavale, i le taumatau). *Eh fah-peh-feh-a ohna oh ahloo eel' m'ligh vah-lehleh (ee leh ah'igh)? Ahloo ee oh. Ahloo sah'oh (ee leh towng-a-vahleh, ee leh towma-tow).*	4. Nā fea vau te haere i te tahua manureva (i te 'oire)? Haere i terā pae. Haere i 'āfaro noa (i tō 'oe pae 'aui, i tō 'oe pae 'atau). *Nah feh-a vow teh highreh ee teh ta-hooa mahnoo-rehva (ee teh 'oyreh)? Highreh ee t'rrah pay. Highreh 'ah-fahro noh-a (ee toh 'oy pay 'ow-ee, ee toh 'oy pay 'a-tow).*

SENTENCES

ENGLISH	NEW GUINEA PIDGIN	FIJIAN
5. Would you take my baggage to the bus, please. There is just one bag. There are two bags and that bundle.	5. Yu karim ol bek bilong mi i go long bas, plis. I gat wanpela bek tasol. I gat tupela bek na dispela karamap. *Yoo kahrim ol bek b'long mee ee go long bahss, pleess. Ee gaht wahnp'la bek tahssol. Ee gaht toop'la bek na dissp'la kahra-mahp.*	5. E rawa beka mo kauta noqu i yaya ki na basi. E dua ga na kato. E rua na kato kei na i oloolo ko ya. *Eh row'mbekka mo ka-oota nonggoo ee yahya kee na mbahssi. Eh ndooa nga na kahto. Eh rrooa na kahto kay na ee ollo-ollo ko yah.*
6. When does the bus go? Show me, please. The bus is late. The bus has already gone.	6. Bas i go wataim? Yu soim mi plis. Bas i bihaintaim. Bas i go pinis. *Bahss ee go wahttighm? Yoo sohm mee pleess. Bahss ee b'highntighm. Bahss ee go pinnis.*	6. E na lako beka e na gauna cava na basi? Yalo vinaka, ni vakaraitaka mada vei au. E sa bera na basi. E sa lako oti na basi. *Eh na lahgo mbek' eh na ngowna thahva na mbahssi? Yallo v'nahka, nee vong-a-ray-tahka mahnda vay ow. Eh sa mbehrra na mbahssi. Eh sa lahgo awtee na mbahssi.*
7. A ticket <u>for one person</u> (for two persons) to ——, please. Two adults and one child. First class. Tourist class.	7. Mi laik i baim tiket <u>long wanpela</u> man (long tupela man) i go long ——, plis. Tupela bikpela na wanpela pikinini. Namba wan klas. Namba tu klas. *Mee lighk ee bighm tikket long wahnp'la mahn (long toop'la mahn) ee go long ——, pleess. Toop'la bikp'la na wahnp'la pikkaninny. Nahmba wahn klahss. Nahmba too klahss.*	7. Yalo vinaka, tikite ni <u>lewe dua</u> (ni lewe rua) ki ——. Rua na uabula ka dua na gone lailai. Matai ni kalasi. Na kalasi ni sara vanua. *Yallo v'nahka, t'keeteh nee lehweh ndooa (nee lehweh rrooa) kee ——. Rrooa na ooa-mboola ka ndooa na ngohneh laylay. Ma-tigh nee ka-lahss'. Na ka-lahssi nee sarra va-nooa.*
8. Excuse me, what time is it? Two o'clock. Ten past two. Half past two. Ten to three.	8. Plis, haumas kilok nau? Em i tu kilok. Em i ten minit bihain long tu kilok. Em i hap pas tu. Ten minit i go bilong painim tri kilok. *Pleess, howmahss killok now? Em ee too killok. Em ee ten minnit b'highn long too killok. Em ee hahp pahss too. Ten minnit ee go b'long pighnim tree killok.*	8. Vosoti au, e sa vica beka na kaloko? E sa rua na kaloko. Sa sivi na rua e na tini na miniti. Sa veimama na rua. Sa vo e tini na miniti me tolu. *V'sottee ow, eh sa vitha mbekka na ka-lokko? Eh sa rrooa na ka-lokko. Sa seevee na rrooa eh na teenee na m'neetee. Sa vay-mahma na rrooa. Sa vo eh teenee na m'neetee meh tolloo.*

354

SENTENCES

TONGAN

5. Fakamolemole mu'a 'o fetuku 'a eku ū me'a kihe pasi. Koe kato pe ia 'e taha. Koe kato 'e ua pea moe kofukofu koena.

Fah-mohleh-mohleh mooa, oh feh-tookoo ehg' oo meh-ah gheea pahssi. Goy kahtto beh ee' eh ta-hh. Goy kahtto eh ooa beh' moy koff'koff' ko-ehna.

6. 'Oku 'alu he fiha 'ae pasi? Fakamolemole 'o fakahinohino mai. 'Oku tomui 'ae pasi. Kuo 'osi 'alu 'ae pasi ia.

Ohg' ahloo eh fee-hah ay pahssi? Fah-mohleh-mohleh oh fah-hinn'-hinno migh. Ohg' toh-mooee ay pahssi. Gw' ohssi ahloo ay pahssi eea.

7. Ha tikite <u>kihe tokotaha</u> (kihe tokoua) ki ———, fakamolemole. Tokoua lalahi pea moe ki'i leka 'e taha. Kalasi 'uluaki. Kalasi 'eve'eva.

Ah teekit' keea tohgo-ta-hh (keea tohgo-ooa) ghee ———, fah-mohleh-mohleh. Tohg' ooa la-la-hh beh' moy g'lehga eh ta-hh. Ka-lahssi ooloo-ahgi. Ka-lahssi ehveh-eh-va.

8. Kātaki, koe fihá 'eni? Koe uá 'eni. Kuo 'osi 'ae ua mo e miniti 'e hongofulu. Kuo haāfe 'ae tolu. 'Oku toe 'ae miniti 'e hongofulu kihe tolu.

Ka-tahkee, goy fee-hah ehnee? Goy wah ehnee. Gw' ohssee ay wah moy m'neetee eh hong-o-fooloo. Gwo hahf' ay tolloo. Ohg' toy ay m'neetee eh hong-o-fooloo gheea tolloo.

SAMOAN

5. Fa'amolemole, e te mafai ona 'avatu la'u 'ato i le pasi. Na'o le 'atopa'u e tasi. E lua 'atopa'u ma le ta'ui.

Fah-mohleh-mohleh, eh t' m'figh ohna a-vahtoo lah'oo ahto eel' pahssi. Nah'o leh ahto-pah'oo eh tahssi. Eh looa ahto-pah'oo ma leh tah'ooi.

6. 'O āfea e alu ai le pasi? Fa'asino mai, fa'amolemole. Ua tuai le pasi. Ua alu le pasi.

O ahfeh-igh ahloo ayl' pahssi? Fah-seeno migh, fah-mohleh- mohleh. Ooa twigh l' pahssi. Oo ahloo l' pahssi.

7. 'O se pepa mo <u>le tagata e to'atasi</u> (mo tagata e to'alua) ———, fa'amolemole. E to'alua tagata matutua ma le tamaitiiti e to'atasi. 'O le vaega numera tasi. 'O le vaega numera lua.

O seh pehpa mo l' t'ngahta eh toh'a-tahssi (mo t'ngahta eh toh'a-looa) ———, fah-mohleh-mohleh. Eh toh'a-looa t'ng-ahta maht'tooa mahl' tahmay-teeti eh toh'a-tahssi. O leh vighng-a noomeh-ra tahssi. O leh vighng-a noomeh-ra looa.

8. Fa'amolemole, o le a le taimi? Ua ta le lua. Sefulu e te'a ai le lua. Ua 'afa le lua. Sefulu i le tolu.

Fah-mohleh-mohleh, ohleh ah l' tighmee? Ooa tah leh looa. S'fooloo eh teh'igh leh looa. Ooa ahfa leh looa. S'fooloo eel' tohloo.

TAHITIAN

5. 'Ia ti'a ia 'oe, e nehenehe ānei tā 'oe e 'āfa'i i tō'u taiha'a i te pereo'o mata'eina'a ra? Hō'ē ana'e iho pūtē taiha'a. E piti pūtē taiha'a 'ē terā pū'ohu.

'Eea tee'a eea 'oy, eh n'heh-n'heh ah-neigh tah 'oy eh 'ahf'eh ee toh'oo, tigh-h'ah ee teh pehreh'oh maht'ehn'ahra? Hoh'eh ahn'eh eeho poo-teh tigh-h'ah 'eh t'rrah poo'hoo.

6. Āfea e haere ai te pereo'o mata'eina'a? Fa'a'ite mai iā'u, 'ia ti'a ia 'oe. 'Ua tāere te pereo'o mata'eina'a. 'Ua reva ē na te pereo'o mataeina'a.

Ah-feh-a eh highreh ay teh pehreh'oh maht'ehn'ah? Fa'eeteh may yah'oo, 'eea tee'a eea 'oy. 'Ooa tighreh t'pehreh'oh maht'ehn'ah. 'Ooa rehva eh na t'pehreh'oh maht'ehn'ah.

7. E tīteti <u>nō te hō'ē ta'ata</u> (nō e piti ta'ata) i ———, 'ia ti'a ia 'oe. E piti ta'ata pa'ari 'ē hō'ē tamari'i. Te tahua mātāmua. Te tahua piti.

Eh tee-tehteh noh teh hoh'eh t'ahta (noh eh pittee t'ahta) ee ———, 'eea tee'a eea 'oy. Eh pittee t'ahta p'ahree 'eh hoh'eh tahmah-ree. Teh ta-hooa mahtah-mooa. Teh ta-hooa pittee.

8. 'Ē'ē, e aha te hora i teie nei? Hora piti. Hō'ē 'ahuru miniti i ma'iri i te hora piti. Hora piti 'ē te 'āfa. 'Ahuru miniti e hora toru ai.

'Eh'eh, eh a-hah teh hohra ee teh-ee-eh neigh? Hohra pittee. Hoh'eh 'a-hooroo m̄ n̄eetee ee ma'eeree ee teh hohra pittee. Hohra pittee 'eh teh 'ahfa. 'A-hooroo m'neetee eh hohra tohroo ay.

SENTENCES

ENGLISH	NEW GUINEA PIDGIN	FIJIAN

9. Take me to a hotel (to the ——— Hotel). Is this (that) the hotel? How far is it?

9. Kisim mi i go long wanpela hotel (long ——— Hotel). Dispela (Dispela long hap) em i dispela hotel? Em i longwe o nogat?
Kissim mee ee go long wahnp'la ho-tell (long ——— Ho-tell). Dissp'la (Dissp'la long hahp) em ee dissp'la ho-tell? Em ee longweh oh nohgaht?

9. Kauti au ki na dua na otela (ki na ——— otela). Sa i koya ogo (oya) na otela? E vakaevei na kena yawa?
Kowtee ow kee na ndooa na oh-tellah (kee na ——— oh-tellah). Sa ee kohya onggo (ohya) na oh-tellah? Eh vong-a-eh-vay na kenna yahwa?

10. Have you a single room (a double room)? May I see the room? I don't like that room. I like this room.

10. Yu gat rum i gat wanpela bet (rum i gat tupela bet)? Mi laik lukim dispela rum. Mi no laikim dispela rum long hap. Mi laikim dispela rum hia.
Yoo gaht room ee gaht wahnp'la bett (room ee gaht toop'la bett)? Mee lighk lookim dissp'la room. Mee no lighkim dissp'la room long hahp. Mee lighkim dissp'la room heea.

10. E tiko beka e dua na rumu ni lewe dua (e dua na rumu ni lewe rua)? E rawa beka meu raica na rumu? Au sega ni vinakata na rumu ko ya. Au vinakata na rumu oqo.
Eh teeko mbek' eh ndooa na rroomoo nee lehweh ndooa (eh ndooa na rroomoo nee lehweh rrooa)? Eh row' mbekka meoo rightha na rroomoo? Ow seng-a nee vinna-kutta na rroomoo ko yah. Ow vinna-kutta na rroom' onggo.

11. Could I have the key of my room, please? Are there any letters for me (for us)?

11. Mi laik yu givim mi ki bilong rum bilong mi, plis. I gat sampela pas i kam long mi (long mipela) o nogat?
Mee lighk yoo givvim mee kee b'long room b'long mee, pleess. Ee gaht sahmp'la pahss ee kahm long mee (long meep'la) oh nohgaht?

11. Yalo vinaka, e rawa beka meu taura na ki ni noqu rumu? E so beka na noqu (neirau) i vola?
Yallo v'nahka, eh row'mbekka meoo towrra na kee nee nonggoo rroomoo? Eh so mbekka na nonggoo (nay-rrow) ee vohla?

12. Could I speak to ———, please? It has to do with ———. It is very important.

12. Mi laik toktok wantaim long ———, plis. Em i toktok long ———. Em i bikpela samting tumas.
Mee lighk tawktawk wahnt'm long ———, pleess. Em ee tawktawk long ———. Em ee bikp'la sahmting too-mahss.

12. E rawa beka meu vosa vei ———? E baleta na ———. E rui ka bibi sara.
Eh row'mbekka meoo vossa vay ———? Eh mba-lehta na ———. Eh rrooi ka mbeembee sarra.

SENTENCES

TONGAN	SAMOAN	TAHITIAN

9. 'Ave au <u>kiha hotele</u> (kihe Hotele ko ———). Koe hotele 'eni ('ena)? Koe ha hono mama'o?
Ahveh ow gheea hoh-tehleh (gheea Hoh-tehleh go ———). Goy hoh-tehleh ehnee (ehna)? Goy ah hohno ma-ma-oh?

9. 'Ave a'u i <u>se fale talimālō</u> (i le fale talimālō 'o ———. 'O le fale talimālō <u>lenei</u> (lenā)? O le a le mamao?
Ahveh ah'oo eess' fahleh tahlee-mah-loh (eel' fahleh tahlee-mah-loh o ———). O leh fahleh tahlee-mah-loh l'neigh (l'nah)? Ohleh ah leh m'mow?

9. 'Āfa'i iā'u <u>i te hōtēra</u> (i te Hōtēra ———). 'O <u>teie</u> (terā) te hōtēra? E fea āteara'a?
'Ah-fah'ee 'ow ee teh hoh-tehrra (ee teh Hoh-tehrra ———). 'Oh teh-ee-eh (t'rrah) teh hoh-tehrra? Eh feh-a ah-teh-a-rah?

10. 'Oku 'i ai <u>ha loki kihe</u> tokotaha (ha loki kihe tokoua)? Teu lava 'o sio he loki? 'Oku 'ikai teu sa'ia he loki. 'Oku 'ou sa'ia he loki ko'eni.
Ohg' ee igh ah lohgi gheea tohgo-ta-hh (ah lohgi gheea tohgo-ooa)? Teeoo lahv' oh seeo eh lohgi? Ohg' ee-kigh teeoo sah-ee' eh lohgi Ohg' oh sah-ee' eh lohgi go-ehnee.

10. E i ai <u>se potu mo se tagata</u> e to'atasi (se potu mo tagata e to'alua)? E mafai ona 'ou va'ai i le potu? 'Ou te lē mana'o i le potu lenā. 'Ou te mana'o i le potu lenei.
Eigh ay s' pohtoo mohss' t'ngahta eh toh'a-tahssi (s' pohtoo mo t'ng-ahta eh toh'a-looa)? Eh m'figh ohna oh va'igh eel' pohtoo? Oh teh leh m'nah'o eel' pohtoo l'nah. Oh t' m'nah'o eel' pohtoo l'neigh.

10. Tē vai ra tā 'oe <u>hō'ē piha</u> (piha e piti ta'ata)? Nehenehe tau e hi'o i te piha? 'Aita vau i au i terā piha. E au vau i teie piha.
Teh vay ra tah 'oy hoh'eh peeha (peeha eh pittee ta'ahta)? N'heh-n'heh tow eh hee'o ee teh peeha? 'Ighta vow ee ow ee t'rrah peeha. Eh ow vow ee teh-ee-eh peeha.

11. Fakamolemole mu'a 'o omai 'ae ki kihoku loki? 'Oku 'i ai ha 'ū tohi <u>kia te au</u> (kia kimautolu)?
Fah-mohleh-mohleh mooa, oh 'migh igh kee ghee-ohg' lohgi? Ohg' ee igh ha oo tohhee gheea teh ow (gheea 'mow-tohloo)?

11. E mafai ona 'aumai le kī o lo'u potu, fa'amolemole? E i ai <u>sa'u</u> (se matou) tusi?
Eh m'figh ohna oh-migh l' kee oh loh'oo pohtoo, fah-mohleh-mohleh? Eigh ay sah'oo (s' mahtoh) toossee?

11. 'Ia ti'a ia 'oe, e hōro'a mai te tāviri o tō'u piha iā'u ra. Tē vai ra ānei te rata <u>na'u</u> (nā māua)?
'Eea tee'a eea 'oy, eh hohroh'ah may teh tah-veeree oh toh'oo peeha yah'oora. Teh vayra-ah-neigh teh rahta nah'oo (nah ma'ooa)?

12. Fakamolemole mu'a pe teu lava 'o lea kia ———? 'Oku kau kihe ———. 'Oku fu'u mahu'inga aupito.
Fah-mohleh-mohleh mooa, beh teeoo lahva oh leh' gheea ———? Ohg' gow ghee hee ———. Ohg' foo ma-hooing' ow-peeto.

12. E mafai ona 'ou talanoa iā ———, fa'amolemole? O se mea e uiga i le ———. E matuā tāua tele.
Eh m'figh ohna oh tahla-noh-a ee-ah ———, fah-mohleh-mohleh? Oh seh meh-a eh weeng-a ee leh ———. Eh m'too-ah tow-a telleh.

12. 'Ia ti'a ia 'oe, e nehenehe ānei tau e parauparau ia ———? E ma'a 'ohipa iti 'e 'ōna ———. E mea faufa'a rahi roa.
'Eea tee'a eea 'oy, eh n'heh-n'heh ah-neigh tow eh p'rrow-p'rrow eea ———? Eh m'ah 'o-hee-pah eetee 'eh 'ohna ———. Eh meh-a fowf'ah rahee roh-a.

SENTENCES

ENGLISH	NEW GUINEA PIDGIN	FIJIAN

13. How much is this?
I would like to buy this, please.
That is too dear.
I don't want it.

13. Dispela i haumas? Mi laik baim dispela, plis. Em i dia tumas. Mi no laik.

Dissp'la ee howmahss? Mee lighk bighm dissp'la, pleess. Em ee deea too-mahss. Mee no lighk.

13. E vica na kena i sau oqo? Yalo vinaka, au via volia oqo. E rui sau levu ko ya. Au sega ni vinakata.

Eh vitha na kenna ee sow onggo? Yallo v'nahka, ow veea volleea onggo. Eh rrooi sow lehvoo ko ya. Ow seng-a nee vinna-kutta.

14. May I wash my hands?
I would like a bath. I need some soap (a towel, hot water).

14. Orait mi wasim han hia? Mi laik waswas. Mi laikim <u>sop</u> (taul, hatwara).

Aw-right mee wahssim hahn heea? Mee lighk wahsswahss. Mee lighkim sohp (towl, hot-wahra).

14. E rawa beka niu savata na ligaqu? Au via sisili. Au kerea e <u>dua na sovu</u> (e dua na tauwelu, e so na wai katakata).

Eh row'mbekka neeoo savahta na ling-ahngg'? Ow veea s'seelee. Ow keh-rreh' eh ndooa na sohvoo (eh ndooa na tow-welloo, eh so na way kutta-kutta).

15. Is the restaurant <u>open</u> (closed)? Could I see the menu? I would like ———.
The bill, please.

15. Haus kaikai i <u>op</u> (i pas)? Mi laik lukim nem bilong ol kaikai long menu. Mi laik ———. Yu bringim bil, plis.

Howss kighkigh ee ohp (ee pahss)? Mee lighk lookim nehm b'long ol kighkigh long meenyoo. Mee lighk ———. Yoo bringim bill, pleess.

15. E <u>dola</u> (sogo) beka na vale ni kana? E rawa niu raica na i vola ni ka me laukana? Au vinakata ———. Yalo vinaka, solia mada mai na bili.

Eh ndohla (song-o) mbekka na vahleh nee kahna? Eh raw'neeoo rraytha na ee vohla nee kah meh loh-kahna? Ow vinna-kutta ———. Yallo v'nahka, solleea mahnda may na beelee.

16. I would like to make a telephone call. Would you call ——— for me?
There is no answer.
I have been cut off.

16. Mi laik toktok long telipon. Mi laik bai yu putim telipon long ——— bai mi toktok wantaim em. Telipon i ring tasol nogat ansa. Swis ating i katim toktok bilong mitupela.

Mee lighk tawktawk long telli-pohn. Mee lighk bigh yoo pootim telli-pohn long ——— bigh mee tawktawk wahnt'm em. Telli-pohn ee ring tahssol nohgaht ahnsa. Swiss ahting ee kahtim tawktawk b'long mee-toop'la.

16. Au via talevoni. E rawa ni ko tauri ——— mada mai vei au? E sega ni saumi mai. Sa tamusuki na noqu vosa.

Ow veea tahleh-vohnee. Eh raw'nee ko towrree ——— mahnda migh vay ow? Eh seng-a nee sohmee migh. Sa tahmoo-sookee na nonggoo vossa.

SENTENCES

TONGAN

13. 'Oku fiha eni?
Fakamolemole mu'a 'oku ou fie
fakatau 'a eni. 'Oku fu'u
mamafa. 'Oku 'ikai teu fiema'u.
Ohg' fee-hah ehnee? Fah-
mohleh-mohleh mooa, ohg'
oh fee' fah'tow ah ehnee.
Ohg' foo ma-mahfa. Ohg' ee-
kigh teeoo feea-mow.

14. Teu lava fanofano hoku
nima? 'Oku ou fiema'u keu
kaukau. Teu fiema'u ae koa (ha
taueli, vai vela).
Teeoo lahva fahn'fahno
hohg' neema? Ohg' oh feea-
mow gheeoo kow-kow. Teeoo
feea-mow igh koh-a (ah tow-
ehlee, vigh vehla).

15. 'Oku ava (mapuni) 'ae fale
kai? Teu lava sio kihe lisi oe
meākai? 'Oku ou fiema'u ae
———. 'E me'a 'a hoku mo'ua
fakamolemole.
Ohg' ahva (ma-poonee) igh
fahleh kigh? Teeoo lahva
seeo gheea lissi oy meh-a-
kigh? Ohg' oh feea-mow igh
———. Eh meh-a ah
hohgoo mo-ooa fah-mohleh-
mohleh.

16. 'Oku ou fiema'u keu
telefoni. Teke lava 'o telefoni
kia ——— ma'aku? 'Oku 'ikai
ke tali mai ia. Na'e tu'usi au ia.
Ohg' oh feea-mow keeoo
tella-fohnee. Tehgeh lahva o
tella-fohnee gheea ———
ma-ahgoo? Ohg' ee-kigh keh
tahlee migh eea. Nigh toossi
ow eea.

SAMOAN

13. O le a le tau o le mea lea?
'Ou te fia fa'atauina le mea
lenei, fa'amolemole. E taugata
tele. 'Ou te le mana'o ai.
Ohleh ah leh tow ohl' meh-a
leh-a? Oh t' feea fah-tow-
eena leh meh-a l'neigh, fah-
mohleh-mohleh. Eh towng-a-
tah telleh. Oh teh leh m'nah'o
igh.

14. E mafai ona fufulu o'u
lima? 'Ou te fia ta'ele. 'Ou te
mana'o i se fasi moli (i se solo
ta'ele, i se vai vevela).
Eh m'figh ohna f'fooloo oh'oo
leema? Oh teh feea tah'ehleh.
Oh t' m'nah'o eess' fahssi
mohlee (ee s' sohloh
tah'ehleh, ee s' vigh v'vehlah).

15. 'O tatala (tapuni) le fale
'aiga? E mafai ona 'ou va'ai i le
menu? 'Ou te mana'o ———.
Totogi, fa'amolemole.
O t'tahlah (tah-poonee) l'
fahleh eighng-a? Eh m'figh
ohna oh va'igh eel' mehnoo?
Oh t' m'nah'o ———.
T'tohngi, fah-mohleh-
mohleh.

16. 'Ou te mana'o e fai la'u
telefoni. E a pe a e telefoni iā
——— mo a'u? E leai se tali
mai. Ua vavae ese ina a'u ma le
laina.
Oh t' m'nah'o eh figh lah'oo
tel'fohnee. Eh ah peh igh tel'-
fohnee ee-ah ——— mo
ah'oo? Eh leh igh s' tahli
migh. Ooa v'vigh ehsseh
eenah ah'oo mahl' layna.

TAHITIAN

13. E hia moni i teie? E
hina'aro vau i te ho'o, 'ia ti'a ia
'oe. E mea ho'o rahi roa. E'ita
vau e hina'aro.
Eh heea mohnee ee teh-ee-
eh? Eh heen'ahrro vow ee teh
ho'oh, 'eea tee'a eea 'oy. Eh
meh-a ho'oh rahee roh-a.
Eh'eeta vow eh heen'ahrro.

14. E nehenehe vau e horoi tō'u
rima? E hina'aro vau e hapu i te
pape. E hina'aro vau ma'a pu'a
iti (tauera, ma'a pape ve'ave'a).
Eh n'heh-n'heh vow eh h'rroy
toh'oo reema? Eh heen'ahrro
vow m'ah poo'a eetee (tow-
ehrra, m'ah pahpeh veh'a-
veh'a).

15. 'Ua mahiti ('ōpani) ānei te
fare tāma'ara'a? Nehenehe tau
e hi'o i te parau mā'a? E
hina'aro vau i ———. E hoa,
f'a'ite mai te moni mā'a.
'Ooa ma-heetee ('oh-pahnee)
ah-neigh teh fahreh
tahma'rah'a? N'heh-n'heh
tow eh hee'o ee teh p'rrow
mah'a? Eh heen'ahrro vow ee
———. Eh hoh-a, fah'eeteh
may t'mohnee mah'a.

16. E hina'aro vau e tāniuniu.
E nehenehe ānei tā 'oe e
tāniuniu ia ———? 'Aita e
pahono. 'Ua tāpūhia mai te
niuniu.
Eh heen'ahrro vow eh tah-
nyoonyoo. Eh n'heh-n'heh
ah-neigh tah 'oy eh tah-
nyoonyoo eea ———?
'Ighta eh pa-hohnoh. 'Ooa
tah-poo-heea may teh
nyoonyoo.

ENGLISH	NEW GUINEA PIDGIN	FIJIAN

17. Could I have <u>some notepaper</u> (some air mail paper, some envelopes)? Where can I buy stamps? How much altogether?

17. Plis mi laikim <u>sampela pepa bilong raitim leta</u> (sampela emel pepa, sampela skin pas). Bai mi baim stem we? Olgeta haumas?

Pleess, mee lighkim sahmp'la pehpa b'long rightim letta (sahmp'la emmehl pehpa, sahmp'la skin pahss). Bigh mee bighm stem weh? Olgetta howmahss?

17. Au kerea <u>e so na pepa</u> (e so na drau ni pepa ni meli, e so na waqanivola)? Au na volia rawa beka evei e so na sitaba? E vica taucoko na kena i sau?

Ow k'rreh-a eh so na pehpa (eh so na ndrow nee pehpa nee mehlee, eh so na wahngga-nee-vohla)? Ow na volleea row'mbek' ey-vay eh so na s'tamba? Eh vith' towthokko na kenna ee sow?

18. I am ill. Where can I see a doctor? Please get a good doctor. Could I have some water?

18. Mi gat sik. Mi go painim dokta we? Plis, yu go tokim dokta, em i kam. Mi laikim wara bilong dring.

Mee gaht sik. Mee go pighnim dokta weh? Pleess, yoo go tawkim dokta, em ee kahm. Mee lighkim wahra b'long dring.

18. Au tauvi mate. Au na kunea beka evei e dua na vuniwai? Yalo vinaka, kauta mai vei au e dua na vuniwai vinaka. E rawa ni dua vei au na wai?

Ow tohvee mahteh. Ow na koo-neh-a mbek' eh-vay eh ndooa na voonee-wigh? Yallo v'nahka, kohta migh vay ow eh ndooa na voonee-wigh v'nahka. Eh raw'nee ndooa vay ow na wigh?

19. May I introduce ———. I am pleased to meet you. My name is ———.

19. Mi laik bai yu bungim ———. Mi amamas long mitim yu. Nem bilong mi em i ———.

Mee lighk bigh yoo boongim ———. Mee ahma-mahss long meetim yoo. Nehm b'long mee em ee ———.

19. Oqo ko ———. Vinaka na bula. Na yacaqu ko ———.

Onggo ko ———. V'nahka na mboolla. Na ya-thanggoo ko ———.

20. Who are you? A friend. I come from ———. Go away!

20. Yu husat? Mi pren. Mi bin kam long ———. Yu raus!

Yoo hoozat? Mee pren. Mee bin kahm long ———. Yoo rowss!

20. O cei beka o kemuni? E dua nomuni tokani. Au lako mai ———. Lako tani!

O thay mbek' o keh-moonee? Eh ndooa no-moonee tok-kahnee. Ow lahgo migh ———. Lahgo tahnee!

21. What is this called? What is this place called? It is called ———.

21. Wanem nem bilong dispela samting? Wanem nem bilong dispela ples? Ol i kolim long ———.

Wahnehm nehm b'long dissp'la sahmting? Wahnehm nehm b'long dissp'la pless? Ol ee kollim long ———.

21. Na cava na yaca ni ka oqo? Na cava na yaca ni vanua oqo? E yacana li ko ———.

Na thahva na yahtha nee ka onggo? Na thahva na yahtha nee va-noo' onggo? Eh ya-thahna lee ko ———.

TONGAN	SAMOAN	TAHITIAN

17. 'Omai mu'a ha 'ū pepa (ha ngaahi 'ū pepa 'ea meili, moha 'ū sila)? Teu lava fakatau ha 'ū sitapa 'ife? 'Oku fiha katoa?

O-migh mooa ah oo peppa (ahng-high oo peppa eh' mehlee, mo' oo seela)? Teeoo lahva fah'tow ha oo seetahpa eefeh? Ohg' feea katoh-a?

17. E mafai ona 'ou maua <u>ni</u> <u>nai pepa</u> (ni pepa mo tusi i le va'alele, ni nai teutusi)? O fea a fa'atau ai fa'ailoga mo tusi? O le a le tau aofa'i?

Eh m'figh ohna oh mow-a nee nigh pehpa (nee pehpa mo toossi eel' vah-lehleh, nee nigh teh-o-toossi)? Oh feh-ah fah-tow wigh fah-ee-lohng-a mo toossi? Ohleh ah leh tow ow-fa'?

17. E roa'a <u>ma'a parau pāpa'i</u> (ma'a parau pāpa'i na te manureva, ma'a vihi rata). I hea vau ho'o ai i te titiro? E hia moni pau roa?

Eh roh-a m'ah p'rrow pahp'ay (m'ah p'rrow pahp'ay nah teh mahnoo-rehva, m'ah v'hee rahta). Ee heh-a vow hoh'o ay ee teh t'teerro? Eh heea mohnee pow roh-a?

18. 'Oku ou puke. Teu lava sio kiha toketa 'ife? Fakamolemole 'o 'omai ha toketa 'oku sai. 'Omai mu'a ha vai?

Ohg' oh pookeh. Teeoo lahva seeo keea tokkeh-tah eefeh? Fah-mohleh-mohleh oh 'migh ah tokkeh-tah ohg' sigh. O-migh moo' ah vigh?

18. Ua 'ou ma'i. O fea e mafai ona 'ou va'ai ai i se fōma'i? Fa'amolemole, se'i 'a'ami se fōma'i agava'a. E mafai ona 'ou maua sina vai?

Ooa oh ma'ee. Oh feh-a eh m'figh ohna oh va'igh igh s' foh-ma'ee? Fah-mohleh-mohleh, seh'ee ah'ahmee s' foh-ma'ee ahng-a-va'. Eh m'figh ohna oh mow-a seena vigh?

18. E ma'i tō'u. I hea vau e hi'o ai i te taote? 'Ia ti'a ia 'oe, 'a hōro'a mai hō'ē taote maita'i. Hina'aro vau ma'a pape.

Eh m'ay toh'oo. Ee heh-a vow eh hee'o ay ee teh towteh? 'Eea tee'a eea 'oy, 'a hohro'a may hoh'eh towteh mayt'ay. Heen'ahrro vow m'ah pahpeh.

19. Mo feiloaki mo ———. 'Oku ou fiefia keu feiloaki mo koe. Ko hoku hingoa ko ———.

Mo faylo-ahkee mo ———. Ohg' oh feea-feea keeoo faylo-ahkee mo koy. Koh'k' hing-wah go ———.

19. 'Ou te fia fa'afeiloa'i atu ———. Ua 'ou fiafia lava e fa'afeiloa'i atu iā te 'oe. 'O lo'u igoa 'o ———.

Oh t' feea fah-feigh-law'ee attoo ———. Ooa oh feea-feea lahva eh fah-feigh-law'ee attoo ee-ah teh oy. Oh loh'oo ee-ngaw-a o ———.

19. E fa'afārerei vau ———. 'Ua māuruuru vau i te fārerei ia 'oe. Tō'u i'oa 'o ———.

Eh fa'fahreh-reigh vow ———. 'Ooa mow-rooroo vow ee teh fahreh-reigh ya 'oy. Toh'oo ee'oh-a 'oh

20. Kohai koe? Koe kaume'a. 'Oku ou ha'u mei ———. 'Alu mama'o!

Ko-high goy? Goy kow-meh-a. Ohg' oh how' may ———. Ahloo ma-mah'!

20. 'O ai 'oe? 'O se uo. 'Ou te sau mai ———. Alu 'ese! O igh oy? O seh woh. Oh teh sow migh ———. Ahloo esseh!*

20. 'O vai 'oe? E hoa. Haere mai vau na ———. 'A haere 'ē!

'Oh vay 'oy? Eh hoh-a. Highreh may vow nah ———. 'A highreh 'eh!

21. Koeha hono ui eni? Koeha hono ui 'ae feitu'u ko'eni? 'Oku ui ko ———.

Koy-hah ho-noh ooi ehnee? Koy-hah ho-noh ooi igh fay-too go-ehnee? Ohg' ooi go ———.

21. O le a le ta'u o le mea lenei? O le a le igoa o lenei nofoāga? E ta'ua 'o le ———.

Ohleh ah leh tah'oo ohleh meh-a l'neigh? Ohleh ah leh ee-ngaw-a oh l'neigh noffo-ahng-a? Eh ta'ooa o leh ———.

21. E aha te i'oa o teie? E aha te i'oa teie vāhi? E pi'ihia ia ———.

Eh hah teh ee'oh-a oh teh-ee-eh? Eh hah teh ee'oh-a teh-ee-eh vahee? Eh pee'heea eea ———.

SENTENCES

ENGLISH	NEW GUINEA PIDGIN	FIJIAN

22. What is the matter?
Don't worry. I am sorry
(glad). I shall give you this.

22. Olsem wanem? Nogut yu
wori. Mi sori (amamas tru). Mi
givim dispela samting long yu.
Olsehm wahnehm? Nohgood
yoo wahree. Mee sorree
(ahma-mahss troo). Mee
givvim dissp'la sahm-ting
long yoo.

22. Na cava na leqa? Kakua ni
leqa. Au rarawa (marau) e na
ka oqori. Au na solia vei
kemuni oqo.
Na thahva na lengga? Ka-
koo' nee lengga. Ow rra-
rrahwa (ma-rrow) eh na ka
ong-gohrri. Ow na solleea
vay keh-moonee onggo.

23. What do you want?
Please sit down. I have to
leave. You must go now.

23. Yu laik wanem samting?
Plis, yu sindaun. Mi mas go. Yu
mas go nau.
Yoo lighk wahnehm
sahmting? Pleess, yoo
sindown. Mee mahss go. Yoo
mahss go now.

23. Na cava ko ni vinakata?
Yalo vinaka, dabe mada. E
dodonu meu sa gole mada. Mo
ni gole sara yani oqo.
Na thahva ko nee vinna-
kutta? Yallo v'nahka,
ndahmbeh mahnda? Eh
ndoh-ndohnoo meoo sa
ngohleh mahnda. Mo nee
ngohleh sarra yannee onggo.

24. I need help. I am in
trouble. Please give this
message to ———.
As soon as possible.

24. Mi laikim sampela halivim.
Mi gat trabel. Plis, yu givim
dispela tok long ———.
Kwiktaim tumas.
Mee lighkim sahmp'la hahli-
vim. Mee gaht trahbell.
Pleess, yoo givvim dissp'la
tawk long ———.
Kwiktighm too-mahss.

24. Au gadreva e dua na
veivuke. Au leqa tiko. Yalo
vinaka, solia na i tukutuku oqo
vei ———. E na kena totolo
duadua ko rawata.
Ow ngan-drrehva eh ndooa
na vay-vookeh. Ow lengga
teeko. Yallo v'nahka, solleea
na ee took'tookoo onggo vay
———. Eh na kenna toh-
tollo ndooa-ndooa ko row'ta.

25. That is very nice
(marvellous). That is bad
(terrible). I have enjoyed
myself very much.

25. Em i nais tumas (nais nogut
tru). Em i nogut (nogut tru). Mi
amamas tru.
Em ee nighss too-mahss
(nighss nohgood troo). Em ee
nohgood (nohgood troo). Mee
ahma-mahss troo.

25. Sa vinaka (vinaka dina)
oqori. Sa ca (ca dina) oqori. Au
sa mai lasa sara vakalevu.
Sa v'nahka (v'nahka ndeena)
ong-gohree. Sa thah (thah
ndeena) ong-gohree. Ow sa
may lahssa sarra vong-a-
lehvoo.

SENTENCES

TONGAN	SAMOAN	TAHITIAN

22. Koeha 'oku ke pehe ai?
'Oua teke tokanga kiha me'a.
'Oku ou loto <u>mamahi</u> (fiefia).
Teu 'oatu 'ae ma'au.
Koy-hah ohg' geh peh-heh
igh? Oh-a tehgeh toh-gahng'
keea me'a. Ohg' oh lohtoh
ma-ma-hh (feea-feea). Teeoo
'wahtoo igh ma-ow.

22. O le a le mea ua tupu? 'Aua
le popole. Ua 'ou <u>salamō</u>
(olioli). E tatau ona 'ou avatu
ina iā te 'oe le mea lenei.
Ohleh ah l' meh-a wa
toopoo? Ow-a l' po-pohleh.
Ooa oh s'l'moh (ohlee-ohlee).
Eh t'tow ohna oh vahtoo eena
ee-ah teh oy l' meh-a l'neigh.

22. E aha te huru? 'Īaha e
pe'ape'a. 'Ua <u>pe'ape'a</u> ('oa'oa)
vau. E hōro'a tu vau i teie.
Eh hah teh hooroo? 'Ee-hah
eh peh'a-peh'a. 'Ooa peh'a-
peh'a ('oh-a-'oh-a) vow. Eh
hohro'ah too vow ee teh-ee-
eh.

23. Koeha 'ae me'a 'oku ke
fiema'u? Fakamolemole 'o
ta'utu hifo. Koau teu 'alu.
Kuopau keke 'alu he taimini.
Koy-hah igh meh-a ahgoo
geh feea-mow? Fah-mohleh-
mohleh oh ta-ootoo heefo.
Go-ow teeoo ahloo. Gwo-pow
gehgeh ahloo eh tigh-meenee.

23. O le a le mea e te mana'o
ai? Fa'amolemole nofo i lalo. E
tatau one 'ou alu. Ua tatau ona
e alu nei.
Ohleh ah l' meh-a eht'
m'n'oy? Fah-mohleh-mohleh
noffo ee lallo. Eh t'tow ohna
oh ahloo. Ooa t'tow ohna eh
ahloo neigh.

23. E aha tā 'oe e hina'aro? 'A
pārahi i raro, 'ia ti'a ia 'oe. E
haere vau. Haere 'oe i teie nei.
Eh hah tah 'oy eh
heen'ahrro? 'A pahrr-hee ee
rrahrro, 'eea tee'a eea 'oy. Eh
highreh vow. Highreh 'oy ee
teh-ee-eh neigh.

24. Teu fiema'u 'ae tokoni.
'Oku ou faingata'a'ia.
Fakamolemole 'oke 'oange 'eku
fekau kia ———. 'Ihe vave
taha.
Teeoo feea-mow igh toh-
gohnee. Ohg' oh fighng-a-
tah-eea. Fah-mohleh-mohleh
ohgeh oh-ahng-eh ehg' feh-
kow gheea ———. Eea
vahveh tah.

24. 'Ou te mana'omia se
fesoasoani. Ua 'ou
fa'alavelavea. Fa'amolemole,
'ave atu le fe'au iā ———.
Fa'avave lava.
Oh t' m'nah'o-meea s' f'so'so-
ahnee. Ooa oh fah-lahveh-la-
veh-a. Fah-mohleh-mohleh,
ahveh attoo l' feh'ow ee-ah
———. Fah-vahveh lahva.

24. Hina'aro vau i te tauturu.
Tei roto vau i te 'ati. 'Ia ti'a ia
'oe, 'a hōro'a tu teie parau ia
———. Te 'oi'oira'a e
nehenehe.
Heen'ahrro vow ee teh tow-
tooroo. Teigh rohtoh vow ee
teh 'ahtee. 'Eea tee'a eea 'oy,
'a hohro'ah too teh-ee-eh
p'rrow eea ———. Teh
'oy'oyrr'ah eh n'heh-n'heh.

25. 'Oku <u>sai 'aupito</u>
(langilangi'ia). 'Oku <u>kovi ia</u>
(palakú). Na'aku ma'u 'ae malie
'ia moe fiefia lahi 'aupito.
Ohg' sigh ow-peeto (lahngi-
lahngi-eea). Ohg' kohvee eea
(pahla-koo). Nahkoo mow
igh mahlee-eh eea moy feea-
feea ligh ow-peeto.

25. Ua <u>matuā mānaia tele</u>
(mānaia tele lava). Ua <u>leaga</u>
(leaga tele lava). Sa 'ou matuā
fiafia tele lava.
Ooa m'too-ah mah-naya
telleh (mah-naya telleh
lahva). Ooa leh-ahng-a (leh-
ahng-a telleh lahva). Sah oh
m'too-ah feea-feea telleh .
lahva.

25. E mea <u>nehenehe roa</u>
(purotu) terā. E mea <u>'ino</u>
(ri'ari'a roa) terā. 'Ua 'oa'oa
rahi roa vau.
Eh meh-a n'heh-n'heh roh-a
(poo-rohtoo) t'rrah. Eh meh-
a 'eeno (ree'a-ree'a roh-a)
t'rrah. 'Ooa 'oh-a-'oh-a rahee
roh-a vow.

VOCABULARY

ENGLISH	NEW GUINEA PIDGIN	FIJIAN
above	antap long	dela
accident, the	bagarap	leqa
address, the	adres	vosa
adult, the	bikpela man	uabula
advertisement, the	toksave	tukutuku ni veivoli
aerogramme, the	leta pas	erokaramu
afraid	pret	rere
after	bihain long	e muri
afternoon, the	apinun	yakavi
again	gen	. . . tale
against	i go long	coqa
agree, to	yesa	vakadonuya
air, the	win	cagi
air conditioner, the	win masin	misini ni cagi batabata
air mail, the	mel long balus	meli kau a macawa
airplane, the	balus	waqavuka
airport, the	ples balus	rara ni waqavuka
alive	. . . i gat laip	bula
all	olgeta	taucoko
all right	orait	vinaka
almost	klostu	voleka
alone	wanpela tasol	taudua
already	yet	oti
also	tu	tale ga
although	maski . . .	dina ga
always	oltaim	veigauna
among	namel long	maliwa
and (between nouns)	na	kei
angry	. . . kros	cudru
animal, the	abus	manumanu
another one (different)	narakain	duatani
another one (more)	narapela	dua tale
answer, to	bekim tok	sauma
antiseptic, the	marasin bilong klinim sua	tatarovi ni jiemu
apartment, the	rum	vale
apple, the	laulau bilong waitman	apolo
approximately	samting olsem	rauta
arm, the	han	liga
army, the	ami	mataivalu
around	nabaut	wavolita
arrive, to	kamap	yaco
art, the	samting tumbuna	i yaloyalo
art gallery, the	haus tambaran	vale ni droini
artificial	. . . man i wokim	bulia na tamata
ask (inquire), to	askim	taroga
at	long	e
attempt, to	traim	sa ga

VOCABULARY

TONGAN	SAMOAN	TAHITIAN
'i 'olunga	i luga	i ni'a
tu'utāmaki	fa'alavelave fa'afuase'i	'ati
tu'asila	tuātusi	i'oa fa'aeara'a
tangata lahi	tagata matua	pa'ari
faka'ali'ali	fa'asalalauga	parau fa'a'ite
tohi 'ea meili	teutusi va'alele	parau rata nō te reva
manavahē	fefe	ri'ari'a
hili	'uma	i muro iho
efiafi	aoauli	tapera'a mahana
toe	toe	fa'ahou
fa'aki ki	aga'i 'i	ti'a 'ore
loto-taha	lotomalie	fa'ati'a
'ea	'ea	mata'i reva
'ea konitisina	masini fa'amālūlū	fa'ahaumārūra'a
'ea meili	meli va'alele	rata nō te reva
vakapuna	va'alele	manureva
mala'e vakapuna	malae va'alele	taura'a manureva
mo'ui	ola	oraora
... kotoa pē	'ātoa	pau roa
sai katoa	lelei	ti'a
meimei	toetoe 'ā	'oi ti'a
toko taha pē	to'atasi	hō'ē
'osi ...	'uma	a'ena
foki mo	fo'i	ato'a
neongo	e ui lava ina	noa atu ā
ma'u ai pē	fāifaipea	ā muri noa atu
'i he lotolotonga 'o	i totonu o	i rotopū
pea	ma	'ē
'ita	ita	'iriā
manu	manu vaefā	'animara
kehe	ma se isi	te tahi 'ē
moetaha	se isi	te tahi
tali	tali 'i	pahono
faito'o tamate siemu	vaimanu'a	tūpohe i te manumanu
loki	potu	piha fa'aeara'a
'āpele	'apu	'āpara
nai	e tusa 'o ...	fātatari'i
nima	lima	rima
tau	'au	nu'u
takatakai 'i	ta'amilo	'ati noa a'e
a'u	taunu'u	tae
faiva	faiva	rāve'a
fale faka'ali'ali-ta	fale māta'aga mō ata	fare hi'ora'a rāve'a
me'a-ngaāhi	fai	... i rāve
fehu'i	fesili	ani
'i	i	i
feinga	taumafai	tamata

VOCABULARY

ENGLISH	NEW GUINEA PIDGIN	FIJIAN
awake	... i no slip	yadra
baby, the	pikinini	gone lailai
back (rear), the	baksait	daku
back (again)	bek	tale
backwards	long bek	ki muri
bad	... nogut	ca
bag, the	bek	kato
baggage, the	kago	i yaya
ballpoint, the	pen bolpoin	peni
bamboo shoots, the	ol pikinini mambu	drauni bitu gone
banana, the	banana	jaina
bank (money), the	beng	baqe
bathe, to	waswas	sili
bathroom, the	ples waswas	vale ni sili
battery, the	bateri	batiri
beach, the	nambis	baravi
beans, the	ol bin	bini
beard, the	mausgras	kumi
beautiful	nais	totoka
because	bilong wanem	baleta
because of	long	e na vuku ni
become, to	kamap	yacova
bed, the	bet	i davodavo
beef, the	abus bulmakau	lewe ni bulumakau
beer, the	bia	bia
before (time)	bipo long taim	ni bera ni
behind	bihain long	e muri
believe, to	bilipim	vakabauta
bell, the	belo	lali kaukamea
best	nambawan	vinaka duadua
better	mobeta	vinaka cake
beyond	narasait long	sivia
bicycle, the	wilwil	basikeli
big	bikpela	levu
bill, the	bil	bili
binoculars, the	glas bilong kapten	vakadodoirairai
bird, the	pisin	manumanu vuka
biscuit, the	biskit	bisikete
black	blakpela	loaloa
blanket, the	blanket	i tutuvi
blood, the	blut	dra
blue	blu	karakarawa
boat, the	bot	waqa
body, the	skin	yago
boiled	... i bin boilim	saqa
book, the	buk	i vola

VOCABULARY

TONGAN	SAMOAN	TAHITIAN
'ā	ala	ara
valevale	pepe	'aiū
tu'a	tua	muri
ki mui	toe sau fo'i	ho'i mai
fakaholomui	'i tua	i muri mai
kovi	leaga	'ino
kato	'ato	pūtē taiha'a
'ū me'a	'ato	taiha'a
polopeni	polopeni	pēni pāpa'i
muka pitu	tatupu o le 'ofe	'ōteo 'ofe
siaine	fa'i	mai'a
pangikē	faletupe	fare moni
kaukau	tā'ele	hopu
loki kaukau	potu tā'ele	piha pape
maka kasa	ma'a uila	'ōfa'i mōri pata
matātahi	matāfaga	tahatai
'ū piini	pī	pipi
kava	'ava	huruhuru ta'a
faka'ofo'ofa	mānaia	nehenehe
koe'uhi	'auā	nō te mea
koe'uhi ko	'ona 'o	nō
hoko	'avea ma	riro
mohenga	moega	ro'i
pulu	fāsipovi	pua'atoro
pia	pia	pia
'i mu'a	'a'o le'i	nā mua a'e
'i he tu'a	i tua	i muri mai
tui	talitonu	ti'aturi
fafangu	logo	oe
lelei taha	silisili ona	maita'i roa a'e
lelei ange	sili atu i lō	maita'i a'e
'i kō atu 'i	i tala atu	i piha'i atu
pasikala	uila	pereo'o tāta'ahi
lahi	telē	rahi
hoku mo'ua	pili	parau tārahu
me'a-faka'ata mata-ua	mea va'ai	hi'o fenua
manupuna	manu lele	manu
pisikete	masi	faraoa pa'apa'a
'uli'uli	uliuli	'ere'ere
sipi kafu	palaniketi	paraitete
toto	toto	toto
lanu-moana	lanumoana	ninamu
vaka	va'a	poti
sino	tino	tino
'osi fakalili	puna	piha'a
tohi	tusi	puta

VOCABULARY

ENGLISH	NEW GUINEA PIDGIN	FIJIAN
boot, the	bikpela su	i vava
born	mama i karim	sucu
both	tupela	ruarua
bottle, the	botol	tavaya
bottle opener, the	op botol	dola ni tavaya
bottom, the	ananit	vuna
box, the	bokis	kato
boy, the	manki	gone tagane
bra, the	banis bilong susu	vakamoko
brake, the	brek	i tatarovi
brave	. . . i no save pret	qaqa
bread, the	bret	madrai
break, to	brukim	voroka
breakfast, the	kaikai long moning	i katalau
bridge, the	bris	i kawakawa
bring, to	kisim . . . i kam	kauta mai
brooch, the	bros	pini
brown	braun	qeleqelea
brush, the	brus	i tataviraki
bundle, the	karamap	i oloolo
bus, the	bas	basi
businessman, the	man bisnis	dau veivoli
busy	. . . i gat wok	osooso
but	tasol	ia
butter, the	bata	bata
button, the	baten	i bulukau
buy, to	baim	volia
cabbage, the	kabis	kaveti
cake, the	kek	keke
call (telephone), the	ring long telipon	talevoni
called, is	nem bilong . . . i	yacana
call out, to	singaut	kaci
camera, the	kamera	i taba
candle, the	kandel	kadrala
captain (of ship), the	kapten	kavetani
car, the	kar	motoka
carefully	isi isi	vakavinaka
cargo, the	kago	i usana
carpet, the	tepik	ibe
carrot, the	karot	kareti
carry, to	karim	kauta
cat, the	pusi	vusi
centimetre, the	sentimita	senitimita
century, the	handet yia	senitiuri
certainly	orait orait	vakaidina
chair, the	sia	i dabedabe

VOCABULARY

TONGAN	SAMOAN	TAHITIAN
puti	se'evae 'u'umi	tia'aputi
fanau'i	fānau	fānaura'a
fakatou	le lua	e piti
hina	fagu	mōhina
me'a-fakaāva-hina	tala fagu	'iriti mōhina
takele	ta'ele	rarora'a
puha	pusa	'āfata
tamasi'i tangata	tama	tamāroa
potisi	papa	tāpe'a titi
me'a ta'ofi	tāofi	tāpe'ara'a
loto-to'a	lototele	itoito
mā	falaoa	faraoa
foa'i	gau	'ōfati
kai-pongipongi	'aiga o le taeao	tāmā'ara'a po'ipo'i
hala-kavakava	ala laupapa	'ē'a turu
'omai	'aumai	'āfa'i mai
pine teuteu	pine	pine 'una'una
melomelo	'ena'ena	ravarava
polosi	pulumu	porōmu
kofukofu	taui	pū'ohu
pasi	pasi	pereo'o mata'eina'a
tangata pisinisi	tamāloa fai pisinisi	ta'ata ho'o tao'a
mo'ua	pisi	'ohipa roa
ka	peita'i	'āre'a
pata	pata	pata
fakama'u	fa'amau	pitopito
fakatau mai	fa'atau mai	ho'o mai
kāpisi	kapisi	pota
keke	keke	faraoa monamona
'ui	vili	pi'i niuniu
ui 'a ... ko	ta'ua 'o le ...	pi'ihia
kaila	'alaga	tūō
me'a-fai-tā	mea pu'eata	pata hoho'a
te'elango	mōliga'o	mōri hinu
'eikivaka	kapeteni	ra'atira
motokā	ta'avale	pereo'o uira
tokanga	fa'aeteete	ha'apa'o maita'i
ūta	uta	tao'a uta
kāpeti	kapeta	vauvau tahua
kāloti	karoti	taroti
fua	'ave	'āfa'i
pusi	pusi	mimi
senitamita	senitimita	tenetimētera
senituli	senituri	tenetere
pau	mautinoa lava	'oia ho'i
sea	nofoa	pārahira'a

ENGLISH	NEW GUINEA PIDGIN	FIJIAN
change (small money), the	senis	veisau
change (money), to	senisim	vukica
change (transport), to	senisim	veisau
cheap	. . . i no dia	voli rawarawa
cheese, the	sis	jisi
cherry, the	sirsen	jeri
chicken, the	kakaruk	toa
chief, the	luluai	turaga
child, the	pikinini	gone lailai
chocolate, the	braunpela loli	jiokeliti
choose, to	kisim long laik	digia
chopsticks, the	sopstik	kau ni kana vakajaina
church, the	haus lotu	vale ni lotu
cigar, the	siga	sika
cigarette, the	sigaret	sikereti
cinema, the	haus piksa	yaloyalo yavala
city, the	biktaun	siti
clean	klin	savasava
clean, to	klinim	vakasavasavataka
clerk, the	kuskus	vunivola
clock, the	kilok	kaloko
close, to	pasim	sogota
closed	. . . pas	sogo
cloth, the	laplap	i sulu
clothes, the	klos	i sulu
coast, the	nambis	baravi
coat, the	kot	kote
coffee, the	kopi	kove
coin, the	mani ain	i lavo siliva
cold	kol	liliwa
cold season (winter), the	taim bilong kol	vula i liliwa
colour, the	kala	roka
comb, the	kom	i seru
come, to	kam	lako mai
comfortable	. . . gut moa	tiko vinaka
commercial	. . . bilong bisnis	baleta na veivoli
company (firm), the	kampani	kabani
complain, to	kotim	didivaka
completely	olgeta	vakatabakidua
conceal, to	haitim	vunia
concert, the	singsing	vukalasalasa
consul, the	tultul	kaunisela
contain, to	holim . . . i stap	tu kina
continue, to	skruim . . . i go	ia tiko
convenient	. . . i mekim isi	veirauti
conversation, the	toktok	veivosaki
cook, to	kukim	vakasaqara

VOCABULARY

TONGAN	SAMOAN	TAHITIAN
toenga silini	sui	moni hu'ahu'a
fetongi	talaina	taui
fetongi	sui	taui i te pereo'o
ma'ama'a	taugōfie	māmā
siisi	sisi	pata pa'ari
seli	sieri	terise
moa	moa	moa
'eiki	ali'i	tāvana
tamasi'i	tamaitiiti	tamari'i
sokaleti	sukalati	totora
fili	filifili	ma'iti
sopisitiki	tui sipuni 'a'ai 'ai Saina	pātia tinitō
fale lotu	falesā	fare pure
sikā	sikā	titā
sikaleti	sikareti	'ava'ava pupuhi
hele'uhila	faletīfaga	teata
kolo lahi	'a'ai	'oire
ma'a	mamā	mā
fakama'a	fa'amamā	horoi
kalake	tagata 'ōfisa	pāpa'i parau
uasi	uati	hora
tāpuni	tāpuni	'ōpani
'osi tāpuni	ua tāpuni	'ōpani
tupenu	'ie	'a'ahu
ū tupenu	'ofu	'ahu
matātahi	talafātai	tahatai
kote	peleue	'ahu pereue
kofi	kofe	taofe
fo'i pa'anga	tinoitupe	moni hu'ahu'a
momoko	mālūlū	to'eto'e
fa'ahita'u momoko	tau mālūlū	'anotau to'eto'e
lanu	lanu	huru pēni
helu	selu	pāhere
ha'u	sau	haere mai
fiemālie	mālū	nanaho
fakapisinisi	fefa'atauina o 'oloa	ho'o tao'a
kautaha	kamupani	taiete
hanu	fa'ameo	fa'ahapa
kakato	'uma	pau roa
fufu'ui	nātia	fa'a'ore
koniseti	koneseti	hīmenera'a
konisela	konesula	tonitera
'oku 'i ai 'i ... 'a	'o lo'o i	fāri'i
hoko atu	faipea	tāmau noa
faingamālie	tatau ai	au
potalanoa	talanoaga	paraparau
ngaohi kai	fa'avela	tunu

VOCABULARY

ENGLISH	NEW GUINEA PIDGIN	FIJIAN
cookie, the	biskit	bisikete
corkscrew, the	skru tuptup	i dola ni tavaya
corner (of room), the	kona	tutu
corner (street), the	kona	tutu
corridor, the	ples wokabaut insait long haus	tadrua
costs, (it)	kastim	... na i sau
cotton, the	katen	vauvau
cotton-wool, the	kapok	vauvau
count, to	kaunim	wilika
country (nation), the	kantri	matanitu
countryside, the	bus	loma ni vanua
course, of!	turait!	vakakina!
courtyard, the	kot	rara
cover, to	karamapim	ubia
crab, the	kuka	qari
cream, the	strongpela susu	kirimu
cross, to	go long hap long	kosova
crowd, the	planti man na meri	lewe vuqa
cup, the	kap	bilo
curry, the	kari	kari
cushion, the	pilo	i lokoloko ni dabedabe
custom (way), the	pasin	i tovo
customs, the	kastam	i vakarau
cut, to	katim	kotiva
dance, to	singsing	meke
dangerous	... i gat samting nogut	rerevaki
dark (colour)	tudak	butobuto
dark (no light)	tudak	butobuto
day, the	de	siga
daytime, the	taim long san	sigalevu
dead	... i dai pinis	mate
dear (expensive)	dia	i sau levu
decide, to	pasim tingting	lewa
deep	godaun tru	titobu
demand, to	singaut long	taroga vakaukaua
dentist, the	dokta bilong tit	dau cavu bati
desert, the	ples wesan	talasiga
diamond, the	daimen	daimani
dictionary, the	buk bilong painim mining	i vola ni vakamacala vosa
die, to	dai pinis	mate
different	arakain	duidui
difficult	... i hatwok	dredre
dinner, the	kaikai long belo	vakayakavi
direction, the	... i makim rot	sala
dirty	doti	dukadukali
do, to	mekim	cakava
doctor, the	dokta	vuniwai

VOCABULARY

TONGAN	SAMOAN	TAHITIAN
pisikete	masi	faraoa pa'apa'a
me'a to'o-'umosi	mea toso momono	hou 'ōroi
tuliki	tulimanu	poro
tuliki	afega	poro porōmu
hala vaha'a loki	'o le polotito	aroā piha
'oku totongi	'o le tau ...	ho'o
filo	vavae	vavai
vavaē	vavae	vavai māhanahana
lau	faitau	tai'o
fonua	atunu'u	'āi'a
'uta	fanua	mata'eina'a
'aua!	'o lea lava!	'au'ae!
loto'ā	lotoā	'āua
'ufi'ufi	ufiufi	tāpo'i
paka	pa'a	pa'apa'a
kilimi	kulimi	ū pa'ari
kolosi	sopo'ia	tātauro
fu'u kakai	motu o tagata	putuputu ra'a
ipu	ipu	taota
kale	kale	mā'a tari
pilo	'aluga	tūru'a na'ina'i
anga	aganu'u	peu
tute	tiute	'aufau tute
tofa'i	tipi	tāpū
hulohula	siva	'ori
fakatu'utamaki	mata'utia	mea ataata
fakapo'upo'uli	taugauli	pōiri
fakapo'uli	pogisā	pōiri
'aho	aso	mahana
taimi 'aho	ao	ao
pekia	oti	pohe
mamafa	taugatā	moni rahi
pehe	filifili	fa'ata'a te mana'o
loloto	loloto	hohonu
tu'utu'uni	poloa'i	ani
tōketā ngaohi-nifo	fōma'i fa'inifo	taote niho
toāfā	toāfa	metepara
taiamoni	taimane	taiamani
tikisinale	lolomi fefiloi	puta 'auvaha
pekia	oti	pohe
kehekehe	'ese'ese	mea 'ē
faingata'a	faigatā	mea fifi
kai 'efiafi	'aiga	tāmā'ara'a ahiahi
feitu'u	ala	terera'a
'uli	'ele'elea	repo
fai	fai	rave
tōketā	fōma'i	taote

VOCABULARY

ENGLISH	NEW GUINEA PIDGIN	FIJIAN
dog, the	dok	koli
don't!	nogat!	kua!
door, the	tua	katuba
doubt, the	tubel	vakatitiqa
down	daun	e ra
dress (woman's), the	klos meri	vinivo
drink, the	dring	gunu
drink, to	dringim	gunuva
drive (car), to	draivim	draivataka
driver, the	draiva	draiva
dry	drai	mamaca
duck, the	pato	ga
during	long taim bilong	e na gauna
dusty	. . . i gat dus	soqosoqoa
duty (obligation), the	wok	i tavi
each	wanpela wanpela	yadua
each other	wanpela narapela	veiyadua
early (before time)	bipotaim	totolo
earrings, the	ol bilas bilong yau	sau
east	hap san i kamap	tokalau
easy	isi	rawarawa
eat, to	kaikaim	kania
egg, the	kiau	yaloka
either . . . or	. . . ating . . .	se . . . se
electric	lektrik	livaliva
elevator, the	lipt	eleveti
embassy, the	haus luluai bilong longwe ples	mata
empty	nating	maca
enemy, the	birua	meca
engine (car), the	ensin	idini
enjoy, to	amamas tru	marautaka
enormous	bikpela tru	vakaitamera
enough	inap	rauta
enter, to	kam insait long	curuma
entrance, the	tua i kam insait	katuba
envelope, the	skin pas	waqa ni vola
equal	wankain	tautauvata
evening, the	apinun	yakavi
everybody	olgeta man	veitamata kece
everything	olgeta samting	veika kece
everywhere	long olgeta ples	veivanua kece
exactly	stret	dodonu
example, for	wankain olsem	kena i vakaraitaki
except	tasol i no gat	vakavo
exhibition, the	so	vakaraitaki ka
exit, the	dua i go ausait	katuba

VOCABULARY

TONGAN	SAMOAN	TAHITIAN
kulī	maile	'uri
'oua 'e ...!	'aua!	'eiaha!
matapā	faitoto'a	'ōpani
tāla'a	fa'alētonu	mana'o 'āpitipiti
hifo	'i lalo	i raro
kofu 'oe fefine	'ofu fafine	'ahu vahine
inu	meainu	inu
inu	inu	inu
faka'uli	fa'auli	fa'ahoro
tangata faka'uli	'aveta'avale	ta'ata fa'ahoro pereo'o
mōmoa	mago	marō
pato	pato	mo'orā
lolotonga 'a	'a'o	i te tau ...
efu	pefua	reporepo
fatongia	tiute	tārahu
taki taha	ta'itasi	tāta'ihō'ē
fe- ... -'aki	le isi i le isi	tetahi i te tahi
tōmua	vave	'oi'oi a'e
mama telinga	tautaliga	tāpe'a tari'a
'isite	sasa'e	hiti'a o te rā
faingofua	faigōfie	'ohie
kai	'ai	'amu
fo'i manu	fua	huero
hala pe 'ia ... ko	po'o ... po'o	te tahi ... te tahi
faka'uhila	uila	uira
lifi	lifi	pereo'o pa'uma
'api 'oe fakafofonga kimuli	sāvali	fare tonitera rahi
maha	gaogao	pau
fili	fili	'enemi
mīsini	afi	mātini
mālie'ia 'i	fa'afiafia	fa'a'ārearea
faka'ulia	lāpo'a	rahi roa
fa'unga	lava	rava'i
hū	ulufale	tomo
hū'anga	faitoto'a	'ūputa
sila	teutusi	vihi rata
tatau	tutusa	ti'a te fāito
efiafi po'uli	afiafi	ahiahi
kakai kotoa	so'o se tasi	pauroa te ta'āta
me'a kotoa	'o mea 'uma lava	te ta'ato'ara'a
'ihe feitu'u kotoa pē	so'o se mea	i te mau vāhi ato'a
fe'ungamālie	tonu	ti'a roa
hangē ko 'eni	fa'aa'oa'o	hoho'a hi'ora'a
tuku kehe	vaganā	maori rā
faka'ali'ali	fa'aaliga	hi'ora'a rē
hū'anga ki tu'a	ulufafo	'ūputa atu

VOCABULARY

ENGLISH	NEW GUINEA PIDGIN	FIJIAN
expect, to	wetim	waraka
explain, to	tok save long	vakamacalataka
eye, the	ai	mata
face, the	pes olgeta	mata
fact, in	em i tru	dina
fail, to	no inap mekim	sega ni raivata
fair (just)	stret	dodonu
fall, to	pundaun	tau
family, the	famili	matavuvale
famous	. . . i gat biknem	rogovaki
fan, the	brum bilong winim pes	iri
far	longwe	yawa
farmer, the	pama	dau teitei
fast	kwik	totolo
fasten, to	pasim	vesuka
festival, the	singsing	sogo
fetch, to	kisim . . . i kam	kauta mai
few, a	wan wan	e vica
field, the	ples kunai	loma ni bai
fight, to	pait	veivala
fill, to	pulapim	vakasinaita
film (for camera), the	pilum	filimu
film (movie show), the	piksa	yaloyalo yavala
finally	pinis tru	e muri sara
find, to	painim pinis	kunea
finish, to	pinisim	vakaotia
fire, the	paia	buka waqa
first	namba wan	i matai
fish, the	pis	ika
flat	stret	tautauvata
flat (tyre), the	taia i plat	qara
floor, the	polo	buturara
flower, the	plaua	senikau
fly, the	lang	lago
fly, to	flai	vuka
follow, to	bihainim	muria
food, the	kaikai	kakana
foot, the	fut	yava
football (game), the	kikbal	veicaqe
for	long	ni
forbidden	. . . tambu	tabu
foreign	. . . bilong longwe ples	tani
forest, the	bus	veikau
forget, to	lusim tingting	guilecava
fork, the	pok	i cula
former	. . . bipo	e liu

VOCABULARY

TONGAN	SAMOAN	TAHITIAN
'amanaki	fa'atalitali	ti'aturi
fakamatala	fa'amatala	fa'ata'a
mata	mata	mata ho'ira'a
fofonga	fofoga	mata
mo'oni	meamoni	'oia mau
hala	pa'ela	'aore i manuia
totonu	tonu	ti'a
tō	pa'ū	topa
fāmili	'āiga	fēti'i
ongoongoa	ta'uta'ua	tu'iro'o
ī	ili	pererau tāhirihiri
mama'o	mamao	ātea
faāma	faifa'ato'aga	ta'ata fa'a'apu
vave	saosaoa	viti viti
fakama'u	fa'amau	tāmau
kātoanga	fa'afiafiaga	'ōroa
'alu 'o 'omai	'a'ami	'āfa'i
si'i	nai	'aita re'a
ngoue	laufanua	fenua fa'a'apu
fuhu	taua'ifusu	moto
fakafonu	fa'atumu	fa'a'ī
filimi	ata	firimu
sio faiva	tīfaga	firimu
faka'osiaki	fa'a'iuga	hōpe'ara'a
'ilo	maua	'itehia
faka'osi ki	fa'auma	fa'aoti
afi	afi	auahi
'uluaki	muamua	mātāmua
ika	i'a	i'a
lafalafa	māfola	pāpū
pā	pā	uaua marū
faliki	fola	tahua
matala'i 'akau	fugālā'au	tiare
lango	lago	ra'o
puna	lele	ma'ue
muimui ki	mulimuli	pe'e
me'akai	mea'ai	mā'a
va'e	vae	'āvae
'akapulu	futipolo	tu'era'a pōpō
ma'a	mo	na
tapu	vavao	'ōpanihia
muli	'ese	rātere
vao	vao	fa'a
ngalo	galo	ha'amo'e
huhu	tui	pātia mā'a
mu'aki	muamua	nā mua

377

VOCABULARY

ENGLISH	NEW GUINEA PIDGIN	FIJIAN
forwards	poret	ki liu
free (vacant)	. . . i no gat man no meri	galala
fresh	nupela	bulabula
fried	, . . . i bin praim	tavuteke
fried rice, the	prairais	raisi tavuteke
friend, the	pren	i tau
from	long	mai
front of, in	ai bilong	e mata ni
frontier, the	arere bilong kantri	i yalayala
frozen	. . . i ais pinis	cevata
fruit, the	pikinini bilong diwai	vua ni kau
full	pulap	sinai
garden, the	gaden	i teitei
gasoline (petrol), the	bensin	benisini
girl, the	meri	gone yalewa
give, to	givim	solia
glad	. . . amamas	marau
glass (drinking), the	glas	bilo
glass (substance), the	glas	iloilo
glove, the	soken bilong han	qa ni liga
go, to	go	lako
go down, to	go daun	lako sobu
go up, to	go antap	lako cake
god, the	god	kalou
gold, the	gol	koula
good	gutpela	vinaka
goods, the	kago	i yau
government, the	gavman	matanitu
gram, the	giram	karamu
grapes, the	ol pikinini bilong rop wain	vaini
grass, the	gras	co
green	grin	karakarawa
grey	gre	roka dravudravua
ground, the	graun	qele
guard, to	sambai long	yadrava
guest, the	pasindia	vulagi
guide, the	man i soim rot	i dusidusi
guidebook, the	buk em i soim rot	vola ni dusidusi
gun, the	gan	dakai
hair, the	gras bilong het	drau ni ulu
haircut, the	katim gras	i koti
hairdresser, the	man i save katim gras bilong het	dau veikoti
ham, the	lek bilong pik	lewe ni vuaka
handbag, the	hanpaus	kato tuberi
handkerchief, the	kankisip	tavoi
harbour, the	pasis	wavu
hard (firm)	hatpela	kaukaua

378

VOCABULARY

TONGAN	SAMOAN	TAHITIAN
ki mu'a	'i luma	i mua mai
'ata'ata	pāganoa	ta'ata 'ore
fo'ou	fou	haumārū
fakapaku	falai	faraipāni
laise fakapaku	alaisa falai	raiti faraipāni
kaume'a	uō	hoa
mei	mai	mai
'i mu'a	i luma	i mua mai
tafa fonua	tuā'oi	'ōti'a
fakamomoko 'o fefeka	fa'a'aisa	pa'ari i te to'eto'e
fo'i 'akau	fuālā'au	mā'a
fonu	tumu	'ī
ngoue	fa'ato'aga	'āua tiare
penisini	kesi	mōrī 'ārahu
ta'ahine	teine	pōti'i
'o'ange	'ave atu	hōro'a
fiefia	fiafia	'oa'oa
ipu sio'ata	ipu mālamalama	hapaina
sio'ata	tioata	hi'o
kofu-nima	tōtini lima	rimarima
'alu	alu	haere
hifo	alu 'i lalo	pou
hake	alu 'i luga	pa'uma
'otua	atua	atua
koula	'auro	pirū
lelei	lelei	maita'i
koloa	'oloa	tao'a
pule'anga	mālō	hau fa'atere
kulemi	karama	tarama
kālepi	vine mata	vine
musie	mutia	matie
lanu-mata	lanumeamata	matie
lanu-lavilavi	'efu'efu	rehu
kelekele	'ele'ele	fenua
le'o	leoleo	tia'i
taha 'a'ahi	mālō	manihini
tangata taki	ta'iala	arata'i
tohi fakahinohino	tusi ta'iala	puta arata'i
me'afana	fana	pupuhi
lou'ulu	lauulu	rouru
kosi	'oti ulu	tāpū rouru
faikosi	'o le tagata 'oti ulu	ta'ata tāpū rouru
hemi	vasāsui	hamu
kato to'oto'o fefine	taga	pūtē rima
holoholo	solosolo	horoi
taulanga	tāulaga	avaroto
fefeka	malō	pa'ari

VOCABULARY

ENGLISH	NEW GUINEA PIDGIN	FIJIAN
hat, the	hat	i sala
have, to	gat	e tiko
he	em	o koya
head, the	het	ulu
headache, the	het i pen	mosi ni ulu
hear, to	harim	rogoca
heart, the	kilok	uto
heavy	hevi	bibi
height, the	longpela bilong en	cere
help, to	halivim	vukea
her (adj.)	. . . bilong em	na nona
here	hia	ke
high	antap	cere
hill, the	maunten	delana
his	. . . bilong em	na nona
hold, to	holim	taura
holy	. . . tambu	tabu
home, at	long haus	e vale
honest	stret	dina
hope, to	hop	nuitaka
horse, the	hos	ose
hospital, the	haus sik	vale ni bula
host, the	bos bilong haus	taukei ni vale
hot (weather)	hat	katakata
hot (heated food, etc.)	hat	katakata
hot season (summer), the	taim bilong san	vula i katakata
hotel, the	haus pasindia	otela
hour, the	aua	aua
house, the	haus	vale
how?	olsem wanem?	vakacava?
how many?	haumas?	e vica?
however (conj.)	tasol	ia
hut, the	haus	i cili
I	mi	au
ice, the	ais	wai ceveta
ice cream, the	aiskrim	aisi kirimu
if	sapos	ke
ill	sik	tauvi mate
immediately	stret nau	vakatotolo
important	. . . i bikpela samting	bibi
impossible	. . . i hat moa	dredre
in	insait long	e
information, the	toksave	i tukutuku
inside	insait	loma
instead of	long halivim	ka sega ni
interesting	. . . i laikim tru	taleitaki
interpreter, the	man i tanim tok	dau vakadewa vosa

VOCABULARY

TONGAN	SAMOAN	TAHITIAN
tatā	pūlou	tāupo'o
'i ai	i ai	na
ne	o ia	'oia
'ulu	ulu	upo'o
ngangau 'ulu	tigā le ulu	'āhoahoa
fanongo	fa'alogo	fa'aro'o
mafu	fatu	māfatu
mamafa	mamafa	teiaha
mā'olunga	mauāluga	teitei
tokoni ki	fesoasoani	tauturu
hono	lana	tāna
'i heni	i'inei	'ū nei
mā'olunga	maualugā	teitei
mo'unga	mauga	'āivi
hono	lana	tāna
pukepuke	tāofi	mau
tapu	pa'ia	mo'a
'i 'api	i le fale	'utuāfare
faitotonu	fa'amaoni	mana'o ti'a
'amanaki lelei	fa'amoemoe	ti'aturi
hōsi	solofanua	pua'arehenua
fale mahaki	falema'i	fare ma'i
tangata 'oku 'o'ona 'a e'api	ali'i talimālō	fatu
mafana	vevela	māhanahana
vela	vevela	māhanahana
fa'ahita'u mafana	tau māfanafana	'anotau māhanahana
hotele	fale talimālō	hōtēra
houa	itūlā	hora
fale	fale	fare
'e fēfē?	fa'apēfea?	nā fea?
toko fiha?	e fia?	e hia?
kaikehe	peita'i ane	āre'a rā
ki'i fale	fale o'o	fare iti
kou	'ou	au
'aisi	'aisa	pape to'eto'e
'aisikilimi	'aisakulimi	pape to'eto'e
kapau	'āfai	mai te mea ē
mahamahaki	ma'i	pohe i te ma'i
leva	loa	i teie nei iho ā
mahu'inga	tāua	faufa'a
'ikai ke lava	lē mafai	ti'a 'ore
'i	i totonu	i roto
ongoongo ke tala	fa'amatalaga	parau fa'a'ite
'i loto	i totonu	i roto
ko e fetongi 'o	'ae lē	'aore . . . ra
fakamānako	mālie	fa'ahiahia
toko taha fakatonu lea	fa'amatala'upu	'auvaha

381

VOCABULARY

ENGLISH	NEW GUINEA PIDGIN	FIJIAN
iron (metal), the	ain	kaukamea
is	stap	tiko
island, the	ailan	yanuyanu
isn't it?	laka?	se vakaevei?
it	em	na ka
jewellery, the	bilas	vatu talei
journey, the	wokabaut	i lakolako
jump, to	kalap	rika
jungle, the	bus	veikau
key, the	ki	ki
kill, to	kilim i dai	vakamatea
kilogram, the	kilogiram	kilokaramu
kilometre, the	kilomita	kilomita
kind (friendly)	gut	yalo vinaka
king, the	king	tui
kiss, to	givim kis	reguca
kitchen, the	haus kuk	vale ni kuro
knife, the	naip	i sele
know, to	save	kila
label, the	namba	i vola
lake, the	raunwara	drano
lamb, the	sipsip	lami
lamp, the	lam	cina
last	bihain tru	otioti
late (behind time)	bihaintaim	bera
later on	bai	e muri
laugh, to	lap	dredrevaka
laundry (clothes), the	klos was	i sulu sava
law, the	lo	lawa
lawyer, the	loman	loya
lead, to	go pas long	liutaka
learn, to	lainim	vulica
least, at	liklik tru	sivia
leave (place), to	lusim	biuta
leave behind, to	larim	biuta
left (hand)	han kais	mawi
leg, the	lek	yava
lemon, the	muli	moli karokaro
lemonade, the	loliwara	wai ni moli
letter (note), the	pas	i vola
letter (character), the	rait	mata ni vola
lettuce, the	letis	letisi
lie, the	giaman	lasu
lie down, to	slip	davo
lift, to	litimupim	laveta
light (colour)	tulait	seavu

VOCABULARY

TONGAN	SAMOAN	TAHITIAN
'ukamea	u'amea	'āuri
ko	ua	e
motu	motu	motu
ē?	ā 'ea?	ānei?
ia	le mea	'oia
siueli	ma'a tāua	tao'a ri'i nehenehe
fononga	malaga	tere
hopo	oso	'ōu'a
vao	vaomatua	ururā'au
kī	kī	tāviri
tāmate'i	fasi	ha'apohe roa
kulemi 'e taha afe	kilokarama	tiro
mita 'e taha afe	kilomita	tiromētera
anga-'ofa	agalelei	maita'i
tu'i	tupu	ari'i
'uma	kisi	'āpā
peito	umukuka	fare tūtu
hele	naifi	tipi
'ilo	iloa	'ite
faka'ilonga	pepa	tāpa'o
ano	vaitūloto	roto
lami	māmoe	fanau'a māmoe
maāma	mōlī	mōri
faka'osi	mulia'i	hōpe'a
tōmui	tuai	tāere
a nainai ange	mulimuli ane	i muri a'e
kata	'ata	'ata
fō	tāgamea	pu'ara'a 'a'ahu
lao	tulāfono	ture
loea	lōia	'auvaha ture
taki	ta'i	fa'atere
ako	a'o	ha'api'i
'ikai si'i hifo 'i	'e la'itiiti	tei iti a'e
tuku	tu'ua	reva
fakatoe	tu'u	vaiho
to'ohema	tauagavale	'aui
va'e	vae	'āvae
lemani	tīpolo	tāporo
lemaneiti	vaitīpolo	rimona
tohi	tusi	rata
mata'itohi	mata'itusi	reta
lētisi	latisi	pota matie
loi	pepelo	ha'avare
tokoto	ta'oto	ta'oto
hiki	si'i	'āfa'i i ni'a
maāma	vāivai	teatea

383

VOCABULARY

ENGLISH	NEW GUINEA PIDGIN	FIJIAN
light (weight)	. . . i no hevi	mamada
lighter (cigarette), the	sigaret laita	vakawaqa ni tavako
like (prep.)	olsem long	vaka
lipstick, the	pen bilong maus	boro ni tebe ni gusu
litre, the	lita	lita
little, a	liklik	vakalailai
live (reside), to	stap	tiko
lock, the	lok	loka
long (size)	longpela	balavu
long (time)	longpela	dede
long ago	bipo tru	gauna makawa
look at, to	lukim	raica
look for, to	painim	vakaraica
lose (mislay), to	lusim	vakayalia
lose (race, etc.), to	kuk	druka
loud	strong	domoilevu
love, to	laikim	domona
low	. . . daun	lolovira
lunch, the	smolpela kaikai	vakasigalevu
machine, the	masin	misini
magazine, the	niuspepa	i vola
make, to	wokim	cakava
malaria, the	malaria	waqaqa
man, the	man	tagane
manager, the	bosman	manidia
mango, the	mango	maqo
many	planti	. . . vuqa
map, the	map	mape
market, the	bung	makete
married	. . . i marit	vakamau
matches, the	masis	masese
means, (it)	i min	kena i balebale
measure, to	makim	vakarautaka
meat, the	abus	lewe
mechanic, the	mekanik	mekeniki
medicine, the	marasin	wai ni mate
meet, to	painim	sotava
melon, the	melen	meleni
menu, the	menu	i vola ni ka me laukana
message, the	tok	i tukuluku
metre, the	mita	mita
middle, the	namel	veimama
midnight	biknait	bogilevu
milk, the	susu	sucu
millimetre, the	milimita	milimita
minute, the	minit	miniti

VOCABULARY

TONGAN	SAMOAN	TAHITIAN
ma'ama'a	māma	māmā
masi penisini	afi penisini	pātē auahi
hange ko	pei	mai
lipisitiki	vali laugutu	'ute'ute 'utu
lita	lita	ritera
si'isi'i	la'itiiti	ri'i
nofo	nofo	noho
loka	loka	rota
lōloa	'umi	roa
fuoloa	'umi	maoro
fuoloa	anamuā	a'e nei
sio ki	va'ai	māta'ita'i
fakasiosio	su'e	pā'imi
mole	lē iloa	mo'e
fo'i	faia'ina	pau
le'o-lahi	leotele	teitei
'ofa kia	alofa	here
mā'ulalo	maualolo	ha'eha'a
kai ho'atā	'aiga a le aoauli	tāmā'ara'a avatea
mīsini	masini	mātini
makasini	tusiata	ve'a
ngaohi	fai	rave
malēlia	fiva Niukini	fīva re'are'a
tangata	tamāloa	ta'ata
pule	pule	ra'atira
mango	mago	vī
lahi	tele	e rave rahi
mape	fa'afanua	hoho'a fenua
māketi	māketi	mātete
'osimali	fa'aipoipo	fa'aipoipo
masi	lā'au afitusi	māti
'oku 'uhinga	uiga	teie te aura'a
fua	fua	fāito
kanomate	fāsipovi	'īna'i
'enisinia	'inisinia	ra'atira huira
vai fai to'o	vai	rā'au
fakataha	feiloa'i	farerei
meleni	meleni	merēni popa'ā
miniū	'o le lisi o 'aiga	tāpura mā'a
fekau	fe'au	parau fa'a'ite
mita	mita	mētera
loto mālie	'ogātotonu	rōpū
tu'uapō	vaeluāpō	tu'ira'a pō
hu'akau	susu	ū
milimita	milimita	mirimētera
miniti	minute	miniti

VOCABULARY

ENGLISH	NEW GUINEA PIDGIN	FIJIAN
mirror, the	glas bilong lukluk	iloilo
mistake, the	rong	cala
moment, the	minit	miniti
monastery, the	haus pater	vale ni bete
money, the	mani	i lavo
month, the	mun	vula
monument, the	makim	i vakananumi
moon, the	mun	vula
more	moa	levu cake
morning, the	moningtaim	mataka
mosque, the	haus lotu bilong ol mahomet	vale ni lotu ni musulamani
mosquito, the	natnat	namu
most	moa tru	duadua
motor-bike, the	motobaik	motovai
mountain, the	maunten	ulu ni vanua
mouth, the	maus	gusu
movie camera, the	kamera piksa	i taba
much	planti	vakalevu
museum, the	haus bilong tumbuna pasin	vale ni yaya makawa
mushroom, the	papai	daliga
music, the	musik	vakatagi
must	mas	e dodonu
mustard, the	mastet	masitedi
my	... bilong mi	na noqu
name, the	nem	yaca
napkin, the	napkin	pikini
narrow	... i no brait	qiqo
natural	... samting tru	sucu kaya
near (not far)	klostu	voleka
near to	klostu long	volekata
need, to	laikim	yaga
needle, the	nil bilong samap	i cula
never	i no gat wanpela taim	sega sara
new	nupela	vou
newspaper, the	niuspepa	niusiveva
next (after)	bihain	dua tale
night, the	nait	bogi
no (adj.)	... i no gat sampela	e sega ...
nobody	i no gat man	e sega ni dua na tamata
noise, the	nois	rorogo
noodles, the	ol nudal	kakana vakawa ni jaina
noon	belo kaikai	sigalevu
north	not	vualiku
not	no	sega
not at all	no ... tasol	sega sara ga
notepaper, the	pepa bilong raitim leta	pepa
nothing	i no gat samting	e sega

386

VOCABULARY

TONGAN	SAMOAN	TAHITIAN
sio'ata	fā'ata	hi'o hipa
hala	sesē	hape
momeniti	itūlā	taime
monasteliō	fale o monike	fare monahi
pa'anga	tupe	moni
māhina	māsina	'āva'e
fakamanatu	ma'a fa'amanatu	pou ha'amana'o
māhina	māsina	'āva'e
lahi ange	sili	rahi a'e
pongipongi	taeao	po'ipo'i
fale lotu faka-Mahometi	'o le fale tāpua'i o moāmeta	fare pure mahōmeta
namu	namu	naonao
lahi taha	aupito	rahi roa a'e
motopaiki	uila afi	pereo'o tahitahi
mo'unga	mauga	mou'a
ngutu	gutu	vaha
me'afaita faiva	mea pu'e ata gāi'oi'oi	patara'a hoho'a teata
lahi	tele	rahi
musiume	falemāta'aga	vāhi hi'ora'a taiha'a tahito
fakamalu-'a-tēvolo	pūlou 'āitu	tari'a 'iore
musika	pesega	'upa'upa
pau	tatau lava	e ti'a
masitati	'ava āluga	muta
hoku	la'u	tā'u
hingoa	igoa	i'oa
napikeni	napekini	tauera tāmā'ara'a
lausi'i	lauitiiti	piriha'o
fakaenatula	tupu fua	natura
ofi	lata mai	fātata
ofi ki	latalata	fātata i
pau	mana'o	e mea hina'arohia
hui-tuitui	nila	nira
'ikai . . . teitei	lē . . . lava	'aita roa atu
fo'ou	fou	'āpī
niusipepa ongoongo	nusipepa	ve'a
hoko	soso'o	i muru iho
pō	pō	pō
'ikai ha taha	leai	'aita roa
'ikai ha toko taha	leai sē isi	'aita e ta'ata
vākē	pisa	māniania
nutolo	lialia	mā'a tihopu
ho'atā	aoauli	avatea
noate	mātū	'apato'erau
'ikai	lē	'aore
mole ke mama'o	leai lava	'aita roa
pepa fai'tohi	pepa tusi	parau pāpa'i
hala ātaāta	leai se mea	'aita

VOCABULARY

ENGLISH	NEW GUINEA PIDGIN	FIJIAN
notice, the	toksave	i vakamacala
now	nau	nikua
number, the	namba	i wiliwili
nurse, the	sista	nasi
nuts, the	ol galip	vua ni kau
obtain, to	kisim	taura
occupied	pulap	tawa
offer, to	mekim ofa	vakacabora
office, the	ofis	vale ni volavola
officer (army), the	ofisa	turaga ni valu
often	planti taim	wasoma
oil, the	wel	waiwai
old (persons)	. . . lapun	qase
old (things)	olpela	makawa
olives, the	pikinini diwai oliv	oliva
on	antap long	e
once	wanpela taim	vakadua
onion, the	anian	varasa
only	. . . tasol	wale ga
open	i op i stap	dola
open, to	opim	dolava
opera, the	kain singsing na danis	vakatasuasua
opposite	arasait	veibasai
or	no	se
orange, the	switmuli	moli
ordered	takim	vakaroti
ordinary	. . . nating	wale
our	bilong mipela	na noda
outside	ausait	tautuba
overcoat, the	kotren	kote ni batabata
owe, to	gat dinau	dinau
oyster, the	kina	civa
pack, to	bungim wantaim	solega
pain, the	pen	mosi
paint, the	pen	i boro
pair, the	tupela	e rua
palace, the	haus bilong king	vale vakatui
paper, the	pepa	veva
parcel, the	karamap	i oloolo
park, the	gaden bilas	rara ni gade
park (car), to	pasim kar	kelea
passport, the	paspot	vasivote
pastry, the	kek	keke
pay, to	peim	sauma
peace, the	gutpela taim	vakacegu
peach, the	prut pis	piji
pearl, the	kiau bilong gam	mata ni civa

VOCABULARY

TONGAN	SAMOAN	TAHITIAN
fakatokanga	fā'aliga	parau fa'a'ite
eni	nei	i teie nei
lau	nūmera	nūmera
neesi	teine tausima'i	utuutu ma'i
niu kelekele	fualā'au	huero
ma'u	maua	roa'a
nofo'i	nōfoia	api
tu'uaki	ofo	pūpū
'ōfisi	'ōfisa	piha tōro'a
'ofisa	'ōfisa	ra'atira fa'ehau
fa'a	faiso'o	pinepine
lolo	suāu'u	hinu
motu'a	matua	rū'au
motu'a	anamuā	tahito
'olive	'ōlive	olive
funga	i luga o	i ni'a
tu'o taha	fa'atasi	hō'ē taime
onioni	aniani	'oniāni
... pē	na'o	... ana'e
ava	matala	mahiti
fakaava	tatala	'iriti
faiva hiva	fa'afiafiaga i pesega	opera
fehāngaaki	fa'afeagai	i mua mai
pe	po'o	'ē 'aore ra
moli	moli	'ānani
'ota	fa'atonuina	poro'i
noa	ta'atele	mātau
homau	la mātou	tā māua
tu'a	i fafo	i rāpae
kote loloa fakamafana	'ofutelē fa'amāfanafana	'ahu rahi
mo'ua kia	'aitālafu	tārahu
tofe	tio	tio
fa'o	teu	pū'ohu
mamahi	tigā	māuiui
vali	vali	pēni
hoa	... e lua	pea
pālasi	maota	aora'i
pepa	pepa	parau
fakamoimoi	āfifi	pū'ohu
pa'aka	malae	'āua
tau	fa'atū	'āua pereo'o
paāsipoōti	tusifolau	parau fa'ati'a
taati	keki	faraoa momona
totongi	totogi	'aufau
melino	filēmū	hau
piisi	pisi	pīti
mata'i tofe	penina	poe

389

VOCABULARY

ENGLISH	NEW GUINEA PIDGIN	FIJIAN
peas, the	hebsen	pisi
pen, the	pen	peni
pencil, the	pensil	penikau
pepper, the	pepa	pepa
perfume, the	sanda	waiwai ni sasaunaki
perhaps	ating	beka
permit, to	larim	vakadonuya
person, the	man no meri	tamata
petrol (gasoline), the	bensin	benisini
pharmacy, the	haus marasin	sitoa ni wai ni mate
photograph, the	poto	i taba
picture, the	piksa	yaloyalo
piece, the	hap	tiki
pillow, the	pilo	i lokoloko
pin, the	pin	pini
pineapple, the	ananas	vadra
pink	ret	piqi
place, the	hap	vanua
plate, the	plet	veleti
platform (railway), the	ples bilong wetim tren	i kelekele
pleasant	switpela	maleka
plum, the	prut plam	palamu
point out, to	mekim long pinga long	dusia
police station, the	plis stesin	siteseni ni ovisa
policeman, the	plisman	ovisa
poor (needy)	. . . rabis	dravudravua
pork, the	abus pik	lewe ni vuaka
porter, the	kagoboi	dau cola i yaya
possible	. . . i ken	rawa
post-box, the	letabokis	kato ni vakacuru i vola
postcard, the	poskat	posikati
post-office, the	haus pos	positovesi
potatoes, the	poteto	pateta
practise, to	traiim	vulica
prawn, the	kindam bilong solwara	ura
present (gift), the	presen	i loloma
president, the	presiden	peresitedi
press (clothes), to	ainim	yayanitaka
pretty	nais	totoka
price, the	pe	i sau
priest, the	pater	bete
prison, the	kalabus	vale ni veivesu
private	. . . tambu long olgeta	vuni
promise, to	promisim	yalataka
province, the	distrik	yasana
public	. . . bilong olgeta man na meri	leive ni vanua

VOCABULARY

TONGAN	SAMOAN	TAHITIAN
pī	pī	pipi iti
peni	peni	tuira
peni vahevahe	penitala	pēni tara
pepa	pepa	pēpa
kaloni	fa'amanogi	mono'i
mahalo	'ātonu	paha
loto kiai	fa'ataga	fa'ati'a
tokotaha	tagata	ta'ata
penisini	kesi	mōri 'ārahu
fale fakatau-vai	falevailā'au	fare rā'au
tā	ata	hoho'a
fakatātā	fa'atusa	hoho'a
konga	fāsimea	pēha'a
pilo	'aluga	tūru'a
pine	pine	pine
fainā	fala 'aina	painapo
pingiki	piniki	tārona
potu	nofoaga	vāhi
peleti	ipu māfolafola	merēti
palepale talianga lēlue	tūlaga	porōmu 'āuri
fakamānako	mālie	hō'ata
palamu	palamu	rama popa'ā
tuhu ki	fa'asino	tohu
fale polisi	fale leoleo	fare mūto'i
polisi	leoleo tamāloa	mūto'i
masiva	mativa	veve
kano'i puaka	fāsi pua'a	pua'a
pota	'o le 'ave 'ato	ta'ata hōpoi
lava	mafai	ti'a
li'anga meili	pusa meli	'āfata rata
pousikaati	posikati	hoho'a rata
pōsiti'ōfisi	falemeli	fare rata
pateta	pateta	'umara pūtete
ako	fa'ata'ita'i	ha'api'i mai
fa'ahinga 'uo iiki	ūla	'ōura pape
me'a'ofa	meaalofa	taiha'a hōro'a
palesiteni	peresitene	peretiteni
haeane'i	'āuli	tā'āuri
faka'ofo'ofa	mānaia	purotu
totongi	tau	moni ho'o
taula'eiki	ositāulaga	perepitero
pilisone	falepuipui	fare 'āuri
'ikai ngofua lihe kakai	tōtino	fa'a'erehia
fakapapau	fōlafola	fafau
vahefonua	itūmālō	mata'eina'a
fakahāhā	mo tagata 'uma	fa'a'ite hua

VOCABULARY

ENGLISH	NEW GUINEA PIDGIN	FIJIAN
pull, to	pulim . . . i kam	dreta
puncture, the	taia i plat	qara
pure	. . . klin	savasava
purple	. . . hap ret	lokaloka
put, to	putim	biuta
quantity, the	haumas	kena levu
queen, the	misis kwin	ranadi
question, the	kwestin	taro
quick	hariap	totolo
quiet	. . . i no gat nois	cegu
race (contest), the	resis	veitau
radio, the	wailis	retio
railway, the	tren	sitima ni vanua
raincoat, the	kotren	kote ni uca
raining, it is	ren i kamdaun	uca
razor, the	masin bilong sep	i toro
read, to	ritim	wilika
ready	redi	vakarau
receive, to	kisim	taura
record (gramophone), the	rekot	veleti ni vakatagi
red	ret	damudamu
register (letter), to	rejistarim	rejistataka
religion, the	lotu	lotu
remember, to	holim long tingting	nanuma
repair, to	wokim gut	vakavinakataka
repeat, to	mekim gen	vakaruataka
reply, to	bekim tok	sauma
rest, to	malolo	vakacegu
restaurant, the	haus kaikai	vale ni kana
result, the	ansa	macala
rice (cooked), the	rais	raisi
rich	. . . i gat planti samting	vutuniyau
right (correct)	stret	dodonu
right (hand)	han sut	matau
ring, the	ring	mama
ripe	. . . mau	dreu
river, the	riva	uciwai
road, the	rot	gaunisala
roast	. . . i bin kukim long aven	vavi
room, the	rum	rumu
run, to	ran	cici
sad	. . . i sori	lomabibi
safe	. . . i stap gut	bula
sailor, the	boskru	kai mua
salt, the	sol	masima
same	wankain	tautauvata

VOCABULARY

TONGAN	SAMOAN	TAHITIAN
fusi'i	toso	huti
pā	pā	pararī
haohaoa	mamā	mā
lanu-vaioleti	violē	vare'au
tuku	tu'u	tu'u
hono lahi	anoano	rahira'a
kuini	tupu tama'ita'i	ari'i vahine
fehu'i	fesili	uira'a
vave	vave	'oi'oi
longo	filēmū	mania
lova	tū'uga	horora'a
letiō	uālesi	niuniu nā te reva
lēlue	ala a'umea	porōmu 'āuri
kote faka'uha	'ofu fa'aua	pereue fa'arari
'oku 'uha	ua timu	e ua
tele	tafi	hahu ta'a
lau	faitau	tai'o
teuteu	sāuni	ineine
ma'u	maua	fāri'i
lēkoti	pu'e leo	pehe 'upa'upa tari'a
kulokula	mūmū	'ute'ute
lesisita'i	puipui	ha'amana
lotu	lotu	ha'apa'ora'a
manatu'i	mānatua	ha'amana'o
monosi	fa'afou	tātā'i
toe fai	toe fai	tāpiti
tali	tali	pahono
mālōlō	mapu	fa'aea
fale kai	fale'aiga	fare tāmā'ara'a
fua	i'uga	hōpe'a
laise	alaisa	raiti
tu'umālie	mau'oloa	'ona
totonu	sa'o	'āfaro
to'omata'u	taumatau	'atau
mama	mama	tāpe'a rima
momoho	pula	para
vaitafe	vaitafe	'ānāvai
hala	ala	porōmu
tunu	tao	tunu umu
loki	potu	piha
lele	momo'e	horo
loto-mamahi	fa'anoanoa	mata 'oto
malu	sao	ora
tangata alutahi	seila	mātarō
māsima	māsima	miti popa'ā
tatau	tutusa	ho'ea

VOCABULARY

ENGLISH	NEW GUINEA PIDGIN	FIJIAN
sandals, the	sandal	i vava
sandwich, the	sanwis	seniwiji
sauce, the	sos	sosi
say, to	tokim	kaya
school, the	skul	koro ni vuli
science, the	save	vakadidike
scissors, the	sisis	i koti
sea, the	solwara	wasawasa
seat, the	sia	i dabedabe
second	namba tu	i karua
second (of time), the	sekon	sekodi
secretary, the	kuskus	sekeriteri
see, to	lukim	raica
seems, (it)	ating . . .	rairai
seldom	sampela taim	vagauna
sell, to	salim	volitaka
send (thing), to	salim	vakauta
separate	. . . abrus	wasea
servant, the	hausboi	dau veiqaravi
service station, the	sevis stesin	sevesiteseni
several	sampela	e vica
sew, to	samapim	cula
shallow	. . . i no daun	vodea
shampoo, the	sop	i sava ni ulu
shave, to	sepim	toro
she	em	o koya
sheet, the	bet laplap	siti
shelter, the	ples bilong hait	i vakaruru
ship, the	sip	waqa
shirt, the	siot	sote
shoe, the	su	i vava
shop, the	stua	sitoa
short	sot	lekaleka
show, to	soim	vakaraitaka
shower, the	waswas	i sisili
side, the	hapsait	yasa
sign, to	raitim nem long	sainitaka
silk, the	slika	silika
silver, the	silva	siliva
since (time)	bihain long	mai na gauna
sing, to	singsing	laga sere
sit, to	sindaun	dabeca
skirt, the	siket	liku
sky, the	heven	lomalagi
sleep, to	slip	moce
slow	slo	berabera
small	liklik	lailai

VOCABULARY

TONGAN	SAMOAN	TAHITIAN
senitolo	se'evae	tia'a
sanuisi	sānuisi	faraoa 'amu'amu
lolo	sosi	miti tereve
pehē	fai atu	parau
fale ako	ā'oga	fare ha'api'ira'a
saienisi	saienisi	'ite
hele kosi	seleulu	pā'oti
tahi	sami	miti
hekeheka'anga	nofoa	pārahira'a
... ua	lona lua	a piti
sekoni	sēkone	tetoni
sēkelitali	failautusi	pāpa'i parau
sio ki	va'ai	'ite
'oku hangē	e peisea'i	e au
tātāāitaha	seāseā	varavara
fakatau atu	fa'atau atu	ho'o atu
fekau	'ave	hāpono
mavahe	'ese'ese	fa'ata'a
sevaniti	'au'auna	tāvini
fale penisini	pamu penisini	fare 'ōperera'a mōrī
ni'ihi	tele	mea rahi
tuitui	su'i	au
'ikai loloto	papa'u	pāpa'u
lolo 'uku ulu	moli fufulu lauulu	pu'a rouru
telekava	sele	hahu
ne	ia	'oia
tupenu kafu	'ie 'afu	'ahu tāpo'i
malu	lafitaga	tāmaru
vaka	va'a	pahi
sote	'ofutino	'ahu 'o'omo
sū	se'evae	tia'a
fale koloa	fale'oloa	fare toa
nounou	pu'upu'u	poto
fakahā	fā'ali	fa'a'ite
saoa	fale ta'ele	ha'ama'irira'a pape
tafa'aki	itū	pae
fakamo'oni hingoa ki	saini	tāpa'o
silika	silika	tirita
siliva	siliva	'ārio
talu mei	talu mai	a'enei
hiva'i	pese	himene
tangutu	nofo	pārahi
piva	sakeke	piritoti
langi	lagi	ra'i
mohe	moe	ta'oto
māmālie	telegese	tāere
ki'i	la'itiiti	iti

VOCABULARY

ENGLISH	NEW GUINEA PIDGIN	FIJIAN
smoke, to	smok	vakatavako
snow, the	ais	uca cevata
soap, the	sop	sovu
socks, the	soken	sitokini
soda water, the	sodawara	wai qaqa
soft	... malomalo	malumu
soldier, the	soldia	sotia
some	sampela	e so
somebody	wanpela man no meri	e dua na tamata
something	wanpela samting	e dua na ka
sometimes	sampela taim	e na so na gauna
somewhere	long sampela hap	e na dua na vanua
soon	kwiktaim	wale ga oqo
sorry	sori	vosota
soup, the	sup	suvu
sour	... i pait olsem muli	gaga
south	saut	ceva
soy sauce, the	soi sos	soya sosi
space, the	spes	maliwa
speak, to	tokim	vosa
spectacles, the	aiglas	mata iloilo
spoon, the	spun	sevuni
sport, the	pilai	qito
square (place), the	ples	loma ni bai ririvi
stairs, the	leta	i kabakaba
stamp (postage), the	stem	sitaba
stand, to	sanap	tucake
star, the	sta	kalokalo
start, to	kirapim	tekivutaka
station (railway), the	tren stesin	siteseni
stay, to	sindaun	tiko
steak, the	mit	lewe ni bulumakau
steep	... i go daun tumas	baba
steering, the	stia	uli
stick, the	kanda	kau
still (adv.)	yet	vakadua
stockings, the	soken	sitokini
stone, the	ston	vatu
storey (floor), the	polo	taba vale
straight on	stret	vakadodonu
strap, the	pasim	i dreke
street, the	rot	sala
streetcar (tram), the	tram	taramu
string, the	string	wa
strong	strongpela	kaukaua
student, the	studen	gone vuli
study, to	lainim	vulica

VOCABULARY

TONGAN	SAMOAN	TAHITIAN
ifi	ulaula	puhipuhi i te 'ava'ava
sinou	kiona	hiona
koa	moli	pu'a
sitōkeni	tōtini	tōtini
vai sota	vai sōtā	tōtā
molū	malū	marū
sōtia	fitafita	fa'ehau
ni'ihi	nai	nā
ha taha	'o se isi	te tahi ta'ata
ha me'a	se mea	hō'ē tao'a
ko e taimi ni'ihi	i nisi aso	te tahi taime
'i ha feitu'u pē	i se isi mea	hō'ē vāhi
vave	vave	fātata roa
loto-mamahi	fa'anoanoa	pe'ape'a
supo	sua	tihopu
mahi	'o'ona	'ava'ava
saute	saute	'apato'a
lolo soi	soi sosi	miti tinitō
'atā	avanoa	ārea
lea	tautala	parau
mata'sio'ata	mata tioata	titi'amata
sēpuni	sipuni	punu tāipu
sipoti	tā'aloga	ha'utira'a
mala'e	sikuea	māhora
sitepu	sitepu	'ē'a
sitapa	fa'ailoga	titiro
tu'u	tū	ti'a
fetu'u	fetū	feti'a
kamata	'āmata	ha'amata
fale lēlue	taunu'uga	pūhapa
nofo	nofo	noho
siteiki	fāsipovi	tāpū pua'atoro
fakalilifa	tofē	matomato
me'a faka'uli	'o le foeuli	fa'aterera'a
tokotoko	lā'au	pēha'a rā'au
. . . pē	pea	. . . noa
sitōkeni	tōtini	tōtini
maka	ma'a	'ōfa'i
fungavaka	fogāfale	tahua
hangatonu	fa'asa'o	'āfaro
leta	fusi	'iri tāpe'a
hala	ala	porōmu
talamu	taramu	'ē'a 'āuri
maea	mānoa	taura
mālohi	mālosi	pūai
tamaioeiki ako	tama ā'oga/teine ā'oga	ta'ata ha'api'i
ako	a'o	ha'api'i

VOCABULARY

ENGLISH	NEW GUINEA PIDGIN	FIJIAN
substance, the	samting	lewena
suddenly	santu	vakasauri
sugar, the	suga	suka
suitcase, the	paus	kato
summit, the	antap	delana
sun, the	san	mata ni siga
sweet	swit	kamikamica
swim, to	swim	qalo
table, the	tebol	teveli
tailor, the	man bilong samapim klos	dau cula i sulu
take, to	kisim	taura
tall	long	balavu
tap, the	kok	vaivo
tape (recording), the	tep	wa ni katoni vosa
tape recorder, the	teprikoda	misini ni katoni vosa
taste, to	traiim	tovolea
tax, the	takis	i vakacavacava
taxi, the	taksi	tekesi
tea (to drink), the	ti	ti
teach, to	skulim	vakavulica
teacher, the	tisa	qase ni vuli
telegram, the	wailis	talekaramu
telephone, the	telipon	talevoni
television, the	bokis wailis wantaim piksa	televiseni
temperature, the	makim hat o kol	tuvaki ni katakata
temple, the	haus lotu	vale ni lotu
than	long	vei
that	dispela	ko ya
theatre, the	haus piksa	vale ni yaloyalo
their	. . . bilong ol	na nodra
then (at that time)	dispela taim	mani
there	long hap	keri
there is	i gat	e tiko
they	ol	ratou
thick	strong	vavaku
thin	bun nating	mamare
thing, the	samting	ka
think, to	tingting	vakasamataka
third	namba tri	i katolu
thirsty	hangre long dring	karamaca
this	dispela	oqo
thread, the	tret	wa ni culacula
through	long namel long	kosova
throw, to	tromweim	viritaka
ticket, the	tiket	tikite
ticket-office, the	tiket ofis	vale ni saumi tikite

VOCABULARY

TONGAN	SAMOAN	TAHITIAN
me'a	'a'ano	tino
fakafokifā	fa'afuase'ia	'oi'oi
suka	suka	tihota
kato	'atopa'u	fāri'i tauiha'a
tumu'aki	tumutumu	tupua'i
la'ā	lā	mahana
melie	suamalie	momona
kakau	'a'au	'au
tēpile	laulau	'amura'a mā'a
tangata tuitui	su'i 'ofu	ta'ata nirara'a 'āhu
to'o	'ave	rave
mā'olunga	'umi	roa
paipa	paipa	fa'atahera'a
tepi	lipine	rīpene 'upa'upa tari'a
misini hiki tepi	la'au pu'e leo	mātini 'upa'upa tari'a
ahiahi'i	tofo	tamata
tukuhau	lāfoga	'aufau
tekisī	ta'avale la'u pasese	pereo'o uira
tī	tī	tī
ako'i	a'oa'o	ha'api'i atu
faiako	faiā'oga	'orometua ha'api'i
mākoni	uālesi	niuniu
telefoni	telefoni	niuniu paraparau
televīsone	televise	'āfata hoho'a paraparau
mafana	māfanafana	huru ve'ave'a
temipale	mālumalu	marae
'i	i lō le	e
ena	lenā	terā
fale faiva	faletīfaga	fare teata
honau	la lātou	tā rātou
toki	i lenā lava itūlā	i reira
'i hē	i ai	i 'ō ra
'oku 'i ai	e i ai	e
nau	lātou	rātou
fuolahi	māfiafia	me'ume'u
fuosi'i	mānifinifi	rairai
me'a	'o le mea	mea
fakakaukau	māfaufau	mana'o
... tolu	vaetoluga	a toru
fieinua	fia inu	po'ihā
... ko eni	lenei	teie
filo	filo	tuaina
'i	i	māiha
hua'i	togi	tāora
tikite	tikite	titeti
'ōfisi tikite	'ōfisa fa'atau pepa	fare titeti

VOCABULARY

ENGLISH	NEW GUINEA PIDGIN	FIJIAN
tie, the	nektait	neketai
time, the	taim	gauna
timetable, the	taimtebol	porokarami
tin opener, the	op tin	i dola
tip (money), the	sevis mani	i vakaqumi
tired	... i les	oca
to	long	ki
tobacco, the	tabak	tavako
today	tude	edaidai
together	wantaim	vata
toilet (men), the	haus pekpek man	vale lailai
toilet (women), the	haus pekpek meri	vale lailai
toilet paper, the	pepa pekpek	i kakavelu
tomato, the	tomato	tomata
tomb, the	hul i planim man longen	i bulubulu
tomorrow	tumora	ni mataka
tonight	tunait	bogi e daidai
too (much)	... tumas	rui
toothbrush, the	bros bilong tit	i masi ni bati
toothpaste, the	sop bilong tit	waiwai ni bati
touch, to	pilim	taura
tourist, the	kam man	sara vanua
towards	long hap i go long	ki
towel, the	taul	tauwelu
tower, the	taua	tawa
town, the	taun	tauni
town hall, the	kaunsel haus	tauna olo
train, the	tren	tereni
tram, the	tram	taramu
translate, to	tanim tok	vakadewataka
travel, to	wokabaut	veilakoyaki
tree, the	diwai	vunikau
trouble, the	trabel	leqa
trousers, the	trausis	tarausese
true	tru	dina
try on, to	traiim	vakatovolea
turn, in	wanpela wanpela	veitaravi
twice	tupela taim	vakarua
typewriter, the	taipraita	taipa
typist, the	taipis	dau taipa
tyre, the	taia	taya
ugly	... i no naispela	rairai ca
umbrella, the	ambrela	i viu
under	ananit long	boto
understand, to	save	kila
unfortunately	tarangu	ka ni rarawa

VOCABULARY

TONGAN	SAMOAN	TAHITIAN
hēkesi	fusiua	tā'amu
taimi	taimi	taime
taimi-tēpile	fua o taimi	tāpura taime
me'a-fakaāva-kapa	tala 'apa	'iriti punu
tipi	meaalofa	moni hōro'a
hela	vāivai	rohirohi
ki	'i	i
tapaka	tapa'a	'ava'ava
he 'aho ni	i le asō	i teie nei mahana
fakataha	fa'atasi	ana'e tāpiti
fale mālōlō	fale'ese tamāloa	fare iti
fale mālōlō	fale'ese fafine	fare iti
pepa fale-mālōlō	pepa fale'ese	parau fare iti
temata	tamato	tōmāti
fonualoto	tia	menema
'apongipongi	taeao	ānānahi
he poó ni	nānei	i teie pō
fu'u	na'uā	rahi roa
polosi nifo	pulumu nifo	porōmu niho
kilimi fufulu nifo	mea fulunifo	pu'a niho
ala	tago	fāfā
taha 'eve'eva	tagata faimalaga	rātere
ki	aga'i 'i	i
taueli	solo	tauera
taua	'olo	fare teitei
kolo	'a'ai	'oire
tauniholo	fale fono	fare hau
lēlue	nofoa afi	pereo'o auahi
talamu	taramu	'ē'a 'āuri
hiki	fa'aliliu	'iriti
fononga	malaga	tere
'akau	lā'au	tumu rā'au
fakahoha'a	fa'alavelave	'aueue
talausese	'ofuvae	piripou
mo'oni	moni	mau
'ahi'ahi	fa'ata'ita'i	tamata
fetongitongi	auaua'i	tata'itahi
tu'o ua	fa'alua	e piti
mīsini taipe	lomitusi	mātini patapata parau
faitaipe	tagata lomitusi	patapata parau
taea	pa'u	uaua
mata-kovi	'auleaga	hā'iri'iri
fakamalu	fa'amalu	fare 'amarara
'i he lalo	i lalo	i raro a'e
'ilo hono 'uhinga	mālamalama	'ua ta'a
pango	leaga 'ua . . .	pāoa

VOCABULARY

ENGLISH	NEW GUINEA PIDGIN	FIJIAN
university, the	univesiti	univesiti
until	inap long	ka yacova
upstairs	antap	cake
urgently	kwiktaim	vakatotolo
usually	. . . save . . .	dau kena i vakarau
valley, the	ples daun	buca
valuable	. . . i kastim planti mani	talei
veal, the	mit bilong pikinini bulmakau	lewe ni bulumakau gone
vegetables, the	sayor	kakana draudrau
very	. . . tumas	sara
view (outlook), the	ples lukluk	ka e saravi
village, the	ples	koro
visit, to	go lukim	sikova
voyage, the	wokabaut long sip	soko
wait for, to	wetim	waraka
waiter, the	boi	dau veiqaravi
walk, to	wokabaut	taubale
wall (of room), the	banis	lalaga
wall (garden, etc.), the	banis	lalaga
want, to	laik	vinakata
war, the	pait	i valu
wash, to	wasim	savata
washbasin, the	dis bilong waswas	siqi
watch, the	hanwas	kaloko ni liga
watch, to	lukim	yadrava
water, the	wara	wai
we	mipela	keitou
weather, the	taim	draki
week, the	wik	macawa
weight, the	skel	kena bibi
well (adv.)	gut	vakavinaka
well (health)	. . . i stap gut	bula vinaka
west	hap san i go daun	ra
wet	. . . i gat wara	suasua
wet season, the	taim bilong ren	vula i uca
wharf, the	bris	wavu
what?	wanem samting?	cava?
wheel, the	wil	yava
when?	wataim?	e naica?
where (is it)?	we?	evei?
where (to)?	·we?	ki vei?
which?	wanem?	e cava?
white	wait	vulavula
who?	husat?	ko cei?
whose?	. . . bilong husat?	nei cei?
why?	bilong wanem?	baleta?
wide	brait	raraba

VOCABULARY

TONGAN	SAMOAN	TAHITIAN
'univesiti	univesitē	ha'api'ira'a teitei roa
'o a'u ki	se'i	e tae atu
'i 'olunga	fogā fale āluga	i ni'a iho
fakavavevave	fa'avave	rū noa
fa'a	e māsani ai	mātau
tele'a	vanu	fa'a
mahu'inga	tāua	tao'a
kano'i pulu-mui	a'ano o le tama'i povi	pua'atoro fanau'a
fo'i 'akau	lā'au 'aina	mā'a fa'a'apu
... 'aupito	matuā	... rahi
mātanga	va'aiga	hi'ora'a
kolo	nu'u	'oire iti
'a'ahi	asi	mata'ita'i
folau	folau	tere
tatali ki	fa'atali	tia'i
tangata tali-tēpile	laulau'aiga	tuati
'alu lalo	savali	haere
holisi	pā	papa'i
'ā maka	pā	patu
fi'e ma'u	mana'o	hina'aro
tau	taua	tama'i
fufulu	fufulu	horoi
pesoni tafitafi	'apa fafano	punu horoira'a
uasi	uati	uāti
tokanga ki	matamata	hi'o
vai	vai	pape
mau	mātou	māua
anga 'o e 'aho	tau	mahana
'uike	vāiaso	hepetoma
fakamamafa	mamafa	teiaha
lelei	lelei	maita'i
lelei	mālosi	maita'i
hihifo	sisifo	to'o'a o te rā
viku	susū	rari
fa'ahita'u 'uha	tau susū	'anotau ua
uafu	uafu	uāhu
hā?	'o le ā?	e aha?
va'e	uili	huira
'afē?	āfea?	āfea?
'i fē?	'o fea?	tei hea?
ki fē?	po'o fea?	i hea?
he fē?	... ai?	tēhea?
hinehina	pa'epa'e	'uo'uo
'a hai?	'o ai?	'o vai?
koe me'a 'a hai?	e ana?	nā vai?
ke hā?	'aiseā?	nō te aha?
fālahi	lautele	'a'ano

VOCABULARY

ENGLISH	NEW GUINEA PIDGIN	FIJIAN
wild	wail	kila
win, to	winim	qaqa
wind, the	win	cagi
window, the	windo	katuba leka
wine, the	wain	waini
wise	. . . i save tumas	vuku
with	wantaim	kei
without	i no gat	sega ni
woman, the	meri	yalewa
wonder, to	tingim . . . o nogat	qoroya
wonderful	. . . nais tumas	veivakurabuitaka
wood (timber), the	diwai	kau
wool, the	gras bilong sipsip	vuti ni sipi
word, the	tok	vosa
work, the	wok	cakacaka
workman, the	wokboi	tamata cakacaka
world, the	graun	vuravura
worse	. . . moa nogut	ca cake
worst	nambawan nogut	ca duadua
worth, to be	kastim	e na yaga . . .
write, to	raitim	vola
wrong	kranki	cala
year, the	yia	yabaki
yellow	yelo	dromodromo
yesterday	asde	nanoa
you	yu	iko
young	yang	cauravau
your	. . . bilong yu	na nomu

VOCABULARY

TONGAN	SAMOAN	TAHITIAN
kaivao	'āivao	'ōviri
mālōhi	mua	rē
matangi	matagi	mata'i
matapā teke	fa'amalama	ha'amāramarama
'uaine	uaina	uaina
poto	poto	pa'ari
'i	ma	mā
ta'e	e aunoa ma	'ore
fefine	fafine	vahine
fifili	se'i iloa	feruri
fakaofo	ofoofogia	hiahia roa
'akau	lā'au	rā'au
fulufulu'i sipi	fulufulu	huruhuru māmoe
lea	'upu	parau
ngāue	galue	'ohipa
tangata ngāue	tagata faigāluega	ta'ata rave 'ohipa
mamani	lalolagi	ao
kovi ange	leaga i lo lē . . .	'ino a'e
kovi taha	sili ona leaga	'ino roa a'e
ko e . . . mahu'ingá	e tusa ma le . . .	hau a'e
tohi	tusi	pāpa'i
hala	sesē	hape
ta'u	tausaga	matahiti
engeenga	sāmasama	re'are'a
'aneafi	ananafi	inānahi
'akoe	'oe	'oe
ki'i	talavou	'āpī
ho'o	lau	tā 'oe

Italics indicate the languages of this book.

AFGHANISTAN Pashto and *Persian.*

ARGENTINA *Spanish.*

AUSTRALIA *English*; aboriginal languages only in remote areas.

BANGLADESH *Bengali,* some *English.*

BELIZE *English.*

BOLIVIA *Spanish.*

BRAZIL *Portuguese.*

BURMA Many local languages, but *Burmese* is spoken by two-thirds of the country. Some *English.*

CHILE *Spanish.*

CHINA *Mandarin* is understood by two-thirds of the country. Among some dozen Chinese dialects the most important are *Cantonese* (Guangdong province); *Hokkien* (Amoy and Fukien province); and Wu (Shanghai area). Tibetan in Tibet. Mongolian languages along northern border.

COLOMBIA *Spanish.*

COOK ISLANDS Generally *English*, with Raratongan and other relatives of New Zealand Maori.

ECUADOR *Spanish.*

FIJI *English* is official; *Fijian* (Bauan dialect) is widespread. Indian minorities speak Gujarati (and generally *Hindi*) or *Tamil.*

FRENCH GUIANA (Guyane Française): *French*, a French creole, and local languages.

FRENCH POLYNESIA (Polynésie Française, comprises Society Islands, Tuamotuan Archipelago and Marquesas): *French*, but *Tahitian* is the majority native language and language of communication. Chinese minority speaks Hakka.

GUAM *English* and Chamorro.

GUATEMALA *Spanish.*

GUYANA Mainly *English* and English creole.

HAWAIIAN ISLANDS (state of U.S.A.): *English*; native Hawaiian now little used.

HONDURAS *Spanish.*

HONG KONG (British colony): *English* (official) and *Cantonese.*

INDIA Some fourteen major languages, but *Hindi* (nearly the same language as *Urdu*) is understood through most of the north, and is official together with *English*, which is known broadly throughout the country. *Bengali* in Calcutta and West Bengal. Gujarati in Bombay and as the general language of commerce. Southern Indian languages are led by *Tamil* (Madras and the state of Tamil Nadu).

INDONESIA Javanese, Balinese and numerous other regional languages, but *Indonesian* (nearly the same language as *Malay*) is generally understood throughout the country.

IRAN *Persian* in various dialects.

JAPAN *Japanese* in various dialects; Ainu locally in north.

KAMPUCHEA *Kampuchean* and minorities of *Vietnamese, Malay, Thai*; some *French.*

KIRIBATI (Gilbert Islands, including Banaba, Ocean Island): *English*, plus local Gilbertese.

KOREA *Korean* with minor dialectal differences, throughout North and South. Some *Japanese*.

LAOS Generally *Lao*, with regional differences of pronunciation. Minority languages among hill tribes. Some *French*.

MACAU (province of Portugal): *Portuguese, Cantonese*, some *English*.

MALAYSIA *Malay*, some *English*. Chinese Malays generally speak *Hokkien*.

MEXICO *Spanish*.

NEW CALEDONIA (Nouvelle-Calédonie): *French* and several local languages.

NEW GUINEA, see PAPUA NEW GUINEA.

NEW ZEALAND *English*; native Maori relatively little used.

NICARAGUA *Spanish*.

PACIFIC ISLANDS, TRUST TERRITORY (includes Carolines, Marshalls and Marianas): Chamorro and some dozen other native languages, but with *English* the language of education.

PAKISTAN *Urdu, English* and *Bengali* (few speakers) are official. Minority languages include *Persian*, Pashto, Panjabi.

PANAMA *Spanish*.

PAPUA NEW GUINEA Some 400 local languages, with *New Guinea Pidgin* as the main language of communication in the north, *English* (and Police Motu) in Papua.

PARAGUAY *Spanish*, Guarani.

PERU *Spanish*, Quechua.

PHILIPPINES *Tagalog* (also called Pilipino) covers about half the country, and is spreading as a language of communication. It is the official language, together with *English*.

SAMOA *English* and *Samoan* in both independent and American Samoa.

SINGAPORE Four official languages are *Mandarin, Malay, Tamil* and *English*. Most Singapore Chinese in fact speak *Hokkien*.

SOLOMON ISLANDS Pidgin, closely related to *New Guinea Pidgin*; some *English*. Numerous local languages.

SRI LANKA (Ceylon): *Sinhalese* is official, but about one-eighth of the country speaks *Tamil. English* commonly understood.

SURINAME Dutch, an English creole called "Taki-taki", and local languages.

TAHITI, see FRENCH POLYNESIA.

TAIWAN (Formosa): Native Taiwanese is a minority language. *Mandarin* is official, *Hokkien* much spoken, *Japanese* widely understood.

THAILAND *Thai* and numerous minority languages.

TIMOR *Indonesian*, plus some *Portuguese* (in the former colony), superimposed on local languages.

TONGA (Friendly Islands): *Tongan*; some *English*.

TUVALU (Ellice Islands): *English*, plus local Ellicean.

URUGUAY *Spanish*.

VANUATU (New Hebrides): Pidgin (comparable with *New Guinea Pidgin*) in a variety known as Beach-la-Mar; some *English* and *French*.

VENEZUELA *Spanish*.

VIETNAM Local languages in central mountain area, elsewhere *Vietnamese* with only minor variations of dialect.

CALENDARS

Every country in the area covered by this book makes use of the Western calendar for commercial purposes. Simply note:

In Thailand and Laos years are reckoned in the "Buddhist era" (Thai *Pŭt-tā' sǎ'gǎ'rǎht*); subtract 543 to get the Western year (*Krit sǎ'gǎ'rǎht*).

In Taiwan years are reckoned from the "founding of the republic"; add 1911 to get the Western year.

In Japan years are numbered from the accession of the reigning emperor; so that 1983 is *Shōwa 58-nen,* the fifty-eighth year of the Shōwa reign (the reign of Hirohito).

There are some twenty other calendars of regional or sectional interest in Asia.

THE MUSLIM CALENDAR crosses national boundaries and determines Muslim religious holidays. It is designed to keep in step with the phases of the moon, independently of the seasons. Reckoned against the Western calendar, it starts about eleven days earlier each year. The years are numbered from the date of Muhammad's flight from Mecca (A.D. 622) and are known as "years of the Hegira" (Malay *Tahun Hijrah,* "TH").

The twelve months of the year, with their numbers of days, are (in Malay language, but recognisably similar elsewhere): Muharram 30, Safar 29, Rabial-awal 30, Rabial-akir 29, Jamadil-awal 30, Jamadil-akir 29, Rejab 30, Sha'aban 29, Ramadan 30, Shawal 29, Dzul-kaedah 30, Dzul-hijjah 29 or 30. The month of Dzul-hijjah has 30 days in eleven years out of each thirty, namely, when the number of the Muslim year, divided by 30, yields remainders 2, 5, 7, 10, 13, 16, 18, 21, 24, 26 or 29.

The year TH 1403 began on 19 October 1982. (Actually, since the preceding night is included, this means 6 p.m. on 18 October.) Some subsequent years (Muslim leap-years starred *) start: *1404** 8.10.83, *1405* 27.9.84, *1406** 16.9.85, *1407* 6.9.86, *1408* 26.8.87, *1409** 14.8.88, *1410* 4.8.89, *1411* 24.7.90, *1412** 13.7.91, *1413* 2.7.92, *1414* 21.6.93, *1415** 10.6.94, *1416* 31.5.95, *1417** 19.5.96.

The month of Ramadan is the "month of fasting" and the month of Shawal the "month of feasting". Muhammad's birthday is celebrated in the month of Rabial-awal. The Muslim holy day each week is Jumaat, 6 p.m. Thursday to 6 p.m. Friday.

Note that Iran, though predominantly Muslim, has a separate calendar (solar, starting with the spring equinox).

SIGNS

In Pakistan, India, Bangladesh, Sri Lanka, Malaysia, Hong Kong, Philippines, Papua New Guinea, Fiji, Tonga and Samoa you can expect that all important signs will be in English or carry English translation.
In New Caledonia and French Polynesia you can expect that they will be in French.

IRAN Read Persian (except numerals) from right to left.

باز	(Bāz)	OPEN
بند	(Band)	CLOSED
خطر	(Khatar)	DANGER
دخانیات ممنوع است	(Dokhāniyat mamnu' ast)	NO SMOKING
ورود	(Varud)	ENTRANCE
خروج	(Kharuj)	EXIT
مستراح ، توالت	(Mostarāh, Tuālet)	TOILET
مردانه ، آقایان	(Mardāna, Āghāyān)	(MEN)
زنانه ، بانوان	(Zanāna, Bānuān)	(WOMEN)
ورود ممنوع	(Varud mamnu' ast)	NO ENTRY, KEEP OUT
پارکینگ ممنوع	(Parking mamnu' ast)	NO PARKING

BURMA

၀င်ပေါက်	(Winbau')	ENTRANCE
ထွက်ပေါက်	(Twe'bpau')	EXIT
ဖွင့်သည်	(Bpwin-de)	OPEN
ပိတ်သည်	(Bpei'dte)	CLOSED
အန္တရာယ်	('Àndǎre)	DANGER
မ၀င်ရ	(Mǎ-win-yà)	NO ENTRANCE KEEP OUT
၌ ၀ဲ: ၎း၌၁ဓ	(Koun-gǎn-yēidanà)	INFORMATION
အိမ်သာ	('Eindha)	TOILET
ကျား:	(Tjā)	(MEN)
မ	(Mà)	(WOMEN)
ဆေး၀ဲ၆ မ ၄ာ ၁က်ရ	(Hseilei' mǎthau'yà)	NO SMOKING
ရ၆	(Ya')	STOP
တန်: ၆ပါ	(Dtànā sī-ba)	FORM QUEUE
ဖိ ၄၆ မ ၆:ရ	(Banna' mǎsi-yà)	NO FOOTWEAR
တိုး:တိုး:	(Dtòundòun)	SILENCE

411

SIGNS

THAILAND

เข้า	(Kàu)	ENTRANCE
ออก	('Ǎwk)	EXIT
เปิด	(Bpǔht)	OPEN
ปิด	(Bpĭt)	CLOSED
อันตราย	('Andta'rahi)	DANGER
ห้ามเข้า	(Hàhm kàu)	NO ENTRANCE
สอบถาม	(Sǎwp-táhm)	INFORMATION
สุขา	(Su'káh)	TOILET
ชาย	(Chahi)	(MEN)
หญิง	(Yíng)	(WOMEN)
ห้ามสูบบุหรี่	(Hàhm sǔup bu'rĭh)	NO SMOKING
หยุด	(Yǔt)	STOP

LAOS

ຢຸດ	(Yūt)	STOP
ຫ້າມເຂົ້າ	(Hàhm kâu)	NO ENTRY
ທາງເຂົ້າ	(Tāhng kâu)	ENTRANCE
ທາງອອກ	(Tāhng 'âwk)	EXIT
ເປີດ	(Bpûht)	OPEN
ປິດ	(Bpĭt)	CLOSED
ຫ້ອງນ້ຳ	(Hâwng nàm)	TOILET
ຜູ້ຊາຍ	(Pûusāhi)	(MEN)
ຜູ້ຍິງ	(Pûu-nyǐng)	(WOMEN)
ອັນຕະລາຍ	(Ǎndtālāhi)	DANGER
ລະວັງໝາຮ້າຍ	(La'wang mǎh hâhi)	BEWARE OF THE DOG
ລະວັງ	(La'wang)	CAUTION
ຫ້າມສູບຢາ	(Hàhm sûup yǎh)	NO SMOKING
ຫ້າມຈອດ	(Hàhm jâwt)	NO PARKING
ບໍ່ຫວ່າງ	(Baw wahng)	OCCUPIED
ຫວ່າງ	(Wahng)	FREE

SIGNS

KAMPUCHEA

ចូល	(Jōl)	ENTRANCE
ចេញ	(Jĕng)	EXIT
របើក	(Bǎak)	OPEN
បិទ	(Bet)	CLOSED
គ្រោះថ្នាក់	(Grúas-tnak)	DANGER
ប្រយ័ត្ន	(Breyat)	CAUTION
ហាម មិនឱ្យចូល	(Haam mĭn 'aoy jōl) ⎱	⎰ NO ENTRANCE
កុំចូល	(Gom jōl) ⎰	⎱ KEEP OUT
បង្គន់	(Bŏnggúan)	TOILET
ប្រុស	(Bros)	(MEN)
ស្រី	(Srey)	(WOMEN)
ហាម មិនឱ្យចត	(Haam mĭn 'aoy jót) ⎱	
កុំចត	(Gom jót) ⎰	NO PARKING
កុំជក់បារី	(Gom júak barey)	NO SMOKING

VIETNAM

NGUY-HIỂM	DANGER
LỐI VÀO	ENTRANCE
LỐI RA	EXIT
ĐÀN ÔNG ⎱ QUÝ ÔNG ⎰	MEN'S TOILET
ĐÀN BÀ ⎱ QUÝ BÀ ⎰	WOMEN'S TOILET
CẤM VÀO	NO ENTRANCE
PHÒNG VẤN-SỰ	INFORMATION
CẤM HÚT THUỐC	NO SMOKING
DỪNG LẠI	STOP
MỞ	OPEN
ĐÓNG CỬA	CLOSED

SIGNS

CHINA Sometimes written vertically, top to bottom; occasionally right to left.

入口	(Rùkǒu)	ENTRANCE
出口	(Chūkǒu)	EXIT
开	(Kāi)	OPEN
关	(Guān)	CLOSED
危险	(Wēixiǎn)	DANGER
闲人免进	(Xián rén miǎn jìn)	NO ENTRANCE KEEP OUT
询问处	(Xúnwènchù)	INFORMATION
厕所	(Cèsuǒ)	TOILET
男	(Nán)	(MEN)
女	(Nǚ)	(WOMEN)
不许吸烟	(Bù xǔ xīyān)	NO SMOKING
停	(Tíng)	STOP

JAPAN Sometimes written vertically, top to bottom; occasionally right to left.

開	(Aite iru)	OPEN
閉	(Shimatte iru)	CLOSED
入口	(Iriguchi)	ENTRANCE
出口	(Deguchi)	EXIT
バス	(Basu)	BUS
男性用トイレ	(Danseiyō toire)	MEN'S TOILET
女性用トイレ	(Joseiyō toire)	WOMEN'S TOILET
危険	(Kiken)	DANGER
禁止	(Kinshi)	PROHIBITED
停止	(Teishi)	STOP
通行禁止	(Tsūkō kinshi)	NO ENTRY
タクシー	(Takushii)	TAXI

SIGNS

KOREA

입 구	(Ipgu)	ENTRANCE
출 구	(Chulgu)	EXIT
화장실	(Hwajang sil)	TOILET
남 자	(Namja)	(MEN)
여 자	(Yŏja)	(WOMEN)
입 장 금 지	(Ipjang gŭmji)	NO ADMITTANCE
주 차 금 지	(Jucha gŭmji)	NO PARKING
들어오지마시오	(Dŭrŏojimasio)	KEEP OUT
금 연	(Gŭmyŏn)	NO SMOKING
위 험	(Wihŏm)	DANGER
차 단	(Chadan)	CLOSED

INDONESIA

MASUK	ENTRANCE
KELUAR	EXIT
BUKA	OPEN
TUTUP	CLOSED
BAHAYA	DANGER
DILARANG MASUK	{ NO ENTRANCE / KEEP OUT
PEMBERITAHUAN } PENERANGAN	INFORMATION
KAMAR KECIL, KAKUS	TOILET
LAKI-LAKI	(MEN)
WANITA	(WOMEN)
DILARANG MEROKOK	NO SMOKING
PERHENTIAN	STOP

SIGNS

	FRENCH	PORTUGUESE	SPANISH
ENTRANCE	Entrée	Entrada	Entrada
EXIT	Sortie	Saida	Salida
OPEN	Ouvert	Aberto	Abierto
CLOSED	Fermé	Encerrado	Cerrado
		Fechado	
DANGER	Danger	Perigo	Peligro
NO ENTRANCE	Entrée interdite	Entrada proibida	Prohibida la entrada
			Prohibido el paso
INFORMATION	Renseignements	Informações	Información
TOILET	Cabinet	Retrete	Servicios
			Retrete
			Baños
(MEN)	Messieurs	Cavalheiros	Caballeros
	Hommes	Homens	
(WOMEN)	Dames	Senhoras	Señoras
NO SMOKING	Défense de fumer	Proibido fumar	Prohibido fumar
	Pas fumeurs		
STOP	Halte	Pare	Alto
		Alto	

FIJI
Imm. Act. 1971 Sect. 9
VISITOR
Nadi 2 6 AUG 1982 Entered
Valid for ONE MONTH only
unless EXTENDED.

J357160

IMMIGRATION

NADI AIRPORT

SABYAI THAILAND

IMMIGRATION DIVISION

Visitor-Permitted to remain until
- 5 OCT 1980

HONG KONG

IMMIGRATION OFFICER
HONG KONG
★ 11 JUL 1980 ★
(1052)
DEPARTED

VISAS

Visitor-Permitted to remain until

18 DEC 1983
IMMIGRATION SERVICE
18 SEP 1983

STATE OF BAHRAIN

STATE OF BAHRAIN

DINAR

21 8121
21 5 18

مطار البحرين الدولي 30

3 MAY 1981
Employment in Bahrain

2 MAY 198
BAHRAIN INTERNATIONAL AIRPORT

ESTADOS UNIDOS MEXICANOS
ACAPULCO. GRO.

2.01
VISA: KUNJUNGAN WISATA
Diizinkan mengadakan satu kali perjalanan ke Indonesia untuk KUNJUNGAN WISATA selama: 30(Tiga Puluh) hari
Good for a single journey to Indonesia for thirty days visit as tourist.

Nama : McMahon, Alice
Name :

Tanggal
Date

Nomor
Number

001989 /WI

25.01.83

Tempat2 yang akan dikunjungi di Indonesia/Place(s) to be visited in Indonesia:
Bali, Java, Sumatera
Berlaku hanya apabila mendarat di Indonesia dalam waktu 3 (tiga) bulan terhitung dari tanggal pemberian/Valid only for landing in Indonesia within three(3) months from the date of issue, if passport

SYDNEY

HS